Design of Embedded Systems Using 68HC12/11 Microcontrollers

Design of Embedded Systems Using 68HC12/11 Microcontrollers

Richard E. Haskell

Computer Science and Engineering Department
Oakland University
Rochester, Michigan 48309

PRENTICE HALL
Upper Saddle River, NJ 07458

Library of Congress Cataloging-in-Publication Data

Haskell, Richard E.
   Design of embedded systems using 68HC12/11 microcontrollers /
Richard E. Haskell
     p. cm.
    ISBN 0-13-083208-1 (pbk.)
    1. Embedded computer systems—Design and construction.
    2. Motorola 68HC11 (Microprocessor)
TK7895.E42H38   1999
004.2'1—dc21   99-16964
                                            CIP

Publisher: *Tom Robbins*
Associate editor: *Alice Dworkin*
Production editor: *Audri Anna Bazlen*
Editor-in-chief: *Marcia Horton*
Executive managing editor: *Vince O'Brien*
Assistant managing editor: *Eileen Clark*
Vice-president of production and manufacturing: *David W. Riccardi*
Art director: *Jayne Conte*
Cover design: *Bruce Kenselaar*
Manufacturing buyer: *Pat Brown*
Marketing manager: *Danny Hoyt*
Editorial assistant: *Dan DePasquale*

© 2000 by Prentice Hall
Prentice-Hall, Inc.
Upper Saddle River, New Jersey 07458

Printed in the United States of America
10 9 8 7 6 5 4 3 2 1

ISBN 0-13-083208-1

Prentice-Hall International (UK) Limited, London
Prentice-Hall of Australia Pty. Limited, Sydney
Prentice-Hall Canada Inc., Toronto
Prentice-Hall Hispanoamericana, S.A., Mexico
Prentice-Hall of India Private Limited, New Delhi
Prentice-Hall of Japan, Inc., Tokyo
Prentice-Hall (Singapore) Pte. Ltd., Singapore
Editora Prentice-Hall do Brasil, Ltda., Rio de Janeiro

To Edie

Contents

Contents

Preface

Many people think of a computer as a PC on a desk with a keyboard and video monitor. However, most of the computers in the world have neither a keyboard nor a video monitor. Rather they are small microcontrollers—a microprocessor, memory, and I/O all on a single chip—that are embedded in a myriad of other products such as automobiles, televisions, VCRs, cameras, copy machines, cellular telephones, vending machines, microwave ovens, medical instruments, and hundreds of additional products of all kinds. This book is about how to program microcontrollers and use them in the design of embedded systems.

A popular microcontroller that has been used in a wide variety of different products is the Motorola 68HC11. Motorola has recently introduced an upgrade of this microcontroller, the 68HC12, that has new, more powerful instructions and addressing modes. This book emphasizes the use of the 68HC12 while at the same time providing information about the 68HC11. It can therefore be used in courses that use both 68HC12 and 68HC11 microcontrollers.

This book is the result of teaching various microcomputer interfacing courses over the past 20 years. While the technology may change, the basic principles of microcomputer interfacing remain largely the same and these basic principles are stressed throughout this book. However, microcomputer interfacing is a subject that is learned only by doing. The courses that I have taught using this material have all been project-oriented courses in which the students design and build real micro-computer interfacing projects.

A definite trend in microcomputer interfacing and in digital design in general is a shift from hardware design to software design. Microcomputer interfacing has always involved both hardware and software considerations. However, the increasingly large-scale integration of the hardware together with sophisticated software tools for designing hardware means that even traditional hardware design is becoming more and more a software activity.

In the past most software for microcomputer interfacing has been written in assembly language. This means that each time a new and better microprocessor comes out the designer must first learn the new assembly language. The advantage of assembly language is that it is "closest to the hardware" and will allow the user to do exactly what he or she wants in the most efficient manner. While some feel that assembly language programs are more difficult to write and maintain than programs written in a high-level language, the major disadvantage of assembly language programs is related to the obsolescence of the microprocessor—when upgrading to a new or different microprocessor, all of the software has to be rewritten! Even when upgrading from a 68HC11 to a 68HC12, which is upward compatible at the source-code level, to get the best performance from the 68HC12 you will need to rewrite the code to use the newer, more powerful instructions and addressing modes.

This has led to a trend of using high-level languages such as C or C++ for microcomputer interfacing. While this helps to solve the obsolescence problem—much of the same high-level code might be reusable with a new microprocessor—high-level languages come with their own problems. The development environment is not always the most convenient. One has to edit the program, compile it, load it, and then run it to test it on the real hardware. This edit-compile-test cycle can be very time consuming for large programs. Without sophisticated run-time debugging tools the debugging of the program on real hardware can be very frustrating. When designing microcomputer interfaces you would like to be as close to the hardware as possible.

What you would like is a computer language with the advantages of both a high-level language and assembly language, with none of the disadvantages. It would be nice if the language were also interactive so that you could sit at your computer terminal and literally "talk" to the various hardware interfaces. The language should also produce compact code so that you can easily embed the code in PROMS or flash memory for a stand-alone system. While you're at it why not embed the entire language in your target system so that you can develop your program "on-line" and even upgrade the program in the field once the product is delivered. Impossible, you say? In fact, just such a language exists for almost any microprocessor you may want to use. The language is Forth and we will use a derivative of it in this book to illustrate how easy microcomputer interfacing can be.

We will use a unique version of Forth called *WHYP* (pronounced *whip*) that is designed for use in embedded systems. WHYP stands for *W*ords to *H*elp *Y*ou *P*rogram. It is a subroutine threaded language which means that WHYP words are just the names of 68HC12(11) subroutines. New WHYP words can be defined simply by stringing previously defined WHYP words together.

A unique feature of Forth—and WHYP—is its simplicity. It is a simple language to learn, to use, and to understand. In fact, in this book we will develop the entire WHYP language from scratch. We will see that WHYP consists of two parts—some 68HC12 subroutines that reside on the target system (typically an evaluation board) and a C++ program that runs on a PC and communicates with the 68HC12 target system through a serial line. In the process of developing the WHYP subroutines on the target system you will learn 68HC12 assembly language programming. When you finish the book you will also know Forth. Previous knowledge of C++ will be helpful in understanding the C++ portion of WHYP that resides on the PC. The complete C++ source code is included on the disk that accompanies this book and in discussed in Chapters 16 and 17. However, these chapters are optional and are not required in order to use WHYP to program the 68HC12.

You will discover that you can develop large software projects using WHYP in a much shorter time than you could develop the same program in either assembly language or C. You might be surprised at the number of industrial embedded systems projects that have been developed in Forth. Many small companies and consultants that use Forth don't talk much about it because many consider it a competitive advantage to be able to develop software in a shorter time than others who program in assembly language or C.

In Chapter 1 you will learn about the architecture of the 68HC12 and how to write a simple assembly language program, assemble it, download it to the target board, and execute it. You will see how to write 68HC12 subroutines in Chapter 2 where you will learn how the system stack works. We will then develop a separate data stack, using the 68HC12 index register, X, as a stack pointer. This data stack will be used throughout the book to pass parameters to and from our 68HC12 subroutines (WHYP words). We will see in Chapter 2 that this makes it possible to access our 68HC12 subroutines interactively, by simply typing the name of the subroutine on the PC keyboard.

In Chapter 3 we will study 68HC12 arithmetic with emphasis on the new 16-bit signed and unsigned multiplication and division instructions available on the 68HC12. We will use these instructions to create WHYP words for all of the arithmetic operations.

The power of WHYP comes from the fact that you can define new WHYP words in terms of previously defined words. This makes WHYP an extensible language in which every time you write a WHYP program you are really extending the language by adding new words to its dictionary. You will learn how to do this in Chapter 4.

In Chapter 5 we will look at the 68HC12 branching and looping instructions and see how we can use them to build some high-level WHYP branching and looping words such as an *IF . . . ELSE . . . THEN* construct and a *FOR . . . NEXT* loop. We will also see in this chapter how we can do recursion in WHYP, that is, how we can have a WHYP word call itself.

After the first five chapters you should have a good understanding of the 68HC12 instructions and how they are used to create the WHYP language. The next six chapters will use WHYP as a tool to explore and understand the I/O capabilities of the 68HC12 (and 68HC11). The important topic of interrupts is introduced in

Chapter 6 and specific examples of using interrupts in conjunction with various I/O functions are given in Chapters 7–11.

Parallel interfacing will be discussed in Chapter 7 where examples will be given of interfacing a 68HC12 to seven-segment displays, hex keypads, and liquid crystal displays. Real-time interrupts are used to program interrupt-driven traffic lights.

Chapter 8 will cover the 68HC12 Serial Peripheral Interface (SPI) where it will be shown how to interface keypads and seven-segment displays using the SPI. The 68HC11 and 68HC12 Analog-to-Digital (A/D) converter is described in Chapter 9 where an example is given of the design of a digital compass.

The 68HC12 programmable timer is discussed in Chapter 10 where examples are given of using output compares, input captures, and the pulse accumulator. Examples of using interrupts include the generation of a pulse train and the measurement of the period of a pulse train. An example of storing hex keypad pressings in a circular queue using interrupts is also included in Chapter 10. As a final example of using interrupts a design is given of a sonar tape measure using the Polaroid ultrasonic transducer.

Chapter 11 deals with the Serial Communication Interface (SCI) which is the module used by the 68HC12 to communicate with the PC.

Chapters 1–11 provide all the basic material needed to program a 68HC12 microcontroller for most applications. These chapters can form the basis of a one-term projects-oriented capstone design course at the senior/graduate level.

The material in Chapters 12 and 13 will be of interest to those who want access to more advanced topics related to programming in WHYP. Chapter 12 describes how to convert ASCII number strings to binary numbers and vice versa. Chapter 13 shows how you can create defining words using the *CREATE ... DOES>* construct. These defining words are used to create jump tables and various data structures in WHYP.

The 68HC12 has special instructions that facilitate the implementation of fuzzy control. Chapter 14 discusses fuzzy control and shows how to design a fuzzy controller using WHYP on a 68HC12.

A number of special topics related to the 68HC12 are covered in Chapter 15 and as mentioned above Chapters 16 and 17 describe the C++ program for that part of WHYP that runs on the PC. The appendices contain the 68HC12 and 68HC11 instruction sets, plus useful information about WHYP, including procedures for installing WHYP on various evaluation boards.

Chuck Moore invented Forth in the late 1960s while programming minicomputers in assembly language. His idea was to create a simple system that would allow him to write many more useful programs than he could using assembly language. The essence of Forth is simplicity—always try to do things in the simplest possible way. Forth is a way of thinking about problems in a modular way. It is modular in the extreme. Everything in Forth is a word and every word is a module that does something useful. There is an action associated with Forth words. The words execute themselves. In this sense they are object oriented. We send words parameters on the data stack and ask the words to execute themselves and send us the answers back on the data stack. We really don't care how the word does it—once we have written it and tested it so we know that it works.

Forth has been implemented in a number of different ways. Chuck Moore's original Forth had what is called an *indirect-threaded* inner interpreter. Other Forths have used what is called a *direct-threaded* inner interpreter. These inner interpreters get executed every time you go from one Forth word to the next, that is, all the time. WHYP is what is called a *subroutine-threaded* Forth. This means that the subroutine calling mechanism that is built into the 68HC12 is what is used to go from one WHYP word to the next. In other words, WHYP words are just regular 68HC12 subroutines. This both simplifies the implementation and speeds up the execution, at the expense of using somewhat more memory. In WHYP a word is compiled as a 3-byte jump-to-subroutine instruction while direct-threaded Forths need to store only the 2-byte address in memory. The inner interpreter takes care of reading the next address and executing the code at that address. Indirect-threaded Forths have an additional level of indirection. The 2-byte address in memory points not to the code to be executed, but to a location containing the address of the code to be executed. WHYP avoids these complications by being subroutine threaded and using the subroutine structure built into the 68HC12.

The way you program in Forth is bottom up—even though you may design the overall solution top down. You define a simple little word (subroutine) and test it out interactively at the keyboard. You put values on the data stack by simply typing them on the screen, separated by spaces, followed by the name of the word. When you press *<enter>*, the word (subroutine) is executed immediately and it leaves the answer(s) on the data stack which you can then display. This will all be explained in detail in the first five chapters of this book.

You should think of WHYP as your personal language that will allow you to write programs for the 68HC12 incrementally and interactively. Because we develop WHYP from scratch in this book there will be no mystery as to how it works. The entire source code—both the assembly language and the C++ parts—are included on the disk that comes with this book. In the true spirit of Forth this will give you complete control over your programming environment. Remember, Forth is an extensible language—and WHYP is your personal language that you will be able to extend and modify to suit your needs.

Acknowledgment

The material in this book is based on many years of teaching Forth in a senior graduate course on embedded systems. My interest in and knowledge of Forth has benefited greatly from the Forth Interest Group (http://www.forth.org/fig.html) and many enjoyable years attending the annual FORML Conference in Pacific Grove, CA, and the annual Rochester Forth Conference in Rochester, NY. Many colleagues and students have influenced the development of this book. Their stimulating discussions, probing questions, and critical comments are greatly appreciated. I wish to thank Darrow F. Dawson of the University of Missouri-Rolla who reviewed the manuscript and made important suggestions that improved the book.

1

Introducing the 68HC12

The 68HC12 is the latest family of Motorola microcontrollers and is a direct descendent of the popular 68HC11. In this book you will learn about both the 68HC11 and the 68HC12 with an emphasis on the newer 68HC12. In the first section of this chapter we will describe what a microcontroller is and how it developed over the years from the early microprocessors. We will then take a close look at the 68HC12 registers that make up the programming model of the processor. We will introduce a number of 68HC12 instructions that are used to access the registers. You will learn how to write a simple assembly language program, assemble it using an assembler, download the machine code into memory on an evaluation board, and finally execute the program. This process cries out for simplification and we will see in succeeding chapters how to develop the language WHYP that will allow you to write and debug your 68HC12 programs in an interactive and direct way.

1.1 FROM MICROPROCESSORS TO MICROCONTROLLERS

A major revolution in the computer industry has taken place in the past 25 years. The making of the first microprocessor was made possible by the remarkable development of integrated circuits during the 1960s. This technology allowed hundreds and then thousands of transistors to be etched onto a single piece of silicon. This led to the design of integrated circuits in which more and more logic elements were incorporated into a single chip. In 1969 Intel undertook a contract to develop a set of integrated circuits that could be used to make a programmable electronic calculator. Instead of developing yet another special-purpose integrated circuit with only a limited function, Intel chose to produce a more general-purpose device, the 4004 microprocessor, that could be programmed to perform many different functions. This first microprocessor had only four data lines over which both address information and data had to be sent to memory devices. Intel put this chip on the market in 1971 as part of a four-chip set that formed a microprogrammable computer. The 4004 had many limitations and the following year Intel introduced the 8008 and two years later the 8080 which became widely used in a host of different applications. In 1975 Motorola produced its first microprocessor—the 6800.

The 6800 had 8 data lines (called a *data bus*) and 16 address lines (called an *address bus*). This means that it could address $2^{16} = 65,536$ different memory addresses, each containing 8 bits, or 1 byte of data. The heart of the 6800 was its CPU, or Central Processing Unit, sometimes referred to as an MPU, or microprocessor unit. The CPU contained the registers and logic to execute the instruction set of the 6800. The 6800 registers included two 8-bit accumulators (*A* and *B*), a 16-bit index register (*X*), a 16-bit stack pointer (*SP*), a 16-bit program counter (*PC*), and an 8-bit condition-code register (*CCR*). Thus, the first microprocessors consisted only of a CPU that could address external memory as shown in Figure 1–1.

The external memory shown in Figure 1–1 consists of Random-Access Memory (RAM), which is read-write memory, Read-Only Memory (ROM), and Input/Output memory (I/O). Typically the I/O memory consists of dedicated special-purpose devices for performing such operations as parallel I/O, serial I/O, timer functions, and Analog-to-Digital (A/D) conversion. These I/O devices contain registers that look like memory locations to the CPU. The RAM in Figure 1–1 could be either Static RAM (SRAM) or Dynamic RAM (DRAM). Dynamic RAM can contain more bytes of memory than static RAM for the same size chip but requires

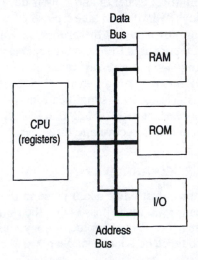

Figure 1–1   A Microprocessor (CPU) Connected to External Memory

additional circuitry to refresh the data periodically to keep it from being lost. Other types of memory devices that might be connected to the address and data buses in Figure 1–1 include Erasable Programmable Read-Only Memory (EPROM), Electrically-Erasable Programmable Read-Only Memory (EEPROM), and flash EEPROM. Both flash EEPROM and EEPROM are nonvolatile memory that will maintain their data when power is removed. Individual bytes can be erased and programmed in EEPROM while flash EEPROMs normally require erasing the entire memory array at one time.

As integrated circuit technology developed over the years, one of the trends has been the development of faster and more complex microprocessors such as the Intel 80x86 and Pentium and the Motorola 680x0 and PowerPC. These microprocessors are used in many of the popular desktop computers used in offices all over the world. Another trend has been to package more and more functionality onto a single chip. The Motorola 6801 was introduced in 1978 and included a small amount of RAM and ROM as well as parallel and serial I/O on a single chip. The following year Motorola introduced an EPROM version of the 6801, the 68701, as well as the first of the low-cost 6805 family of microcontrollers.

The first 68HC11 was introduced by Motorola in 1985. This 8-bit microcontroller (the A8 part) contained on a single chip the CPU11 microprocessor, 8 Kbytes of ROM, 256 bytes of RAM, 512 bytes of EEPROM, up to 38 parallel I/O lines, a 16-bit timer that includes three input captures and five output compares, a synchronous Serial Peripheral Interface (SPI), an asynchronous Serial Communications Interface (SCI), and an 8-channel, 8-bit A/D converter. Since 1985 over five dozen different 68HC11 parts have been introduced by Motorola. These parts differ in the types and amounts of on-board resources that are included in the chip.

A block diagram of a typical 68HC11 is shown in Figure 1–2. In the single-chip mode the entire program is stored in the ROM or EPROM and the only contact

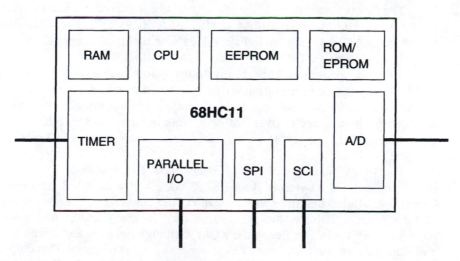

Figure 1–2   Block Diagram of a 68HC11

with the outside world is through the various peripheral lines connected to the timer, parallel I/O, SPI, SCI, or A/D converter. The 68HC11 can also operate in an expanded multiplexed mode in which the parallel I/O lines become multiplexed address and data buses that can be used to address external memory. The amount of on-board resources for several of the 68HC11 parts are listed in Table 1–1. In this table the '711 parts have EPROM instead of ROM. These parts can be programmed by the user and erased under ultraviolet light. The I/O column lists the maximum number of I/O lines when these lines are not being used for some other purpose such as a timer function, serial I/O, or A/D converter. In addition to the resources listed, all parts have SPI and SCI serial interfaces. The timer on all but the 'A8 part can be configured to have either three input captures and five output compares, or four input captures and four output compares. These timer functions will be described in detail in Chapter 10. The 68HC11 microcontroller has been used in a wide variety of applications including those listed in Table 1–2.

Motorola has introduced other families of microcontrollers including the 68HC3xx family based on the 32-bit 68020 (CPU32) and the MPC500 series of microcontrollers based on the PowerPC. The 68HC16 microcontroller fits somewhere between the 68HC11 and the 68HC332.

In 1997 Motorola introduced the 68HC12 as an enhanced 68HC11. It is upward compatible with the 68HC11 (but not at the object code level). It has a greatly enhanced central processing unit (CPU12) that has several new instructions and addressing modes designed to make it easier to support higher-level languages. Programs can run significantly faster on a 68HC12 for several reasons. The typical clock speed has been increased from 2 MHz on a 68HC11 to 8 MHz on a 68HC12. The number of clock cycles required to execute many of the instructions has been reduced on the 68HC12. In addition, the new instructions and addressing modes require fewer clock cycles to perform the same task. This means that not only do programs run faster, but they also take up less memory space.

The first two members of the 68HC12 family of microcontrollers introduced by Motorola are the MC68HC812A4 and the MC68HC912B32. The block diagram of the MC68HC812A4 is shown in Figure 1–3. Note that it contains 1 Kbyte of SRAM and 4 Kbytes of EEPROM. There is no ROM or EPROM that would normally hold the application program. This chip is designed to be used with external memory and for that purpose nonmultiplexed address and data buses are provided. The data bus is 16-bits wide and on-chip memory mapping allows expansion of the normal 64-Kbyte address space to over 5 Mbytes. Note in Figure 1–3 that this chip contains an 8-channel A/D converter, an enhanced timer interface, two SCI ports, and one SPI port.

The block diagram of the MC68HC912B32 is shown in Figure 1–4. Note that it contains 32 Kbytes of flash EEPROM, 1 Kbyte of RAM, and 768 bytes of EEPROM. It also has the same 8-channel A/D converter as the MC68HC812A4. The MC68HC912B32 is designed to be used in the single-chip mode with the program residing in the flash EEPROM, although ports A and B can be used as a multiplexed address and data bus to access external memory. This chip has only a single SCI port but has an additional four-channel Pulse-Width Modulator

Table 1–1 Selected 68HC11 Parts

Part No.	ROM/EPROM	RAM	EEPROM	I/O	Timer	A/D
68HC11A8	8K	256	512	38	3 IC, 5 OC	Yes
68HC11D0	0	192	0	14	3/4 IC, 4/5 OC	No
68HC711D3	4K	192	0	32	3/4 IC, 4/5 OC	No
68HC711E9	12K	512	512	38	3/4 IC, 4/5 OC	Yes
68HC711K4	24K	768	640	62	3/4 IC, 4/5 OC	Yes

Table 1–2 Applications of the 68HC11 Microcontroller

Consumer

Televisions	Home Video Game Systems
VCRs	Compact Disc Players
Cable Boxes	Digital Audio Systems
Camcoders	Digital Radio
Cameras	Appliances
Security Systems	

Office Automation

Modems	Tape Drives
Typewriters	Monitors
Smart Furniture	Keyboards
Hard Disk Drives	Scanners

Communications

Handheld Radios	Telephone Switching
Cellular Telephones	Analog Telephones
Cordless Telephones	Answering Machines
Digital Telephones	Pagers

Industrial Control and Instrumentation

Elevators	Fire Control
Traffic Control	Security Systems
Meter Reading	Lighting Control
ATM Machines	Noise Control
Vending Machines	Gas Furnaces
Card Readers	Blood Pressure Monitors
Bar Code Readers	Blood Analyzers
Manufacturing Tracking	Glucose Monitors
Process Control	Gas Analyzers

Automotive

Instrument Displays	Cruise Control
Injection Systems	Active Suspension
Emission Control	Anti-lock Braking Systems (ABS)
Engine Control	Air Bags
Climate Control	Automatic Seat Belts

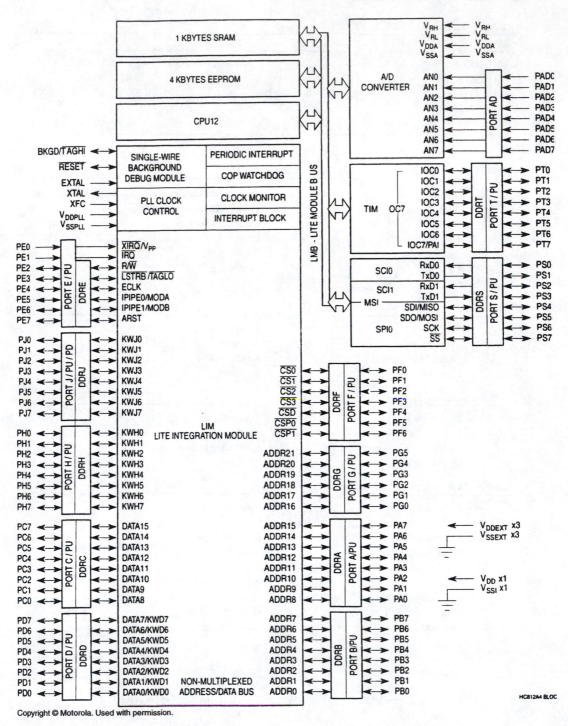

Figure 1–3   Block Diagram of the MC68HC812A4

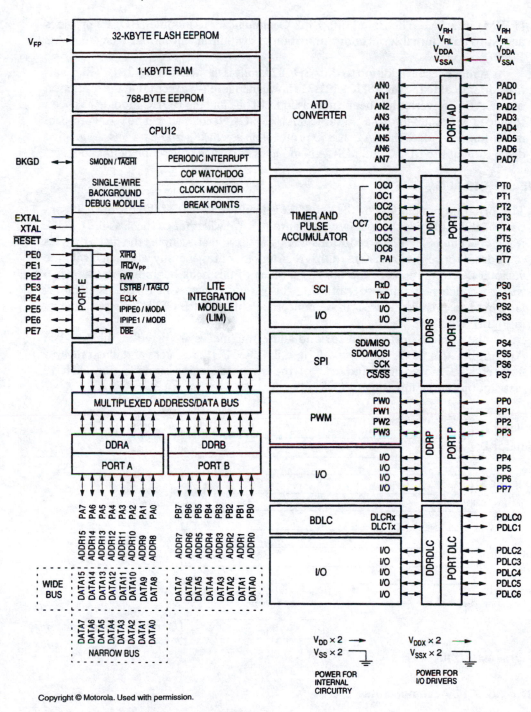

Copyright © Motorola. Used with permission.

Figure 1–4   Block Diagram of the MC68HC912B32

(PWM) interface. The Byte Data Link Communications module (BDLC) provides access to an external serial communication bus within an automobile using the SAE J1850 protocol.

A more recent addition to the 68HC12 family is the MC68HC912BC32 that is almost identical to the MC68HC912B32 shown in Figure 1–4 except that the resolution of the A/D converter has been increased to 10 bits and the BDLC module has been replaced with the Motorola Scalable CAN (MSCAN) controller. The CAN protocol is tending to replace the SAE J1850 protocol on a vehicle serial data bus. A detailed discussion of the BDLC and MSCAN modules are beyond the scope of this book.

1.2 THE 68HC12 REGISTERS

The programming model of the 68HC12 is identical to that of the 68HC11. It consists of the set of registers shown in Figure 1–5. We will refer to these as the CPU12 registers. The 68HC12 also contains a register block that occupies the first 512 bytes of address space. The registers in this register block are generally associated with the various I/O operations of the 68HC12. Much of this book beginning in Chapter 6 will be concerned with programming the various registers in this register block. However, in this section we will be concerned only with the CPU12 registers shown in Figure 1–5.

The 68HC12 instruction set and addressing modes are listed in Table A–1 in Appendix A. In this section we will describe the CPU12 registers and illustrate how data can be moved into and out of these registers using some of the 68HC12 instructions and addressing modes.

| Accumulator A | A | B | Accumulator B |
| Accumulator D | D | | |

Index register X	IX
Index register Y	IY
Stack Pointer	SP
Program counter	PC

| | S X H I N Z V C | Condition code register |

Figure 1–5   The 68HC12 Registers

1.2.1 The 68HC12 Accumulators

The 68HC12 has two 8-bit accumulators, A and B, that can be combined into the single 16-bit accumulator D. That is, A is the upper 8-bits of D and B is the lower 8-bits of D. The accumulators are used for storing intermediate results and for performing arithmetic and logical operations. The following are some of the instructions involving accumulators A, B, and D.

LOAD AND STORE INSTRUCTIONS

LDAA	Load A from memory
LDAB	Load B from memory
LDD	Load D from memory
STAA	Store A to memory
STAB	Store B to memory
STD	Store D to memory

TRANSFER AND EXCHANGE INSTRUCTIONS

TAB	Transfer A to B
TBA	Transfer B to A
EXG A,B	Exchange A and B

ADDITION AND SUBTRACTION INSTRUCTIONS

ABA	Add B to A
ADDA	Add memory to A
ADDB	Add memory to B
ADCA	Add memory with carry to A
ADCB	Add memory with carry to B
ADDD	Add memory to D
SBA	Subtract B from A
SUBA	Subtract memory from A
SUBB	Subtract memory from B
SBCA	Subtract memory with borrow from A
SBCB	Subtract memory with borrow from B
SUBD	Subtract memory from D

DECREMENT AND INCREMENT INSTRUCTIONS

DECA	Decrement A
DECB	Decrement B
INCA	Increment A
INCB	Increment B

COMPARE AND TEST INSTRUCTIONS

CBA	Compare A to B
CMPA	Compare A to memory
CMPB	Compare B to memory
CPD	Compare D to memory
TSTA	Test A for zero or minus
TSTB	Test B for zero or minus

BOOLEAN LOGIC INSTRUCTIONS

ANDA	AND A with memory
ANDB	AND B with memory

EORA	Exclusive OR A with memory
EORB	Exclusive OR B with memory
ORAA	OR A with memory
ORAB	OR B with memory

CLEAR, COMPLEMENT, AND NEGATE INSTRUCTIONS

CLRA	Clear A
CLRB	Clear B
COMA	One's complement A
COMB	One's complement B
NEGA	Two's complement A
NEGB	Two's complement B

SHIFT AND ROTATE INSTRUCTIONS

LSLA	Logic shift left A
LSLB	Logic shift left B
LSLD	Logic shift left D
LSRA	Logic shift right A
LSRB	Logic shift right B
LSRD	Logic shift right D
ASLA	Arithmetic shift left A
ASLB	Arithmetic shift left B
ASLD	Arithmetic shift left D
ASRA	Arithmetic shift right A
ASRB	Arithmetic shift right B
ROLA	Rotate left A through carry
ROLB	Rotate left B through carry
RORA	Rotate right A through carry
RORB	Rotate right B through carry

STACKING INSTRUCTIONS

PSHA	Push A
PSHB	Push B
PSHD	Push D
PULA	Pull A
PULB	Pull B
PULD	Pull D

Some of the instructions in the above list describe an operation involving a memory location. Where in memory the data reside is determined by the addressing mode. In general, several different addressing modes can be used with each memory access instruction as shown in Table A–1 in Appendix A. We will discuss addressing modes in more detail later in this chapter and in Chapter 2.

1.2.2   Index Registers, *X* and *Y*

The index registers X and Y are 16-bit registers that are used for several different purposes. They can be used in a manner similar to the accumulators for temporary storage when moving 16-bit data to and from memory. The following are some of the instructions involving index registers X and Y.

LOAD AND STORE INSTRUCTIONS

LDX	Load X from memory
LDY	Load Y from memory
STX	Store X to memory
STY	Store Y to memory
LEAX	Load effective address into X
LEAY	Load effective address into Y

TRANSFER AND EXCHANGE INSTRUCTIONS

EXG X,Y	Exchange X and Y
XGDX	Exchange D with X
XGDY	Exchange D with Y

ADDITION AND SUBTRACTION INSTRUCTIONS

ABX	Add B to X
ABY	Add B to Y

DECREMENT AND INCREMENT INSTRUCTIONS

DEX	Decrement X
DEY	Decrement Y
INX	Increment X
INY	Increment Y

COMPARE AND TEST INSTRUCTIONS

CPX	Compare X to memory
CPY	Compare Y to memory

STACKING INSTRUCTIONS

PSHX	Push X
PSHY	Push Y
PULX	Pull X
PULY	Pull Y

The main use of the index registers X and Y is in conjunction with various modes of addressing. An addressing mode is what specifies where a particular data item is to be found. For example, the instruction *LDAA #$10* is an example of the *immediate addressing mode*. This means that the value $10 immediately follows the opcode in memory. The $ sign means that 10 is a hexadecimal value. The # sign means that it is immediate addressing. One of the most important addressing modes associated with the index registers X and Y is indexed addressing. For example, the instruction

```
LDAA 0,X
```

means load into accumulator A the byte in memory at the address that is in index register X. We say that X is pointing to a byte in memory. The zero in the above instruction is a displacement that gets added to the value of X. For example, the instruction *LDD 4,X* will load two bytes of memory into accumulator D ($A{:}B$). The byte at address $X+4$ will be loaded into accumulator A and the byte at address $X+5$ will be loaded into accumulator B.

1.2.3 Stack Pointer, *SP*

The stack is a region of memory that is set aside for storing temporary data. The stack pointer, *SP*, is a 16-bit register that contains the address of the top of the stack. The stack is used by the 68HC12 to save the return address when a subroutine is called. It is also used to save register values when an interrupt occurs.

The stack can be used to save the contents of registers A, B, X, and Y using the instructions *PSHA*, *PSHB*, *PSHX*, and *PSHY*. These values are removed from the stack using the instructions *PULA*, *PULB*, *PULX*, and *PULY*.

As we will see WHYP uses two stacks, a data stack and a return stack. The WHYP return stack is the same as the system stack and uses register *SP* as the stack pointer. The WHYP data stack uses index register X as the stack pointer. A 16-bit value in D is pushed on the WHYP data stack using the instruction

```
STD 2,-X
```

where the operand 2,-X indicates auto predecrement indexed addressing. In this case, the value in index register X is predecremented by 2 before the value in D is stored at the new location pointed to by X. Thus, to push D on the WHYP data stack the index register, X, is first decremented by 2 and then D is stored at this new address in X.

68HC11 Note:

The auto predecrement indexed addressing mode is not available in the 68HC11. Therefore, the equivalent of the 68HC12 instruction *STD 2,-X* would have to be written as the three 68HC11 instructions

```
DEX
DEX
STD 0,X
```

The following are some of the instructions involving the stack pointer, *SP*.

LOAD AND STORE INSTRUCTIONS

LDS	Load SP from memory
STS	Store SP to memory
LEAS	Load effective address into SP

TRANSFER AND EXCHANGE INSTRUCTIONS

TSX	Transfer SP to X
TSY	Transfer SP to Y
TXS	Transfer X to SP
TYS	Transfer Y to SP
EXG X,SP	Exchange X and SP

DECREMENT AND INCREMENT INSTRUCTIONS

DES	Decrement SP
INS	Increment SP

COMPARE AND TEST INSTRUCTIONS

CPS	Compare SP to memory
CPY	Compare Y to memory

1.2.4 Program Counter, *PC*

The program counter, *PC*, is a 16-bit register that contains the address of the next instruction to be executed. When an instruction is executed, the program counter is automatically incremented the number of times needed to point to the next instruction. 68HC12 instructions may be from 1 to 6 bytes long. Therefore, the program counter may be incremented by 1 to 6 depending upon the instruction being executed.

Some instructions cause the program counter to change to some new value rather than simply be incremented. These include the branching, jump, and subroutine instructions. We will discuss subroutines in Chapter 2 and branching instructions in Chapter 5.

1.2.5 The Condition Code Register

The 68HC12 has a Condition Code Register (*CCR*) that contains five status flags or condition codes and three control flags. The five status flags are the carry flag (*C*), the zero flag (*Z*), the negative flag (*N*), the overflow flag (*V*), and the half carry flag (*H*). The three control flags are the interrupt mask flag (*I*), the X-interrupt mask flag (X), and the stop disable flag (S). Each flag is 1 bit in the condition code register. The location of each flag is shown in Figure 1–6.

Any of the bits in the condition code register (with the exception of the X bit) can be set using the 68HC12 instruction *ORCC*. This instruction will perform a logical OR of the *CCR* with a byte mask in memory (immediate addressing) containing a 1 in the bit locations to be set. Any of the bits in the condition code register can be cleared using the 68HC12 instruction *ANDCC*. This instruction will perform a logical AND of the *CCR* with a byte mask in a memory containing a 0 in the bit locations to be cleared.

We will now look at the meaning of each bit in the condition code register.

Carry (C)   The carry flag is bit 0 of the condition code register. It can be considered to be an extension of a register, or memory location operated on by an instruction. The carry bit is changed by three different types of instructions. The first are arithmetic instructions. These include the addition instructions *ADDA, ADDB, ADDD, ADCA* (add with carry), *ADCB*, and *ABA* (add B to A), the subtraction instructions *SUBA, SUBB, SUBD, SBCA* (subtract with carry from A), *SBCB*, and *SBA* (subtract B from A), and the compare instructions *CMPA, CMPB, CBA, CPD, CPX*, and *CPY*. The carry bit is also changed by the multiplication instructions, *MUL, EMUL*, and *EMULS*, the five division instructions, *IDIV, IDIVS, EDIV, EDIVS*, and *FDIV*, the negate instructions, *NEG, NEGA*, and *NEGB*, and the decimal adjust instruction, *DAA*.

The second group of instructions that can change the carry bit are the shifting and rotating instructions such as *ASL, ASLA, ASLB, ASR, ASRA, ASRB, LSL, LSLA, LSLB, LSR, LSRA, LSRB, LSRD, ROL, ROLA, ROLB, ROR, RORA*, and *RORB*.

Finally, the carry bit can be set to 1 with the instruction *SEC* (set carry) and cleared to zero with the instruction *CLC* (clear carry). These instructions which are valid for the 68HC11 get translated to the 68HC12 instructions *ORCC #$01* and *ANDCC #$FE*, respectively.

Zero Flag (Z)   The zero flag is bit 2 of the condition code register. This flag is set to 1 when the result of an instruction is zero. If the result of an instruction is not zero, the Z flag is cleared to zero. This Z flag is tested by the branching instruction

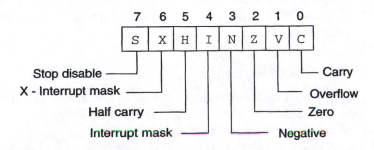

Figure 1–6   The 68HC12 Condition Code Register

BEQ (branch if equal to zero, $Z = 1$) and *BNE* (branch if not equal to zero, $Z = 0$). These branching instructions are described in Chapter 5.

Negative Flag (*N*)   The negative flag is bit 3 of the condition code register. Negative numbers are stored in 68HC12 computers using the two's complement representation. In this representation a negative number is indicated when bit 7 (the leftmost bit) of a byte is set to 1. When the result of an instruction leaves the sign bit set (bit 7 of a byte or bit 15 of a word), the *N* flag is set to 1. If the result of an instruction is positive, (the sign bit is 0), the *N* flag is cleared to 0. The *N* flag is tested by the branching instruction *BMI* (branch if minus, $N = 1$) and *BPL* (branch if plus, $N = 0$). These branching instructions are described in Chapter 5.

Overflow Flag (*V*)   The overflow flag is bit 1 of the condition code register. It is set any time the result of a signed (two's complement) operation is out of range. The *V* flag is tested by the branching instructions *BVS* (branch if overflow set, $V = 1$) and *BVC* (branch if overflow clear, $V = 0$).

Half-Carry (*H*)   The half-carry flag is bit 5 of the condition code register. It contains the carry from bit 3 to bit 4 resulting from an 8-bit addition or subtraction operation. The half-carry flag is used by the microprocessor when performing Binary-Coded Decimal (BCD) addition. As a programmer you normally don't need to worry about the half-carry flag.

Interrupt Mask Flag (*I*)   The interrupt mask flag is bit 4 of the condition code register. When it is set to 1, hardware interrupts are masked and the 68HC12 will not respond to an interrupt. When the *I* flag is cleared to 0, interrupts are enabled and the 68HC12 will service hardware interrupts.

The *I* flag is set to 1 with the instruction *SEI* (set interrupt mask) and is cleared to zero with the instruction *CLI* (clear interrupt mask). The 68HC12 translates these two instructions to *ORCC #$10* and *ANDCC #$EF*, respectively. A detailed discussion of interrupts will be given in Chapter 6.

X-Interrupt Mask Flag (*X*)   The *X*-interrupt mask flag is bit 6 of the condition code register. This bit is set to 1 by a hardware reset at which point hardware interrupts entering the *XIRQ* pin of the microprocessor are masked. The *X* flag can be cleared to 0 with the instruction *ANDCC #$BF* after which *X*-interrupts are enabled. The 68HC11 can use the instruction *TAP* (which gets translated to *TFR A,CCR* in the 68HC12) to clear the *X* flag. The *X*-interrupt mask cannot be set by software. Therefore, once the *X* bit has been cleared to zero, the *XIRQ* is essentially a nonmaskable interrupt. A detailed discussion of interrupts will be given in Chapter 6.

Stop Disable Flag (*S*)   The stop disable flag is bit 7 of the condition code register. If this bit is set to 1, the *STOP* instruction is disabled. If this bit is cleared to 0, the *STOP* instruction is enabled. When this bit is set, the *STOP* instruction is treated as a no operation (*NOP*) instruction. The *STOP* instruction is used to conserve power by stopping the internal clocks. An external interrupt is needed to start the clocks again.

1.3 WRITING PROGRAMS FOR THE 68HC12

In the last section we introduced some of the instructions that operate on the 68HC12 registers shown in Figure 1–5. In this section we will show how to write a simple assembly language program, assemble it, download it to an evaluation board, and execute it. We will then look at how this programming process might be made interactive.

1.3.1 Editing and Assembling an .ASM File

Let's begin by writing a simple assembly language program that will add and sub-tract two 16-bit numbers. If we look in Table A–1 in Appendix A we see that the only instruction that will add 16-bit numbers is *ADDD* and the only instruction that will subtract 16-bit numbers is *SUBD*. Therefore, one of our 16-bit numbers must be in *D* and the other must be in some memory location. We will use immediate addressing which means that the data are in the program immediately following the instruction opcode.

To write the assembly language program use any convenient editor such as *EDIT* and type in the program shown in Figure 1–7 and save it in the file chap1a.asm. We begin by defining two variables, *SUM* and *DIFF*, where we will store the answers. The assembler directive, *DW* (define word), will reserve 16 bits (2 bytes) and the 0 following *DW* will initialize the contents to zero. The statement *ORG $800* will force the address of *SUM* to be at the hex address $800. The statement *ORG $810* will cause the code for the program to begin at address $810.

```
; Example 1 - Chapter 1

        ORG  $800
SUM     DW      0
DIFF    DW      0
        ORG  $810
EX1
        LDD     #1234
        ADDD    #5678
        STD     SUM             ;add 1234+5678
        LDD     #5678
        SUBD    #1234
        STD     DIFF            ;subtract 5678-1234
        END
```

Figure 1–7   A 68HC12 Program to Add and Subtract Two 16-bit Numbers

The file chap1a.asm must now be assembled using a 68HC12 assembler. A convenient one to use is AS12 from Motorola, but any assembler will do. To use AS12 from a DOS prompt, type

```
as12 chap1a.asm >chap1a.lst
```

This will assemble the program shown in Figure 1–7 and produce the listing file, chap1a.lst, shown in Figure 1–8.

Note in Figure 1–8 that the machine code for all the instructions is displayed in hex on the left-hand side of the listing. The first column displays the address. Note that the address of *SUM* is $800 and the address of *DIFF* is $802. This is because *SUM* uses up 2 bytes. The program starts at address $810. The first instruction is *LDD #1234* which loads the decimal value 1234 into *D*. The machine code for this instruction is *cc 04 d2*. The byte *cc* is the opcode for this instruction and the 16-bit hex value 04d2 is the hex equivalent of the decimal number 1234 and is stored immediately following the opcode *cc*. The pound sign, #, in the assembly language instruction signifies immediate addressing.

The next instruction, *ADDD #5678*, will add the decimal value 5678 to the contents of *D*. Note that the opcode for *ADDD* is *c3* and the hex equivalent of 5678 is 162e and is stored immediately following the opcode *c3*. The instruction *STD SUM* will store the contents of *D*, which now contains the result of the addition, in the variable *SUM* at memory location $800. This is an example of the *extended* addressing mode in which the 16-bit address of the memory location ($0800) appears in the machine code of the instruction (7c 08 00).

The next three instructions behave in a similar fashion, first loading the decimal value 5678 into *D*, then subtracting the decimal value 1234 from *D*, and finally storing the difference in the variable *DIFF*.

```
                              ; Example 1 - Chapter 1
0800                              ORG $800
0800 00 00          SUM       DW      0
0802 00 00          DIFF      DW      0
0810                              ORG $810
                    EX1
0810 cc 04 d2                 LDD     #1234
0813 c3 16 2e                 ADDD    #5678
0816 7c 08 00                 STD     SUM       ;add 1234+5678
0819 cc 16 2e                 LDD     #5678
081c 83 04 d2                 SUBD    #1234
081f 7c 08 02                 STD     DIFF      ;subtract 5678-1234
                              END
```

Figure 1–8   The File chap1a.lst Produced by Assembling the Program in Figure 1–8

1.3.2   Downloading and Executing the Program

When you assembled the program in Figure 1–7, it produced not only the .LST listing file shown in Figure 1–8 but it also produced the .S19 file, chap1a.s19, shown in Figure 1–9.

This file contains information about the machine code shown at the left of Figure 1–8. Each line in Figure 1–9 begins with either S0, S1, or S9. The first line begins with S0 and contains header information. The last line begins with S9 and indicates that it is the last line in the file. All lines that begin with S1 are to be downloaded to the target evaluation board. The two characters following S1 represent an 8-bit byte whose value is the number of bytes to download from that line. This number is 07 in the second line of Figure 1–9 and is followed by 7 bytes (2 characters each). The first 2 bytes are the address 0800 (indicated in bold in Figure 1–9). This is followed by 4 bytes of 00 to be loaded into memory starting at address 0800. The last byte in the line (F0) is a checksum.

The third line in Figure 1–9 will download 16 data bytes representing the first 16 bytes of the machine code in Figure 1–8 and store them in memory starting at address 0810. Note that the total number of bytes downloaded from that line is $13 = 19. This includes 2 bytes for the address 0810, 16 data bytes, and 1 checksum. The fourth line in Figure 1–9 will download the last two bytes (08 02) of the machine code in Figure 1–8 starting at address 0820.

As an example of downloading this .S19 file into an evaluation board we will consider the M68HC12A4EVB evaluation board from Motorola. This board contains the MC68HC812A4 microcontroller together with 16 Kbytes of external RAM and 32 Kbytes of external EPROM. This external EPROM contains the D-Bug12 program from Motorola that we will use to download our code and execute the program. The evaluation board is connected to your PC through one of the serial COM ports.

To communicate with the evaluation board you need to execute some type of communications program on the PC. Any number of standard communications programs will do, but we have included one on the disk that comes with this book. The program is called HOST.EXE and it is a C++ program whose source listing is included on the disk. It can be used to quickly download .S19 files to your evaluation board. To use it, make sure that power is supplied to the evaluation board and that it is connected to one of the serial ports on your PC. Type *host* from the DOS prompt as shown in Figure 1–10. If you press the *<enter>* key (or the reset button on the evaluation board) you should get the > prompt. If not, you may not be connected to COM1. You can switch to COM2 by pressing function key F10 (and selecting 2).

```
S014000046696C653A206368617031612E61736D0A6A
S1070800000000000F0
S1130810CC04D2C3162E7C0800CC162E8304D27CC2
S10508200802C8
S9030000FC
```

Figure 1–9   The File chap1a.s19 Produced by Assembling the Program in Figure 1–8

Once you have the prompt, type *load*. This is a D-Bug 12 command that is waiting for you to download your .S19 file. To do this, press function key F6. You will be asked to enter the .s19 filename to download. Type `chap1a.s19` and press *<enter>*. The file will be downloaded as shown in Figure 1–10. You can verify that the bytes were downloaded by using the D-Bug 12 command *md* (memory display) as shown in Figure 1–11. In this case we display three rows of 16 bytes each. The first row starts at address $800 and the last row starts at address $820.

We can use the D-Bug 12 trace command *t* to execute one instruction at a time starting at address $810. The trace command will execute the instruction whose address is in the program counter, *PC*. We therefore need to make sure that the program counter is set to $810. The D-Bug 12 command *rd* (register display) will display the contents of all registers as shown in Figure 1–12. This shows the value of the program counter, *PC*, to be 0000. To change it to 810 use the D-Bug 12 command *rm* (register modify) as shown in Figure 1–12. The current value of *PC* will be displayed after which you can type 810. If you press *<enter>* the current value of the stack pointer, *SP*, will be displayed and you can change that value. Pressing *<enter>* will proceed through all of the registers. We will change only the program counter value so you can exit the *rm* command by typing a period followed by *<enter>*. Typing the

```
C:\WHYP\WHYP12\ASM>host

Terminal host...9600 baud
(Press F10 to check/change COM port)
(Press F6 to download .S19 file)
(Press F4 to download .S19 file with * handshake)
(Press <Esc> to exit HOST)


>load


Enter .s19 filename to download: chap1a.s19

Getting data...
S014000046696C653A206368617031612E61736D0A6A
S107080000000000F0
S1130810CC04D2C3162E7C0800CC162E8304D27CC2
S10508200802C8
S9030000FC
.
Finished downloading...*
>
```

Figure 1–10   Downloading a .S19 file Using HOST.EXE

```
>md 800 820

0800  00 00 00 00 - 52 00 80 02 - 09 00 28 18 - 90 00 83 00     ....R.....(.....
0810  CC 04 D2 C3 - 16 2E 7C 08 - 00 CC 16 2E - 83 04 D2 7C     ......|........|
0820  08 02 00 00 - 0C 00 40 00 - 42 00 08 00 - 10 00 0C 08     ......@.B.......
```

Figure 1–11   Displaying Memory Using the D-Bug 12 Command *md*

```
>rd

 PC     SP     X      Y     D = A:B    CCR = SXHI NZVC
0000   0A00   0000   0000     11:5C          1001 0000
>rm

PC=0000 810

SP=0A00 .

>rd

 PC     SP     X      Y     D = A:B    CCR = SXHI NZVC
0810   0A00   0000   0000     11:5C          1001 0000
>
```

Figure 1–12   Displaying and Changing the Contents of the Program Counter, PC

rd command again verifies that the program counter has been changed to 0810 as shown in Figure 1–12.

You can now single-step through each instruction by typing *t* (followed by <*enter*>) as shown in Figure 1–13. This trace command will execute the instruction whose address is in the program counter and then display the contents of all registers. Note that after executing the instruction *LDD #1234* at address $810 the value in *D* is $04D2 which is the hex equivalent of the decimal number 1234 (see Figure 1–8). Also note that the program counter has been incremented to $0813 which is the address of the next instruction, *ADDD #$162E*, which is displayed on the screen following the register values.

After stepping through each of the six instructions in Figure 1–8 as shown in Figure 1–13, the sum and difference values should be stored in the variables *SUM* and *DIFF* at addresses $800 and $802. You can verify this by using the D-Bug 12 command *mdw* (memory display word) as shown in Figure 1–14. Note that the sum $1B00 (decimal 6912) is stored at address $800 and the difference $115C (decimal 4444) is stored at address $802.

Let's review the program we wrote in Figure 1–7 to see how we might make it more useful. The purpose of the program was to add and subtract two 16-bit numbers. But the numbers we are adding and subtracting are built into the program using the immediate addressing mode. This is inconvenient because if we want to

```
>t

 PC      SP      X       Y       D = A:B     CCR = SXHI NZVC
 0813   0A00   0000    0000        04:D2            1001 0000
 0813   C3162E           ADDD    #$162E
>t

 PC      SP      X       Y       D = A:B     CCR = SXHI NZVC
 0816   0A00   0000    0000        1B:00            1001 0000
 0816   7C0800            STD    $0800
>t

 PC      SP      X       Y       D = A:B     CCR = SXHI NZVC
 0819   0A00   0000    0000        1B:00            1001 0000
 0819   CC162E           LDD     #$162E
>t

 PC      SP      X       Y       D = A:B     CCR = SXHI NZVC
 081C   0A00   0000    0000        16:2E            1001 0000
 081C   8304D2           SUBD    #$04D2
>t

 PC      SP      X       Y       D = A:B     CCR = SXHI NZVC
 081F   0A00   0000    0000        11:5C            1001 0000
 081F   7C0802            STD    $0802
>t

 PC      SP      X       Y       D = A:B     CCR = SXHI NZVC
 0822   0A00   0000    0000        11:5C            1001 0000
 0822   00               BGND
>
```

Figure 1–13   Single-Stepping through the Instructions in Figure 1–8

```
>mdw 800 810

0800   1B00 115C - 5200 8002 - 0900 2818 - 9000 8300     ...\R.....(.....
0810   CC04 D2C3 - 162E 7C08 - 00CC 162E - 8304 D27C     ......|........|

>
```

Figure 1–14   Displaying Memory Using the D-Bug 12 Command *mdw*

add and subtract different numbers we need to write a completely new program! We might consider storing the numbers to be added and subtracted in memory locations described by variables as we did for the answers *SUM* and *DIFF*. However, this raises the questions of where these variables should be and how will we get the values to be added and subtracted into these variables?

Since the operations we are trying to perform are addition and subtraction, perhaps we should think about writing two subroutines, *plus(a, b, s)* and *minus(a, b, d)* in which we pass in the parameters *a* and *b* and receive back the sum, $s = a + b$, from *plus* and the difference, $d = a - b$, from *minus*. But this now raises the question as to how we should pass the parameters to the subroutines. One possibility is to use registers. Some microprocessors have several general-purpose registers which would make this a viable option. However, as we have seen, the 68HC12 can use only the *D* register for 16-bit arithmetic operations. One of the operands must be in memory.

This gets us back to the idea of having both operands plus the answer in memory. But how can we do this without using named variable locations and in such a way that a subroutine can get at the data easily? One common way that programs pass data to and from subroutines is by way of a stack. We saw in Section 1.2 that the 68HC12 has a system stack whose top is pointed to by the stack pointer, *SP*. This stack is typically used to hold return addresses and to save register values during subroutine and interrupt calls. We will find it convenient to introduce a second stack, called a *data stack,* that will hold the data values we want to pass to and from subroutines. We will introduce such a stack for our addition and subtraction problem in the next chapter.

1.4 ADDRESSING MODES

Addressing modes determine the address where the data associated with instructions are located. This address is called the *effective address*. Examples of immediate addressing and extended addressing were illustrated in Figure 1–7. All of the 68HC12 addressing modes are listed in Table 1–3. Only the first six addressing modes in Table 1–3 are available on the 68HC11. (On the 68HC11 the relative addressing and indexed addressing use only 8-bit offsets.)

The 68HC12 has added the seven new addressing modes shown in the bottom half of Table 1–3. In addition, the 68HC12 allows 5-bit, 9-bit, and 16-bit constant offsets in the indexed addressing mode. The constant offset is added to *X*, *Y*, *SP*, or *PC* to compute the effective address. For example, if *X* contains the value $1234, then the instruction *LDD* -2,*X* will store the value in *D* at address $1234 minus 2 or $1232. This will store the contents of *A* at $1232 and the contents of *B* at $1233. Similarly, the instruction *JSR* 0,*Y* will jump to a subroutine at the address stored in *Y*.

The predecrement indexed addressing mode computes the effective address by first decrementing *X*, *Y*, or *SP* by a value of 1 to 8. For example, if *X* contains the value $1234, then the instruction *STAA 1,-X* will first decrement *X* by 1 to $1233 and then store the value of *A* at address $1233.

As a second example, consider the *MOVW* instruction which is of the form

```
MOVW source,dest
```

and moves a word (16-bits) from the effective address *source* to the effective address *dest*. (There is also a *MOVB* instruction which moves an 8-bit byte.) The addressing mode for *source* can be either immediate, extended, or indexed, and the addressing mode for *dest* can be either extended or indexed.

For example, suppose that *X* contains the value $1234 and the word $5678 is stored at address $1234 as shown in Figure 1–15. Then after executing the instruction *MOVW 0, X, 2,-X* the value at address $1234 (0,*X*) will be copied to address $1232

Table 1–3   68HC12 Addressing Modes

Addressing Mode	Description	Examples
Inherent	Data location is inherent in instruction	INX DECB
Immediate	Data immediately follow the opcode	LDAA #$2C LDD #$1234
Direct	Data are on page zero given by an 8-bit address ($00-$FF)	STAA $FC STD $34
Extended	Data are in memory given by a 16-bit address ($0000-$FFFF)	STAB $1234 STX $0848
Relative	Opcode is followed by an 8-bit or 16-bit relative offset from PC	BNE -$2B LBEQ $0452
Indexed (constant offset)	5-bit, 9-bit, or 16-bit constant offset from X, Y, SP, or PC	LDD -2,X JSR 0,Y
Indexed (predecrement)	Auto predecrement X, Y, or SP by 1–8	STAA 1,-X MOVW 0,X,2,-X
Indexed (preincrement)	Auto preincrement X, Y, or SP by 1–8	LDAB 1,+Y STD 2,+X
Indexed (postdecrement)	Auto postdecrement X, Y, or SP by 1–8	STD 2,X- LDAA 4,Y-
Indexed (postincrement)	Auto postincrement X, Y, or SP by 1–8	LDD 2,X+ STAA 1,X+
Indexed (accumulator offset)	Add contents of A, B, or D to X, Y, SP, or PC	ADDA B,X STX D,Y
Indexed-Indirect (16-bit offset)	Address of data located at 16-bit constant offset from X, Y, SP, or PC	LDAA [0,Y] JSR [0,Y]
Indexed-Indirect (D accumulator offset)	Address of data located at X, Y, SP, or PC plus the value in D	ADDA [D,X] JSR [D,Y]

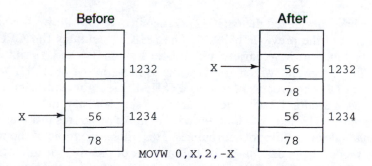

Figure 1–15   Effects of Executing the Instruction *MOVW 0,X,2,-X*

(2,-*X*) and *X* will now be equal to $1232 as shown in Figure 1–15. As we will see in the next chapter, this is equivalent to duplicating the top 16-bit element on a data stack.

The preincrement indexed addressing mode computes the effective address by first incrementing *X*, *Y*, or *SP* by a value of 1 to 8. For example, if *Y* contains the value $1234, then the instruction *LDAB 1,+Y* will first increment *Y* by 1 to $1235 and then load in to *B* the value at address $1235.

The postdecrement indexed addressing mode computes the effective address by using the value in *X*, *Y*, or *SP* (equivalent to *0,X*, for example) and then decrementing *X*, *Y*, or *SP* by a value of 1 to 8. For example, if *X* contains the value $1234, then the instruction *STD 2,X-* will store the value of *D* at address $1234 and then decrement *X* by 2 to $1232.

The postincrement indexed addressing mode computes the effective address by using the value in *X*, *Y*, or *SP* (equivalent to *0,X*, for example) and then incrementing *X*, *Y*, or *SP* by a value of 1 to 8. For example, if *X* contains the value $1234, then the instruction *LDD 2,X+* will load the value at address $1234 into *D* and then increment *X* by 2 to $1236.

The accumulator offset indexed addressing mode computes the effective address by adding the value of *A*, *B*, or *D* to *X*, *Y*, *SP*, or *PC*. For example, if *X* contains the value $1234 and *B* contains the value $12, then the instruction *ADDA B,X* will add the byte at address $1246 (*X+B*) to the value in *A* and leave the sum in *A*.

The 16-bit constant offset indexed indirect addressing mode adds a 16-bit constant offset to *X*, *Y*, *SP*, or *PC* to compute the address that contains the effective address. For example, if *Y* contains the value $1234 and if the value $5678 is stored at address $1234, then the instruction *LDAA [0,Y]* will load *A* with the byte at address $5678.

The *D* accumulator offset indexed indirect addressing mode adds the value in *D* to *X*, *Y*, *SP*, or *PC* to compute the address that contains the effective address. For example, consider the instruction *ADDA [D,X]*. If *X* contains the value $1234 and *D* contains the value $2345, then the value at $3579 ($1234+$2345) will contain the address of the byte that is added to accumulator *A*.

1.5 SUMMARY

In this chapter we have introduced the 68HC12 microcontroller and shown how it is an enhanced version of the previous 68HC11. The 68HC12 contains the CPU12 microprocessor together with a variety of on-board memory and peripheral resources. The CPU12 registers, which are the same as those in the 68HC11, were described in Section 1.2. The process of writing a 68HC12 assembly language program was illustrated in Section 1.3 with the example of a simple program to add and subtract 16-bit numbers. This led us to look for ways to make programs more useful by writing reusable code in the form of subroutines. This will be the topic of the next chapter in which we develop a data stack for the purpose of passing parameters to and from our 68HC12 subroutines. This will lead us to the development of our stack-based programming language, WHYP.

EXERCISES

Exercise 1.1

a. Draw a memory map for a 68HC812A4 operating in the single-chip mode indicating the starting and stopping addresses of the I/O register block, the internal RAM, and the internal EEPROM.

b. Draw a memory map for a 68HC912B32 operating in the single-chip mode indicating the starting and stopping addresses of the I/O register block, the internal RAM, the internal EEPROM, and the internal flash memory.

Exercise 1.2

Consider the following 68HC12 code that is in the file example2.asm.

```
;          Example 2 - Chapter 1
           ORG  $800
JACK       DW        $1234
JILL       DW        $5678
MARY       DW        $0808
JOE        DW        $080A
           ORG  $810
EX2
           LDD       JACK
           LDY       MARY
           STD       0,Y
           STD       6,Y
           LDD       JILL
           LDX       JOE
           STD       0,X
           STD       2,X
           END
```

a. After these eight instructions are executed, what will be the contents of the 16 bytes from $800–$80F?

b. Assemble the file example2.asm, make a .LST file, and download the .S19 file to the 68HC12.

c. Change the program counter, *PC*, to $810 and single-step the eight instructions using the trace command, *T*.

d. Use the memory display command, *MD*, to view the contents of memory locations $800–$80F. Compare these with your answers in part (a).

Exercise 1.3

Consider the following 68HC12 code that is in the file example3.asm.

```
;          Example 3 - Chapter 1
           ORG  $800
JACK       DW        $ABCD
JILL       DW        $7777
MARY       DW        $0808


           ORG  $810
EX2
           LDD       JACK
           LDX       JILL
           LDY       MARY
           STD       2,Y+
           STX       2,Y+
           STX       2,Y+
           STD       2,Y+
           END
```

a. After these seven instructions are executed, what will be the contents of the 16 bytes from $800–$80F? Indicate any bytes whose value you may not know.

b. Assemble the file example3.asm, make a .LST file, and download the .S19 file to the 68HC12.

c. Change the program counter, *PC*, to $810 and single-step the seven instructions using the trace command, *T*.

d. Use the memory display command, *MD*, to view the contents of memory locations $800–$80F. Compare these with your answers in part (a).

Exercise 1.4

Consider the following 68HC12 code that is in the file example4.asm.

```
;           Example 4 - Chapter 1
            ORG  $800
JACK        DW         $1122
JILL        DW         $3344
MARY        DW         $0810


            ORG  $810
EX2
            LDD        JACK
            LDY        JILL
            LDX        MARY
            STD        2,-X
            STY        2,-X
            END
```

a. After these five instructions are executed, what will be the contents of the 16 bytes from $800–$80F? Indicate any bytes whose value you may not know.

b. Assemble the file example4.asm, make a .LST file, and download the .S19 file to the 68HC12.

c. Change the program counter, *PC*, to $810 and single-step the five instructions using the trace command, *T*.

d. Use the memory display command, *MD*, to view the contents of memory locations $800–$80F. Compare these with your answers in part (a).

Exercise 1.5

Consider the following 68HC12 code that is in the file example5.asm.

```
;           Example 5 - Chapter 1
            ORG  $800
MARY        DW         $0810

            ORG  $810
EX2
            LDD        #$2468
            LDX        MARY
            STD        2,-X
            MOVW       0,X,2,-X
            END
```

    a. Indicate what happens when each of these four instructions is executed.

    b. Assemble the file `example5.asm`, make a .LST file, and download the .S19 file to the 68HC12.

    c. Change the program counter, *PC*, to $810 and single-step the four instructions using the trace command, *T*.

    d. Use the memory display command, *MD*, to view the contents of memory locations $800–$80F after each of the last two instructions is executed. Compare these results with your answers in part (a).

Exercise 1.6

Consider the following 68HC12 code that is in the file `example6.asm`.

```
;           Example 6 - Chapter 1
            ORG $800
MARY        DW          $0810

            ORG $810
EX2
            LDD         #$2468
            LDX         MARY
            STD         2,-X
            LDD         #$1369
            STD         2,-X
            MOVW        2,X,2,-X
            END
```

    a. Indicate what happens when each of these six instructions is executed.

    b. Assemble the file `example6.asm`, make a .LST file, and download the .S19 file to the 68HC12.

    c. Change the program counter, *PC*, to $810 and single-step the four instructions using the trace command, *T*.

    d. Use the memory display command, *MD*, to view the contents of memory locations $800–$80F after each of the *STD* and *MOVW* instructions are executed. Compare these results with your answers in part (a).

Exercise 1.7

Consider the following 68HC12 code that is in the file `example7.asm`.

```
;           Example 7 - Chapter 1
            ORG $800
MARY        DW          $0810

            ORG $810
EX2
            LDD         #$1234
            LDX         MARY
            STD         2,-X
            STD         2,-X
            LDD         0,X
            STAB        0,X
            STAA        1,X
            END
```

    a. Indicate what happens when each of these seven instructions is executed.

    b. Assemble the file `example7.asm`, make a .LST file, and download the .S19 file to the 68HC12.

    c. Change the program counter, *PC*, to $810 and single-step the seven instructions using the trace command, *T*.

    d. Use the memory display command, *MD*, to view the contents of memory locations $800–$80F after each of the *STD*, the *STAB*, and the *STAA* instructions are executed. Compare these results with your answers in part (a).

Exercise 1.8

Consider the following 68HC12 code that is in the file `example8.asm`.

```
;            Example 8 - Chapter 1
             ORG $800
MARY         DW          $0810

             ORG $810
EX2
             LDD         #$1234
             LDX         MARY
             STD         2,-X
             LDD         #$5678
             STD         2,-X
             MOVW        0,X,2,-X
             MOVW        4,X,2,X
             MOVW        0,X,4,X
             END
```

    a. Indicate what happens when each of these eight instructions is executed.

    b. Assemble the file `example8.asm`, make a .LST file, and download the .S19 file to the 68HC12.

    c. Change the program counter, *PC*, to $810 and single-step the eight instructions using the trace command, *T*.

    d. Use the memory display command, *MD*, to view the contents of memory locations $800–$80F after each of the *STD* and *MOVW* instructions are executed. Compare these results with your answers in part (a).

2

Subroutines and Stacks

In the last chapter we saw that it would be useful to write subroutines for our addition and subtraction problem in which we could pass parameters to the subroutines on a data stack. We will show how we can do this in this chapter. We begin by looking at the 68HC12 system stack in Section 2.1 and the instructions used to push and pull (pop) values from the stack. In Section 2.2 we will see how 68HC12 subroutines work and how the system stack is used to save subroutine return addresses. Then in Section 2.3 we will show how to create a data stack using index register X as the stack pointer. This data stack can be used to pass parameters to subroutines. Finally in Section 2.4 we will describe a method for making calls to subroutines interactive. This will involve saving the names of subroutines on the PC and sending the address of the subroutine to the 68HC12 when its name is typed on the keyboard. This will lead directly to the way in which our interactive programming language WHYP works.

2.1 THE SYSTEM STACK

The stack is a group of memory locations in which temporary data can be stored. A stack is different from any other collection of memory locations in that data are put on and taken from the *top* of the stack. The process is similar to stacking dinner plates on top of one another, where the last plate put on the stack is always the first one removed from it. We sometimes refer to this as a *Last-In-First-Out* or LIFO stack. In this section we will describe the 68HC12 system stack. In Section 2.3 we will create our own data stack.

The memory address corresponding to the top of the stack (the last full location) is stored in the stack pointer, *SP*. When data are put on the stack, the stack pointer is *decremented*. This means that the stack grows *backward* in memory. As data values are put on the stack, they are put into memory locations with lower addresses. Data can be put on and taken off the stack using the *push* and *pull* instructions given in Table 2–1.

When pushing one of the 8-bit registers, *A*, *B*, or *CCR*, on the stack, the following operation takes place:

1. The stack pointer, *SP*, is decremented by 1.
2. The contents of the 8-bit register are stored at the address in *SP*.

When pushing one of the 16-bit registers, *D*, *X*, or *Y*, on the stack, the following operation takes place:

1. The stack pointer, *SP*, is decremented by 2.
2. The contents of the 16-bit register are stored at the address in *SP*. (The high byte is stored at *SP* and the low byte is stored at *SP*+1.)

When pulling (sometimes referred to as popping), one of the 8-bit registers, *A*, *B*, or *CCR*, off the stack, the following operation takes place:

1. The value at the address stored in *SP* is loaded into the 8-bit register.
2. The stack pointer is incremented by 1.

Table 2–1 Push and Pull Instructions

Mnemonic	Function
PSHA	Push A
PSHB	Push B
PSHC	Push CCR
PSHD	Push D
PSHX	Push X
PSHY	Push Y
PULA	Pull A
PULB	Pull B
PULC	Pull CCR
PULD	Pull D
PULX	Pull X
PULY	Pull Y

> **68HC11 Note:**
>
> When values are pushed on the stack in the 68HC12, the stack pointer is first decremented and then the data are stored at the new location of *SP*. However, in the 68HC11 the data are first stored at the current *SP* location and then the stack pointer is decremented. Thus, in the 68HC12 the stack pointer points to the last full location on the stack, while in the 68HC11 it points to the next free location on the stack.

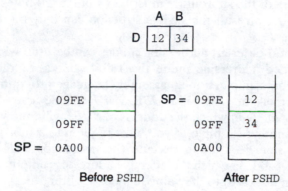

Figure 2–1   Pushing D on the Stack

When pulling one of the 16-bit registers, *D*, *X*, or *Y*, off the stack, the following operation takes place:

1. The value at the address stored in *SP* is loaded into the 16-bit register. (The byte at *SP* is loaded into the high byte and the byte at *SP*+1 is loaded into the low byte.)
2. The stack pointer is incremented by 2.

As an example, suppose that the stack pointer, *SP*, contains the value $0A00 and the *D* register contains the value $1234. After executing the instruction *PSHD* the value $1234 will be stored at address $09FE as shown in Figure 2–1. If the two instructions *PULB* and *PULA* are now executed in that order, then *B* will end up containing $12, *A* will end up containing $34, and the stack pointer, *SP*, will contain $0A00 again.

2.2   SUBROUTINES

A subroutine is a segment of code that is normally written to perform a particular function or task. A subroutine is called by executing a *JSR* (jump to subroutine) or *BSR* (branch to subroutine) instruction. A subroutine is exited by executing a *return* *from subroutine* (*RTS*) instruction. This will cause the program to return to the instruction following the *JSR* or *BSR* instruction that called the subroutine.*

The computer knows where to go when an *RTS* instruction is executed because it stored the return address on the stack when the *JSR* or *BSR* instruction was executed. The *RTS* instruction just pops the value on top of the stack into the program counter.

The *BSR* instruction uses relative addressing. It is a 2-byte instruction in which the second byte is a relative (two's complement) offset that gets added to the address of the next instruction to compute the subroutine address. This means that the address of the subroutine must be within ±128 bytes from the location of the *BSR* call. As a result the *BSR* instruction can only be used when calling nearby subroutines.

Several different addressing modes can be used with the *JSR* instruction. In the extended addressing mode the 16-bit address of the subroutine follows the opcode. For example, if in an assembly language program the label of a subroutine is *SUB1*, then the instruction *JSR SUB1* will be assembled using this extended addressing mode in which the address of *SUB1* will follow the *JSR* opcode.

As another example, if you want to jump to a subroutine whose address is in index register *Y*, you can execute the instruction *JSR 0,Y*. This is an indexed addressing mode in which the effective address is computed by adding a signed 5-bit offset (0 in this case) to the value in index register *Y*.

To see how subroutine calls work, type in the example program shown in Figure 2–2 and save it in a file called chap2a.asm. Assemble the program using the steps described in Section 1.3.1 to obtain the listing file shown in Figure 2–3 and the .S19 file chap2a.s19.

This program firsts jumps to subroutine *SUB1* at address $809. This subroutine loads *D* with the hex value $1234 and then jumps to subroutine *SUB2* address $810. This subroutine transfers the contents of *D* to *X* and then returns to address $80f

```
; Example 2 - Chapter 2

        ORG  $800
EX2
        JSR     SUB1
        LDD     #$5678
        JSR     SUB2
SUB1
        LDD     #$1234
        JSR     SUB2
        RTS
SUB2
        TFR     D,X
        RTS
```

Figure 2–2   Example Illustrating Subroutine Calls

*The 68HC12 also has a *CALL* instruction that calls a subroutine in expanded memory. To return from such a subroutine, one uses the *RTC* (return from call) instruction. We will not use the *CALL* and *RTC* instructions in this book.

```
                              ; Example 2.1 - Chapter 2

0800                                  ORG    $800
                       EX2
0800  16 08 09                        JSR    SUB1
0803  cc 56 78                        LDD    #$5678
0806  16 08 10                        JSR    SUB2
                       SUB1
0809  cc 12 34                        LDD    #$1234
080c  16 08 10                        JSR    SUB2
080f  3d                              RTS
                       SUB2
0810  b7 45                           TFR    D,X
0812  3d                              RTS
```

Figure 2–3   The Listing File, *chap2a.lst*

which is the statement following the call to *SUB2* in *SUB1*. This itself is another *RTS* instruction that will return to address $803 in the main program.

To watch all this happen, download the file chap2a.s19 to the 68HC12 evaluation board following the steps described in Section 1.3.2. You can verify and view the downloaded instructions by using the D-Bug 12 command *asm* (assembler/ disassembler) as shown in Figure 2–4. Pressing *<enter>* goes from one instruction to the next. Type a period (followed by *<enter>*) to exit the *asm* command.

To single-step through the instructions shown in Figure 2–3, set the program counter to $800 using the *rm* command as described in Section 1.3.2. Then you can step through the instructions using the *t* command as shown in Figure 2–5. Note that when the *JSR SUB1* instruction at location $800 is executed, the program jumps to address $809 and the stack pointer is decremented by two because the return address was pushed on the stack. The next two instructions will load the value $1234 into *D* and then jump to subroutine *SUB2* at address $810. At this point the value of *SP* is $09FC because two return addresses are now on the stack ($803 and $80F). The instruction at address $810 will transfer the contents of *D* to *X* and then the *RTS* instruction at address $812 will return to address $80F by popping that address from the stack into the program counter.

```
>asm 800

0800   160809      JSR   $0809                    >
0803   CC5678      LDD   #$5678                   >
0806   160810      JSR   $0810                    >
0809   CC1234      LDD   #$1234                   >
080C   160810      JSR   $0810                    >
080F   3D          RTS                            >
0810   B745        TFR   D,X                      >
0812   3D          RTS                            >.
```

Figure 2–4   Using the D-Bug12 *asm* Command

```
>rd

 PC    SP     X       Y      D = A:B    CCR = SXHI NZVC
0800  0A00   0000    0000     00:00           1001 0000
>t

 PC    SP     X       Y      D = A:B    CCR = SXHI NZVC
0809  09FE   0000    0000     00:00           1001 0000
0809  CC1234         LDD    #$1234
>t

 PC    SP     X       Y      D = A:B    CCR = SXHI NZVC
080C  09FE   0000    0000     12:34           1001 0000
080C  160810         JSR    $0810
>t

 PC    SP     X       Y      D = A:B    CCR = SXHI NZVC
0810  09FC   0000    0000     12:34           1001 0000
0810  B745           TFR    D,X
>t

 PC    SP     X       Y      D = A:B    CCR = SXHI NZVC
0812  09FC   1234    0000     12:34           1001 0000
0812  3D             RTS
>t

 PC    SP     X       Y      D = A:B    CCR = SXHI NZVC
080F  09FE   1234    0000     12:34           1001 0000
080F  3D             RTS
>t

 PC    SP     X       Y      D = A:B    CCR = SXHI NZVC
0803  0A00   1234    0000     12:34           1001 0000
0803  CC5678         LDD    #$5678
>t

 PC    SP     X       Y      D = A:B    CCR = SXHI NZVC
0806  0A00   1234    0000     56:78           1001 0000
0806  160810         JSR    $0810
>t

 PC    SP     X       Y      D = A:B    CCR = SXHI NZVC
0810  09FE   1234    0000     56:78           1001 0000
0810  B745           TFR    D,X
>t

 PC    SP     X       Y      D = A:B    CCR = SXHI NZVC
0812  09FE   5678    0000     56:78           1001 0000
0812  3D             RTS
>t

 PC    SP     X       Y      D = A:B    CCR = SXHI NZVC
0809  0A00   5678    0000     56:78           1001 0000
0809  CC1234         LDD    #$1234
>
```

Figure 2–5 Single-Stepping the Instructions in Figure 2–3

```
; subroutine example
subname
        pshb                ; save B
        pshx                ; save X
        ----
        ----                ; instructions that
        ----                ; change B and X
        ----
        ----
        pulx                ; restore X
        pulb                ; restore B
        rts
```

Figure 2–6   Saving and Restoring Registers in a Subroutine

The *RTS* instruction at address $80F will now return to address $803 by popping this address from the stack into the program counter. The instruction at address $803 will load the value $5678 into *D* and then the instruction at address $806 will jump to subroutine *SUB2* at address $810 pushing its return address ($809) on the stack. This time a different value in *D* will be transferred to *X* and the *RTS* instruction at address $812 will this time return to address $809. At this point the stack pointer is back at its initial value of $0A00. The program needs to stop here because we are at the beginning of subroutine *SUB1* and we did not get here with a *JSR* instruction. Therefore, no return address is on the stack, so if we continue to single-step instructions, the *RTS* instruction will try to pop a nonexistent return address from the stack.

A program segment that calls a subroutine may be using a certain register, say *B*, for a particular purpose, such as a counter. If the subroutine changes the value of *B*, then an error will occur in the calling program. To prevent this from happening a subroutine should save the values of registers that it modifies by pushing them on the stack at the beginning of the subroutine. Then they must be popped from the stack, in reverse order, at the end of the subroutine before the *RTS* instruction is executed. It is important to remember that the return address is on the stack and this is the address that is popped by the *RTS* instruction. Therefore, the same number of bytes must be popped from the stack at the end of a subroutine as were pushed onto the stack at the beginning of the subroutine. The structure of a typical subroutine is shown in Figure 2–6.

2.3   A DATA STACK

In Figure 2–1 we saw how the instruction *PSHD* would push the contents of *D* onto the system stack. We would like to make our own data stack that we can use to pass parameters to subroutines. We will use the index register *X* as a stack pointer. To push the value in *D* onto this data stack we need to first decrement *X* by 2 and then store the value of *D* at the new memory location pointed to by *X*. The auto predecrement indexed addressing mode allows us to do this in a single instruction. Thus, the instruction

```
STD 2,-X
```

will push *D* onto our data stack as shown in Figure 2–7.

To pop the value on the data stack shown in Figure 2–7 into *Y* we can use the instruction

```
LDY 2,X+
```

which uses the auto postincrement indexed addressing mode. This instruction first loads *Y* with the value pointed to by *X* (at address $096E in Figure 2–7) and then increments *X* by 2. We will always push and pop only 16-bit values on our data stack. Thus, from a logical point of view we can think of our stack as being 16 bits wide.

We are now in a position to write subroutines that will expect certain items on the data stack and leave results on the same data stack. Suppose we want to add the top two (16-bit) items on the data stack and replace them with the 16-bit sum. We can indicate this with a "stack picture" of the form (*before--after*) in which *before* is a list of items on the stack (top of the stack to the right) *before* the subroutine is called, and *after* is a list of items on the stack *after* the subroutine is called. For example, the stack picture for a subroutine that adds two 16-bit numbers, *n1* and *n2*, and leaves the sum, *n3* on the data stack can be written as

```
( n1 n2 -- n3 )       where n3 = n1 + n2
```

The subroutine PLUS shown in Figure 2–8 will do this.

The execution of each instruction in Figure 2–8 and its effect on the data stack is shown in Figure 2–9 where the width of the data stack is 16 bits. It is assumed that the two numbers $162E and $04D2 have been pushed on the data stack before the subroutine *PLUS* is called. The first instruction, *LDD 2,X+*, will load the value on top of the stack (pointed to by *X*), $04D2, into *D* and then increment *X* by 2. *X* is now pointing to the value $162E which is now on top of the stack. The fact that the value $04D2 is still in its old location is immaterial. The top of the stack is always

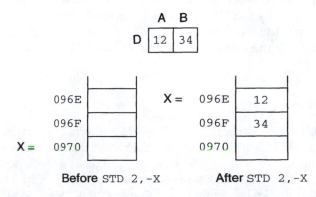

Figure 2–7 Using *X* as a Stack Pointer for a Data Stack

```
;            + ( n1 n2 -- n1+n2 )
PLUS
             LDD     2,X+
             ADDD    0,X
             STD     0,X
             RTS
```

Figure 2–8   A Subroutine to Add Two Numbers on the Data Stack

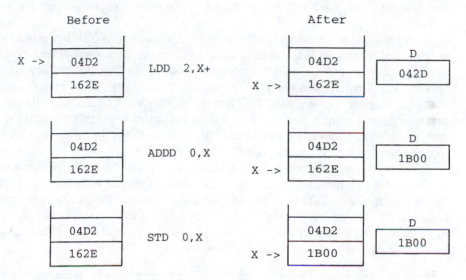

Figure 2–9   Executing the Instructions in Figure 2–8

pointed to by X and any memory locations at lower memory addresses are no longer considered to be on the stack.

The second instruction in Figure 2–9, *ADDD 0,X*, will add the value pointed to by X, $162E, to the current value in D, $04D2, and leave the sum, $1B00, in D. The third instruction in Figure 2–9 will store the value in D, $1B00, at the memory location pointed to by X. It replaces the value $162E and becomes the only value left on the stack. Thus, the two original values on the data stack, $162E and $04D2, have been replaced by their sum, $1B00.

A similar subroutine, *MINUS*, shown in Figure 2–10 will expect two numbers, *n1* and *n2* on the data stack. *n2* is on the top of the stack. The subroutine will subtract *n2* from *n1* and leave the difference on the stack. Note that initially X is pointing to *n2* on top of the stack. The instruction *LDD 2,X* will load the value of *n1* at $X+2$ into D. The instruction *SUBD 2,X+* will subtract the value at X (*n2*) from the value in D (*n1*) and leave the difference in D. The value of X will then be incremented by 2 so that it is now pointing to the value *n1* on the data stack. The last instruction, *STD 0,X*, will store the value in D in the address pointed to by X. That is,

```
;           - ( n1 n2 -- n1-n2 )
MINUS
        LDD      2,X
        SUBD     2,X+
        STD      0,X
        RTS
```

Figure 2–10   A Subroutine to Subtract Two Numbers on the Data Stack

the difference, *n1* − *n2*, will replace the value of *n1* as the only value left on the data stack.

We have now developed subroutines, *PLUS* and *MINUS*, that expect values on the data stack and leave their answer on the same data stack. There is still the question of how the values get on the data stack in the first place. They could get there in any number of ways. For example, the program shown in Figure 2–11 consists of a main program called *EX2* and the subroutine *PLUS*. The main program first sets the data stack pointer, *X*, and then uses index register *Y* to push the decimal values 5678 and 1234 on the data stack. It then jumps to the subroutine *PLUS* to do the addition and finally pops the sum back into *Y*.

It may seem as if we haven't progressed very far from the similar example in Chapter 1 in which the values to be added were stored as immediate values in the program. After all, they are still immediate values in the main program in Figure 2–11. However, the subroutine *PLUS* is normally called after the values to be added have been pushed on the data stack by other subroutines. This will become apparent in succeeding chapters.

```
; Example 2.2 - Chapter 2          File: chap2b.asm
        ORG      $800
EX2
        LDX      #$0970      ;set the data stack pointer
        LDY      #5678
        STY      2,-X        ;push 5678 on data stack
        LDY      #1234
        STY      2,-X        ;push 1234 on data stack
        JSR      PLUS        ;add them
        LDY      2,X+        ;pop sum into Y


PLUS
        LDD      2,X+
        ADDD     0,X
        STD      0,X
        RTS
```

Figure 2–11   A Program to Call the Subroutine *plus*

There is yet another way that data can be pushed onto the data stack—and that is directly from the PC keyboard in an interactive manner. We will describe how this can be done in the following section.

2.4 MAKING SUBROUTINES INTERACTIVE

Let's assume that the subroutines *PLUS* and *MINUS* shown in Figures 2–8 and 2–10 have been assembled and stored in memory in the 68HC12. Now suppose that we write a C++ program that will be executed on the PC. In this C++ program we will maintain a dictionary of subroutine names and their addresses. We don't have to use the usual kinds of subroutine names that must begin with letters but can use any characters we want. For example, we will call the subroutine *PLUS+* and the sub-routine *MINUS−*. If we type the name of the subroutine (e.g., +) the program will send the address of *PLUS* to the 68HC12 over the serial line. A small kernel pro-gram running on the 68HC12 will read this address and jump to the subroutine at that address. Therefore, to execute the subroutine *PLUS* we simply type + on the keyboard and press *<enter>*. To execute the subroutine *MINUS* we would just type − on the keyboard and press *<enter>*.

The programming language WHYP (pronounced "whip") that we will develop in this book works in just this way. WHYP stands for *Words* to *Help You Program* and consists of a collection of 68HC12 subroutines each of which is given a name (word). Over 125 different subroutines are initially stored in the 68HC12 and a dic-tionary containing their names and addresses is maintained in a C++ program run-ning on the PC. When you type any of these subroutine names, its address is sent to the 68HC12 which immediately executes the subroutine.

The next question is how do we get data values pushed onto our data stack? Suppose we type the number 1234 on the keyboard and press *<enter>*. The C++ program will first search the dictionary to see if 1234 is the name of one of the sub-routines in the 68HC12. In this case it isn't so it will then check to see if it is a valid number in the current base. The base can be either decimal or hex. The default is decimal, but you can change to hex by typing *hex*. (You switch back to decimal by typing *decimal.*) In this case 1234 is a valid decimal number and so WHYP pushes this number onto the data stack. It does this by first sending the address of a sub-routine called *TPUSH* to the 68HC12 followed by the number 1234. When the subroutine *TPUSH* is executed, it reads the number 1234 from the serial port and pushes it onto the data stack.

Therefore, if we run WHYP and type

```
1234 5678 +
```

and press *<enter>*, first 1234 will be pushed on the data stack, then 5678 will be pushed on the data stack, and then the subroutine *PLUS* will be executed, leaving the sum on the data stack. The WHYP word "dot" (.), just a single period, will display the value on the top of the data stack and pop the value from the stack.

Therefore, if you type

```
1234 5678 + .
```

the sum 6912 will be displayed on the screen.

If you are using the M68HC12A4EVB evaluation board from Motorola, you can try this by loading WHYP12.S19 into your evaluation board using HOST.EXE and executing the program starting at address $4000. (To see how to load WHYP into other evaluation boards, see Appendix C.) Press <Esc> to exit HOST and then execute WHYP12.EXE from the DOS prompt by just typing *WHYP12* followed by <*enter*>. Make sure that the files WHYP12.HED and WHYP12.CFG are in the subdirectory containing WHYP12.EXE.

A sample session of using WHYP in this interactive mode is shown in Figure 2–12. The entries shown in boldface are what you type. The WHYP prompt is *ok*. The WHYP word .*S* will display the contents of the data stack nondestructively. That is, all of the values remain on the stack. Note that WHYP words are case insensitive; thus, .*S* and .*s* are the same WHYP word.

```
>g 4000

Exiting HOST

C:\WHYP\WHYP12>whyp12
Using WHYP12.HED
Communicating with COM1
68HC12 WHYP12 - Version 4.6
Press <Esc> or type BYE to exit
ok
1234 5678 + . 6912 ok
5678 1234 - . 4444 ok
1234 5678 + hex . 1b00 ok
decimal ok
5678 1234 - hex . 115c ok
1234 5678 .s
S:[2] 1234 5678 ok
+ .s
S:[1] 68ac ok
```

Figure 2–12   A Sample Interactive Session Using WHYP

2.5 STACK MANIPULATION WORDS

We saw in the previous section that WHYP can be used to execute 68HC12 subroutines, in the form of WHYP words, interactively. The WHYP words expect certain items on the data stack before the word is called and leave other words on the data stack after the word (subroutine) is executed. It is sometimes necessary to move the items on the stack around so they are in the proper order before a particular word is called. WHYP has a number of stack manipulation words to make this easy to do.

For example, the word *DUP* will duplicate the top element on the data stack as shown in Figure 2–13. The 68HC12 subroutine shown in Figure 2–14 will perform this operation. Note that it consists of a single *MOVW* (move word) instruction.

As described in Section 1.4 the *MOVW* instruction (there is also a *MOVB*, move byte, instruction) is of the form

```
movw    source,dest
```

where *source* and *dest* can be one of any number of addressing modes. In Figure 2–14 the source operand is *0,X* which means that the data are at the memory location pointed to by X. This data word (162E in Figure 2–13) is moved to the memory location described by the operand *2,-X* which means decrement *X* by 2 and then store the data at this new value of *X*. This produces the *DUP* operation shown in Figure 2–13.

The WHYP word *SWAP* will swap the top two elements on the data stack as shown in Figure 2–15. This can be implemented with the 68HC12 subroutine shown in Figure 2–16. Note that *D* is first loaded with the item on top of the stack, *w2*. Then the item at location *X+2*, (*w1*) is moved to the location at *X*. Finally, the value in *D* (*w2*) is moved to the location at *X+2*.

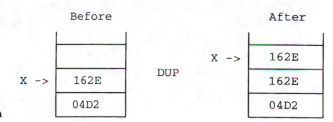

Figure 2–13   The DUP Operation

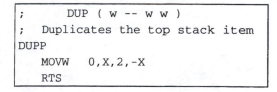

Figure 2–14   68HC12 Code for DUP

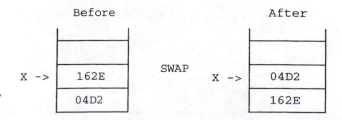

Figure 2–15   The SWAP Operation

```
;       SWAP ( w1 w2 -- w2 w1 )
; Exchange top two stack items.
SWAP
    LDD 0,X
    MOVW 2,X,0,X
    STD 2,X
    RTS
```

Figure 2–16 68HC12 Code for SWAP

The WHYP word DROP shown in Figure 2–17 discards the top element on the stack by incrementing the data stack pointer by 2 as shown in Figure 2–18.

As a final example, the WHYP word *OVER* copies the second element on the stack to the top as shown in Figure 2–19. Note that it can be implemented with the single 68HC12 instruction

```
movw    2,X,2,-X
```

as shown in Figure 2–20. The source operand, *2,X*, points to the second stack item, *w1*, and the destination operand, *2,-X*, pushes this item on top of the stack.

A list of all the WHYP stack manipulation words is given in Box 2–1. Using the examples in Figures 2–13 through 2–20, you should be able to write the 68HC12 subroutines for all the words in Box 2–1 (see Exercises 2.7 and 2.8). The words *2DUP*, *2SWAP*, *2DROP*, and *2OVER* are used primarily when dealing with 32-bit, or double, numbers. Double numbers use two 16-bit stack locations and will be described in detail in Chapter 3 (see Section 3.1.2).

Notice that the word *FLIP* operates on a single 16-bit value on top of the stack and exchanges its upper and lower byte. The 68HC12 subroutine for FLIP is shown in Figure 2–21.

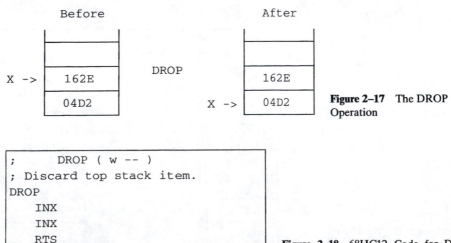

Figure 2–17 The DROP Operation

```
;       DROP ( w -- )
; Discard top stack item.
DROP
    INX
    INX
    RTS
```

Figure 2–18 68HC12 Code for DROP

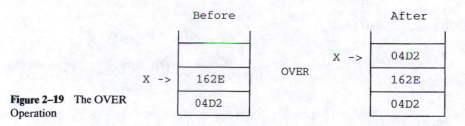

Figure 2–19   The OVER Operation

```
;         OVER ( w1 w2 -- w1 w2 w1 )
;  Copy second stack item to top
OVER
     MOVW  2,X,2,-X
     RTS
```

Figure 2–20   68HC12 Code for OVER

```
;         FLIP     ( ab -- ba )      flip bytes
FLIP
     LDD    0,X
     STAB   0,X               ;bb
     STAA   1,X               ;ba
     RTS
```

Figure 2–21   68HC12 Code for FLIP

Box 2–1   WHYP Stack Manipulation Words

DUP   (n-- n n)
Duplicates the top element on the stack.

SWAP   (n1 n2 — n2 n1)
Interchanges the top two elements on the stack.

DROP   (n --)
Removes the top element from the stack.

OVER   (n1 n2 -- n1 n2 n1)
Duplicates the second element on the stack.

TUCK   (n1 n2 -- n2 n1 n2)
Duplicates the top element on the stack under the second element.
This is equivalent to SWAP OVER.

ROT   (n1 n2 n3 -- n2 n3 n1)
Rotates the top three elements on the stack. The third element becomes the first element.

-ROT   (n1 n2 n3 -- n3 n1 n2)
Rotates the top three elements on the stack backwards.
The top element is rotated to third place.

(*continued*)

Box 2–1 *(continued)*

NIP   (n1 n2 -- n2)
Removes the second element from the stack. This is equivalent to SWAP DROP.

2DUP   (n1 n2 -- n1 n2 n1 n2)
Duplicates the top two elements on the stack.

2SWAP   (n1 n2 n3 n4 -- n3 n4 n1 n2)
Interchanges the top two numbers on the stack with the third and fourth numbers on the stack.

2DROP   (n1 n2 --)
Removes the top two elements from the stack.

2OVER   (n1 n2 n3 n4 -- n1 n2 n3 n4 n1 n2)
Duplicates the fourth and third elements on the stack.

PICK   (n1 -- n2)
Duplicates the value at position n1 from the top of the stack (not counting n1). The top of the stack corresponds to n1 equal to 0.
0 PICK is the same as DUP
1 PICK is the same as OVER

ROLL   (n --)
Rotates the value at position n (not counting n) to the top of the stack. n must be greater than 0.
1 ROLL is the same as SWAP
2 ROLL is the same as ROT

FLIP   (ab -- ba)
Exchanges the bytes of the top element on the stack.

You should test all of the words in Box 2–1 by running WHYP, putting three numbers on the data stack by typing in their values, and then using the WHYP word *.s* to see what is on the stack. Recall that the WHYP word *.s* will display the contents of the data stack without removing the elements on the stack. An example of testing some of these words is shown in the interactive WHYP session shown in Figure 2–22.

The WHYP word *SP@* (-- *a*) (pronounced "S-P-fetch") will push the current value of the data stack pointer (*X*) onto the data stack. The WHYP word *SP!* (*a* --) (pronounced "S-P-store") will set the data stack pointer to the value that is currently on the data stack. The 68HC12 subroutines for these two words are shown in Figure 2–23. Note that the *SP* in these words refers to the *data stack* pointer, and not the 68HC12 system stack pointer, *SP*, of the same name. As we will see in the next section the 68HC12 system stack is the same as the WHYP *return stack,* for which we use *RP* for the name of the stack pointer.

```
C:\WHYP\WHYP12\>whyp12
Using WHYP12.HED
Communicating with COM1
68HC12 WHYP12 - Version 4.6
Press <Esc> or type BYE to exit
ok
2 5 7 .s
S:[3] 2 5 7 ok
swap .s
S:[3] 2 7 5 ok
rot .s
S:[3] 7 5 2 ok
tuck .s
S:[4] 7 2 5 2 ok
3 pick .s
S:[5] 7 2 5 2 7 ok
nip .s
S:[4] 7 2 5 7 ok
3 roll .s
S:[4] 2 5 7 7 ok
drop .s
S:[3] 2 5 7 ok
-rot .s
S:[3] 7 2 5 ok
```

Figure 2–22   Examples of Testing Stack Words Using .*S*

```
;         SP@ ( -- a )"SP-fetch"
; Push the current data stack pointer.
SPAT

        TFR    X,Y              ;Y = X = a
        STY    2,-X             ;push on data stack
        RTS


;         SP! ( a -- )"SP-store"
; Set the data stack pointer.
SPSTO
        LDX    0,X              ;X = a
        RTS
```

Figure 2–23   Definition of the WHYP Words SP@ and SP!

2.6   THE RETURN STACK

When you type a number, it is put on the data, or parameter, stack. All of the arithmetic operations and words such as *DUP*, *ROT*, *DROP*, *SWAP*, and *OVER* operate on numbers that are on the data stack.

WHYP also has a second stack called the *return stack*. The return stack is the same as the 68HC12 system stack and is used by the 68HC12 to store the return address when a subroutine is called. It is also used by certain WHYP words such as *DO*.

You can also use the return stack *if you are careful*. You can move a number from the data stack to the return stack temporarily if you are sure to move it back before the end of a subroutine. Otherwise, as we discussed in Section 2.2, the proper return address will not be on top of the return stack, and the 68HC12 will not be able to find its way back to the next word to execute.

The WHYP word >R (n --) (pronounced "to-R") will pop n from the data stack and push it onto the return stack as shown in Figure 2–24. For example,

```
3 >R
```

moves 3 to the top of the return stack and leaves the parameter stack unchanged. Other WHYP words that use the return stack, *R*, are shown in Box 2–2.

The 68HC12 subroutines that implement the first four words in Box 2–2 are given in Figure 2–25. Note, for example, how >R is implemented. This subroutine will be called with the jump to subroutine instruction *JSR TOR*. This will, of course, push the return address on the (return) stack. We must therefore first save this return address by popping it off the stack into *Y* using the instruction *PULY*. We then

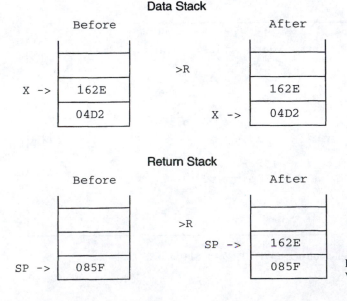

Figure 2–24   Operation of the Word >R ("to-R")

```
;         >R ( w -- )        ( R:    -- w )     "to-R"
; Push the data stack to the return stack.
TOR
          PULY                          ;save return addr
          LDD      2,X+                 ;D = w
          PSHD                          ;push D on ret stack
          PSHY                          ;restore return addr
          RTS


;         R> ( -- w )         ( R: w -- )       "from-R"
; Pop the return stack to the data stack.
RFROM
          PULY                          ;save return addr
          PULD                          ;D = ret stack val, w
          STD      2,-X                 ;push w on data stack
          PSHY                          ;restore return addr
          RTS


;         R@     ( -- w )  ( R: w -- w )  "R-fetch"
; Copy top of return stack to the data stack.
RAT
          TFR      SP,Y                 ;SP -> Y
          LDD      2,Y                  ;D = ret stack val, w
          STD      2,-X                 ;push w on data stack
          RTS


;         R>DROP ( -- )     ( R: w -- )   "from-R-DROP"
RFDROP
          PULY                          ;save return addr
          PULD                          ;pop w
          PSHY                          ;restore return addr
          RTS
```

Figure 2-25 68HC12 Code for Return Stack Words

load *D* with the value on top of the data stack and pop the data stack. Then we push *D* onto the return stack. This is the value we want left on the return stack when we exit the subroutine *TOR*. We must therefore push the return address that we saved in *Y* back on the return stack, using the instruction *PSHY*, so that when the instruction *RTS* is executed the program will return to the proper address and the value from the top of the data stack will be left on top of the return stack.

A similar implementation occurs for the word *R>* which pops the top of the return stack to the data stack. *>R* and *R>* typically work in pairs just as *PSHD* and *PULD* do. *>R* pushes the top of the data stack to *R* and *R>* pulls the top of *R* into the top of the data stack.

Box 2–2   WHYP Return Stack Words

>R	(n --)	(R: -- n)	("to-R")

Pops the top element of the data stack and pushes it onto the return stack.

R>	(-- n)	(R: n --)	("from-R")

Pops the top element of the return stack and pushes it onto the data stack.

R@	(-- n)	(R: n -- n)	("R-fetch")

Copies the top element of the return stack to the top of the parameter stack.

R>DROP	(--)	(R: n --)	("from-R-DROP")

Pops the top element of the return stack and throws it away.

RP@	(-- n)	(R: --)	("RP-fetch")

Pushes the current RP (system SP) to the data stack.

RP!	(n --)	(R: --)	("RP-store")

Sets the return stack pointer (the system SP).

The word *R@* copies the top of the return stack to the data stack without popping it from the return stack. Therefore, this word can be used as often as one wishes without having to match it to a *>R* instruction as we normally have to do with *R>*.

Sometimes it is necessary just to discard the value on top of the return stack. The word *R>DROP* does this with a single word that is equivalent to the two words *R>* and *DROP*.

The WHYP word *RP@* (-- a) (pronounced "R-P-fetch") will push the current value of the return stack pointer (*SP*) onto the data stack. The WHYP word *RP!* (a --) (pronounced "R-P-store") will set the return stack pointer to the value that is currently on the data stack. The 68HC12 subroutines for these two words are shown in Figure 2–26. Note that the value pushed on the data stack by *RP@* is the value of the return stack pointer before the subroutine *RPAT* is called (which will push a return address on the stack). Also note that in the subroutine *RPSTO* (for *RP!*) the instruction *PULD* pops the return address from one return stack location, but the instruction *PSHD* at the end of the subroutine pushes this return address onto a different return stack location because the value of the 68HC12 stack pointer, *SP*, has been changed in the subroutine! After returning from this subroutine, the value of *SP* will be the address *a* that was on the data stack when *RP!* was called.

We saw that the WHYP word *.S* can be used to display the contents of the data stack nondestructively. Similarly, the word *.R* can be used to display the contents of the return stack nondestructively. An example of running WHYP12 and using *.S* and *.R* to see the behavior of the return stack words, *>R*, *R@*, and *R>* is shown in Figure 2–27.

```
;          RP@    ( -- a )          "RP-fetch"
; Push the current RP (system SP) to the data stack.
RPAT
        PULD                    ;save return addr
        TFR     SP,Y            ;SP -> Y
        STY     2,-X            ;push Y to data stack
        PSHD                    ;restore return addr
        RTS


;          RP!      ( a -- )    "RP-store"
; Set the return stack pointer (the system SP).
RPSTO
        PULD                    ;save return addr
        LDY     2,X+            ;Y=a
        TFR     Y,SP            ;Y -> SP, SP = a
        PSHD                    ;restore return addr
        RTS
```

Figure 2–26   68HC12 Code for WHYP Words RP@ and RP!

```
C:\WHYP\WHYP12>whyp12
Using WHYP12.HED
Communicating with COM1
68HC12 WHYP12 - Version 4.6
Press <Esc> or type BYE to exit
ok
1 2 3 .s .r
S:[3] 1 2 3
R:[0] ok
>r .s .r
S:[2] 1 2
R:[1] 3 ok
r@ .s .r
S:[3] 1 2 3
R:[1] 3 ok
r> .s .r
S:[4] 1 2 3 3
R:[0] ok
```

Figure 2–27   Examples of Testing Return Stack Words Using .R

2.7 SUMMARY

In this chapter we have shown how the system stack is implemented in the 68HC12 and how you can make your own data stack using an index register as the stack pointer. We have seen how subroutines are called and how data can be passed to and from a subroutine using a data stack. We showed how subroutines can be made interactive by sending their address to the 68HC12 from a program running on the PC. This is the basis of the programming language WHYP that we introduced by looking at how various stack manipulation words can be implemented in 68HC12 assembly language. Finally, we noted that the WHYP return stack is the same as the 68HC12 system stack and we introduced a number of WHYP words that can be used to access the return stack.

In addition to the WHYP words given in Boxes 2–1 and 2–2 we also introduced the WHYP words shown in Box 2–3.

In the next chapter we look at additional 68HC12 arithmetic instructions and see how they can be used to write new WHYP words.

Box 2–3   Other WHYP Words Introduced in Chapter 2

`+`   `( n1 n2 -- n3 )`   `( "plus" )`
Adds top two elements on data stack and leaves the sum. $n3 = n1 + n2$.

`-`   `( n1 n2 -- n3 )`   `( "minus" )`
Subtracts top element from second element on data stack and leaves the difference. $n3 = n1 - n2$.

`SP@`   `( -- a )`   `( "SP-fetch" )`
Pushes the current data stack pointer (index register X) onto the data stack.

`SP!`   `( a -- )`   `( "SP-store" )`
Sets the data stack pointer, X, to the value on top of the data stack.

`.`   `( n -- )`   `( "dot" )`
Pops the top element on the data stack and display it value on the PC screen.

`.S`   `( -- )`   `( "dot-S" )`
Displays the contents of the data stack nondestructively.

`.R`   `( -- )`   `( "dot-R" )`
Displays the contents of the return stack nondestructively.

`HEX`   `( -- )`
Changes display mode to hexadecimal.

`DECIMAL`   `( -- )`
Changes display mode to decimal.

EXERCISES

Exercise 2.1

Draw a diagram similar to Figure 2–9 that will illustrate the operation of the subroutine *minus* shown in Figure 2–10.

Exercise 2.2

The program shown in Figure 2–11 is given in the file chap2b.asm.

a. Assemble the file chap2b.asm, make a .LST file, and download the .S19 file to the 68HC12.
b. Change the program counter, *PC*, to $800 and single-step the instructions using the trace command, *T*, until just before the instruction *JSR PLUS* is to be executed.
c. Use the memory display command, *MD*, to view the contents of memory locations $960–$96F. What values have been pushed on the data stack?
d. Continue to single-step the instructions using the trace command, *T*, until the instruction *LDY 2,X+* has been executed.
e. Use the memory display command, *MD*, to view the contents of memory locations $960–$96F. What value is now on top of the data stack?

Exercise 2.3

Modify the program shown in Figure 2–11 to use the subtraction subroutine shown in Figure 2–10 and repeat the steps given in Exercise 2.2.

Exercise 2.4

a. Write a 68HC12 assembly language program that will
   1. Load register *D* with the value $1234.
   2. Load register *X* with the value $5678.
   3. Push *D* on the system stack.
   4. Push *X* on the system stack.
   5. Pop the top of the stack (16 bits) into *D*.
   6. Pop the top of the stack (16 bits) into *X*.
b. Assemble your program, make a .LST file, and download the .S19 file to the 68HC12.
c. Single-step the instructions in your program using the trace command, *T*.

Exercise 2.5

Use WHYP in the interpretive mode to compute the following in decimal:

a. 2648 + 8634
b. 7429 − 2739
c. 2739 + 836
d. 5839 − 7253

Exercise 2.6

Use WHYP in the interpretive mode to compute the following in hex:

a. 3AC5 + 82F3
b. D5F2 − 835A
c. 6E38 + 52B7
d. 17A5 − 48CB

Exercise 2.7

Write 68HC12 subroutines that will implement the following WHYP words. Compare your results with the corresponding subroutines given in the file WHYP12.ASM in Appendix D.

   a. SWAP (n1 n2 -- n2 n1)
   b. TUCK (n1 n2 -- n2 n1 n2)
   c. ROT (n1 n2 n3 -- n2 n3 n1)
   d. -ROT (n1 n2 n3 -- n3 n1 n2)
   e. NIP (n1 n2 -- n2)

Exercise 2.8

Write 68HC12 subroutines that will implement the following WHYP words. Compare your results with the corresponding subroutines given in the file WHYP12.ASM in Appendix D.

   a. 2DUP (n1 n2 -- n1 n2 n1 n2)
   b. 2SWAP (n1 n2 n3 n4 -- n3 n4 n1 n2)
   c. 2DROP (n1 n2 --)
   d. 2OVER (n1 n2 n3 n4 -- n1 n2 n3 n4 n1 n2)

Exercise 2.9

Use the WHYP word *.S* to test each of the words in Box 2–1 (see Figure 2–22).

Exercise 2.10

Use the WHYP words *.S* and *.R* to test each of the words in Box 2–2 (see Figure 2–27).

Exercise 2.11

Define a WHYP word *3DUP (a b c -- a b c a b c)* using the WHYP word *PICK*.

3

68HC12 Arithmetic

In this chapter we will look in more detail at the 68HC12 arithmetic instructions. These will include addition, subtraction, multiplication, and division instructions. We will also investigate the increment and decrement instructions as well as the shift and rotate instructions. We will use these instructions to create new WHYP words including ones that operate on 32-bit, or double, numbers.

3.1 ADDITION AND SUBTRACTION

As we saw in Chapter 1 the 68HC12 addition and subtraction instructions are those shown in Table 3–1. We used the *ADDD* and *SUBD* instructions in Chapter 2 to define our WHYP words + and −. This worked because we were adding and subtracting 16-bit numbers. If we want to add and subtract 32-bit numbers, we will have to do it in pieces where we add the carry. But note from Table 3–1 that there is no "add memory with carry to *D*" instruction. You can only add memory with carry to either of the 8-bit registers, *A* or *B*. The same is true if you want to subtract with a borrow. In Section 3.1.2 we will see how to use these instructions to add and subtract 32-bit numbers. However, we will first look at the increment and decrement instructions.

Table 3–1   Addition and Subtraction Instructions

Addition Instructions

Mnemonic	Function
ABA	Add B to A
ADDA	Add memory to A
ADDB	Add memory to B
ADCA	Add memory with carry to A
ADCB	Add memory with carry to B
ADDD	Add memory to D
ABX	Add B to X
ABY	Add B to Y

Subtraction Instructions

Mnemonic	Function
SBA	Subtract B from A
SUBA	Subtract memory from A
SUBB	Subtract memory from B
SBCA	Subtract memory with borrow from A
SBCB	Subtract memory with borrow from B
SUBD	Subtract memory from D

3.1.1   Increment and Decrement Instructions

The 68HC12 increment and decrement instructions are shown in Table 3–2. The increment instruction adds 1 to the designated memory location or register. The decrement instruction subtracts 1 from the designated memory location or register.

Table 3–2   Increment and Decrement Instructions

Increment Instructions

Mnemonic	Function
INC	Increment memory by 1
INCA	Increment A by 1
INCB	Increment B by 1
INS	Increment SP by 1
INX	Increment X by 1
INY	Increment Y by 1

Decrement Instructions

Mnemonic	Function
DEC	Decrement memory by 1
DECA	Decrement A by 1
DECB	Decrement B by 1
DES	Decrement SP by 1
DEX	Decrement X by 1
DEY	Decrement Y by 1

```
;          1+           ( n -- n+1 )
ONEP

           LDD          0,X
           ADDD         #1
           STD          0,X
           RTS


;          2+           ( n -- n+2 )
TWOP

           LDD          0,X
           ADDD    ·    #2
           STD          0,X
           RTS
```

Figure 3–1   68HC12 Code for 1+ and 2+

The *INC* and *DEC* instructions can increment or decrement only a single byte in memory. The WHYP word *1+ (n -- n+1)* will increment the 16-bit value on top of the data stack by 1 and the WHYP word *2+ (n -- n+2)* will increment the 16-bit value on top of the data stack by 2 as shown by the 68HC12 subroutines in Figure 3–1. In a similar way, the WHYP words *1− (n -- n−1)* and *2− (n -- n−2)* will decrement the 16-bit value on top of the data stack by 1 and 2, respectively.

3.1.2 Double Numbers

A double number is a 32-bit integer that is stored as two 16-bit words on the stack with the HI-word on top of the stack as shown in Figure 3–2.

The stack picture of a double number will be indicated as

```
( d -- )
```

The WHYP word *D. (d --)* can be used to print the value of a double number on the screen. The following two words will add and subtract double numbers:

D+   (d1 d2 -- d3)   (d3 = d1+d2)
            Add two double numbers leaving a double sum.
D−   (d1 d2 -- d3)   (d3 = d1−d2)
            Subtract two double numbers leaving a double difference.

Remember that *d1*, *d2*, and *d3* are all 32-bit numbers made up of 4 bytes each. The double number *d2* is on top of the data stack with the data stack pointer, *X*, pointing

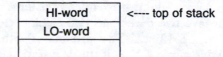

Figure 3–2   A Double Word Consists of Two 16-bit Words

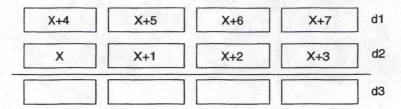

Figure 3–3   Adding and Subtracting Double Words

```
;         D+  ( d1  d2  --  d3 )
DPLUS
          LDAA    7,X
          ADDA    3,X
          STAA    7,X
          LDAA    6,X
          ADCA    2,X
          STAA    6,X
          LDAA    5,X
          ADCA    1,X
          STAA    5,X
          LDAA    4,X
          ADCA    0,X
          STAA    4,X
          LEAX    4,X
          RTS
```

Figure 3–4   68HC12 Code for D+

to its high byte as shown in Figure 3–3. Note that $X+4$ points to the high byte of *d1*. To add these two 32-bit numbers we must add each byte separately, because only registers A and B have an "add with carry" instruction. The 68HC12 subroutine shown in Figure 3–4 will implement the WHYP word $D+$.

The subroutine *DPLUS* in Figure 3–4 first adds the two least significant bytes (pointed to by $X+7$ and $X+3$) and stores the result in $X+7$. This addition may have produced a carry so the next two bytes (pointed to by $X+6$ and $X+2$) must be added with the instruction *ADCA*. The same procedure is used with the two most significant bytes so that after all four bytes have been added, the 32-bit sum is in the four bytes previously occupied by *d1* ($X+4$ to $X+7$). Inasmuch as we want to make this value the new top of the stack we need to drop the four bytes from X to $X+3$. We can do this by adding 4 to index register X. We could use four *INX* instructions, but we can save two bytes and two clock cycles by using the *load effective address* instruction, *LEAX 4,X*. This will load X with the effective address associated with the addressing mode *4,X*. But this is just $X+4$ which is what we want.

```
;                  D-  ( d1 d2 -- d3 )
DMINUS
                LDAA      7,X
                SUBA      3,X
                STAA      7,X
                LDAA      6,X
                SBCA      2,X
                STAA      6,X
                LDAA      5,X
                SBCA      1,X
                STAA      5,X
                LDAA      4,X
                SBCA      0,X
                STAA      4,X
                LEAX      4,X
                RTS
```

Figure 3–5 68HC12 Code for D−

The 68HC12 code for the double subtraction word, $D-$, works in a similar way and is shown in Figure 3–5. The only difference is that it used the *SUBA* and *SBCA* instructions instead of *ADDA* and *ADCA*.

3.1.3 Displaying Single and Double Numbers on the Screen

A single number is a 16-bit number which may be thought of as an unsigned number in the range 0 to 65,535 ($0000–$FFFF) or as a two's complement signed number in the range −32,768 to +32,767 ($8000–$7FFF). To display the *signed* version of the number on top of the data stack, you use the WHYP word "dot" (.) introduced in Chapter 2. To display the *unsigned* version of the number on top of the data stack, you use the WHYP word *U.* ("U-dot").

A double number is a 32-bit number which may be thought of as an unsigned number in the range 0 to 4,294,967,295 ($00000000–$FFFFFFFF) or as a two's complement signed number in the range −2,147,483,648 to +2,147,483,647 ($80000000–$7FFFFFFF). To display the *signed* version of the double number on top of the data stack, you use the WHYP word *D.* ("D-dot") and to display the *unsigned* version of the double number on top of the data stack, you use the WHYP word *UD.* ("U-D-dot"). These words are summarized in Box 3–1.

If you're curious about how these display words work, the 68HC12 code for the word *U.* is shown in Figure 3–6. When you type *U.*, this is the code that is executed on the 68HC12. It loads accumulator *A* with a 2 and sends this value to the PC by calling the subroutine *OUTPUT*, which is part of the WHYP12 kernel. This subroutine sends the value 2 out the serial port to the PC. It then executes the kernel subroutine *TPOP* which pops the top of the data stack and sends the value out the serial port to the PC. Meanwhile, the C++ program running on the PC, having received a 2 from the 68HC12, uses this as an opcode which tells it to read another 16-bit value from the serial port and display it on the screen as an unsigned number.

```
;            U. ( n -- )                      ;print unsigned number
UDOTT
             LDAA    #2                        ;opcode = 2
             JSR     OUTPUT                    ;send to host
             JSR     TPOP                      ;send top of stack
             RTS
```

Figure 3–6 68HC12 Code for U.

Box 3–1   WHYP Words to Display Numbers on the Screen

.   (n --)   ("dot")
               Pop the top element on the data stack and display its signed value on the
               PC screen.

U.   (u --)   ("U-dot")
               Pop the top element on the data stack and display its unsigned value on
               the PC screen.

D.   (d --)   ("D-dot")
               Pop the top double number on the data stack and display its signed value
               on the PC screen.

UD.   (ud --)   ("U-D-dot")
               Pop the top unsigned double number on the data stack and display its
               unsigned value on the PC screen.

Similar code to that in Figure 3–6 (with different opcodes) will be executed for the other three words in Box 3–1 and the C++ program on the PC will take the appropriate action to display a signed or unsigned single or double number.

We saw in Chapter 2 that to push a value onto the data stack you just need to type the number on the PC keyboard. It was assumed there that the value you type in is a single number that will fit in 16 bits. Suppose you want to type a double number that will take up two 16-bit words on the data stack. There are two ways to do this. If the number itself will, in fact, fit into 16-bits, then you must include a decimal point at the end of the number. For example, if you type

```
5.  .s
```

then the two words 5 0 will appear on the data stack as shown in Figure 3–7. On the other hand, if the number you type is greater than 65535, then the use of the trailing decimal point is optional. For example, if you are in HEX and type

```
12345678 .s
```

then the two words 5678 1234 will appear on the data stack as shown in Figure 3–7.

Note in Figure 3–7 that "dot" (.) will display signed numbers in the range −32,768 to +32,767 ($8000–$7FFF) and U. will display unsigned numbers in the

```
C:\WHYP\WHYP12>whyp12
Using WHYP12.HED
Communicating with COM1
68HC12 WHYP12 - Version 4.6
Press <Esc> or type BYE to exit
ok
5. .s
S:[2] 5 0 ok                     \ double number
d. 5 ok
hex ok
12345678 .s
S:[2] 5678 1234 ok               \ double number
d. 12345678 ok
decimal ok
32767 . 32767 ok
32768 . -32768 ok                \ . displays signed numbers
32768 u. 32768 ok
-1 . -1 ok
-1 u. 65535 ok
-1. d. -1 ok                     \ decimal numbers display - sign
-1. ud. 4294967295 ok
hex ok
-1 . ffffffff ok                 \ hex numbers do not display - sign
-1 u. ffff ok
-1. d. ffffffff ok
-1. ud. ffffffff ok
ffffffff .s                      \ out of range as signed number
S:[2] ffffffff 7fff ok
d. 7fffffff ok                   \ max positive signed 32-bit number
-ffff .s
S:[1] 1 ok
. 1 ok
-80000000 .s
S:[2] 0 ffff8000 ok
d. 80000000 ok
80000000 .s                      \ out of range as signed number
S:[2] ffffffff 7fff ok
d. 7fffffff ok
```

Figure 3–7   Examples of Displaying Single and Double Numbers

range 0 to 65,535 ($0000–$FFFF). In the *DECIMAL* mode, a negative sign is displayed for signed numbers. On the other hand, in the *HEX* mode all numbers are displayed in two's complement signed format with 16-bit numbers sign-extended to 32 bits.

Also note that 32-bit numbers entered from the keyboard must be in the range −2,147,483,648 to +2,147,483,647 ($80000000–$7FFFFFFF). If you try to enter a number greater than +2,147,483,647, it will be truncated to $7FFFFFFF. If you try to enter a number less than −2,147,483,648, it will be truncated to $80000000. Note that −1. will be stored as the 32-bit number $FFFFFFFF.

3.2 MULTIPLICATION

The 68HC12 has the three multiply instructions shown in Table 3–3. The instruction *EMUL* will multiply two 16-bit *unsigned* numbers in *D* and *Y* and leave the 32-bit *unsigned* product in *Y:D*.

The WHYP word *UM** ("U-M-star") will multiply two 16-bit *unsigned* numbers on the data stack and leave the 32-bit *unsigned* product on the data stack. The 68HC12 subroutine shown in Figure 3–8 uses the instruction *EMUL* to implement *UM**. Note that the high word of the product (in *Y*) is left on top of the data stack.

The instruction *EMULS* given in Table 3–3 will multiply two 16-bit *signed* numbers in *D* and *Y* and leave the 32-bit *signed* product in *Y:D*. The WHYP word *M** ("M-star"), defined by the 68HC12 subroutine shown in Figure 3–9, will multiply two 16-bit *signed* numbers on the data stack and leave the 32-bit *signed* product on the data stack.

The WHYP word * ("star") will multiply two 16-bit *signed* numbers on the data stack and leave the 16-bit *signed* product on the data stack. Of course, the result will be correct only if the product will fit into 16 bits. This means that the product must be in the range −32,768 to +32,767. How can we define the word *? It turns out that the 16-bit signed multiplication, *, is just *UM* DROP*. That is, if you multiply

Table 3–3 Multiply Instructions

Mnemonic	Function	Operation
EMUL	16 × 16 multiply (unsigned)	(D) x (Y) => Y:D
EMULS	16 × 16 multiply (signed)	(D) x (Y) => Y:D
MUL	8 × 8 multiply (unsigned)	(A) x (B) => A:B

```
;      UM*      ( u u -- ud )    16 x 16 = 32
;      Unsigned multiply. Return double product.
UMSTA
       LDD      2,X+
       LDY      2,X+
       EMUL
       STD      2,-X
       STY      2,-X
       RTS
```

Figure 3–8 68HC12 Code for UM*

```
;         M*          ( n n -- d )   16 x 16 = 32
;         Signed multiply. Return double product.
MSTAR
          LDD      2,X+
          LDY      2,X+
          EMULS
          STD      2,-X
          STY      2,-X
          RTS
```

Figure 3–9   68HC12 Code for M*

```
;         *           ( n n -- n )    16 x 16 = 16
;         Signed multiply. Return single product.
;         Same as UM* DROP;
STAR
          LDD      2,X+
          LDY      2,X+
          EMUL
          STD      2,-X
          RTS
```

Figure 3–10   68HC12 Code for *

two 16-bit unsigned numbers and then throw away the upper 16 bits of the 32-bit product, the remaining 16 bits will be the 16-bit signed product if you consider the two inputs to be 16-bit signed numbers. This may not be obvious at first, but if you try some examples you will see how it works. For example, $FFFF times $FFFF (unsigned) is $FFFE0001. If you drop the high word, you have 0001 which is the product of −1 ($FFFF) times −1 ($FFFF). The 68HC12 subroutine shown in Figure 3–10 uses the instruction EMUL to implement the WHYP word *.

The instruction *MUL* given in Table 3–3 will multiply two 8-bit *unsigned* numbers in A and B and leave the 16-bit *unsigned* product in D. This is the only multiply instruction that the 68HC11 has. As a result, to multiply two 16-bit numbers and obtain a 32-bit product you need to call *MUL* four times using the long multiplication method shown in Figure 3–11. In this figure A, B, C and D are 8-bit values. Multiplying B by D will produce the 16-bit value $BDH:BDL$. Similarly, $A \times D = ADH:ADL$, $C \times B = CBH:CBL$ and $C \times A = ACH:ACL$. The 32-bit product will be $P1:P2:P3:P4$ where $P1 = ACH$ (with a possible carry from P2), $P2 = ADH + CBH + ACL$ (with a possible carry from P3), $P3 = BDH + ADL + CBL$ and $P4 = BDL$. This is the method used to implement the WHYP word $UM*$ in WHYP11.

Sometimes it is necessary to multiply a double number (32 bits) by a single number (16 bits) and obtain a double number result. Of course, in general, if you multiply a 32-bit number by a 16-bit number you could get as much as a 48-bit

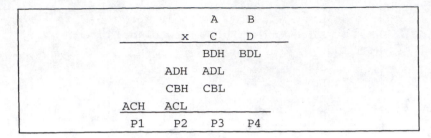

Figure 3–11   Method for Multiplying Two 16-bit Numbers on a 68HC11

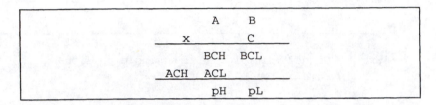

Figure 3–12   Method for Multiplying a 32-bit Number by a 16-bit Number

```
;           DUM*      ( ud un -- ud )     32 x 16 = 32
;           Unsigned multiply of double number by single number.
;           Returns a double unsigned number, pcL pcH.
;           A B x C = pH pL   (drop high 16 bits of product, ACH)
;           pL = BCL, pH = BCH + ACL
DUMST
      LDD       0,X                 ;D = un (C)
      LDY       2,X                 ;Y = udH (A)
      EMUL                          ;Y = ACH, D = ACL
      STD       2,X                 ;save ACL
      LDD       0,X                 ;D = un (C)
      LDY       4,X                 ;Y = udL (B)
      EMUL                          ;Y = BCH, D = BCL
      STD       4,X                 ;save pL = BCL
      TFR       Y,D                 ;D = BCH
      ADDD      2,X                 ;D = BCH+ACL = pH
      STD       2,X                 ;save pH
      LEAX      2,X                 ;fix data stack
      RTS
```

Figure 3–13   68HC12 Code for *DUM**

product. However, in many cases you will know that the result can't exceed 32-bits, even though it will be greater than 16-bits.

Suppose that *A*, *B*, and *C*, are 16-bit numbers. Then we can represent the multiplication of the 32-bit number *A:B* by the 16 bit number *C* as shown in Figure 3–12. In this figure, multiplying *B* times *C* gives the 32-bit result *BCH:BCL*. Multiplying *A*

```
C:\WHYP\WHYP12>whyp12
Using WHYP12.HED
Communicating with COM1
68HC12 WHYP12 - Version 4.6
Press <Esc> or type BYE to exit
ok
4 6 * . 24 ok
-5 7 * . -35 ok
-8 -4 * . 32 ok
3 -9 * . -27 ok
hex ok
ffff ffff um* ud. fffe0001 ok
decimal ok
-1234 4321 m* d. -5332114 ok
123456. 25 dum* d. 3086400 ok
```

Figure 3–14   Examples of Using the WHYP Multiplication Words

times *C* gives the 32-bit result *ACH:ACL*. Adding these two partial products, shifted by 16-bits as shown, will produce the complete 48-bit product. However, we are going to drop the *ACH* and limit the result to 32 bits. The low word of this product will be *pL* = *BCL* and the high word will be *pH* = *BCH* + *ACL*. Therefore, we can define the WHYP word, *DUM* (ud un -- ud)*, to do this multiplication and implement it with the 68HC12 subroutine shown in Figure 3–13.

You should run WHYP and try some examples of using the multiplication words *, *UM**, *M**, and *DUM**. Some examples are shown in Figure 3–14.

3.3 DIVISION

The five 68HC12 divide instructions are given in Table 3–4. Only the instructions *FDIV* and *IDIV* are available on the 68HC11. The 68HC12 has introduced a signed 16-bit divide instruction, *IDIVS*, as well as both unsigned and signed extended divide instructions, *EDIV* and *EDIVS*, that take a 32-bit dividend. In all cases the quotient is 16 bits which means that overflow can occur if the divisor is too small. In this section we will see how we can make WHYP words that will allow us to perform division interactively and also how to do division that will leave a 32-bit quotient so that no overflow can occur. We will look at each of the 68HC12 division instructions and see what WHYP words we can make from them. We begin with the 16-bit signed divide instruction, *IDIVS*.

3.3.1 16-bit Signed Division: IDIVS

As shown in Table 3–4 the instruction *IDIVS* will divide the signed contents of *D* by the signed contents of *X* and leave the quotient in *X* and the remainder in *D*. An attempt to divide by zero will set the carry bit in the *CCR* and if the signed quotient is outside the range −32,768 to +32,767, then the overflow bit in the *CCR* will be set.

Table 3–4 Divide Instructions

Mnemonic	Function	Operation
EDIV	32 × 16 divide (unsigned)	(Y:D) / (X) => Y Remainder => D
EDIVS	32 × 16 divide (signed)	(Y:D) / (X) => Y Remainder => D
FDIV	16 × 16 fractional divide	(D) / (X) => X Remainder => D
IDIV	16 × 16 integer divide (unsigned)	(D) / (X) => X Remainder => D
IDIVS	16 × 16 integer divide (signed)	(D) / (X) => X Remainder => D

It turns out that there is only one case in which overflow will occur. It is when you try to divide $-32,768$ ($8000) by -1 ($FFFF). The result is $+32,768$ which is outside the range $-32,768$ to $+32,767$.

The WHYP word */MOD (n1 n2 -- r q)* will divide the signed 16-bit dividend, *n1*, by the signed 16-bit divisor, *n2*, and leave the remainder, *r*, and quotient, *q*, on the data stack. The 68HC12 subroutine shown in Figure 3–15 will implement */MOD*.

Note in Figure 3–15 that the data stack pointer, *X*, must first be pushed on the return stack because it needs to be used in the *IDIVS* instruction. *D* and *X* are then loaded with *n1* and *n2* and the *IDIVS* instruction is executed. If the divisor, *n2*, is zero, or if an overflow occurs, then both the remainder, *r*, and the quotient, *q*, are set to $FFFF. Otherwise, their computed values are put on the data stack.

```
;          /MOD       ( n1 n2 -- r q )    16/16 = 16:16
;          Signed divide of a single by a single.
;          Return remainder and quotient.
SMOD
           PSHX                   ;save data stack pointer
           LDD        2,X         ;D = n1
           LDX        0,X         ;X = n2
           IDIVS                  ;X = q, D = r
           TFR        X,Y         ;Y = q
           BCS        SM1         ;if div by 0
           BVC        SM2         ; or overflow
SM1        LDD        #$FFFF      ; set r and q to $FFFF
           LDY        #$FFFF
SM2        PULX                   ;restore data stack pointer
           STD        2,X         ;put r on data stack
           STY        0,X         ;put q on data stack
           RTS
```

Figure 3–15 68HC12 Code for */MOD*

Examples of using the WHYP word, /*MOD*, are shown in Figure 3–16. Note that the sign of the remainder is the same as the sign of the dividend. This is what we call *symmetric division* in which the quotient is truncated toward zero. Note in all cases the quotient times the divisor plus the remainder is equal to the dividend.

Symmetric division is not the only possibility. In fact, many Forth language implementations use what is called *floored division* in which the quotient is rounded toward minus infinity and the sign of the remainder is the same as the sign of the divisor. The results of floored division for the same example used in Figure 3–16 are shown in Table 3–5. Note how the quotient is rounded toward minus infinity and how the sign of the remainder is the same as the sign of the divisor. While the second and third results in Table 3–5 may seem strange to you, they are fine because all we need is the divisor times the quotient plus the remainder to be equal to the dividend.

Most divide instructions built into microprocessors use symmetric division including the *IDIVS* instruction in the 68HC12. Therefore, our /*MOD* instruction in Figure 3–15 uses symmetric division.

The *IDIVS* instruction can also be used to create the WHYP words / (*n1 n2 -- q*) ("slash") and *MOD* (*n1 n2 -- r*) which return only the quotient and remainder, respectively. The 68HC12 subroutine for implementing / is shown in Figure 3–17 and

```
C:\WHYP\WHYP12>whyp12
Using WHYP12.HED
Communicating with COM1
68HC12 WHYP12 - Version 4.6
Press <Esc> or type BYE to exit
ok
26 7 /mod . . 3 5 ok
-26 7 /mod . . -3 -5 ok
26 -7 /mod . . -3 5 ok
-26 -7 /mod . . 3 -5 ok
 ok
-32768 -1 /mod . . -1 -1 ok   \ only overflow case
-123 0 /mod . . -1 -1 ok      \ divide by zero
```

Figure 3–16   Examples of Using the WHYP Word /*MOD*

Table 3–5   Floored Division

Dividend	Divisor	Quotient	Remainder
26	7	3	5
−26	7	−4	2
26	−7	−4	−2
−26	−7	3	−5

```
;        /       ( n n -- q )      16/16 = 16
;        Signed divide of a single by a single.
;        Return quotient.
SLASH
         PSHX
         LDD     2,X
         LDX     0,X
         IDIVS
         TFR     X,Y
         BCS     SL1
         BVC     SL2
SL1      LDD     #$FFFF
         LDY     #$FFFF
SL2      PULX
         LEAX    2,X
         STY     0,X
         RTS
```

Figure 3–17 68HC12 Code for /

```
;        MOD       ( n n -- r )      16/16 = 16
;        Signed divide of a single by a single.
;        Return remainder.
MOD
         PSHX
         LDD     2,X
         LDX     0,X
         IDIVS
         TFR     X,Y
         BCS     MD1
         BVC     MD2
MD1      LDD     #$FFFF
MD2      PULX
         LEAX    2,X
         STD     0,X
         RTS
```

Figure 3–18 68HC12 Code for *MOD*

the subroutine for implementing *MOD* is shown in Figure 3–18. Examples of using the WHYP words / and *MOD* are shown in Figure 3–19.

3.3.2 Extended Unsigned Division: *EDIV*

As shown in Table 3–4 the instruction *EDIV* will divide the unsigned 32-bit number in $Y{:}D$ by the unsigned 16-bit number in X and leave the quotient in Y and the remainder in D. An attempt to divide by zero will set the carry bit in the *CCR* and if

```
C:\WHYP\WHYP12>whyp12
Using WHYP12.HED
Communicating with COM1
68HC12 WHYP12 - Version 4.6
Press <Esc> or type BYE to exit
ok
3546 5 / . 709 ok
-7654 6 / . -1275 ok
345 0 / . -1 ok            \ divide by zero
3546 5 mod . 1 ok
-7654 6 mod . -4 ok
-26 -7 mod . -5 ok
```

Figure 3–19   Examples of Using the WHYP Words / and *MOD*

the unsigned quotient is greater than 65,535 ($FFFF), then the overflow bit in the *CCR* will be set.

The WHYP word *UM/MOD (ud un--ur uq)* will divide the unsigned 32-bit dividend, *ud*, by the unsigned 16-bit divisor, *un*, and leave the remainder, *ur*, and quotient, *uq*, on the data stack. The 68HC12 subroutine shown in Figure 3–20 will implement *UM/MOD*.

Examples of using *UM/MOD* are shown in Figure 3–21. Note that if you divide by zero or if the quotient is larger than 65535, then both the quotient and remainder

```
;       UM/MOD    ( udl udh un -- ur uq )   32/16 = 16:16
;       Unsigned divide of a double by a single.
;       Return remainder and 16-bit quotient.
UMMOD
        PSHX
        LDY     2,X
        LDD     4,X
        LDX     0,X
        EDIV
        BCS     UM1            ;if div by 0
        BVC     UM2            ; or overflow
UM1     LDD     #$FFFF         ; rem = $FFFF
        LDY     #$FFFF         ; quot = $FFFF
UM2     PULX
        LEAX    2,X
        STD     2,X
        STY     0,X
        RTS
```

Figure 3–20   68HC12 Code for *UM/MOD*

```
C:\WHYP\WHYP12>whyp12
Using WHYP12.HED
Communicating with COM1
68HC12 WHYP12 - Version 4.6
Press <Esc> or type BYE to exit
ok
1234567. 100 um/mod u. u. 12345 67 ok
12345. 0 um/mod u. u. 65535 65535 ok          \ divide by 0
654321 10 um/mod u. u. 65432 1 ok
654321 2 um/mod u. u. 65535 65535 ok          \ overflow
```

Figure 3–21 Examples of Using the WHYP Word *UM/MOD*

```
;        MU/MOD   ( ud un -- urem udquot )
;        Unsigned divide of a double by a single.
;        Return remainder and double quotient.
MUMOD
        LDD     0,X
        STD     2,-X              ; dup un
        PSHX
        LDD     4,X               ;D = udH
        LDY     #0                ;0:udH / un
        LDX     0,X
        EDIV                      ;Y = quotH, D = remH
        BCC     MU1               ;if div by 0
        PULX
        LEAX    2,X
        LDD     #$FFFF            ; rem, quot = $FFFF
        STD     0,X
        STD     2,X
        STD     4,X
        RTS
MU1     PULX
        STY     2,X               ;quotH
        STD     4,X               ;remH
        LDY     4,X               ;Y = remH
        LDD     6,X               ;D = udL
        PSHX
        LDX     0,X               ;X = un
        EDIV                      ;Y = quotL, D = remL
        PULX
        STD     6,X               ;remL
        STY     4,X               ;quotL
        LEAX    2,X
        RTS
```

Figure 3–22 68HC12 Code for *MU/MOD*

```
C:\WHYP\WHYP12>whyp12
Using WHYP12.HED
Communicating with COM1
68HC12 WHYP12 - Version 4.6
Press <Esc> or type BYE to exit
ok
1234567. 10 mu/mod ud. u. 123456 7 ok
12345678. 10 mu/mod ud. u. 1234567 8 ok
12345678. 0 mu/mod ud. u. 4294967295 65535 ok \ divide by 0
hex ok
12345678 100 mu/mod ud. u. 123456 78 ok
```

Figure 3–23   Examples of Using the WHYP Word *MU/MOD*

will be set to 65535 ($FFFF). To eliminate this overflow problem we need a word that will divide an unsigned double number by an unsigned single number and leave a double (32-bit) quotient and a 16-bit remainder. The WHYP word *MU/MOD* (*ud un -- urem udquot*) shown in Figure 3–22 will do this.

The subroutine in Figure 3–22 calls the instruction *EDIV* twice to perform multiple-word division. When doing long division, you divide the divisor into the "high part" of the dividend to get the "high part" of the quotient. The "high remainder" becomes part of the remaining dividend that is divided by the divisor to yield the "low part" of the quotient and the final remainder. In particular, if *ud* is a 32-bit numerator with high word *udH* and low word *udL*, then to divide *ud* by the 16-bit denominator *un*, first divide *0:udH/un* to give *quotH* and *remH*. Then divide *remH:udL/un* to give *quotL* and *remL*. The subroutine shown in Figure 3–22 performs just this long division.

Examples of using the WHYP word *MU/MOD* are shown in Figure 3–23. Note that an overflow no longer exists because the quotient will always fit into 32 bits. Only when you try to divide by zero will the quotient be $FFFFFFFF and the remainder $FFFF.

3.3.3 Extended Signed Division: *EDIVS*

As shown in Table 3–4 the instruction *EDIVS* will divide the signed 32-bit number in *Y:D* by the signed 16-bit number in *X* and leave the quotient in *Y* and the remainder in *D*. An attempt to divide by zero will set the carry bit in the *CCR* and if the signed quotient is outside the range −32,768 ($8000) to +32,767 ($7FFF), then the overflow bit in the *CCR* will be set.

The WHYP word *M/MOD* (*d n -- r q*) will divide the signed 32-bit dividend, *d*, by the signed 16-bit divisor, *n*, and leave the remainder, *r*, and quotient, *q*, on the data stack. The 68HC12 subroutine shown in Figure 3–24 will implement *M/MOD*. Examples of using *M/MOD* are shown in Figure 3–25.

It is sometimes necessary to multiply two 16-bit signed numbers, *n1* and *n2*, and then divide the product by another 16-bit signed number, *n3*, to produce a 16-bit

```
;       M/MOD        ( dl dh n -- r q )      32/16 = 16:16
;       Signed divide of a double by a single.
;       Return remainder and quotient.
MMOD
        PSHX
        LDY     2,X
        LDD     4,X
        LDX     0,X
        EDIVS
        BCS     MM1
        BVC     MM2
MM1     LDD     #$FFFF
        LDY     #$FFFF
MM2     PULX
        LEAX    2,X
        STD     2,X
        STY     0,X
        RTS
```

Figure 3–24   68HC12 Code for *M/MOD*

```
C:\WHYP\WHYP12>whyp12
Using WHYP12.HED
Communicating with COM1
68HC12 WHYP12 - Version 4.6
Press <Esc> or type BYE to exit
ok
-1234567. 100 m/mod . . -12345 -67 ok
1234567. -100 m/mod . . -12345 67 ok
-1234567. -100 m/mod . . 12345 -67 ok
-1234567. 10 m/mod . . -1 -1 ok          \ overflow
1234567. 0 m/mod . . -1 -1 ok            \ divide by 0
```

Figure 3–25   Examples of Using the WHYP Word *M/MOD*

result, *n4*. To maintain the best accuracy, the product *n1**n2 should be a 32-bit inter-mediate value. The WHYP word */ (*n1 n2 n3 -- n4*) whose 68HC12 implementation is shown in Figure 3–26 will do this. Note that the instruction *EMULS* is used to multiply *n1* by *n2*, leaving the 32-bit product in *Y:D*. This 32-bit product is then di-vided by *n3* using the instruction *EDIVS*. Examples of using the WHYP word */ are shown in Figure 3–27.

```
;            */       ( n1 n2 n3 -- n4 ) n4 = n1*n2/n3
;         "star-slash"
;           Signed multiply-divide  n1*n2 double
STARSL
        PSHX
        LDD      4,X
        LDY      2,X
        EMULS
        LDX      0,X
        EDIVS
        BCS      SS1
        BVC      SS2
SS1     LDY      #$FFFF
SS2     PULX
        LEAX     4,X
        STY      0,X
        RTS
```

Figure 3–26   68HC12 Code for */

```
C:\WHYP\WHYP12>whyp12
Using WHYP12.HED
Communicating with COM1
68HC12 WHYP12 - Version 4.6
Press <Esc> or type BYE to exit
ok
20000 50 100 */ . 10000 ok
20000 50 10 */ . -1 ok          \ overflow
20000 50 0 */ . -1 ok           \ divide by 0
```

Figure 3–27   Examples of Using the WHYP Word */

3.3.4 Integer and Fractional Divide: *IDIV* and *FDIV*

The instructions *IDIV* and *FDIV* were the only divide instructions provided in the 68HC11. The newer 68HC12 divide instructions described above, *IDIVS*, *EDIV*, and *EDIVS*, are more useful and reduce the need to use *IDIV* and *FDIV*. However, we will describe both of these instructions and then show how we can use both of them to produce the same result as *EDIV*.

The Instruction *IDIV*   As shown in Table 3–4 the instruction *IDIV* will divide the unsigned contents of D by the unsigned contents of X and leave the quotient in X and the remainder in D. An attempt to divide by zero will set the carry bit in the *CCR*. The overflow bit, V, in the *CCR* will always be cleared to zero because as long as the divisor is a nonzero value, the quotient will always fit into 16 bits.

```
; IDIV      ( num denom -- rem quot )
;                   Integer divide 16 by 16
IDIVV
        PSHX
        LDD     2,X
        LDX     0,X
        IDIV                        ;X=quot,D=rem
        TFR     X,Y
        BCC     ID1                 ;div by 0
        LDD     #$FFFF              ;quot already $FFFF
ID1     PULX
        STD     2,X
        STY     0,X
        RTS
```

Figure 3–28   68HC12 Code for WHYP Word *IDIV*

The WHYP word *IDIV (num denom -- rem quot)* shown in Figure 3–28 can be used to test the behavior of the instruction *IDIV*. It will divide the unsigned 16-bit numerator, *num*, by the unsigned 16-bit denominator, *denom*, and leave the remainder, *rem*, and quotient, *quot*, on the data stack. We might have called this word *U/MOD* because it is just the unsigned version of the word */MOD* described in Section 3.3.1.

The WHYP word *U/ (n1 n2 -- q)* ("U-slash") is an unsigned 16-bit divide that just leaves the quotient on the data stack. Its 68HC12 implementation, using the instruction, *IDIV*, is shown in Figure 3–29. Examples of using *IDIV* and *U/* are shown in Figure 3–30.

The Instruction *FDIV*, Fractional Divide   As shown in Table 3–4 the instruction *FDIV* will divide the unsigned contents of *D* by the unsigned contents of *X* and

```
;       U/      ( u1 u2 -- q )    16/16 = 16
;       Unsigned divide of a single by a single.
;       Return quotient.
USLASH
        PSHX
        LDD     2,X
        LDX     0,X
        IDIV
        TFR     X,Y
        PULX
        LEAX    2,X
        STY     0,X
        RTS
```

Figure 3–29   68HC12 Code for *U/*

```
C:\WHYP\WHYP12>whyp12
Using WHYP12.HED
Communicating with COM1
68HC12 WHYP12 - Version 4.6
Press <Esc> or type BYE to exit
ok
78 5 idiv . . 15 3 ok
54321 100 idiv u. u. 543 21 ok
53 0 idiv . . -1 -1 ok                        \ divide by 0
78 5 u/ . 15 ok
54321 100 u/ . 543 ok
3456 5 u/ . 691 ok
55 5 u/ . 11 ok
34 0 u/ . -1 ok                               \ divide by 0
```

Figure 3–30   Examples of Using the WHYP Words *IDIV* and *U/*

leave the quotient in *X* and the remainder in *D*. An attempt to divide by zero will set the carry bit in the *CCR*. The instruction *FDIV* is a fractional divide in which it is assumed that the numerator is less than the denominator. If the numerator is greater than or equal to the denominator, then the overflow bit, *V*, in the *CCR* will be set.

The WHYP word *FDIV (num denom -- rem quot)* shown in Figure 3–31 can be used to test the behavior of the instruction *FDIV*. It will divide the unsigned 16-bit numerator, *num*, by the unsigned 16-bit denominator, *denom*, and leave the remainder, *rem*, and quotient, *quot*, on the data stack. Examples of using *FDIV* are shown in Figure 3–32.

```
;     FDIV              ( num denom -- rem quot )
;                       Fractional divide 16 by 16
FDIVV
        PSHX
        LDD       2,X
        LDX       0,X
        FDIV                ;X=quot,D=rem
        TFR       X,Y
        BCS       FD1       ;if div by 0
        BVC       FD2       ; or numer > denom
FD1     LDD       #$FFFF    ; rem = $FFFF
        LDY       #$FFFF    ; quot = $FFFF
FD2     PULX
        STD       2,X
        STY       0,X
        RTS
```

Figure 3–31   68HC12 Code for WHYP Word *FDIV*

```
C:\WHYP\WHYP12>whyp12
Using WHYP12.HED
Communicating with COM1
68HC12 WHYP12 - Version 4.6
Press <Esc> or type BYE to exit
ok
1 2 fdiv u. u. 32768 0 ok
hex ok
1 2 fdiv u. u. 8000 0 ok
1 4 fdiv u. u. 4000 0 ok
3 4 fdiv u. u. c000 0 ok
1 3 fdiv u. u. 5555 1 ok
2 3 fdiv u. u. aaaa 2 ok
5 2 fdiv u. u. ffff ffff ok    \ numer > denom
7 0 fdiv u. u. ffff ffff ok    \ div by 0
```

Figure 3–32   Examples of Using the WHYP Word *FDIV*

When dividing two integers using *FDIV*, the radix point of the quotient is to the left of bit 15. That is, the entire 16-bit quotient can be considered to be a binary fraction. This is easier to see in HEX, as shown by the examples in Figure 3–32. For example, 1 divided by 2 produces the quotient $8000 which represents the binary value 0.1. Similarly, 1 divided by 4 produces the quotient $4000 which represents the binary value 0.01, and 3 divided by 4 produces the quotient $C000 which represents the binary value 0.11.

The instruction *FDIV* is equivalent to multiplying the numerator by 2^{16} (shifting left 16 bits) and then performing a 32 by 16 integer division. Thus, for example, 1 divided by 2 becomes $10000 divided by 2, which shifts the numerator right one bit producing $8000.

Note from the examples in Figure 3–32 that 1 divided by 3 produces the quotient $5555 with a remainder of 1. This can be verified by noting that $5555 times 3 is $FFFF plus 1 is $10000. Similarly, 2 divided by 3 produces the quotient $AAAA with a remainder of 2 which can be verified by noting that $AAAA times 3 is $1FFFE plus 2 is $20000.

A 68HC11 Version of *UM/MOD*   As noted in the previous section the instruction *FDIV* is equivalent to shifting the numerator left 16 bits and then performing a 32 by 16 integer division. This gives us a method for writing a subroutine for *UM/MOD* (*ud un — ur uq*) that will work on the 68HC11. For *UM/MOD* to give a valid 16-bit quotient, the high byte of the numerator must be less than denominator—otherwise, the quotient won't fit into 16 bits. This means that we can first divide the high word of the numerator by the divisor using *FDIV* to get a fractional quotient and a fractional remainder. We then divide the low word of the numerator plus the fractional remainder by the denominator which gives an integer quotient and integer remainder. This is the final remainder, *ur*. The final quotient, *uq*, is the sum of the integer quotient from *IDIV* and the fractional quotient from

```
;        UM/MOD   ( udl udh un -- ur uq )
;        32 / 16 = 16 quot 16 rem
UMMOD
         PSHX
         PULY
         PSHY                    ;Y = X
         DEY
         DEY                     ;temp storage
         LDD     4,Y             ;D = udh
         LDX     2,Y             ;X = un
         FDIV                    ;X = qf  D = rf
         STX     0,Y             ;save qf
         ADDD    6,Y             ;D = (udl + rf)
         LDX     2,Y             ;X = un
         IDIV                    ;X = q  D = rem
         STD     6,Y             ; urem - - -
         PSHX
         PULA
         PULB                    ;D = q
         ADDD    0,Y             ;D = q + qf = uq
         STD     4,Y             ;urem uquot - -
         PULX
         INX
         INX                     ; urem uquot
         RTS
```

Figure 3–33   68HC11 Code for *UM/MOD* Using *FDIV* and *IDIV*

FDIV. The 68HC11 subroutine shown in Figure 3–33 will implement *UM/MOD* using *FDIV* and *IDIV* in this manner.

All other WHYP divide words for the 68HC11 can be derived from *UM/MOD*. If you are interested in how this is done, you can consult the 68HC11 assembly language source code in the file WHYP11.ASM.

3.4 SHIFT AND ROTATE INSTRUCTIONS

The 68HC12 shift and rotate instructions are listed in Table 3–6. These instructions are used to move bits left or right in a memory byte or in registers *A*, *B*, or *D*. There are three categories of shift and rotate instructions: logical shift, arithmetic shift, and rotate. We will look at each of these three categories of instructions.

3.4.1 Logical Shift Instructions

The logical shift instructions shift all bits in a memory location or register one bit left or right. The bit shifted out goes into the carry bit and a zero is shifted in.

Table 3–6   Shift and Rotate Instructions

Logical Shift Instructions

Mnemonic	Function
LSL	Logic Shift Left Memory
LSLA	Logic Shift Left A
LSLB	Logic Shift Left B
LSLD	Logic Shift Left D
LSR	Logic Shift Right Memory
LSRA	Logic Shift Right A
LSRB	Logic Shift Right B
LSRD	Logic Shift Right D

Arithmetic Shift Instructions

Mnemonic	Function
ASL	Arithmetic Shift Left Memory
ASLA	Arithmetic Shift Left A
ASLB	Arithmetic Shift Left B
ASLD	Arithmetic Shift Left D
ASR	Arithmetic Shift Right Memory
ASRA	Arithmetic Shift Right A
ASRB	Arithmetic Shift Right B

Rotate Instructions

Mnemonic	Function
ROL	Rotate Left Memory Through Carry
ROLA	Rotate Left A Through Carry
ROLB	Rotate Left B Through Carry
ROR	Rotate Right Memory Through Carry
RORA	Rotate Right A Through Carry
RORB	Rotate Right B Through Carry

Logic Shift Left   The instructions *LSL*, *LSLA*, and *LSLB* will cause the eight bits in memory byte, accumulator *A* or accumulator *B* to be shifted one bit to the left. The leftmost bit (bit 7) will be shifted into the carry bit. A zero will be shifted into the rightmost bit (bit 0). The operation is shown in Figure 3–34.

You can also shift the bits in *D* left one bit using the instructions *LSLD* shown in Figure 3–35.

Logic Shift Right   The instructions *LSR*, *LSRA*, and *LSRB* will cause the eight bits in memory byte, accumulator *A* or accumulator *B* to be shifted one bit to the right. The rightmost bit (bit 0) will be shifted into the carry bit. A zero will be shifted into the leftmost bit (bit 7). A picture of what this instruction does is shown in Figure 3–36.

You can also shift the bits in *D* right one bit using the instructions *LSRD* as shown in Figure 3–37.

Figure 3–34 The Logic Shift Left
Instructions: *LSL, LSLA, LSLB*

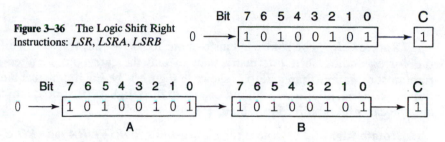

Figure 3–35 The Logic Shift Left Instruction, *LSLD*

Figure 3–36 The Logic Shift Right
Instructions: *LSR, LSRA, LSRB*

Figure 3–37 The Logic Shift Right Instruction, *LSRD*

Figure 3–38 Arithmetic Shift Right
Instructions: *ASR, ASRA, ASRB*

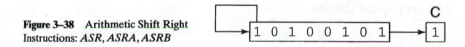

3.4.2 Arithmetic Shift Instructions

The arithmetic shift left instructions *ASL, ASLA, ASLB,* and *ASLD* are identical to the corresponding logic shift left instructions *LSL, LSLA, LSLB,* and *LSLD,* shown in Figures 3–34 and 3–35. However, the arithmetic shift right instructions, *ASR, ASRA,* and *ASRB,* differ from the corresponding logic shift right instructions, *LSR, LSRA,* and *LSRB* shown in Figure 3–36 in that the sign bit (the leftmost bit) remains the same. This means that if the sign bit is a 1 (corresponding to a negative number), this 1 will continually be shifted to the right. A picture of what this instruction does is shown in Figure 3–38.

There is no arithmetic shift right instruction for register *D.* To perform an arithmetic shift right operation on register *D* you must combine the *ASRA* instruction with a rotate instruction as described in Section 3.4.4.

3.4.3 Rotate Instructions

The rotate instructions rotate the bits in a memory byte or accumulators *A* or *B* through the carry bit.

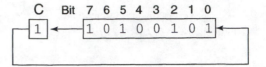

Figure 3–39 The Rotate Left
Instructions: *ROL, ROLA, ROLB*

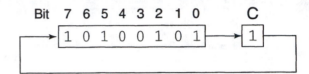

Figure 3–40 The Rotate Right
Instructions: *ROR, RORA, RORB*

Rotate Left   The rotate left instructions *ROL, ROLA*, and *ROLB* differ from the corresponding shift left instructions in that the carry bit is shifted into the rightmost bit rather than a zero as shown in Figure 3–39. Each time that the instruction is executed, all bits are shifted one bit to the left. Bit 7 is shifted into the carry and the carry bit is shifted into bit 0.

Rotate Right   The rotate right instructions *ROR, RORA*, and *RORB* are just the opposite of rotate left. As shown in Figure 3–40, each bit is shifted one bit to the right. Bit 0 is shifted into the carry and the carry bit is shifted into bit 7.

3.4.4 Shifting 16-bit Words

We saw in Section 3.4.2 that there is no 68HC12 instruction to arithmetic shift right for register *D*. We can, however, perform this operation by using the two instructions, *ASRA* and *RORB*. The *ASRA* instruction will perform the operation shown in Figure 3–38 on the upper byte of *D* where bit 0 of *A* will move into the carry bit. The instruction *RORB* will then move this carry bit into bit 7 of *B* as shown in Figure 3–40. The net effect will be an arithmetic shift right operation on register *D*.

Shifting bits in a register or memory location one bit to the left is equivalent to multiplying by 2. The WHYP word 2* (*n* -- 2**n) shown in Figure 3–41 will multiply the number on top of the data stack by 2 by first shifting the low byte left using the instruction *ASL 1,X* and then rotating left the high byte using the instruction *ROL 0,X*. This is a faster way to multiply by 2 than to type 2 *.

Shifting bits in a register or memory location one bit to the right is equivalent to dividing by 2. An arithmetic shift right operation will perform a signed division while a logical shift right operation will perform an unsigned division. The WHYP word 2/ (*n* -- *n*/2) shown in Figure 3–41 will divide the signed number on top of the data stack by 2 by first arithmetic shifting the high byte right using the instruction *ASR 0,X* and then rotating right the low byte using the instruction *ROR 1,X*.

Similarly, the WHYP word U2/ (*u* -- *u*/2), shown in Figure 3–41, will divide the unsigned number on top of the data stack by 2 by first logic shifting the high byte right using the instruction *LSR 0,X* and then rotating right the low byte using the instruction *ROR 1,X*.

```
;         2*        ( n -- 2*n )
TWOT
          ASL     1,X                      ;arith shift left
          ROL     0,X
          RTS


;         2/        ( n -- n/2 )
TWOS
          ASR     0,X                      ;arith shift right
          ROR     1,X
          RTS


;         U2/       ( u -- u/2 )
U2S
          LSR     0,X
          ROR     1,X                      ;logic shift right
          RTS
```

Figure 3–41   68HC12 Code for the WHYP Words *2**, *2/*, and *U2/*

All the shift and rotate instructions discussed in this section have shifted by one bit. Sometime you would like to shift more than one bit. For example, you might want to shift the low byte on top of the data stack to the high byte and fill the low byte with zeros. You can do this by typing

```
8 LSHIFT
```

where the WHYP word *LSHIFT (n1 n2 -- n3)* will shift left the bits in *n1 n2* times. The 68HC12 subroutine, *LSHIFT*, shown in Figure 3–42, will implement this WHYP word. Note that *n2* is loaded into *Y* and then the equivalent of *2** in Figure 3–41 is executed *n2* times. Index register *Y* is decremented until it reaches zero. The branching instruction *BNE* (branch not equal) will branch back to the label *LS1* as long as *Y* is not equal to zero. We will discuss branching instructions in detail in Chapter 5.

The WHYP word *RSHIFT (n1 n2 -- n3)* will logic shift right the bits in *n1 n2* times. For example, if you type

```
8 RSHIFT
```

then the high byte of the number on top of the data stack will be shifted into the low byte and the high byte will be filled with zeros. The 68HC12 subroutine for implementing *RSHIFT* is also shown in Figure 3–42.

3.5 SUMMARY

In addition to the WHYP words given in Box 3–1 for displaying numbers on the screen this chapter also discussed the arithmetic WHYP words given in Box 3–2.

```
;        LSHIFT       ( n1 n2 -- n3 )
;                  Left shift bits of n1 n2 times
LSHIFT
        LDY    2,X+              ;Y = n2
LS1     ASL    1,X               ;arith shift left
        ROL    0,X               ; n2 bits
        DEY
        BNE    LS1
        RTS


;        RSHIFT       ( n1 n2 -- n3 )
;                  Right shift bits of n1 n2 times
RSHIFT
        LDY    2,X+              ;Y = n2
RS1     LSR    0,X               ;logic shift right
        ROR    1,X               ; n2 bits
        DEY
        BNE    RS1
        RTS
```

Figure 3–42   68HC12 Code for the WHYP Words *LSHIFT* and *RSHIFT*

Box 3–2   Arithmetic WHYP Words

+   (n1 n2 -- n3)   ("plus")
          Adds top two elements on data stack and leaves the sum. $n3 = n1 + n2$.

−   (n1 n2 -- n3)   ("minus")
          Subtracts top element from second element on data stack and leaves the
          difference. $n3 = n1 - n2$.

D+   (d1 d2 -- d3)   ("D-plus")
          Adds top two double numbers on data stack and leaves the double sum.
          $d3 = d1 + d2$.

D−   (d1 d2 -- d3)   ("D-minus")
          Subtracts top double number from second double number on data stack
          and leaves the difference. $d3 = d1 - d2$.

1+   (n -- n+1)
          Increments the top of the stack by 1.

2+   (n -- n+2)
          Increments the top of the stack by 2.

1−   (n -- n−1)
          Decrements the top of the stack by 1.

2−   (n -- n−2)
          Decrements the top of the stack by 2.

(continued)

Box 3–2 (*continued*)

UM*	`( u1 u2 -- ud )`	

Unsigned multiply. Leaves the 32-bit product, u1*u2, on the stack.

M*   `( n1 n2 -- d )`
Signed multiply. Leaves the 32-bit product, n1*n2, on the stack.

*   `( n1 n2 -- n3 )`
Leaves the 16-bit product, n1*n2, on the stack.

DUM*   `( ud un -- ud )`
Unsigned multiply of 32 × 16. Leaves the 32-bit product, ud*un, on the stack.

/MOD   `( n1 n2 -- rem quot )`
Divides signed 16-bit n1 by signed 16-bit n2 and leaves the signed 16-bit quotient over the signed remainder on the stack.

/   `( n1 n2 -- quot )`
Divides signed 16-bit n1 by signed 16-bit n2 and leaves the signed 16-bit quotient, n1/n2, on the stack.

MOD   `( n1 n2 -- rem )`
Leaves on the stack the remainder of dividing signed 16-bit n1 by signed 16-bit n2.

UM/MOD   `( ud un -- urem uquot )`
Divides 32-bit unsigned ud by 16-bit unsigned un and leaves the 16-bit unsigned quotient over the 16-bit unsigned remainder on the stack.

MU/MOD   `( ud un -- urem udquot )`
Divides 32-bit unsigned ud by 16-bit unsigned un and leaves the 32-bit unsigned quotient over the 16-bit unsigned remainder on the stack.

M/MOD   `( d n -- rem quot )`
Divides 32-bit signed d by 16-bit signed n and leaves the 16-bit signed quotient over the 16-bit signed remainder on the stack.

*/   `( n1 n2 n3 -- n4 )`
Leaves n4 = n1*n2/n3, on the stack. Keeps n1*n2 as an intermediate 32-bit value.

U/   `( u1 u2 -- uquot )`
Divides 16-bit unsigned u1 by 16-bit unsigned u2 and leaves the 16-bit unsigned quotient, u1/u2, on the stack.

IDIV   `( u1 u2 -- rem quot )`
Divides unsigned 16-bit u1 by unsigned 16-bit u2 and leaves the unsigned 16-bit quotient over the unsigned 16-bit remainder on the stack.

FDIV   `( u1 u2 -- rem quot )`
Fractional division. Divides unsigned 16-bit u1 by unsigned 16-bit u2 and leaves the unsigned 16-bit quotient over the unsigned 16-bit remainder on the stack. u1 must be less than u2.

(*continued*)

Box 3–2 (*continued*)

2*	(n -- n*2) Multiplies the top of the stack by 2 by performing an arithmetic shift left one bit.
2/	(n -- n/2) Divides the top of the stack by 2 by performing an arithmetic shift right one bit.
U2/	(u -- u/2) Divides the unsigned value on top of the stack by 2 by performing a logic shift right one bit.
LSHIFT	(n1 n2 -- n3) Shifts bits of n1 left n2 times.
RSHIFT	(n1 n2 -- n3) Shifts bits of n1 right n2 times.

We showed how all of the WHYP words in Box 3–2 can be implemented using 68HC12 instructions. We saw that WHYP words are just the names of 68HC12 subroutines. In the next chapter we will see how you can write your own 68HC12 subroutines by defining new WHYP words in terms of already existing WHYP words.

EXERCISES

Exercise 3.1

Use WHYP in the interpretive mode to compute the following in decimal:

  a. 264857 + 863425
  b. 742916 − 282739
  c. 142739 + 258367
  d. 275839 − 726153

Exercise 3.2

Use WHYP in the interpretive mode to compute the following in hex:

  a. 273AC5 + 8A52F3
  b. 7CD5F2 − 2F835A
  c. B6E3A82 + 29752B7
  d. 5E17A5 − A748CB

Exercise 3.3

Use WHYP in the interpretive mode to compute the following in decimal:

  a. 4857 * 3425
  b. 742916 / 282
  c. 42739 * 58367
  d. 275839 / 153

Exercise 3.4

Use WHYP in the interpretive mode to compute the following in hex:

   a. 3AC5 * 8A52
   b. D5F2 / 83
   c. B6E3A82 * 29752B7
   d. A5E17A5 / 48CB

Exercise 3.5

Use WHYP in the interpretive mode to compute the following in decimal:

   a. −4857 * 3425
   b. 742916 / −282
   c. −42739 * 58367
   d. −275839 / 153

Exercise 3.6

Use WHYP in the interpretive mode to compute the following in hex:

   a. 3AC5 * −8A52
   b. −D5F2 / 83
   c. −B6E3A82 * 29752B7
   d. A5E17A5 / −48CB

Exercise 3.7

Use the WHYP words *LSHIFT* and *RSHIFT* to perform the following multiplications and divisions:

   a. 3A * 23
   b. D5F2 / 25
   c. E3 * 26
   d. A5E1 / 28

Exercise 3.8

An imaging system measures the diameter of ball bearings in pixel_units (0 - 1024). Write a WHYP word called *volume (D -- dvol)* that expects the diameter, *D*, on the data stack and leaves the volume of the ball bearing, *dvol*, (in pixel_units^3) as a double number. *Hint*: The volume is given by $\pi D^3/6$ and π can be approximated by 355/113. To maintain maximum accuracy, you should perform as many multiplications in the numerator as possible before dividing without exceeding 32 bits.

Exercise 3.9

What is the difference between the WHYP words *UM/MOD* and *MU/MOD*? Try some examples in both *HEX* and *DECIMAL* using .*S* to display the data stack.

4

WHYP—An Extensible Language

In previous chapters we have seen that WHYP allows us to give names to 68HC12 subroutines and then to execute these subroutines interactively from the PC keyboard. Data values are passed to and from these subroutines (WHYP words) on a data stack that is separate from the system (return) stack. If every time we want to make a WHYP word we have to write a 68HC12 subroutine, then WHYP would be of limited value. However, in this chapter we will see how you can define new WHYP words in terms of previously defined words and automatically add these words to the dictionary. This makes WHYP an extensible language in which each word that you define adds a new word to the language.

In Chapter 5 we will see how we can use the 68HC12 branching instructions to define WHYP words that will allow you to write WHYP words that contain branches and loops. You will then be able to write WHYP programs to perform any function you want on the 68HC12.

4.1 A CLOSER LOOK AT WHYP

As we have seen in Chapters 2 and 3, each word in WHYP is the name of a 68HC12 subroutine. There are over 125 such small subroutines that are stored in the file WHYP12.S19 that you download to the 68HC12 evaluation board. The names and addresses of all of these subroutines are given in the file `WHYP12.HED` (see Appendix E) which must be in the same directory as the program `WHYP12.EXE`. The evaluation board or target system is connected to a PC through an asynchronous serial line as shown in Figure 4–1.

The names of all WHYP words (subroutines) are stored in a dictionary that is maintained in the PC. We want to be able to "talk" to the target system by typing a WHYP word on the PC and having the corresponding WHYP subroutine execute on the target system. We do this by sending the address of the subroutine over the serial line to the target system. A small kernel program is running on the target system that waits for an address to be received on the serial line and then executes the subroutine at that address. It is this kernel program that you execute when you type *G 4000* after downloading `WHYP12.S19` to the evaluation board. The code for this kernel looks something like that shown in Figure 4–1, namely,

```
LOOP    BSR INWDY
        JSR 0,Y
        BRA LOOP
```

The subroutine *INWDY* waits for two bytes to be received in the serial port and stores this 16-bit address in index register *Y*. The statement *JSR 0,Y* then jumps to the subroutine whose address is in *Y*. The *BRA* (branch always) instruction always branches back to the label *LOOP*. We will discuss branching instructions in detail in Chapter 5.

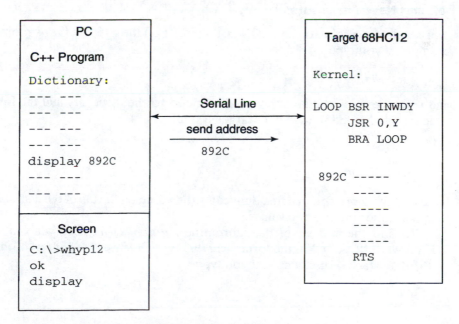

Figure 4–1   The Structure of WHYP

The actual WHYP kernel is given in the listing of `WHYP12.ASM` in Appendix D. The only difference from the loop shown in Figure 4–1 is the addition of an acknowledge signal that is sent back to the PC after the WHYP subroutine is executed.

4.2 DEFINING NEW WHYP WORDS

You can define your own WHYP words, made up of other WHYP words, by using the WHYP word : (colon) in the following form:

```
: <name>   --- --- --- --- ;
```

where the colon (:) begins the definition, *<name>* is the name of your WHYP word, --- --- are the WHYP words making up your definition, and the semicolon (;) ends the definition.

Note that new WHYP words are defined in terms of previously defined words. This is the way WHYP works. New, more powerful words are continually being defined. When you have finished, your entire main program will be just one word. The words you define are stored in the WHYP dictionary along with all the predefined WHYP words. They become part of the WHYP language and are treated just like any other WHYP word. The WHYP interpreter cannot tell the difference between words that you define and words that come as part of the language. This means that every WHYP application program is really a specialized language that is designed to solve a particular problem!

4.2.1 Defining New Words Interactively

You can define a colon definition by just typing it on the screen at the *ok* prompt. For example, if you type

```
: squared DUP * ;
```

and press *<enter>*, the name *squared* is added to the dictionary and the following code is downloaded to the HC12 target system:

```
16 4104   JSR DUP
16 4337   JSR *
3D        RTS
```

Note that the word *squared* first duplicates the value on the top of the data stack and then multiplies the top two values.

To find the address of the subroutine *squared* in memory, you can use the WHYP word "tick" (') in the form ' *<name>* which leaves the address of the word on the data stack. For example, if you type

```
HEX
' squared u.
```

the address $5000 will be displayed, as shown in Figure 4–2.

```
C:\WHYP\WHYP12>whyp12
Using WHYP12.HED
Communicating with COM1
68HC12 WHYP12 - Version 4.6
Press <Esc> or type BYE to exit
ok
: squared DUP * ; ok
hex ok
' squared u. 5000 ok
5000 20 dump
          0  1  2  3  4  5  6  7  8  9  A  B  C  D  E  F
5000   16 41 04 16 43 37 3D FF FF FF FF FF FF FF FB FF    A  C7=........
5010   FF FF FF FF FF FF DB FF FF EF FF FF FF FF FF FF    ...............
ok
decimal ok
5 squared . 25 ok
: cubed DUP squared * ; ok
hex ok
' cubed u. 5007 ok
5000 20 dump
          0  1  2  3  4  5  6  7  8  9  A  B  C  D  E  F
5000   16 41 04 16 43 37 3D 16 41 04 16 50 00 16 43 37    A  C7= A  P  C7
5010   3D FF FF FF FF FF DB FF FF EF FF FF FF FF FF FF    =..............
ok
decimal ok
5 cubed . 125 ok
```

Figure 4–2   Example of Defining New WHYP Words Using Colon Definitions

You can verify that the 68HC12 code for the subroutine *squared* has been downloaded to address $5000 by typing

```
5000 20 DUMP
```

as shown in Figure 4–2. The WHYP word *DUMP (addr len --)* can be used to display a block of memory of length *len* starting at address *addr*. The value of *len* is the number of bytes to display; however, *DUMP* always displays multiples of 16 bytes. For example, a hex length of $20 will display 32 bytes, or two rows of 16 bytes each. Notice that the (printable) ASCII characters associated with each memory byte are displayed to the right of each line. The memory addresses displayed by *DUMP* are always in hexadecimal, so it is generally useful to switch to *HEX* before using *DUMP*.

Note that the seven bytes of the subroutine *squared* (16 41 04 16 43 37 3D) are stored in memory at addresses $5000–$5006. The address of the subroutine *squared* ($5000) is stored in the dictionary on the PC and is associated with the name *squared*. When you type *squared,* this address will be sent to the target system and the subroutine for *squared* will be executed. Therefore, if you now type

```
DECIMAL
5 squared .
```

the value 25 will be displayed on the screen as shown in Figure 4–2.

When you typed the colon definition for *squared* and pressed *<enter>*, the code for *squared* was downloaded to the address of the current *target dictionary pointer*, *tdp*. The default value of *tdp* is set to 5000 in the configuration file, WHYP12.CFG, as shown in Figure 4–3. This configuration file is read each time you run WHYP12 on the PC. You can change the default value of *tdp* in this .CFG file to have new WHYP words loaded at a different location. Alternatively, you can press function key F9 to change the value of *tdp*. This will display the current value of *tdp* and offer you a chance to enter a new hex value. Pressing *<enter>* without entering a new value will keep the current value unchanged.

After each byte is downloaded to the target system, the value of *tdp* is automatically incremented. Therefore, *tdp* always points to the next available memory location in the target system. If you press function key F9 after defining *squared* as described above, the current value of *tdp* will be $5007. This is where the next word defined will be loaded.

If you now type a new colon definition for *cubed*,

```
: cubed DUP squared * ;
```

the name *cubed* is added to the dictionary and the following code is downloaded starting at address $5007 as shown in Figure 4–2.

```
WHYP12.HED
tdp        5000
vdp        800
TORG       4000
HEDBASE    4000
RAMBASE    0900
INCHAR     32
OUTPUT     3B
TPUSH      44
TPOP       4D
INWDY      58
INWDX      61
STOREW     6A
TBLKST     75
SNDSUB     8B2
EESTART    1000
EESTOP     1FFF
last       be
rts_code   31
set_flags  -1
```

Figure 4–3   The File WHYP12.CFG

```
16 4104   JSR DUP
16 5000   JSR squared
16 4337   JSR *
3D        RTS
```

Note that all WHYP words are case insensitive. You can type either *dup* or *DUP*. Generally, in writing a program we will define all new words in lowercase (such as *squared*) but will write built-in WHYP words such as *DUP* in uppercase. This is just a matter of taste so as to easily tell which words are newly defined and which are built into the language.

4.2.2 *SEE* and *SHOW*

The WHYP words *SEE* and *SHOW* can be used to decompile any WHYP word to see how it is defined. For example, if you type

```
see squared
```

then

```
squared
        DUP * ;
```

will be displayed, as shown in Figure 4–4. *SEE* is meant to decompile WHYP words that are defined as colon definitions. If the WHYP word is one of the built-in

```
see squared
squared
            DUP * ;
ok
show squared
squared
 16 41   4
 16 43 37 3D
ok
see cubed
cubed
            DUP squared * ;
ok
show cubed
cubed
 16 41   4
 16 50   0
 16 43 37 3D
ok
```

Figure 4–4 Illustrating the Use of *SEE* and *SHOW*

subroutines such as *DUP* or *ROT*, then *SEE* will just display its machine code (with the *RTS* instruction represented by the semicolon).

To see the machine code of a colon definition, you can use the word *SHOW*. For example, if you type

```
show squared
```

then the machine code of *squared* will be displayed with each *JSR* instruction on a separate line as shown in Figure 4–4. The results of applying *SEE* and *SHOW* to the word cubed are also shown in Figure 4–4.

4.2.3 Single-Stepping through Colon Definitions

Once you define a colon definition such as *squared* or *cubed*, you can test it interactively as we did in Figure 4–2. If this process produces incorrect results, you will need to debug your subroutine. One way to do this is to use the *Trace* command in D-Bug 12 as described in Chapter 1. The problem with this is that this command will show you the contents of all CPU12 registers, while what you really want to see is what is on the data stack and return stack after you execute each WHYP word making up your colon definition. The WHYP word *STEP* allows you to do this.

To use the word *STEP* you first put on the data stack whatever the word you are testing needs. Then type *STEP* followed by the word to be tested. For example, to single-step through the word *squared*, you would type

```
5 step squared
```

as shown in Figure 4–5. When you type this line, the definition of *squared* is displayed (as with the word *SEE*) followed by the current contents of the data and

```
ok
5 step squared
squared
          DUP  *  ;
S:[1] 5
R:[0]
 DUP
S:[2] 5 5
R:[0]
 *
S:[1] 19
R:[0]
Exit single step
ok
. 25 ok
```

Figure 4–5 Single-Stepping through the Word *squared*

```
ok
5 step cubed
cubed
        DUP squared * ;
S:[1] 5
R:[0]
 DUP
S:[2] 5 5
R:[0]
 squared
S:[2] 5 19
R:[0]
 *
S:[1] 7D
R:[0]
Exit single step
ok
. 125 ok
```

Figure 4–6   Single-Stepping through the Word *cubed*

return stack and the name of the next word to be executed (in this case *DUP*). Pressing the space bar will execute this next word and display the new contents of the data and return stack followed by the name of the next word to be executed. Pressing the space bar will continue to execute one word at a time until the end of the subroutine, at which point the single-step mode is exited and the *ok* prompt returns. You can quit the single-step mode at any point by pressing the *q* key.

An example of single-stepping the word *cubed* is shown in Figure 4–6. Note that when single-stepping, the stack values are always displayed in hex, even if you are currently in the decimal mode.

4.2.4   Loading WHYP Words from a File

In Section 4.2.1 you typed the colon definitions for *squared* and *cubed* directly in WHYP from the *ok* prompt. You will normally want to type all of the colon definitions in a file using any text editor. You can then load these colon definitions into the target system at the same time using the WHYP word *LOAD*. For example, Figure 4–7 shows the contents of the file SQUARE.WHP which is included on the disk with this book. This is the form in which you will normally write your programs.

In this file the backslash, \, indicates a comment. Everything following a backslash, until the end of the line, is ignored. You can also include comments between parentheses. However, inasmuch as everything in WHYP is a word, the word "paren" (is a WHYP word that treats everything to the closing paren) as a comment. Therefore, there *must* be a space after the (. We will normally use parentheses to indicate the stack picture associated with each colon definition.

```
\      Colon definition examples

: squared            ( n -- n**2 )    \ compute the square of n
                     DUP * ;          \ multiply top of stack by itself


: cubed              ( n -- n**3 )     \ compute the cube of n
                     DUP               \ n n
                     squared           \ n n**2
                     * ;               \ n**3
```

Figure 4-7   Contents of the File SQUARE.WHP

Normally you will include several **WHYP** words on a single line, as shown in the definition of *squared* in Figure 4–7. We call such grouping of WHYP words a *phrase*. Your phrases should be small enough so that you can understand what is happening on the data stack. Sometimes it is helpful to indicate what is on the stack as comments at the end of each line as we show for the word *cubed* in Figure 4–7. However, this word is simple enough that we would normally put all three words on one line.

Once you have created the file SQUARE.WHP shown in Figure 4–7, you can load all words in the file by typing

```
load square.whp
```

as shown in Figure 4–8. This will produce the same effect as when you typed in the words at the *ok* prompt in Figure 4–2. Note that after all the words in the file have

```
C:\WHYP\WHYP12>whyp12
Using WHYP12.HED
Communicating with COM1
68HC12 WHYP12 - Version 4.6
Press <Esc> or type BYE to exit
ok
load square.whp
\      Colon definition examples

: squared            ( n -- n**2 )    \ compute the square of n
                     DUP * ;          \ multiply top of stack by itself

: cubed              ( n -- n**3 )     \ compute the cube of n
                     DUP               \ n n
                     squared           \ n n**2
                     * ;               \ n**3

Current value of target dp is 5011
ok
```

Figure 4-8   Loading WHYP Words from the File SQUARE.WHP

been loaded, the current value of the target dictionary pointer, *tdp*, is displayed. In this case it is $5011 which will be the next available location as shown in Figure 4–2. It is useful to check this value to make sure it is still a valid memory address. When you load in a large file, you may fill up a particular segment of RAM (or EEPROM) in which case some of the words won't be in memory at all!

At this point the words *squared* and *cubed* have been loaded into memory and their names are in the dictionary. Therefore, you can execute them with statements such as

```
5 squared .
```

and

```
6 cubed .
```

4.2.5   CR and ."

As another example of defining words using colon definitions, consider the WHYP words given in Box 4–1. The WHYP word *CR* will produce a carriage return on the PC screen. This word just sends the ASCII code for *CR* ($0D) to the PC. The WHYP C++ program running on the PC will then perform a carriage return.

The WHYP word ." ("dot-quote") will print a string on the PC consisting of all the characters between ." and a closing ". (Remember that there must be a space after ."). The word ." must be in a colon definition.

As an example, define the following words:

```
: bar        ( -- )              \ print a bar
             CR ." ******" ;
```

Type *bar*.

```
: post       ( -- )              \ print a post
             CR ." *"
             CR ." *"
             CR ." *" ;
```

Type *post*.

```
: C          ( -- )              \ print a C
             bar post bar cr ;
```

Box 4–1   Some WHYP I/O Words

```
CR           ( -- )    ( "carriage return" )
             Produces a "carriage return" and line feed on the screen.

."           ( -- )    ( "dot-quote" )
             Prints a string consisting of characters to closing ".
```

Type *C*.

```
: E          ( -- )           \ print an E
      bar post bar post bar cr ;
```

Type *E*.

This example illustrates how new WHYP words are defined in terms of previously defined words.

4.3 VARIABLES

The code for the words *squared* and *cubed* gets loaded into memory at the address pointed to by *tdp* as described above. This memory may be in RAM or EEPROM. Eventually, you may move these words to the EPROM in one of the 68HC11 parts such as the 68HC711E9, or to the flash memory in the 68HC912B32, or to an external EPROM or flash memory. At this point these bytes cannot be changed. Therefore, variables, or any data that must be changed during the execution of the program, must be in RAM and cannot be in the memory pointed to by the target dictionary pointer, *tdp*. We use another *variable dictionary pointer*, *vdp*, to point to the memory (in RAM) that will store variables. The default value of *vdp* is given as $800 in the third line of the .CFG file shown in Figure 4–3. You can change this default value in the .CFG file or you can change *vdp* within WHYP by pressing function key F8 in the same way that you change *tdp* by pressing function key F9.

The WHYP word *VARIABLE* is a defining word used to define variable names. If you type

```
VARIABLE my.name
```

then WHYP will create a new dictionary entry called *my.name* and will store the following code in the target system at the address *tdp:*

```
16 451E          JSR (LIT)
0800             0800
3D               RTS
```

This is the code that will be executed when you type *my.name*. To find the address of this code you can type

```
' my.name u.
```

as shown in Figure 4–9.

The value of *vdp* was $0800 before defining *my.name*. This value is stored in the target memory following the instruction *JSR (LIT)*. This instruction will put on the data stack the 16-bit value following this instruction (in this case $0800, the address of the variable *my.name*). Therefore, if you were to type

```
my.name .
```

the address of *my.name* (800) would be displayed on the screen as shown in Figure 4–9. Therefore, executing the name of a *VARIABLE* puts its address on the data stack.

```
C:\WHYP\WHYP12>whyp12
Using WHYP12.HED
Communicating with COM1
68HC12 WHYP12 - Version 4.6
Press <Esc> or type BYE to exit
ok
VARIABLE my.name ok
hex ok
' my.name u. 5000 ok
5000 20 dump
          0  1  2  3  4  5  6  7  8  9  A  B  C  D  E  F
5000   16 45 1E 08 00 3D FF FF FF FF FF FF FF FF FB FF     E   =.........
5010   FF FF FF FF FF FF DB FF FF EF FF FF FF FF FF FF        ................
ok
my.name . 800 ok
```

Figure 4-9   Example of Using a WHYP *VARIABLE*

```
;            (LIT)    ( -- n )
;                     Runtime routine for single literals
LIT
        PULY                    ;Y -> number
        LDD   0,Y               ;Push number
        STD   2,-X              ;on data stack
        INY                     ;jump over number
        INY
        PSHY
        RTS
```

Figure 4-10 68HC12
Code for *(LIT)*

The way that the WHYP word *(LIT)* ("paren-LIT") works is shown by its 68HC12 implementation in Figure 4–10. Note that the "return address" that was automatically pushed on the system stack when *JSR (LIT)* was executed is popped into *Y*. But this is just the address of the number $800 that follows the instruction *JSR (LIT)*. The value at this address ($800) is loaded into *D* and pushed onto the data stack. Then *Y* is incremented by 2 to jump over the number and this address is pushed onto the system stack so that the *RTS* instruction will jump to this address.

4.3.1 Fetch and Store

To write data to a variable you use the WHYP word *!* ("store") defined in Box 4–2. To read data from a variable, you use the WHYP word *@* ("fetch") also defined in Box 4–2. For example,

        7 my.name !

will store the value 7 in the variable *my.name*, and

        my.name @ .

will read the value 7 from the variable *my.name* and print it on the screen as shown in Figure 4–11.

Box 4–2   RAM Memory Access Words

!	(n addr --)	("store")

Stores the 16-bit value of *n* at address *addr*.

@	(addr -- n)	("fetch")

Reads the value at address *addr* and puts it on the data stack.

C!	(c addr --)	("C-store")

Stores the Least Significant Byte (LSB) of the value on top of the stack at address *addr*.

C@	(addr -- c)	("C-fetch")

Reads the byte at address *addr* and leaves it as the Least Significant Byte (LSB) on top of the stack.

+!	(n addr --)	("plus-store")

Adds *n* to the value at address *addr*.

2!	(d addr --)	("2-store")

Stores the 32-bit value of *d* at address *addr*.

2@	(addr -- d)	("2-fetch")

Reads the double number at address *addr* and puts it on the data stack.

```
C:\WHYP\WHYP12>whyp12
Using WHYP12.HED
Communicating with COM1
68HC12 WHYP12 - Version 4.6
Press <Esc> or type BYE to exit
ok
VARIABLE my.name   ok
hex ok
my.name . 800 ok
7 my.name ! ok
800 10 dump
       0  1  2  3  4  5  6  7  8  9  A  B  C  D  E  F
0800  00 07 86 80 52 00 80 02 09 00 28 18 90 00 83 00    ..R .  ( . .
ok
my.name @ . 7 ok
12 my.name c! ok
34 my.name 1+ c! ok
800 10 dump
       0  1  2  3  4  5  6  7  8  9  A  B  C  D  E  F
0800  12 34 86 80 52 00 80 02 09 00 28 18 90 00 83 00    4..R .  ( . .
ok
my.name c@ . 12 ok
my.name 1+ c@ . 34 ok
```

Figure 4–11   Example of Using "fetch" and "store"

Notice that the 16-bit value $0007 is stored in memory locations $800 and $801. Thus, the word *!* ("store") always stores a word, or two bytes, in memory, and the word @ ("fetch") will always fetch two bytes from memory. If you want to access a single byte, you can use the words *C@* ("C-fetch") and *C!* ("C-store") to fetch and store a single byte as shown by the examples in Figure 4–11.

The 68HC12 subroutine that implements the WHYP word *!* ("store") is shown in Figure 4–12. Note that the address, *a*, is popped from the data stack into *Y* and then the word, *w*, is popped from the data stack and moved to the address pointed to by *Y*.

The 68HC12 subroutine that implements the WHYP word @ ("fetch") is also shown in Figure 4–12. Note that the address, *a*, is loaded from the data stack into *Y* and then the word, *w*, is moved from this address pointed to by *Y* to the data stack. In this case the address is on the data stack before @ is executed and the word at that address is left on the stack after @ is executed.

The 68HC12 subroutine that implements the WHYP word *C!* ("C-store") is also shown in Figure 4–12. Note that the byte address, *b*, is popped from the data

```
;       !       ( w a -- )
STORE
        LDY     2,X+            ;Y=a, pop data stack in Y
        MOVW    2,X+,0,Y        ;store w at a
        RTS


;       @       ( a -- w )
AT
        LDY     0,X             ;Y = a
        MOVW    0,Y,0,X         ;w = @Y
        RTS


;       C!      ( c b -- )
CSTOR
        LDY     2,X+            ;Y=b
        LDD     2,X+            ;D = c
        STAB    0,Y             ;store c at b
        RTS


;       C@      ( b -- c )
CAT
        LDY     0,X             ;Y=b
        CLRA
        LDAB    0,Y
        STD     0,X
        RTS
```

Figure 4–12   68HC12 Code for *!*, @, *C!*, and *C@*

stack into *Y* and then the word containing the character, *c*, is popped from the data stack into *D*. Only the lower byte of this word (which is now in *B*) is stored at the address pointed to by *Y*.

The 68HC12 subroutine that implements the WHYP word *C@* ("C-fetch") is also shown in Figure 4–12. Note that the byte address, *b*, is loaded from the data stack into *Y* and then the byte, *b*, is loaded into *B* from this address pointed to by *Y*. Accumulator *A*, the high byte of *D*, is cleared to zero, and then *D* is pushed onto the data stack. Note that elements on the data stack always contain 16 bits, but in this case the character, *c*, is stored in the low byte of the word on the data stack.

Another useful WHYP word shown in Box 4–2 is *+!* (*n addr* --) ("plus-store") that adds *n* to the value at address *addr*. For example, to increment the value stored in the variable *my.name* by 1, you could type

```
1 my.name +!
```

The 68HC12 subroutine that implements the WHYP word *+!* ("plus-store") is shown in Figure 4–13. Note that the address, *addr,* is popped from the data stack into *Y* and then the value at address, *addr*, is loaded into *D*. The value of *n* (still on the data stack) is added to *D* and popped from the data stack. This result is then stored at the address, *addr*, pointed to by *Y*.

Suppose you want to create a double variable that contains a 32-bit value. If you type

```
VARIABLE dname
```

WHYP will create the dictionary entry *dname* that contains a single 16-bit value at the RAM address *dname*, as described above. The variable dictionary pointer, *vdp*, will have been incremented by 2 to point to the next available RAM location. The WHYP word *VALLOT* will add *n* bytes to the variable dictionary pointer, *vdp*, where *n* is the value on the data stack when *VALLOT* is executed. Thus,

```
2 VALLOT
```

will add 2 bytes, or one word to the variable dictionary pointer, *vdp*. Thus, a double variable called *dname* can be created by typing

```
VARIABLE dname        2 VALLOT
```

The WHYP words *2!* (*d addr* --) and *2@* (*addr* -- *d*), shown in Box 4–2, can be used to store and fetch double numbers from a double variable. For example,

```
123456 dname 2!
```

```
;         +!      ( n addr -- )      add n to @addr
PSTORE
          LDY     2,X+              ;Y = addr
          LDD     0,Y               ;D = @addr
          ADDD    2,X+              ;add n to @addr
          STD     0,Y
          RTS
```

Figure 4–13   68HC12 Code for *+!*

```
;        2!    ( d a  -- )              store double word
         LDY    2,X+                   ;Y = a
         MOVW   2,X+,2,Y+              ;store dH
         MOVW   2,X+,0,Y              ;store dL
         RTS


;        2@    ( a -- d )              fetch double word
         LDY    2,X+                   ;Y = a
         MOVW   2,Y,2,-X              ;push dL on data stack
         MOVW   0,Y,2,-X              ;push dH on data stack
         RTS
```

Figure 4–14   68HC12 Code for *2!* and *2@*

will store the double number 123456 in the double variable *dname*. To print the value in *dname* you could type

```
dname 2@ d.
```

The 68HC12 subroutine that implements the WHYP word *2!*("2-store") is shown in Figure 4–14. Note that the address, *a*, is popped from the data stack into *Y* and then the high word, *dH*, is popped from the data stack and moved to the address pointed to by *Y*. Then *Y* is incremented by 2 and the low word, *dL*, is popped from the data stack and moved to the address pointed to by *Y*.

The 68HC12 subroutine that implements the WHYP word *2@* ("2-fetch") is also shown in Figure 4–14. Note that the address, *a*, is popped from the data stack into *Y* and then the two words *dL* (at *Y*+2) and *dH* (at *Y*), are pushed onto the data stack.

4.3.2   System Variables

There are two system variables, *SP0* and *RP0*, that are used in the WHYP kernel as shown in Figure 4–15. The system variable *SP0* contains the value of the data stack pointer for an empty stack. Thus,

```
SP0 @
```

will return the address of the data stack pointer when nothing is on the stack. The system variable *RP0* contains the value of the return stack pointer for an empty stack.

```
STACK    EQU      RAMBASE+$100        ;system (return) stack
DATSTK   EQU      RAMBASE+$80         ;data stack
****** WHYP System Variables ******
SP0      EQU      RAMBASE             ;initial data stack pointer
RP0      EQU      RAMBASE+$02         ;initial return stack pointer
```

Figure 4–15   The System Variables *SP0* and *RP0*

```
;          DEPTH ( -- n )                    return #items on stack
DEPTH
          STX      2,-X                    ;save data stack ptr
          LDD      SP0
          SUBD     0,X                     ;#bytes = SP0 - X
          ASRA
          RORB                             ;D = #stack items
          STD      0,X                     ; if neg, underflow
          RTS
```

Figure 4–16   68HC12 Code for *DEPTH*

As noted in Chapter 2, the WHYP word *SP@*, defined in Box 2–3, returns the address of the last item pushed on the data stack. That is, it is the current value of the data stack pointer. Similarly, the WHYP word *RP@*, defined in Box 2–3, returns the address of the last item pushed on the return stack.

The WHYP word *DEPTH* returns the number of items on the data stack. The 68HC12 subroutine that implements *DEPTH* is shown in Figure 4–16. Note that since each element on the data stack is a word that contains two bytes, the number of bytes on the stack must be divided by 2 to give the number of words on the data stack.

4.3.3 Arrays

Suppose you want to create an array that contains five 16-bit values. If you type

```
VARIABLE my.array
```

WHYP will create the dictionary entry *my.array* that contains a single 16-bit value at the RAM address *my.array* as described above. Then typing

```
8 VALLOT
```

will add 8 bytes, or four words, to the variable dictionary pointer, *vdp*. The array created in RAM will then look like that shown in Figure 4–17. The WHYP word *VHERE* puts the current value of *vdp* on the data stack. Therefore, if you type

```
VHERE .
```

my.array	my.array[0]
my.array + 2	my.array[1]
my.array + 4	my.array[2]
my.array + 6	my.array[3]
my.array + 8	my.array[4]
	vdp -->

Figure 4–17 Array Elements Contain Two Bytes Each

the current value of *vdp* will be displayed on the screen. (This value can also be seen by pressing function key F8.)

To print the value of *my.array[3]*, you could type

```
my.array 3 2* + @ .
```

which fetches the value from address *my.array* + 6. This may look a little awkward. You could clean it up by defining an *array fetch* word called *A@ (ix addr -- n)* that expects the array index and array address on the data stack, and then fetches the 16-bit value at address *addr + 2*ix*. The definition of *A@* would be

```
: A@        ( ix addr -- n )
            SWAP 2* + @ ;
```

To print the value of *my.array[3]*, you could then type

```
3 my.array A@ .
```

In Chapter 13 we will see how we can use a defining word to define arrays in such a way that you can just type

```
3 my.array @ .
```

to print the value of *my.array[3]*. We will also see in Chapter 13 how you can type

```
1234 3 my.array !
```

to store the value 1234 in *my.array[3]*.

4.4   CONSTANTS

The WHYP word *CONSTANT* is a defining word that lets you define constants. For example, if you type

```
25 CONSTANT quarter
```

then WHYP will create a new dictionary entry called *quarter* and will store the following code in the target system at the address *tdp*:

```
16 451E       JSR (LIT)
0019          0019
3D            RTS
```

Note that this is similar to what happens when you define a variable. However, instead of the address of a variable being stored following the instruction *JSR (LIT)*, the value of the constant (in this case, $0019 = 25$) is stored there. Therefore, if you type

```
quarter .
```

```
HEX
0024    CONSTANT   PORTH
0025    CONSTANT   DDRH
0028    CONSTANT   PORTJ
0029    CONSTANT   DDRJ


FF DDRH C!
00 DDRJ C!
3A PORTH C!
PORTJ C@ .
```

Figure 4–18 Examples of Using
*CONSTANT*s

the value 25 will be printed on the screen. The value stored in *CONSTANT*s are
16-bit signed numbers.

Constants are often used to define fixed addresses such as the addresses of registers in the 68HC12 register block. The words *C@* and *C!* can then be used to read
and write data to these registers as illustrated in Figure 4–18.

4.4.1 Tables

A table is like a constant array. As such it can be stored in EEPROM and EPROM
as well as RAM. This means that you sometimes want to create a table that gets
stored at the address of the target dictionary pointer, *tdp*. To do this we use the
WHYP word *CREATE* which works in a similar way as *CONSTANT* except that no
space is reserved for the constant value. For example, if you type

```
CREATE table
```

you will create a dictionary entry called *table* and the address of *table* (its *CFA*, or
code field address) will contain the instruction *JSR DOVAR* as shown in Figure 4–19
as well as the example given in Figure 4–20.

Note from the example shown in Figure 4–20 that the CFA of *table* is $5000.
The WHYP word *HERE* puts the current value of *tdp* on the data stack. After cre-
ating *table*, the value of *tdp* is $5003 which is called the *parameter field address*, or
PFA, of *table* as shown in Figure 4–19.

Executing *table* will execute the instruction *JSR DOVAR* which has the effect
of putting the PFA shown in Figure 4–19 on the data stack. This is illustrated in
Figure 4–20.

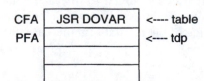

Figure 4–19 Example of Creating a
Table Using *CREATE*

```
C:\WHYP\WHYP12>whyp12
Using WHYP12.HED
Communicating with COM1
68HC12 WHYP12 - Version 4.6
Press <Esc> or type BYE to exit
ok
CREATE table ok
hex ok
' table u. 5000 ok
5000 10 dump
          0  1  2  3  4  5  6  7  8  9  A  B  C  D  E  F
5000  16 46 AA FF FF FF FF FF FF FF FF FF FF FF FF    F..............
ok
' dovar u. 46aa ok
here u. 5003 ok
table u. 5003 ok
5 , 8 , 23 , ok
5000 10 dump
          0  1  2  3  4  5  6  7  8  9  A  B  C  D  E  F
5000  16 46 AA 00 05 00 08 00 23 FF FF FF FF FF FF    F.      #.......
ok
here u. 5009 ok
 ok
: @table 2* table + @ ; ok
2 @table . 23 ok
```

Figure 4–20   Example of Creating a Table Using *CREATE*

At this point the target dictionary pointer, *tdp*, contains the value of the *PFA* of *table*. The WHYP word comma (,), defined in Box 4–3, will store the value on the data stack at the location pointed to by the target dictionary pointer, *tdp*; that is, at the next available location in the target memory. Therefore, if you type

```
5 , 8 , 23 ,
```

as shown in Figure 4–20, the table shown in Figure 4–21 will be created in the target memory as shown in Figure 4–20. You could now define a new word called @*table* as

---

Box 4–3   WHYP Words to Insert Data into Target Memory

,	(n --) ("comma")
	Stores the value *n* at the location pointed to by the target dictionary pointer, *tdp*, and increments *tdp* by 2. Will comma data into EEPROM.
C,	(c --) ("C-comma")
	Stores the byte *c* at the location pointed to by the target dictionary pointer, *tdp*, and increments *tdp* by 1. Will C-comma data into EEPROM.

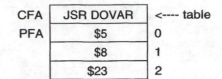

Figure 4–21 Example of Creating a
Table Using *CREATE*

```
: @table    ( ix -- n )
            2* table        \ 2*ix pfa
            + @ ;           \ @(pfa + 2*ix)
```

Figure 4–22 Definition of *@table* to Retrieve Words from a Table

shown in Figure 4–22. This word expects an index on the data stack and returns the
16-bit value at that index in the table. For example, *2 @table* will return $23 to the
top of the stack as shown in Figure 4–20.

Note that the WHYP word comma (,) increments the target dictionary pointer,
tdp, by 2. The dictionary pointer, *tdp*, can also be incremented by *n* bytes by using
the WHYP word *ALLOT (n --)* in the same way that *VALLOT* increments the
variable dictionary pointer, *vdp*, as described in Section 4.3.3.

Character (ASCII) data can be stored in one byte. The word *C,* ("C-comma"),
defined in Box 4–3, will store the Least Significant Byte (LSB) of the value on top of
the data stack at *tdp*. You can create a table containing byte values rather than word
values by typing

```
CREATE table 5 C, 8 C, 23 C,
```

You can then define a word called *C@table* as shown in Figure 4–23. *2 C@table* will
then return $23 to the top of the stack. Note the difference between *C@table* defined
in Figure 4–23 and *@table* defined in Figure 4–22.

You may have wondered why the program doesn't run into the data when the
instruction *JSR DOVAR* in Figure 4–21 is executed. After all, the *JSR* instruction
puts the address of the next instruction on the system stack. This is just the PFA
value shown in Figure 4–21. The 68HC12 assembly language code for *DOVAR* is
shown in Figure 4–24. The first instruction, *PULY*, will pop the value of *PFA* from
the system stack and put it in index register *Y*. The next instruction then pushes this
value of *PFA* onto the WHYP data stack. (Remember that index register *X* is the
WHYP data stack pointer.) The *RTS* instruction at the end of *DOVAR* in Figure 4–24 doesn't go back to the *PFA* in Figure 4.21 where the data are because this
return address was popped from the system stack by the *PULY* instruction. Rather
the *RTS* instruction will pop the next return address from the system stack, which
will be the return address of the instruction that jumped to the subroutine *table*. The
program will therefore jump to the word following *table*.

```
:  C@table       ( ix -- c )
                 table + C@ ;
```

Figure 4–23   Definition of *C@table* to Retrieve Bytes from a Table

```
;         DOVAR      ( -- a )              (leave pfa on data stack)
                                           ;Run time code for CREATE
DOVAR
          PULY                             ;get return addr (pfa)
          STY     2,-X                     ;push on data stack
          RTS                              ;return one level up
```

Figure 4–24   68HC12 Code for *DOVAR*

4.5   EEPROM

As we saw in Chapter 1 the MC68HC812A4 has 4 Kbytes of EEPROM and the MC68HC912B32 has 768 bytes of EEPROM (see Figures 1–3 and 1–4). This electrically erasable programmable read-only memory is a nonvolatile memory that can be used to store program code or table values that are changed infrequently. Writing data to the EEPROM requires a special procedure in which the byte must first be erased (the erased state is $FF) and then programmed with the new value to be stored at that address. Both the erasure and programming procedure require a high voltage (derived from the internal V_{DD} supply using a charge pump) to be applied for 10 milliseconds. Thus, writing data to the EEPROM is much slower than writing data to RAM. Data can be read from the EEPROM at normal speeds. The EEPROM has a minimum erase/program life of 10,000 cycles.

The EEPROM starts at address $1000 in the MC68HC812A4 and at address $0D00 in the MC68HC912B32. These default addresses can be mapped to any 4-Kbyte boundary by using the I/O register *INITEE* shown in Figure 4–25. The 4 bits *EE[15:12]* represent the upper 4 bits of the 16-bit EEPROM address. On reset these bits are set to 0001 in the 'A4 part (corresponding to address $1000) and to 0000 in the 'B32 part (corresponding to address $0D00). The *EEON* bit in the *INITEE* register in Figure 4–23 is set to 1 on reset which enables the

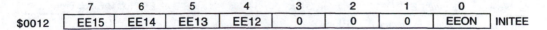

	7	6	5	4	3	2	1	0	
$0012	EE15	EE14	EE13	EE12	0	0	0	EEON	INITEE

EE[15:12]: Internal EEPROM map position
          Upper four bits of 16-bit EEPROM address.

EEON: Internal EEPROM On (Enable)
        0 – Disable EEPROM
        1 – Enable EEPROM (Default on reset)

Figure 4–25   The EEPROM Initial Position Register

	7	6	5	4	3	2	1	0	
$00F1	1	BPROT6	BPROT5	BPROT4	BPROT3	BPROT2	BPROT1	BPROT0	EEPROT

BPROT[6:0]:   EEPROM Block Protection
        0 – Associated EEPROM block can be programmed and erased.
        1 – Associated EEPROM block cannot be programmed and erased.

Figure 4–26   The MC68HC812A4 EEPROM Block Protect Register

	7	6	5	4	3	2	1	0	
$00F1	1	1	1	BPROT4	BPROT3	BPROT2	BPROT1	BPROT0	EEPROT

BPROT[4:0]:   EEPROM Block Protection
        0 – Associated EEPROM block can be programmed and erased.
        1 – Associated EEPROM block cannot be programmed and erased.

Figure 4–27   The MC68HC912B32 EEPROM Block Protect Register

EEPROM and puts it in the memory map determined by the *EE[15:12]* bits. Writing a 0 to the *EEON* bit will disable the EEPROM.

The starting and stopping addresses of the EEPROM must be included as the entries *EESTART* and *EESTOP* in the file WHYP12.CFG as shown in Figure 4–3. Certain blocks of memory within the EEPROM address space can be protected from accidental writes or erasure by using the *EEPROT* register shown in Figure 4–26 for the MC68HC812A4 and in Figure 4–27 for the MC68HC912B32. The blocks protected by each bit are shown in Tables 4–1 and 4–2.

On reset, all of the *BPROT* bits are set to 1, meaning that all bytes in the EEPROM are protected and cannot be written to or erased. Therefore, before the EEPROM can be used, at least some of the *BPROT* bits in the *EEPROT* register must be cleared to zero. At the beginning of the WHYP12 kernel the statement

```
CLR EEPROT ;enable EEPROM writes
```

will enable writes to all bytes in the EEPROM.

Table 4–1   4-Kbyte EEPROM Block Protection

Bit Name	Block Protected	Block Size
BPROT6	$1000 to $17FF	2048 Bytes
BPROT5	$1800 to $1BFF	1024 Bytes
BPROT4	$1C00 to $1DFF	512 Bytes
BPROT3	$1E00 to $1EFF	256 Bytes
BPROT2	$1F00 to $1F7F	128 Bytes
BPROT1	$1F80 to $1FBF	64 Bytes
BPROT0	$1FC0 to $1FFF	64 Bytes

Table 4–2   768-Byte EEPROM Block Protection

Bit Name	Block Protected	Block Size
BPROT4	$0D00 to $0DFF	256 Bytes
BPROT3	$0E00 to $0EFF	256 Bytes
BPROT2	$0F00 to $0F7F	128 Bytes
BPROT1	$0F80 to $0FBF	64 Bytes
BPROT0	$0FC0 to $0FFF	64 Bytes

4.5.1   Erasing the EEPROM

Erasing and programming the EEPROM is controlled by the *EEPROG* register shown in Figure 4–28. To erase any part of the EEPROM, the *ERASE* bit in the *EEPROG* register must be set to 1. To erase a single byte, you set the *BYTE* bit to 1. To bulk erase the entire EEPROM array, you would clear both the *BYTE* and *ROW* bits to zero. The *EELAT* bit must also be set to 1 for programming and erasure.

	7	6	5	4	3	2	1	0	
$00F3	BULKP	0	0	BYTE	ROW	ERASE	EELAT	EEPGM	EEPROG

BULKP: Bulk Erase Protection
        0 – EEPROM can be bulk erased .
        1 – EEPROM is protected from being bulk or row erased.
        (Default on reset)

BYTE: Byte and Aligned Word Erase
        0 – Bulk or row erase is enabled
        1 – One byte or one aligned word erase only.
        Has no effect when ERASE = 0.

ROW: Row or Bulk Erase (when BYTE = 0)
        0 – Erase entire EEPROM array.
        1 – Erase only one 32-byte row.
        Has no effect when ERASE = 0.

ERASE: Erase Control
        0 – EEPROM configured for programming.
        1 – EEPROM configured for erasure.

EELAT: EEPROM Latch Control
        0 – EEPROM set up for normal reads.
        1 – EEPROM address and data bus latches set up for programming or erasing. Can only write to if EEPGM = 0.

EEPGM: Program and Erase Enable
        0 – Disables program/erase voltage to EEPROM
        1 – Applies program/erase voltage to EEPROM

Figure 4–28   The EEPROM Control Register

The following steps are used to erase a single byte:

1. Write a 1 to the *BYTE*, *ERASE*, and *EELAT* bits in the *EEPROG* register.
2. Write any byte to the EEPROM address to be erased.
3. Write a 1 to the *EEPGM* bit in the *EEPROG* register.
4. Delay 10 milliseconds.
5. Write a 0 to the *EEPGM* bit in the *EEPROG* register.
6. Write a 0 to the *EELAT* bit in the *EEPROG* register to set normal read mode.

The subroutine shown in Figure 4–29 will erase a single byte at the address in register *Y*. Note that it is important to follow steps 3–5 above in which the *EEPGM* bit is first set to 1, delay for 10 milliseconds, and then the *EEPGM* bit is brought to 0 before the *EELAT* bit is cleared. This is necessary because the other bits in the *EEPROG* register cannot be changed when the *EEPGM* bit is set.

The subroutine *DLY10* shown in Figure 4–30 will delay for 10 milliseconds. This subroutine just executes the two instructions

```
DL1     DEX
        BNE     DL1
```

```
;          ERASE BYTE AT ADDRESS Y
BYTEE
        LDAB    #$16
        STAB    EEPROG          ;set to byte erase mode
        STAB    0,Y             ;write any data to addr to erase
        LDAB    #$17
        STAB    EEPROG          ;turn on high voltage
        JSR     DLY10           ;10 msec delay
        LDAB    #$16
        STAB    EEPROG          ;turn off hi voltage
        CLR     EEPROG          ;clear EELAT bit
        RTS
```

Figure 4–29 Subroutine to Erase the Byte at Address in *Y*

```
;          10MS.DELAY ( -- )      ; 8 MHz clock
DLY10                             ; 4*N + 12 = 80000
        PSHX                      ; 2 cycles
        LDX     #19997            ; 2    "      N = 19997
DL1     DEX                       ; 1    "
        BNE     DL1               ; 3    "
        PULX                      ; 3    "
        RTS                       ; 5    "
```

Figure 4–30 Subroutine to Delay 10 Milliseconds

```
;          ERASE.BULK          ( -- )
BULKE
         LDAB      #$06
         STAB      EEPROG              ;set to bulk erase mode
         STAB      EESTART             ;write any data to EEPROM
         LDAB      #$07
         STAB      EEPROG              ;turn on high voltage
         BSR       DLY10               ;10 msec delay
         LDAB      #$06
         STAB      EEPROG              ;turn off high voltage
         LDAB      #$00
         STAB      EEPROG              ;clear EELAT bit
         RTS
```

Figure 4–31   Subroutine to Erase Entire Unprotected EEPROM

19,997 times. Inasmuch as *DEX* takes 1 clock cycle and *BNE* takes 3 clock cycles (see Table A–1 in Appendix A), then this loop will take $19,997 \times 4 = 79,988$ clock cycles. The other instructions in this subroutine take a total of 12 clock cycles for a total of 80,000 clock cycles. Each cycle of an 8-MHz clock takes 0.125 microseconds. Therefore, 80,000 clock cycles will take 10 milliseconds. The WHYP word *10MS.DELAY* will execute this subroutine.

The subroutine shown in Figure 4–31 will bulk erase all of the unprotected blocks in the entire EEPROM array. It follows steps similar to those for byte erase except that both the *BYTE* and *ROW* bits in the *EEPROG* register are zero. The WHYP word *ERASE.BULK* will execute this subroutine.

4.5.2 Programming the EEPROM

A byte in the EEPROM must first be erased (set to $FF) before it is programmed. The programming process will write zeros to the appropriate bits in the byte. The following steps are used to program a single byte:

1. Write a 1 to the *EELAT* bit in the *EEPROG* register.
2. Write the byte to the EEPROM address to be programmed.
3. Write a 1 to the *EEPGM* bit in the *EEPROG* register.
4. Delay 10 milliseconds.
5. Write a 0 to the *EEPGM* bit in the *EEPROG* register.
6. Write a 0 to the *EELAT* bit in the *EEPROG* register to set normal read mode.

The subroutine *EESTA* shown in Figure 4–32 will write the byte in accumulator *A* to the EEPROM address in index register *Y*. The subroutine first checks to see if the value at address *Y* is already an $FF. If it is not, the byte is erased by calling the subroutine *BYTEE* given in Figure 4–29. The subroutine then programs the byte by following the six steps given above.

```
;       EEPROM PROGRAMMING ROUTINES
;       STORE BYTE A AT ADDRESS Y
EESTA
        PSHA                        ;save byte
        LDAA    0,Y                 ;if @addr != FF
        CMPA    #$FF
        BEQ     EEB1
        BSR     BYTEE               ;erase byte
EEB1    PULA                        ;get byte
        LDAB    #$02
        STAB    EEPROG              ;set EELAT bit
        STAA    0,Y                 ;store data to EEPROM addr
        LDAB    #$03
        STAB    EEPROG              ;set EEPGM bit (EELAT=1)
        JSR     DLY10               ;10 msec delay
        LDAB    #$02
        STAB    EEPROG              ;turn off hi voltage
        CLR     EEPROG              ;clear EELAT bit
        RTS


;       STORE WORD D AT ADDRESS Y AND Y+1
EESTD
        PSHB
        BSR     EESTA
        INY
        PULA
        BSR     EESTA
        RTS
```

Figure 4–32   Subroutines to Program a Byte and a Word in the EEPROM

The subroutine *EESTD* shown in Figure 4–32 will write the word in register *D* to the EEPROM addresses *Y* and *Y*+1. It does this by calling the subroutine *EESTA* twice, the first time with the value in *A* (the high byte of *D*) and the second time with the value in *B* (the low byte of *D*) that was first pushed on the system stack and later popped into *A*.

The WHYP words *EEC!* (*c addr* --) and *EE!* (*n addr* --), defined in Box 4–4, can be used to write bytes and words to the EEPROM. Their 68HC12 implementations are shown in Figure 4–33. Examples of using these EEPROM memory access words are shown in Figure 4–34.

4.5.3 Storing WHYP Programs in the EEPROM

You can write your WHYP colon definitions directly into EEPROM by changing the value of the target dictionary pointer, *tdp*, to an address in the EEPROM using

```
;          EEC!   ( c addr -- )
EECST
        LDY      2,X+
        LDD      2,X+
        TBA
        JSR      EESTA
        RTS


;          EE!    ( n addr -- )
EEST
        LDY      2,X+
        LDD      2,X+
        JSR      EESTD
        RTS
```

Figure 4–33   68HC12 Code for *EEC!* and *EE!*

```
C:\WHYP\WHYP12>whyp12
Using WHYP12.HED
Communicating with COM1
68HC12 WHYP12 - Version 4.6
Press <Esc> or type BYE to exit
ok
hex ok
1000 10 dump
         0  1  2  3  4  5  6  7  8  9  A  B  C  D  E  F
1000  11 12 34 FF FF FF FF FF FF FF FF FF FF FF FF FF    4.............
ok
erase.bulk ok
1000 10 dump
         0  1  2  3  4  5  6  7  8  9  A  B  C  D  E  F
1000  FF FF FF FF FF FF FF FF FF FF FF FF FF FF FF FF    ...............
ok
55 1000 eec! ok
1000 10 dump
         0  1  2  3  4  5  6  7  8  9  A  B  C  D  E  F
1000  55 FF FF FF FF FF FF FF FF FF FF FF FF FF FF FF  U...............
ok
6789 1001 ee! ok
1000 10 dump
         0  1  2  3  4  5  6  7  8  9  A  B  C  D  E  F
1000  55 67 89 FF FF FF FF FF FF FF FF FF FF FF FF FF  Ug..............
ok
```

Figure 4–34   Examples of Using EEPROM Memory Access Words

```
C:\WHYP\WHYP12>whyp12
Using WHYP12.HED
Communicating with COM1
68HC12 WHYP12 - Version 4.6
Press <Esc> or type BYE to exit
ok
erase.bulk ok
hex ok
1000 20 dump
         0  1  2  3  4  5  6  7  8  9  A  B  C  D  E  F
1000   FF FF FF FF FF FF FF FF FF FF FF FF FF FF FF FF  ................
1010   FF FF FF FF FF FF FF FF FF FF FF FF FF FF FF FF  ................
ok
   <press function key F9>
Current value of target dp is 5000
Enter a new hex value for tdp (5000): 1000
Value of tdp is 1000
load square.whp
\       Colon definition examples

: squared        ( n -- n**2 )    \ compute the square of n
                 DUP * ;          \ multiply top of stack by itself

: cubed          ( n -- n**3 )    \ compute the cube of n
                 DUP             \ n n
                 squared         \ n n**2
                 * ;             \ n**3

Current value of target dp is 1011
ok
1000 20 dump
         0  1  2  3  4  5  6  7  8  9  A  B  C  D  E  F
1000   16 41 08 16 43 3B 3D 16 41 08 16 10 00 16 43 3B    A  C;= A    C;
1010   3D FF FF FF FF FF FF FF FF FF FF FF FF FF FF FF  =...............
ok
decimal ok
5 squared . 25 ok
5 cubed . 125 ok
save.headers
Enter a filename for header names: square.hed
ok
```

Figure 4–35   Example of Loading a WHYP Program into EEPROM

Box 4–4   EEPROM Memory Access Words

EEC!   (c addr --) ("E-E-C-store")
          Stores the Least Significant Byte (LSB) of the value on top of the stack at the EEPROM address *addr*.

EE!   (n addr --) ("E-E-store")
          Stores the 16-bit value of *n* at the EEPROM address *addr*.

ERASE.BULK   (--)
          Erases the entire EEPROM by storing $FF in all EEPROM addresses.

key F9. If you do this and then load a *.WHP* file containing colon definitions, then these words will be compiled into the EEPROM memory as illustrated by the example in Figure 4–35.

Inasmuch as the subroutines for the words *squared* and *cubed* in Figure 4–35 have been downloaded into EEPROM, these bytes will remain in memory when power is removed from the chip. However, the names *squared* and *cubed* will be lost from the dictionary when you exit the WHYP program. This is because each time WHYP is run all dictionary entries are loaded into the PC memory from the .HED file given as the first line in the *.CFG* file shown in Figure 4–3. If you want the words *squared* and *cubed* whose code you stored in the EEPROM to be added to WHYP permanently, you can type the word *save.headers* as shown in Figure 4–35. This will ask you to enter a new file name for the header names. In Figure 4–35 we typed square.hed for this file name. The beginning of this file is shown in Figure 4–36.

This file contains all the WHYP names that were in the file WHYP12.HED but has added the new names *squared* and *cubed*. Note that the names are listed in reverse order from the names in WHYP12.HED and that the addresses are now the absolute addresses rather than the relative addresses. The word *save.headers* always writes the names and addresses of all words in the dictionary with the most recently defined word written first. Note that the addresses of *squared* and *cubed* are their addresses in the EEPROM.

```
cubed             1007
squared           1000
calc.output       48d0
firerules         48b6
fill.weights      48a2
SNDSUB            4895
DUMP              487b
CMOVE>            47be
CMOVE             47aa
MOVE              4796
-----             ----
```

Figure 4–36   Beginning of the File SQUARE.HED Saved in Figure 4–33

```
SQUARE.HED
tdp         5000
vdp         800
TORG        4000
HEDBASE 0000
RAMBASE 0900
INCHAR   35
OUTPUT   3E
TPUSH    47
TPOP     50
INWDY    5B
INWDX    64
STOREW   6D
TBLKST   78
SNDSUB   88f
EESTART 1000
EESTOP   1FFF
last        be
rts_code      34
set_flags   -1
```

Figure 4–37   The File WHYP12.CFG Modified to Use SQUARE.HED

The file SQUARE.HED can be used when you run WHYP12 by modifying the file WHYP12.CFG as shown in Figure 4–37. The two changes from Figure 4–3 are to replace WHYP12.HED with SQUARE.HED in the first row and to change the value of *HEDBASE* in row 5 from 4000 to 0000. The addresses in the *.HED* file get added to *HEDBASE* to produce the absolute address. Inasmuch as the file SQUARE.HED contains the absolute addresses of the words, then *HEDBASE* must be set to 0000.

The examples so far in this book have assumed that you load the file WHYP12.S19 into RAM. However, you may find it more convenient to permanently load WHYP into EPROM or flash memory. The method for doing this is described in Appendix C.

Note that although there is room in the internal EEPROM of the 68HC812A4 to store WHYP, this is not a good idea because bytes in the EEPROM cannot be read while the *EEPGM* bit in the *EEPROG* register is set (see Figure 4–28). This means that you can't program other parts of the EEPROM from a program that is running in the EEPROM itself.

4.6 SUMMARY

In addition to the WHYP words given in Boxes 4–1–4–4, the words given in Box 4–5 were also discussed in this chapter.

Box 4–5   Other WHYP Words Introduced in Chapter 4

:	(--) ("colon")

Used to define a new WHYP word using the following format:
: *<name>* --- --- --- ;

;	(--) ("semi-colon")

Used to end a colon definition.

'	(-- cfa) ("tick" -- a single quote)

The statement ' *<name>* will leave the CFA of *<name>* on the data stack.

ALLOT   (n --)
Allocates *n* bytes of memory by incrementing *tdp* by *n*.

DUMP   (addr len --)
Displays a block of memory of length *len* starting at address *addr*. The value of *len* is the number of bytes to display; however, *DUMP* always displays multiples of 16 bytes.

SEE   (--)
SEE <name> will decompile the WHYP definition of *<name>*.

SHOW   (--)
SHOW <name> will display the machine code of *<name>*.

STEP   (<name_stack> --)
STEP <name> will single-step through the WHYP words making up *<name>*.
The data stack must contain the values expected by *<name>* before *STEP* is called.
Pressing the space bar single-steps the next instruction. Pressing *q* quits *STEP*.

LOAD   (--)
LOAD <filename> will load the file *<filename>* containing colon definitions.

VARIABLE   (--)
VARIABLE <name> will define *<name>* to be a variable.

DEPTH   (-- n)
Returns the number of items on the data stack.

VALLOT   (n --)
Allocates *n* bytes of RAM memory by incrementing *vdp* by *n*.

CONSTANT   (n --)
n CONSTANT <name> will define *<name>* to be a constant with value *n*.

CREATE   (--)
CREATE <name> will add *<name>* to the dictionary and compile a *JSR DOVAR* at its CFA. Executing *<name>* will put its PFA on the data stack.

(continued)

Box 4–5   (*continued*)

```
HERE        ( -- n )
```
Puts the current value of the target dictionary pointer, *tdp*, on the data stack.

```
VHERE       ( -- n )
```
Puts the current value of the variable dictionary pointer, *vdp*, on the data stack.

```
10MS.DELAY  ( -- )
```
Produces a 10-millisecond delay.

```
\           ( -- n )       ("backslash")
```
All characters following \ to the end of the line are treated as a comment.

```
(           ( -- n )       ("paren")
```
All characters between (and a closing) are treated as a comment.

In this chapter we saw how to use colon definitions to define new WHYP words in terms of previously defined WHYP words. We also learned how to define variables and constants and how to create arrays and tables. Finally we learned how to program and erase the 68HC12 EEPROM and we saw how we can load our WHYP programs directly into the EEPROM.

In the next chapter we will learn how to write programs that contain branches and loops.

EXERCISES

Exercise 4.1

Make sure the dictionary pointer, *tdp*, is pointing to some free RAM location called *RAMSTART* by pressing function key F9.

The file `square.whp` contains the following two colon definitions:

```
: squared DUP * ;
: cubed DUP squared * ;
```

Load this file into your 68HC12 board.

a. What is the address of *squared*? (Type hex ' squared u.)
b. What code makes up the subroutine *squared*?
c. What is the address of the subroutine *cubed*? (Type ' cubed u.)
d. What code makes up the subroutine *cubed*?
e. What is the address of the subroutine *DUP*?
f. What is the address of the subroutine **?
g. Dump the code starting at the address of *DUP*. What 68HC12 instructions make up the subroutine *DUP*?

h. What code makes up the subroutine *?

i. Single-step through 8 `squared`.

j. Single-step through 8 `cubed`.

Exercise 4.2

Use function key F9 to change the target dictionary pointer, *tdp*, to the address of the first byte in the EEPROM. Repeat Exercise 4.1 by loading the file `square.whp` into the EEPROM.

Exercise 4.3

Define a WHYP word *tomiles (ft -- mi ft)* to convert feet to miles and feet. Note that 1 mile = 5280 ft.

Exercise 4.4

Write a WHYP program that will display your first or last name in large letters at the center of the screen. *Hint*: The screen displays 25 lines, each containing 80 characters. The following WHYP words allow you to position the cursor before writing characters:

```
dark ( -- )            Clear the screen and put the cursor at top-left corner.
at (col row -- )       Move the cursor to specified column and row. Upper-left
                       corner is col = 1, row = 1.
```

The following instructions put a block F at the center of screen:

```
: newBar         ." *****" ;
: newPost        ."  *  " ;
: new-F
        dark
        38 10 at newBar
        38 11 at newPost
        38 12 at newBar
        38 13 at newPost
        38 14 at newPost
        38 15 at newPost
        cr ;
```

Instead of having to specify the location of the character explicitly in the instruction we can use variables to store the location, so that a character can be placed anywhere on the screen.

```
variable x
variable y

: newLine
        x @ y @ at            \ move cursor to (x,y) location
        1 y +!                \ increment y for next line
        ;

: F       newLine newBar
          newLine newPost
          newLine newBar
          newLine newPost
          newLine newPost
          newLine newPost
          ;
```

To place F on the screen, we must first specify its location by typing, for example,

```
30 x ! 10 y ! F
```

```
: F-demo
            dark
            0 x ! 0 y ! F
            70 x ! 10 y ! F
            10 x ! 18 y ! F
            40 x ! 15 y ! F
            ;
```

Example: Define a new instruction which clears the screen and put a message "FORTH" at the center of the screen with block characters.

```
: bar           newLine ." *****" ;
: post          newline ." *     " ;
: triad1        newline ." ***   " ;
: sides         newline ." * *   " ;
: tetra         newline ." ****  " ;
: duo1          newline ." **    " ;
: duo2          newline ." * *   " ;
: duo3          newline ." * *   " ;
: center        newline ." *     " ;

: F       bar post bar post post post ;
: O       triad1 sides sides sides sides triad1 ;
: R       tetra sides tetra duo2 duo3 sides ;
: T       bar center center center center center ;
: H       sides sides bar sides sides sides ;

: FORTH dark
            25 x ! 10 y ! F
            32 x ! 10 y ! O
            39 x ! 10 y ! R
            46 x ! 10 y ! T
            53 x ! 10 y ! H
            ;
```

Exercise 4.5

Define the three variables, X, Y, and Z and store the values \$1122 in X, \$3344 in Y, and \$5566 in Z.

    a. Use $C@$ to display the bytes at $X+1$ and Z.
    b. Use $2@$ to display the double words at X and Y.

Exercise 4.6

Put the numbers 2, 4, 6, 8, 10 on the data stack. Use the word *DEPTH* to show how many elements are on the data stack after each of the following words are executed:

    a. OVER
    b. 3 PICK
    c. 4 ROLL
    d. NIP

Exercise 4.7

    a. Create a byte array called *c.array* containing 5 bytes.
    b. Store the following hex values in the 5 bytes of the array: 11, 22, 33, 44, 55.
    c. Write a WHYP word called *.c (ix --)* that will print the value in *c.array[ix]*. Test the word by displaying each value.

Exercise 4.8

The following example was given in the book *Mastering Forth* by A. Anderson and M. Tracy (Brady, 1984). It is a program for a "change optimizer" that will take a collection of coins and tell you how the amount can be realized with the smallest number of coins. Note that we can solve this problem without using any branching instructions, which aren't introduced until the next chapter!

    a. Type in the following colon definitions:

```
: CHANGE         0 ;
: QUARTERS      25 * + ;
: DIMES         10 * + ;
: NICKELS        5 * + ;
: PENNIES          + ;
: INTO          25 /MOD CR ." QUARTERS"
                10 /MOD CR ." DIMES"
                 5 /MOD CR ." NICKELS"
                        CR ." PENNIES" ;
```

    b. Type the following statement:
       CHANGE 2 QUARTERS 7 DIMES 13 NICKELS 133 PENNIES INTO
    c. Put the statements in part (b) into a colon definition and single-step through the word observing the values on the data stack at each step.

Exercise 4.9

    a. Create a table called *baud* that contains the 12 baud rates listed in Table 11–1 in Chapter 11.
    b. Define a WHYP word called *.baud (ix --)* that will expect an index value, *ix*, (0–11) on the data stack and display the corresponding baud rate on the screen.

Exercise 4.10

    a. Find the starting address of the internal EEPROM on your microcontroller. Dump out the first 16 bytes on the screen.
    b. Use *EEC!* to store the value $55 in the first byte of the EEPROM.
    c. Use *EE!* to store the value $1234 in the second and third bytes of the EEPROM.
    d. Use the *DUMP* word to verify that the values were written to the EEPROM.

5

Branching and Looping

A computer program achieves its apparent power by being able to conditionally branch to different parts of a program. The 68HC12 microprocessor uses branch instructions for this purpose. A conditional branch instruction can cause a branch in the program to occur, depending upon the state of one or more of the bits in the condition code register. In this chapter we will look at the 68HC12 instructions related to branching and see how they can be used to implement WHYP words for producing branches and loops.

5.1 68HC12 BRANCH INSTRUCTIONS

The 68HC12 has a large number of branch instructions. There are two major categories: short branch and long branch instructions. When writing assembly language programs you would normally use the short branch instructions. However, we will see that it is convenient to use the long branch instructions when compiling high-level WHYP branching instructions. We will first look at short conditional branch instructions that test only a single bit in the condition code register. We will then explore the difference between unsigned and signed branch instructions.

5.1.1 Short Conditional Branch Instructions

The instructions shown in Table 5–1 test the state of one of the flags in the condition code register. Other branching instructions, which will be described in later sections, test some combination of the status flags.

A branching instruction will cause a branch to occur if the branch test is true. For example, the branching instruction *BEQ* (branch if equal zero) will cause a branch in the program if the Z flag in the condition code register is 1. This will be the case if the result of the previous instruction produced a result of zero.

The conditional branch instructions shown in Table 5–1 are all two bytes long. The first byte is the opcode and the second byte is the *relative displacement* of the branch destination. This is the two's complement number that must be added to the address of the next instruction to obtain the address of the instruction to be executed if the branch test is *true*. If the branch test is *false*, then the instruction following the branch instruction is executed. This is illustrated in Figure 5–1 where *BI* is the address of the branch instruction and *BI*+2 is the address of the next instruction. Note that if $Z = 1$ when the *BEQ* instruction is executed, the program will branch to the address formed by adding the displacement (06) to the address of the next instruction (5014), that is, to address 501A = 5014 + 06.

If a branching instruction branches backward in memory, the displacement must be negative. It is just the two's complement of the number of bytes between the

Table 5–1 Simple Short Conditional Branch Instructions

Operation	Mnemonic	Branch Test
Branch if equal zero	BEQ	Z = 1
Branch if not equal zero	BNE	Z = 0
Branch if plus	BPL	N = 0
Branch if minus	BMI	N = 1
Branch if carry clear	BCC	C = 0
Branch if carry set	BCS	C = 1
Branch if overflow set	BVS	V = 1
Branch if overflow clear	BVC	V = 0

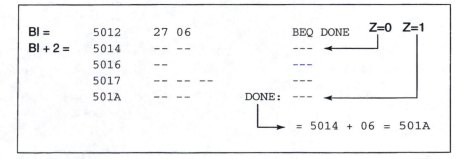

Figure 5–1 The displacement (06) in a branch instruction is added to *BI*+2 to obtain the destination address of the branch.

address of the next instruction ($BI + 2$) and the branch destination address. These displacements are automatically calculated by the assembler.

As an example of calculating a branch displacement, suppose a branch instruction is to branch backward -8 bytes from the address of the next instruction. Since -8 is represented as a two's complement hexadecimal number by $F8, the branch displacement will be F8 as shown in Figure 5–2. Note that this subtraction is done by subtracting the address of the next instruction ($BI + 2$) from the destination address. The result, $FFF8, is the 16-bit hexadecimal representation of -8_{10}. When a two's complement 8-bit hexadecimal number such as $F8 is stored as a 16-bit number, the sign bit (1 in this case) is extended to the left through the high-order byte. Thus, $F8 and $FFF8 both represent the negative number -8_{10}. When using a short branch instruction, the displacement $F8 is used; when using a long branch instruction, the displacement $FFF8 is used.

Note that since the branch displacement for the short branch instructions given in Table 5–1 is a single 8-bit byte, a short branch instruction can branch forward only a maximum of 127 bytes ($7F) and backward a maximum of -128 bytes ($80). The counting of these bytes always begins at the address of the instruction *following* the branch instruction. At first this may seem like a serious limitation. Actually it is not. In fact, the 68HC11 has only short branch instructions. Well-written assembly language programs should not need to branch conditionally more than ±127 bytes. Branches should take place within small program segments or subroutines. If you need to perform lots of instructions within a loop, for example, you should use subroutine calls to make the program more modular. This will make the program much easier to debug and maintain.

In the unlikely event that you do need to branch conditionally more than ±127 bytes you can use the 68HC12 long branch instructions. Each of the instructions in Table 5–1 has a long branch equivalent. For example, the instruction *LBEQ* (long branch if equal to zero) uses the test $Z = 1$ just as the instruction *BEQ* does. However, this instruction uses a 16-bit signed displacement rather than an 8-bit displacement. This means that the branching displacement can range from

```
              500C      --           LOOP1:   ---
              500D      -- --                  ---
              500F      -- -- --                ---
   BI =       5012      26 F8                  BNE LOOP1
   BI + 2 =   5014      -- --                   ---
              5016      -- -- --
                                         500C   LOOP1
                                        -5014   BI + 2
                                         FFF8
```

Figure 5–2 Negative branches can be found by subtracting the address of the next instruction from the destination address.

−32,768 ($8000) to +32,767 ($7FFF). The opcodes for the long branch instructions are two bytes long so that these long branch instructions use a total of four bytes and execute slower than the short branch instructions. The long branch instructions can be useful when writing compilers as we will illustrate in Section 5.2.3.

5.1.2 Unconditional Branch and Jump Instructions

The instructions in Table 5–1 are *conditional* jump instructions that may or may not cause a branch to occur depending upon the value of one of the bits in the condition code register. Sometimes you may want to jump no matter what. This is called an unconditional branch or jump. Three different versions of unconditional branch and jump instructions are shown in Table 5–2.

The short *BRA* (branch always) instruction has an 8-bit displacement as an operand. This is the same two's complement displacement described above for conditional branch instructions. It will allow an unconditional jump a maximum of 127 bytes forward or −128 bytes backward.

If you need to jump a further distance, you can use the long branch always instruction, *LBRA*. This requires a two-byte operand which represents a 16-bit two's complement number that must be added to the address of the next instruction to obtain the destination address.

Both the short and long *branch always* instructions in Table 5–2 use a *relative* displacement in the instruction. Since this is the number that is *added* to the address of the following instruction, it is independent of the destination offset address. This means that if the entire program is moved within the memory, this relative displacement does not change. The use of relative displacements for determining a destination address will allow you to write *position-independent code*. This means that a program can be moved to any location in memory and still run.

The *JMP* instruction shown in Table 5–2 will jump unconditionally to the effective address determined by the particular addressing mode used in the operand. This could be an absolute address (extended addressing) or some form of indexed addressing.

Table 5–2 Unconditional Branch and Jump Instructions

Operation	Mnemonic	Operand
Short Branch Always	BRA	8-bit displacement
Long Branch Always	LBRA	16-bit displacement
Jump	JMP	<effective address>

5.1.3 Branching Examples

The following examples will illustrate short branching on the state of the Z, N, C, and V condition codes.

Branching on the Zero Flag Z   The subroutine for the WHYP word *LSHIFT* that was introduced in Chapter 3 (see Figure 3–42) is shown in Figure 5–3 including its machine code. Index register Y is loaded with the value $n2$ (the number of times

```
                        ;       LSHIFT       ( n1 n2 -- n1 )
                        ;       Left shift bits of n1 n2 times
                        LSHIFT
44be ed 31                      LDY       2,X+            ;Y = n2
44c0 68 01              LS1 ASL           1,X             ;arith shift left
44c2 65 00                      ROL       0,X             ; n2 bits
44c4 03                         DEY
44c5 26 f9                      BNE       LS1
44c7 3d                         RTS
```

Figure 5–3   Example of Using the *BNE* Branch Instruction

to shift all bits in *n1* left). The instruction *DEY* will decrement *Y* and set the *Z* flag if *Y* is equal to zero. Note from Table A–1 in Appendix A that the instruction *DEY* affects only the *Z* flag in the condition code register. The *BNE* instruction in Figure 5–3 will branch to the label *LS1* if the *Z* flag is 0, that is, if *Y* is not equal to zero. When *Y* becomes zero, the *BNE* test will fail and the program will continue with the *RTS* instruction. In this way the two instructions *ASL 1,X* and *ROL 0,X* are executed exactly *n2* times.

Note that the displacement of the *BNE* instruction, $F9, is a negative number and therefore gets sign extended to $FFF9. It is then added to the address of the next instruction, $44C7, to produce the destination address, $44C0.

The subroutine *EESTA* that was introduced in Figure 4–32 in Chapter 4 is shown with its machine code in Figure 5–4. The instruction *CMPA #$FF* at address $409F compares accumulator *A* to the immediate value $FF. This compare instruction will subtract $FF from the contents of accumulator *A* and set the flags in the

```
                        ;       EEPROM PROGRAMMING ROUTINES
                        ;       STORE BYTE A AT ADDRESS Y
                        EESTA
409c 36                         PSHA                      ;save byte
409d a6 40                      LDAA      0,Y             ;if @addr != FF
409f 81 ff                      CMPA      #$FF
40a1 27 02                      BEQ       EEB1
40a3 07 16                      BSR       BYTEE           ;erase byte
40a5 32                 EEB1 PULA                         ;get byte
40a6 c6 02                      LDAB      #$02
40a8 5b f3                      STAB      EEPROG          ;set EELAT bit
40aa 6a 40                      STAA      0,Y             ;store data to EEPROM addr
40ac c6 03                      LDAB      #$03
40ae 5b f3                      STAB      EEPROG          ;set EEPGM bit (EELAT=1)
40b0 16 40 d8                   JSR       DLY10           ;10 msec delay
40b3 c6 02                      LDAB      #$02
40b5 5b f3                      STAB      EEPROG          ;turn off hi voltage
40b7 79 00 f3                   CLR       EEPROG          ;clear EELAT bit
40ba 3d                         RTS
```

Figure 5–4   Example of Using the BEQ Branch Instruction

condition code register accordingly. The difference is not stored anywhere. In this case, if *A* is equal to $FF, the *Z* flag will be set to 1 and the *BEQ* instruction will branch to label *EEB1* at address $40A5. On the other hand, if *A* is not equal to $FF (meaning that the byte at address *Y* is not erased), then the *Z* flag will be zero, the *BEQ* test will fail, and the branch will not occur. In this case the next instruction, *BSR BYTEE*, will be executed which will branch to the subroutine, *BYTEE*, that will erase the byte.

Note that the relative displacement at address $40A2 is $02. This is a positive displacement that gets added to the address of the next instruction, $40A3, to produce the destination address $40A5, the address of the label *EEB1*.

It is important to know which flags in the condition code register are altered by the instruction immediately preceding a branch instruction. You can find this information in Table A–1 in Appendix A. At the right side of each instruction is an indication of what happens each bit in the condition code register. A triangle (Δ) means that that bit is affected by the instruction. A dash (−) means that bit is unchanged by the instruction.

Note that the *DEY* instruction in Figure 5–3 affects only the *Z* flag. Therefore, only the branch instructions *BNE* and *BEQ* can be used following a *DEY* instruction. On the other hand, the *CMPA* instruction affects the *N*, *Z*, *V*, and *C* flags in the condition code register. Therefore, all of the branch instructions shown in Table 5–1 can be used following a compare instruction.

As another example of using the *BEQ* instruction, consider the subroutine *NEGATE* shown in Figure 5–5. This subroutine implements the WHYP word *NEGATE (n -- -n)* which takes the two's complement of the value on top of the data stack. The 68HC12 instruction *NEG* will take the two's complement of a byte. But we need to take the two's complement of a 16-bit word. If we negate the low byte and it is nonzero, then we just have to complement (one's complement) the high byte. But if the low byte is zero, then we need to take the two's complement of the high byte.

Note that the instruction *NEG 1,X* will negate the low byte and set the *Z* flag if this low byte is zero. The *BEQ* instruction then branches to the instruction *NEG 0,X* which negates the high byte. If the low byte is not zero, then the *BEQ* instruction does not branch and the one's complement of the high byte is computed using the instruction *COM 0,X*. Note that this subroutine has two *RTS* instructions, one in each branch taken by the *BEQ* instruction.

```
                          ;        NEGATE   ( n -- -n )
                          NEGATE
446e 60 01                        NEG     1,X           ;negate low byte
4470 27 03                        BEQ     NG1           ;if not zero
4472 61 00                        COM     0,X           ;complement high byte
4474 3d                           RTS
4475 60 00                NG1     NEG     0,X           ;else, negate high byte
4477 3d                           RTS
```

Figure 5–5   68HC12 Code for the WHYP Word *NEGATE*

Branching on the Negative Flag N As shown in Table 5–1 the two instructions *BPL* (branch if plus) and *BMI* (branch if minus) will branch on the state of the negative flag, N. As an example, the 68HC12 implementation of the WHYP word *ABS* (n -- $|n|$), which takes the absolute value of the element on top of the data stack, is shown in Figure 5–6. The first instruction is *TST 0,X* which tests the high byte of n by subtracting the value $00 from it. If n is negative, the sign bit of the high byte will be 1 and the *TST* instruction will set the N flag in the condition code register. If n is not negative, the N flag will not be set and the *BPL* instruction will branch to the *RTS* instruction at the label *AB2*. If n is negative, then the *BPL* instruction will fail and n is negated using essentially the same code as in Figure 5–5.

An example of a subroutine that uses the *BMI* instruction is the subroutine that implements the WHYP word "S-to-D", $S>D$ (n -- d), shown in Figure 5–7. This word sign extends the single 16-bit word, n, on top of the stack to a double 32-bit word, d. If the sign bit of n is 1, then the high word of d will be $FFFF, while if the sign bit if n is 0, then the high word of d will be $0000. Note that the sign bit is tested using the *TST* instruction again and the *BMI* instruction will branch to *SD1* if the N flag is 1, meaning that the sign bit was set. In this case, the value $FFFF that has been loaded into D will be pushed onto the data stack as the high word of d. On the other hand, if the *BMI* test fails (meaning that the sign bit of n was not set), then D is loaded with $0000 before pushing this value onto the data stack.

```
                    ;       ABS     ( n -- |n| )
                    ABS
4478 e7 00                  TST     0,X         ;if negative
447a 2a 09                  BPL     AB2         ;negate:
447c 60 01                  NEG     1,X         ;negate low byte
447e 27 03                  BEQ     AB1         ;if not zero
4480 61 00                  COM     0,X         ;complement high byte
4482 3d                     RTS
4483 60 00          AB1     NEG     0,X         ;else, negate high byte
4485 3d             AB2     RTS
```

Figure 5–6   68HC12 Code for the WHYP Word *ABS*

```
                    ;       S>D  ( n -- d )     sign extend single to double
                    STOD
4513 cc ff ff               LDD     #$FFFF      ;negative extend
4516 e7 00                  TST     0,X         ;if n positive
4518 2b 03                  BMI     SD1
451a cc 00 00               LDD     #$0000      ;extend zeros
451d 6c 2e          SD1     STD     2,-X        ;else extend 1's
451f 3d                     RTS
```

Figure 5–7   68HC12 Code for the WHYP Word *S>D*

```
                       ;    UM/MOD     ( udl udh un -- ur uq )    32/16 = 16:16
                       ;    Unsigned divide of a double by a single.
                       ;    Return mod and quotient.
                       UMMOD
435a 34                      PSHX
435b ed 02                   LDY      2,X
435d ec 04                   LDD      4,X
435f ee 00                   LDX      0,X
4361 11                      EDIV
4362 25 02                   BCS      UM1            ;if div by 0
4364 28 06                   BVC      UM2            ; or overflow
4366 cc ff ff     UM1  LDD      #$FFFF         ; rem = $FFFF
4369 cd ff ff          LDY      #$FFFF         ; quot = $FFFF
436c 30           UM2  PULX
436d 1a 02                   LEAX     2,X
436f 6c 02                   STD      2,X
4371 6d 00                   STY      0,X
4373 3d                      RTS
```

Figure 5–8   Example of Branching on the Carry and Overflow Flags

Branching on the Carry and Overflow Flags, *C* and *V*   As a final example that includes branches on both the carry and overflow flags, consider the subroutine *UMMOD* shown in Figure 5–8, which was introduced in Chapter 3 (see Figure 3–20) for implementing the WHYP word *UM/MOD (ud un -- ur uq)*. Recall that the *EDIV* instruction divides (unsigned) *Y:D* by *X*, leaving the quotient in *Y* and the remainder in *D*. If a division by zero is attempted, then the carry bit, *C*, in the condition code register is set. This is tested immediately after the *EDIV* instruction by the *BCS* instruction. If the carry is set, meaning a division by zero was attemped, then the branch to label *UM1* is taken and the remainder and quotient are both set to $FFFF.

If the carry was not set, then the *BVC* instruction is executed. The branch instructions do not change any values in the condition code register so that even though the instruction *BCS* has been executed, if the overflow bit was set by the *EDIV* instruction, it will still be set. It will be set if the quotient is greater than $FFFF, in which case the *BVC* (branch on overflow clear) test will fail and the next instructions, which set the remainder and quotient to $FFFF, will be executed. If neither the carry nor the overflow bits are set then the *BVC* instruction will branch to *UM2* and the remainder and quotient computed by *EDIV* will be pushed onto the data stack.

5.1.4   Bit-Condition Branch Instructions

The 68HC12 has two bit-condition branch instructions that are given in Table 5–3. The *BRCLR* instruction will branch if selected bits in a particular memory location are zero. The bits are selected by setting corresponding bits in a mask to 1.

Table 5–3 Bit-Condition Branch Instructions

Operation	Mnemonic	Branch Test
Branch if Selected Bits Clear	BRCLR	(M) & (mask) = 0
Branch if Selected Bits Set	BRSET	!(M) & (mask) = 0

```
FD80              CODE_START:
                            -----
FD89 4F6F0103       BRCLR    PORTAD, $01, DB12:;if bit 0 of PORTAD is 1
FD8D 061000                  JMP   EESTART    ;then jump to start of EEPROM
FD90              DB12:                        ;else stay in D-Bug12
```

Figure 5–9 A Portion of the DB12 Startup Code

The *BRCLR* instruction will then branch if the logical AND of the memory location with the mask is zero. The general form of the instruction is

```
BRCLR opr,msk,rel
```

where *opr* is the addressing mode for the memory location to be tested, *msk* is the mask value, and *rel* is the label of the branch destination address.

The *BRSET* instruction shown in Table 5–3 will branch if selected bits in a particular memory location are 1. In this case the *BRSET* instruction will branch if the logical AND of the one's complement of the memory location with the mask is zero.

An example of using the *BRCLR* instruction is shown in Figure 5–9 which is a portion of the D-Bug12 startup code in the M68HC12A4EVB evaluation board. The *BRCLR* instruction at address $FD89 checks bit 0 of the *PORTAD* register and if this bit is 0, then the program branches to the label *DB12* at address $FD90. On the other hand if bit 0 of *PORTAD* is 1, then the *JMP EE_START* instruction at address $FD8D is executed which will jump to address $1000, the first byte in the EEPROM. This provides a way to jump to a program stored in EEPROM on reset. You can usually change bit 0 of *PORTAD* using a jumper on the evaluation board. For example, jumper W20 provides this function on the M68HC12A4EVB evaluation board. By using this method you can make a turnkey system in which your program is executed when you press the RESET button. In Appendix C we describe how to store the WHYP kernel in an EPROM or flash memory and how you can make a turnkey system that will execute your main word.

5.1.5 Unsigned and Signed Branch Instructions

The conditional branch instructions given in Table 5–1 are the ones most commonly used. In fact, you can get by using only these. However, sometimes it is convenient to use the additional conditional branch instructions given in Tables 5–4 and 5–5. You must, however, be careful. It is very easy to make a mistake when using these conditional branch instructions. The instructions in Table 5–4 must only be used when you are thinking about *unsigned* numbers, that is, 8-bit numbers with decimal

Table 5–4   Conditional Jump Instructions to Use Following a
Comparison of Unsigned Numbers

Operation	Mnemonic	Branch Test
Branch if Higher	BHI	C or Z = 0
Branch if Lower or Same	BLS	C or Z = 1
Branch if Higher or Same	BHS	C = 0
Branch if Lower	BLO	C = 1

Table 5–5   Conditional Jump Instructions to Use Following a Comparison of
Signed Numbers

Operation	Mnemonic	Branch Test
Branch if Greater Than or Equal	BGE	N xor V = 0
Branch if Less Than	BLT	N xor V = 1
Branch if Greater Than	BGT	Z or (N xor V) = 0
Branch if Less than or Equal	BLE	Z or (N xor V) = 1

values between 0 and 255 ($00–$FF), or 16-bit numbers with decimal values between 0 and 65,535 ($0000–$FFFF).

The branching instructions in Table 5–5 must only be used when you are thinking about *signed* numbers, that is, 8-bit signed numbers with decimal values between −128 ($80) and +127 ($7F), or 16-bit signed numbers with decimal values between −32,768 ($8000) and +32,767 ($7FFF).

It is very easy to confuse the instructions in Tables 5–4 and 5–5. This can lead to execution errors that are sometimes hard to find. For example, suppose accumulator B is used as a counter and you want to go through a loop 200_{10} ($C8) times. You might think that the loop shown in Figure 5–10 will work.

It won't! The branching instruction *BLT LOOP* will fail the first time. This is because the value of B is 1 and the value of $C8 is not 200_{10} but is $−56_{10}$. Remember that the *BLT* instruction (and all the instructions in Table 5–5) consider all numbers to be two's complement *signed* numbers. Inasmuch as 1 (the value of B) is greater than $−56_{10}$, the instruction *BLT* will not branch.

The instruction you really want to use is *BLO* (branch if lower). This instruction, and all instructions in Table 5–4 treat all numbers as unsigned numbers, so that $C8 is considered to be 200_{10} and not $−56_{10}$.

In Table 5–4 note that the instructions *BHS* and *BLO* test only the carry flag and are the same as *BCC* and *BCS*, respectively. All other instructions in Tables 5–4 and 5–5 use branch tests that involve more than one flag in the condition code register.

```
            CLRB              ;set B = 0
    LOOP    INCB              ;increment B
            CMPB    #$C8      ;compare B to C8H
            BLT     LOOP      ;loop if B < 200
```

Figure 5–10   How many times is the instruction INCB executed?

```
                        ;         MIN      (n1 n2 -- min )
                   MIN
445c ed 31              LDY       2,X+           ;Y = n2
445e ad 00              CPY       0,X            ;if n2 < n1
4460 2c 02              BGE       MIN1
4462 6d 00              STY       0,X            ;leave n2 on stack
4464 3d            MIN1 RTS                      ;else leave n1


                        ;         MAX      (n1 n2 -- max )
                   MAX
4465 ed 31              LDY       2,X+           ;Y = n2
4467 ad 00              CPY       0,X            ;if n2 > n1
4469 2f 02              BLE       MX1
446b 6d 00              STY       0,X            ;leave n2 on stack
446d 3d            MX1  RTS                      ;else leave n1
```

Figure 5–11   68HC12 Code for the WHYP Words *MIN* and *MAX*

As an example of using signed branch instructions, consider the 68HC12 subroutines for the WHYP words *MIN (n1 n2 -- min)* and *MAX (n1 n2 -- max)*, shown in Figure 5–11. The word *MIN* will leave the minimum of *n1* and *n2* on the data stack and the word *MAX* will leave the maximum of *n1* and *n2* on the data stack.

The numbers *n1* and *n2* on the data stack in Figure 5–11 are signed two's complement numbers. This means that we need to do signed comparisons. In the *MIN* subroutine, *n2* is popped into *Y* which is then compared with *n1* (still on the stack). If *n2* is greater than or equal to *n1*, then the *BGE* instruction branches to the *RTS* instruction which will leave *n1* (the minimum value) on the data stack. On the other hand, if *n2* is less than *n1*, then the *BGE* test fails and the instruction *STY 0,X* will store *n2* (the minimum value) on the data stack.

The instruction *BLE* is used in a similar way in the *MAX* subroutine in Figure 5–11 to leave the maximum of *n1* and *n2* on the data stack.

5.2   WHYP BRANCHING AND LOOPING WORDS

All computer languages must have some way of producing a conditional branch (if...then) and implementing loops. WHYP uses the following well-structured constructs:

```
IF ... ELSE ... THEN
FOR ... NEXT
BEGIN ... AGAIN
BEGIN ... UNTIL
BEGIN ... WHILE ... REPEAT
DO ... LOOP
```

These instructions work somewhat differently than they do in other languages. The words *IF*, *UNTIL* and *WHILE* are WHYP words that expect a true/false flag to be on top of the data stack when the words are executed. A false flag has a value of 0. A true flag has a value of −1 ($FFFF). The WHYP words *TRUE* and *FALSE* are constants that push −1 and 0, respectively, on the data stack when executed.

5.2.1 WHYP Conditional Words

The flag used by branching and looping words may be generated in any way, but the usual way is to use some type of conditional expression that leaves a flag on the data stack. The WHYP conditional words are given in Box 5–1.

As an example, the word "less than," $< (n1\ n2 -- f)$, will leave a true flag on the data stack if $n1$ is less than $n2$. The 68HC12 subroutine for the word $<$ is shown in Figure 5–12. Index register Y is first loaded with the true flag and $n2$ is popped into D from the top of the data stack. This value of $n2$ is then compared with $n1$ which is still on top of the data stack. If $n2$ is greater than $n1$, then the BGT instruction will branch to the label $LT1$ where the true flag in Y will be stored on the top of the data stack, because $n1$ will be less than $n2$. On the other hand, if $n2$ is less than or equal to $n1$, then the BGT test will fail and Y will be loaded with the false flag before storing it on top of the data stack.

Box 5–1   WHYP Conditional Words

The following WHYP conditional words produce a true/false flag:

`<`	`( n1 n2 -- f )`	(`"less-than"`)

flag, f, is true if n1 is less than n2.

`>`	`( n1 n2 -- f )`	(`"greater-than"`)

flag, f, is true if n1 is greater than n2.

`=`	`( n1 n2 -- f )`	(`"equals"`)

flag, f, is true if n1 is equal to n2.

`<>`	`( n1 n2 -- f )`	(`"not-equal"`)

flag, f, is true if n1 is not equal to n2.

`<=`	`( n1 n2 -- f )`	(`"less-than or equal"`)

flag, f, is true if n1 is less than or equal to n2.

`>=`	`( n1 n2 -- f )`	(`"greater-than or equal"`)

flag, f, is true if n1 is greater than or equal to n2.

`0<`	`( n -- f )`	(`"zero-less"`)

flag, f, is true if n is less than zero (negative).

`0>`	`( n -- f )`	(`"zero-greater"`)

flag, f, is true if n is greater than zero (positive).

`0=`	`( n -- f )`	(`"zero-equals"`)

flag, f, is true if n is equal to zero.

The following conditional words compare two unsigned numbers on the stack.

`U<`	`( u1 u2 -- f )`	(`"U-less-than"`)

flag, f, is true if u1 is less than u2.

`U>`	`( u1 u2 -- f )`	(`"U-greater-than"`)

flag, f, is true if u1 is greater than u2.

`U<=`	`( u1 u2 -- f )`	(`"U-less-than or equal"`)

flag, f, is true if u1 is less than or equal to u2.

`U>=`	`( u1 u2 -- f )`	(`"U-greater-than or equal"`)

flag, f, is true if u1 is greater than or equal to u2.

```
;          < ( n1 n2 -- t )
; Return true if n1 is less than n2.
LT
          LDY      #$FFFF          ;true
          LDD      2,X+            ;D = n2
          CPD      0,X             ;if n2 <= n1
          BGT      LT1
          LDY      #0              ;set false
LT1       STY      0,X             ;set flag
          RTS
```

Figure 5–12   68HC12 Code for the WHYP Word <

```
;          U< ( u1 u2 -- t )
; Return true if u1 is less than u2.
ULT
          LDY      #$FFFF          ;true
          LDD      2,X+            ;D = u2
          CPD      0,X             ;if u2 <= u1
          BHI      ULT1
          LDY      #0              ;set false
ULT1      STY      0,X             ;set flag
          RTS
```

Figure 5–13   68HC12 Code for the WHYP Word $U<$

The word "U-less-than," $U<$ ($u1$ $u2$ -- f), will leave a true flag on the data stack if the unsigned number $u1$ is less than the unsigned number $u2$. The 68HC12 subroutine for the word $U<$ is shown in Figure 5–13. Note that the only difference between this subroutine and that in Figure 5–12 is that the branch instruction BGT (signed) has been replaced with BHI (unsigned).

5.2.2 WHYP Logical Words

The WHYP logical operators are given in Box 5–2. The word $INVERT$ performs a one's complement (i.e., it flips all the bits) of the value on top of the data stack. For example, if, in HEX, you type

```
FFFF INVERT
```

the value 0 will be left on top of the stack.

On the other hand, the word NOT is a logical NOT whose definition is 0=. For example, if you type

```
TRUE NOT
```

the value 0 (FALSE) will be left on top of the stack. Note that NOT and $INVERT$ are the same only for the values −1 (TRUE) and 0 (FALSE).

Box 5–2   WHYP Logical Operators

INVERT	(n -- 1's_comp) Leaves the bitwise 1's complement of n on top of the stack.
NOT	(n -- not) Leaves the logical NOT of n on top of the stack. NOT is equivalent to 0=.
AND	(n1 n2 -- and) Leaves n1 AND n2 on top of the stack. This is a bitwise AND.
OR	(n1 n2 -- or) Leaves n1 OR n2 on top of the stack. This is a bitwise OR.
XOR	(n1 n2 -- xor) Leaves n1 XOR n2 on top of the stack. This is a bitwise XOR.

Note that the words *AND*, *OR*, and *XOR* perform bitwise logical operations. For example, if, in HEX, you type

```
48 0F AND
```

the value $0008 will be left on top of the stack. If, in HEX, you type

```
80 45 OR
```

the value $00C5 will be left on top of the stack. If, in HEX, you type

```
AAAA FFFF XOR
```

the value 5555 will be left on top of the stack. Note that this last case is the same as

```
AAAA INVERT
```

The 68HC12 subroutine that implements the WHYP word *AND* is given in Figure 5–14. Note that there is no 68HC12 *ANDD* instruction, only *ANDA* and *ANDB* instructions. Therefore, we first pop *n2* into *D* (*A:B*) and then AND the high byte (*A*) and low byte (*B*) separately. Similar subroutines for *OR* and *XOR* use the 68HC12 instructions *ORAA*, *ORAB*, *EORA*, and *EORB*.

```
;       AND ( n1 n2 -- and )
;       Bitwise AND.
ANDD
        LDD     2,X+        ;pop n2 into D
        ANDA    0,X
        STAA    0,X
        ANDB    1,X
        STAB    1,X
        RTS
```

Figure 5–14   68HC12 Code for the WHYP Word *AND*

5.2.3 IF . . . ELSE . . . THEN

The WHYP *IF* statement works somewhat differently than an *IF* statement in other languages. A typical *IF . . . THEN . . . ELSE* statement that you may be familiar with works like this:

> IF <cond> THEN <true statements> ELSE <false statements>

In WHYP the *IF* statement works like this:

> <cond> IF <true statements> ELSE <false statements> THEN

Note that a *true/false* flag must be on top of the data stack when the *IF* word is executed. If a *true* flag is on top of the data stack, then the <*true statements*> are executed. If a *false* flag is on top of the data stack, then the <*false statements*> are executed. After the <*true statements*> or <*false statements*> are executed, the words following *THEN* are executed. Executing *IF* removes the flag from the top of the data stack. The *ELSE* clause is optional.

The *IF* word must be used within a colon definition. As an example, suppose you type in the two colon definitions shown in Figure 5–15.

If you type

```
                    TRUE iftest


true statements
next statements
```

will be displayed on the screen. If you type

```
                    FALSE iftest
next statements
```

```
: iftest        ( f -- )
                IF
                     CR ." true statements"
                THEN
                     CR ." next statements" CR ;

: if.else.test  ( f -- )
                IF
                     CR ." true statements"
                ELSE
                     CR ." false statements"
                THEN
                     CR ." next statements" CR ;
```

Figure 5–15 Words to Test the *IF . . . ELSE . . . THEN* Statement

will be displayed on the screen. If you type

```
TRUE if.else.test
```

```
true statements
next statements
```

will be displayed on the screen. If you type

```
FALSE if.else.test
```

```
false statements
next statements
```

will be displayed on the screen.

As an example of using the *IF . . . ELSE . . . THEN* statement, consider the colon definition of the word *hex2asc* shown in Figure 5–16. This word assumes a hex number (0–9, A–F) on the stack and returns the ASCII equivalent ($30–$39, $41–$46) of the hex number on the stack. You can load this word from the file HEX2ASC.WHP that is on the disk with this book. If you go to *HEX* and type

```
7 hex2asc .
```

then 37 will be printed on the screen. Similarly, typing

```
B hex2asc .
```

will print 42 on the screen.

If you decompile *hex2asc* by typing

```
see hex2asc
```

you will get the result shown in Figure 5–17. If you also use the word *show*, you will see that the WHYP words shown in Figure 5–17 are equivalent to the 68HC12 machine code shown in Figure 5–18 where we have added the assembly language mnemonics for each instruction.

```
HEX

: hex2asc    ( n -- asc )
            0F AND        \ mask upper nibble
            DUP 9 >       \ if n > 9
            IF
              37 +        \   add $37
            ELSE
              30 +        \ else add $30
            THEN ;
```

Figure 5–16   Colon Definition of the Word *HEX2ASC*

```
ok
see hex2asc
hex2asc
         (LIT)   0   F AND DUP (LIT)   0   9
         > LBEQ   0   C (LIT)   0 37 + LBRA   0   8 (LIT)   0 30
         + ;
ok
```

Figure 5–17 Decompiling the Word *HEX2ASC* in Figure 5–16

```
ok
show hex2asc
hex2asc
  16 45 22  0  F                HEX2ASC   JSR (LIT)   0F
  16 41 F3                                JSR AND
  16 41  8                                JSR DUP
  16 45 22  0  9                          JSR (LIT)   9
  16 42 6A                                JSR >
  EC 31                                   LDD 2,X+            IF
  18 27  0  C                             LBEQ +12
  16 45 22  0 37                          JSR (LIT)   37
  16 42 E2                                JSR +
  18 20  0  8                             LBRA +8             ELSE
  16 45 22  0 30                          JSR (LIT)   30
  16 42 E2                                JSR +
  3D                                      RTS                 THEN
ok
```

Figure 5–18 68HC12 Machine Code Produced by Compiling the Word *HEX2ASC*

Note that the *IF* statement gets compiled as *LDD 2,X+* followed by a long branch equal instruction (*LBEQ*) with the displacement $000C. This means that the flag on top of the data stack is popped into *D* and if this flag is zero (false), then a branch of +12 bytes forward from the address of the next instruction is taken. This will branch to the instruction *JSR (LIT) 30* which is the first instruction in the *ELSE* clause. If the flag were true, then the *LBEQ* branch test would fail and the instructions following *IF* would be executed. Note that the word *ELSE* gets compiled as a long branch always instruction (*LBRA*) with the displacement $0008. This means that after the statements following *IF* are executed, the *ELSE* clause is skipped and the program jumps to the *RTS* instruction.

5.2.4 *FOR . . . NEXT* Loop

The *FOR . . . NEXT* loop must be used within a colon definition and has the following general form:

```
n FOR <WHYP statements> NEXT
```

This *FOR . . . NEXT* loop will execute *<WHYP statements>* n times.

As an example of using the *FOR . . . NEXT* loop, type in the colon definition

```
: stars for ." *" next ;
```

as shown in Figure 5–19. Notice that if you then type

```
<n> stars <enter>
```

then *n* stars will be displayed.

When the statement *FOR* is executed, it moves the value on the parameter stack to the return stack. Each time *NEXT* is executed, it decrements the value on

```
C:\WHYP\WHYP12>whyp12
Using WHYP12.HED
Communicating with COM1
68HC12 WHYP12 - Version 4.6
Press <Esc> or type BYE to exit
ok
: stars for ." *" next ; ok
5 stars *****ok
10 stars **********ok
2 stars **ok
: pattern 10 for cr r@ stars next cr ; ok
pattern
**********
*********
********
*******
******
*****
****
***
**
*
ok
```

Figure 5–19   Examples of Using the *FOR . . . NEXT* Loop

the return stack and if this value is not equal to zero, the program branches back to the statement following *FOR*.

Recall from Box 2–2 in Chapter 2 that the WHYP word *R@* will copy the value from the return stack to the parameter stack. You can use this to find out how far a *FOR . . . NEXT* loop has progressed. For example, if you execute the word *pattern* given by

```
: pattern      ( -- )
               10 FOR
                   CR R@ stars
               NEXT
               CR ;
```

then the pattern shown in Figure 5–19 will be displayed on the screen. The words *stars* and *pattern* are included in the file stars.whp that is on the disk accompanying this book.

To understand how the *FOR . . . NEXT* loop works, you can decompile stars by typing

```
see stars
```

and see the machine code generated by typing

```
show stars
```

as shown in Figure 5–20 where we have added the assembly language mnemonics to the 68HC12 machine code.

```
ok
see stars
stars
          >R (.")  1 2A DONEXT R>DROP ;
ok
show stars
stars
  16 41 B1           JSR   >R                FOR
  16 45 C7  1 2A     JSR   (.") 1 '*'
  B7 76              TSY                      NEXT
  EC 40              LDD   0,Y
  83  0  1           SUBD  #1
  6C 40              STD   0,Y
  26 F0              BNE   -16
  16 41 C4           JSR   R>DROP
  3D                 RTS
ok
```

Figure 5–20   68HC12 Instructions Generated by the Word *stars*

Note that the word *FOR* compiles to *JSR >R* which will move the top of the parameter stack to the return stack (see Box 2–2). The word *NEXT* compiles the 68HC12 instructions from *TSY* to *JSR R>DROP* in Figure 5–20. This code will decrement the top of the return stack (the same as the system stack) and then execute the *BNE* instruction with a displacement of −16. This will branch to the address of the first instruction after *FOR*. When the top of the return stack gets decremented to zero, the *BNE* instruction fails and the next instruction *JSR R>DROP* ("from-R-drop") is executed. This instruction removes the top of the return stack and discards it.

A *FOR . . . NEXT* Delay Loop   Consider the following delay loop:

```
: delay      ( -- )
    20000 FOR NEXT ;
```

How long does this word take to execute? In this section we will show how to calculate the time required to execute this word.

Figure 5–21 shows the 68HC12 assembly language instructions making up the word *delay* together with the number of clock cycles required to execute each instruction, where *N* is the number of times the *FOR . . . NEXT* loop is executed. The clock cycle values for the three *JSR* instructions include 4 clock cycles for the *JSR* instruction plus the total clock cycles for each 68HC12 instruction in the subroutines *(LIT)*, *>R*, and *R>DROP* as given in Figure 5–22. These clock cycles can be found in the 68HC12 instruction set in Appendix A.

```
ok
: delay 20000 for next ; ok
see delay
delay
        (LIT) 4E 20 >R DONEXT R>DROP ;
ok
show delay
delay                                              #clock cycles
  16 45 22 4E 20           JSR (LIT) 20000            4+17 = 21
  16 41 B1         FOR     JSR >R                     4+15 = 19
  B7 76            DONEXT  TSY                         1
  EC 40                    LDD  0,Y                    3
  83  0  1                 SUBD #1                     2
  6C 40                    STD  0,Y                    2
  26 F5                    BNE  -16                    3
                                                      11 * N
  16 41 C4                 JSR R>DROP                  4+13 = 17
  3D                       RTS                         5
ok
                           JSR delay                   4
                                                      62 + 11*N
```

Figure 5–21   Calculating the Number of Clock Cycles in a *FOR . . . NEXT* Delay Loop

```
;        (LIT)    ( -- n )
;              Runtime routine for single literals
LIT
        PULY            3           ;Y -> number
        LDD     0,Y     3           ;Push number
        STD     2,-X    2           ;on data stack
        INY             1           ;jump over number
        INY             1
        PSHY            2
        RTS             5
                       ――
                       17


;        >R ( w -- )              ( R:  -- w )
; Push the data stack to the return stack.
TOR
        PULY            3           ;save return addr
        LDD    2,X+      3           ;D = w
        PSHD            2           ;push D on ret stack
        PSHY            2           ;restore return addr
        RTS             5
                       ――
                       15


;        R>DROP           ( R: sys -- )
RFDROP
        PULY            3           ;save return addr
        PULD            3           ;pop sys
        PSHY            2           ;restore return addr
        RTS             5
                       ――
                       13
```

Figure 5–22   Calculating the Number of Clock Cycles in Delay Loop Subroutines

Including the call to the subroutine *delay* itself, the total number of clock cycles is

```
#clock_cycles = 62 + 11*N
```

Assuming an 8-MHz clock, the delay in microseconds will be

```
8 MHz clock: #µs = #clock_cycles/8
              = 7.75 + 1.375*N
```

Using $N = 20000$, this gives a value of 27500.75 μs or about 27.5 milliseconds. To delay a specified number of microseconds (>10) you would use a value of N given by

```
N = (#µs - 7.75)/1.375
```

```
ok
: 50ms.delay 36358 FOR NEXT ; ok
: 1s.delay 20 FOR 50ms.delay NEXT ;
: 10s.delay 200 FOR 50ms.delay NEXT ;
```

Figure 5–23   Generating Longer Delay Loops

For example, to delay 50 milliseconds, you would use a value of N equal to

$$N = (50000 - 7.75)/1.375 = 36358$$

The maximum delay you can get from this single *FOR . . . NEXT* loop is a little over 90 milliseconds using a value of $N = 65,535$.

To get longer delays you can use nested *FOR . . . NEXT* loops. For example, to get a 1-second delay, you can call a 50-millisecond delay 20 times and to get a 10-second delay you can call a 50-millisecond delay 200 times as shown in Figure 5–23.

If you try the delay loops in Figure 5–23 on the M68HC12A4EVB, you may find that the 10-second delay takes about 17 seconds! This is because the default startup code adds one wait state to each access of external RAM making programs in this RAM run approximately 40 percent slower than if they were run on fast RAMs without wait states. If this is the case, then you can adjust the value, 36358, used in *50ms.delay* by multiplying it by 10/17.

It is also interesting to note that the total number of clock cycles for a 68HC11 running code equivalent to that shown in Figure 5–21 is equal to 127 + 23*N. This means that a 68HC11 will take over twice as many clock cycles to execute the same instructions as will a 68HC12. Coupled with the fact that the 68HC12 runs at 8 MHz instead of 2 MHz for the 68HC11 means that you can expect the same program to run about eight times faster on a 68HC12 than on a 68HC11.

5.2.5   *BEGIN . . . AGAIN*

The BEGIN . . . AGAIN loop must be used within a colon definition and has the following general form:

```
BEGIN <WHYP statements> AGAIN
```

The *<WHYP statements>* in the *BEGIN . . . AGAIN* loop execute endlessly. For example, if after defining the words *stars* and *pattern* in Figure 5–19 the word *stars.forever* shown in Figure 5–24 is executed, then the star pattern will be displayed endlessly on the screen until the reset button is pressed or power is removed from the microcontroller. (Press *<Esc>* a couple of times to exit WHYP.) An endless loop is usually a bad thing in computer programs run on a desktop computer. However, in an embedded system it is often appropriate to use a *BEGIN . . . AGAIN* loop for the main outer loop of a program. You expect the device to work as long as it is turned on. The word *stars.forever* is included in the file stars.whp.

```
: stars.forever        ( -- )
                       BEGIN
                         pattern
                       AGAIN ;
```

Figure 5–24 Sample Word That Uses *BEGIN . . . AGAIN*

```
ok
show stars.forever
stars.forever
                                      BEGIN
  16 50 17        JSR pattern
  18 20           LBRA            AGAIN
  FF F9           -7
  3D              RTS
ok
```

Figure 5–25 68HC12 Instructions Generated by the Word *stars.forever*

To understand how the *BEGIN . . . AGAIN* loop works, the code compiled for the word *stars.forever* is shown in Figure 5–25. The word *BEGIN* does not compile any code; it just remembers where it is during compilation so that it can compute the displacement for the *LBRA* instruction at *AGAIN*. The word *AGAIN* compiles the long branch instruction *LBRA* which is followed by a two's complement displacement. This displacement, $FFF9 (or −7), branches back −7 bytes from the address of the next instruction. This is just the address of the first word after *BEGIN*, in this case the address of *JSR pattern*.

5.2.6 *BEGIN . . . UNTIL*

The *BEGIN . . . UNTIL* loop must be used within a colon definition and has the following general form:

```
BEGIN <WHYP statements> <flag> UNTIL
```

If the *<flag>* is FALSE, the program branches back to the word following *BEGIN*. If the *<flag>* is TRUE, the program continues with the word following *UNTIL*. Executing *UNTIL* removes the flag from the top of the data stack.

As an example of using the *BEGIN . . . UNTIL* loop, consider the word *rows.of.stars* shown in Figure 5–26. This word expects a number *n* on the data stack and then displays *n* rows of stars, each containing one more star than the previous row. You can try this word by loading the file stars.whp which contains this word. Examples of executing this word are shown in Figure 5–27.

```
: stars            ( n -- )
                   FOR
                     ." *"
                   NEXT ;

: rows.of.stars ( n -- )
                   1              \ n i
                   BEGIN
                     CR DUP stars \ n i
                     1+           \ n i+1
                     2DUP <       \ n i+1 f
                   UNTIL          \ n i+1
                   2DROP CR ;
```

Figure 5–26   An Example of Using *BEGIN . . . UNTIL*

```
ok
5 rows.of.stars
*
**
***
****
*****
ok
15 rows.of.stars
*
**
***
****
*****
******
*******
********
*********
**********
***********
************
*************
**************
***************
ok
```

Figure 5–27   Examples of Executing the Word *rows.of.stars*

The word *rows.of.stars* in Figure 5–26 begins by pushing a 1 on the data stack. This will be an index, i, that specifies how many stars to plot in each row. The *BEGIN . . . UNTIL* loop begins by plotting i stars on a new line and then incrementing i by 1. The statements *2DUP* < will produce a true flag if $n < i+1$. That is, it only becomes true when i has been incremented to n. This will occur after n rows have been plotted. At this point the program will exit the *BEGIN . . . UNTIL* loop. There will still be two elements on the data stack which are then dropped by the statement *2DROP*.

Using the words *see* and *show*, you can see what 68HC12 instructions are generated by the word *rows.of.stars* as shown in Figure 5–28 where we have again added the assembly language mnemonics to the 68HC12 machine code.

Just as in the *BEGIN . . . AGAIN* loop, the word *BEGIN* does not compile any code but just remembers where it is during compilation so that it can compute the displacement for the *LBEQ* instruction at *UNTIL*. Note that just as with the *IF* statement, the *UNTIL* statement gets compiled as *LDD 2,X+* followed by a long branch equal instruction (*LBEQ*) with the displacement $FFE8. This means that the flag on top of the data stack is popped into D and if this flag is zero (false), then a branch of -24 bytes backward from the address of the next instruction is taken. This will branch to the instruction *JSR CR* which is the first instruction following *BEGIN*. If the flag were true, then the *LBEQ* branch test would fail and the word following *UNTIL* would be executed.

```
see rows.of.stars
rows.of.stars
        (LIT)   0   1 CR DUP stars
        1+ 2DUP < LBEQ FF E8 2DROP
        CR ;
ok
show rows.of.stars
rows.of.stars
 16 45 22  0   1            JSR   (LIT)  0001
                                                        BEGIN
 16 46 4E                   JSR   CR
 16 41  8                   JSR   DUP
 16 50  0                   JSR   stars
 16 44 86                   JSR   1+
 16 41 4F                   JSR   2DUP
 16 42 3F                   JSR   <
 EC 31                      LDD   2,X+               UNTIL
 18 27 FF E8                LBEQ  -24
 16 41 4A                   JSR   2DROP
 16 46 4E                   JSR   CR
 3D                         RTS
ok
```

Figure 5–28   68HC12 Instructions Generated by the Word *rows.of.stars*

5.2.7   *BEGIN . . . WHILE . . . REPEAT*

The *BEGIN . . . WHILE . . . REPEAT* loop must be used within a colon definition and has the following general form:

```
BEGIN <words> <flag> WHILE <words> REPEAT
```

If the *<flag>* is TRUE, the words between *WHILE* and *REPEAT* are executed, and then a branch is taken to the word following *BEGIN*. If the *<flag>* is FALSE, the program branches to the word following *REPEAT*. Executing *WHILE* removes the flag from the top of the data stack.

As an example, consider the algorithm shown in Figure 5–29 to compute the factorial of *n*. The WHYP word, *factorial*, shown in Figure 5–30 will compute this factorial. This word is in the file fact.whp.

Note that the stack arrangement must be the same at the words *BEGIN* and *REPEAT* for the *WHILE* loop to work properly. Note also that whereas the algorithm given in Figure 5–29 uses the three variables *x*, *i* and *n*, the WHYP implementation uses no variables at all! This is characteristic of WHYP. You will find that you use far fewer variables than in other languages. Parameters are just passed from one WHYP word to the next on the data stack. You may be tempted to introduce a lot of variables as you do in other languages and then use lots of @ and *!* operations when none are really needed. Words like *factorial* in Figure 5–30 just expect a number on the data stack and it will leave the answer on the same data stack. This word can then be used in other words as needed.

```
                    x = 1
                    i = 2
                    WHILE (i <= n)
                       {
                         x = x * i
                         i = i + 1
                       }
                    factorial = x
```

Figure 5–29   Algorithm to Compute the Factorial of *n*

```
: factorial      ( n -- n! )
                 1 2 ROT                    \ x i n
                 BEGIN                      \ x i n
                    2DUP <=                 \ x i n f
                 WHILE                      \ x i n
                    -ROT TUCK               \ n i x i
                    * SWAP                  \ n x' i
                    1+ ROT                  \ x' i' n
                 REPEAT                     \ x i n
                 2DROP ;                    \ x
```

Figure 5–30   WHYP Word to Compute the Factorial of *n*

Study the WHYP code in Figure 5–30 and make sure you understand how it is related to the algorithm in Figure 5–29. At first it may seem more complicated, but we have eliminated all variables and you only have to figure out how to write it once. After that you can just add it to the dictionary by loading it and then compute factorials interactively as shown in Figure 5–31.

To see what 68HC12 instructions are generated by the word *factorial*, we can use the words *see* and *show* as shown in Figure 5–32 where again we have added the assembly language mnemonics to the 68HC12 machine code.

Just as in the *BEGIN . . . UNTIL* loop the word *BEGIN* does not compile any code but just remembers where it is during compilation so that it can compute the displacement for the *LBRA* instruction at *REPEAT*. Note that the *WHILE* statement gets compiled with the same statements as *IF* and *UNTIL*. In this case the *LBEQ* instruction has a displacement $0016 (+22). This means that if the flag on top of the data stack is false, then a branch of +22 bytes forward from the address of the next instruction is taken. This will branch to the instruction *JSR 2DROP* which is the first instruction following *REPEAT*. If the flag were true then the *LBEQ* branch test would fail and the words following *WHILE* would be executed.

The word *REPEAT* compiles the long branch instruction *LBRA* followed by the displacement, $FFDE (−34). This will cause an unconditional branch back −34 bytes from the address of the next instruction, which is just the address of the first word after *BEGIN*, in this case the address of *JSR 2DUP*.

```
load fact.whp
\         Example of BEGIN...WHILE...REPEAT

: factorial      ( n -- n! )
                 1 2 ROT              \ x i n
                 BEGIN                \ x i n
                   2DUP <=            \ x i n f
                 WHILE                \ x i n
                   -ROT TUCK          \ n i x i
                   * SWAP             \ n x' i
                   1+ ROT             \ x' i' n
                 REPEAT               \ x i n
                 2DROP ;              \ x

Current value of target dp is 5033
ok
3 factorial . 6 ok
5 factorial . 120 ok
0 factorial . 1 ok
```

Figure 5–31 Examples of Loading and Executing the Word *factorial*

```
see factorial
factorial
            (LIT)   0   1 (LIT)   0   2 ROT 2DUP
            <= LBEQ   0 16 -ROT TUCK *
            SWAP 1+ ROT LBRA FF DE 2DROP ;
ok
show factorial
factorial
 16 45 22   0   1               JSR   (LIT)   0001
 16 45 22   0   2               JSR   (LIT)   0002
 16 41 1E                       JSR   ROT                 BEGIN
 16 41 4F                       JSR   2DUP
 16 42 88                       JSR   <=
 EC 31                          LDD   2,X+                WHILE
 18 27   0 16                   LBEQ  +22
 16 41 2B                       JSR   -ROT
 16 41 3D                       JSR   TUCK
 16 43 3B                       JSR   *
 16 41   D                      JSR   SWAP
 16 44 86                       JSR   1+
 16 41 1E                       JSR   ROT
 18 20 FF DE                    LBRA  -34                 REPEAT
 16 41 4A                       JSR   2DROP
 3D                             RTS
```

Figure 5–32 68HC12 Instructions Generated by the Word *factorial*

Sine and Arcsine   As another example of a *BEGIN . . . WHILE . . . REPEAT* loop, consider the word *ASIN (n -- angle)* shown in Figure 5–33.

This word finds the arcsine of a value *n* and returns an angle between 0 and 90 degrees. The value *n* is an integer between 0 and 10000, representing numbers between 0 and 1.0. These numbers are stored in a table of sine values, called *SINTBL*, for angles between 0 and 90 degrees as shown in Figure 5–33. The word *ASIN* searches through this table for a value greater than *n* and then rounds to the nearest degree. Examples of executing the word *ASIN* are shown in Figure 5–34.

The table, *SINTBL*, shown in Figure 5–33 can be used to find the *sine* or *cosine* of any angle between 0 and 90° (remember cos θ = sin(90° − θ). For example, if *a* is an angle between 0 and 90, then the WHYP words *sin (a -- s)* and *cos (a -- c)* can be defined as shown in Figure 5–35.

Inasmuch as the sine and cosine of any angle between 0 and 360° is related to the sine and cosine between 0 and 90°, the table, *SINTBL*, shown in Figure 5–33 can be used to find the sine or cosine of any angle (see Exercise 5.18).

If the angle is given to the nearest tenth of a degree, then we can use linear interpolation to find the sine value from the table, *SINTBL*, given in Figure 5–33.

```
\        Sine table                File: SINE.WHP

DECIMAL

CREATE SINTBL
        00000 , 00175 , 00349 , 00524 , 00698 ,      \ 00 - 04
        00872 , 01045 , 01219 , 01392 , 01571 ,      \ 05 - 09
        01736 , 01908 , 02079 , 02250 , 02419 ,      \ 10 - 14
        02588 , 02756 , 02924 , 03090 , 03256 ,      \ 15 - 19
        03420 , 03584 , 03746 , 03907 , 04076 ,      \ 20 - 24
        04226 , 04384 , 04540 , 04695 , 04848 ,      \ 25 - 29
        05000 , 05150 , 05299 , 05446 , 05592 ,      \ 30 - 34
        05736 , 05878 , 06018 , 06157 , 06293 ,      \ 35 - 39
        06428 , 06561 , 06691 , 06820 , 06947 ,      \ 40 - 44
        07071 , 07193 , 07314 , 07431 , 07547 ,      \ 45 - 49
        07660 , 07771 , 07880 , 07986 , 08090 ,      \ 50 - 54
        08192 , 08290 , 08387 , 08480 , 08572 ,      \ 55 - 59
        08660 , 08746 , 08829 , 08910 , 08988 ,      \ 60 - 64
        09063 , 09135 , 09205 , 09272 , 09336 ,      \ 65 - 69
        09397 , 09455 , 09511 , 09563 , 09613 ,      \ 70 - 74
        09659 , 09703 , 09744 , 09781 , 09816 ,      \ 75 - 79
        09848 , 09877 , 09903 , 09925 , 09945 ,      \ 80 - 84
        09962 , 09976 , 09986 , 09994 , 09998 ,      \ 85 - 89
        10000 ,                                      \ 90


\        ARCSIN
                                    \ n = 0 - 10000
: ASIN        ( n -- angle )        \ angle = 0 - 90 degrees
              SINTBL SWAP 0 -ROT            \ 0 pfa n
              BEGIN
                 OVER @ OVER <              \ 0 add n (val<n)
              WHILE
                 SWAP 2+ SWAP               \ cnt add+2 n
                 ROT 1+ -ROT                \ cnt+1 add+2 n
              REPEAT
              2DUP SWAP @ - ABS             \ angle add n dela
              -ROT SWAP 2- @ - ABS >        \ angle f
              IF
                 1-                         \ round down
              THEN ;
```

Figure 5–33   Contents of the File *sine.whp*

```
ok
0 asin . 0 ok
10000 asin . 90 ok
7071 asin . 45 ok
1234 asin . 7 ok
1238 asin . 7 ok
1380 asin . 8 ok
5000 asin . 30 ok
5150 asin . 31 ok
5100 asin . 31 ok
5075 asin . 31 ok
5074 asin . 30 ok
```

Figure 5–34   Examples of Executing the Word *asin* in Figure 5–33

```
: SIN          ( a -- s )              \ angle = 0 - 90 degrees
               2* SINTBL + @ ;         \ s = 0 - 10000


: COS          ( a -- c )              \ angle = 0 - 90 degrees
               90 SWAP -
               2* SINTBL + @ ;         \ c = 0 - 10000
```

Figure 5–35   Defining the Sine and Cosine of an Angle between 0 and 90°

This process is simplified by using the 68HC12 table lookup and interpolate instructions shown in Table 5–6. The instruction *TBL* uses an indexed addressing mode referenced by X, Y, SP, or PC to point to a byte in the table at memory location M. Accumulator B contains the fractional index value (on a scale of 0 to 255) between memory locations M and $M+1$. The instruction *TBL* then linearly interpolates the values stored at memory locations M and $M+1$ and stores the result in accumulator A as shown in Table 5–6. The extended table lookup instruction, *ETBL*, performs a similar function for a table containing 16-bit values and stores the result in D.

The WHYP words *B.LOOKUP (addr frac -- interp)* and *W.LOOKUP (addr frac -- interp)*, shown in Figure 5–36, make it easy to use the *TBL* and *ETBL* instructions. As an example, the word *SIN10 (a -- s)*, shown in Figure 3–37, uses the table, *SINTBL*, in Figure 5–33 to find the sine of an angle, a, where a is a number

Table 5–6   Table Lookup and Interpolate Instructions

Mnemonic	Function	Operation
TBL	Linearly interpolate 8-bit table	$(M) + [(B) \times ((M+1) - (M))] => A$
ETBL	Linearly interpolate 16-bit table	$(M : M+1) + [(B) \times ((M+2 : M+3) - (M : M+1))] => D$

```
;        B.LOOKUP    ( addr frac -- interp )    ;8-bit table lookup wrapper
BLOOKUP
        LDD    2,X+
        LDY    0,X
        TBL    0,Y
        TAB
        LDAA   #0
        STD    0,X
        RTS


;        W.LOOKUP    ( addr frac -- interp )    ;16-bit table lookup wrapper
WLOOKUP
        LDD    2,X+
        LDY    0,X
        ETBL   0,Y
        STD    0,X
        RTS
```

Figure 5–36 WHYP Words for Using the 68HC12 Instructions *TBL* and *ETBL*

```
: SIN10        ( a -- s )          \ angle = 0 - 900 tenths of a degree
        10 IDIV                    \ tenths angle
        SWAP 256 10 */             \ angle frac
        SWAP 2* SINTBL +           \ frac addr
        SWAP W.LOOKUP ;            \ s = 0 - 10000
```

Figure 5–37 Defining the Sine of Angles to a Tenth of a Degree

between 0 and 900, representing an angle between 0 and 90° to the nearest tenth of a degree.

A similar word called *COS10 (a -- c)* could be defined to find the cosine of an angle between 0 and 90° to the nearest tenth of a degree. However, care must be taken in this case when using the word *W.LOOKUP* because you will effectively be indexing backward in the table, *SINTBL*, in Figure 5–33 (see Exercise 5.19).

The words *SIN10 (a -- s)* and *COS10 (a -- c)* can be extended to find the sine or cosine of any angle between 0 and 360° to the nearest tenth of a degree (see Exercise 5.20).

5.2.8 *DO . . . LOOP*

The WHYP *DO* loop must be defined inside a colon definition. To see how it works, define the following word:

```
: dotest          ( limit index -- )
                  DO
                    I .
                  LOOP ;
```

Then if you type

```
5 0 dotest
```

the values 0, 1, 2, 3, 4 will be printed on the screen. Try it.

The *DO* loop works as follows. The word *DO* takes the top two values (*limit* and *index*) from the top of the parameter stack and moves them to the return stack. At this point the two values are no longer on the parameter stack. The word *LOOP* adds one to the index value and compares the result to the limit value. If the incremented index value is less than the limit value, then a branch is taken to the word following *DO*. If the incremented index value is equal to the limit value, then the two values are removed from the return stack and the word following *LOOP* is executed.

The WHYP word *I* copies the index value from the return stack to the top of the parameter stack. Therefore, the execution of the above example can be illustrated as follows:

```
5              \ 5
0              \ 5 0
DO
I              \ ix   ( ix = 0,1,2,3,4)
.
LOOP
```

Note that the limit value must be one greater than the largest index value you want. For example,

```
: test          ( -- )
                11 1 DO
                    I .
                LOOP ;
```

will print out the values

```
1 2 3 4 5 6 7 8 9 10
```

The word *rows.of.stars (n --)* given in Figure 5–26 using a *BEGIN . . . UNTIL* loop can be written using a *DO . . . LOOP* as shown in Figure 5–38. Note that the loop will execute *n* times and because the index starts at zero, the value *I* must be incremented by 1 to plot the correct number of stars.

The Word *LEAVE*   The WHYP word *LEAVE* can be used to exit a *DO* loop prematurely. It is normally used within an *IF* statement inside the *DO* loop. The word *LEAVE* causes the immediate exit from the *DO* loop. (The address of the word following *LOOP* has been stored as the third word on the return stack.)

```
: stars              ( n -- )
                 FOR
                     ." *"
                 NEXT ;

: rows.of.stars ( n -- )
                 0 DO
                     CR I 1+ stars
                 LOOP
                 CR ;
```

Figure 5–38   An Example of Using the DO . . . LOOP

As an example, the word *find.n (imax n -- ff | index tf)* will search for a specific value, *n*, in a table containing *imax* elements and return the index of the value (i.e., its position in the table) under a true flag if the value is found; otherwise, a false flag will be left on top of the data stack. The WHYP statement

```
CREATE TABLE
     9600 , 4800 , 2400 , 1200 , 600 , 300 , 150 , 75 ,
```

will create the table shown in Figure 5–39 in the target memory.

The number of values in the table is *imax* (8 in this case). The value to be searched for is *n*. These two values will be on the stack when *find.n* is executed. The colon definition of *find.n* is given in Figure 5–40.

Study this definition until you see how it works. In general, when using a *DO* loop, the stack picture should be the same after executing *DO* as it is after executing *LOOP*. You will often need to *DUP* some stack value(s) inside a *DO* loop and then *DROP* something after you leave the loop. Note in this case how the *ROT* before *LEAVE* is used to set up the stack so that the final *DROP* will leave the true flag on top of the stack.

CFA	JSR DOVAR	<---- TABLE
PFA	9600	0
	4800	1
	2400	2
	1200	3
	600	4
	300	5
	150	6
	75	7 = imax−1

Figure 5–39   Table to Be Searched by *find.n*

```
: find.n    ( imax n -- ff | index tf )
              0 SWAP ROT              \ 0 n imax
              0 DO                    \ 0 n
                DUP I TABLE           \ 0 n n ix pfa
                SWAP 2* +             \ 0 n n pfa+2*ix
                @ =                   \ 0 n f
                IF                    \ 0 n
                    DROP I TRUE       \ 0 ix tf
                    ROT LEAVE         \ ix tf 0
                THEN
              LOOP                    \ 0 n
              DROP ;                  \ 0 | ix tf
```

Figure 5–40   *find.n* will search a table for a value *n*.

5.3   RECURSION IN WHYP

The WHYP word *RECURSE* within the colon definition of a word will cause the word to call itself. You can use this word to implement algorithms involving recursion.

For example, we wrote a word called *factorial (n -- n!)* in Figure 5–30 that computed the factorial of *n*. However, the factorial of *n*, can be defined as

    n! = n * (n - 1)!

That is, *n!* is defined in terms of *(n – 1)!*. This is an example of a recursive definition. Following this definition, a WHYP word *fact (n -- n!)* to compute *n!* can be defined as shown in Figure 5–41.

To understand how the word defined in Figure 5–41 works, note that the word *RECURSE* executes the entire subroutine *fact* again. But this word expects a number, *n*, on the data stack and leaves its factorial, *n!*, on the stack. Therefore, if *(n−1)* is on the stack and *fact* is called, it will leave *(n−1)!* on the stack. Multiplying this value by *n* will produce the value of *n!*.

```
: fact      ( n -- n! )
              ?DUP                \ n n | 0
              IF                  \ n
                DUP 1-            \ n n-1
                RECURSE *         \ n*(n-1)!
              ELSE
                1                 \ 1
              THEN ;
```

Figure 5–41   Computing the Factorial on *n* Using Recursion

Of course, there must be a limiting case in which we provide the actual answer. In this case, a value of $n = 0$ will, by definition, produce a value of $0! = 1$. Therefore, at the beginning of the word we use *?DUP (n -- n n | 0)* which will duplicate the top of the stack only if the value is nonzero. If it is zero, then it does not duplicate the top of the stack and just leaves the zero on the stack. This will act as a false flag for the *IF* statement and therefore the *ELSE* phrase will be executed which will leave the value 1 on the stack.

Type in this definition of *fact* and then test the word by typing

```
4 FACT  .
```

This should produce the value 24. Note that in this case the word *fact* will actually be executed five times. To see how the word *fact* actually calculates the factorial, insert the word *.S* in the three locations shown in Figure 5–42. The first *.S* at the beginning of the word will display the stack each time the word is called. The second *.S* is at the end of the *IF* clause and the last *.S* is at the end of the *ELSE* clause. Typing

```
4 FACT
```

will produce the results shown in Figure 5–42.

The first five rows are from the first *.S*. Note that each time the word *recurse* is executed, the new value of $n-1$ is left on the stack. Only when this value gets to zero does the *ELSE* clause get executed which leaves a 1 on the stack. The last four rows in Figure 5–42 are from the *.S* at the end of the *IF* clause after the word (*) gets executed. It gets executed once for each *recurse* that took place. That is, it multiplies the 1 by 2 by 3 by 4 to produce the final value of 24.

Using the words *see* and *show*, we can decompile the word *fact* as shown in Figure 5–43 where we have added the 68HC12 assembly language mnemonics. Note

```
ok
:  fact .s ?dup if dup 1- recurse * .s else 1 .s then ; ok
4 fact
S:[1] 4
S:[2] 4 3
S:[3] 4 3 2
S:[4] 4 3 2 1
S:[5] 4 3 2 1 0
S:[5] 4 3 2 1 1
S:[4] 4 3 2 1
S:[3] 4 3 2
S:[2] 4 6
S:[1] 24 ok
```

Figure 5–42 Example Demonstrating Recursion

```
ok
see fact
fact
          ?DUP LBEQ  0  F DUP 1- BSR EF * LBRA  0  5
          (LIT)  0  1 ;
ok
show fact
fact
 16 41 9E                      JSR   ?DUP
 EC 31 18 27  0  F             LBEQ +15
 16 41  8                      JSR   DUP
 16 44 96                      JSR   1-
 7 EF                          BSR  -17         RECURSE (BSR FACT)
 16 43 3B                      JSR   *
 18 20  0  5                   LBRA +5
 16 45 22  0  1                JSR   (LIT) 1
 3D                            RTS
ok
```

Figure 5–43   68HC12 Instructions Generated by the word *fact*

that the statement *RECURSE* gets compiled as a branch to subroutine (*BSR*) to the word *fact* itself. This means that each time *RECURSE* is executed the subroutine fact will be called again. When writing recursive subroutines it is important that each call to *RECURSE* have the appropriate value(s) on the data stack.

   As the factorial example has shown, recursion can sometimes be used as an alternative to loops. As we have seen, recursion can use considerable stack space in the process of carrying out the calculation. Using loops is generally more efficient than using recursion. However, there are certain algorithms that are most easily described in terms of recursion.

5.4 SUMMARY

In this chapter we have studied the 68HC12 branching instructions and showed how they can be used to implement the WHYP branching and looping words summarized in Box 5–3. In addition to the WHYP words given in Boxes 5–1 – 5–3, the words given in Box 5–4 were also discussed in this chapter.

   In the first five chapters we have examined the 68HC12 instruction set and have seen how we can write 68HC12 subroutines in the form of words that pass parameters on a data stack. This extensible language, WHYP, allows us to develop code in an incremental and interactive way. In the next six chapters we will use WHYP to explore the various I/O modules that are built into the 68HC12.

Box 5–3   WHYP Branching and Looping Words

```
IF...ELSE...THEN
        <flag> IF <true statements> ELSE <false statements> THEN

FOR...NEXT
        n FOR <WHYP statements> NEXT
        Execute <WHYP statements> n times.

BEGIN...AGAIN
        BEGIN <words> AGAIN
        Execute <words> forever.

BEGIN...UNTIL
        BEGIN <words> <flag> UNTIL
        Execute <words> until <flag> is true.

BEGIN...WHILE...REPEAT
        BEGIN <words1> <flag> WHILE <words2> REPEAT
        Execute <words1>; if <flag> is true, execute <words2>
        and branch back to <words1>;
        if <flag> is false, exit loop.

DO...LOOP
        <limit> <index> DO <WHYP statements> LOOP
        Execute <WHYP statements> as long as <index> is less than <limit>;
        LOOP increments <index> by 1.
```

Box 5–4   Other WHYP Words Introduced in Chapter 5

MIN	(n1 n2 -- n3) Leaves the smaller of *n1* and *n2* on the stack.
MAX	(n1 n2 -- n3) Leaves the larger of *n1* and *n2* on the stack.
NEGATE	(n -- -n) Changes the sign of *n*.
ABS	(n -- |n|) Leaves the absolute value of *n* on the stack.
S>D	(n -- d) Sign extends a single to a double.
LEAVE	(--) Immediately exits a *DO* loop.
RECURSE	(--) Executes the current word recursively.
?DUP	(n -- n n | 0) Duplicates the top of the stack only if *n* is nonzero.
B.LOOKUP	(addr frac -- interp) 8-bit table lookup wrapper
W.LOOKUP	(addr frac -- interp) 16-bit table lookup wrapper

EXERCISES

Exercise 5.1

Following the examples shown in Figures 5–12 and 5–13, write 68HC12 subroutines for the other WHYP conditional words shown in Box 5–1. Compare your results with those given in the file WHYP12.ASM in Appendix D.

Exercise 5.2

Following the example shown in Figure 5–14, write 68HC12 subroutines for the WHYP logical operators *OR* and *XOR* shown in Box 5–2. Compare your results with those given in the file WHYP12.ASM in Appendix D.

Exercise 5.3

Write a WHYP word called *new.rows.of.stars (n --)* that will display *2n* rows of stars. Each row in the first *n* rows should contain one more star than the preceding row, starting with one star in row 1 (see Figure 5–27). Each row in the second *n* rows should contain one less star than in the preceding row starting with *n* stars and ending with one star in the last row.

Exercise 5.4

Write a WHYP word called *baud (rate --)* that expects a baud rate from the table shown in Figure 5–39 and will store the table index value in the variable, *BAUD_INDEX*, if the baud rate is in the table. Use the word *find.n* given in Figure 5–40.

Exercise 5.5

Define a WHYP word called *DOUBLED (bal int --)* that expects a starting balance and interest rate on the data stack and prints out a table containing the year and balance for 20 years or until the starting balance has doubled, whichever occurs first. Test the program by typing

```
1000 6 DOUBLED
```

Exercise 5.6

A magic number is a three-digit number having the property that the sum of the cubes of the digits is equal to the number itself.

a. Write a WHYP word called *STRIP (n -- units tens hunds)* that expects a number between 100 and 999 on the data stack and returns each of the three digits.

b. Write a WHYP word called *SUMCUBE (n1 n2 n3 -- sum_of_cubes)* that returns the sum of the cubes of the top three values on the stack. *Hint: SUMECUBE* can call *CUBE* given by

```
: CUBE ( n -- n**3 )
        DUP DUP * * ;
```

c. Write a WHYP word called *MAGIC.NOS (--)* that will print out all magic numbers between 100 and 999.

Exercise 5.7

The Fibonacci sequence is a sequence of numbers in which each number (starting with the third) is the sum of the two immediately preceding numbers. Thus, the beginning of the sequence looks like this

```
1 1 2 3 5 8 13 21 34
```

Define a WHYP word called *fib* (*n* --) that will print the Fibonacci sequence for all values less than *n*. Test your word by typing

```
1000 fib
```

Exercise 5.8

The *N*th Fibonacci number is given by

```
FIB(N) = FIB(N-1) + FIB(N-2)
```

a. Write a WHYP word called *FIBN* (*n1* -- *n2*) that will find the *N*th number in a Fibonacci sequence *using recursion*. Start counting with zero. Thus,

```
FIBN(4) = 5 and FIBN(6) = 13
```

b. Write a second word called *FIB2 (n* --) that will call *FIBN* and print out the Fibonacci sequence for all numbers less than *n* (just as was done in Exercise 5.7).

Exercise 5.9

Create a table called weights that contains the following values:

```
75 135 175 115 220 235 180 167
```

Define a WHYP word called *heaviest (pfa* -- *max.value*) that will put the maximum value from the table on the top of the stack. If you type

```
weights heaviest .
```

the value 235 should be printed on the screen.

Exercise 5.10

Define a WHYP word called *2SUM (n1 n2 n3* -- *sum*) that will accept three test scores from the stack and return the sum of the two highest scores. For example,

```
15 19 13 2SUM
```

will print 34.

Exercise 5.11

The Newton-Raphson method uses successive approximations for finding roots of the equation $f(x) = 0$. If the *i*th approximation is given by x_i, then the i + first approximation is given by

$$x_{i+1} = x_i - \frac{f(x_i)}{f'(x_i)} \tag{5.1}$$

To find the square root of N we need to solve the equation $f(x) = x^2 - N = 0$. Taking the derivative $f'(x) = 2x$, and substituting into (5.1), we find that

$$x_{i+1} = \frac{\frac{N}{x_i} + x_i}{2}$$

   a. Write a WHYP word called *sqrt (n -- n')* that expects a single word *n* on the stack and leaves the square root of *n*, *n'*, on the stack. Note that the maximum positive value of *n* is 32767. Use an initial guess of x_i of 60 and iterate five times. Test the word by taking the square root of several values including 400.

   b. Write a WHYP word called *dsqrt (d -- n')* that expects a double word *d* on the stack and leaves the 16-bit square root of *d*, *n'*, on the stack. Use an initial guess of x_i of 127 and iterate seven times. Test the word by taking the square root of several double-word values including 40,000.

   c. Write a WHYP word called *cuberoot (d -- n')* that expects a double word *d* on the stack and leaves the 16-bit cube root of *d*, *n'*, on the stack. Test the word by taking the cube root of several double-word values including 3375. and 8,000,000. *Hint:* The word *3DUP (a b c -- a b c a b c)* is equivalent to (see Exercise 2.11) 2 PICK 2 PICK 2 PICK.

Exercise 5.12

Consider the word *fact (n -- n!)* shown in Figure 5–41 that computes the factorial using recursion.

   a. How large a value of *n* can you use in *fact* before the result overflows 16 bits?

   b. Write a new word called *dfact (n -- d)* that will compute the factorial of *n* and leave the result as a double number. How large a value of *n* can you now use before you overflow 32 bits? *Hint:* Use *DUM** from Chapter 3.

Exercise 5.13

Define a WHYP word *?LEAP (year -- flag)* that will accept a year (16-bit number) on the data stack and leave a flag indicating whether the year is a leap year or not.

```
Examples:    1985 ?LEAP .  will print 0
             1984 ?LEAP .  will print -1 indicating a leap year
             1900 ?LEAP .  will print 0
```

Hint: A year is a leap year if it is divisible by 4 but not by 100, or if it is divisible by 400.

Exercise 5.14

The Greatest Common Divisor (GCD) of two integer numbers is the largest number which can fully divide both the numbers. The most famous method to find the GCD of two numbers *GCD(m,n)* is due to the ancient mathematician Euclid:

```
If m>n, find GCD(n,m)
If m=0, GCD(m,n)=n
Otherwise, GCD(m,n)=GCD(m, n MOD m)
```

Translating this algorithm to WHYP, we have

```
: GCD ( m n -- gcd )
        BEGIN   2DUP >          \ if m>n, exhange m and n
                IF SWAP THEN
                OVER            \ if m=0, exit loop
        WHILE   OVER MOD        \ else, replace n by n mod m
        REPEAT                  \ repeat until m=0
        SWAP DROP               \ discard m, which is 0
    ;
```

Write a word for *GCD (m n -- gcd)* using *recursion*. Test the routine by typing

```
123  456  GCD .
865  245  GCD .
475  150  GCD .
```

Exercise 5.15

The value of x^n can be written as $x^n = x*x^{n-1}$. Write a WHYP word called

```
power ( x n -- xⁿ )
```
(shown as) $power\ (\ x\ n\ --\ x^n\ )$

that expects x and n on the data stack and computes x^n using *recursion*.

Exercise 5.16

Assume that you have created a table, called *table*, that contains 15 single-word values. Write a WHYP word called *?in.table (val -- f)* that will expect a 16-bit value *val* on the data stack and will leave a true flag if the value *val* is in the table and a false flag if *val* is not in the table.

Exercise 5.17

The following words will produce a random number between 0 and FFFF hex.

```
VARIABLE seed        1234 seed !
: rand ( -- rand# )
        seed @ 5421 *
        1+ DUP seed ! ;
```

Each time *rand* is called, a new "random" number between 0 and 65,535 will be produced. To get a random integer between 0 and $N-1$ you could write

```
: random ( N -- random# )      \ rand# between 0 and N-1
        rand SWAP MOD ;
```

This turns out to produce numbers that are not very random because it is equivalent to taking *random#* from the low bits of *rand#* (i.e., the random number is the remainder when you divide *rand#* by N). A better result is obtained if you take *random#* from the high bits of *rand#* (i.e., the "excess bits" beyond 16 bits produced when you multiply *rand#* by N). Write a new version of *random (N -- random#)* that will produce a random integer between 0 and $N-1$ by taking this value from the high bits in the random number produced by *rand*.

Exercise 5.18

a. Write a WHYP word called *sin360 (a -- s)* that will compute the sine, s, of an angle, a, between 0 and 360° using the table, *SINTBL*, shown in Figure 5–33. Note that in each of the four quadrants the sine of the angle, a, is given by

$\sin (a)$	$a \leq 90°$
$\sin (180 - a)$	$90° < a \leq 180°$
$-\sin (a - 180)$	$180° < a \leq 270°$
$-\sin (360 - a)$	$270° < a < 360°$

b. Write a WHYP word called *cos360 (a -- s)* that will compute the cosine, *c*, of an angle, *a*, between 0 and 360°.

Exercise 5.19

Write a WHYP word called *cos10 (a -- c)* that will compute the cosine, *c*, of an angle, *a*, where *a* is a number between 0 and 900, representing an angle between 0 and 90° to the nearest tenth of a degree. Use the table, *SINTBL*, in Figure 5–33 and the fact that cos θ = sin(90° − θ). Remember that in the word *W.LOOKUP (addr frac -- intrp)* the address, *addr*, is the lower address of the interpolated range. For a solution, see the file sine.whp.

Exercise 5.20

a. Write a WHYP word called *sin3600 (a -- s)* that will compute the sine, *s*, of an angle, *a*, between 0 and 360° where *a* represents tenths of a degree (0–3600). *Hint:* See Exercise 5.18 and use the word *W.LOOKUP* (see Figure 5–36).

b. Write a WHYP word called *cos3600 (a -- c)* that will compute the cosine, *c*, of an angle, *a*, between 0 and 360° where *a* represents tenths of a degree (0–3600). *Hint:* See Exercises 5.18 and 5.19.

6

Interrupts

Hardware interrupts allow external events to interrupt the normal execution of a program and instead execute an interrupt service routine, after which the execution of the original program is picked up where it left off. The addresses of the interrupt service routines are called *interrupt vectors*. These interrupt vectors are stored in a special table in memory. When a particular interrupt occurs, the address of the interrupt service routine is looked up in the interrupt vector table and control is transferred to that address. In this chapter we will

- Describe the kinds of interrupts available on the 68HC12 and the 68HC11 in Sections 6.1 and 6.2, respectively.
- Show how interrupt vectors can be mapped to RAM locations in Section 6.3.
- Show how interrupt service routines can be written in WHYP in Section 6.4.
- Explore the use of real-time interrupts in Section 6.5 including an example of producing a fixed time delay.
- Show how interrupt service routines can be written in assembly language in Section 6.6.

6.1 68HC12 INTERRUPTS

There are 25 different sources of interrupts on a 68HC812A4 and 23 on a 68HC912B32. These interrupts are divided into two categories: nonmaskable and maskable. The maskable interrupts can be masked by setting the I-bit in the condition code register. Nonmaskable interrupts cannot be masked. We will discuss nonmaskable interrupt in Section 6.1.1 and maskable interrupts in Section 6.1.2.

6.1.1 68HC12 Nonmaskable Interrupts

There are six 68HC12 nonmaskable interrupts shown in Table 6–1. Each interrupt source has a 16-bit vector address that holds the address (interrupt vector) of the code to be executed when the interrupt occurs.

The nonmaskable interrupts shown in Table 6–1 are listed in order of priority. If more than one interrupt occurs at the same time, the interrupt with the highest priority will be serviced first. We will briefly describe each of these nonmaskable interrupts in turn.

Reset   When the *RESET* pin on a 68HC12 goes low, normal microprocessor functions are suspended. When this pin returns high, the microprocessor will set bits *X* and *I* in the condition code register and start executing instructions starting at the address stored at $FFFE–$FFFF. The 68HC12 has a Power-On Reset (POR) circuit that causes the reset signal to be asserted internally after power (5 volts) has been applied to the processor.

It is necessary for addresses $FFFE–$FFFF to be in some type of nonvolatile memory (ROM, EPROM, or Flash memory) so that a valid reset vector will be at that address. Of course, the memory it points to must also be in nonvolatile memory so that some meaningful code will be executed when you turn on the processor.

COP (Computer Operating Properly)   The two COP (Computer Operating Properly) interrupt sources shown in Table 6–1 are used to help detect both hardware and software errors. When the clock monitor is enabled [by setting the *CME* bit in the *COP Control Register* (*COPCTL*)] special circuitry will produce a reset if the clock stops or its frequency falls below about 500 KHz.

The COP Failure Reset is a watchdog timer that will produce a reset if a special sequence ($55 followed by $AA) isn't written to the *Arm/Reset COP Timer Register* (*COPRST*) within a specified time. You would include this operation as part of

Table 6–1 68HC12 Nonmaskable Interrupts

Vector Address	Interrupt Source
$FFFE–$FFFF	Reset
$FFFC–$FFFD	COP Clock Monitor Fail Reset
$FFFA–$FFFB	COP Failure Reset
$FFF8–$FFF9	Unimplemented Instruction Trap
$FFF6–$FFF7	SWI
$FFF4–$FFF5	XIRQ

your software when you know that certain portions of code must be executed within a certain time. A COP failure would be an indication that your software is not operating properly. We will look at an example of using this feature in Chapter 15.

Unimplemented Instruction Trap   All 1-byte opcodes in the 68HC12 are valid except $18 which requires a second byte to form the complete opcode. Only 54 of the 256 possible second bytes are valid. If your program tries to execute one of these invalid 2-byte opcodes, the program will trap to the address stored in $FFF8–$FFF9.

Software Interrupts (SWI)   A software interrupt occurs when you execute the *SWI* instruction. This will cause the instructions at the address stored in $FFF6–$FFF7 to be executed. Before this happens the return address (the address following the *SWI* instruction) is pushed on the stack together with registers *Y, X, A, B*, and *CCR*, as shown in Figure 6–1. After pushing these values on the stack the interrupt mask, *I*, in the condition code register, *CCR*, is set to 1. This will prevent any maskable interrupts from being processed while in the software interrupt routine. The *I* bit can be cleared to zero by either executing the *CLI* (clear interrupt mask) instruction or by executing the *RTI* (return from interrupt) instruction. The *RTI* instruction is executed at the end of all interrupt service routines. It will pop from the stack all of the values shown in Figure 6–1. This will include the *CCR* register which may have had the *I* bit cleared to zero if interrupts had been enabled before the *SWI* instruction was executed. A similar sequence occurs for maskable hardware interrupts which we will describe in Section 6.1.2.

When the *RTI* instruction is executed, the return address on the stack is popped into the program counter. The program will therefore continue at the point in the program where the interrupt occurred. For a software interrupt this would be the statement following the *SWI* instruction.

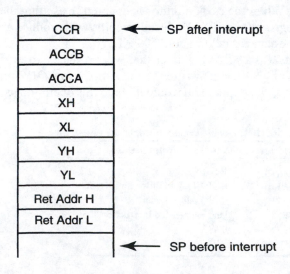

Figure 6–1 | CCR   ← SP after interrupt
ACCB
ACCA
XH
XL
YH
YL
Ret Addr H
Ret Addr L
         ← SP before interrupt

Figure 6–1 Register Stacking for Interrupts

Nonmaskable Interrupt Request (*XIRQ*)   The *XIRQ* is pin *PE0* on the 68HC12. The *XIRQ* interrupt is a pseudo-nonmaskable interrupt that is associated with the *X* bit in the *CCR*. After reset, this bit is set which inhibits interrupts when the *XIRQ* pin goes low. However, software can clear the *X* bit in the *CCR* by using the instruction *ANDCC #$BF*. Once this bit has been cleared, it cannot be set to 1 again by software. Thus, at this point the interrupt becomes nonmaskable.

When an *XIRQ* interrupt occurs by a high to low signal on pin *PE0*, the current instruction is completed and then the registers shown in Figure 6–1 are pushed on the stack. The return address will be the value in the program counter, that is, the address of the instruction following the one being executed when the interrupt occurs. This will be the address returned to after the interrupt service routine is executed. The *XIRQ* interrupt service routine address is stored in the vector address $FFF4–$FFF5 (see Table 6–1). After all registers shown in Figure 6–1 are pushed on the stack, both the *I* bit and the *X* bit in the *CCR* are set. This means that another *XIRQ* interrupt cannot occur during the execution of an *XIRQ* interrupt service routine. Executing the *RTI* instruction at the end of the interrupt service routine will pop the registers shown in Figure 6–1 off the stack, including the *CCR* register which will have its *X* bit cleared. At that point a new *XIRQ* interrupt can occur.

6.1.2   68HC12 Maskable Interrupts

The maskable interrupts available on the 68HC812A4 are shown in Table 6–2 and those available on the 68HC912B32 are shown in Table 6–3. The differences in the

Table 6–2   68HC812A4 Maskable Interrupts

Vector Address	Interrupt Source
$FFF2–$FFF3	IRQ or Key Wake Up D
$FFF0–$FFF1	Real-Time Interrupt
$FFEE–$FFEF	Timer Channel 0
$FFEC–$FFED	Timer Channel 1
$FFEA–$FFEB	Timer Channel 2
$FFE8–$FFE9	Timer Channel 3
$FFE6–$FFE7	Timer Channel 4
$FFE4–$FFE5	Timer Channel 5
$FFE2–$FFE3	Timer Channel 6
$FFE0–$FFE1	Timer Channel 7
$FFDE–$FFDF	Timer Overflow
$FFDC–$FFDD	Pulse Accumulator Overflow
$FFDA–$FFDB	Pulse Accumulator Input Edge
$FFD8–$FFD9	SPI Serial Transfer Complete
$FFD6–$FFD7	SCI 0
$FFD4–$FFD5	SCI 1
$FFD2–$FFD3	ATD
$FFD0–$FFD1	Key Wakeup J (stop wakeup)
$FFCE–$FFCF	Key Wakeup H (stop wakeup)

Table 6–3 68HC912B32 Maskable Interrupts

Vector Address	Interrupt Source
$FFF2–$FFF3	IRQ
$FFF0–$FFF1	Real-Time Interrupt
$FFEE–$FFEF	Timer Channel 0
$FFEC–$FFED	Timer Channel 1
$FFEA–$FFEB	Timer Channel 2
$FFE8–$FFE9	Timer Channel 3
$FFE6–$FFE7	Timer Channel 4
$FFE4–$FFE5	Timer Channel 5
$FFE2–$FFE3	Timer Channel 6
$FFE0–$FFE1	Timer Channel 7
$FFDE–$FFDF	Timer Overflow
$FFDC–$FFDD	Pulse Accumulator Overflow
$FFDA–$FFDB	Pulse Accumulator Input Edge
$FFD8–$FFD9	SPI Serial Transfer Complete
$FFD6–$FFD7	SCI 0
$FFD4–$FFD5	Reserved
$FFD2–$FFD3	ATD
$FFD0–$FFD1	BDLC

two are that the 'A4 part has key wakeup interrupts (described in Chapter 15) and a second SCI1 interrupt. On the other hand, the 'B32 part has a BDLC interrupt.

All of the interrupts shown in Tables 6–2 and 6–3 are maskable interrupts that are inhibited when the *I* bit in the *CCR* is set (using the *SEI* instruction). To enable all of these maskable interrupts you must clear the *I* bit in the *CCR* by executing the *CLI* instruction. In addition, each interrupt source will have a local enable bit that must be set in one of the I/O registers in order to enable that particular interrupt. For example, to enable pin *PE1* as an IRQ interrupt, you must set bit *IRQEN* (bit 6) in the *Interrupt Control Register*, *INTCR*, shown in Figure 6–2.

The maskable interrupts shown in Tables 6–2 and 6–3 are listed in order of priority. If more than one interrupt occurs at the same time, the interrupt with the highest priority will be serviced first. These all have a lower priority than the nonmaskable interrupts shown in Table 6–1.

Any of the maskable interrupts shown in Tables 6–2 and 6–3 can be assigned the highest priority (among the maskable interrupts) by writing the low byte of its vector address to the *Highest Priority I Interrupt Register*, *HPRIO*, shown in Figure 6–3. For example, to make Timer Channel 2 the highest priority, you would store an $EA, the low byte of its vector address, $FFEA, in the *HPRIO* register. The remaining interrupts will maintain their relative priority.

When a maskable interrupt occurs, a process similar to that for the *XIRQ* interrupt occurs. The vector addresses shown in Tables 6–2 and 6–3 contain the starting addresses of the instructions that are executed when the corresponding interrupt occurs. When a hardware interrupt occurs, the current instruction is completed and

	7	6	5	4	3	2	1	0	
$001E	IRQE	IRQEN	DLY	0	0	0	0	0	INTCR

IRQE: IRQ Select Edge Sensitive Only (read anytime, write once)
          0 – IRQ responds to low-level on pin PE1 (default)
          1 – IRQ responds only to falling edges on pin PE1

IRQEN: External IRQ Enable (read and write anytime)
          0 – Pin PE1 not connected to IRQ interrupt logic
          1 – Pin PE1 connected to IRQ interrupt logic (default)

DLY: Enable Oscillator Start-Up Delay on Exit from STOP (read anytime, write onc
          0 – No stabilization delay imposed on exit from STOP
          1 – Stabilization delay is imposed on exit from STOP (default)

Figure 6–2   The Interrupt Control Register

	7	6	5	4	3	2	1	0	
$001F	1	1	PSEL5	PSEL4	PSEL3	PSEL2	PSEL1	0	HPRIO

PSEL[5:1]: Priority select bits to form low byte of vector address of maskable interrupt
           with highest priority (default is F2: IRQ)

Figure 6–3   The Highest Priority I Interrupt Register

then the registers shown in Figure 6–1 are pushed on the stack after which the *I* bit
in the *CCR* is set to prevent new hardware interrupts from occurring.

All interrupt service routines must end with the *RTI* (return from interrupt)
instruction. This will cause all of the registers shown in Figure 6–1 to be popped
from the stack. The return address on the stack is popped into the program counter
causing the program to continue at the point in the program where the interrupt
occurred with all of the registers returned to the values they had when the interrupt
occurred.

6.2 68HC11 Interrupts

The interrupts available on a typical 68HC11, the 68HC711E9, are shown in
Table 6–4. These are basically a subset of the interrupts shown in Tables 6–1–6–3
for the 68HC12. The main difference is that the input captures and output compares
are mostly confined to separate pins, and therefore separate interrupts, on the
68HC11. The basic interrupt process is the same as on the 68HC12. One difference
is that when the registers shown in Figure 6–1 are pushed on the stack, the 68HC11
stack pointer is decremented after the value is pushed on the stack rather than
before. That is, on a 68HC11 the stack pointer always points to the next available
memory location (see note at the end of Section 2.1).

Table 6–4   68HC711E9 Interrupts

Vector Address	Interrupt Source
$FFFE–$FFFF	Reset
$FFFC–$FFFD	COP Clock Monitor Fail Reset
$FFFA–$FFFB	COP Failure Reset
$FFF8–$FFF9	Illegal Opcode Trap
$FFF6–$FFF7	SWI
$FFF4–$FFF5	XIRQ
$FFF2–$FFF3	IRQ
$FFF0–$FFF1	Real-Time Interrupt
$FFEE–$FFEF	Timer Input Capture 1
$FFEC–$FFED	Timer Input Capture 2
$FFEA–$FFEB	Timer Input Capture 3
$FFE8–$FFE9	Timer Output Compare 1
$FFE6–$FFE7	Timer Output Compare 2
$FFE4–$FFE5	Timer Output Compare 3
$FFE2–$FFE3	Timer Output Compare 4
$FFE0–$FFE1	Timer Input Capture 4/Output Compare 5
$FFDE–$FFDF	Timer Overflow
$FFDC–$FFDD	Pulse Accumulator Overflow
$FFDA–$FFDB	Pulse Accumulator Input Edge
$FFD8–$FFD9	SPI Serial Transfer Complete
$FFD6–$FFD7	SCI Serial System

6.3   INTERRUPT VECTOR JUMP TABLES

The vector addresses shown in Tables 6–1–6–4 are typically in nonvolatile memory such as EPROMs or write-protected flash memory. If you are the one who programs the EPROM, then you can just store the address of your interrupt service routines in the appropriate vector addresses between $FFCE and $FFFF. However, it is usually more convenient to map these addresses to corresponding addresses in RAM where you can store the address of your interrupt routine at any time. There are several different ways to do this.

6.3.1   68HC711E9

For example, the 68HC11 BUFFALO monitor maps the vector addresses $FFD6–$FFFF to a vector jump table at addresses $00C4–$00FF, where each entry in the jump table is a 3-byte JMP instruction to the interrupt service routine. If you are programming WHYP in the EPROM of a 68HC711E9, you can use a similar approach by using the assembly language code shown in Listing 6–1 to store values in the vector addresses $FFD6–$FFFF.

Note that at the very top of memory the starting address of the WHYP kernel, $D000, is stored in addresses $FFFE and $FFFF. This is the reset interrupt vector which means that on power-on or when you press the reset button on the evaluation board, the reset pin on the 68HC11 will go low and produce a reset interrupt. This

Listing 6–1   INTVECE9.LST File for Interrupt Vectors

```
0001 e000              ROMBS     EQU     $D000
0002 e000              WHYP      EQU     $D000
0003
0004 00c4                        ORG     $00C4
0005                   *** Vector jump table ***
0006 00c4              JSCI      RMB     3
0007 00c7              JSPI      RMB     3
0008 00ca              JPAIE     RMB     3
0009 00cd              JPAO      RMB     3
0010 00d0              JTOF      RMB     3
0011 00d3              JTOC5     RMB     3
0012 00d6              JTOC4     RMB     3
0013 00d9              JTOC3     RMB     3
0014 00dc              JTOC2     RMB     3
0015 00df              JTOC1     RMB     3
0016 00e2              JTIC3     RMB     3
0017 00e5              JTIC2     RMB     3
0018 00e8              JTIC1     RMB     3
0019 00eb              JRTI      RMB     3
0020 00ee              JIRQ      RMB     3
0021 00f1              JXIRQ     RMB     3
0022 00f4              JSWI      RMB     3
0023 00f7              JILLOP    RMB     3
0024 00fa              JCOP      RMB     3
0025 00fd              JCLM      RMB     3
0026
0027 ffd6                        ORG     ROMBS+$2FD6
0028                   *** Vectors ***
0029 ffd6 00 c4        VSCI      FDB     JSCI
0030 ffd8 00 c7        VSPI      FDB     JSPI
0031 ffda 00 ca        VPAIE     FDB     JPAIE
0032 ffdc 00 cd        VPAO      FDB     JPAO
0033 ffde 00 d0        VTOF      FDB     JTOF
0034 ffe0 00 d3        VTOC5     FDB     JTOC5
0035 ffe2 00 d6        VTOC4     FDB     JTOC4
0036 ffe4 00 d9        VTOC3     FDB     JTOC3
0037 ffe6 00 dc        VTOC2     FDB     JTOC2
0038 ffe8 00 df        VTOC1     FDB     JTOC1
0039 ffea 00 e2        VTIC3     FDB     JTIC3
0040 ffec 00 e5        VTIC2     FDB     JTIC2
0041 ffee 00 e8        VTIC1     FDB     JTIC1
0042 fff0 00 eb        VRTI      FDB     JRTI
0043 fff2 00 ee        VIRQ      FDB     JIRQ
0044 fff4 00 f1        VXIRQ     FDB     JXIRQ
0045 fff6 00 f4        VSWI      FDB     JSWI
0046 fff8 00 f7        VILLOP    FDB     JILLOP
0047 fffa 00 fa        VCOP      FDB     JCOP
0048 fffc 00 fd        VCLM      FDB     JCLM
0049 fffe d0 00        VRST      FDB     WHYP
```

will cause the contents of $FFFE and $FFFF ($D000 in this case) to be loaded into the program counter so that execution of the WHYP kernel will begin at address $D000.

The remaining 20 interrupt vectors shown in Listing 6–1 are addresses between $00C4 and $00FD stored at addresses $FFD6–$FFFD. Note that the value of each of these interrupt vectors is three bytes more than the preceding one. This means that the "interrupt service routine" for each one can be only three bytes long. In fact, this is enough room for only a jump instruction of the form *JMP INTSER*, where *INTSER* is the address of the real interrupt service routine. We will see in Section 6.4 how to write WHYP words to store the address of an interrupt service routine in this interrupt vector jump table.

6.3.2   D-Bug12

A different approach to interrupt vector jump tables is taken on 68HC12 microcontrollers that use Motorola's D-Bug12 monitor/debugger program. The addresses stored in the vector address table $FFCE–$FFFF are addresses that are still in EPROM or flash memory. Code is executed for each interrupt which will cause an interrupt service routine to be executed whose address has been stored in the user vector addresses listed in Tables 6–5–6–7. Note that these are RAM addresses between $0B0E–$0B39.

Before jumping to the address at the user vector address, the D-Bug12 code checks to make sure that this user address is not $0000. If it is (meaning that the user forgot to store the address of the interrupt service routine in the user vector address), then an error message is printed on the screen.

Note in Table 6–5 that the reset (and COP resets) do not have RAM user vector addresses. A reset will execute the D-Bug12 monitor/debugger program. However, this program has a mechanism (on Motorola evaluation boards) for allowing a user program to be executed on a reset. The program checks bit 0 of Port AD, and if it is 1 then the program jumps to the first byte in the internal EEPROM where you can include a jump to your program. You can normally set a jumper on the evaluation board to make bit 0 of Port AD high.

Table 6–5   68HC12 Nonmaskable User Interrupts

Vector Address	Interrupt Source	User Vector Address
$FFFE–$FFFF	Reset	*
$FFFC–$FFFD	COP Clock Monitor Fail Reset	*
$FFFA–$FFFB	COP Failure Reset	*
$FFF8–$FFF9	Unimplemented Instruction Trap	$0B38–$0B39
$FFF6–$FFF7	SWI	$0B36–$0B37
$FFF4–$FFF5	XIRQ	$0B34–$0B35

Table 6-6   68HC812A4 Maskable User Interrupt Vectors

Vector Address	Interrupt Source	User Vector Address
$FFF2-$FFF3	IRQ or Key Wake Up D	$0B32-$0B33
$FFF0-$FFF1	Real-Time Interrupt	$0B30-$0B31
$FFEE-$FFEF	Timer Channel 0	$0B2E-$0B2F
$FFEC-$FFED	Timer Channel 1	$0B2C-$0B2D
$FFEA-$FFEB	Timer Channel 2	$0B2A-$0B2B
$FFE8-$FFE9	Timer Channel 3	$0B28-$0B29
$FFE6-$FFE7	Timer Channel 4	$0B26-$0B27
$FFE4-$FFE5	Timer Channel 5	$0B24-$0B25
$FFE2-$FFE3	Timer Channel 6	$0B22-$0B23
$FFE0-$FFE1	Timer Channel 7	$0B20-$0B21
$FFDE-$FFDF	Timer Overflow	$0B1E-$0B1F
$FFDC-$FFDD	Pulse Accumulator Overflow	$0B1C-$0B1D
$FFDA-$FFDB	Pulse Accumulator Input Edge	$0B1A-$0B1B
$FFD8-$FFD9	SPI Serial Transfer Complete	$0B18-$0B19
$FFD6-$FFD7	SCI 0	$0B16-$0B17
$FFD4-$FFD5	SCI 1	$0B14-$0B15
$FFD2-$FFD3	ATD	$0B12-$0B13
$FFD0-$FFD1	Key Wakeup J (stop wakeup)	$0B10-$0B11
$FFCE-$FFCF	Key Wakeup H (stop wakeup)	$0B0E-$0B0F

Table 6-7   68HC912B32 Maskable User Interrupt Vectors

Vector Address	Interrupt Source	User Vector Address
$FFF2-$FFF3	IRQ	$0B32-$0B33
$FFF0-$FFF1	Real-Time Interrupt	$0B30-$0B31
$FFEE-$FFEF	Timer Channel 0	$0B2E-$0B2F
$FFEC-$FFED	Timer Channel 1	$0B2C-$0B2D
$FFEA-$FFEB	Timer Channel 2	$0B2A-$0B2B
$FFE8-$FFE9	Timer Channel 3	$0B28-$0B29
$FFE6-$FFE7	Timer Channel 4	$0B26-$0B27
$FFE4-$FFE5	Timer Channel 5	$0B24-$0B25
$FFE2-$FFE3	Timer Channel 6	$0B22-$0B23
$FFE0-$FFE1	Timer Channel 7	$0B20-$0B21
$FFDE-$FFDF	Timer Overflow	$0B1E-$0B1F
$FFDC-$FFDD	Pulse Accumulator Overflow	$0B1C-$0B1D
$FFDA-$FFDB	Pulse Accumulator Input Edge	$0B1A-$0B1B
$FFD8-$FFD9	SPI Serial Transfer Complete	$0B18-$0B19
$FFD6-$FFD7	SCI 0	$0B16-$0B17
$FFD4-$FFD5	Reserved	$0B14-$0B15
$FFD2-$FFD3	ATD	$0B12-$0B13
$FFD0-$FFD1	BDLC	$0B10-$0B11

6.4 WRITING WHYP INTERRUPT SERVICE ROUTINES

When a hardware interrupt occurs; the 68HC12 checks the interrupt mask *I* bit in the condition code register shown in Figure 1–6 in Chapter 1. If this bit is set to 1, then hardware interrupts are masked and no interrupt processing takes place. This bit is set to 1 with the 68HC12 instruction *SEI* (which actually translates to *ORCC #$10*, object code = $1410). The WHYP word *SEI* will compile this object code in-line using the C++ function *sei()*, shown in Figure 6–4. If the *I* bit in the condition

```
//      SEI
void    sei()
        {
        if(compile)
            dict12.tcomma(0x1410);        // compile SEI 1410
        else
            cout << "SEI must be in colon definition ";
        }

//      CLI
void    cli()
        {
        if(compile)
            dict12.tcomma(0x10ef);        // compile CLI 10EF
        else
            cout << "CLI must be in colon definition ";
        }

//      INT:
void    int_colon()
        {
        int int_stack;
        int_stack = RAMBASE + 0x30;
        colon();                          // make header
        dict12.tccomma(0xce);             // LDX #(RAMBASE+$30)
        dict12.tcomma(int_stack);
        }

//      RTI;
void    rti_semis()
        {
        compile = false;
        dict12.tccomma(0x0b);      // compile RTI
        dict12.fix_size();
        }
```

Figure 6–4 The WHYP Interrupt Words

code register is cleared to 0, then hardware interrupts are enabled so that interrupt processing can takes place. This bit is cleared to 0 with the 68HC12 instruction *CLI* (which actually translates to *ANDCC #$EF*, object code = $10EF). The WHYP word *CLI* will compile this object code in-line using the C++ function *cli()*, shown in Figure 6–4.

If a hardware interrupt occurs with the *I* bit cleared, then all 68HC12 registers are pushed on the system stack in the order shown in Figure 6–1. The *I* bit is then set to mask interrupts while in the interrupt service routine. At the end of an interrupt service routine the 68HC12 instruction *RTI* (return from interrupt, opcode = $0B) is executed. This instruction will pop all the registers shown in Figure 6–1 from the system stack and therefore return the program to the place and state that it was in before the interrupt occurred. Note that the popped condition code register will have the *I* bit cleared and therefore interrupts are automatically enabled again.

High-level WHYP words can be used for interrupt service routines if you use the WHYP words *INT:* and *RTI;* instead of the usual colon and semicolon to define your word. The word *RTI;* will compile the opcode for *RTI* ($0B) in-line using the C++ function *rti_semis()*, as shown in Figure 6–4.

The word *INT:* (see Figure 6–4) first makes a header just as in a regular colon definition by calling the C++ function *colon()*. It then compiles in-line the machine code for the 68HC12 instruction *LDX #$0930* (assuming *RAMBASE* = $0900). This changes the WHYP data stack pointer to $0930 which is a separate data stack area used only for interrupts. It is necessary to do this because when an interrupt occurs there is no way of knowing if the *X* index register might have been pushed on the stack and the current value of *X* is not the WHYP data stack pointer at all. Note that it is not possible to nest hardware interrupts when they are written as high-level WHYP words. Each interrupt must run, uninterrupted, to completion. This is usually not a problem because the *I* bit in the *CCR* will be set to mask any other interrupt from occurring until the current interrupt service routine has been completed. The only way to overcome this would be to include a *CLI* instruction within the interrupt service routine. But you *cannot* do this if you write your interrupt service routines in WHYP. Later in this chapter we will see how to write interrupt service routines in assembly language. But first we will look at an example of writing interrupt service routines in WHYP on a 68HC12 and 68HC11.

6.5 REAL-TIME INTERRUPTS

Sometimes it is useful to produce periodic interrupts at a constant rate. If the periodic time between interrupts is approximately 1, 2, 4, 8, 16, 32, or 65 milliseconds then the Real-Time Interrupt (RTI) can be used. The periodic rate is set using bits *RTR[2:0]* in the *Real-Time Interrupt Control Register* (*RTICTL*) as shown in Figure 6–5. At each timeout the *RTIF* flag in the *Real-Time Interrupt Flag Register* (*RTIFLG*) is set and an interrupt will occur if the RTIE bit in the RTICTL register is set as shown in Figure 6–5.

An example of using the real-time interrupt is given by the program shown in Listing 6–2. The constants at the beginning of the program define the addresses for

	7	6	5	4	3	2	1	0	
$0014	RTIE	RSWAI	RSBCK	0	RTBYP	RTR2	RTR1	RTR0	RTICTL

RTIE: Real Time Interrupt Enable
          0 – RTIF interrupts disabled
          1 – RTIF interrupts enabled

RSWAI: RTI and COP Stop While in Wait
          0 – RTI and COP continue running in wait
          1 – RTI and COP disabled when in wait

RSBCK: RTI and COP Stop While in Background Debug Mode
          0 – RTI and COP continue running in background mode
          1 – RTI and COP disabled when in background mode

RTBYP: Real Time Interrupt Divider Chain Bypass
          0 – Divider chain functions normally
          1 – Divider chain bypassed

RTR[2:0]: RTI Interrupt Rate Select

RTR[2:0]	Time-Out Period M = 8.0 MHz
0 0 0	OFF
0 0 1	1.024 ms
0 1 0	2.048 ms
0 1 1	4.096 ms
1 0 0	8.196 ms
1 0 1	16.384 ms
1 1 0	32.768 ms
1 1 1	65.536 ms

	7	6	5	4	3	2	1	0	
$0015	RTIF	0	0	0	0	0	0	0	RTIFLG

RTIF: Real Time Interrupt Flag
          0 – Cleared by writing a 1 to bit position 7
          1 – Set to 1 when timeout occurs (causes interrupt if RTIE set in RTICTL)

Figure 6–5   Real-Time Interrupt Registers in a 68HC12

the two real-time registers, *RTICTL* and *RTIFLG*, shown in Figure 6–5. Also the user vector address associated with the real-time interrupt, $0B30, is defined as the constant *RTI.IVEC* (see Table 6–6 or Table 6–7).

The word *RTIF.CLR* will clear the *RTIF* flag by writing a 1 to bit 7 of the *RTIFLG* register. The word *RTI.SET32* will enable RTI interrupts by setting bit 7 of the *RTICTL* register and will set the RTI rate to 32.77 milliseconds by setting bits *RTR[2:0]* in the *RTICTL* register to 110. Similar words can be created to set the rate to one of the other values shown in Figure 6–5. The word *RTI.INT.DISABLE* disables RTI interrupts by clearing bit 7 of the *RTICTL* register.

The interrupt service routine *RTI.INTSER* shown in Listing 6–2 is written in WHYP by using *INT:* and *RTI;* as described in Section 6.3 (see Figure 6–4). Note that this interrupt routine simply increments the contents of a variable called *TICKS*

Listing 6–2   Real-time Interrupt

```
\        Real-time Interrupt       File: RTI.WHP
VARIABLE         TICKS
HEX
0B30    CONSTANT   RTI.IVEC
0014    CONSTANT   RTICTL
0015    CONSTANT   RTIFLG

        ( Use real-time interrupt for delay )

: RTIF.CLR       ( -- )            \ clear RT1 flag
                 80 RTIFLG C! ;
: RTI.SET32      ( -- )            \ enable interrupts and
                 86 RTICTL C! ;   \ set RTI rate to 32.77 msec
: RTI.INT.DISABLE       ( -- )
                 0 RTICTL C! ;


INT: RTI.INTSER    ( -- )         \ increment TICKS
                 1 TICKS +!
                 RTIF.CLR
RTI;
: SET.RTI.INTVEC        ( -- )
                 [ ' RTI.INTSER ] LITERAL
                 RTI.IVEC ! ;
DECIMAL
: TICK.DELAY     ( n -- )                    \ delay n ticks
                 >R TICKS @           \ ticks0
                 BEGIN
                    TICKS @ OVER -     \ ticks0 elapsed
                    R@ U>=
                 UNTIL
                 R> 2DROP ;
: RTI.OFF        ( -- )
                 SEI
                 RTI.INT.DISABLE ;
: RTI.ON         ( -- )
                 SEI
                 RTI.SET32
                 SET.RTI.INTVEC
                 CLI ;
DECIMAL
```

and then clears the *RTIF* flag. This means that every 32 ms the value of *TICKS* will increase by 1.

The address of the interrupt service routine *RTI.INTSER* is stored in the interrupt vector table by executing the word *SET.RTI.INTVEC* shown in Listing 6–2. Note that the first line in this word is

```
[ ' RTI.INTSER ] LITERAL
```

The WHYP words [("left-bracket") and] ("right-bracket"), when used inside a colon definition, turn the compiler off and on, respectively. This means that all the words between [and] are executed immediately when the word is compiled rather than being compiled into the word. In this case the words ' *RTI.INTSER* will put the address of the interrupt service routine, *RTI.INTSER*, on the data stack. The WHYP word *LITERAL* will compile a literal of the number on top of the data stack. What gets compiled into memory is a *JSR (LIT)*, followed by the address of *RTI.INTSER* (see Section 4.3 and Figure 4–10). Therefore, when the word *SET.RTI.INTVEC* is executed, the net effect of the statement

```
[ ' RTI.INTSER ] LITERAL
```

is to put the address of *RTI.INTSER* on the data stack. The last line in the word *SET.RTI.INTVEC* is

```
RTI.IVEC !
```

which will then store the address of *RTI.INTSER* in the user vector address, $0B30.

The word *TICK.DELAY (n --)* in Listing 6–2 will delay *n* ticks (where 1 tick is 32 ms). Note that this word first reads an initial value of *TICKS* (*ticks0*) and then continually reads the contents of *TICKS* and computes the elapsed time (in ticks) since *ticks0*. It continues to loop until the elapsed number of ticks is equal to or greater than *n*.

You can test this program by loading the file `RTI.WHP` and then typing *RTI.ON*. At this point interrupts should be occurring and incrementing the variable TICKS every 32 milliseconds. Every time you type

```
TICKS @ .
```

you should get a different answer. If you type

```
33 TICK.DELAY
```

it should take about 1 second for the *ok* prompt to appear.

6.5.1 Real-Time Interrupt on a 68HC11

The real-time interrupt on a 68HC11 works in a similar way to the real-time interrupt on a 68HC12. However, the 68HC11 does not have real-time control and flag registers. Instead it uses parts of the timer registers, *TMSK2*, *TFLG2*, and *PACTL*, as shown in Figure 6–6. These timer registers will be described in more detail in Chapter 10.

	7	6	5	4	3	2	1	0	
$1024	TOI	RTII	PAOVI	PAII	0	0	PR1	PR0	TMSK2

RTII: Real Time Interrupt Enable
             0 – RTIF interrupts disabled
             1 – RTIF interrupts enable

	7	6	5	4	3	2	1	0	
$1025	TOF	RTIF	PAOVF	PAIF	0	0	0	0	TFLG2

RTIF: Real Time (Periodic) Interrupt Flag
             0 – Cleared by writing a 1 to bit position 6
             1 – Set to 1 when timeout occurs (causes interrupt if RTII set in TMSK2)

	7	6	5	4	3	2	1	0	
$1026	DDRA7	PAEN	PAMOD	PEDGE	DDRA3	I4/O5	RTR1	RTR0	PACTL

RTR[1:0]:   RTI Interrupt Rate Select

RTR[1:0]	periodic rate
0 0	4.096 ms
0 1	11.192 ms
1 0	16.384 ms
1 1	32.768 ms

Figure 6–6   Timer Registers Used for Real-Time Interrupts on a 68HC11

Note that real-time interrupts are enabled by setting bit 6 (*RTII*) of *TMSK2* and the real-time interrupt flag, *RTIF*, is bit 6 of TFLG2. Only four different time-out periods are available on the 68HC11 which are selected by the two bits *RTR[1:0]* in the *PACTL* register.

There is one other change you would have to make to the program in Listing 6–2 to have it run on a 68HC11. Recall from Listing 6–1 that the interrupt vectors are mapped to the user RAM addresses shown in Table 6–8. The RAM address for the real-time interrupt is $00EB. But this is a 3-byte location where a *JMP* instruction to the interrupt service routine must be inserted. This means that we can't just store the address of the interrupt service routine at the address *RTI.IVEC* but must insert a *JMP* opcode before the address. A way to do this is shown in Figure 6–7 where we have modified the word *SET.RTI.INTVEC* in Listing 6–2 to include the word

```
: SET.INTVEC    ( intser.addr jmp.tbl.addr -- )
                7E OVER C!                \ JMP opcode
                1+ ! ;
```

Note that this word first stores the opcode for *JMP* ($7E) at the jump table address and then stores the address of the interrupt service routine at the address following the *JMP* opcode. With these changes the real-time interrupt program shown in Listing 6–2 should run on a 68HC11. (See Exercise 6.1.)

Table 6–8   68HC711E9 Interrupt Jump Table

Vector Address	Interrupt Source	User Jump Table
\$FFFE–\$FFFF	Reset	main
\$FFFC–\$FFFD	COP Clock Monitor Fail Reset	\$00FD
\$FFFA–\$FFFB	COP Failure Reset	\$00FA
\$FFF8–\$FFF9	Illegal Opcode Trap	\$00F7
\$FFF6–\$FFF7	SWI	\$00F4
\$FFF4–\$FFF5	XIRQ	\$00F1
\$FFF2–\$FFF3	IRQ	\$00EE
\$FFF0–\$FFF1	Real-Time Interrupt	\$00EB
\$FFEE–\$FFEF	Timer Input Capture 1	\$00E8
\$FFEC–\$FFED	Timer Input Capture 2	\$00E5
\$FFEA–\$FFEB	Timer Input Capture 3	\$00E2
\$FFE8–\$FFE9	Timer Output Compare 1	\$00DF
\$FFE6–\$FFE7	Timer Output Compare 2	\$00DC
\$FFE4–\$FFE5	Timer Output Compare 3	\$00D9
\$FFE2–\$FFE3	Timer Output Compare 4	\$00D6
\$FFE0–\$FFE1	Timer Input Capture 4/Output Compare 5	\$00D3
\$FFDE–\$FFDF	Timer Overflow	\$00D0
\$FFDC–\$FFDD	Pulse Accumulator Overflow	\$00CD
\$FFDA–\$FFDB	Pulse Accumulator Input Edge	\$00CA
\$FFD8–\$FFD9	SPI Serial Transfer Complete	\$00C7
\$FFD6–\$FFD7	SCI Serial System	\$00C4

```
HEX
00EB   CONSTANT  RTI.IVEC


                \ set interrupt vector in EVB jump table
: SET.INTVEC ( intser.addr jmp.tbl.addr -- )
          7E OVER C!               \ JMP opcode
          1+ ! ;


: SET.RTI.INTVEC    ( -- )
             [ ' RTI.INTSER ] LITERAL
             RTI.IVEC SET.INTVEC ;
```

Figure 6–7   The Word *SET.INTVEC* Inserts a *JMP* Opcode

6.6 WRITING ASSEMBLY LANGUAGE INTERRUPT SERVICE ROUTINES

The time it takes to execute an interrupt service routine is an important parameter when designing interrupt-driven software. If interrupts occur faster than they can be executed, then you may both miss some interrupts and not have any time left to do other things. One way to find the time required to execute an interrupt service routine is to look up the number of clock cycles required by each instruction. We have done that in Figure 6–8 for the interrupt service routine, *RTI.INTSER*, given in Listing 6–2. Note, for example, that the subroutine *(LIT)* takes 17 clock cycles as shown in Figure 5–22 in Chapter 5. The *JSR* instruction takes an additional 4 clock cycles. You can verify the times for the other subroutines in a similar manner (see Exercise 6.3).

An alternate and easier way to find the time required to execute an interrupt service routine is to measure it directly using the built-in 68HC12 timer. A way to do this easily in WHYP will be shown in Chapter 10.

The interrupt service routine shown in Figure 6–8 takes 148 clock cycles to execute. Using an 8-MHz clock, this will take 148/8 = 18.5 μs to execute. This is less than 2 percent of the shortest RTI period of 1.024 ms given in Figure 6–5. However, if the source of this interrupt were an external square wave, then in order not to miss any interrupts, the frequency of the square wave would need to be less than 1/18.5 μs ≈ 54 KHz.

It is always a good idea to keep interrupt service routines as short as possible. Sometimes it may be necessary to write the interrupt service routine in assembly language so that it will execute as fast as possible. As an example, the interrupt service routine shown in Figure 6–8 that just increments the variable, *TICKS*, can be written in assembly language, as shown in Figure 6–9. Note that this interrupt service routine takes only 19 clock cycles rather that the 148 shown in Figure 6–8. This means that with an 8-MHz clock it will execute in 19/8 ≈ 2.4 μs. This is nearly eight times faster that the same routine written in WHYP. Recall that we saw in Section 5.2.4 that the same program will run about eight times faster on a 68HC12 than on a 68HC11. Therefore, as a general rule we can conclude that a program written in WHYP on a 68HC12 will run about as fast as the same program written in assembly language on a 68HC11. This is the price we pay for having a rapid prototyping environment in which we can access our subroutines interactively from the keyboard.

```
INT: RTI.INTSER      ( -- )             \ increment TICKS
                 1 TICKS +!
                 RTIF.CLR
RTI;
                                             #clock cycles
  CE 09 30           LDX   #$0930
  16 45 1B 00 01     JSR   (LIT) 0001        4+17 = 21
  16 50 00           JSR   TICKS             4+22 = 26
  16 44 AE           JSR   +!                4+17 = 21
  16 50 18           JSR   RTIF.CLR          4+66 = 70
  0B                 RTI                            8
                                                  148
```

Figure 6–8 Computing the Time Required to Execute the Interrupt Service Routine

```
*          Real-time Interrupt       File: RTI.ASM

RTIFLG          EQU       $0015

                ORG       $0810
TICKS           DW        0

                ORG       $4C00
RTI_INTSER                                    #clock cycles
                LDY       TICKS                    3
                INY                                1
                STY       TICKS                    3
                LDAA      #$80                     1
                STAA      RTIFLG                   3
                RTI                                8
                                                  19
```

Figure 6–9   The Interrupt Service Routine, *RTI_INTSER*, Written in Assembly
Language

However, we can really have the best of both worlds. In most large programs it is usually only a small part of the code that takes up most of the time. You can always write specific interrupt service routines or other subroutines in assembly language and give them WHYP names. You just need to add the names of these routines to the file WHYP12.HED together with their offset addresses relative to *TORG* to make them part of the WHYP dictionary.

For example, to use the interrupt service routine in Figure 6–9 instead of the one in Figure 6–8 in the program in Listing 6–2 you only need to do the following:

1. Delete the interrupt service routine (from *INT:* to *RTI;*) in Listing 6–2.
2. Delete the statement *VARIABLE TICKS* at the beginning of Listing 6–2 and add the statement *0810 CONSTANT TICKS* following the word *HEX*. This will give the variable *TICKS* the same address assigned in Figure 6–9.
3. Add the line *RTI.INTSER C00* at the beginning of the file WHYP12.HED. When WHYP12 is run, this will put *RTI.INTSER* in the dictionary with an address of $4C00 (assuming you are using the 'A4 board with *TORG* = $4000).
4. Assemble the file RTI.ASM shown in Figure 6–9 and download the resulting file, RTI.S19, to the 68HC12 using *HOST*.
5. Execute WHYP on the 68HC12, run WHYP12 on the PC, and load the modified file, RTI.WHP, shown in Listing 6–2. Typing *RTI.ON* will turn on the real-time interrupts using the assembly language interrupt service routine shown in Figure 6–9.

6.7 SUMMARY

This chapter described the use of interrupts on the 68HC12 and 68HC11. The interrupt vectors are given in Tables 6–1 – 6–3 for the 68HC12 and in Table 6–4 for the 68HC11. These interrupt vectors can be mapped to RAM locations as shown in Tables 6–5 – 6–7 for the 68HC12 and in Listing 6–1 for the 68HC11.

Interrupt service routines can be written in WHYP by using the words *INT:* and *RTI;* to define the word instead of the normal colon and semicolon. An example of using this technique was given for the case of real-time interrupts used to produce a fixed time delay. A method was described for writing interrupt service routines in assembly language and incorporating these routines in WHYP programs.

New WHYP words that were introduced in this chapter are given in Box 6–1.

Box 6–1   WHYP Words Introduced in this Chapter

[	(--) (*"left-bracket"*) Turns off the compiler within a colon definition.
]	(--) (*"right-bracket"*) Turns on the compiler within a colon definition.
LITERAL	(n --) Compile *n* as a literal within a colon definition. Compiles *JSR (LIT)* followed by *n*.
CLI	(--) Compiles the opcode for *CLI* ($10EF) in-line within a colon definition.
SEI	(--) Compiles the opcode for *SEI* ($1410) in-line within a colon definition.
INT:	(--) Used in place of : to define a high-level WHYP word that is an interrupt service routine.
RTI;	(--) Used to end a high-level WHYP word defined using *INT:*. Compiles the opcode for the *RTI* instruction ($0B) in-line.

EXERCISES

Exercise 6.1

Modify the program shown in Listing 6–2 so that it will work for real-time interrupts on the 68HC11.

Exercise 6.2

Use the D-Bug12 commands *MD* (memory display), *MDW* (memory display word), and *ASM* to examine the interrupt vectors in Tables 6–1 – 6–3 for your system and to disassemble the code that is executed when a particular interrupt occurs.

Exercise 6.3

Verify the number of clock cycles for each subroutine call in Figure 6–8. Note that the instruction *JSR TICKS* will cause a jump to the subroutine

```
JSR (LIT) 0800
RTS
```

which will cause the address of *TICKS* (0800) to be put on the data stack.

Exercise 6.4

Write a WHYP program using real-time interrupts that will print the message "Another five seconds" on a new line on the PC screen every 5 seconds. *Hint:* Use a RTI time-out period of 16.384 ms and count 305 interrupts to produce 5 seconds.

Exercise 6.5

Write a WHYP program using real-time interrupts that will print a row of stars of the type shown in Figure 5–27 about every quarter of a second on the screen. The number of stars in each row should increase from one to ten and then back to one. This pattern should be repeated indefinitely.

7

Parallel Interfacing

In this chapter we will show, by means of several examples, how you can write WHYP programs to control external devices using parallel interfacing. In Section 7.1 we will investigate how the ports on the 68HC12 and 68HC11 can be used for parallel I/O. Simple examples of using these parallel ports for inputs and outputs will be described in Section 7.2. Two different types of seven-segment displays will be discussed in Section 7.3. We will show three different ways to read a keypad in Section 7.4. In Section 7.5 we will develop some WHYP words that will allow you to write information on a liquid crystal display. Finally, we show how interrupts can be used to control traffic lights in Section 7.6.

7.1 PARALLEL I/O PORTS

As shown in Figures 1–3 and 1–4 in Chapter 1, different members of the 68HC12 family of microcontrollers have different parallel I/O ports. The same is true for the 68HC11 family of microcontrollers. In this section we will describe the parallel I/O ports associated with the MC68HC812A4, the MC68HC912B32, and the MC68HC711E9 microcontrollers. We will consider each of these microcontrollers separately.

7.1.1 The MC68HC812A4 Parallel Ports

The MC68HC812A4 registers associated with parallel I/O are listed in Table 7–1. Each of these ports (except *PORTAD*) has a data register and a data direction register of the type shown in Figure 7–1. Each pin of an I/O port can be either an input or an output depending on the bits in the corresponding data direction register as shown in Figure 7–1.

The hexadecimal port address as well as the address of the data direction register for each I/O port are indicated in Table 7–1. Note that *PORTAD* is an input-only port and has no data direction register.

Each I/O port has an alternate or special optional function which is indicated in Table 7–1. We will consider many of these alternate functions in detail in later chapters. When the pins of an I/O port are not being used for its alternate function, they can be used as general-purpose I/O pins.

Table 7–1   Parallel Ports in the MC68HC812A4

Name	Port Addr	DDR Addr	Alternate Function
PORTA	0000	0002	High address byte in expanded mode
PORTB	0001	0003	Low address byte in expanded mode
PORTC	0004	0006	High data byte in expanded mode
PORTD	0005	0007	Low data byte in expanded mode
PORTE	0008	0009	External bus control signals
PORTF	0030	0032	Chip selects
PORTG	0031	0033	Memory expansion
PORTH	0024	0025	Key wakeup
PORTJ	0028	0029	Key wakeup
PORTS	00D6	00D7	Serial I/O
PORTT	00AE	00AF	Timer
PORTAD	006F	Input only	A/D converter

Port Data Register

7	6	5	4	3	2	1	0	
Px7	Px6	Px5	Px4	Px3	Px2	Px1	Px0	PORTx

Port Data Direction Register

7	6	5	4	3	2	1	0	
DDx7	DDx6	DDx5	DDx4	DDx3	DDx2	DDx1	DDx0	DDRx

DDx[7:0]:   Data Direction for Port x
0 – Input
1 – Output

Figure 7–1   Registers Associated with Parallel I/O Ports

There are three normal operating modes for the 68HC12:

- Normal expanded wide mode
- Normal expanded narrow mode
- Normal single-chip mode

In addition, there are four special operating modes that are usually used for factory testing and system development. We will consider only the three normal operating modes in this book.

The M68HC12A4EVB evaluation board from Motorola is factory configured to operate in the normal expanded wide mode. This means that Ports A and B are used for a 16-bit address bus and Ports C and D are used for a 16-bit data bus. Therefore, Ports A, B, C, and D will not be available for general-purpose parallel I/O operations in this mode. You can free up Port D for general-purpose I/O by switching to the normal expanded narrow mode (by installing jumpers on the board) in which Port C is used as an 8-bit data bus.

In the normal expanded modes, Port E is used for external bus control signals including a read/write line and the E clock signal. Pins $PE0$ and $PE1$ are interrupt input signals.

Port F contains seven bits that can be used as chip select signals. On the M68HC12A4EVB evaluation board bit 5 of Port F is used as a chip select that covers the address range $8000 to $FFFF and bit 4 of Port F is used as a chip select that covers the address range $0000 to $7FFF. The other five bits of Port F can be used as general-purpose I/O pins.

Port G contains six bits that can be used to expand the address space of the 68HC12 to over 5 Mbytes of memory. If the address space of your system is $0000 to $FFFF, then the six bits of Port G can be used as general-purpose I/O pins.

Ports H and J are two eight-bit ports that can be used for general-purpose I/O. Each pin in Ports H and J is associated with the key wakeup feature of the 68HC812A4 which will be described in Chapter 15.

The eight bits of Port S are associated with serial I/O. Bits 0–3 are used by the two SCI ports that will be described in Chapter 11. One of these SCI ports will be used to communicate with the PC. Bits 4–7 are used by the SPI port that will be described in Chapter 8. Port S bits that are not used for SCI or SPI functions can be used as general-purpose I/O pins.

Port T is an 8-bit port whose pins are associated with a timer module. The operation of this timer module will be described in detail in Chapter 10. When not used for timer functions, the bits of Port T can be used as general-purpose I/O pins.

The eight bits of Port AD are inputs that are associated with an eight-channel analog-to-digital converter that will be described in detail in Chapter 9. When not using the A/D converter, the bits of Port AD can be used as general-purpose inputs.

The 68HC812A4 registers associated with parallel I/O are listed in Box 7–1 where we have written WHYP constants that associate the register's address with its name. This listing is in the file PIOA4.WHP which you can load at the beginning of a

Box 7–1   Parallel I/O Registers—68HC812A4

```
\        PIOA4.WHP
\        68HC12 registers for Parallel I/O - MC68HC812A4


HEX
0000     CONSTANT        PORTA       \ I/O Port A
0001     CONSTANT        PORTB       \ I/O Port B
0002     CONSTANT        DDRA        \ Data Direction for Port A
0003     CONSTANT        DDRB        \ Data Direction for Port B
0004     CONSTANT        PORTC       \ I/O Port C
0005     CONSTANT        PORTD       \ I/O Port D
0006     CONSTANT        DDRC        \ Data Direction for Port C
0007     CONSTANT        DDRD        \ Data Direction for Port D
0008     CONSTANT        PORTE       \ I/O Port E
0009     CONSTANT        DDRE        \ Data Direction for Port E
0024     CONSTANT        PORTH       \ I/O Port H
0025     CONSTANT        DDRH        \ Data Direction for Port H
0028     CONSTANT        PORTJ       \ I/O Port J
0029     CONSTANT        DDRJ        \ Data Direction for Port J
002D     CONSTANT        PUPSJ       \ Port J Pull-up/Pulldown Select
002E     CONSTANT        PULEJ       \ Port J Pull-up/Pulldown Enable
0030     CONSTANT        PORTF       \ I/O Port F
0031     CONSTANT        PORTG       \ I/O Port G
0032     CONSTANT        DDRF        \ Data Direction for Port F
0033     CONSTANT        DDRG        \ Data Direction for Port G
006F     CONSTANT        PORTAD      \ Input Port AD
00AE     CONSTANT        PORTT       \ I/O Port T
00AF     CONSTANT        DDRT        \ Data Direction for Port T
00D6     CONSTANT        PORTS       \ I/O Port S
00D7     CONSTANT        DDRS        \ Data Direction for Port S
```

program to include the names of these I/O ports in the WHYP dictionary. Alternatively, you can include the *CONSTANT* statements for only the port names that you use in your program.

7.1.2   The MC78HC912B32 Parallel Ports

The MC68HC912B32 registers associated with parallel I/O are listed in Table 7–2. Note that there are fewer parallel I/O ports in the MC68HC912B32 than there were in the MC68HC812A4. In the expanded mode, the MC68HC912B32 uses Ports A and B as a multiplexed address and data bus. In the single-chip mode, Ports A and B are available for general-purpose I/O.

In the normal expanded modes, Port E is used for external bus control signals as with the MC68HC812A4. In the single-chip mode, bits *PE2–PE7* can be used as

Table 7–2 Parallel Ports in the MC68HC912B32

Name	Port Addr	DDR Addr	Alternate Function
PORTA	0000	0002	High addr/data byte in expanded mode
PORTB	0001	0003	Low addr/data byte in expanded mode
PORTE	0008	0009	External bus control signals
PORTP	0056	0057	Pulse-width modulator
PORTS	00D6	00D7	Serial I/O
PORTT	00AE	00AF	Timer
PORTDLC	00FE	00FF	Byte data link communications module
PORTAD	006F	Input only	A/D converter

general-purpose I/O pins. Pins *PE0* and *PE1* are always inputs and can be used to produce interrupts as was described in Chapter 6.

Port P can be used as a general-purpose 8-bit I/O port. Bits *PP0–PP3* are also used as part of the pulse-width modulator module to be described in Chapter 15.

Bits *PS2–PS3* of Port S are two general-purpose I/O pins. Bits 0–1 are used by the SCI port that will be described in Chapter 11. This SCI port will normally be used to communicate with the PC. Bits *PS4–PS7* are used by the SPI port that will be described in Chapter 8. These bits can be used as general-purpose I/O pins when not using the SPI function.

Box 7–2   Parallel I/O Registers—68HC912B32

```
\              PIOB32.WHP
\              68HC12 registers for Parallel I/O - MC68HC912B32


HEX
0000           CONSTANT          PORTA        \ I/O Port A
0001           CONSTANT          PORTB        \ I/O Port B
0002           CONSTANT          DDRA         \ Data Direction for Port A
0003           CONSTANT          DDRB         \ Data Direction for Port B
0008           CONSTANT          PORTE        \ I/O Port E
0009           CONSTANT          DDRE         \ Data Direction for Port E
0056           CONSTANT          PORTP        \ I/O Port P
0057           CONSTANT          DDRP         \ Data Direction for Port P
006F           CONSTANT          PORTAD       \ Input Port AD
00AE           CONSTANT          PORTT        \ I/O Port T
00AF           CONSTANT          DDRT         \ Data Direction for Port T
00D6           CONSTANT          PORTS        \ I/O Port S
00D7           CONSTANT          DDRS         \ Data Direction for Port S
00FE           CONSTANT          PORTDLC      \ I/O Port DLC
00FF           CONSTANT          DDRDLC       \ Data Direction for Port DLC
```

　　　　Port DLC is a 7-bit register that can be used as seven general-purpose I/O pins. Bits 0 and 1 are associated with the Byte Data Link Communications module (BDLC) which is designed to provide easy access to a J1850 serial communication bus used in the automotive industry.

　　　　Port T and Port AD are associated with the same timer module and A/D converter as in the MC68HC812A4.

　　　　The file `PIOB32.WHP` containing WHYP constants defining the 68HC912B32 registers associated with parallel I/O is shown in Box 7–2 on page 187.

7.1.3　The MC68HC711E9 Parallel Ports

As an example of a 68HC11 part, consider the MC68HC711E9 whose registers associated with parallel I/O are listed in Table 7–3. Note that there are only five ports: A, B, C, D, and E. We will consider each of these ports separately. The following discussion will also apply to the 68HC11A8 and 68HC11D3 parts.

Table 7–3　Parallel Ports in the MC68HC711E9

Name	Port Addr	DDR Addr	Alternate Function
PORTA	1000	3 in-3 out-2 i/o	Timer
PORTB	1004	Output only	High address byte in expanded mode
PORTC	1003	1007	Low addr/data byte in expanded mode
PORTCL	1005	1007	Port C Latched
PORTD	1008	1009	Serial I/O
PORTE	100A	Input only	A/D converter

Port A　The registers associated with parallel I/O on Port A are shown in Figure 7–2. In register *PORTA* pins *PA0–PA2* are always inputs and pins *PA4–PA6* are always outputs. Pin *PA7* can be either an input or an output depending on the value of bit 7 (*DDRA7*) in the *PACTL* register as shown in Figure 7–1. For the 'E9 and 'D3 parts, pin *PA3* can be either an input or an output depending on the value of bit 3 (*DDRA3*) in the *PACTL* register as shown in Figure 7–2. For the 'A8 part, pin *PA3* is always an input.

　　　　The pins of Port A can also be used for a variety of timer functions. The other bits of the *PACTL* register shown in Figure 7–2 refer to these timer functions which will be described in Chapter 10.

Port B　Port B is always on output on the 'A8 and 'E9 parts. However, the 'D3 part has a data direction register, *DDRB* ($0006), that can be used to make each pin of Port B either an input or an output. In the expanded multiplexed mode, Port B provides the high-order address outputs (*ADDR8–ADDR15*). In this mode Port B cannot be used for parallel I/O. However, on the 'A8 and 'D3 EVB boards, the 68HC24 port expansion chip is used to get back Ports B and C so that they can be used for parallel I/O. This port expansion chip provides Port B and Port C in a transparent fashion so they still have the same addresses as in the single-chip mode.

Port A Data

	7	6	5	4	3	2	1	0	
$1000	PA7	PA6	PA5	PA4	PA3	PA2	PA1	PA0	PORTA

Pulse Accumulator Control

	7	6	5	4	3	2	1	0	
$1026	DDRA7	PAEN	PAMOD	PEDGE	DDRA3	I4/O5	RTR1	RTR0	PACTL

DDRA7:   Data Direction for Bit 7 of Port A
          0 – Input
          1 – Output

DDRA3:   Data Direction for Bit 3 of Port A
          0 – Input
          1 – Output

Figure 7–2 Registers Associated with Parallel I/O on Port A

The use of Port B in simple and full handshaking will be discussed in the following section on Port C.

Port C   Each pin of Port C can be either an input or an output depending on the bits in the data direction register, *DDRC*, as shown in Figure 7–1. In the expanded multiplexed mode the Port C pins are a multiplexed low-order address/data bus.

In addition to the Port C data register, *PORTC*, there is a Port C data latched register, *PORTCL*, as indicated in Table 7–3. The pins *STRA* and *STRB* are available in the single-chip mode on the 'A8 and 'E9 parts. Inputs to Port C will be latched in the *PORTCL* register on any active edge of *STRA*. The active edge (rising or falling) is defined by the *EGA* bit in the parallel I/O control register, *PIOC*, shown in Figure 7–3. An active edge on *STRA* also sets the *STAF* bit in *PIOC*. This *STAF* bit is cleared by a read of the *PIOC* register followed by a read of the *PORTCL* register.

The *STRA* pin is an input and the *STRB* pin is an output. In the simple handshake mode (*HNDS* = 0 in *PIOC*), a write to *PORTB* causes the *STRB* pin to pulse for two E-clock periods. The *INVB* bit in *PIOC* determines if *STRB* is pulsed high (*INVB* = 1) or low (*INVB* = 0).

The full handshake mode (*HNDS* = 1) can be either input handshake (*OIN* = 0) or output handshake (*OIN* = 1). Input handshaking is used when the MCU wants to read some external data. The MCU first asserts *STRB* to tell the external device that it is ready. The external device then puts the data on Port C and pulses the *STRA* input. The active edge on *STRA* latches the data into *PORTCL*. In the interlocked mode (*PLS* = 0) an active edge on *STRA* also de-asserts *STRB*. A read of the *PORTCL* register causes *STRB* to be asserted again, telling the external device that

Parallel I/O Control

	7	6	5	4	3	2	1	0	
$1002	STAF	STAI	CWOM	HNDS	OIN	PLS	EGA	INVB	PIOC

STAF: Strobe A Interrupt Status Flag
          0 – No edge on STRA
          1 – Selected edge on STRA

STAI: Strobe A Interrupt Enable Mask
          0 – STAF does not request interrupt
          1 – STAF requests interrupt

CWOM: Port C Wired-OR Mode
          0 – Port C outputs are normal CMOS outputs
          1 – Port C outputs are open-drain outputs

HNDS: Handshake Mode
          0 – Simple strobe mode
          1 – Full input or output handshake mode

OIN: Output or Input Handshake Select (HNDS = 1)
          0 – Input handshake
          1 – Output handshake

PLS: Pulsed/Interlocked Handshake Operation (HNDS = 1)
          0 – Interlocked handshake
          1 – Pulsed handshake

EGA: Active Edge for Strobe A
          0 – falling edge
          1 – rising edge

INVB: Invert Strobe B
          0 – Active level is logic zero
          1 – Active level is logic one

Figure 7–3 The Parallel I/O Control Register

the MCU is ready to receive more data. In the pulsed mode ($PLS = 1$), $STRB$ remains asserted for only two E-clock periods.

Output handshaking ($HNDS = 1$ and $OIN = 1$) is used when the MCU wants to output data to some external device. The MCU first writes the data to $PORTCL$. This will assert $STRB$ to tell the external device that the data are available on Port C. The external device reads the data on Port C and then pulses the $STRA$ input to tell the MCU that it has read the data. In the interlocked mode ($PLS = 0$),

```
Box 7-3    Parallel I/O Registers—68HC11
\          PIO11.WHP
\          68HC11 registers for Parallel I/O
HEX
1000       CONSTANT        PORTA        \ I/O Port A
1002       CONSTANT        PIOC         \ Parallel I/O Control Register
1003       CONSTANT        PORTC        \ I/O Port C
1004       CONSTANT        PORTB        \ Output Port B
1005       CONSTANT        PORTCL       \ Alternate Latched Port C
1007       CONSTANT        DDRC         \ Data Direction for Port C
1008       CONSTANT        PORTD        \ I/O Port D
1009       CONSTANT        DDRD         \ Data Direction for Port D
100A       CONSTANT        PORTE        \ Input Port E
```

an active edge on *STRA* de-asserts *STRB*. A write to the *PORTCL* register causes *STRB* to be asserted again, telling the external device that more data are available. In the pulsed mode (*PLS* = 1) *STRB* remains asserted for only two E-clock periods.

Port D   Pins *PD0–PD5* can be either inputs or outputs on the 'A8 and 'E9 parts using the data direction register, *DDRD*, (see Table 7–3). The 'D3 part also has *PD6* and *PD7* implemented as either inputs or outputs. (These two pins are *STRA* and *STRB* on the 'A8 and 'E9 parts).

Port D is normally used for the SPI and SCI interfaces. These will be described in detail in Chapters 8 and 11, respectively.

Port E   The pins of Port E are all inputs and are also used for the 8-channel A/D converter discussed in detail in Chapter 9.

The file PIO11.WHP containing WHYP constants defining the 68HC711E9 registers associated with parallel I/O is shown in Box 7–3.

7.2 USING PARALLEL PORTS

Parallel ports are often used for simple I/O such as turning on LEDs or reading switch inputs. In this section we will look at how you can do this using WHYP on a 68HC12 or 68HC11.

7.2.1 Using Parallel Port Outputs

A *Light Emitting Diode* (LED) emits light when current flows through it in the positive direction as shown in Figure 7–4. Current flows through the LED when the voltage on the *anode* side (the wide side of the triangle) is made higher than the voltage on the *cathode* side (the straight line connected to the point of the triangle). When current flows through a lighted LED, the forward voltage across the LED is

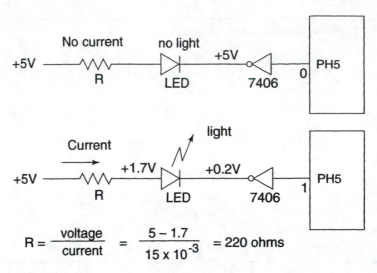

Figure 7–4 Turning On a LED by Storing a 1 in *PH5*

typically about +1.5 volts. We can turn an LED on and off using a port output pin of the 68HC812A4 with the circuit shown in Figure 7–4. When the pin output is low, the output of the inverter is high (+5 volts) and no current can flow through the LED and therefore no light will be emitted. If we bring the port output pin high, the output of the inverter goes low (assume about 0.2 volt) and current will flow from the +5-volt power supply through the resistor *R* and the LED. The resistor is used to limit the amount of current that flows through the LED. A typical current would be 15 milliamps or 15×10^{-3} amps. Using Ohm's law we can compute the resistor size needed as shown in Figure 7–4.

In Figure 7–4 the LED is connected through an inverter to bit 5 of Port H (*PH5*). We have assumed that bit 5 of data direction register *H*, *DDRH*, has been set to 1 so that *PH5* is an output. To turn on the LED, you need to set bit *PH5* high. Let's try to write a 68HC12 subroutine called *HI* that will expect a bit number and address on the WHYP data stack such that if you type

```
5 PORTH HI
```

then bit 5 of Port H will be set to 1.

To do this we need to create a mask with bit 5 set and all other bits zero. This mask will be $\$00100000 = 32_{10}$. The byte at *PORTH* must then be read, ORed with the mask, and written back to *PORTH*. This process will leave all other bits in *PORTH* unchanged. The subroutine *HI* shown in Figure 7–5 will do this. Note that it first pops the address on top of the data stack into *Y* and the bit number into *D* (the bit number will then be in *B*).

The subroutine *MASK* shown in Figure 7–5 will take the bit number in *B* as an input and return the corresponding mask in *B*. It does this by using a lookup table containing the eight possible masks. Note that the statement *BSR MSK1* will push the address of the table onto the system stack. The instruction *PULY* at the label *MSK1* will then pop this address into *Y*. The value of *B* is added to this address to index into the table and then the byte at the resulting address is loaded into *B*.

In the subroutine *HI* this mask in *B* is pushed onto the data stack. Note that in this case only one byte is pushed onto the data stack so that the instruction *ORAA 1,X+* will OR the value in *A* with this byte mask and then pop the mask from the data stack. The resulting value in *A* is then stored back at the address pointed to by *Y*.

The WHYP word *LO (b# addr --)*, whose 68HC12 subroutine is shown in Figure 7–5, will clear bit number *b#* of the byte at address *addr* to 0. It does this by

```
;        MASK      8-bit byte
;        INPUT: B = bit no.
;        OUTPUT; B = mask = 2^bit#
MASK
        PSHY                        ;save Y
        BSR       MSK1
        DB        1
        DB        2
        DB        4
        DB        8
        DB        16
        DB        32
        DB        64
        DB        128
MSK1    PULY                        ;addr of DB  1
        ABY
        LDAB      0,Y               ;get mask
        PULY                        ;restore Y
        RTS


;        HI        ( b# addr -- )
;        set bit number b# of byte at address addr to 1
HI
        LDY       2,X+              ;Y = addr
        LDD       2,X+              ;B = b#
        BSR       MASK              ;B = mask
        STAB      1,-X              ;push B on data stack
        LDAA      0,Y               ;A = @Y
        ORAA      1,X+              ;OR with mask and pop mask
        STAA      0,Y               ;store back at addr
        RTS
```

Figure 7–5 WHYP Bit Testing and Setting Words

```
;        LO       ( b# addr -- )
;        clear bit number b# of byte at address addr to 0
LO
         LDY      2,X+                   ;Y = addr
         LDD      2,X+                   ;B = b#
         BSR      MASK                   ;B = mask
         COMB                            ;complement mask
         STAB     1,-X                   ;push B on data stack
         LDAA     0,Y                    ;A = @Y
         ANDA     1,X+                   ;AND with mask and pop mask
         STAA     0,Y                    ;store back at addr
         RTS


;        ?HI      ( b# addr -- f )
;        leave a true flag if bit number b# of byte
;        at address addr is high
QHI
         LDY      2,X+                   ;Y = addr
         LDD      2,X+                   ;B = b#
         BSR      MASK                   ;b = mask
         STAB     1,-X                   ;push B on data stack
         LDAA     0,Y                    ;A = @Y
         ANDA     1,X+                   ;AND with mask and pop mask
         BEQ      QH1                    ;if not zero
         LDD      #$FFFF                 ; leave true flag
         BRA      QH2
QH1      LDD      #$0000                 ;else leave false flag
QH2      STD      2,-X                   ;push flag on stack
         RTS
```

Figure 7–5   (*continued*)

finding the mask as in *HI* and then complementing the mask so that a 0 is located at bit number *b#* with all other bits 1. This complemented mask is then ANDed with the byte at address *addr* to force bit number *b#* to zero.

Having turned on the LED shown in Figure 7–4, you can turn it off by typing

```
5 PORTH LO
```

7.2.2 Using Parallel Port Inputs

Figure 7–6 shows one way to read a switch using port *PH2*. The pins associated with port H can be configured as either inputs or outputs. This is done by setting the corresponding bits in the data direction register for port H, *DDRH*, as was shown in Figure 7–1. A zero bit in the *DDRH* will configure the corresponding pin in port H

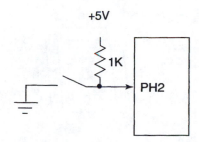

Figure 7-6 Interfacing a Switch to *PH2*

to be an input, while a one bit in the *DDRH* will configure the corresponding pin in port H to be an output. For example, the statements

```
HEX
F0 DDRH C!
```

will make pins 0–3 of port H inputs and pins 4–7 of port H outputs.

Having made *PH2* an input, you could define the following word to check to see if the switch is open:

```
: ?open      ( -- f )
             2 PORTH ?HI ;
```

The WHYP word *?HI (b# addr -- f)* whose 68HC12 subroutine is shown in Figure 7–5 will leave a true flag on the data stack if bit number *b#* of the byte at address *addr* is high. Note that when the switch is open the value at *PH2* will be pulled up to 5 volts by the 1K pull-up resistor in Figure 7–6. When the switch is closed, the value at *PH2* will be zero. Therefore, from the definition of *?HI* in Figure 7–5, the word *?open* will leave a true flag (−1 or $FFFF) on the data stack if the switch is open and a false flag (0) if the switch is closed.

7.3 SEVEN-SEGMENT DISPLAYS

The operation of a Light Emitting Diode (LED) was described in Section 7.2.1 and a way to interface it to a parallel port was shown in Figure 7–4. Seven LEDs can be arranged in a pattern to form different digits as shown in Figure 7–7. Digital watches use similar seven-segment displays using liquid crystals rather than LEDs. Liquid crystal displays will be described in Section 7.5. The red digits on digital clocks are LEDs. Seven-segment displays come in two flavors: common anode and common cathode. A common anode seven-segment display has all of the anodes tied together as shown in Figure 7–7. A common cathode seven-segment display would have all the cathodes tied together. In Figure 7–7 we should really connect a separate resistor to each of the seven LEDs so that each lighted LED would have the same current and therefore the same brightness. For experimental purposes, it is easier to cheat and put a single resistor from the common anode to +5 volts. This will mean that an 8, which has all LEDs lit, will be dimmer (because the current is split

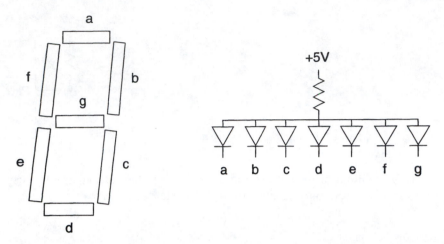

Figure 7–7   A seven-segment display contains seven Light Emitting Diodes (LEDs).

between all eight LEDs) than a 1 which has only two LEDs lit. We will look at examples of using both common anode and common cathode seven-segment displays.

7.3.1 Common-Anode Displays

The seven-segment display shown in Figure 7–7 comes in an integrated package, called a MAN 72 with three common anode pins and separate pins for each segment *a–g*, as shown in Figure 7–8. These seven segment pins can be connected to the outputs of 7406 inverters with the inputs connected to the seven output pins *PH0–PH6* using the pinouts shown in Figure 7–8. *PH7* can optionally be used to control the decimal point, *dp*, of the MAN 72. All three anode pins on the MAN 72 should be connected through a 220-Ω resistor to +5 volts. Then by bringing different output lines, *PH0–PH6*, high, we can form any digit by lighting the appropriate LEDs.

To display any hex digit *n* on the seven-segment display we can define the WHYP word *.led (n --)*, shown in Figure 7–9. Note that we create a table in which each byte is the code to store in *PORTH* to display a particular hex digit. For example, an 8 would have all seven segments on and therefore the values *PH6–PH0* will be 1111111, or $7F. Similarly, a 4 will have segments *b, c, f, g* on, or 0110011 = $33. The hex values, *B* and *D*, are displayed as lowercase letters, *b.* and *d.*, with a decimal point so that they can be distinguished from an 8 and 0. Note that the 6 has all segments except *b* lit to distinguish it from the lowercase *b*.

The word *.led (n --)* adds the value *n* to the address of the table *7seg*. (Remember that if you use *CREATE 7seg*, then the word *7seg* will leave the address of the *pfa*, or the first entry in the table, on the data stack.) This byte

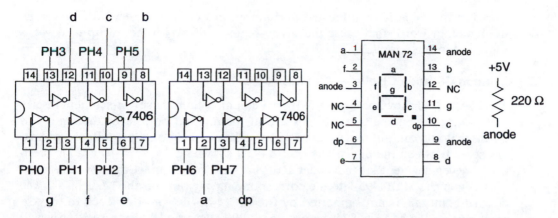

Figure 7–8   Connecting the MAN 72 Common Anode Seven-Segment Display

```
HEX                 \ File: LED.WHP

FF PORTH C!                     \ Port H outputs

CREATE 7seg
        7E C,     \ 0
        30 C,     \ 1
        6D C,     \ 2
        79 C,     \ 3
        33 C,     \ 4
        5B C,     \ 5
        5F C,     \ 6
        70 C,     \ 7
        7F C,     \ 8
        7B C,     \ 9
        77 C,     \ A
        9F C,     \ b.
        4E C,     \ C
        BD C,     \ d.
        4F C,     \ E
        47 C,     \ F

: .led            ( n -- )
                  7seg + C@        \ get 7seg code
                  PORTH C! ;       \ store in Port H
```

Figure 7–9   Using a Table to Display a Hex Digit on an LED

stored in the table is then fetched and stored in *PORTH*. The word *.led* can be used in other words that cause the seven-segment display to count up or down as suggested in Exercise 7.2.

7.3.2 Common-Cathode Displays—The MC14495-1

The MAN 6780 shown in Figure 7–10 is a common cathode seven-segment display that has the advantage that the pins are at the top and bottom of the digit. This means that you can put two or more of these side by side on a protoboard without any space between the digits. The MC14495-1 shown in Figure 7–10 is a hexadecimal-to-seven-segment latch/decoder ROM/driver. You connect the seven segment pins *a–g* on the MC14495-1 to the corresponding *a–g* pins on the MAN 6780. The decimal point, *dp*, is not supported by the MC14495-1. Note that each of the segment pins on the MAN6780 is an anode. A 290-Ω current-limiting resistor is built into each *a–g* output pin of the MC14495-1 driver. The two common cathode pins on the MAN 6780 can just be connected to ground.

To display a hex value between 0 and *F* on the MAN 6780, we must latch this hex value into the MC14495-1 through the *D-C-B-A* inputs. When the latch enable pin, *LE*, on the MC14495-1 is low, the current values on the *D-C-B-A* inputs will not affect the digit displayed on the MAN 6780. When LE goes from zero to one, the current *D-C-B-A* inputs will be latched into the chip and decoded to provide the proper *a–g* segment outputs. At this point the MAN 6780 will display the hex digit and will continue to display this digit as long as *LE* is high regardless of the values on the *D-C-B-A* inputs.

This means that we can control multiple seven-segment displays on a common four-line bus connected to the *D-C-B-A* inputs of all MC14495-1 chips. A separate signal must then be connected to the *LE* pin of each MC14495-1. For example, suppose we want to display a two-digit hex number on two MAN 6780 displays. Each

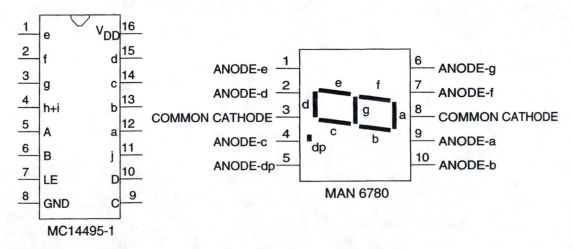

Figure 7–10   Connecting the MAN6780 Common Cathode Seven-Segment Display

```
HEX

: .digit          ( dig# n -- )
                  30 OR PORTH C!        \ keep old values displayed
                  4 +                   \ get bit# for LE
                  DUP PORTH LO          \ bring LE low
                  PORTH HI ;            \ bring LE high to display digit
```

Figure 7–11   Displaying One of Two Digits Using the MC14495-1

MAN 6780 will have its own MC14495-1 connected as shown in Figure 7–10. Connect *PH0–PH3* to A–D on each MC14495-1. Connect *PH4* to the *LE* pin of digit 0 (rightmost) and *PH5* to the *LE* pin of digit 1 (leftmost). The word *.digit (dig# n --)*, shown in Figure 7–11, will display the hex digit *n* (0–F) on the seven-segment display number *dig#* (0 or 1).

Note that the first line in *.digit* in Figure 7–11 ORs the value of *n* (0–F) with $30. This will ensure that *PH4* and *PH5* will be high when *n* is stored in *PH0–PH6*. This will not change either of the two displayed digits. At this point the digit number, *dig#* (0 or 1) is on the stack. Adding 4 to this value in the second line will produce the bit number of *PORTH* that is connected to the *LE* pin of the corresponding digit. Bringing *LE* low in line 3 of Figure 7–11 will cause the hex value *n* on *PH0–PH3* to enter the latch of the selected MC14494-1. Bringing the *LE* pin back high in the last line in Figure 7–11 will cause this value of *n* to be latched in the chip and decoded. This will cause the digit to be displayed on the MAN6780.

The word *.digit* can be used in other words that will display a two-digit hex value that can then count from $00 to $FF (see Exercise 7.3).

7.4   KEYPAD INTERFACING

There are several ways to determine which key in a keypad is pressed. Keypads come in two common configurations. In the first, each key acts as a switch between a particular row and column of an *n*-row by *m*-column grid array. We will look at how to decode such a keypad in Section 7.4.1. The second configuration is when one side of each key switch is common. A method of decoding this type of keypad using a 74154 decoder will be described in Section 7.4.3. Special chips are available to simplify the interfacing of keypads. We will look at one such chip, the 74C922 16-Key Encoder, in Section 7.4.2.

7.4.1   4 × 4 Hex Keypad

Consider a 4 × 4 keypad connected to Port J of a 68HC811A4 as shown in Figure 7–12. Pins *PJ0–PJ3* are configured as outputs and pins *PJ4–PJ7* are configured as inputs. These four inputs are pulled up to 5 volts with the four pull-up resistors. You can optionally enable internal pull-up or pull-down devices on input

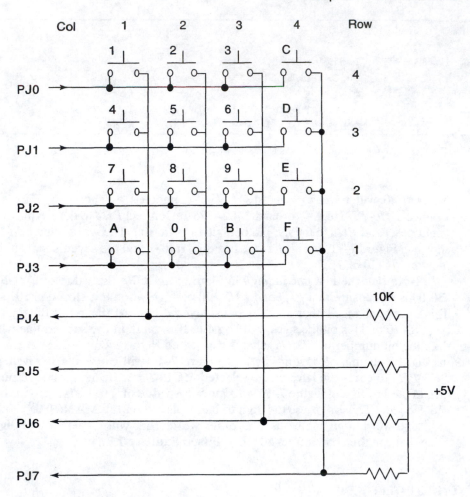

Figure 7–12   Connecting a 4 × 4 Keypad to Port J

pins of Port J of a 68HC811A4 by setting bits in the *PUPSJ* and *PULEJ* registers
shown in Figure 7–13. Writing $F0 to both *PUPSJ* and *PULEJ* will enable pull-up
devices on pins *PJ4–PJ7* as indicated in Figure 7–12. Thus, if all the key switches
are open, the four bits *PJ4–PJ7* will all be read as 1's. If a zero is written to only
one of the rows *PJ0–PJ3*, then a key in that row that is pressed will cause the
input connected to its column to go low. This can be read by the MCU to
determine which key has been pressed.

For example, suppose that *PJ1* is brought low while *PJ0*, *PJ2*, and *PJ3* are high.
That is, a 1101, or $D, is written to the low nibble of Port J. If Port J is then read and
the high nibble, *PJ4–PJ7*, is not $F, then either key 4, 5, 6, or D must have been
pressed. If *PJ4* is low, that is, Port J reads $ED, then key 4 was pressed. If *PJ5* is low,
that is, Port J reads $DD, then key 5 was pressed. If *PJ6* is low, that is, Port J reads
$BD, then key 6 was pressed. If *PJ7* is low, that is, Port J reads $7D, then key D was

Port J Pull-Up/Pulldown Select Register

	7	6	5	4	3	2	1	0	
$002D	Bit 7	6	5	4	3	2	1	Bit 0	PUPSJ

PUPSJ[7:0]:   Port J Pull-Up/Pull-Down Select (Initialize before enabling with PULEJ)
0 – Pulldown selected for associated Port J pin
1 – Pull-up selected for associated Port J pin

Port J Pull-Up/Pull-Down Enable Register

	7	6	5	4	3	2	1	0	
$002E	Bit 7	6	5	4	3	2	1	Bit 0	PULEJ

PUPSJ[7:0]:   Port J Pull-Up/Pull-Down Enable
0 – No pull-up/pulldown device for associated Port J pin
1 – Enable pull-up/pulldown device for associated Port J pin

Figure 7–13   Registers Associated with Parallel I/O on Port J

pressed. In a similar way we could determine the key codes for all 16 keys and store them in a table called *keycodes* as shown in Figure 7–14.

The WHYP word *?keypad (-- ff | n tf)* given in Figure 7–14 will check to see if a key is being pressed and return either a false flag (if no key is being pressed) or a true flag over the hex value of the key being pressed. Note that this word reads each of the 16 codes in the table *keycodes*, stores the code in *PORTJ*, and then reads back the contents of *PORTJ*. The key value is found when the read back value is equal to the key code.

The WHYP word *keypad (-- n)* shown in Figure 7–15 will wait for a key to be pressed and return the hex value of the key pressed.

Once you obtain a keypad value using the word *keypad*, you usually want to do something with this value such as display the hex digit on a seven-segment display. If, for example, you want to display the value of the first key pressed on digit 1 using the word *.digit* in Figure 7–11 and then display the value of the second key pressed on digit 0, you could run into a problem. After displaying the first value on digit 1, if your finger were still pressing the key, the program would display this same value on digit 0. You need to be able to wait until you have released your finger before waiting to press another key. The word *wait.for.keyup* in Figure 7–15 will do this. The word *main.keypad* in Figure 7–15 will display any key you press on the seven-segment display shown in Figure 7–8.

Sometimes the switches making up a keypad will have a tendency to bounce when they are pressed. That is, when contact is first made, it may open momentarily before closing for good. This could lead to thinking that the key was up (and therefore continuing the program) when it really wasn't. In such a situation a digit might inadvertently get displayed twice. To solve this problem, key switches are debounced, either in hardware or software. The software solution is to delay for about

```
load PIOA4.WHP
HEX
: init.key        ( -- )              \ PJ0-PJ3 outputs
                  0F DDRJ C!          \ PJ4-PJ7 inputs
                  F0 PUPSJ C!         \ PJ4-PJ7 pullups
                  F0 PULEJ C! ;       \ enable pullups

CREATE keycodes            \ key   row      col
        D7 C,              \ 0      1        2
        EE C,              \ 1      4        1
        DE C,              \ 2      4        2
        BE C,              \ 3      4        3
        ED C,              \ 4      3        1
        DD C,              \ 5      3        2
        BD C,              \ 6      3        3
        EB C,              \ 7      2        1
        DB C,              \ 8      2        2
        BB C,              \ 9      2        3
        E7 C,              \ A      1        1
        B7 C,              \ B      1        3
        7E C,              \ C      4        4
        7D C,              \ D      3        4
        7B C,              \ E      2        4
        77 C,              \ F      1        4
DECIMAL

: ?keypad         ( -- ff | n tf )
                  0 keycodes          \ ff pfa
                  16 0 DO             \ ff pfa
                     DUP I + C@       \ ff pfa code
                     DUP PORTJ C!     \ ff pfa code
                     PORTJ C@ =       \ ff pfa flag
                     IF               \ ff pfa
                        DROP I TRUE   \ ff n tf
                        ROT LEAVE     \ n tf ff
                     THEN
                  LOOP                \ ff pfa
                  DROP ;
```

Figure 7–14 Scanning a 4 × 4 Keypad

10 ms after a key pressing is sensed. If the key is read again and it is the same value as before, then you can conclude that the key has stopped bouncing and the correct value has been read. In Figure 7–16 the WHYP word *getkey (-- n)* will wait for a key to be pressed, including debounce, and return the hex value of the key pressed. Note

```
: keypad          ( -- n )
                  BEGIN
                     ?keypad
                  UNTIL ;


: wait.for.keyup  ( -- )
                  BEGIN
                     ?keypad
                  WHILE
                     DROP
                  REPEAT ;


: main.keypad     ( -- )
                  init.key
                  BEGIN
                     keypad
                     .led
                     wait.for.keyup
                  AGAIN ;
```

Figure 7–15 Displaying Keys Pressed on the Seven-Segment Display

```
DECIMAL

: getkey          ( -- n )
                  BEGIN
                     keypad           \ n1
                     10MS.DELAY       \ debounce
                     keypad           \ n1 n2
                     OVER <>          \ n1 f
                  WHILE
                     DROP
                  REPEAT ;


: wait.for.keyup     ( -- )
                  BEGIN
                     BEGIN
                        ?keypad
                     WHILE
                        DROP
                     REPEAT
                     10MS.DELAY       \ debounce
                     ?keypad
                  WHILE
                     DROP
                  REPEAT ;
```

Figure 7–16 Including the Effects of Debounce When Reading a Keypad

that this word reads the keypad twice, separated by a 10-ms delay, until the two values are the same. The WHYP word *wait.for.keyup (--)* shown in Figure 7–16 will wait for a key to be released, including the effects of debounce.

7.4.2 The 74C922 16-Key Encoder

The MM74C922 is a 16-key encoder that can be used to read the value of a key pressed on a 4 × 4 keypad. Figure 7–17 shows how to connect the MM74C922 to a common 4 × 4 keypad in which the row signals, *Y1–Y4*, and column signals, *X1–X4*, are on a ribbon cable attached to the keypad. These lines are connected to the corresponding pins on the MM74C922.

The MM74C922 chip shown in Figure 7–17 performs the same sort of scanning operation done by the software in Figure 7–14. The data out pins, *A–D*, are connected to the inputs *PJ0–PJ3*, and the *DATA AV* pin is connected to pin *PJ7*, as shown in Figure 7–17.

The MM74C922 continually scans the 16-key keypad until a key is pressed. It then brings the *DATA AV* pin (connected to *PJ7*) high, indicating that data are available on the output pins *A–D*. These pins can be read into Port J. The value of the key code is the small digit shown at the top of each key in Figure 7–17. The key labels are the bold digits shown on each key in Figure 7–17. The table *keytbl* shown in Figure 7–18 relates the key label to key code (index into the table).

The *DATA AV* pin on the MM74C922 will go low when you release the key. It would be more convenient if you could use an edge-sensitive input to the 68HC12 that would set a flag on a positive edge of *DATA AV*. We will see in Chapter 10 that pins in the timer module can be used as edge-sensitive inputs. In that chapter we will show how to interface the MM74C922 16-key encoder using such edge-sensitive inputs.

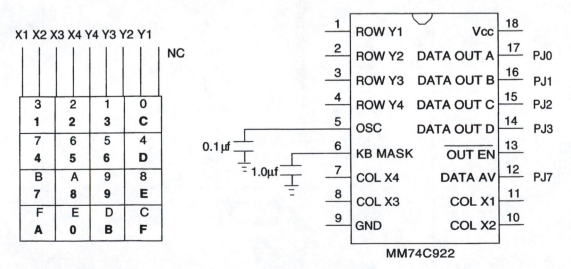

Figure 7–17 Interfacing the MM74C922 16-Key Encoder to a Keypad

```
HEX

CREATE keytbl
        C C, 3 C, 2 C, 1 C, D C, 6 C, 5 C, 4 C,
        E C, 9 C, 8 C, 7 C, F C, B C, 0 C, A C,

: init.key      ( -- )
                00 DDRJ C! ;        \ Port J inputs

: getkey2       ( -- n )     \ Read hex value from keypad
                BEGIN
                   7 PORTJ ?HI
                UNTIL
                PORTJ C@
                0F AND
                keytbl + C@ ;
```

Figure 7–18   WHYP Words to Read a Keypad Using the MM74C922 16-Key Encoder

The WHYP word *getkey2 (-- n)* given in Figure 7–18 will wait for a key to be pressed and return the hex value of the key pressed. Note that the word *init.key* in Figure 7–18 initializes Port J as inputs. The word *getkey2 (-- n)* waits for bit 7 of Port J to go high and then reads the key code from the low nibble of *PORTJ*. It then uses this key code value to index into *keytbl* to read the key value *n*. Debouncing is taken care of internally in hardware, using the $1.0\mu f$ capacitor connected to *KB MASK* pin of the MM74C922.

In Section 10.4 we will show how the *DATA AV* signal in Figure 7–17 can be connected to pin *PT7/PAI* where a rising edge (resulting from pressing a key) will set a flag in the pulse accumulator module (see Figure 10–16). In Section 10.7 we will show how to interface the keypad shown in Figure 7–17 using interrupts.

7.4.3 Interfacing a 16 × 1 Hex Keypad Using a 74154 Decoder

In this section we will give an example of using the pulsed handshaking mode on a 68HC711E9 as described in Section 7.1.3. A 16-switch keypad in which one side of each switch is tied together can be interfaced to a 74154 4-to-16 decoder chip, as shown in Figure 7–19. Note that the common side of each switch is pulled high to +5 volts. This means that if all switches are open, the *STRA* signal will be high. If a particular hex value, say $5 = 0101$, is output on *PB0–PB3* to the A–D inputs of the 74154 and the *STRB* signal is pulsed low, the corresponding output 5 will pulse low while all other outputs remain high. If switch 5 is closed, this will cause *STRA* to pulse low, setting bit 7 (*STAF*) in the *PIOC* register. Knowing the value on *PB0–PB3* when this occurs will tell you which key is pressed.

The WHYP word *?keypad (-- ff | n tf)* given in Figure 7–20 will check to see if a key is being pressed and return either a false flag (if no key is being pressed) or a

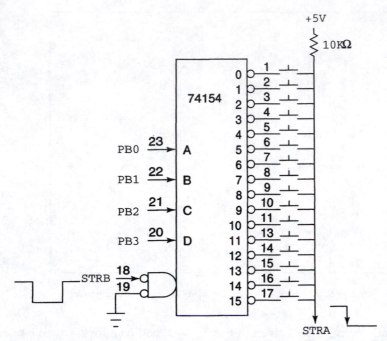

Figure 7–19   Interfacing a 16 × 1 Hex Keypad to a 68HC711E9 Using a 74154

```
DECIMAL

: init.key       ( -- )
                 0 PIOC C! ;      \ pulse STRB lo, falling edge of STRA


: ?keypad        ( -- ff | n tf )
                 0                          \ ff
                 16 0 DO                    \ ff
                     I PORTB C!             \ ff          pulses STRB low
                     7 PIOC ?HI             \ ff flag
                     IF                     \ ff
                         PORTCL C@ DROP     \ clear STAF
                         DROP I TRUE        \ n tf
                         LEAVE              \ n tf
                     THEN                   \ ff
                 LOOP ;
```

Figure 7–20   Scanning a 16 × 1 Keypad

true flag over the hex value of the key being pressed. Note that this word stores each of the 16 key values ($0–$F) in *PORTB* which automatically pulses *STRB* low. It then checks to see if the *STAF* bit in the *PIOC* register has been set, indicating that *STRA* went low. If it is, then the key has been found and its value is the current index value I in the DO loop. Note that $PORTCL$ has to be read to clear the $STAF$ flag.

We used the outputs of Port B on a 68HC11 to control the 74154 in Figure 7–19. We did this to illustrate the use of $STRB$ to pulse the enable pin on the 74154 low. It is important to keep the enable pin on the 74154 high during the time that the input values $A–D$ are changing to avoid an erroneous value causing $STRA$ to go low. This would cause you to think you have read the wrong key. Also note that $STRA$ is an edge-sensitive input that sets the $STAF$ bit (bit 7) in the $PIOC$ register. The 68HC12 family members (and the 68HC11D3) do not have $STRA$ and $STRB$ pins. If you want to use edge-sensitive inputs, you can use pins in the timer module (input captures or pulse accumulator input) as will be described in Chapter 10 or key wakeup pins on Ports H and J as will be described in Chapter 15.

7.5   LIQUID CRYSTAL DISPLAYS

A Liquid Crystal Display (LCD) is a common type of display used in a variety of applications such as watches, calculators, and laptop computers. Its big advantage is that it uses much less power than an LED and therefore can be used in battery-powered applications. An LCD consists of a liquid crystal material sandwiched between two conducting plates. An AC voltage applied between the two conductors will cause the reflectance (or transmittance) of the liquid crystal to change, making a character visible. LCD displays come in a variety of configurations.

For example, the Varitronix, Ltd. Model MDL-16166 displays one line of 16 characters. This display and many other common ones use a built-in Hitachi HD44780 LCD Controller/Driver that performs all of the functions needed to drive the LCD and provides an easy interface to a microcontroller using an 8-bit data bus, $DB0–DB7$, and three control signals, RS, R/W, and E. The relationships between RS, R/W, and E are shown in Figure 7–21. The signal, RS, can be thought of as a

RS	R/W	E	Operation
0	0	⌐\	Write instruction code
0	1	/‾\	Read busy flag and address counter
1	0	⌐\	Write data
1	1	/‾\	Read data

Figure 7–21   Relationships between RS, R/W, and E

register select signal that selects either the LCD control register ($RS = 0$) or the LCD data register ($RS = 1$). The read/write signal R/W is 1 for a read operation and 0 for a write operation. Data or instruction codes are written on the falling edge of E, and E must be high for a read operation.

The HD44780 has its own instruction set shown in Table 7–4. (For a complete data sheet, go to `http://www.hitachi.com/`.) The first eight are instruction codes that are written to the LCD control register with $RS = 0$ and $R/W = 0$, as shown in Figure 7–21. The last entry in Table 7–4 shows the format of the busy flag and address counter when reading from the LCD control register with $RS = 0$ and $R/W = 1$, as shown in Figure 7–21.

Table 7–4   HD44780 Instruction Set

Instruction	DB7	DB6	DB5	DB4	DB3	DB2	DB1	DB0	Description
Clear display	0	0	0	0	0	0	0	1	Clears display & returns cursor to home. Sets I/D=1 in Entry Mode.
Return home	0	0	0	0	0	0	1	×	Returns cursor to home position (Address 0) Set DD RAM address to zero.
Entry mode set	0	0	0	0	0	1	I/D	S	I/D=1: increment cursor; S=0: normal ; I/D=0: decrement cursor; S=1 shift display.
Display ON/OFF control	0	0	0	0	1	D	C	B	Sets ON/OFF all display (D), cursor (C), and blink of cursor (B).
Cursor or display shift	0	0	0	1	S/C	R/L	×	×	S/C=1: display shift; S/C=0: cursor move; R/L=1: shift right; R/L=0: shift left.
Function set	0	0	1	DL	N	F	×	×	DL=1: 8 bits; DL=0: 4 bits; N=1: 2 line; N=0: 1 line; F=1: 5×10 dots; F=0; 5×7 dots.
Set the CG RAM address	0	1	CG RAM address						Sets the CG RAM address, after which CG RAM data is sent and received.
Set the DD RAM address	1	DD RAM address							Sets the DD RAM address, after which DD RAM data is sent and received.
Read busy flag & address	BF	Address counter							Read busy flag (BF) and address counter contents.

The HD44780 contains a 128-byte data display memory (DD RAM) that contains the ASCII codes of the characters being displayed on the LCD display. This DD RAM address is set (address 0 is the display home position) using the *Set the DD RAM address* instruction. After this is done, subsequent data writes will write the ASCII code of the character to be displayed to the DD RAM address (and display the character) and then increment the DD RAM address so that the next character will be displayed in the next location.

The HD44780 also contains a 64-byte character-generator memory (CG RAM) that can be used to change the font of up to 16 different characters. We will not consider this feature in this book, but if you are interested you can consult an HD44780 data sheet.

The data bus *DB0–DB7* on the HD44780 can be connected directly to a microcontroller's data bus and the controller can be wired up to respond to reads and writes to a particular series of addresses (see Exercise 7.6). The HD44780 can also be connected to the parallel I/O ports on a microcontroller and then software can be written to produce the control signals shown in Figure 7–21. This will be the approach we take in this section.

The diagram in Figure 7–22 shows how we can connect an LCD display to a 68HC812A4 using Ports H and J. Any suitable parallel I/O ports could be used on other microcontrollers. A 20-KΩ potentiometer is used to control the contrast of the displayed digits.

Listing 7–1 gives some WHYP words that will allow you to display characters on an LCD. Note that the words *RS*, *R/W*, and *E.* are defined to leave a bit number plus the address of *PORTJ* on the stack so that statements such as *RS LO* and *RS HI* will set *RS* low and high (see Figure 7–5). We also use the word *E.* rather than *E* because *E* is a hex digit.

The words >*intstr (n --)* and >*data (n --)* can be used to write an instruction or data to the LCD. These words first wait for the busy flag to go low, indicating that all internal operations in the LCD have been completed. The data *n* are then stored in *PORTH* and the *R/W* line is brought low, indicating a write operation. *RS* is brought low for an instruction and high for data. Then the *E.* signal is brought high, then low.

The word *busy.wait* will wait for the busy flag to go to zero. Note that the busy flag is bit 7 on the data bus when a read operation is performed with *RS* = 0. Also note that *E.* must be high when the busy flag is read.

Normally the LCD will initialize itself on power up. However, this does not always happen. In this case you can initialize it in software using the somewhat strange procedure given in the word *init.lcd (--)* shown in Listing 7–1. One problem is that the busy flag cannot be checked before the LCD is initialized. Therefore, the word >*instr* described above won't work. We've included a similar word called >*inst (n --)* that is the same as >*instr (n --)* except that the word *busy.wait* is replaced with the word *.1ms.delay* which just delays for 0.1 ms to give the busy flag time to become zero. Note that the word *init.lcd* also requires a 4.1-ms delay. These two delay routines just use *FOR . . . NEXT* delay loops as described in Section 5.2.4.

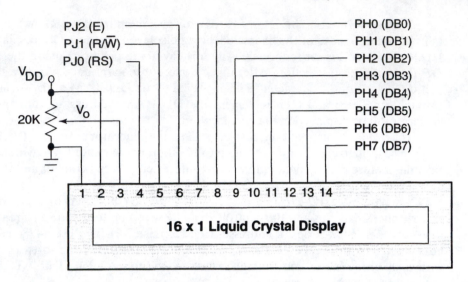

Figure 7–22 Interfacing to a Liquid Crystal Display

Listing 7–1   LCD

```
\       Liquid Crystal Display
\       Data byte: PORTH
\       Control: PORTJ   RS: PJ0 R/W: PJ1 E: PJ2

LOAD HEX2ASC.WHP
HEX

: RS            ( -- )              \ L: instr; H: data
                0 PORTJ;

: R/W           ( -- )              \ H: read; L: write
                1 PORTJ;

: E.            ( -- )              \ Enable signal: H->L
                2 PORTJ;

: .1ms.delay ( -- )
                67 FOR NEXT ;

: 4.1ms.delay ( -- )
                2976 FOR NEXT ;

: lcd.setup    ( -- )
                FF DDRH C!      \ Port H outputs
                07 DDRJ C!      \ PJ0-P2 outputs
                R/W LO
                RS LO
                E. LO ;

\ Used during LCD initialization when busy flag cannot be checked
: >inst         ( n -- )                \ write lcd instruction
```

Listing 7–1   (continued)

```
                  .1ms.delay            \ wait for busy = 0
                  PORTH C!
                  R/W LO
                  RS LO
                  E. HI E. LO ;

: busy.wait       ( -- )                \ wait for busy flag to go to zero
                  00 DDRH C!            \ make Port H inputs
                  R/W HI
                  RS LO
                  BEGIN
                     E. LO E. HI
                     PORTH C@           \ read port H
                     E. LO
                     80 AND NOT         \ until bit 7 is zero
                  UNTIL
                  R/W LO
                  FF DDRH C! ;          \ make Port H outputs

: >instr          ( n -- )              \ write lcd instruction
                  busy.wait             \ wait for busy = 0
                  PORTH C!
                  R/W LO
                  RS LO
                  E. HI E. LO ;

: >data           ( n -- )              \ write lcd data
                  busy.wait             \ wait for busy = 0
                  PORTH C!
                  R/W LO
                  RS HI
                  E. HI E. LO ;

: init.lcd        ( -- )
                  30 >inst              \ set function, 8 bit, 1 line
                  4.1ms.delay
                  30 >inst              \ set function, 8 bit, 1 line
                  .1ms.delay
                  30 >inst              \ set function, 8 bit, 1 line
                  30 >inst              \ set function, 8 bit, 1 line
                  8 >inst               \ display off, cursor on, blink
                  1 >inst               \ clear display
                  6 >inst               \ entry mode set, inc cursor
                  F >inst               \ display on, cursor on, blink
                  80 >inst ;            \ set DD RAM addr to 0000000

: clear.lcd       ( -- )
                  1 >instr
                       4.1ms.delay ;

: hex>lcd         ( hex -- )
                  HEX2ASC >data ;
```

The word >*instr (n --)* can be used to execute any of the instructions shown in Table 7–4. For example, *1 >instr* will clear the display, as shown in the definition of the word *clear.lcd*.

The word >*data (n --)* is used to send ASCII values to the display data RAM. If your data are in the form of a hex value (as, for example, by reading a hex keypad), you must first convert this value to an ASCII value using the WHYP word *HEX2ASC* described in Section 5.2.3 (see Figure 5–16). Note that at the beginning of Listing 7–1 we have included the statement *LOAD HEX2ASC.WHP*. The word *hex>lcd (hex --)*, shown in Listing 7–1, will display a hex value on the LCD by first converting the hex value to ASCII and then writing it in the DD RAM using >*data*.

Other examples of using WHYP to write data on an LCD are considered in Exercises 7.5–7.8 and 13.9.

7.6 INTERRUPT-DRIVEN TRAFFIC LIGHTS

Consider the set of traffic lights shown in Figure 7–23. The lights are assumed to be at a four-way intersection with one street going north–south and the other road going east–west. To simulate these traffic lights in the lab we could use colored LEDs and connect them to Port H as shown in Figure 7–4 in Section 7.2.1. We will connect the east–west lights to *PH1–PH3* and the north–south lights to *PH4–PH6*.

We can use real-time interrupts (see Section 6.5) to continually cycle through the six states shown in Table 7–5. Note that when the light on one street is red and the light on the other street is green, we will delay 5 seconds. (Assume very fast cars so that we won't have to wait all day in the lab!) We will delay 1 second on a yellow–red or red–red combination.

The idea will be to use interrupts so that the entire operation will be carried out in the background with no need for the CPU to intervene to keep the traffic lights going. The same idea can be used to cycle through any set of states that you can change by writing to an output port such as Port H.

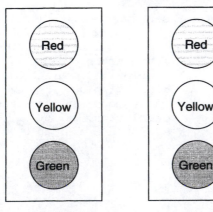

North - South   East - West

Figure 7–23 Six colored LEDs can represent a set of traffic lights

Table 7–5   Traffic Light States

State	North–South	East–West	Delay (sec.)
1	Green	Red	5
2	Yellow	Red	1
3	Red	Red	1
4	Red	Green	5
5	Red	Yellow	1
6	Red	Red	1

We begin by making a table that represents the six states shown in Table 7–5. This table is called *LIGHTS* in the program shown in Listing 7–2. The first byte in the table is the number of states (6). This is followed by a pointer to the next state. This pointer is an index into the table. It is initialized to 2, which means that it is pointing to the byte at index 2 in the table, which is the hex value $18. This is the binary value 00011000 which will be written out to Port H. The bits in Port H will be assigned to the colored LEDs according to the bit positions _RYGRYG_. Thus the hex value $18 will turn on the green north–south light and the red east–west light.

Listing 7–2   Traffic Lights Using Real-time Interrupt

```
\    TABLE DRIVEN TRAFFIC LIGHTS          File: TRAFFIC.WHP
\    using RTI interrupts

HEX
0014    CONSTANT RTICTL
0015    CONSTANT RTIFLG
0024    CONSTANT PORTH
0025    CONSTANT DDRH
0B30    CONSTANT RTI.IVEC

VARIABLE DTIME
CREATE LIGHTS
\        Lights table         _RYGRYG_ = Port H
         6        C,          \ number of states
         2        C,          \ pointer to next state
         18       C,          \ 00011000
         5 1F *   C,          \ 5 sec. delay - $1F = 31 ticks per second
         28       C,          \ 00101000
         1F       C,          \ 1 sec. delay
         48       C,          \ 01001000
         1F       C,          \ 1 sec. delay
         42       C,          \ 01000010
         5 1F *   C,          \ 5 sec. delay
         44       C,          \ 01000100
         1F       C,          \ 1 sec. delay
         48       C,          \ 01001000
         1F       C,          \ 1 sec. delay
```

(*continued*)

Listing 7–2 (continued)

```
: RTIF.CLR          ( -- )            \ clear RT1 flag
               80 RTIFLG C! ;

: RTI.SET32         ( -- )
               06 RTICTL C! ; \ set RTI rate to 32.768 msec

: RTI.INT.ENABLE        ( -- )
               7 RTICTL HI ;

: RTI.INT.DISABLE       ( -- )
               7 RTICTL LO ;

INT: RTI.INTSER     ( -- )
               DTIME @ 1-                       \ ticks
               DUP 0=
               IF                               \ ticks
                  DROP LIGHTS DUP 1+ C@         \ pfa ptr
                  DUP 2 PICK C@                 \ pfa ptr ptr cnt
                  2* 1+                         \ pfa ptr ptr ptrmax
                  >
                  IF                            \ pfa ptr
                     DROP 2                     \ cycle back
                  THEN                          \ pfa ptr
                  2DUP + DUP C@ PORTH C!        \ pfa ptr addr
                  1+ C@                         \ pfa ptr ticks
                  ROT 1+                        \ ptr ticks pfa+1
                  ROT 2+ SWAP C!                \ update ptr
               THEN
               DTIME !
               RTIF.CLR
RTI;

: SET.RTI.INTVEC           ( -- )
               [ ' RTI.INTSER ] LITERAL
               RTI.IVEC ! ;

: INIT.TRAFFIC ( -- )
               FF DDRH C!                        \ Port H outputs
               RTI.SET32                         \ set RTI rate to 32.768 ms
               SET.RTI.INTVEC                    \ set interrupt vector
               RTI.INT.ENABLE                    \ enable RTI interrupts
               1 DTIME ! ;                       \ start on 1st interrupt

: MAIN.TRAFFIC ( -- )
               SEI
               INIT.TRAFFIC
               CLI ;

: TURNOFF
               SEI
               0 PORTH C!                        \ turn off leds
               RTI.INT.DISABLE ;

DECIMAL
```

The next entry in the table is the delay time measured in ticks. A tick will be the time between interrupts. We want the traffic light to delay 1 second and 5 seconds. We need to have the number of ticks for a 5-second delay fit in eight bits. Thus, the delay for one tick must be at least 5/255 = 0.0196 seconds, or 19.6 ms. Therefore, from Figure 6–5 we will choose an RTI timeout period of 32.768 ms. The number of ticks for a 1-second delay will be 1/0.032768 = 30.52. Therefore, in the table we will store the value $1F = 31 for a 1-second delay and 5*$1F for a 5-second delay. The rest of the table stores a pair of bytes for each state: the byte to be written to Port H and the delay value for that state.

The variable *DTIME* defined at the beginning of the program in Listing 7–2 is used to hold the number of ticks before a time-out that will move to the next state. This value is set to 1 in the word *INIT.TRAFFIC* so that a state change will occur on the first interrupt.

The interrupt service routine, *RTI.INTSER*, shown in Listing 7–2, starts by decrementing the value of *DTIME*. If the decremented value is not zero, then the *IF* statement is skipped and the decremented tick value is stored in *DTIME*. Finally, the *RTIF* flag is cleared by writing a 1 to bit 7 of *RTIFLG*.

If the decremented value of *DTIME* is equal to zero in the interrupt service routine, then the *IF* statement is executed. The *pfa* of *LIGHTS* (the address of the first byte in the table) and the value of the pointer to the next state, *ptr*, are put on the data stack in the first line following *IF*.

The pointer value, *ptr*, is then compared to the number of states (*cnt*) times 2 plus 1 which is the index value of the last byte in the table. If the pointer value (which later gets incremented by 2 for each state change) has exceeded the length of the table, then it gets reset to 2 in the inner *IF...THEN* statement.

The pointer value is then added to the address of *LIGHTS* (*pfa*) to produce the address of the byte to write to Port H. This byte is fetched and stored in Port H. The number of delay ticks is then fetched from the next address. The value of the pointer is then updated by adding 2 to the contents of *pfa*+1. Following the *THEN* statement, the current value of the delay ticks is stored in *DTIME*.

The word *INIT.TRAFFIC* sets the data direction register of Port H for all outputs, sets the RTI time-out rate to 32.768 ms, stores the interrupt vector, enables RTI interrupts, and initializes *DTIME* to 1.

Note that the main program in *MAIN.TRAFFIC* just disables interrupts, calls *INIT.TRAFFIC*, and then clears the interrupt mask to enable interrupts. At this point WHYP can go on and do other things with the traffic lights continually changing on their own. To turn the traffic lights off, you can execute the word *TURNOFF* in Listing 7–2. This word disables all interrupts and turns off all the LEDs by writing a 0 to Port H.

7.7   SUMMARY

In this chapter we have learned how to use parallel I/O ports to interface seven-segment displays, hex keypads, and LCD displays to 68HC12(11) microcontrollers. We also saw, using a traffic light example, how real-time interrupts can be used to

---

Box 7–4   WHYP Port Bit Set and Test Words

HI   (b# addr --)
         Set bit number *b#* of the byte at address *addr* to 1.

LO   (b# addr --)
         Clear bit number *b#* of the byte at address *addr* to 0.

?HI   (b# addr -- f)
         Leave a *true* flag on the data stack if bit number *b#* of the byte at address *addr* is high.

---

produce an arbitrary sequence of events on the parallel ports. We saw in Boxes 7–1 – 7–3 how to use the WHYP *CONSTANT* statement to define the names of the parallel I/O ports. We also introduced the WHYP words given in Box 7–4 for setting and testing individual bits in a byte.

Parallel I/O allows us to send and receive multiple bytes at a time. However, this can be expensive in terms of using up the available I/O pins. An alternative is to use a single pin and send the data one bit at a time. This is called serial I/O and we will look at the first of two types of serial I/O methods available on a 68HC12 in the next chapter.

EXERCISES

Exercise 7.1

Connect all eight bits of Port H (or some other parallel port) to eight LEDs (a bar LED is convenient) using the connection shown in Figure 7–4.

  a. Define a WHYP word called *ON (n --)* that will turn on LED number *n* (0–7).
  b. Define a WHYP word called *OFF (n --)* that will turn off LED number *n* (0–7).
  c. Define a WHYP word called *DLY (--)* that will delay about 0.25 seconds.
  d. Define a WHYP word called *ONOFF (n -- n+1)* that will turn off LED number *n*, turn on LED number *n*+1, and then delay about 0.25 seconds.
  e. Define a WHYP word called *8BLINK (--)* that will turn each LED on, in sequence, for 0.25 seconds. Use *ONOFF*.
  f. Define a WHYP word called *TEST1 (--)* that will call *8BLINK* five times.
  g. Define a WHYP word called *TEST2 (--)* that will toggle LEDs 3 and 4 on and off (with a 0.25-second delay) five times. When LED 3 is on, LED 4 is off, and vice versa.

Exercise 7.2

Using the MAN72 7-segment display shown in Figure 7–8 and the word *.led* given in - Figure 7–9.

  a. Write a WHYP word called *counter (--)* that will count from 0 to F on the seven-segment display with about a 0.25-second delay between counts. *Hint:* Use a *FOR ... NEXT* delay loop as described in Section 5.2.4.
  b. Write a WHYP word called *keep.counting (--)* that will continually count from 0 to F.
  c. Write a WHYP word called *count.down (--)* that will count down from F to 0 on the seven-segment display with a 0.25-second delay between counts.

d. Write a WHYP word called *bug (--)* that will cause a single segment of the seven-segment display to be lit for 0.25 seconds before another single segment is lit. Continually display the following segment sequence:

```
a b g e d c g f
```

Exercise 7.3

Using the word *.digit (dig# n --)* given in Figure 7–11,

    a. Write a WHYP word called *.hex (c --)* that will display the hex value of the byte *c* (00–FF) on the 2-digit seven-segment displays.

    b. Write a WHYP word called *count.up (--)* that will count up from 00 to FF on the 2-digit seven-segment displays with a 0.25-second delay between counts. *Hint:* Use a *FOR . . . NEXT* delay loop as described in Section 5.2.4.

Exercise 7.4

Using the MM72C922 setup shown in Figure 7–17 and the words given in Figure 7–18, write a WHYP word called *main.keypad2 (--)* that will display the hex value of the key pressed on seven-segment display shown in Figure 7–8.

Exercise 7.5

Write a subroutine called *query (--)* that will enter decimal digits (0–9) typed on the keypad and store them in a buffer called *buffin*. As each character is typed, it should be displayed on the LCD and the cursor should be advanced to the right. The key, *B*, should back up the cursor and erase the last digit displayed on the LCD. Exit the subroutine *query* when the *E* key is pressed.

Exercise 7.6

The Axiom CME12A4 Development Board has an LCD connector that allows you to connect an LCD display directly to the data bus. The LCD control register is at address $3F0 for a write (instruction) and at address $3F2 for a read (busy flag). The LCD data register is at address $3F1 for a data write and at address $3F3 for a data read.

    The Axiom CME12B32 Development board has a similar LCD connector. The LCD control register is at address $270 and the LCD data register is at address $271.

    a. Write the WHYP words *>instr (n --)* and *>data (n --)* that will write instructions and data, respectively, to one of these LCD displays.

    b. Write the WHYP words *init.lcd (--)*, *clear.lcd (--)*, and *hex>lcd (hex --)* corresponding to the same words in Listing 7–1 that will work with one of these LCD displays.

Exercise 7.7

The Axiom CME-11A8 is a single-board computer that uses the 68HC11A8 microcontroller. It has an LCD connector that allows you to connect an LCD display directly to the data bus. The LCD control register is at address $B5F0 and the LCD data register is at address $B5F1.

    a. Write the WHYP words *>instr (n --)* and *>data (n --)* that will write instructions and data, respectively, to this LCD display.

    b. Write WHYP words *init.lcd (--)*, *clear.lcd (--)*, and *hex>lcd (hex --)* corresponding to the same words in Listing 7–1 that will work with this LCD display.

Exercise 7.8

Modify the LCD setup for the program written in Exercise 7.5 such that new characters are always displayed in the rightmost position on the LCD display and displayed characters are shifted to the left as in a normal calculator.

Exercise 7.9

The Axiom CME-11A8 is a single-board computer that uses the 68HC11A8 microcontroller. It has a keypad connector that allows you to connect a 4 × 4 keypad of the type shown in Figure 7–12 to Ports D and E. The output rows (Axiom calls these the columns), *PJ3–PJ0*, in Figure 7–12 are connected to *PD5–PD2* of Port D. The input columns (Axiom calls these the rows), *PJ4–PJ7*, in Figure 7–12 are connected to *PE0–PE3*. Instead of the pull-up resistors shown in Figure 7–12 the Axiom keypad interface uses pull-down resistors. This means that open keys will read zero rather than one. Therefore, instead of writing a 0 to a given row, you would write a 1 with all other rows zero.

The keypad sold by Axiom has the keys C, D, E, and F, in Figure 7–12 labeled A, B, C, and D, respectively. Keys A and B in Figure 7–12 are labeled * and #, respectively.

Modify the program shown in Figure 7–14 such that the word *?keypad (-- ff | n tf)* will work with the Axiom keypad connected to the CME-11A8 single-board computer.

Exercise 7.10

The Axiom CME12A4 Development Board is a single-board computer that uses the 68HC812A4 microcontroller. It has a keypad connector that allows you to connect a 4 × 4 keypad of the type shown in Figure 7–12 to Port H. The output rows (Axiom calls these the columns), *PJ3–PJ0*, in Figure 7–12 are connected to *PH3–PH0* of Port H. The input columns (Axiom calls these the rows), *PJ4–PJ7*, in Figure 7–12 are connected to *PH4–PH7*. Open keys will read 1 in *PH4–PH7* as in Figure 7–12. Therefore, you will write a 0 to test a given row as was done in Figure 7–14.

The keypad sold by Axiom has the keys C, D, E, and F, in Figure 7–12 labeled A, B, C, and D, respectively. Keys A and B in Figure 7–12 are labeled * and #, respectively.

Modify the program shown in Figure 7–14 such that the word *?keypad (-- ff | n tf)* will work with the Axiom keypad connected to the CME12A4 Development Board.

Exercise 7.11

The Axiom CME12B32 Development Board is a single-board computer that uses the 68HC912B32 microcontroller. It has a keypad connector that allows you to connect a 4 × 4 keypad of the type shown in Figure 7–12 to Ports S and P. The output rows (Axiom calls these the columns), *PJ3–PJ0*, in Figure 7–12 are connected to *PS7–PS4* of Port S. The input columns (Axiom calls these the rows), *PJ4–PJ7*, in Figure 7–12 are connected to *PP4–PP7* of Port P. Open keys will read 1 in *PP4–PP7*, as in Figure 7–12. Therefore, you will write a 0 to test a given row as was done in Figure 7–14.

The keypad sold by Axiom has the keys C, D, E, and F, in Figure 7–12 labeled A, B, C, and D, respectively. Keys A and B in Figure 7–12 are labeled * and #, respectively.

Modify the program shown in Figure 7–14 such that the word *?keypad (-- ff | n tf)* will work with the Axiom keypad connected to the CME12B32 Development Board.

Exercise 7.12

Interface a keypad using the MM74C922 16-key encoder shown in Figure 7–17 to a 68HC11 microcontroller (see Section 7.1.3). Connect the four DATA OUT A–D lines to *PC0–PC3* and connect the DATA AV pin to *STRA* on the 68HC11. Modify the WHYP words given in Figure 7–18 for this new configuration.

Exercise 7.13

Write a program using interrupts that will cause the "bug" sequence on a seven-segment display described in Exercise 7.2(d) to be displayed continually in the background.

Exercise 7.14

Write a program using interrupts that will interface the keypad shown in Figure 7–19 to a 68HC12. Use the IRQ interrupt by connecting the common side of the switches to pin *PE1*. Use pins from Port J for the inputs to the 74154.

8

The Serial Peripheral Interface (SPI)

Two different methods of serial communications are available on 68HC12 (and 68HC11) microcontrollers. The first is the Serial Peripheral Interface (SPI) that will be described in this chapter. The second is the Serial Communications Interface (SCI) that will be covered in Chapter 11. The SPI is a synchronous serial interface in which a clock signal is sent along with the data signal. The SCI is an asynchronous serial interface that uses start and stop bits to synchronize each transmitted character.

In this chapter we will look at the 68HC12 and 68HC11 registers used to program the SPI and then describe its use by means of several examples. A method of reading a keypad using the SPI with a pair of 74164 shift registers will be described in Section 8.2. The MC144499 Four-Digit Seven-Segment Display Driver can control four separate seven-segment displays using the SPI as described in Section 8.3. The 68HC11E9 EVBU contains the MC68HC68T1 Real-Time Clock on the board. This chip has a serial interface that is connected to the SPI port on the 68HC11. We will describe the operation of this chip in Section 8.4. Several other chips that have SPI interfaces are described in the exercises at the end of the chapter. These include a D/A converter, EEPROMs, a digital potentiometer, and a voice record/playback ChipCorder.

8.1 OPERATION OF THE SPI

The SPI is a synchronous serial interface in which data in an 8-bit byte can be shifted in and/or out one bit at a time. It can be used to communicate with a serial peripheral device or with another microcontroller with an SPI interface. The SPI system in the 68HC12 contains the four signals shown in Table 8–1. The system can operate in either a master or slave mode. When communicating with a peripheral device, the 68HC12 SPI will operate as the master. When one 68HC12 (the master) is connected to a second 68HC12 (the slave), the four SPI signals will be connected as shown in Figure 8–1.

In the master, the bits are sent out of the *MOSI* (master-out-slave-in) pin and received in the *MISO* (master-in-slave-out) pin. In the slave the bits are received in the *MOSI* (master-out-slave-in) pin and sent out the *MISO* (master-in-slave-out) pin. The bits to be shifted out are stored in the SPI data register, *SP0DR*, and are sent out most significant bit (bit 7) first, as shown in Figure 8–1. (In the 68HC12 the bits can be sent out least significant bit first by setting the *LSBF* bit in the SPI Control Register 1 as described below.) At the same time that bit 7 is being shifted out, the *MOSI* pin in the master a bit from bit 7 of the slave is being shifted into bit 0 of the master via the *MISO* pin. This bit will eventually end up in bit 7 of the master after eight clock pulses or shifts. The clock, which controls how fast the bits are shifted out of and into *SP0DR*, is the signal *SCK* at *PS6*. The frequency of this clock can be controlled by the SPI baud rate register, *SP0BR*, as will be described below. The SS (slave-select) pin must be low to select a slave. This signal can come from any pin on the master, including its *SS* pin when it is configured as an output.

The SPI can be used to communicate with a peripheral device that has an interface in the form of a shift register. This could be another 68HC12 or 68HC11

Table 8–1 68HC12 SPI Signals

Pin	SPI signal	Name
PS4	MISO	Master-In-Slave-Out
PS5	MOSI	Master-Out-Slave-In
PS6	SCK	Serial Clock
PS7	SS	Slave Select

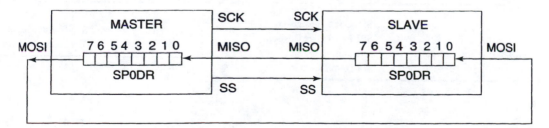

Figure 8–1 Two SPI Modules Connected in a Master-Slave Configuration

SPI port, as shown in Figure 8–1, or a peripheral device designed to receive and/or transmit this type of data. Such devices include the MC144499 4-Digit Seven-Segment Display Driver, the 74165 shift register, and the MC68HC68T1 Real-Time Clock, all of which will be described in detail in this chapter. We will first look at how to program the SPI registers to perform serial data transfers.

8.1.1 The SPI Registers

The registers associated with the SPI are shown in Table 8–2 for the 68HC12 and in Table 8–3 for the 68HC11. Note that the 68HC12 has added a second control register and a separate baud rate register. An SPI transmission (and/or reception) is always initiated by the master (in our case the 68HC12 or 68HC11 we are programming). The peripheral device (which could be another 68HC12/11) is called the slave.

The master initiates a transfer by storing a byte in the SPI data register. The bits are shifted out of *SP0DR* most significant bit (bit 7) first and received in the least significant bit (bit 0), as shown in Figure 8–1.

The clock which controls how fast the bits are shifted out of and into *SP0DR* is the serial clock, *SCK*. The frequency of this clock can be controlled by the SPI baud rate register, *SP0BR*, shown in Figure 8–2. Eight different frequencies can be selected with bits *SPR2:SPR0*, as indicated in Table 8–4. The 68HC11 does not have an SPI baud rate register. Rather it uses two bits, *SPR1:SPR0*, in its SPI control register to select the clock frequency. With only two bits, you can select only the four frequencies shown in Table 8–5.

The SPI Control Register 1, *SP0CR1*, is shown in Figure 8–3. The two bits *CPOL* and *CPHA* control the polarity and phase of the clock. If *CPOL* = 0, the clock idles low and data are shifted in and out on the rising edge of the clock if *CPHA* = 0 and on the falling edge of the clock if *CPHA* = 1. If *CPOL* = 1, the clock idles high and data are shifted in and out on the falling edge of the clock if *CPHA* = 0 and on the rising edge of the clock if *CPHA* = 1. If *CPHA* = 1, the *SS* slave select line can remain low during successive transfers. On the other hand, if *CPHA* = 0 the *SS* line must be deasserted and reasserted between each successive byte of data transferred.

Table 8–2 SPI Registers in the 68HC12

Name	Register Addr	Description
SP0CR1	00D0	SPI Control Register 1
SP0CR2	00D1	SPI Control Register 2
SP0BR	00D2	SPI Baud Rate Register
SP0SR	00D3	SPI Status Register
SP0DR	00D5	SPI Data Register

Table 8–3 SPI Registers in the 68HC11

Name	Register Addr	Description
SPCR	1028	SPI Control Register
SPSR	1029	SPI Status Register
SPDR	102A	SPI Data Register

	7	6	5	4	3	2	1	0	
$00D2	0	0	0	0	0	SPR2	SPR1	SPR0	SP0BR

Figure 8–2 SPI Baud Rate Register

Table 8–4   68HC12 SPI Clock Rate Selection

SPR[2:0]	Divide E Clock by	Frequency ($E = 8$ MHz)
0 0 0	2	4.0 MHz
0 0 1	4	2.0 MHz
0 1 0	8	1.0 MHz
0 1 1	16	500 kHz
1 0 0	32	250 kHz
1 0 1	64	125 kHz
1 1 0	128	62.5 kHz
1 1 1	256	31.3 kHz

Table 8–5   68HC11 SPI Clock Rate Selection

SPR[1:0]	Divide E Clock by	Frequency ($E = 2$ MHz)
0 0	2	1.0 MHz
0 1	4	500 kHz
1 0	16	125 kHz
1 1	32	62.5 kHz

	7	6	5	4	3	2	1	0	
$00D0	SPIE	SPE	SWOM	MSTR	CPOL	CPHA	SSOE	LSBF	SP0CR1

SPIE: Serial Peripheral Interrupt Enable
            0 – SPI interrupts disabled
            1 – SPI interrupts enabled

SPE: Serial Peripheral System Enable
            0 – SPI disabled
            1 – SPI enabled

SWOM: Port S Wired-OR Mode (affects PS[4:7] pins)
            0 – Normal CMOS outputs
            1 – Open-drain outputs

MSTR: Master/Slave Mode Select
            0 – Slave mode
            1 – Master mode

CPOL: Clock Polarity
            0 – SCK pin idles low (data not being transferred)
            1 – SCK pin idles high (data not being transferred)

CPHA: Clock Phase
            0 – SS line must be deasserted and reasserted between each successive byte
            1 – SS line may remain active low between successive byte transfers

SSOE: Slave Select Output Enable (master mode only)
            0 – General-purpose output if DDRS7 = 1
            1 – SS output mode if DDRS7 = 1

LSBF: Least-Significant Bit Enable
            0 – Data transferred most-significant bit first
            1 – Data transferred least-significant bit first

Figure 8–3   SPI Control Register 1

	7	6	5	4	3	2	1	0	
$00D3	SPIF	WCOL	0	MODF	0	0	0	0	SP0SR

SPIF: SPI Transfer Complete Flag
0 – Cleared by SP0SR read with SPIF set, followed by SP0DR access
1 – set upon completion of data transfer between processor and external device

WCOL: Write Collision
0 – No write collision
1 – Write collision

MODF: Mode Fault
0 – No mode fault
1 – Mode fault

Figure 8–4   SPI Status Register

To use the SPI, the *SPE* bit in the control register *SP0CR1* must be set to 1 and to use the SPI as the master the *MSTR* bit must be set to 1. Setting the *SPIE* bit will enable interrupts which will cause a hardware interrupt to occur when a byte data transfer has been completed.

When the eight bits have been completely shifted out of (and/or into) the *SP0DR*, the *SPIF* flag (bit 7) in the SPI status register, *SP0SR*, shown in Figure 8–4, is set to 1. This bit is cleared by reading the status register, *SP0SR*, followed by accessing the data register, *SP0DR*.

The SPI control register in the 68HC11, *SPCR*, is the same as the 68HC12 register, *SP0CR1*, shown in Figure 8–3, except that bits 0 and 1 contain the two baud rate select bits, *SPR1* and *SPR0*, given in Table 8–5. The bits *SSOE* and *LSBF* in Figure 8–3 are available only in the 68HC12. The *SSOE* bit can enable an *SS* output mode in a master in which the *SS* output automatically goes low during each SPI

	7	6	5	4	3	2	1	0	
$00D1	0	0	0	0	PUPS	RDS	0	SPC0	SP0CR2

PUPS: Pull-Up Port S Enable
0 – No internal pull-ups on port S
1 – All port S input pins have an active pull-up device

RDS: Reduce Drive of Port S
0 – Normal port S output drivers
1 – Reduced drive capability on all port S outputs for lower power and less noise

SPC0:   Serial Pin Control 0
0 – Normal operation
1 – Bidirectional mode

Figure 8–5   SPI Control Register 2

transmission and then goes high during each idling state so that external devices are deselected. If the *LSBF* bit is set, then data are transferred least significant bit first rather than the more normal most significant bit first.

The SPI status register in the 68HC11, *SPSR*, is the same as the 68HC12 SPI status register shown in Figure 8–4. The 68HC12 SPI Control Register 2, for which there is no counterpart in the 68HC11, is shown in Figure 8–5. There are three bits in this control register that enable internal pull-ups on port S inputs, reduce the drive capability on port S outputs, and enable a bidirectional mode. In the bidirectional mode a single pin (*MOSI* for a master and *MISO* for a slave) can be used for both input and output.

8.1.2 Programming the SPI in WHYP

Basic WHYP words for programming the SPI port are given in the file SPI.WHP, shown in Figure 8–6. (A similar file called SPI11.WHP contains the same words for

```
\        Serial Peripheral Interface
HEX
00D0   CONSTANT    SP0CR1            \ SPI Control Register
00D2   CONSTANT    SP0BR             \ SPI Baud Rate Register
00D3   CONSTANT    SP0SR             \ SPI Status Register
00D5   CONSTANT    SP0DR             \ SPI Data Register

: SPI.INIT     ( -- )               \ Initialize SPI port
               40 PORTS C!          \ SS lo, sclk lo, MOSI hi
               E2 DDRS C!           \ SS lo when DDRS7 set
               04 SP0BR C!          \ 250 KHz (/32)
               54 SPCR C! ;         \ CPHA = 1, CPO; = 0

: ?SPI.DONE    ( -- f )             \ Is SPI data sent?
               7 SP0SR ?HI ;

: SEND.SPI     ( c -- )
               SP0DR C!             \ send char
               BEGIN
                   ?SPI.DONE        \ wait till sent
               UNTIL ;

: SS.HI        ( -- )               \ set SS high
               7 PORTS HI ;

: SS.LO        ( -- )               \ set SS low
               7 PORTS LO ;
```

Figure 8–6 Basic WHYP SPI Words in File SPI.WHP

the 68HC711E9 or 68HC11A8.) The word *SPI.INIT* will initialize the SPI port as a master and set the clock rate to $E/32$, where E is the frequency of the 68HC12 clock. If $E = 8$ MHz, then $E/32$ will be 250 KHz. Notice that the data direction register for Port S must set *PS5* (*MOSI*), *PS6* (*SCK*), and *PS7* (*SS*) as outputs.

The WHYP word *?SPI.DONE (-- f)* returns a true flag when bit 7 of the SPI status register, *SP0SR*, is set to 1, that is, when a byte transfer is complete. The WHYP word *SEND.SPI (c --)* will send a byte out the *MOSI* pin and wait for the transfer to be complete. Finally, the words *SS.HI* and *SS.LO* set the *SS* pin (*PS7*) high and low.

To send a byte of data out the SPI *MOSI* pin, you just need to put the byte on the data stack and then execute the WHYP word *SEND.SPI*, shown in Figure 8–6. Note that when you execute *SEND.SPI*, a new byte will come into the SPI data register, *SP0DR*, from *PS4* (*MISO*). This may or may not be meaningful data depending on whether *PS4* is connected to some peripheral. Similarly, the byte you send out the *MOSI* pin may or may not be meaningful depending on whether *PS5* is connected to some peripheral. We will give several examples of using the SPI in various configurations in the following sections.

8.2   KEYPAD INTERFACING WITH 74165 SHIFT REGISTERS

Keypad interfacing was described in Section 7.4. The basic WHYP word developed was *?keypad (-- ff | n tf)* which checked to see if a key was being pressed and returned a false flag if no key was being pressed and returned a true flag over the hex key value if a key was being pressed. A version of this word for a 4 × 4 keypad was given in Figure 7–14 and a version for a 16 × 1 keypad was given in Figure 7–20. The 16 × 1 keypad was interfaced with a 74154 decoder chip as shown in Figure 7–19. This used the lower nibble of Port B in a 68HC11. In this section we will show how the SPI can be used to read this same 16 × 1 hex keypad by using 74165 shift registers.

A 16 × 1 hex keypad (or any collection of 16 switches) can be connected to two 74165 shift registers, as shown in Figure 8–7. In this case one side of each switch is connected to ground. The 74165 is an 8-bit parallel in/serial out shift register. The other side of each switch is connected to one of the parallel inputs (*A–H*) of the shift register. If pin 1 (*SH/$\overline{L}$ D*) of the 74165 is brought low, the values on the eight parallel inputs are latched into the shift register. When the *SH/$\overline{L}$ D* pin is high and the *CLK INH* pin is low, then on the rising edge of the *CLK* input the eight bits in the shift register are shifted one bit to the right. Bit *A* is shifted to *B*, *B* to *C*, and so on. Bit *G* is shifted to *H* which shows up on the serial output pin, Q_H. In Figure 8–7 the output Q_H of the lower 74165 is connected to the serial input pin, *SER*, of the upper 74165. The output Q_H of the upper 74165 is connected to the *MISO* pin of the *SPI* port in the 68HC12 (or 68HC11).

In Figure 8–7 the SPI signal *SCK* is connected to each *CLK* pin of the two 74165 chips and the SPI signal *SS* is connected to each *SH/$\overline{L}$ D* pin of the two 74165 chips. Note that the *MOSI* pin of the SPI port is not connected to anything. We are only interested in receiving bytes in the *MISO* pin. To do this, of course, we must

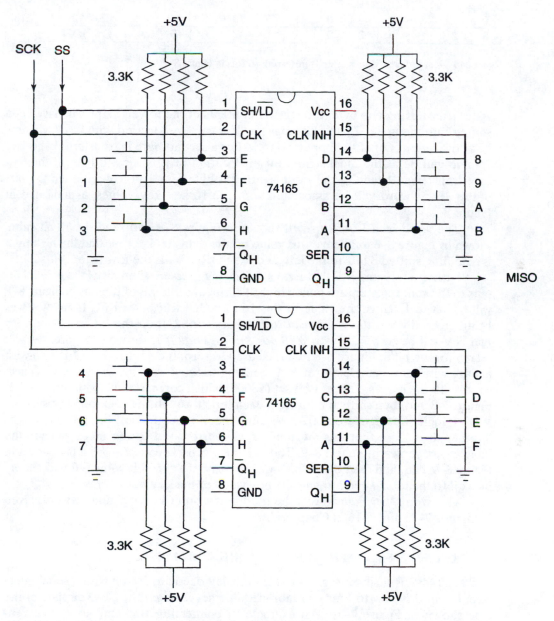

Figure 8–7   Connecting a 16 × 1 Hex Keypad to Two 74165 Shift Registers

write a dummy value (say zero) to the SPI data register, *SP0DR*, and it will be shifted out the unconnected *MOSI* pin at the same time that the desired byte is being shifted in the *MISO* pin.

Notice in Figure 8–7 that pin *H* of the upper 74165 (key 3) will be the first bit shifted out. This will end up in the most significant bit of the first byte transferred.

0	1	2	3	4	5	6	7	8	9	10	11	12	12	14	15
3	2	1	0	8	9	A	B	7	6	5	4	C	D	E	F

Figure 8–8   Keypad Hex Values after Transferring 16 Bits in Figure 8–7

After transferring one byte, the register contents of the lower 74165 will have been shifted into the upper 74165 shift register. The value associated with key 7 will now be at the output Q_H of the upper 74165. After a second byte is transferred, this key 7 value will be at the most significant bit location of this second byte. If the first byte transferred becomes the most significant byte of a 16-bit word, then the bits of this 16-bit word will be associated with the 16 hex key values, as indicated in Figure 8–8.

The word *read.16shift (-- n)*, shown in Figure 8–9 will read the 16-bit value shown in Figure 8–8 and leave this value on the data stack. Note that the high byte is read first, shifted 8 bits to the left, and then ORed with the low byte.

Note from Figure 8–7 that if no key is being pressed, then all of the parallel inputs to the shift registers are pulled high. This means that all of the bits in Figure 8–8 will be set to 1. Thus, the value of this 16-bit value will be $FFFF. If any key was being pressed when the word *read.16shift* is executed, then the bit associated with that key will be zero. The word *?bit.pos (n -- ff | bit# tf)*, shown in Figure 8–9, will search for the bit in Figure 8–8 that is cleared to zero. It does this by ANDing n with a mask with only a single bit set and checking to see if that bit was zero. The mask starts with the most significant bit set ($8000) which corresponds to bit number 0 in Figure 8–8 and then shifts the bit right each time through the DO loop by using the WHYP logic shift right word *U2/*. We label the most significant bit in Figure 8–8 as 0 rather than 15 so that this bit number will correspond to the index value in the table *keytbl* shown in Figure 8–9. The WHYP word *?keypad (-- ff | n tf)*, shown in Figure 8–9, can then read the 16-bit value of n and if a zero bit value is found, simply index into the table *keytbl* to find the hex value of the key being pressed.

This word *?keypad* can then be used in the other keypad-related words given in Figures 7–15 and 7–16 in Chapter 7.

8.3   FOUR-DIGIT SEVEN-SEGMENT DISPLAY USING A MC14499

The MC14499 is a seven-segment LED display decoder/driver with a serial interface. It can drive up to four common-cathode seven-segment LED displays of the type shown in Figure 7–10. An example of connecting this chip to three seven-segment displays (#2, #3, and #4) is shown in Figure 8–10. A fourth display (#1) could be added by connecting the base of its common-cathode select transistor to pin 11 of the MC14499.

The digits are displayed by sending a 4-bit code for each digit. The hex codes $0–$9 will display the decimal digits 0–9 as expected. However, only the hex code $A will, in fact, display its hex value A. The hex code $F displays a blank and the hex code $E displays a dash. The other hex codes, $B–$D, display a vertical line,

```
\          Hex keypad decoding using 74165 chips and SPI

LOAD SPI.WHP
HEX

: spi.key.init  ( -- )
                SPI.INIT
                SS.HI ;                   \ shift mode

: read.16shift  ( -- n )
                SS.LO                     \ latch data
                SS.HI
                0 SEND.SPI                \ get high byte
                SP0DR C@
                8 LSHIFT
                0 SEND.SPI                \ get low byte
                SP0DR C@ OR ;

: ?bit.pos      ( n -- ff | bit# tf )
                0 SWAP                    \ ff n
                8000                      \ ff n mask
                10 0 DO                   \ loop 16 times
                   2DUP AND               \ ff n m n'
                   0=
                   IF                     \ ff n m
                      DROP I TRUE         \ ff n b# tf
                      2SWAP LEAVE         \ b# tf ff n
                   THEN
                   U2/                    \ ff n m'
                LOOP
                2DROP ;

CREATE keytbl
                3 C, 2 C, 1 C, 0 C,
                8 C, 9 C, A C, B C,
                7 C, 6 C, 5 C, 4 C,
                C C, D C, E C, F C,

: ?keypad       ( -- ff | n tf )
                read.16shift
                ?bit.pos
                IF
                   keytbl + C@
                   TRUE
                ELSE
                   FALSE
                THEN ;
```

Figure 8–9 Scanning a 16 × 1 Keypad Using the SPI

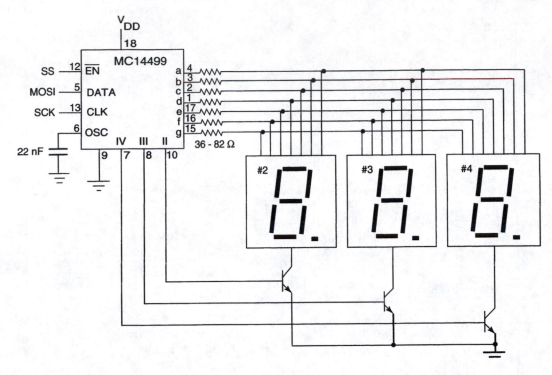

Figure 8–10   Connecting the MC14499 to Three Common-Cathode Seven-Segment Displays

two vertical lines, and a U, respectively. Therefore, the three-digit display shown in Figure 8–10 would be useful for displaying decimal values between 000 and 999.

The four 4-bit codes are sent serially from the *MOSI* pin of the SPI port to the *DATA* pin of the MC14499. They are sent as two bytes (most significant bit first) with the code for digit #1 sent first and the code for digit #4 sent last. Thus, for example, to display the number 345 in Figure 8–10, we would send the 16-bit value 1111001101000101. The first nibble, 1111, would display a blank on digit #1 if it were connected.

The *SCK* pin on the SPI port is connected to the *CLK* pin on the MC14499. The *EN* signal (pin 12) on the MC14499 is connected to the *SS* pin on the SPI port. This signal must be low to shift data into the MC14499. When this signal is brought high, the 16-bit data that were shifted in are loaded into a latch. At this point the digits are displayed as the digit codes are multiplexed into a segment decoder that drives the seven-segment outputs. Each digit is turned on in sequence (controlled by an internal oscillator) by turning on the transistor connected to its common-cathode pin. Although only a single digit is really on at one time, they all appear to be on because they are refreshed fast enough (> 60 Hz) so that your eye integrates the display over time. Each digit is on one-fourth of the time. The MC14499 does all of this work for you. All you have to do is send it the 16-bit value representing the four digit codes.

The WHYP word *.4leds (n--)*, shown in Figure 8–11, will display the 16-bit number *n* as a four-digit decimal number (0000–9999) on up to four seven-segment LEDs. If the number is less than four digits, leading blanks will be displayed. Suppose the number *n* is the decimal number 345. As described above, we need to send two bytes to the MC14499. The first byte will contain the eight bits 11110011 (a blank and a 3) and the second byte will contain the eight bits 01000101 (a 4 and a 5). The first problem is to convert the decimal number 345 (which will be stored in the computer as the hex value $159) to these two digit-code bytes.

The file STRING.WHP that is loaded at the beginning of Figure 8–11 includes a WHYP word called "paren-U." *(U.) (u -- addr len)* that converts an unsigned 16-bit number to an ASCII string and leaves the address and length of the string on the data stack. The details of how this word works are described in Chapter 12. For now, we can just use the word. If you load the file STRING.WHP and type

```
345 (U.)
```

the number 345 will be converted to the three-character ASCII string shown in Figure 8–12 and the address, *A*, and length 3 will be left on the data stack.

The *FOR . . . NEXT* loop in the word *.4leds* in Figure 8–11 will store as many leading blanks ($0F) as necessary (0 to 3) so as to produce a four-byte string. For the

```
\       4 LEDs Using the MC14499 Decoder/Driver with Serial Interface
\       File: SPILED.WHP


LOAD SPI.WHP
LOAD STRING.WHP
DECIMAL


: pack2          ( addr -- c )
                 DUP C@
                 4 LSHIFT              \ addr c1
                 SWAP 1+ C@            \ c1 c2
                 15 AND OR ;


: .4leds         ( n -- )
                 SS.LO
                 10 BASE !
                 (U.) 4 SWAP -         \ addr #blanks
                 FOR                   \ addr
                    1- 15 OVER C!      \ store F for blank
                 NEXT
                 DUP pack2 SEND.SPI    \ 1st digit
                 2+ pack2 SEND.SPI     \ 2nd and 3rd digit
                 SS.HI ;
```

Figure 8–11   Displaying Four Seven-Segment LEDs Using the MC14499

A | 33 | '3'
34 | '4'
35 | '5'

A | 0F | blank
33 | '3'
34 | '4'
35 | '5'

Figure 8–12 Bytes Created by Typing *345 (U.)*

Figure 8–13 Character String (Lower Nibble) to Send to the MC14499

number 345, the three bytes shown in Figure 8–12 will be transformed to the four bytes shown in Figure 8–13 at the end of the *FOR . . . NEXT* loop and the address, *A*, will be on top of the stack.

We now want to send the four lower nibbles in Figure 8–13 to the MC14499. The word *pack2 (addr -- c)*, shown in Figure 8–11, will pack the lower nibbles of the two bytes starting at address *addr* into a single byte and leave this byte on the data stack. For example, if the address *A* in Figure 8–13 is on the stack, then *pack2* will produce the byte $F3. If the address A+2 is on the stack, then *pack2* will produce the byte $45. These two bytes are sent to the MC14499 by the two *SEND.SPI* words in the word *.4leds* in Figure 8–11. Note that when the word *SS.HI* at the end of *.4leds* is executed, the three-digit number 345 will be displayed.

The setup shown in Figure 8–10 will be used in Chapter 9 to display the degrees (0–360) of a digital compass.

8.4   THE 68HC68T1 REAL-TIME CLOCK

The MC68HC68T1 Real-Time Clock plus RAM is a 16-pin chip that is mounted on the M68HC11EVBU board. It has *MOSI, MISO, SCK*, and *SS* pins that are designed to interface directly to the corresponding SPI pins on a 68HC11 (or 68HC12). The chip contains a clock/calendar and a 32-byte general-purpose RAM. The address map is shown in Figure 8–14 and the Clock/RAM registers are shown in Figure 8–15. Although this chip can be connected to any SPI port, we will describe its operation as it exists on the M68HC11EVBU board.

The details of the clock control register are shown in Figure 8–16. The clock crystal on the EVBU board is a 32.768 KHz crystal so that bits 4 and 5 of *T1CCR* must both be set to 1. Also the *START* bit must be set to 1 to start the clock. Therefore, writing a $B0 to *T1CCR* (address $B1) will start the clock. The WHYP word *T1.INIT* in Figure 8–17 will do this.

The WHYP word *!T1(data addr --)*, shown in Figure 8–17, will store the byte *data* at the T1 address *addr*. This is done by first bringing *SS* high, then sending the address followed by sending the byte of data, and finally bringing *SS* low. Note that the *SPIF* bit is cleared by doing a dummy read of *SPDR* (the SPI status register, *SPSR*, was read in the word *SEND.SPI*).

The WHYP word *@T1 (addr -- byte)* will read a byte of data from the T1 address *addr*. Note that it does this by first sending the address and then sending a

	HEXADECIMAL				HEXADECIMAL
	$00		SECONDS		$20
32 BYTES GENERAL-PURPOSE USER			MINUTES		$21
	T		HOURS		$22
	H		DAY OF THE WEEK		$23
RAM	R		DATE OF THE MONTH		$24
	U		MONTH		$25
READ ADDRESSES ONLY			YEAR		$26
	$1F				
	$20		NOT USED		$27
			NOT USED		$28
			NOT USED		$29
			NOT USED		$2A
	T		NOT USED		$2B
	H		NOT USED		$2C
CLOCK/CALENDAR	R		NOT USED		$2D
	U		NOT USED		$2E
READ ADDRESSES ONLY			NOT USED		$2F
			STATUS REGISTER		$30
			CLOCK CONTROL REGISTER		$31
	$32		INTERRUPT CONTROL REGISTER		$32

					HEXADECIMAL
	$33				
	T				
	H		SECONDS		$A0
NOT USED	R		MINUTES		$A1
	U		HOURS		$A2
	$7F		DAY OF THE WEEK		$A3
	$80		DATE OF THE MONTH		$A4
32 BYTES GENERAL-PURPOSE USER	T		MONTH		$A5
	H		YEAR		$A6
RAM	R		NOT USED		$A7
	U		SECONDS ALARM		$A8
WRITE ADDRESSES ONLY	$9F		MINUTES ALARM		$A9
	$A0		HOURS ALARM		$AA
			NOT USED		$AB
	T		NOT USED		$AC
	H		NOT USED		$AD
CLOCK/CALENDAR	R		NOT USED		$AE
	U		NOT USED		$AF
WRITE ADDRESSES ONLY			NOT USED		$B0
			CLOCK CONTROL REGISTER		$B1
	$B2		INTERRUPT CONTROL REGISTER		$B2

Figure 8–14   MC68HC68T1 Address Map

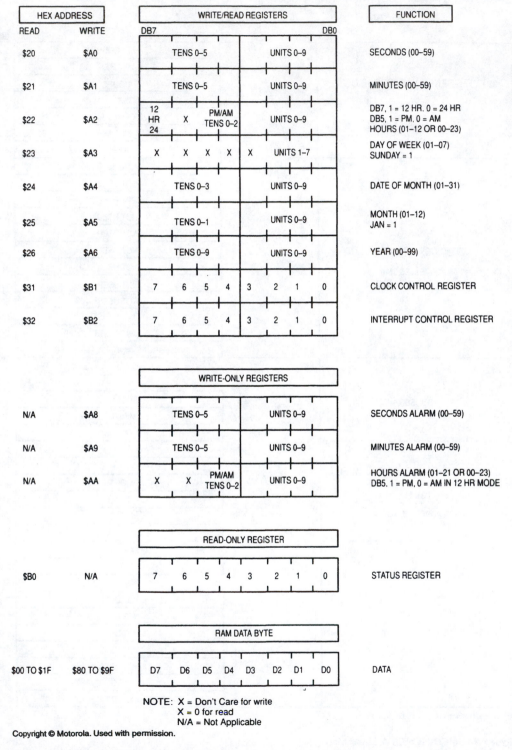

Figure 8–15   MC68HC68T1 Clock/RAM registers

	7	6	5	4	3	2	1	0	
$B1	START	LINE	XTAL1	XTAL0	50HZ	CLK2	CLK1	CLK0	T1CCR

START: Start/Stop bit
           0 – Stop clock
           1 – Start clock

LINE: LINE/XTAL
           0 – XTAL$_{in}$ pin is source of time update
           1 – clock uses 50/60 Hz LINE input

XTAL1, XTAL0:   Crystals Selects

XTAL[1:0]	Crystal Frequency
0 0	7.194304 MHz
0 1	2.097152 MHz
1 0	1.048576 MHz
1 1	32.768 kHz

50HZ: Input LINE frequency
           0 – 60 Hz
           1 – 50 Hz

CLK[2:0]: Square-wave frequency output selects
           0 – XTAL frequency

Figure 8–16 The MC68HC68T1 Clock Control Register

dummy value of zero which will cause the byte from the T1 chip to be sent into the *MISO* pin of the SPI port. This byte is then read from the SPI data register, *SPDR*, using *C@*.

Note from Figures 8–14 and 8–15 that seconds, minutes, and hours are stored as BCD numbers in addresses $A0, $A1, and $A2, respectively. These are write-only addresses. The same bytes are read from addresses $20, $21, and $22. The WHYP word *SET.TIME (hr min sec --)* will store a particular time in the clock. Since these are BCD numbers, you must actually give hex values for hours, minutes, and seconds. For example, to set the time to 10:35:42, you would type

```
HEX
10 35 42 SET.TIME
```

Similarly, the WHYP word *.TIME (--)* will print the time on the screen. Again you must be in HEX to display the proper time.

The words shown in Figure 8–17 are included in the file T1.WHP. If you have a M68HC11EVBU evaluation board running WHYP (see Appendix C), you can test these words by typing

```
\          MC68HC68T1 Real-Time Clock plus RAM
LOAD SPI11.WHP
HEX

: !T1          ( data addr -- )
               SS.HI
               SEND.SPI                \ send addr
               SEND.SPI                \ send data
               SS.LO
               SPDR C@ DROP ;          \ clear SPIF


: T1.INIT      ( -- )
               B0 B1 !T1 ;             \ start clock


: @T1          ( addr -- byte )
               SS.HI
               SEND.SPI                \ send addr
               0 SEND.SPI              \ send dummy byte to get data
               SS.LO
               SPDR C@ ;               \ clear SPIF and get byte


: SET.TIME     ( hr min sec -- )
               A0 !T1 A1 !T1 A2 !T1 ;


: .TIME        ( -- )
               20 @T1 21 @T1 22 @T1 . . . ;
```

Figure 8–17 WHYP Words for the MC68HC68T1 Real-Time Clock

```
LOAD T1.WHP
HEX
SPI.INIT
T1.INIT
10 35 42 SET.TIME
.TIME
```

Similar words could be written to set and read the date (see Exercise 8.1).

8.5 SUMMARY

This chapter has described the operation of the Serial Peripheral Interface (SPI) that is a standard module on all 68HC11 and 68HC12 microcontrollers. We developed some basic WHYP words for accessing the SPI port. These words are included in the files SPI.WHP (for the 68HC12) and SPI11.WHP (for the 68HC11) and are summarized in Box 8–1.

Several examples of using the SPI port were presented in this chapter. These included a method of reading a keypad using the SPI with a pair of 74164 shift registers in Section 8.2, interfacing to the MC144499 Four-Digit Seven-Segment

---

Box 8–1   WHYP SPI Words—File: SPI.WHP

```
SPI.INIT        ( -- )
                Initializes the SPI port with a clock rate of E/32.
SS.HI           ( -- )
                Sets the SS line (PS7) high.
SS.LO           ( -- )
                Sets the SS line (PS7) low.
SEND.SPI        ( c -- )
                Sends the 8-bit byte, c, out the MOSI (PS5) pin.
```

Display Driver in Section 8.3, and interfacing to the MC68HC68T1 Real-Time Clock in Section 8.4. For additional applications, see the exercises at the end of this chapter.

The other method of serial communications on a 68HC12, the SCI port, will be described in Chapter 11. In the next chapter we will see how analog voltages can be measured on the 68HC12 (and 68HC11).

EXERCISES

Exercise 8.1

a. Define a WHYP word called *SET.DATE (mo day yr --)* that will set the date in the MC68HC68T1 Real-Time Clock plus RAM with serial interface. For example,

```
HEX
2 19 98 SET.DATE
```

will set the date of Feb. 19, 1998.

b. Define a WHYP word called *.DATE (--)* that will print the date stored in the MC68HC68T1 Real-Time Clock plus RAM with serial interface in the format *mo day yr*. For example,

```
HEX
.DATE
```

would print

```
2 19 98
```

Exercise 8.2

The MAX7219/MAX7221 from MAXIM are serial interfaced LED display drivers that are similar to the MC14499 shown in Figure 8–10 except that they can drive up to eight common-cathode seven-segment LED displays. The data sheet can be found on http://www.maxim-ic.com. Write WHYP words that can be used to display a 16-bit integer as a decimal number between 0 and 65535 on five seven-segment displays using the MAX7219/MAX7221 chip.

Exercise 8.3

The Motorola MC144110 is a digital-to-analog converter with serial interface. A simplified block diagram is shown below. The full data sheet can be downloaded from `http://mot2.mot-sps.com/cgi-bin/dlsrch`. The MC144110 actually contains six D/A converters with separate *Rx OUT* and *Qx OUT* pins. However, only the outputs from the first D/A converter are shown in the diagram. The *R1 OUT* pin is a direct output that can be fed to a high-impedance input. The *Q1 OUT* pin is a buffered output (using an emitter-follower) that can feed low-impedance circuits.

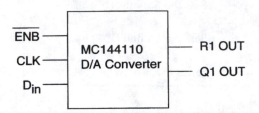

You can interface the MC144110 to a 68HC12 SPI port by connecting the SPI *SS* signal to the *ENB* pin, the *SCK* signal to the *CLK* pin, and the *MOSI* pin to the D_{in} pin. When *ENB* is low, 6-bit data are shifted into D_{in}, MSB first. The last byte shifted in determines the output *R1 OUT* and *Q1 OUT*. Therefore, to use only this single output, input a single byte with the 6 bits in the 6 high bits of the byte. Each bit is latched on the falling edge of the clock that can idle either high or low.

a. Write a WHYP word called *INIT.D/A* (--) that will initialize the SPI port for interfacing to the MC144110.

b. Write a WHYP word called *DACONV* (n --) that will output an analog voltage on *R1 OUT* and *Q1 OUT* proportional to the lower 6 bits of n (0–63).

c. Write a WHYP word called *6DACONV* (n1 n2 n3 n4 n5 n6 --) that will output an analog voltage on all six D/A outputs with *n1* output on *R1 OUT* and *n6* output on *R6 OUT*. Note that a total of 36 bits must be shifted in with *n1* shifted in last. These 36 bits must be packed into 4.5 bytes.

Exercise 8.4

Using the sine table, *SINTBL*, given the file `SINE.WHP` (see Figure 5–33), write a WHYP word called *sinewave* (--) that will produce a 60-Hz sine wave using the MC144110 D/A converter described in Exercise 8.3. Factor the problem by writing appropriate small WHYP words that go into the word *sinewave*. Estimate the highest frequency sine wave you can generate using your WHYP words.

Exercise 8.5

The 74164 shown to the right is an 8-bit serial in/parallel out shift register. Data can be shifted in either pins *A* or *B* when the other pin is high. Data are shifted on the rising edge of the *CLK* input. A low level on either *A* or *B* inhibits data from being shifted in.

a. Explain how you could interface this chip to the 68HC12 SPI port and use it as a seven-segment decoder connected to the MAN 72 shown in Figure 7–8.

b. Write a WHYP word called *.sled* (n --) similar to that shown in Figure 7–9 that will display a hex digit on the seven-segment display.

```
       ___∪___
 1  ─┤ A    Vcc ├─ 14
     │   74164   │
 2  ─┤ B     QH ├─ 13
     │             │
 3  ─┤ QA     QG ├─ 12
     │             │
 4  ─┤ QB     QF ├─ 11
     │             │
 5  ─┤ QC     QE ├─ 10
     │             │
 6  ─┤ QD    CLR ├─ 9
     │             │
 7  ─┤ GND   CLK ├─ 8
     └───────────┘
```

Exercise 8.6

Microchip Technology Inc. make a series of bus serial EEPROMs that use the SPI interface to read and write bytes. For example, the 25C320 is a 32 Kbit (4096 bytes) EEPROM available in the eight-pin package shown below. The full data sheet can be downloaded from http://microchip.com/10/Lit/Memory/SPI/index.htm.

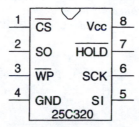

You can interface the 25C320 to a 68HC12 SPI port by connecting the SPI *SS* signal to the *CS* pin, the *SCK* signal to the *SCK* pin, the *MOSI* signal to the *SI* pin, and the *MISO* signal to the *SO* pin. When *CS* is low, 8-bit data are shifted into *SI*, MSB first. Each bit is latched on the rising edge of the clock that idles low. Table 8–6 lists the six instructions used to read and write data to the EEPROM.

Table 8–6   25C320 Instruction Set

Instruction	Format	Description
WREN	00000110	Set the write enable latch (enables writes)
WRDI	00000100	Reset the write enable latch (disables writes)
RDSR	00000101	Read status register
WRSR	00000001	Write status register
READ	00000011	Read data from memory starting at selected address
WRITE	00000010	Write data to memory starting at selected address

    a. Write a WHYP word called *INIT.EEPROM (--)* that will initialize the SPI port for interfacing to the 25C320.

    b. Write a WHYP word called *READ (addr -- byte)* that will read the byte at address, *addr*, and leave the value, *byte*, on the data stack. To read a byte you must send the *READ* instruction followed by a 16-bit address (high byte first) in the range $0000–$0FFF. You must then send a dummy value, such as $00, to shift the byte from the EEPROM into the SPI data register.

    c. After one byte is shifted out using the word *READ* in part (b), the internal address pointer is incremented to the next higher address. Additional bytes can be shifted out by providing more clock pulses. Write a WHYP word called *READ.NEXT (-- byte)* that will read the byte at the next address.

    d. Before any data can be written to the EEPROM, a write enable sequence must take place. This consists of bringing *CS* low, sending the *WREN* instruction, and bringing *CS* back high again. Write a WHYP word called *WRITE.ENABLE (--)* that will execute this write enable sequence.

e. Write a WHYP word called *WRITE (c addr --)* that will write the byte, *c*, at address, *addr*. To write a byte you must first execute a write enable sequence as in part (d), then bring *CS* low, send the WRITE instruction, followed by a 16-bit address (high byte first) in the range $0000–$0FFF, followed by the data byte to write, and then bring *CS* high.

f. After sending the address in part (e), up to 32 bytes can be written to the same page, where a page starts on a 32-byte boundary. Write a WHYP word called *WRITE.BLOCK (from.addr #bytes to.addr --)* that will write #*byte* (up to 32 bytes) from a buffer at address *from.addr* to the EEPROM starting at address *to.addr*.

Exercise 8.7

The Analog Devices AD7376 is a ±15-V operation digital potentiometer. A simplified block diagram is shown below.

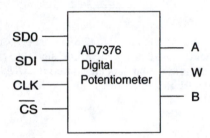

You can go to `http://www.analog.com/product/Product_Center.html` to download the full data sheet. The fixed resistance between *A* and *B*, R_{AB}, can be either 10 kΩ, 50 kΩ, 100 kΩ, or 1 MΩ. The output *W* is the "wiper" that causes the resistance between *W* and *B* to be given by the equation

$$R_{WB}(D) = (D/128) \times R_{AB} + R_W$$

where *D* is 7-bit data that have been shifted into *SDI* and R_W is the wiper contact resistance equal to 120 Ω.

You can interface the AD7376 to a 68HC12 SPI port by connecting the SPI *SS* signal to the *CS* pin, the *SCK* signal to the *CLK* pin, the *MOSI* signal to the *SDI* pin, and the *MISO* signal to the *SD0* pin. When *CS* is low, 8-bit data are shifted into *SDI*, MSB first. Each bit is latched on the rising edge of the clock that idles low. The *SD0* pin can be connected to the *SDI* pin of a second AD7376 to daisy-chain multiple variable resistors.

a. Write a WHYP word called *INIT.R (--)* that will initialize the SPI port for interfacing to the AD7376.

b. Write a WHYP word called *R (n --)* that will cause the resistance between *W* and *B* to be *n* ohms. Assume that R_{AB} = 10 kΩ, so that *n* should be between 0 and 10,000.

Exercise 8.8

The ISD4004 ChipCorder is a series of single-chip voice record/playback devices. A simplified block diagram is shown below. The full data sheet can be downloaded from

http://www.isd.com/product/chipcorder. These devices can store voice recordings of 8-, 10-, 12-, and 16-minute durations. The recordings are stored directly in analog
format using a unique multilevel storage technology. Table 8–7 lists the ten instructions used
to read and write data to the ChipCorder.

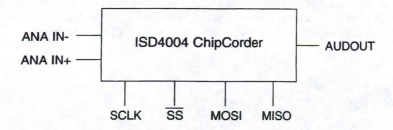

Table 8–7   ISD4004 Instruction Set

Instruction	Opcode Address	Description
POWERUP	00100XXX	**Power-Up**
SETPLAY	11100XXX	**Initialize playback from address <A15–A0>**
	<A15–A0>	
PLAY	11110XXX	**Playback from current address**
SETREC	10100XXX	**Initialize a record operation from address <A15–A0>**
	<A15–A0>	
REC	10110XXX	**Record from current address**
SETMC	11101XXX	**Initialize message cueing from address <A15–A0>**
	<A15–A0>	
MC	11111XXX	**Perform a message cue**
STOP	0X110XXX	**Stop current operation**
STOPWRDN	0X01XXXX	**Stop current operation and enter stand-by mode**
RINT	0X110XXX	**Read interrupt status bits**

You can interface the ISD4004 to a 68HC12 SPI port by connecting the SPI *SS* signal to the
SS pin, the *SCK* signal to the *SCLK* pin, the *MOSI* signal to the *MOSI* pin, and the *MISO*
signal to the *MISO* pin. When *SS* is low, 8-bit data are shifted into *MOSI*, LSB first. Each bit
is latched on the rising edge of the clock that idles low.

Recall that the 68HC12 SPI module normally shifts out a byte most significant bit first.
However, the ISD4004 must receive its data *least significant bit* first. This means, for example,
that when sending the data for the *SETPLAY* instruction, bit *A0* of the address must be sent
first and the most significant bit of the opcode (1) must be sent last.

a. Write a WHYP word called *INIT.ChipCorder (--)* that will initialize the SPI port for
interfacing to the ISD4004. Remember to set the *LSBF* bit (bit 0) in the SPI control
register shown in Figure 8–3 so that the data will be transferred least significant bit
first.

b. Write a WHYP word called *RECORD (--)* that will allow you to record a message (starting at address 00) by connecting a microphone to the ANA IN+ and ANA IN- pins. To enter the record mode you must send the *POWERUP* command, delay 25 ms, send the *POWERUP* command, send the *SETREC* command with address 00, and send the *REC* command.

c. Write a WHYP word called *PLAY (--)* that will play from address 00. To enter the playback mode, you must send the *POWERUP* command, delay 25 ms, send the *SET-PLAY* command with address 00, and send the *PLAY* command.

9

Analog-to-Digital Converter

In this chapter we will investigate the Analog-to-Digital (A/D) converter that is part of 68HC11 and 68HC12 microcontrollers. Most members of the 68HC11 family of microcontrollers (the 'D3 part is a notable exception) have an eight-channel A/D converter that is associated with Port E. The 68HC12 extended the capabilities of this A/D converter and made it part of Port AD. We will start in Section 9.1 by looking at the general process of converting an analog voltage to a digital value using the method of successive approximation. We will then look, in Section 9.2, at the A/D converter as implemented in the 68HC11 and will develop WHYP words to access the A/D converter. We will then see in Section 9.3 how this A/D converter has been extended in the 68HC12 and will develop additional WHYP words to take advantage of these new features. Finally, in Section 9.4 we will use the A/D converter in the design of a digital compass.

9.1 Analog-to-Digital Conversion

A/D converters transform an analog voltage within a given voltage range into a corresponding digital number. For example, you might convert a voltage between 0 and 5 volts to an 8-bit binary number between 00000000 and 11111111. This represents a decimal number between 0 and 255. In this case, a change in the Least

Significant Bit (LSB) of 1 corresponds to a change in voltage of 5 V/256 = 19.5 mV. This quantization error, or step size, is inherent in any type of A/D conversion. We can minimize this error by using more bits. For example, a 10-bit A/D converter will have a step size between 0 and 5 volts of $5 V/2^{10} = 5 V/1024 = 4.9$ mV.

There are a number of different methods used for performing A/D conversions. One of the most popular, and the one used in the 68HC12 and 68HC11 microcontrollers, is the method of successive approximation. We will illustrate this method by using a 4-bit conversion in which the step size between 0 and 5 volts will be $5 V/2^4 = 5 V/16 = 0.3125$ V. For n bits the method of successive approximation requires n steps. The method is essentially a binary search as shown in Figure 9–1 for 4 bits.

Suppose that the input analog voltage to convert is $V_{in} = 3.5$ V. The first step is to guess the mid-range voltage of 2.5 V corresponding to the binary number 1000. That is, we just set the most significant bit. If this voltage (2.5 V) is less than the voltage V_{in}, then we want to keep this bit, because we know the input voltage is greater than 2.5 V. We then add the next most significant bit and try 1100, or 3.75 V, in step 2. This voltage is greater than 3.5 V so we have overshot the mark and must discard this bit. Setting the next bit means that we will try the value 1010, or 3.125 V in step 3. This value is less than 3.5 V so we will keep this bit. Finally, we will set the last (least significant) bit and try 1011, or 3.4375 V in step 4. This is still less than 3.5 V so we keep this bit. We are now finished and our converted value is 1011 which really represents 3.4375 V, but is within our error margin of 0.3125 V.

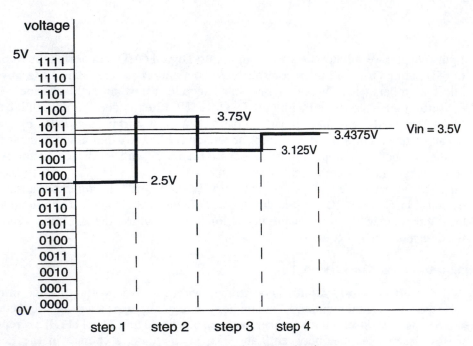

Figure 9–1   Illustrating the Method of Successive Approximation

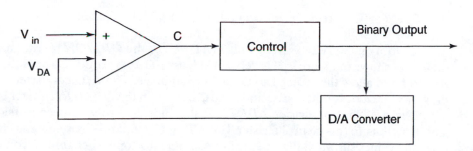

Figure 9–2   Implementing the Method of Successive Approximation

The successive approximation method illustrated in Figure 9–1 can be implemented using a comparator and D/A converter as shown in Figure 9–2. Assuming a 4-bit A/D converter as shown in Figure 9–1, the control circuit will first put out the binary value 1000. The D/A converter will convert this value to V_{DA} = 2.5 V. Because this value is less than V_{in} = 3.5 V, the output, C, of the comparator will be 1. This tells the control circuit to keep this bit and output the value 1100 in the second step, as shown in Figure 9–1. This time the value of V_{DA} = 3.75 V is greater than V_{in} = 3.5 V, and therefore the output, C, of the comparator will be 0. This tells the control circuit to throw away this bit and to output the value 1010 in step 3. This bit is kept as is the last bit as shown in Figure 9–1.

The 68HC12 and 68HC11 use a charge-redistribution technique to implement an eight-channel, 8-bit successive approximation A/D converter. This technique samples and stores the voltage at the beginning of the conversion and therefore no external sample and hold circuitry is needed.

9.2   THE 68HC11 A/D CONVERTER

Port E of the 68HC11 can be used as an eight-channel A/D converter. (The 'D3 part does not have a port E and therefore does not have this A/D converter.) The pins on port E can also be used as general-purpose input pins (for example, to read switch values as described in Section 7.2.2).

The A/D converter is an 8-bit successive approximation converter that converts an analog voltage to a digital value between \$00 and \$FF (0–255 decimal). The analog input values to the A/D converter must have a voltage in the range V_{RH} to V_{RL}, where V_{RH} and V_{RL} are 68HC11 pins normally connected to +5 volts and ground, respectively. The A/D converter will convert a voltage between V_{RH} and V_{RL} to an 8-bit digital value between 0 and 255. As we will see in Section 9.4 the value of V_{RL} can be greater than 0 volts and V_{RH} can be less than +5 volts to increase the sensitivity (bits per volt) of the conversion.

The A/D converter always takes four consecutive readings, each one typically taking 32 E clock cycles. Therefore, the time required to perform an A/D conversion is 128 E clock cycles, or 64 μs for a 2-MHz clock. During this time you can convert either a single channel four times, or four channels once.

The 68HC11 registers associated with the A/D converter are shown in Table 9–1.

To turn on the A/D converter, bit 7 (*ADPU*) of the *OPTION* register must be set to 1, as shown in Figure 9–3. A delay of at least 100 μs is required after setting the *ADPU* bit to allow the analog bias voltages to stabilize. The A/D converter will use the system E clock for the conversion if the *CSEL* bit in the *OPTION* register is zero.

The A/D control register, *ADCTL*, is shown in Figure 9–4. A conversion begins by writing to this control register. Bits *CD*, *CC*, *CB*, and *CA* select the channel using the values shown in Figure 9–5. For example, to convert channel 2 you would store a 2 in *ADCTL*. This will set the *SCAN* and *MULT* bits to 0 which means that four consecutive conversions of channel 2 will take place. The four results will be stored in the four result registers, *ADR1*, *ADR2*, *ADR3*, and *ADR4*. Bit 7 (*CCF*) of the control register will be set to 1 when all four result registers contain valid conversion results. This *CCF* bit is cleared to 0 by a write to the control register, *ADCTL*, which will start a new conversion.

If *MULT* = 1 (and *SCAN* = 0) in the control register in Figure 9–4, then a single separate conversion is done on each of four separate channels. As indicated in Figure 9–5, if *CD* and *CC* are both zero in *ADCTL*, then channels 0–3 are converted. If *CD* = 0 and *CC* = 1, then channels 4–7 are converted. When *MULT* = 1, the *CB* and *CA* bits in *ADCTL* have no effect.

If *SCAN* = 1, then conversions continue after the fourth conversion, with the fifth conversion stored in *ADR1* (overwriting the result of the first conversion), the

Table 9–1 A/D Converter Registers in the 68HC11

Name	Register Addr	Description
ADCTL	1030	A/D Control Register
ADR1	1031	A/D Result Register 1
ADR2	1032	A/D Result Register 2
ADR3	1033	A/D Result Register 3
ADR4	1034	A/D Result Register 4
OPTION	1039	System Configuration Options

	7	6	5	4	3	2	1	0	
$1039	ADPU	CSEL	IRQE	DLY	CME	0	CR1	CR0	OPTION

ADPU: A/D Power Up
              0 – A/D charge pump off
              1 – A/D charge pump on -- delay required before using A/D system

CSEL: Clock Select
              0 – A/D system uses the system E clock (must be above 750 KHz)
              1 – A/D system uses internal R-C clock source (about 1.5 MHz)

Figure 9–3 Setting the ADPU bit of the Option register turns on the A/D converter.

7	6	5	4	3	2	1	0	
CCF	0	SCAN	MULT	CD	CC	CB	CA	ADCTL

$1030

CCF: Conversions Complete Flag (read only)
               0 – cleared by a write to ADCTL which starts a new conversion
               1 – set when all four A/D result registers contain valid conversion results

SCAN: Continuous Scan Control
               0 – four requested conversions fill four result registers once
               1 – conversions continue in a round-robin fashion

MULT: Multiple-Channel/Single-Channel Control
               0 – performs 4 consecutive conversions on a single channel
               1 – performs a separate conversion for each of four channels

CD, CC, CB, CA :   Channel Selects

Figure 9–4   The A/D Control Register

CD	CC	CB	CA	Channel Signal	MULT = 1
0	0	0	0	PE0	ADR1
0	0	0	1	PE1	ADR2
0	0	1	0	PE2	ADR3
0	0	1	1	PE3	ADR4
0	1	0	0	P34	ADR1
0	1	0	1	PE5	ADR2
0	1	1	0	PE6	ADR3
0	1	1	1	PE7	ADR4
1	0	0	0	Reserved	ADR1
1	0	0	1	Reserved	ADR2
1	0	1	0	Reserved	ADR3
1	0	1	1	Reserved	ADR4
1	1	0	0	V_H	ADR1
1	1	0	1	V_L	ADR2
1	1	1	0	1/2 V $_H$	ADR3
1	1	1	1	Reserved	ADR4

Figure 9–5   The A/D Channel Assignments

sixth conversion stored in $ADR2$, and so on. If $MULT = 0$, then these continuous conversions will be performed on the single selected channel, while if $MULT = 1$, then the continuous conversions will be performed on the selected group of four channels.

9.2.1 WHYP Words for the 68HC11 A/D Converter

WHYP words for accessing the 68HC11 A/D converter are included in the file ATD11.WHP that is shown in Listing 9–1. The register names given in Table 9–1 are defined as *CONSTANTs* at the beginning of the file.

Listing 9–1   68HC11 A/D Converter

```
\               68HC11 Analog-to-Digital Converter -- File: ATD11.WHP
HEX

1030        CONSTANT     ADCTL        \ A/D Control Register
1031        CONSTANT     ADR1         \ A/D Result Register 1
1032        CONSTANT     ADR2         \ A/D Result Register 2
1033        CONSTANT     ADR3         \ A/D Result Register 3
1034        CONSTANT     ADR4         \ A/D Result Register 4
1039        CONSTANT     OPTION       \ System Configuration Options

: ADCONV.ON        ( -- )
                   80 OPTION C!         ( Set ADPU )
                   5 FOR NEXT ;         ( Wait at least 100 µsec.)


: ADCONV.OFF       ( -- )
                   0 OPTION C! ;        ( Clear ADPU )


: WAIT.FOR.CONV    ( -- )
                   BEGIN
                     7 ADCTL ?HI
                   UNTIL ;

: AVG4             ( -- n )              \ Average 4 values in ADR1 - ADR4
                   0 ADR1 1-
                   4 FOR                 \ sum addr
                     DUP R@ + C@         \ sum addr val
                     ROT + SWAP          \ sum addr
                   NEXT
                   DROP 4 / ;

: ADCONV           ( ch# -- val )        \ Avg 4 readings from channel ch#
                   ADCONV.ON
                   8 MOD ADCTL C!        \ ch# < 8; SCAN=0   MULT=0
                   WAIT.FOR.CONV
                   AVG4 ADCONV.OFF ;
```

Listing 9–1   (*continued*)

```
: GET.4VALUES        ( -- val4 val3 val2 val1 )  \ read 4 a/d regs
                     ADR1 1-
                     4 FOR                  \ addr1
                       DUP R@ + c@ SWAP \ valn addr1
                     NEXT
                     DROP ;


: ADCONV03            ( -- val3 val2 val1 val0 )  \ Convert 1st 4 channels
                     ADCONV.ON
                     10 ADCTL C!
                     WAIT.FOR.CONV
                     GET.4VALUES ADCONV.OFF ;


: ADCONV47            ( -- val3 val2 val1 val0 )  \ Convert 2nd 4 channels
                     ADCONV.ON
                     14 ADCTL C!
                     WAIT.FOR.CONV
                     GET.4VALUES ADCONV.OFF ;
DECIMAL
```

The WHYP words *ADCONV.ON* and *ADCONV.OFF*, shown in Listing 9–1, will turn the A/D converter on and off by setting and clearing the ADPU bit in Figure 9–3. The WHYP word *wait.for.conv (--)*, given in Listing 9–1, will wait for the *CCF* bit in Figure 9–4 to be set to 1.

In Listing 9–1 the WHYP word *ADCONV (ch# -- val)* will perform four conversions of a single channel, whose channel number is on the data stack, and leave the average of these four values on the data stack. It first turns the A/D converter on and then starts the conversion by storing the channel number (mod 8) in the control register, *ADCTL*. It then waits for the conversion to be completed, averages the four readings with the word *AVG4*, and then turns off the A/D converter.

It is often a good idea to average four consecutive readings of an A/D converter in order to minimize any noise in the signal that may cause the readings to jump around a little. The WHYP word *AVG4 (-- n)*, shown in Listing 9–1, averages the values stored in the four result registers, *ADR1–ADR4*. Note that when the *FOR* statement is executed the first time, the value 4 is put on the return stack and the top of the data stack will contain the address of *ADR1–1*. Each time the word *R@* is executed, it copies the value on the return stack to the data stack. The first time through the loop this value will be 4, which when added to the address of *ADR1–1*, gives the address of *ADR1+3*, or the address of the result register *ADR4*. The value in this register is read and added to the sum (initialized to zero) on the bottom of the data stack. When *NEXT* is executed, it decrements the top of the return stack (the first time the 4 becomes a 3) and, if this value is nonzero, branches back to the word following *FOR*. The second time through the *FOR . . . NEXT* loop the contents of *ADR3* is added to the sum; the third time the contents of *ADR2* is added to the sum; and the fourth time the contents of *ADR1* is added to the sum. This sum is then divided by 4 to give the average of the four values.

The word *ADCONV03 (-- val3 val2 val1 val0)*, shown in Listing 9–1, will perform a single conversion of the four channels, 0–3, and leave all four values on the data stack. The value from channel 0 (*PE0*) will be on top of the data stack. The WHYP word *ADCONV47 (-- val7 val6 val5 val4)* will perform a single conversion of the four channels, 4–7, and leave all four values on the data stack. The value from channel 4 (*PE4*) will be on top of the stack.

The word *GET.4VALUES (-- val4 val3 val2 val1)*, shown in Listing 9–1, will read the values from the four result registers, *ADR4*, *ADR3*, *ADR2*, and *ADR1*, and store these results on the data stack. Note that in the *FOR . . . NEXT* loop the value from *ADR4* is read first.

9.3   THE 68HC12 A/D CONVERTER

Compared with the 6 registers (see Table 9–1) associated with the A/D converter in the 68HC11, there are 14 registers associated with the A/D converter in the 68HC12, as shown in Table 9–2. There are actually additional registers reserved for future enhancements of the A/D converter. For example, there are reserved ATD control registers 0 and 1 at addresses $0060 and $0061. Also note that there are 8 A/D result registers instead of the 4 in the 68HC11 and these 8 registers are at even addresses starting at address $0070. The corresponding odd addresses starting at address $0071 are reserved, to be used to expand the A/D converter beyond 8-bit resolution, as it has been (to 10 bits) in the MC68HC912BC32. The names of the A/D result registers, *ADRxH*, identify them as the *high* byte of the result.

Table 9–2   A/D Converter Registers in the 68HC12

Name	Register Addr	Description
ATDCTL2	0062	ATD Control Register 2
ATDCTL3	0063	ATD Control Register 3
ATDCTL4	0064	ATD Control Register 4
ATDCTL5	0065	ATD Control Register 5
ATDSTAT	0066	ATD Status Register (H)
ATDSTATL	0067	ATD Status Register (L)
ADR0H	0070	A/D Result Register 0
ADR1H	0072	A/D Result Register 1
ADR2H	0074	A/D Result Register 2
ADR3H	0076	A/D Result Register 3
ADR4H	0078	A/D Result Register 4
ADR5H	007A	A/D Result Register 5
ADR6H	007C	A/D Result Register 6
ADR7H	007E	A/D Result Register 7

The 68HC12 A/D converter can be operated in either a four conversion mode (as in the 68HC11) or in an eight conversion mode depending on bit S8CM in the *ATDCTL5* register, shown in Figure 9–6.

The *ATDCTL5* control register shown in Figure 9–6 is similar to the *ADCTL* control register in the 68HC11 (see Figure 9–4) except that the conversion complete flag, *CCF*, has been moved to a new 16-bit status register, shown in Figure 9–7.

	7	6	5	4	3	2	1	0	
$0065	0	S8CM	SCAN	MULT	CD	CC	CB	CA	ATDCTL5

S8CM: Select 8 Channel Mode
         0 – Conversion sequence consists of four conversions
         1 – Conversion sequence consists of eight conversions

SCAN: Continuous Scan Control
         0 – four requested conversions fill four result registers once
         1 – conversions continue in a round-robin fashion

MULT: Multiple-Channel/Single-Channel Control
         0 – performs 4 or 8 consecutive conversions on a single channel
         1 – performs a separate conversion for each of four or eight channels

CD, CC, CB, CA :   Channel Selects

Figure 9–6   The 68HC12 ATD Control Register 5

	7	6	5	4	3	2	1	0	
$0066	SCF	0	0	0	0	CC2	CC1	CC0	ATDSTAT

	7	6	5	4	3	2	1	0	
$0067	CCF7	CCF6	CCF5	CCF4	CCF3	CCF2	CCF1	CCF0	ATDSTATL

SCF: Sequence Complete Flag
           0 – if AFFC = 0, cleared by a write to ATDCTL5 which starts a new conversion
               if AFFC = 1, cleared after the first result register is read
           1 – set when a four or eight conversion sequence is complete

CC[2:0]:   Conversion Counter for current (4 or 8 conversion) sequence
           3-bit number = channel number currently being converted

CCF[7:0]: Conversions Complete Flag (read only)
           0 – cleared by a write to ADCTL which starts a new conversion
           1 – set when all four A/D result registers contain valid conversion results

Figure 9–7   The 68HC12 ATD Status Register

There are, in fact, eight conversion complete flags, *CCFx*, one for each of the eight channels. Normally, we are interested in when an entire sequence consisting of four or eight conversions has been completed. The sequence complete flag, *SCF*, shown in Figure 9–7, is used to test this condition.

The *ADPU* bit used to enable the A/D converter has been moved from the *OPTION* register in the 68HC11 to the new *ATDCTL2* control register, shown in Figure 9–8. This control register also contains an *AFFC* bit which, when set, will cause the *CCF* flags to be cleared automatically when a result register is read (see Figure 9–7).

There are no interrupts associated with the A/D converter on the 68HC11. However, it is possible to produce a hardware interrupt on the 68HC12 when the A/D conversion sequence is complete. This interrupt is enabled with the *ASCIE* bit in the *ATDCTL2* control register, shown in Figure 9–8. The interrupt vector addresses associated with this ATD interrupt are shown in Tables 6–6 and 6–7 in Chapter 6.

If *MULT* = 1, *S8CM* = 0, and *SCAN* = 0 in the *ATDCTL5* control register in Figure 9–7, then a single separate conversion is done on each of four separate channels just as in the 68HC11 as shown in Figure 9–9. On the other hand, if *MULT* = 1 and *S8CM* = 1, then a single separate conversion can be done on each of the eight separate channels with the results stored in the eight A/D result registers, as indicated in Figure 9–10.

	7	6	5	4	3	2	1	0	
$0062	ADPU	AFFC	AWAI	0	0	0	ASCIE	ASCIF	ATDCTL2

ADPU: A/D Power Up
0 – A/D disabled
1 – A/D enabled

AFFC: A/D Fast Flag Clear All
0 – A/D flag clearing operates normally
1 – Uses fast clear sequence for A/D conversion complete flags
(Any access to result register will cause the associated CCF to clear automatically.)

AWAI: A/D Wait Mode
0 – A/D continues to run in wait mode
1 – A/D stops to save power in wait mode

ASCIE: A/D Sequence Complete Interrupt Enable
0 – A/D interrupt disabled
1 – A/D interrupt (on sequence complete) enabled

ASCIF: A/D Sequence Complete Interrupt Flag
0 – No A/D interrupt occurred
1 – A/D sequence complete

Figure 9–8 The 68HC12 ATD Control Register 2

CD	CC	CB	CA	Channel Signal	MULT = 1
0	0	0	0	AN0	ADR0
0	0	0	1	AN1	ADR1
0	0	1	0	AN2	ADR2
0	0	1	1	AN3	ADR3
0	1	0	0	AN4	ADR0
0	1	0	1	AN5	ADR1
0	1	1	0	AN6	ADR2
0	1	1	1	AN7	ADR3
1	0	0	0	Reserved	ADR0
1	0	0	1	Reserved	ADR1
1	0	1	0	Reserved	ADR2
1	0	1	1	Reserved	ADR3
1	1	0	0	V_H	ADR0
1	1	0	1	V_L	ADR1
1	1	1	0	$(V_H + V_L)/2$	ADR2
1	1	1	1	Reserved	ADR3

Figure 9–9 The 68HC12 A/D Channel Assignments (S8CM = 0)

CD	CC	CB	CA	Channel Signal	MULT = 1
0	0	0	0	AN0	ADR0
0	0	0	1	AN1	ADR1
0	0	1	0	AN2	ADR2
0	0	1	1	AN3	ADR3
0	1	0	0	AN4	ADR4
0	1	0	1	AN5	ADR5
0	1	1	0	AN6	ADR6
0	1	1	1	AN7	ADR7
1	0	0	0	Reserved	ADR0
1	0	0	1	Reserved	ADR1
1	0	1	0	Reserved	ADR2
1	0	1	1	Reserved	ADR3
1	1	0	0	V_H	ADR4
1	1	0	1	V_L	ADR5
1	1	1	0	$(V_H + V_L)/2$	ADR6
1	1	1	1	Reserved	ADR7

Figure 9–10 The 68HC12 A/D Channel Assignments (S8CM = 1)

Listing 9–2   (*continued*)

```
                    ROT + SWAP              \ sum addr
            NEXT
            DROP 4 / ;

: ADCONV        ( ch# -- val )      \ Avg 4 readings from channel ch#
            ADCONV.ON
            8 MOD ATDCTL5 C!        \ ch# < 8; SCAN=0  MULT=0
            WAIT.FOR.CONV
            AVG4 ADCONV.OFF ;


: GET.4VALUES ( -- val4 val3 val2 val1 )        \ read 4 a/d regs
            ADR0H 2-
            4 FOR                               \ addr1
                DUP R@ 2* + C@ SWAP             \ valn addr1
            NEXT
            DROP ;


: ADCONV03      ( -- val3 val2 val1 val0 )      \ Convert 1st 4 channels
            ADCONV.ON
            10 ATDCTL5 C!
            WAIT.FOR.CONV
            GET.4VALUES ADCONV.OFF ;


: ADCONV47      ( -- val3 val2 val1 val0 )      \ Convert 2nd 4 channels
            ADCONV.ON
            14 ATDCTL5 C!
            WAIT.FOR.CONV
            GET.4VALUES ADCONV.OFF ;


DECIMAL
```

The word *ADCONV.ON* sets the *ADPU* and *AFFC* bits in the *ATDCTL2* control register, shown in Figure 9–8. The word *WAIT.FOR.CONV* tests the *SCF* bit (bit 7) in the ATD status register, *ATDSTAT*, shown in Figure 9–7.

The words *AVG4* and *GET.4VALUES* differ from the corresponding words in Listing 9–1 in that the initial address put on the stack is *ADR0H-2* and the *FOR . . . NEXT* loop index, *R@*, is multiplied by 2 due to the fact that the result register addresses are two bytes apart.

The other words, *ADCONV*, *ADCONV03*, and *ADCONV47*, are the same as for the 68HC11 in Listing 9–1 except that *ATDCTL5* has replaced *ADCTL*. By setting the *S8CM* bit in the *ATDCTL5* control register (see Figure 9–6) you could write a word called *ADCONV07* that would convert all eight channels (see Exercise 9.1).

9.4　DESIGN OF A DIGITAL COMPASS

A small analog Hall-effect transducer (No. 1525) is produced by Dinsmore Instrument Company (`http://dinsmoregroup.com/dico/`) that can be used to sense the direction of the horizontal component of the earth's magnetic field. The sensor has six leads: four for power and ground and two output channels, *A* and *B*. These six leads can be connected as shown in Figure 9–11. The two outputs, *A* and *B*, are quadrature encoded sinusoidal waves whose relative phase depends on the orientation of the sensor with respect to the earth's magnetic field, as shown in Figure 9–12. The output voltages vary from a minimum of about 2.1 volts (*MinAD*) to about 2.9 volts (*MaxAD*). These two signals are fed to channels 2 and 3 of the 68HC11's or 68HC12's A/D converter. The two potentiometers shown in Figure 9–11 can be used to set V_{RL} to about 2 volts and V_{RH} to about 3 volts. Although this is a little out of the A/D specs, it seems to work and means that the 1-volt range between 2 and 3 volts will be converted to the total 8-bit range from 0 to 255.

The WHYP code for the digital compass is shown in Listing 9–3. The *A* and *B* voltages are read using the word *read.A/D (-- A B)*. The values *A* and *B* are signed values relative to the zero, or DC, level of the sine waves. This DC value is continually measured by keeping track of the maximum and minimum voltages read in the two variables *MaxAD* and *MinAD*. The variable *Amp* contains the amplitude of the sine waves, *MaxAD − dc*.

For maximum accuracy it is best to use the nearly linear regions of the curves shown as heavy lines in Figure 9–12. These are the regions in which small degree

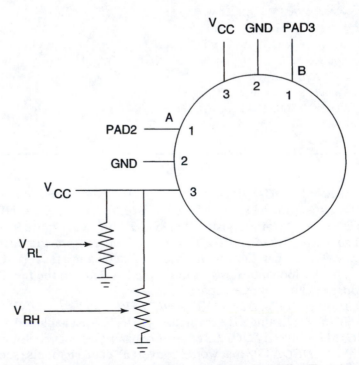

Figure 9–11　Connections to the Dinsmore Analog Hall-Effect Transducer

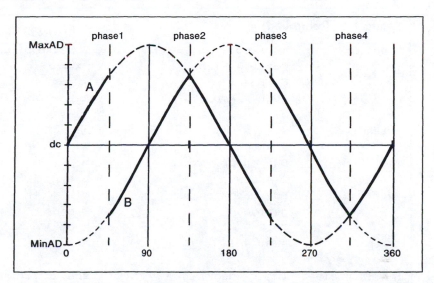

Figure 9–12 Quadrature Encoded Output of Dinsmore Hall-Effect Compass Transducer

changes produce the largest voltage change. The word *read.compass (-- deg)* in Listing 9–3 determines which of the four phases in Figure 9–12 the reading is in by comparing the signs of *A* and *B*. Once the phase is determined, the appropriate curve to use (corresponding to the heavy lines in Figure 9–12) is determined in the words *phasex* ($x = 1 - 4$) by comparing the absolute values of *A* and *B*. The arcsine WHYP word *ASIN* from the file SINE.WHP is used to compute the degree.

Listing 9–3   Digital Compass

```
\        Digital compass          File: COMPASS.WHP
LOAD SPILED.WHP        \ Fig. 7.11
LOAD SINE.WHP          \ Fig. 5.33
LOAD ATD.WHP           \ Listing 8.2

VARIABLE Amp               \ max amplitude of sin wave
VARIABLE MaxAD             \ max A/D reading
VARIABLE MinAD             \ min A/D reading
DECIMAL

\  Compass Using Dinsmore Analog Hall-Effect Sensor

: check.maxmin  ( n -- )                   \ update MaxAD & MinAD
                DUP MaxAD @ MAX            \ n mx
                MaxAD !                    \ n
                MinAD @ MIN                \ mn
                MinAD ! ;
```

(continued)

Listing 9–3   (*continued*)

```
: get.dc          ( -- dc )                  \ 0 value of sine waves
                  MaxAD @ MinAD @            \ mx mn
                  OVER + 2/                  \ mx dc
                  TUCK - Amp ! ;             \ Amp = MaxAD - dc


: read.A/D        ( -- A B )
                  3 ADCONV                   \ b
                  DUP check.maxmin           \ b
                  2 ADCONV                   \ b a
                  DUP check.maxmin           \ b a
                  get.dc                     \ b a dc
                  TUCK -                     \ b dc A
                  -ROT - ;                   \ A B


: ASIN.scale      ( n -- deg )               \ scaled arc sine
                  10000 Amp @ DUP 0=         \ make sure Amp <> 0
                  IF                         \ if Amp = 0
                      DROP OVER              \ take arcsine of 1
                  THEN
                  */ ASIN ;


: ACOS.scale      ( n -- deg )               \ scaled arc cosine
                  ASIN.scale 90 SWAP - ;


: phase1          ( A B -- deg )
                  ABS 2DUP <
                  IF
                      DROP ASIN.scale
                  ELSE
                      NIP ACOS.scale
                  THEN ;
: phase2          ( A B -- deg )
                  2DUP >
                  IF
                      NIP ASIN.scale 90 +
                  ELSE
                      DROP ACOS.scale 90 +
                  THEN ;


: phase3          ( A B -- deg )
                  SWAP ABS 2DUP >
                  IF
```

Listing 9–3 (*continued*)

```
                        NIP ASIN.scale 180 +
                ELSE
                    DROP ACOS.scale 180 +
                THEN ;


: phase4        ( A B -- deg )
                2DUP <
                IF
                    NIP ABS ASIN.scale 270 +
                ELSE
                    DROP ABS ACOS.scale 270 +
                THEN ;


: read.compass  ( -- deg )
                read.A/D                    \ A B
                2DUP XOR 0<
                IF                          \ phase 1 or 3
                    2DUP >
                    IF
                        phase1
                    ELSE
                        phase3
                    THEN
                ELSE                        \ phase 2 or 4
                    2DUP + 0>
                    IF
                        phase2
                    ELSE
                        phase4
                    THEN
                THEN ;

: compass       ( -- )
                SPI.INIT
                0 MaxAD !
                255 MinAD !
                BEGIN
                    read.compass
                    359 SWAP - .4leds
                    5000 FOR NEXT
                AGAIN ;
```

The degree value (0–359) is displayed on three common-cathode seven-segment displays using the Motorola MC14499 Decoder/Driver with Serial Interface chip described in Section 8.3.

9.5 SUMMARY

In this chapter we have learned how the eight-channel A/D converters on the 68HC11 and 68HC12 work. We developed the WHYP words shown in Box 9–1 for reading the analog values on any of the eight channels. These words are available in the files `ATD11.WHP` for the 68HC11 and `ATD.WHP` for the 68HC12.

Box 9–1 WHYP A/D Converter Words File: ATD.WHP

ADCONV   (ch# -- val)
              Averages four readings from channel *ch#* and leaves the result on the data stack.

ADCONV03   (-- val3 val2 val1 val0)
              Converts channels 0–3 once each and leaves all four values on the data stack.

ADCONV47   (-- val7 val6 val5 val4)
              Converts channels 4–7 once each and leaves all four values on the data stack.

Finally in this chapter we designed a digital compass using a Hall-effect sensor that uses two channels of the A/D converter to measure the analog voltages of two quadrature sine waves. Other types of analog sensors that can be used to measure temperature, pressure, light intensity, and acceleration are described in the exercises at the end of this chapter.

EXERCISES

Exercise 9.1

a. Write a WHYP word called *8channel.adconv* (--) that will convert all eight channels of the A/D converter once and leave all values in the eight A/D result registers.

b. Write a WHYP word called *ADCONV07* (-- val7 val6 val5 val4 val3 val2 val1 val0) that will convert all eight channels of the A/D converter and leave all eight values on the data stack.

Exercise 9.2

The LM35A from National Semiconductor is a 3-pin (power, ground, and output) precision centigrade temperature sensor that produces an analog output equal to 0 mV + 10.0 mV/°C. A complete data sheet can be downloaded from `http://www.nsc.com/`. Assume that this output is connected to pin *PAD3* of Port AD through an op-amp (e.g., the MC33272A from Motorola or the AD522 High Accuracy Data Acquisition Instrumentation Amplifier from Analog Devices) in such a way that an op-amp output of 0 to 5 volts corresponds to a temperature range of −30°C to +40°C.

a. Write a WHYP word called *degreeC (-- n)* that will leave the temperature, in degrees Celsius (Centigrade) on the data stack.

b. Write a WHYP word called *degreeF (-- n)* that will leave the temperature, in degrees Fahrenheit on the data stack. To convert Celsius to Fahrenheit multiply by 9/5 and add 32.

Exercise 9.3

A thermistor is a solid-state device whose resistance is a function of temperature. The resistance of a Negative Temperature Coefficient (NTC) thermistor varies inversely proportional to temperature while the resistance of a Positive Temperature Coefficient (PTC) thermistor increases linearly with a temperature change. However, for a given temperature change, the change in resistance is larger for an NTC thermistor than it is for a PTC thermistor. The resistance of a thermistor can produce a corresponding voltage using a simple Wheatstone bridge circuit or voltage divider. For more detailed information on thermistors and how to use them to measure temperature, you can see the Web site http://www.thermistor.com/.

Assume that an NTC thermistor is used to measure temperature using a simple voltage divider. The thermistor is calibrated by measuring ten different temperatures between some minimum and maximum temperature. These temperature values and the corresponding A/D converter input (0–255) are stored in two tables called *TEMP* and *ADVAL*.

Write a WHYP word called *get.temp (-- temp)* that will read an A/D value, look it up in the table *ADVAL*, and find the corresponding temperature in the table *TEMP*. Perform linear interpolation between the two closest values in the table.

Exercise 9.4

The TSL250 is a light-to-voltage optical sensor from Texas Instruments that can be used to measure light intensity. Its spectral responsivity is above 0.5 for wavelengths between about 450 and 950 nm with a maximum responsivity at about 880 nm. The sensor includes a photodiode and transimpedance amplifier in a single package with three pins: power, ground, and output voltage (typically 2 volts). A detailed data sheet can be downloaded from http://www.ti.com/sc/docs/schome.htm.

Assume that the TSL250 is connected to channel 3 of the 68HC12 A/D converter. Write a WHYP word called *turn.on.lights (--)* that will turn on lights (by setting bit 1 in Port H high) when the output of the TSL250 falls below 1 volt.

Exercise 9.5

The ADXL05 from Analog Devices is a ±1 g to ±5 g single-chip accelerometer. It uses an internal sensor in which an applied acceleration in a particular direction causes the center plates of a string of capacitors to move relative to fixed outer plates. The device comes in a 10-pin circular package less than 10 mm in diameter. Using three external capacitors, three external resistors, and an external trim pot, you can make the output voltage vary from 0.5 volt (−1 g) to 4.5 volts (+1 g) with 0 g corresponding to 2.5 volts. You can go to http://www.analog.com/product/Product_Center.html to download a complete data sheet.

Write a WHYP word called *get.g (-- n)* that will leave the acceleration, in milli-g, on the data stack, that is, a value of 1000 corresponds to 1 g.

Exercise 9.6

The ADXL05 described in Exercise 9.5 can be used to measure tilt by measuring the component of the earth's gravity. If the sensitive axis of the ADXL05 is oriented parallel to the earth's surface (i.e., horizontal), then the output voltage will be 2.5 V (0 g). A tilt by an angle θ to the horizontal will cause the voltage to change to V_{out} given by

$$V_{out} = scale\_factor\ (V/g) \times 1g \times \sin\theta + zero\_g\_output$$

For a *zero_g_output* voltage of 2.5 V and a *scale_factor* of 2 V/g, the angle θ is given by

$$\theta = arcsin\ [(V_{out} - 2.5)/2]$$

Write a WHYP word called *level (-- angle)* that will leave the tilt angle, in tenths of a degree, on the data stack. *Hint:* Use the arcsin table in Figure 5–33 and linearly interpolate to the nearest tenth of a degree.

Exercise 9.7

The MPX2100 from Motorola is a four-pin (power, ground, $+V_{out}$, and $-V_{out}$) 100-kPa pressure sensor consisting of a strain gauge and thin-film resistor network on a single chip. The output voltage varies linearly from 0 to 40 mV as the pressure differential varies from 0 to 100 kPa (0 to 14.5 PSI). A complete data sheet can be downloaded from `http://mot2.mot-sps.com/cgi-bin/dlsrch`. Assume that this output is connected to pin PAD2 of Port AD through an op-amp (e.g., the MC33272A from Motorola or the AD522 High Accuracy Data Acquisition Instrumentation Amplifier from Analog Devices) in such a way that an op-amp output of 0 to 5 volts corresponds to a pressure range of 0 to 100 kPa.

    a. Write a WHYP word called *pressure_kPa (-- n)* that will leave the pressure, in kPa, on the data stack.

    b. Write a WHYP word called *pressure_PSI (-- n)* that will leave the pressure, in PSI, on the data stack.

Exercise 9.8

The MPX4115A from Motorola is a Manifold Absolute Pressure (MAP) sensor consisting of a strain gauge, thin-film resistor network, and op-amp on a single chip. It is designed to measure absolute air pressure in applications such as engine control, aviation altimeters, and weather barometers. The output voltage varies linearly from 0.2 to 4.8 V as the absolute pressure varies from 15 to 115 kPa (2.2 to 16.7 PSI). A complete data sheet can be downloaded from `http://mot2.mot-sps.com/cgi-bin/dlsrch`. Assume that this output is connected to pin *PAD3* of Port AD.

    a. Write a WHYP word called *map_kPa (-- n)* that will leave the pressure, in kPa, on the data stack.

    b. Write a WHYP word called *map_PSI (-- n)* that will leave the pressure, in PSI, on the data stack.

Exercise 9.9

Modify the digital compass program shown in Listing 9–3 so as to display the compass output on an LCD display (see Section 7.5).

Exercise 9.10

Modify the digital compass program shown in Listing 9–3 so that the user can predefine a particular direction. The output will consist of turning on one of the following three LEDs: GO_LEFT, GO_RIGHT, or GO_STRAIGHT.

Exercise 9.11

Modify the program for the digital compass given in Listing 9–3 so that it will use real-time interrupts and the A/D interrupt. Read the compass value every 32.768 ms. The real-time interrupt, RTI, should start the A/D conversion and the ATD sequence complete interrupt (see Figure 9–8) can be used to determine when the A/D conversion has been completed.

Exercise 9.12

A fuel tank level measuring device consists of a rod 20 cm long that pivots at one end on a potentiometer and has a float on the other end such that the angle of the rod to the horizontal is $-45°$ when the tank is empty and $+45°$ when the tank is full. Assume that the potentiometer is connected to *PAD2* of a 68HC12 in such a way that the voltage at *PAD2* varies from 0 to 5 volts as the rod rotates from $-45°$ to $+45°$. Write a 68HC12 program using WHYP that will read the A/D converter value at *PAD2* every 32.77 ms (using a real-time interrupt) and display the height value of the float (proportional to the fuel level in the tank) on a seven-segment or LCD display.

10

Timers

Timers are an important part of microcontroller interfacing. They can be used to produce delays, measure time intervals such as pulse widths, create various output waveforms such as pulse-width modulated signals, count the number of events, and other similar activities. The 68HC11 and 68HC12 have sophisticated timer systems that can easily be programmed to perform all of the above functions. Very often timers are used in conjunction with hardware interrupts. In fact, 12 of the 25 hardware interrupts on the 68HC12 (20 on the 68HC11) are associated with the timer subsystem. In this chapter we will examine the operation of the 68HC11 and 68HC12 programmable timers and look at a number of examples. After describing the basic operation of the programmable timer subsystem in Section 10.1, we will look at output compares in Section 10.2, input captures in Section 10.3, and the pulse accumulator in Section 10.4. We will show how the timer can be used to measure the execution time of an interrupt service routine in Section 10.5. A circular queue data structure is introduced in Section 10.6 and used in Section 10.7 to store keypad pressings in response to an interrupt. An example of using interrupts to generate a pulse train is given in Section 10.8 and another example of using interrupts to measure the period of a pulse train is given in Section 10.9. Finally, in Section 10.10 we design a sonar tape measure using the Polaroid ultrasonic transducer.

10.1 THE 68HC12 PROGRAMMABLE TIMER

The 68HC12 has a fairly sophisticated timer subsystem associated with Port T. The 68HC12 registers associated with the timer are shown in Table 10–1. All timer functions are based around a single, free-running 16-bit up-counter, *TCNT*, shown in Figure 10–1. The address of *TCNT* ($0084) is the address of the high byte of *TCNT*. The contents of *TCNT* should be accessed as a word so as to read the real 16-bit value stored in *TCNT*. If you define *TCNT* to be the constant $0084 by typing

```
HEX
0084      CONSTANT  TCNT
```

Table 10–1 Timer Registers in the 68HC12

Name	Register Addr	Description
TIOS	0080	Timer Input Capture/Output Compare Select
CFORC	0081	Timer Compare Force Register
OC7M	0082	Output Compare 7 Mask Register
OC7D	0083	Output Compare 7 Data Register
TCNT	0084	Timer Count Register
TSCR	0086	Timer System Control Register
TCTL1	0088	Timer Control Register 1
TCTL2	0089	Timer Control Register 2
TCTL3	008A	Timer Control Register 3
TCTL4	008B	Timer Control Register 4
TMSK1	008C	Timer Interrupt Mask Register 1
TMSK2	008D	Timer Interrupt Mask Register 2
TFLG1	008E	Timer Interrupt Flag Register 1
TFLG2	008F	Timer Interrupt Flag Register 2
TC0	0090	Timer Input Capture /Output Compare Register 0
TC1	0092	Timer Input Capture /Output Compare Register 1
TC2	0094	Timer Input Capture /Output Compare Register 2
TC3	0096	Timer Input Capture /Output Compare Register 3
TC4	0098	Timer Input Capture /Output Compare Register 4
TC5	009A	Timer Input Capture /Output Compare Register 5
TC6	009C	Timer Input Capture /Output Compare Register 6
TC7	009E	Timer Input Capture /Output Compare Register 7
PACTL	00A0	Pulse Accumulator Control Register
PAFLG	00A1	Pulse Accumulator Flag Register
PACNT	00A2	16-bit Pulse Accumulator Count Register

$0084	Bit 15	14	13	12	11	10	9	Bit 8	TCNT (High)
$0085	Bit 7	6	5	4	3	2	1	Bit 0	TCNT (Low)

Free-running 16-bit counter
Clock input is MCLK (8 MHz) prescaled by 1, 2, 4, 8, 16, or 32 according to bits
PR2:PR0 in TMSK2

Figure 10–1 Timer Counter

then you can read the counter at any time by typing

```
TCNT @
```

Note from the definition of @ shown in Figure 4–12 that the *MOVW* instruction will access both bytes of *TCNT* at the same time.

If you try reading *TCNT* in this way, you will find that it always reads zero. You must first enable the timer by setting bit 7 of the timer system control register, *TSCR*, shown in Figure 10–2. Thus, if you type

```
HEX
0086  CONSTANT TSCR
80 TSCR C!
```

then every time you type

```
TCNT @ u.
```

you will display a new counter value.

The value of *TCNT* is incremented at a rate that depends on the three bits, *PR2: PR0*, in register *TMSK2*, shown in Figure 10–3. The default rate is the microprocessor module clock, *MCLK*, prescaled by 1. If this clock rate is 8 MHz, then *TCNT* will increment once every 125 ns. This means that the counter will overflow (go from $FFFF to $0000) every 8.192 ms. By changing these three bits in *TMSK2*, you can divide the clock rate by 2, 4, 8, 16, or 32. These bits may be changed at any time; however, the change will not take effect until the next time that all prescaled counter stages are zero.

	7	6	5	4	3	2	1	0	
$0086	TEN	TSWAI	TSBCK	TFFCA	0	0	0	0	TSCR

TEN: Timer Enable
         0 – Timer disabled, including the counter
         1 – Timer enabled, counter free running

TSWAI: Timer Stops While in Wait
         0 – Timer continues to run during wait
         1 – Timer disabled when MCU is in the wait mode

TSBCK: Timer Stops While in Background Mode
         0 – Timer continues to run while in background mode
         1 – Timer disabled when MCU is in background mode

TFFCA: Timer Fast Flag Clear All
         0 – Normal timer flag clearing
         1 – Fast timer flag clearing (see technical data sheet)

Figure 10–2 The Timer System Control Register

	7	6	5	4	3	2	1	0	
$008D	TOI	0	TPU	TDRB	TCRE	PR2	PR1	PR0	TMSK2

PR[2:0]:   Timer Prescaler Select

PR[1:0]	Prescaler	1 count time (MCLK = 8 MHz)	overflow time (MCLK = 8 MHz)
000	1	0.125 μs	8.192 ms
001	2	0.25 μs	16.384 ms
010	4	0.5 μs	32.768 ms
011	8	1.0 μs	65.536 ms
100	16	2.0 μs	131.07 ms
101	32	4.0 μs	262.14 ms
110	Reserved		
111	Reserved		

PR[2:0] can be read or written anytime.

Figure 10–3   Setting the Timer Count Time

When the timer overflows, the *TOF* bit of *TFLG2* (timer interrupt flag register 2) is set to 1, as shown in Figure 10–4. This flag is cleared by writing a 1 to bit 7 (*TOF*) of *TFLG2*. Although this may seem strange, it is the standard way of clearing flags in the 68HC12.

Each pin of Port T can be selected to act as either an input capture or an output compare. This selection is done by setting the bits in the timer input capture/output compare select register, *TIOS*, shown in Figure 10–5. We will discuss output compare in Section 10.2 and input capture in Section 10.3. First we will look at the 68HC11 timer registers.

	7	6	5	4	3	2	1	0	
$008F	TOF	0	0	0	0	0	0	0	TFLG2

TOF: Timer Overflow Interrupt Flag
        0 – Cleared by writing a 1 to bit position 7
        1 – Set to 1 when counter rolls over from $FFFF to $0000

Figure 10–4   The timer overflow interrupt flag is bit 7 of TFLG2.

PORT T	IOC7	IOC6	IOC5	IOC4	IOC3	IOC2	IOC1	IOC0
Pin	PT7	PT6	PT5	PT4	PT3	PT2	PT1	PT0

	7	6	5	4	3	2	1	0	
$0080	IOS7	IOS6	IOS5	IOS4	IOS3	IOS2	IOS1	IOS0	TIOS

IOS[7:0]:   Input Capture or Output Compare Channel Designator
             0 – The corresponding channel is an input capture
             1 – The corresponding channel is an output compare

Figure 10–5   Selecting Pins of Port T to Be Either an Input Capture or an Output Compare

10.1.1 The 68HC11 Timer Registers

The timer registers on the 68HC11 are shown in Table 10–2. They are similar to those on the 68HC12 with some notable changes. First of all, the free-running counter, *TCNT*, on the 68HC11 is always on so there is no timer system control register used to enable the timer.

Secondly, the timer channels are associated with pins on Port A and some of the pins are designated as output compares while others are designated as input captures. For example, the 68HC711E9 can have four or five output compares and three or four input captures, as shown in Figure 10–6. Pins *PA0–PA2* are always input captures and pins *PA4–PA7* are always output compares. Pin *PA3* can be either an input capture or an output compare depending on bit *I4/O5* of the *PACTL* register, as shown in Figure 10–6.

Another difference in the 68HC11 timer is that the rate at which *TCNT* is incremented depends on only two bits in register *TMSK2*, as shown in Figure 10–7. The default rate is the microprocessor clock rate E. If this clock rate is 2 MHz, then *TCNT* will increment once every 500 ns. This means that the counter will overflow (go from \$FFFF to \$0000) every 32.768 ms. By changing the two bits in *TMSK2*, you can divide the clock rate by 4, 8, or 16. However, unlike the 68HC12, these bits can be changed only during the first 64 μs after reset.

PORT A	OC1/PAI	OC2	OC3	OC4	IC4/OC5	IC1	IC2	IC3
Pin	PA7	PA6	PA5	PA4	PA3	PA2	PA1	PA0

	7	6	5	4	3	2	1	0	
\$1026	DDRA7	PAEN	PAMOD	PEDGE	DDRA3	I4/O5	RTR1	RTR0	PACTL

I4/O5:   Input Capture 4 / Output Compare 5 Flag
            0 – PA3 is Output Compare 5 pin
            1 – PA3 is Input Capture 4 pin

Figure 10–6 Output Compares and Input Captures on the 68HC711E9

	7	6	5	4	3	2	1	0	
\$1024	TOI	RTII	PAOVI	PAII	0	0	PR1	PR0	TMSK2

PR[1:0]:   Timer Prescaler Select

PR[1:0]	Prescaler	1 count time (E clock = 2 MHz)	overflow time (E clock = 2 MHz)
0 0	1	0.5 μs	32.768 ms
0 1	4	2.0 μs	131.07 ms
1 0	8	4.0 μs	262.14 ms
1 1	16	8.0 μs	524.29 ms

PR[1:0] can only be written once within 64 clock cycles after reset.

Figure 10–7 Setting the Timer Count Time in the 68HC11

Table 10–2   Timer Registers in the 68HC11

Name	Register Addr	Description
CFORC	100B	Compare Force Register
OC1M	100C	OC1 Action Mask Register
OC1D	100D	OC1 Action Data Register
TCNT	100E	Timer Counter Register
TIC1	1010	Input Capture 1 Register
TIC2	1012	Input Capture 2 Register
TIC3	1014	Input Capture 3 Register
TOC1	1016	Output Compare 1 Register
TOC2	1018	Output Compare 2 Register
TOC3	101A	Output Compare 3 Register
TOC4	101C	Output Compare 4 Register
TI405	101E	Input Capture 4/Output Compare 5 Reg
TCTL1	1020	Timer Control Register 1
TCTL2	1021	Timer Control Register 2
TMSK1	1022	Timer Interrupt Mask Register 1
TFLG1	1023	Timer Interrupt Flag Register 1
TMSK2	1024	Timer Interrupt Mask Register 2
TFLG2	1025	Timer Interrupt Flag Register 2
PACTL	1026	Pulse Accumulator Control Register
PACNT	1027	Pulse Accumulator Count Register

10.2 OUTPUT COMPARES

As described in Section 10.1, the timer port on a 68HC12 (Port T) can be configured to have up to eight output compares. The 68HC12 has eight 16-bit timer input capture/output compare registers, TCx, as shown in Figure 10–8. Note, for example, that the address of $TC2$ is \$0094–\$0095 and the address of $TC7$ is \$009E–\$009F (see Table 10–1).

When the value of the free-running counter, $TCNT$, is equal to the value stored in one of the output compare registers, the corresponding output compare channel flag, CxF, in the timer interrupt flag register, $TFLG1$, is set as shown in Figure 10–9. Note that this flag is cleared by writing a 1 to the corresponding bit

$009y	Bit 15	14	13	12	11	10	9	Bit 8	TCx (High)
$009y+1	Bit 7	6	5	4	3	2	1	Bit 0	TCx (Low)

Figure 10–8   Timer Input Capture/Output Compare Register x (y = 2x)

	7	6	5	4	3	2	1	0	
$008E	C7F	C6F	C5F	C4F	C3F	C2F	C1F	C0F	TFLG1

C0F–C7F: Channel x Flag

0 – Cleared by writing a 1 to corresponding bit position

1 – Set to 1 when counter matches output compare x value

Figure 10–9   The Output Compare Channel Flags

position. Thus, for example, the following WHYP word will clear bit 6, *C6F*, of *TFLG1*:

```
HEX
: C6F.CLR          ( -- )                    \ Clear C6F - bit 6 - in TFLG1
                   40 TFLG1 C! ;
```

Recall from Section 5.2.4 that we used a *FOR . . . NEXT* loop to produce 1 second- and 10-second delays (see Figure 5–23). However, these delays were not very accurate due to wait states inserted when accessing external memory. We will now use output compares to define the WHYP word *S.DELAY (n --)*, shown in Listing 10–1 that will delay for exactly *n* seconds without any errors. Listing 10–1 is contained in the file *oc_delay.whp*.

Listing 10–1   Delay Using Output Compare

```
\ Delay using 68HC12 output compare timer functions. File: OC_DELAY.WHP

HEX

0080    CONSTANT TIOS          \ Timer Input Cap./Output Comp. Select
0084    CONSTANT TCNT          \ Timer Counter Register
0086    CONSTANT TSCR          \ Timer System Control Register
008D    CONSTANT TMSK2         \ Timer Interrupt Mask Register 2
008E    CONSTANT TFLG1         \ Timer Interrupt Flag Register 1
009C    CONSTANT TC6           \ Timer Output Compare Register 6

\       Use output compare 6 for a 25 msec delay

: TIMER.INIT     ( -- )        \ Initialize timer
                 40 TIOS C!    \ select output compare 6
                 32 TMSK2 C!   \ div by 4: 2 MHz timer clock
                 80 TSCR C! ;  \ enable timer

: C6F.CLR        ( -- )        \ Clear C6F - bit 6 - in TFLG1 )
                 40 TFLG1 C! ;

DECIMAL

: 25.MSEC        ( cnt -- cnt' )\ wait 25 msec.
                 50000 +       \ add 50000 to prev cnt
                 DUP TC6 !     \ store in output compare 6 reg
                 C6F.CLR       \ clear output compare 6 flag
                 BEGIN         \ wait for timeout
                    6 TFLG1 ?HI
                 UNTIL ;

: S.DELAY        ( n -- )      \ delay n seconds
                 TIMER.INIT
                 40 *          \ no. of 25.msec delays
                 TCNT @ SWAP   \ cnt #
                 FOR
                    25.MSEC
                 NEXT
                 DROP ;
```

The word *TIMER.INIT (--)* in Listing 10–1 will select channel 6 (*PT6*) of Port T as an output compare, divide MCLK by 4 so that the timer is incremented every 0.5 μs, and then enable the timer. The word *25.MSEC (cnt -- cnt')*, shown in Listing 10–1, will produce a delay of 25 milliseconds. It expects a timer count value on the stack. This represents the current value of *TCNT*. A value of 50000 (25 ms at 0.5 μs per count) is then added to *cnt* to form the value *cnt'* which is stored in the output compare register, *TC6*. The *BEGIN ... UNTIL* loop then waits for the value in *TCNT* to become equal to the value in *TC6* at which point bit 6 of *TFLG1* will be set to 1. The value of *cnt'* is left on the stack so that if the word *25.MSEC* is executed again, another 25 ms will elapse. By calling this word 40 times, a delay of exactly 1 second will be produced. The word *S.DELAY (n --)*, shown in Listing 10–1, simply calls the word *25.MSEC* 40 * *n* times.

10.2.1   Pulse Train Example

The eight output compares, *OC0–OC7*, are associated with pins *PT0–PT7* of Port T, as shown in Figure 10–5. As described above, when the free-running counter, *TCNT*, matches the value in one of the output compare registers, *TCx*, shown in Figure 10–8, the corresponding output compare flag, *CxF*, in *TFLG1* is set as shown in Figure 10–9. When this occurs, it is possible to cause the output of *PT0–PT7* to change. In this way we can produce output waveforms on pins 0–7 of Port T.

In addition to the registers shown in Figures 10–8 and 10–9, the registers shown in Figure 10–10 also are used for output compares. Output compare 7 can control the outputs of any of the pins *PT0–PT7*. On the other hand output compares 0–6 can control only their own output pins. The output compare 7 mask register, *OC7M*, and the output compare 7 data register, *OC7D*, are used by output compare 7 to control the outputs on pins *PT0–PT7*. Setting an output compare mask, *OC7Mx*, in *OC7M* will enable the corresponding output pin *x*. If this mask bit is set, then the contents of the corresponding bit, *OC7Dx*, in *OC7D* will determine whether pin *x* of Port T will go high or low on a successful match of output compare 1. For example, if *OC7M6* is set to 1 and *OC7D6* is cleared to 0, then on a successful match of output compare 7 (*TC7*) the value on *PT6* will go low.

It is possible to have output compare 7 (*TC7*) and output compare 6 (*TC6*) both control the output of pin *PT6* at the same time. The way that *TC6* controls pin *PT6* is determined by the two bits, *OM6* and *OL6*, in register *TCTL1* as shown in Figure 10–10. For example, if *OM6* = 1 and *OL6* = 1, then pin *PT6* will be set to 1 on a successful match of output compare 6.

As an example, suppose we want to generate the waveform shown in Figure 10–11 on pin *PT6*. We can arrange for a match on output compare 7 to cause the signal to go from high to low, and a match on output compare 6 to cause the signal to go from low to high. Note that the width of the negative-going pulse can be as short as one timer clock period (125 ns) because we will have loaded values into both *TC7* and *TC6* before the counter hits them both in succession. The WHYP word *PULSE* shown in Listing 10–2 will generate this waveform.

The word *TINIT* in Listing 10–2 will first select channels 6 and 7 of Port T as output compares, divide MCLK by 4 so that the timer is incremented every 0.5 μs,

	7	6	5	4	3	2	1	0	
$0082	OC7M7	OC7M6	OC7M5	OC7M4	OC7M3	OC7M2	OC7M1	OC7M0	OC7M

OC7M7–OC7M0 Output Compare 7 Masks
        0 – TC7 is disabled for the corresponding port T pin
        1 – TC7 is enabled to control the corresponding port T pin

	7	6	5	4	3	2	1	0	
$0083	OC7D7	OC7D6	OC7D5	OC7D4	OC7D3	OC7D2	OC7D1	OC7D0	OC7D

If OC7Mx is set, data in OC7Dx is output to port T, bit x on successful TC7 compares.

	7	6	5	4	3	2	1	0	
$0088	OM7	OL7	OM6	OL6	OM5	OL5	OM4	OL4	TCTL1

	7	6	5	4	3	2	1	0	
$0089	OM3	OL3	OM2	OL2	OM1	OL1	OM0	OL0	TCTL2

OM[0:7]:   Output Mode
OL[0:7]:   Output Level

OMx	OLx	Action taken on successful TCx compare
0	0	Timer disconnected from output pin logic
0	1	Toggle OCx output line
1	0	Clear OCx output line to 0
1	1	Set OCx output line to 1

Figure 10–10   Additional Registers Used for Output Compares

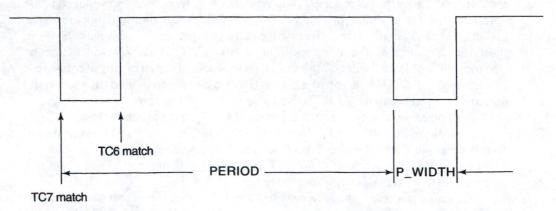

Figure 10–11 Pulse Train

and then enable the timer. It will then store the current counter value in *TC6* and *TC7* and then set pin *PT6* to go low on a *TC7* match and high on a *TC6* match. In the *BEGIN . . . AGAIN* loop of *PULSE*, the value stored in the variable *PERIOD* is added to the current value in *TC7*. This means that the next *TC7* match will occur

Listing 10–2   Pulse Train Using Output Compares

```
\         Pulse train using output compares 7 and 6. File: PULSE.WHP
HEX

0080      CONSTANT TIOS           \ Timer Input Cap.\Output Comp. Select
0082      CONSTANT OC7M           \ Output Compare 7 Mask Register
0083      CONSTANT OC7D           \ Output Compare 7 Data Register
0084      CONSTANT TCNT           \ Timer Counter Register
0086      CONSTANT TSCR           \ Timer System Control Register
0088      CONSTANT TCTL1          \ Timer Control Register 1
008D      CONSTANT TMSK2          \ Timer Interrupt Mask Register 2
008E      CONSTANT TFLG1          \ Timer Interrupt Flag Register 1
009C      CONSTANT TC6            \ Timer Output Compare Register 6
009E      CONSTANT TC7            \ Timer Output Compare Register 7

DECIMAL
VARIABLE  P_WIDTH   6625 P_WIDTH !
VARIABLE  PERIOD    17500 PERIOD !
HEX

: TINIT              ( -- )
                     C0 TIOS C!            \ select output compares 6 & 7
                     32 TMSK2 C!           \ div by 4: 2 MHz timer clock
                     80 TSCR C!            \ enable timer
                     TCNT @ DUP TC6 ! TC7 ! \ init cnt in TC6 & TC7
                     6 OC7M HI             \ pulse train out PT6
                     6 OC7D LO             \ PT6 goes low on TC7 match
                     4 TCTL1 HI 5 TCTL1 HI ; \ set PT6 high on TC6 match

: CLR.C76            ( -- )                \ clear both C7F and C6F
                     C0 TFLG1 C! ;

: PULSE              ( -- )
                     TINIT
                     BEGIN
                        TC7 @ CLR.C76
                        PERIOD @ +
                        DUP TC7 !          \ TC7new = TC7old + PERIOD
                        P_WIDTH @ + TC6 !  \ TC6 = TC7new + P_WIDTH
                        BEGIN              \ wait for PT6 to go low on
                           6 TFLG1 ?HI     \ TC7 match and the high on
                        UNTIL              \ TC6 match
                     AGAIN ;
DECIMAL
```

one period later. The new value stored in *TC6* will be the new value stored in *TC7* plus the value in the variable *P_WIDTH*. The *BEGIN* ... *UNTIL* loop then waits for bit 6 of *TFLG1* to be set. This will occur on a match of *TC6*, at which point pin *PT6* goes high. It will have already gone low on the match of *TC7* (which will have set bit 7 of *TFLG1*). At the beginning of the *BEGIN* ... *AGAIN* loop, both bits 7 and 6 of *TFLG1* are cleared by the word *CLR.C76*.

In Section 10.8 we will see how to generate this same pulse train using interrupts. This will eliminate the *BEGIN...AGAIN* and *BEGIN...UNTIL* loops in the word *PULSE* is Listing 10–2. Therefore, the pulse train will be generated in the background in such a way that WHYP will be able to do other things while the pulse train is being generated.

10.2.2 Output Compares on a 68HC11

As shown in Table 10–2 and Figure 10–6, the 68HC11 has only four (or five) output compares associated with pins *PA3–PA7* of Port A. The registers used for output compares in the 68HC11 are shown in Figure 10–12. Output compare 1 (associated

PORT A	OC1/PAI	OC2	OC3	OC4	IC4/OC5	IC1	IC2	IC3
Pin	PA7	PA6	PA5	PA4	PA3	PA2	PA1	PA0

	7	6	5	4	3	2	1	0	
$1023	OC1F	OC2F	OC3F	OC4F	I405F	IC1F	IC2F	IC3F	TFLG1

OC1F–OC5F: Output Compare x Flag
        0 – Cleared by writing a 1 to corresponding bit position
        1 – Set to 1 when counter matches output compare x value

	7	6	5	4	3	2	1	0	
$100C	OC1M7	OC1M6	OC1M5	OC1M4	OC1M3	0	0	0	OC1M

OC1M7–OC1M3 Output Compare Masks
        0 – OC1 is disabled for the corresponding port A pin
        1 – OC1 is enabled to control the corresponding port A pin

	7	6	5	4	3	2	1	0	
$100D	OC1D7	OC1D6	OC1D5	OC1D4	OC1D3	0	0	0	OC1D

If OC1Mx is set, data in OC1Dx is output to port A, bit *x* on successful OC1 compares.

	7	6	5	4	3	2	1	0	
$1020	OM2	OL2	OM3	OL3	OM4	OL4	OM5	OL5	TCTL1

OM[2:5]:   Output Mode
OL[2:5]:   Output Level
        Note: OC5 functions only if the I4/O5 bit in the PACTL register is clear.

OMx	OLx	Action taken on successful OCx compare
0	0	Timer disconnected from output pin logic
0	1	Toggle OCx output line
1	0	Clear OCx output line to 0
1	1	Set OCx output line to 1

Figure 10–12 Registers Used for Output Compare in the 68HC11

with pin *PA7*) plays the same role as output compare 7 in the 68HC12. Note that output compare 2 is associated with pin *PA6*, output compare 3 is associated with pin *PA5*, and output compare 4 is associated with pin *PA4*. This makes it a little more confusing than in the 68HC12. Note that the register *TFLG1* in the 68HC11 contains separate flags for the output compares and the input captures (except bit *I4O5F* which is used for either depending on how pin *PA3* is selected). Except for these pin association differences, the output compares on the 68HC11 can be used in a similar way as that shown in Listings 10–1 and 10–2 for the 68HC12. (See Exercises 10.1 and 10.2.)

10.3 INPUT CAPTURE

The eight pins of Port T can be selected as input capture lines by clearing the appropriate bits in the *TIOS* register, as shown in Figure 10–5. When configured for an input capture, the corresponding input capture/output compare register, *TCx*, shown in Figure 10–8, is used to capture the current counter value, *TCNT*, when a rising or falling edge (or both) occurs on the associated pin *TPx*. When this occurs, the corresponding input capture channel flag, *CxF*, in the timer flag register, *TFLG1*, is set as shown in Figure 10–13. Note that this flag is cleared by writing a 1 to the corresponding bit position. The two bits *EDGxB* and *EDGxA* in timer control registers, *TCTL3* and *TCTL4*, are used to select the capture edge, as shown in Figure 10–13.

For example, suppose that the width of a single pulse connected to pin *PT2* is to be measured. Timer input capture 2 can be used for this purpose. The WHYP

	7	6	5	4	3	2	1	0	
$008E	C7F	C6F	C5F	C4F	C3F	C2F	C1F	C0F	TFLG1

C0F–C7F: Channel x Flag
   0 – Cleared by writing a 1 to corresponding bit position
   1 – Set each time a selected active edge is detected on the ICx input line

	7	6	5	4	3	2	1	0	
$008A	EDG7B	EDG7A	EDG6B	EDG6A	EDG5B	EDG5A	EDG4B	EDG4A	TCTL3

	7	6	5	4	3	2	1	0	
$008B	EDG3B	EDG3A	EDG2B	EDG2A	EDG1B	EDG1A	EDG0B	EDG0A	TCTL4

EDGxB, EDGxA: Input Capture Edge Control

EDGxB	EDGxA	Configuration
0	0	Capture disabled
0	1	Capture on rising edges only
1	0	Capture on falling edges only
1	1	Capture on any edge (rising or falling)

Figure 10–13 Registers Used for Input Capture

word *pulse.width (-- n)*, shown in Listing 10–3, will do this and leave the width (in microseconds) on the data stack. Setting bit 5 of *TCTL4* low and bit 4 of *TCTL4* high will cause *TC2* to be captured on the rising edge of the signal on pin *PT2*, as shown in Figure 10–13. A 1 is written to bit 2 of register *TFLG1* to make sure that the *C2F* flag is cleared. Then the program waits for the rising edge of the pulse to occur by waiting for the *C2F* flag in register *TFLG1* to be set.

When this occurs, the current counter value is captured in *TC2* whose value, *t1*, is read and put on the data stack. After clearing the *C2F* flag, bits 4 and 5 in *TCTL4* are set to 0 and 1, respectively, so as to capture the counter value on the next falling

---

Listing 10–3   Measuring Pulse Width Using Input Capture

```
\ Use input capture to measure width of single pulse. File: PWIDTH.WHP
\ Polling mode -- no interrupts
\ Use TC2 -- signal on PT2
HEX

0080      CONSTANT TIOS          \ Timer Input Cap.\Output Comp. Select
0084      CONSTANT TCNT          \ Timer Counter Register
0086      CONSTANT TSCR          \ Timer System Control Register
008B      CONSTANT TCTL4         \ Timer Control Register 4
008D      CONSTANT TMSK2         \ Timer Interrupt Mask Register 2
008E      CONSTANT TFLG1         \ Timer Interrupt Flag Register 1
0094      CONSTANT TC2           \ Timer Input Capture Register 2

: TIC.INIT      ( -- )
                0 TIOS C!              \ select all input captures
                33 TMSK2 C!            \ div by 8: 8 MHz timer clock
                80 TSCR C! ;           \ enable timer

: PULSE.WIDTH   ( -- n )               \ Measure width n of pulse
                TIC.INIT               \ initialize timer input capture
                5 TCTL4 LO             \ capture on rising edge
                4 TCTL4 HI
                04 TFLG1 C!            \ clear C2F flag
                BEGIN
                  2 TFLG1 ?HI          \ wait for rising edge
                UNTIL
                TC2 @                  \ t1
                04 TFLG1 C!            \ clear C2F flag
                5 TCTL4 HI             \ capture on falling edge
                4 TCTL4 LO
                BEGIN
                  2 TFLG1 ?HI          \ wait for falling edge
                UNTIL
                TC2 @                  \ t1 t2
                04 TFLG1 C!            \ clear C2F flag
                SWAP - ;               \ width = (t2 - t1)

DECIMAL
```

edge of the signal on pin *PT2*. This is done by waiting for the *C2F* flag to be set again at which point the contents of *TC2* will contain the counter time, *t2*, corresponding to the falling edge of the pulse. The difference $(t2 - t1)$ is the width of the pulse and this value is left on the data stack.

10.3.1   Input Captures on a 68HC11

The 68HC11 has three 16-bit timer input capture registers, *TIC1–TIC3*, associated with pins *PA2–PA0*, as shown in Table 10–2 and Figure 10–6. The 'E9 and 'D3 parts can also use pin *PA3* as a fourth input capture if the I4/O5 bit in the *PACTL* register is set to 1, as shown in Figure 10–6. In this case the *TI4O5* register shown in Table 10–2 serves as the input capture register.

The four input capture flags are in bits 0–3 of register *TFLG1*, as shown in Figure 10–14. The two edge selection bits, *EDGxB* and *EDGxA*, are all contained in register, *TCTL2*, as shown in Figure 10–14. Using these registers, you could modify the program shown in Listing 10–3 to measure the width of a pulse connected to pin *PA1* on a 68HC11. (See Exercise 10.3.)

	7	6	5	4	3	2	1	0	
$1023	OC1F	OC2F	OC3F	OC4F	I405F	IC1F	IC2F	IC3F	TFLG1

IC1F–IC4F: Input Capture x Flag
       0 – Cleared by writing a 1 to corresponding bit position
       1 – Set each time a selected active edge is detected on the ICx input line

	7	6	5	4	3	2	1	0	
$1021	EDG4B	EDG4A	EDG1B	EDG1A	EDG2B	EDG2A	EDG3B	EDG3A	TCTL2

EDGxB, EDGxA: Input Capture Edge Control
       Note: IC4 functions only if the I4/O5 bit in the PACTL register is set to 1.

EDGxB	EDGxA	Configuration
0	0	Capture disabled
0	1	Capture on rising edges only
1	0	Capture on falling edges only
1	1	Capture on any edges

Figure 10–14   Registers Used for Input Capture in a 68HC11

10.4   PULSE ACCUMULATOR

The pulse accumulator input, *PAI*, is an input to pin *PT7*. The pulse accumulator system is enabled by setting bit *PAEN* in the *pulse accumulator control register*, *PACTL*, as shown in Figure 10–15. The *pulse accumulator count register*, *PACNT*, is a 16-bit register that can contain a count of the number of external input events on the *PAI* input. Alternatively, it can contain a count of the number of clock pulses (M-clock/64) that occur during the time that the *PAI* input is gated (either high or low).

| $00A2 | Bit 15 | 14 | 13 | 12 | 11 | 10 | 9 | Bit 8 | PACNT (High) |
| $00A3 | Bit 7 | 6 | 5 | 4 | 3 | 2 | 1 | Bit 0 | PACNT (Low) |

16-bit read/write register contains count of external input events at PAI input, or accumulated count of gated input (MCLK / 64 = 8 µsec; overflow = 0.524 sec.).

| | 7 | 6 | 5 | 4 | 3 | 2 | 1 | 0 | |
| $00A0 | 0 | PAEN | PAMOD | PEDGE | CLK1 | CLK0 | PAOVI | PAI | PACTL |

PAEN: Pulse Accumulator System Enable
          0 – Pulse Accumulator disabled
          1 – Pulse Accumulator enabled

PAMOD: Pulse Accumulator Mode
          0 – Event Counter
          1 – Gated time accumulation

PEDGE: Pulse Accumulator Edge Control

PAMOD	PEDGE	Action on Clock
0	0	PAI falling edge increments the counter
0	1	PAI rising edge increments the counter
1	0	A zero on PAI inhibits counting
1	1	A one on PAI inhibits counting

CLK1, CLK0: Clock Select Register

CLK1	CLK0	Selected Clock
0	0	Use timer prescaler clock as timer counter clock
0	1	Use PACLK as input to timer counter clock
1	0	Use PACLK/256 as timer counter clock frequency
1	1	Use PACLK/65536 as timer counter clock frequency

PAOVI: Pulse Accumulator Overflow Interrupt Enable
          0 – Pulse Accumulator Overflow Interrupts inhibited
          1 – Pulse Accumulator Overflow Interrupts enabled

PAI: Pulse Accumulator Input Edge Interrupt Enable
          0 – Pulse Accumulator Input Edge Interrupts inhibited
          1 – Pulse Accumulator Input Edge Interrupts enabled

| | 7 | 6 | 5 | 4 | 3 | 2 | 1 | 0 | |
| $00A1 | 0 | 0 | 0 | 0 | 0 | 0 | PAOVF | PAIF | PAFLG |

PAOVF: Pulse Accumulator Overflow Flag
          0 – Cleared by writing a 1 to bit position 1
          1 – Set to 1 when counter rolls over from $FFFF to $0000

PAIF: Pulse Accumulator Input Edge Flag
          0 – Cleared by writing a 1 to bit position 0
          1 – Set to 1 when a selected edge is detected at the PT7/PAI input pin

Figure 10–15 Registers Used for the Pulse Accumulator

The *PAMOD* bit in the *PACTL* register determines whether the pulse accumulator is in the event counter mode or the gated time accumulation mode, as shown in Figure 10–15. If the *PAMOD* bit is 0, then the pulse accumulator is in the event counter mode and the *PEDGE* bit in the *PACTL* register determines whether the counter is incremented on the falling edge or the rising edge of the *PAI* signal. On the other hand if the *PAMOD* bit is 1, then the pulse accumulator is in the gated time accumulation mode and the *PEDGE* bit in the *PACTL* register determines whether the counter is inhibited by a 0 or 1 on the *PAI* input.

When a selected edge is detected on the *PA7/PAI* input pin, the *PAIF* bit in the *pulse accumulator flag register, PAFLG*, is set as shown in Figure 10–15. This can be used in situations where you might want to detect a rising or falling edge.

For example, Figure 7–17 in Section 7.4.2 showed how to interface a hex keypad using the MM74C922 encoder. The program shown in Figure 7–18 will read the hex value from the keypad when connecting pin 12 of the MM74C922 encoder to pin *PJ7* of the 68HC12. This program checks the level of pin *PJ7* which is only high as long as you hold the key pressed. Alternatively, we could connect pin 12 of the MM74C922 encoder to the *PT7/PAI* pin of the 68HC12. Then the program shown in Figure 10–16 can be used to read the hex value of the keypad. In this case the *PAIF*

```
HEX
00A0    CONSTANT    PACTL
00A1    CONSTANT    PAFLG
00A2    CONSTANT    PACNT
0028    CONSTANT    PORTJ
0029    CONSTANT    DDRJ


CREATE keytbl
        C C,  3 C,  2 C,  1 C,  D C,  6 C,  5 C,  4 C,
        E C,  9 C,  8 C,  7 C,  F C,  B C,  0 C,  A C,


: init.key    ( -- )
              00 DDRJ C!      \ Port J inputs
              1 PACTL LO      \ interrupts disabled
              0 PACTL LO      \ polled mode
              5 PACTL LO      \ event counter
              4 PACTL HI      \ rising edge of PA7
              6 PACTL HI      \ enable PA


: getkey2     ( -- n )       \ Read hex value from keypad
              BEGIN                     \ wait for rising
                  0 PAFLG ?HI           \ edge of PA7
              UNTIL
              01 PAFLG C!               \ clear PAIF flag
              PORTJ C@
              keytbl + C@ ;
```

Figure 10–16   Using the Pulse Accumulator to Read the Keypad in Figure 7–17

flag in the *PAFLG* register will be set when you press the key and cause the *PAI* input pin to go high. Compare the program in Figure 10–16 with that in Figure 7–18.

10.4.1   The Pulse Accumulator on a 68HC11

The pulse accumulator on the 68HC11 is similar to that on the 68HC12 except that the pulse accumulator count register is only an 8-bit register as shown in Figure 10–17. The pulse accumulator control register, *PACTL*, contains only the bits *PAEN*, *PAMOD*, and *PEDGE*, as shown in Figure 10–17. The *PAOVI* and *PAI* bits are in the *TMSK2* register and the flags *PAOVF* and *PAIF* are in the *TFLG2* register, as shown in Figure 10–17.

Except for these changes the pulse accumulator in the 68HC11 operates in the same fashion as described above for the 68HC12. In particular, you could interface the pulse accumulator to the MM74C922 encoder and decode a hex keypad using a program similar to the one shown in Figure 10–16. (See Exercise 10.5.)

10.5   TIMING INTERRUPT SERVICE ROUTINES

When writing interrupt service routines, it is important to have some idea of how long an interrupt service routine takes to execute. Interrupts may be missed if the interrupt service routine takes too long. In Section 6.6 we showed how to calculate the number of clock cycles required to execute an interrupt service routine. In WHYP it is fairly easy to measure how long an interrupt routine will take. As an example, consider the traffic lights problem described in Section 7.6. To measure the time it takes to execute the interrupt routine, *RTI.INTSER*, given in Listing 7–2, make a copy of `TRAFFIC.WHP` (call it, say, `TRAFFIC2.WHP`) and do the following:

1. Add the following two constants at the beginning of the program:

```
0084 CONSTANT TCNT
0086 CONSTANT TSR
```

2. Comment out the line *INT: RTI.INTER (--)* by preceding it with a backslash. Replace it with the following statement:

```
: test TCNT @
```

3. Comment out the line *RTI;* at the end of the interrupt routine by preceding it with a backslash. Replace it with the following statement:

```
TCNT @ SWAP - . ;
```

4. Comment out all the lines in the definition of the word *SET.RTI.INTVEC* by preceding them with a backslash. In the word *INIT.TRAFFIC* comment out the line *SET.RTI.INTVEC* by preceding it with a backslash.

5. Add the following WHYP definition before the word *DECIMAL* at the end of the program:

```
: TEST.SETUP            ( -- )
          80 TSCR C!          \ enable timer
          1 DTIME ! ;         \ set DTIME = 1
```

	7	6	5	4	3	2	1	0	
$1027	Bit 7	6	5	4	3	2	1	Bit 0	PACNT

8-bit read/write register contains count of external input events at PAI input, or accum count of gated input (E-clock / 64 = 32 µsec; overflow = 8.192 msec.).

	7	6	5	4	3	2	1	0	
$1026	DDRA7	PAEN	PAMOD	PEDGE	DDRA3	I4/O5	RTR1	RTR0	PACTL

PAEN: Pulse Accumulator System Enable
         0 – Pulse Accumulator disabled
         1 – Pulse Accumulator enabled

PAMOD: Pulse Accumulator Mode
         0 – Event Counter
         1 – Gated time accumulation

PEDGE: Pulse Accumulator Edge Control

PAMOD	PEDGE	Action on Clock
0	0	PAI falling edge increments the counter
0	1	PAI rising edge increments the counter
1	0	A zero on PAI inhibits counting
1	1	A one on PAI inhibits counting

	7	6	5	4	3	2	1	0	
$1025	TOF	RTIF	PAOVF	PAIF	0	0	0	0	TFLG2

PAOVF: Pulse Accumulator Overflow Interrupt Flag
         0 – Cleared by writing a 1 to bit position 5
         1 – Set to 1 when counter rolls over from $FF to $00

PAIF: Pulse Accumulator Input Edge Interrupt Flag
         0 – Cleared by writing a 1 to bit position 4
         1 – Set to 1 when a selected edge is detected at the PA7/PAI input pin

	7	6	5	4	3	2	1	0	
$1024	TOI	RTII	PAOVI	PAI	0	0	PR1	PR0	TMSK2

PAOVI: Pulse Accumulator Overflow Interrupt Enable
         0 – Pulse Accumulator Overflow Interrupts inhibited
         1 – Pulse Accumulator Overflow Interrupts enabled

PAI: Pulse Accumulator Input Edge Interrupt Enable
         0 – Pulse Accumulator Input Edge Interrupts inhibited
         1 – Pulse Accumulator Input Edge Interrupts enabled

Figure 10–17   Registers Used for Pulse Accumulator on a 68HC11

6. Load `TRAFFIC2.WHP` and type

```
TEST.SETUP
TEST
```

The value displayed on the screen will be the number of timer ticks that occurred between the beginning and end of the interrupt service routine. When tested on a 68HC812A4 evaluation board, this value was 1177. Note that by setting *DTIME* to 1, most of the words inside the outer *IF* statement will be executed. Recall that the default value of the timer clock period is 1 divided by the M-clock frequency. For an 8-MHz clock this is 0.125 μsec. Therefore, the time required to execute the interrupt service routine is 1177 $\times$ 0.125 = 147 microseconds. This is less that 1 percent of the 16.384 milliseconds between interrupts. Therefore, the traffic lights changing in the background will not noticeably affect whatever other programs the 68HC12 might be running.

10.6 A CIRCULAR QUEUE DATA STRUCTURE

A circular queue is a useful data structure to use when you need to store characters read in an interrupt service routine. The queue can then be read as necessary without missing any of the received characters. We will use a queue to store data read from a keypad using interrupts in Section 10.7. As another example we will also use a queue to store characters received in the SCI port in Section 11.4.

In this section we will develop WHYP words for maintaining the *circular queue* shown in Figure 10–18. Multiple values can be stored in this queue before they are removed (in the same order they were stored). Therefore, characters will not be lost if they are received faster than they are removed. Of course, if the queue is full and another character is received, it will be lost.

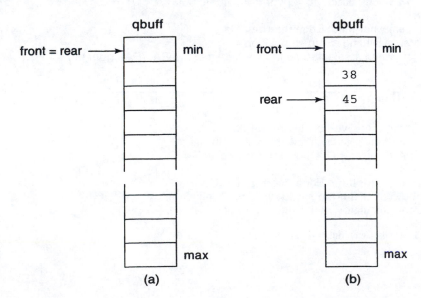

Figure 10–18 A Circular Queue: (a) Empty; (b) Containing Two Values

The queue is defined to be a buffer called *QBUFF* containing *QSIZE*+2 bytes (see Listing 10–4). The address of the first byte in the queue is stored in the variable *QMIN* and the address of the last byte is stored in the variable *QMAX*. The pointers

---

Listing 10–4   A Circular Queue

```
\ Queue Data Structure           File: QUEUE.WHP
\  For storing byte characters
16  CONSTANT   QSIZE
VARIABLE       FRONT
VARIABLE       REAR
VARIABLE       QMIN
VARIABLE       QMAX
VARIABLE       QBUFF   QSIZE VALLOT
VARIABLE       QBUFFEND

: INITQ         ( -- )
                QBUFF FRONT !
                QBUFF REAR  !
                QBUFF QMIN  !
                QBUFF QSIZE + 1+ QMAX ! ;

: CHECKQ          ( -- n tf | ff )
                FRONT @ DUP REAR @ =
                IF
                    DROP FALSE
                ELSE                      \ front
                    1+                    \ front+1
                    DUP QMAX @ >
                    IF
                        DROP QMIN @
                    THEN
                    DUP FRONT !
                    C@ TRUE               \ n tf
                THEN ;

: QSTORE        ( c -- )
                REAR @ 1+                 \ c rear+1
                DUP QMAX @ >
                IF
                    DROP QMIN @           \ c rear
                THEN
                DUP FRONT @ =
                IF
                    1-                    \ queue full
                    DUP QMIN @ <
                    IF
                        QMAX @ REAR !
                    THEN
                    2DROP
                ELSE
                    DUP REAR !
                    C!                    \ store c at REAR
                THEN ;
```

```
inc rear
if rear > max
then rear = min
if front = rear
then queue is full
        dec rear
        if rear < min
        then rear = max
else store value at    rear
```

Figure 10–19   Algorithm to Store a Value in the Circular Queue in Figure 10–18

```
if front = rear
then queue is empty (set false flag)
else  inc front
        if front > max
        then front = min
        read byte at front
        set true flag
```

Figure 10–20   Algorithm to Check Queue for a Value

FRONT and *REAR* are initialized to *QMIN* in the WHYP word *INITQ* (--) in Listing 10–4. To store a value in the queue, the pointer *REAR* is incremented and the value is stored at *REAR*. However, when *REAR* exceeds *QMAX*, it must wrap around to *QMIN*. If *REAR* ever runs into *FRONT*, then the queue is full and we will back up *REAR* and not store the new value. The complete algorithm for storing a value in the queue is given in Figure 10–19 and is implemented by the WHYP word *QSTORE* (c --) in Listing 10–4 which stores the character on top of the data stack in the queue.

To read a value from the queue, the pointer *FRONT* is incremented and that value is read. This will guarantee that the first value stored in the queue will be the first one read from the queue. The queue will be empty any time that *FRONT* = *REAR*. The algorithm to check the queue is given in Figure 10–20 and is implemented by the WHYP word *CHECKQ* (-- n tf | ff) in Listing 10–4.

10.7   KEYPAD INTERFACING USING INTERRUPTS

The interfacing of a 4 × 4 keypad using the 74C922 16-key encoder chip was described in Section 7.4.2 and shown in Figures 7–17 and 7–18. It would be useful to be able to produce a hardware interrupt every time you press a key. You could then store the hex values of the keys pressed in a queue and display the values at a slower rate than the keys are being pressed.

We showed in Figure 10–16 how pin *PT7/PAI* of the pulse accumulator could be used to interface the keypad using the MM74C922 encoder chip. Listing 10–5 shows how that program can be modified to use the pulse accumulator input edge interrupt. Note that this interrupt is enabled by setting the *PAI* bit (bit 0) of the *PACTL* register as shown in Figure 10–15 in Section 10.4.

Listing 10–5   Keypad Input Using the Pulse Accumulator Interrupt

```
\ Keypad input using 74922 encoder chip with interrupts
\ Uses Pulse Accumulator Input Edge to detect data available

LOAD LED.WHP            \ for .led (FIG. 7.9)
LOAD QUEUE.WHP          \ for INITQ, CHECKQ, and QSTORE
LOAD OC_DELAY.WHP       \ for s.delay

HEX
0B1A     CONSTANT PAIE.IVEC    \ pulse accum. input edge interrupt vector

CREATE keytbl
        C C, 3 C, 2 C, 1 C, D C, 6 C, 5 C, 4 C,
        E C, 9 C, 8 C, 7 C, F C, B C, 0 C, A C,

: init.key     ( -- )
            00 DDRC C!        \ PC0-PC3 inputs
            TMSK2 5 LO        \ overflow interrupt disabled
            TMSK2 4 HI        \ input edge interrupt enabled
            PACTL 5 LO        \ event counter
            PACTL 4 HI        \ rising edge of PA7
            PACTL 6 HI        \ enable PA

INT:    paie.intser
            PORTJ C@                    \ read 74923 chip data
            0F AND
            keytbl + C@                 \ index into table
            qstore                      \ & store key value in queue
            01 PAFLG C!                 \ clear PAIF flag

RTI;

: set.paie.intvec    ( -- )
            [ ' paie.intser ] LITERAL
            PAIE.IVEC ! ;

: main.pa      ( -- )
            SEI
            init.key
            INITQ
            set.paie.intvec
            CLI
            BEGIN
              BEGIN
                CHECKQ
              UNTIL
            .led
            2 s.delay
            AGAIN ;
```

The interrupt service routine, *paie.intser*, shown in Listing 10–5 reads the value from Port J and uses it as an index into the table *keytbl* from which the key value is read and stored in a queue. The *PAIF* flag in *PAFLG* is cleared by writing a 1 to bit 0 of *PAFLG*. Note that in the word *set.paie.intvec (--)* in Listing 10–5 the address of the interrupt service routine, *paie.intser*, is stored in the *PAIE.IVEC* user vector address ($0B1A) in Table 6–7.

The word *main.pa*, shown in Listing 10–5, will first initialize the registers and the queue, set up the *PAIE* interrupt vector, and then enable interrupts by clearing the interrupt mask bit in the condition code register with the instruction *CLI*. It will then wait for a key to be pressed by continually checking the queue until the interrupt routine has deposited a key value in the queue. When this happens, the value is displayed on a seven-segment display using the word *.led (n --)* defined in Figure 7–9. Note that the words in Figure 7–9 are loaded into memory at the beginning of the program in Listing 10–5 using the statement *LOAD LED.WHP*.

After displaying the key value on the seven-segment display, a 2-second delay is implemented using the word *s.delay (n --)* defined in Listing 10–1. (This word is loaded into memory at the beginning of the program in Listing 10–5 using the statement *LOAD OC_DELAY.WHP*.) This means that if you keep pressing different keys before the 2 seconds is up, they won't be lost, but rather the interrupt routine will store their values in the queue. When the 2-second delay is up, the next key will automatically be displayed for 2 seconds. This illustrates how hardware interrupts can be used to prevent time-critical data from being lost.

10.8   PULSE TRAIN USING INTERRUPTS

The program given in Listing 10–2 in Section 10.2.1 produced the pulse train shown in Figure 10–21. Note that the word *PULSE* in Listing 10–2 includes a *BEGIN . . . AGAIN* loop and thus no other programs can be executed while the pulse train is being generated. It should be clear, however, that most of the time is being spent in the *BEGIN . . . UNTIL* loop waiting for bit 6 of *TFLG1* to go high. If

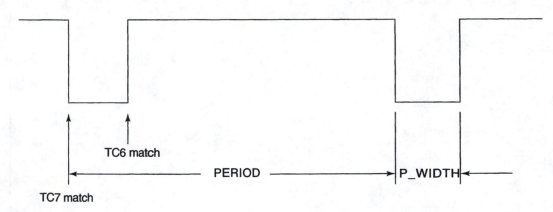

Figure 10–21   Pulse Train

we use an interrupt to detect when bit 6 of *TFLG1* goes high, then we should be able to generate the pulse train in the background while leaving time for the 68HC12 to execute other programs at the same time.

To enable timer interrupts, we must set the appropriate bits in *TMSK1* and/or *TMSK2*, as shown in Figure 10–22. In the case of the pulse train shown in Figure 10–21, we want an interrupt to occur on a *TC6* output compare match. Therefore, we must set bit 6 in *TMSK1*. A program for producing the pulse train using interrupts is shown in Listing 10–6.

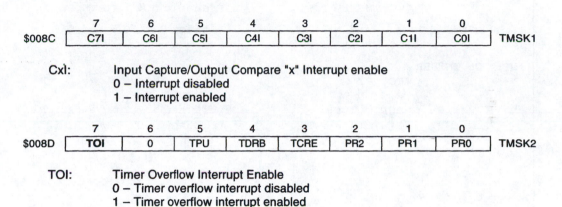

	7	6	5	4	3	2	1	0	
$008C	C7I	C6I	C5I	C4I	C3I	C2I	C1I	C0I	TMSK1

CxI: Input Capture/Output Compare "x" Interrupt enable
        0 – Interrupt disabled
        1 – Interrupt enabled

	7	6	5	4	3	2	1	0	
$008D	TOI	0	TPU	TDRB	TCRE	PR2	PR1	PR0	TMSK2

TOI: Timer Overflow Interrupt Enable
        0 – Timer overflow interrupt disabled
        1 – Timer overflow interrupt enabled

Figure 10–22   Enabling Timer Interrupts

Listing 10–6   Pulse Train Using Interrupts

```
\       Pulse train using output compares 7 and 6. File: PULSEI.WHP
HEX

0080    CONSTANT    TIOS      \ Timer Input Cap.\Output Comp. Select
0082    CONSTANT    OC7M      \ Output Compare 7 Mask Register
0083    CONSTANT    OC7D      \ Output Compare 7 Data Register
0084    CONSTANT    TCNT      \ Timer Counter Register
0086    CONSTANT    TSCR      \ Timer System Control Register
0088    CONSTANT    TCTL1     \ Timer Control Register 1
008C    CONSTANT    TMSK1     \ Timer Interrupt Mask Register 1
008D    CONSTANT    TMSK2     \ Timer Interrupt Mask Register 2
008E    CONSTANT    TFLG1     \ Timer Interrupt Flag Register 1
009C    CONSTANT    TC6       \ Timer Output Compare Register 6
009E    CONSTANT    TC7       \ Timer Output Compare Register 7
0B22    CONSTANT    TC6.IVEC  \ Timer Channel 6 interrupt vector

DECIMAL
VARIABLE P_WIDTH      6625 P_WIDTH !
VARIABLE PERIOD      17500 PERIOD !
HEX
```

(continued)

Listing 10–6 *(continued)*

```
: TINIT              ( -- )
                     C0 TIOS C!              \ select output compares 6 & 7
                     30 TMSK2 C!             \ div by 1: 8 MHz timer clock
                     80 TSCR C!              \ enable timer
                     TCNT @ DUP TC6 ! TC7 !  \ init cnt in TC6 & TC7
                     6 OC7M HI               \ pulse train out PT6
                     6 OC7D LO               \ PT6 goes low on TC7 match
                     4 TCTL1 HI 5 TCTL1 HI   \ set PT6 high on TC6 match
                     40 TMSK1 C! ;           \ enable TC6 interrupts

: CLR.C76            ( -- )                  \ clear both C7F and C6F
                     C0 TFLG1 C! ;

INT: TC6.INTSER      ( -- )
                     TC7 @
                     PERIOD @ +
                     DUP TC7 !               \ TC7new = TC7old + PERIOD
                     P_WIDTH @ + TC6 !       \ TC6new = TC7new + P_WIDTH
                     CLR.C76


RTI;

: SET.TC6.INTVEC     ( -- )
                     [ ' TC6.INTSER ] LITERAL
                     TC6.IVEC ! ;

: PULSEI             ( -- )
                     SEI
                     TINIT
                     SET.TC6.INTVEC
                     CLI ;


DECIMAL
```

The interrupt service routine, *TC6.INTSER*, given in Listing 10–6 will be executed on each rising edge of the pulse train shown in Figure 10–21. This routine computes new values for the output compare registers, *TC7* and *TC6*, based on the period and pulse width stored in the variables *PERIOD* and *P_WIDTH*, respectively. Note that the interrupt service routine should be completed not only before another interrupt occurs (a rising edge of the pulse train) but also before the next falling edge of the pulse train. It is the interrupt routine that stores the new output compare register values. The new value for *TC7* must be stored before the timer counter reaches this new value.

We can measure the time it takes to execute the interrupt service routine, *TC6.INTSER*, by using the same method described above in Section 10.5 for the traffic light program. Doing this yields a value of 648 timer counts, or

648×0.125 μsec $= 81$ μsec. For a 50 percent duty cycle (high time $=$ low time) this would mean that the smallest allowable period value would be $648 \times 2 = 1296$. This corresponds to a maximum frequency of about 6 KHz.

Keeping the value of the variable *PERIOD* constant and varying the value of *P_WIDTH* will produce a pulse-width modulated signal. Such a signal is often used to vary the speed of a DC motor. The higher percent of the period time that is high, the higher the speed of the motor.

The interrupt occurs on the rising edge of the pulse train, shown in Figure 10–21, and the pulse must stay high at least until the interrupt routine has finished executing. The low time can be as short as we want because we set both output compare registers in the interrupt routine. For a given period we should probably keep the low time shorter than the high time. This would mean that this setup could produce signals with duty cycles between 50 percent and 100 percent. To produce signals with duty cycles between 0 percent and 50 percent we should change the setup so that the interrupt occurs on the falling edge rather than the rising edge and the signal remains low for at least half of the period time.

The 68HC912B32 has a separate pulse-width modulator subsystem that will be described in Chapter 15.

10.9 MEASURING THE PERIOD OF A PULSE TRAIN USING INTERRUPTS

Suppose we want to measure the period of a pulse train of the type shown in Figure 10–21. In principle, this should be a simple matter. For example, we could use input capture 1 on pin *PT1* and capture the timer count value on each rising edge of the pulse train. The difference between the time captured on two consecutive rising edges would be proportional to the period. However, at divide by 1 (the default) the timer overflows approximately every 8 milliseconds (see Figure 10–3) which would limit the period of the pulse train to this value. Note that the overflow itself is not a problem for periods less than 8 ms. For example, suppose that the period is equal to $4000 ticks of the timer counter, *TCNT*. If the first edge occurs at a *TCNT* value of $E000 and the second edge occurs at a *TCNT* value of $2000, then the difference will be $2000 - $E000 = $4000 (where the final borrow is ignored due to the rollover).

However, if the real period is equal to $24000 *TCNT* ticks and the two consecutive rising edges read $E000 and $2000, then the period will still be computed as $4000 because *TCNT* is only a 16-bit register. What has happened is that the timer, *TCNT*, has rolled over three times instead of just once. We can keep track of the number of *TCNT* rollovers by using a timer overflow interrupt. If this timer overflow interrupt increments a variable *OVCNT*, then this value of *OVCNT* can be considered to be the high word of a 32-bit timer count where the value of *TCNT* contains the low word.

A program to measure the period of a pulse train input in *PT1* (*TC1*) is shown in Listing 10–7. On each rising edge of the pulse train, the latest 32-bit period is stored in the double variable *DPERIOD*. Note that *DPERIOD* is declared by using the word *VARIABLE* and then allocating an additional 2 bytes with the statement *2 VALLOT* (see Section 4.3.3).

Listing 10–7   Measuring the Period of a Pulse Train

```
\         Measuring the period of a pulse train. File: PERIOD.WHP
HEX
0080    CONSTANT   TIOS        \ Timer Input Cap.\Output Comp. Select
0084    CONSTANT   TCNT        \ Timer Counter Register
0086    CONSTANT   TSCR        \ Timer System Control Register
008B    CONSTANT   TCTL4       \ Timer Control Register 4
008C    CONSTANT   TMSK1       \ Timer Interrupt Mask Register 1
008D    CONSTANT   TMSK2       \ Timer Interrupt Mask Register 2
008E    CONSTANT   TFLG1       \ Timer Interrupt Flag Register 1
008F    CONSTANT   TFLG2       \ Timer Interrupt Flag Register 2
0092    CONSTANT   TC1         \ Timer Input Capture Register 1
0B2C    CONSTANT   TC1.IVEC    \ Timer Channel 1 interrupt vector
0B1E    CONSTANT   TO.IVEC     \ Timer overflow interrupt vector


VARIABLE         OVCNT              \ timer overflow count
VARIABLE         OVCNT.OLD          \ old timer overflow count
VARIABLE         TC1.OLD            \ old TC1
VARIABLE         DPERIOD 2 VALLOT   \ double word period dH dL


: INIT.IC       ( -- )
                00 TIOS C!         \ select input capture 1
                30 TMSK2 C!        \ div by 1: 8 MHz timer clock
                80 TSCR C!         \ enable timer
                3 TCTL4 LO
                2 TCTL4 HI         \ rising edge of TC1
                02 TFLG1 C!        \ clear any old flags
                80 TFLG2 C!
                7 TMSK2 HI         \ enable TOI interrupt
                1 TMSK1 HI ;       \ enable TC1 interrupt


\       Timer overflow interrupt routine
INT: TO.INTSER  ( -- )
                1 OVCNT +!         \ inc OVCNT
                80 TFLG2 C!        \ clear TOF

RTI;


\       Input capture 1 interrupt routine
INT: TC1.INTSER ( -- )
                TC1.OLD @ OVCNT.OLD @      \ ic.o ov.o
                TC1 @ DUP TC1.OLD !        \ ic.o ov.o ic
                OVCNT @ DUP OVCNT.OLD !    \ ic.o ov.o ic ov
                2SWAP D-                   \ spL spH
                DPERIOD 2!                 \ store period in DPERIOD
                02 TFLG1 C!                \ clear C1F
RTI;
```

Listing 10–7   (continued)

```
\       Set interrupt vectors
: SET.TO.INTVEC         ( -- )
                [ ' TO.INTSER ] LITERAL
                TO.IVEC ! ;

: SET.TC1.INTVEC        ( -- )
                [ ' TC1.INTSER ] LITERAL
                TC1.IVEC ! ;

\       Main program
: MAIN ( -- )
                SEI                             \ set interrupt flag
                SET.TO.INTVEC                   \ set interrupt vectors
                SET.TC1.INTVEC
                INIT.IC                         \ init input capture
                CLI ;                           \ clear interrupt flag

DECIMAL
```

As an example, suppose that on the first rising edge of a pulse train the variable *OVCNT* contains the value $0012 and *TCNT* has a value of $E000. If on the next rising edge the variable *OVCNT* contains the value $0015 and *TCNT* has a value of $2000, then the elapsed time will be $00152000 − $0012E000 = $00024000. It will take almost 9 minutes for the variable *OVCNT* to roll over. Therefore, this method can measure the period of *very* low frequency pulse trains.

Note that the program in Listing 10–7 contains two interrupt service routines. The routine *TO.INTSER* simply increments the variable *OVCNT* each time the timer counter, *TCNT*, overflows and then clears the *TOF* flag. The routine *TC1.INTSER* gets executed on each rising edge of the signal on pin *PT1*. It first fetches the 32-bit timer count from the last rising edge which is stored in the two variables *TC1.OLD* (low word) and *OVCNT.OLD* (high word). It then reads the current 32-bit timer count from *TC1* (low word) and *OVCNT* (high word) and then saves these in *TC1.OLD* and *OVCNT.OLD*, respectively. The old 32-bit count is then subtracted from the current 32-bit count and this double word is stored in the double variable *DPERIOD*. Recall that the WHYP word *2!* (*nL nH addr --)* stores the double word *nL nH* at address *addr*. Finally the *C1F* flag in *TFLG1* is cleared.

Note that the main program in Listing 10–7 simply sets the two interrupt vectors, initializes the registers, and then enables the interrupts. The interrupt routines will continually maintain the most recent period value in the double variable *DPERIOD* in the background. Other WHYP words can use the word *2@* to access *DPERIOD* at any time to find out the latest period value. Recall, however, the definition of *2@* (*a -- d)*, shown in Figure 4–14. If an interrupt occurs in the middle of this word, then it is possible that the value of *DPERIOD* will be changed by the interrupt service routine leading to an erroneous value returned by 2@. To prevent this you should disable interrupts while reading *DPERIOD* by using a word such as *get.dperiod (-- d)* defined as

```
: get.dperiod          ( -- d )
                       SEI DPERIOD 2@ CLI ;
```

10.10 THE POLAROID ULTRASONIC TRANSDUCER

An ultrasonic ranging system is available from Polaroid Corporation. It consists of an acoustical transducer and a ranging circuit board. The transducer transmits a sequence of ultrasonic pulses and receives a reflected echo from a target as shown in Figure 10–23. The ranging board has an input pin called *INIT* which is brought high to start a transmitted pulse. A reflected echo is indicated by the *ECHO* pin on the ranging board going high, as shown in Figure 10–24.

We can interface the ranging board to the 68HC12 by connecting the *INIT* pin to *PT6* (and use output compare 6) and the *ECHO* pin to *PT1* (and use input capture 1) as shown in Figure 10–23. We will illustrate the use of the ultrasonic ranging system by designing an ultrasonic tape measure that will record the distance to an object by just aiming the transducer at the object.

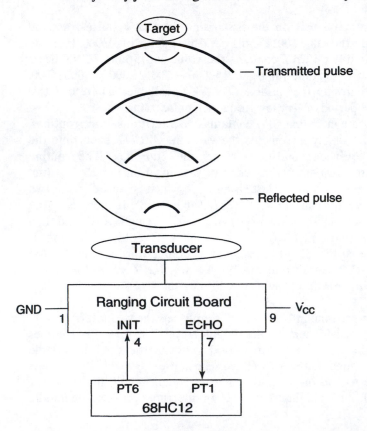

Figure 10–23 Block Diagram of Ultrasonic Ranging System

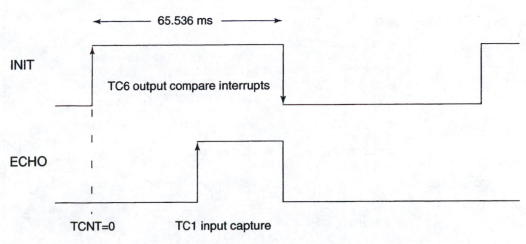

Figure 10–24   Waveforms of Ultrasonic Ranging System

The transducer can measure distances up to about 36 feet. Since the speed of sound is approximately 1.125 ft/ms or 13.5 in/ms (at 20°C), then sound will travel a distance of 36 feet in about 32 ms so that a round trip will take about 64 ms. If we set the timer prescalar to 8, then the timer will roll over every 65.536 ms (see Figure 10–3). If we set up output compare 6 to toggle *PT6* on each match of *TC6*, then we can produce the *INIT* signal shown in Figure 10–24.

A program for the ultrasonic tape measure is shown in Listing 10–8. Output compare 6 is set up to toggle *PT6* and produce an interrupt on each timer match. The value of *TC6* is set to zero so that the match will always occur when *TCNT* rolls over from $FFFF to $0000. Inasmuch as *PT6* is connected to the *INIT* signal on the

---

Listing 10–8   Ultrasonic Tape Measure

```
\        Ultrasonic tape measure   File: SONAR.WHP
LOAD SPILED.WHP         \ for .leds and SPI words (Fig. 7.11)
HEX

0080    CONSTANT TIOS          \ Timer Input Cap.\Output Comp. Select
0084    CONSTANT TCNT          \ Timer Counter Register
0086    CONSTANT TSCR          \ Timer System Control Register
0088    CONSTANT TCTL1         \ Timer Control Register 1
008B    CONSTANT TCTL4         \ Timer Control Register 4
008C    CONSTANT TMSK1         \ Timer Interrupt Mask Register 1
008D    CONSTANT TMSK2         \ Timer Interrupt Mask Register 2
008E    CONSTANT TFLG1         \ Timer Interrupt Flag Register 1
0092    CONSTANT TC1           \ Timer Input Capture Register 1
009C    CONSTANT TC6           \ Timer Output Compare Register 6
0B22    CONSTANT TC6.IVEC      \ Timer Channel 6 interrupt vector

VARIABLE DISTANCE
VARIABLE ECHO
```

(continued)

Listing 10–8   (*continued*)

```
: init.sonar     ( -- )
                 F0 TIOS C!            \ PT6 output, PT1 input
                 80 TSCR C!            \ enable timer
                 03 TMSK2 C!           \ 1 MHz timer clock
                 5 TCTL1 LO            \ toggle PT6 (TC6)
                 4 TCTL1 HI
                 0 TC6 !               \ sync to TCNT
                 6 TMSK1 HI            \ enable TC6 int
                 3 TCTL4 LO            \ rising edge of PT1
                 2 TCTL4 HI ;
INT: TC6.INTSER ( -- )                 \ int on both edges
                 6 PORTT ?HI           \ if rising edge
                 IF
                     02 TFLG1 C!       \ clear C1F flag
                 ELSE                  \ if falling edge
                     1 TFLG1 ?HI       \ if echo
                     IF
                         TC1 @         \ get distance
                         DISTANCE !    \  & save it
                         TRUE ECHO !   \  echo=true
                     ELSE              \ else
                         FALSE ECHO !  \  echo=false
                     THEN
                 THEN
                 40 TFLG1 C!           \ clear OC2F flag
RTI ;
: SET.TC6.INTVEC        ( -- )
                 [ ' TC6.INTSER ] LITERAL
                 TC6.IVEC ! ;
: ?distance      ( -- n tf | ff )
                 ECHO @
                 IF
                     DISTANCE @
                     TRUE
                 ELSE
                     FALSE
                 THEN ;
: sonar.tape     ( -- )
                 init.sonar
                 SPI.INIT
                 BEGIN
                     ?distance
                     IF                \ if echo
                         135 20000 */  \ convert to inches
                         .4leds        \ display distance
                     ELSE
                         SS.LO         \ else
                         EE SEND.SPI   \ display dashes
                         EE SEND.SPI
                         SS.HI
                     THEN
                 AGAIN ;
```

ranging circuit board, then a new ultrasonic pulse will be transmitted on each rising edge of *PT6* when the value of *TCNT* will be zero. This means that if there is an echo and a rising edge of *PT1* stores the value of *TCNT* in *TC1*, this value will be the total elapsed time since the pulse was transmitted.

The interrupt service routine shown in Listing 10–8 will be executed on both the rising and falling edge of *PT6*. The routine first checks to see if it was a rising edge. If it was, then this means that an ultrasonic pulse is being sent. The *C1F* flag of input compare 1 is cleared so that we can determine if an echo occurs before the next falling edge of *PT6*. When a falling edge of *PT6* occurs, the *ELSE* part of the interrupt service routine, *TC6.INTSER*, in Listing 10–8 is executed. This will check the *C1F* flag in *TFLG1* to see if an echo occurred. If it did, then the distance value is read from *TC1* and stored in the variable *DISTANCE* and a *TRUE* flag is stored in the variable *ECHO*. If an echo did not occur, then a *FALSE* flag is stored in the variable *ECHO*.

The word *?distance (-- n tf | ff)*, shown in Listing 10–8, just checks the values in the variables *ECHO* and *DISTANCE* and will return a false flag if an echo has not occurred within the 65.536-ms time-out time. Otherwise, it will return a true flag over the echo time *n* corresponding to the total elapsed time from *INIT* going high to *ECHO* going high. Since each tick corresponds to 1.0 μs, then *n*/1000 would be the total elapsed time in milliseconds.

The word *sonar.tape (--)* in Listing 10–8 will continually read the distance from the transducer to the target using the word *?distance (-- n tf | ff)* and display this value on the three-digit seven-segment display shown in Figure 8–10. The total distance in inches corresponding to the total elapsed time, *n*, can be calculated by multiplying *n* by 135 (13.5 inches/ms) and dividing by 10,000. Dividing by 20,000 instead of 10,000 will give the distance to the object in inches. This is the value that is computed in the word *sonar.tape* in Listing 10–8 and displayed on the three seven-segment displays shown in Figure 8–10 using the word *.4leds* given in Figure 8–11.

10.11   SUMMARY

In this chapter we have seen that the timer subsystem can be used to produce delays, measure time intervals such as pulse widths, and create output waveforms such as pulse-width modulated signals. The 68HC912B32 has a separate pulse-width modulator module designed specifically for producing pulse-width modulated signals. We will discuss this module in Chapter 15. We looked at output compares in Section 10.2, input captures in Section 10.3, and the pulse accumulator in Section 10.4.

Several examples of using interrupts were given in this chapter including interfacing a keypad using interrupts in Section 10.7, generating a pulse train in Section 10.8, measuring the period of a pulse train in Section 10.9, and designing an ultrasonic tape measure in Section 10.10.

A circular queue data structure was defined in Section 10.6. This data structure provides a useful place to store data that are read in an interrupt service routine.

The following files contain the examples of using the timer functions that were discussed in this chapter:

OC_DELAY.WHP   (see Listing 10–1)

> Uses an output compare to define the WHYP word *s.delay (n --)* that will delay *n* seconds.

PULSE.WHP   (see Listing 10–2)

> Uses two output compares to define the WHYP word *pulse (--)* that will produce a pulse train out pin *PT6*.

PWIDTH.WHP   (see Listing 10–3)

> Uses an input capture to define the WHYP word *pulse.width (-- n)* that will measure the width of a single pulse coming in pin *PT2* and leave the width in microseconds on the data stack.

QUEUE.WHP   (see Listing 10–4)

> Defines the words *INITQ (--)*, *CHECKQ (-- n tf | ff)*, and *QSTORE (c --)* to implement a circular queue.

KEYINT.WHP   (see Listing 10–5)

> Uses the pulse accumulator interrupt to detect a keypad pressing.

PULSEI.WHP   (see Listing 10–6)

> Uses an output compare interrupt to generate a pulse train.

PERIOD.WHP   (see Listing 10–7)

> Uses overflow and input capture interrupts to measure the period of a pulse train.

SONAR.WHP   (see Listing 10–8)

> Uses an output compare interrupt and an input capture interrupt to design an ultrasonic tape measure using the Polaroid ultrasonic transducer.

Examples of using the timer module to measure light intensity (using a light-to-frequency converter) and acceleration (using a dual-axis accelerometer with digital output) are given in the exercises at the end of this chapter.

EXERCISES

Exercise 10.1

Modify Listing 10–1 such that the word *S.DELAY (n --)* will work on a 68HC11 using output compare 2.

Exercise 10.2

Modify Listing 10–2 so as to generate the pulse train shown in Figure 10–10 by using output compares 1 and 2 on a 68HC11.

Exercise 10.3

Modify Listing 10–3 so as to measure the width of a positive pulse on pin *PA1* of a 68HC11.

Exercise 10.4

Modify Listing 10–3 so as to measure the width of a negative-going pulse (high-low-high) on pin PT2 of a 68HC12.

Exercise 10.5

Modify the program shown in Figure 10–16 so that it will work with the pulse accumulator of a 68HC11.

Exercise 10.6

The TSL245 is an infrared light-to-frequency converter from Texas Instruments that can be used to measure light intensity. Its spectral responsivity is above 0.5 for wavelengths between about 850 and 1000 nm with a maximum responsivity at about 920 nm. The sensor includes a photodiode and current-to-frequency converter in a single package with three pins: power, ground, and output. The output is a square wave (50 percent duty cycle) with a frequency (between 1 Hz and 500 KHz) directly proportional to light intensity. See the Web site `http://www.ti.com/sc/docs/schome.htm.` to download a detailed data sheet.

    a. Write a WHYP word called *light1 (-- n)* that will leave a frequency value between 0 and 65,535 on the data stack which is proportional to the light level. Use an input capture to measure the instantaneous period of the square wave.

    b. Write a WHYP word called *light2 (-- n)* that will leave a frequency value between 0 and 65,535 on the data stack which is proportional to the light level. Use the pulse accumulator to count the number of cycles of the square wave that occur in a second.

Exercise 10.7

The TSL230 is a programmable light-to-frequency converter from Texas Instruments that can be used to measure light intensity. Its spectral responsivity is above 0.5 for wavelengths between about 450 and 950 nm with a maximum responsivity at about 760 nm. The sensor includes a photodiode and current-to-frequency converter in the single dual-in-line package shown below.

```
       1 |￣￣￣￣￣￣￣| 8
      ---| S0      S3 |---
       2 |           | 7
      ---| S1      S2 |---
       3 |           | 6
      ---| OE     OUT |---
       4 |           | 5
      ---| GND    Vcc |---
         |_____|
            TSL230
```

If S3 and S2 are both low, the output is a pulse train with a frequency (between 1 Hz and 1 MHz) directly proportional to light intensity. For a given light level the output frequency can be scaled (divided by) 2, 10, or 100 by setting pins S3 and S2 as shown in the table on the next page. The light sensitivity can also be increased by setting pins S1 and S0 as shown in the table on the next page. See the Web site `http://www.ti.com/sc/docs/schome.htm.` to download a detailed data sheet.

S1	S0	Sensitivity
L	L	Power Down
L	H	1x
H	L	10x
H	H	100x

S3	S2	Frequency Scaling (divide-by)
L	L	1
L	H	2
H	L	10
H	H	100

Assume that S0-S3 are connected to *PH0-PH3* or Port H.

a. Write a WHYP word called *light.on* (*n* --) that will turn the sensor on with a sensitivity determined by *n*. (*n* = 0 − 3 corresponds to power down, 1x, 10x, and 100x, respectively).

b. Write a WHYP word called *output.scale* (*n* --) that will scale the output frequency by 1, 2, 10, and 100 for values of *n* = 0 − 3.

c. Write a WHYP word called *light1* (-- *n*) that will leave a frequency value between 0 and 65,535 on the data stack which is proportional to the light level. Use an input capture to measure the instantaneous period of the square wave.

d. Write a WHYP word called *light2* (-- *n*) that will leave a frequency value between 0 and 65,535 on the data stack which is proportional to the light level. Use the pulse accumulator to count the number of cycles of the square wave that occur in a second.

Exercise 10.8

The ADXL202 from Analog Devices is a ±2 g dual-axis accelerometer with digital output. See Exercise 9.5 for a description of the ADXL05 single-axis accelerometer with analog output. The ADXL202 uses a similar technology as the ADXL05 for each of two perpendicular axes. The output for each axis is a pulse train in which the duty cycle is proportional to the acceleration. The device comes in a 14-pin DIP with the *x*-axis of acceleration along the length of the chip with the *y*-axis perpendicular to *x* in the plane of the chip. You can go to http://www.analog.com/product/Product_Center.html to download a complete data sheet.

The period of the output waveform for both channels is determined by a single resistor R_{set}. The period, *T2*, given by $R_{set}(\Omega)/125$ MΩ, is typically between 0.5 ms and 10 ms. The high time of the pulse train is *T1*. A duty cycle of 50 percent (*T1* = 0.5 × *T2*) corresponds to 0 g. The acceleration is given by

```
A(g) = (T1/T2 - 0.5)/12.5%
```

Write a WHYP word called *get.xyg* (-- *x y*) that will leave the accelerations along the *x*- and *y*-axes, in milli-g, on the data stack. That is, a value of 1000 corresponds to 1 g.

Exercise 10.9

The ADXL202 described in Exercise 10.8 can be used to measure dual-axis tilt by measuring the component of the earth's gravity. If the *x*- and *y*-axes of the ADXL202 are both oriented parallel to the earth's surface (i.e., horizontal), then the output duty cycle of both will be 50 percent (0 g). A tilt of the ADXL202 will produce an *x*-acceleration, A_x, and a *y*-acceleration, A_y, that can be measured using the formula given in Exercise 10.8. From these measured values between −1 g and +1 g the angles, *pitch* and *roll*, can be computed from

$$pitch = \arcsin(A_x/1 \text{ g})$$
$$roll = \arcsin(A_y/1 \text{ g})$$

Write a WHYP word called *tilt (-- pitch roll)* that will leave the tilt angles, *pitch* and *roll*, in tenths of a degree, on the data stack. *Hint:* Use the arcsin table in Figure 5–33 and linearly interpolate to the nearest tenth of a degree.

Exercise 10.10

The ADXL202 described in Exercises 10.8 and 10.9 can be used to measure 360° of tilt by orienting the chip on a vertical plane. For example, if the *x*-axis is vertical (pointing down toward the earth's surface) and the *y*-axis is horizontal (parallel to the earth's surface), then the *x*-acceleration will be −1 g and the *y*-acceleration will by 0 g. As the chip is rotated in the vertical plane, the *x*-acceleration will increase toward zero and the *y*-acceleration will increase toward +1 g. In fact, as the chip is rotated through 360°, the accelerations A_x and A_y will vary as sinusoidal quadrature signals of the type shown in Figure 9–12 where *B* corresponds to the *x*-acceleration curve and *A* corresponds to the *y*-acceleration curve.

Write a WHYP word called *wheel (-- angle)* that will measure the *x*- and *y*-accelerations of an ADXL202 mounted on the surface of a wheel and leave the orientation of the wheel (0–360°) on the data stack.

Exercise 10.11

Write a program to generate the two waveforms shown below.

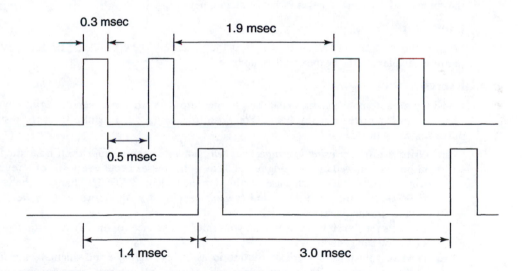

Exercise 10.12

Motor speeds can be measured using a Hall-effect sensor. A Hall-effect switch produces a digital output that goes low when the south pole of an external magnet is close to the sensor and goes high when the magnet is removed. An internal magnet Hall-effect speed sensor provides a digital output pulse when gear or thread teeth move past the sensor. See the Web site http://www.sensorsolutionscorp.com/ for more information on Hall-effect sensors.

a. Assume a single magnet is mounted on a wheel connected to the shaft of a motor. Write a WHYP word called *RPM (-- n)* that will measure the speed of the motor in RPM using a Hall-effect switch.

b. Assume that a wheel has eight teeth evenly spaced on its circumference. Write a WHYP word called *SPEED (-- n)* that will measure the speed of the motor in RPM using a Hall-effect speed sensor.

Exercise 10.13

Incremental optical encoders can be used to measure the direction and angle through which a shaft is rotated. A typical incremental encoder will have two square wave outputs (channels A and B) that are in phase quadrature. If the shaft is rotating clockwise, then the square wave from channel B will lead channel A by 90°. On the other hand if the shaft is rotating counterclockwise, then the square wave from channel A will lead channel B by 90°. See the Web site `http://www.opticalencoder.com/` for more information on incremental optical encoders.

Assume you have an incremental optical encoder with 360 counts per revolution that is connected to a dial that can move from 0 to 360°. Write a program that will measure the angle of the dial at any time. You must initialize the count to zero when the dial is at 0° and then keep track of both positive and negative counts.

Exercise 10.14

Add a switch to the ultrasonic tape measure (see Listing 10–8) that will allow you to display the measured distances in either inches or centimeters.

Exercise 10.15

Modify the program in Listing 10–8 so that the distance will be displayed on four seven-segment displays to the nearest tenth of an inch.

Exercise 10.16

Consider an automobile crank signal used to measure RPM that consists of a square wave with one missing pulse per revolution. You wish to generate such a pulse train for testing purposes using the 68HC12.

a. Write a program *using interrupts* that will generate such a pulse train consisting of 35 pulses followed by a missing pulse. That is, the pulses occur every 10° of a revolution. Let the width of each pulse be stored in the variable *WIDTH*. Changing the value of *WIDTH* will change the period (always keeping it a square wave) and therefore change the simulated value of RPM.

b. Measure the time it takes to execute your interrupt service routine. What is the highest RPM you can generate?

c. Rewrite your interrupt service routine in assembly language and calculate the time it takes to execute. What is the highest RPM you can generate using this assembly language interrupt service routine?

Exercise 10.17

You want to generate an output square wave (approx. 60 Hz) on pin *PT3* of Port T. The square wave is to be generated "in the background" with as little software intervention as possible. Using the real-time interrupt, write a WHYP interrupt service routine called *square.intser* that will toggle *PT3* every 8.196 ms. Write all the other WHYP words needed to set up this interrupt service routine and start the square wave.

Exercise 10.18

a. Redo Exercises 10.8, 10.9, and/or 10.10 using interrupts to measure the duty cycle of the x- and y-axes signals of the ADXL202 accelerometer.

b. Redo Exercise 10.6 using interrupts to measure the frequency of the TSL245 infrared light-to-frequency converter.

c. Redo Exercise 10.7 using interrupts to measure the frequency of the TSL230 programmable light-to-frequency converter.

Exercise 10.19

The figure below shows a hacksaw blade clamped to a base and connected near the base to a solenoid with a piece of wire. By activating the solenoid with a square wave near the hacksaw blade's resonance frequency, the hacksaw blade can be made to oscillate back and forth in a wide arc (typically several oscillations per second).

A ten-segment bar LED is mounted on the top of the hacksaw blade, as shown. By turning on just the right set of LEDs in sequence, you can write a message in the air, for example WHYP as shown in the figure. By making the message scroll from right to left you can write any long message, such as your name, in the air!

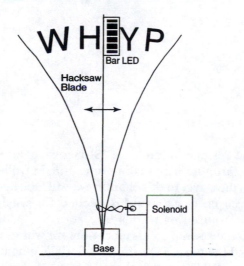

a. Write an interrupt service routine that will generate a square wave to be applied to the solenoid. Make the frequency variable by pressing a key so that you can adjust it to obtain the widest swing of the hacksaw blade.

b. Write a WHYP program that will scroll your name from right to left in the air. The bit maps for a standard character set are included on your disk in the file charset.asm. The corresponding .S19 file takes up 4 Kbytes of memory. These bit maps give the *horizontal* rows of a character as you would use on a screen. You will need to change these to corresponding *vertical* columns to use on your bar LED.

11

The Serial Communication Interface (SCI)

The 68HC12 Serial Peripheral Interface (SPI) was described in Chapter 8. This was an example of *synchronous* serial communication in which a clock signal was sent from the master to the slave. In this chapter we will look at *asynchronous* serial communication in which no clock signal is needed for synchronization. Rather each character is resynchronized by means of a start bit. After looking at the general format of asynchronous serial communication, we will show how it is implemented in the 68HC12 (and the 68HC11) using the Serial Communication Interface (SCI). We will then develop WHYP words that will make it easy to communicate using the SCI port.

11.1 ASYNCHRONOUS SERIAL I/O

There are two basic types of serial communication: *synchronous* and *asynchronous*. In synchronous communication data are normally sent in blocks that often contain error checking. The timing is controlled by a standard clock at both the transmitter and receiver ends. On the other hand, the timing for asynchronous communication is handled one character at a time and while the clocks at the transmitter and receiver must be approximately the same, they are resynchronized with each character. Because each character requires these additional synchronizing bits, asynchronous communication is slower than synchronous communication. However, it is simpler to implement and is in widespread use. In this chapter we will consider only asynchronous communication.

Asynchronous serial communication uses a *start bit* to tell when a particular character is being sent. This is illustrated in Figure 11–1 which shows the transmitted waveform when the character "*T*" (ASCII code = $54) is sent with odd parity. Before a character is sent the line is in the high, or *mark*, state. The line is then brought low (called a *space*) and held low for a time τ called the bit time. This first space is called the *start bit*. It is typically followed by seven or eight data bits. The least significant bit *D0* is transmitted first. For example, in Figure 11–1, the seven bits corresponding to the ASCII code $54 (the character "*T*") are sent starting with *D0*. These seven bits are followed by a *parity bit*. This bit is set to a 1 or a 0 such that the sum of the number of 1's transmitted is either even or odd. We have used odd parity in Figure 11–1. Since three 1's were sent (*D2*, *D4*, and *D6*) the parity bit is zero. Often a character is sent with no parity and eight data bits. The parity bit is followed by one or two stop bits which are always high (a *mark*). The next character will be indicated by the presence of the next start bit. As we will see later in this chapter the 68HC12 SCI can send either eight or nine data bits.

The reciprocal of the bit time is called the *baud rate*. Some common baud rates used in serial communication are given in Table 11–1. We will see in Section 11.2.1 how to set the baud rate used by the 68HC12 SCI port. We use a baud rate of 9600 baud when communicating with the target system from the PC using WHYP.

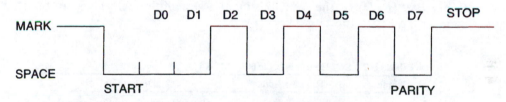

Figure 11–1   ASCII Code 54H = 1010100 ("T") Sent with Odd Parity

Table 11–1   Common Asynchronous Serial Baud Rates

Baud Rate	Bit Time (msec)	No. of STOP Bits	Char. Time (msec)	Char./Sec
110	9.09	2	100.00	10
300	3.33	1	33.33	30
600	1.67	1	16.67	60
1200	0.833	1	8.33	120
2400	0.417	1	4.17	240
4800	0.208	1	2.08	480
9600	0.104	1	1.04	960
14400	0.069	1	0.69	1440
19200	0.052	1	0.52	1920
28800	0.035	1	0.35	2880
38400	0.026	1	0.26	3840

11.2   THE 68HC12 SCI INTERFACE

The 68HC812A4 has two separate SCI modules, SCI0 and SCI1, whose registers are shown in Table 11–2. The eight registers in the first half of the table are associated with SCI0 and the eight identical registers in the second half of the table are associated with SCI1. The 68HC912B32 has only a single SCI port, SCI0, and therefore has only the eight SCI registers in the first half of Table 11–2.

A functional block diagram of the serial communication interface is shown in Figure 11–2. The main function of the SCI is to transform parallel data from the 68HC12 into serial data and send it out through the transmit data pin TxD, and to receive serial data through the receive data pin RxD and transform it to parallel data that can be read by the 68HC12.

The signals TxD (pins $PS1$ or $PS3$) and RxD (pins $PS0$ or $PS2$) are generally connected to a 25-pin or 9-pin "D" connector through an EIA-232-D (formally RS-232C) driver/receiver chip. This driver/receiver transforms the logic 0 (0 volts) and logic 1 (5 volts) signals to +12 volts and −12 volts, respectively. (Sometimes +5 volts and −5 volts are used.) This allows for more noise immunity when sending the signals over a long distance. Pin 2 on the "D" connector is normally the "transmit" pin TxD, and pin 3 is the "receive" pin RxD. But if a straightthrough cable is connected from the serial port on a PC to your target HC12 board, then the PC's "transmit" pin (pin 2) will be connected to the target board's "transmit" pin. However, we want the PC's TxD to be connected to the target board's RxD. If the target board has only one serial connector, its pin 2 will normally be connected to pin $PS0$ (RxD) of the 68HC12 so that a straightthrough cable can be used to connect the PC to the target board.

Table 11–2   SCI Registers in the 68HC812A4

Name	Register Addr.	Description
SC0BDH	00C0	SCI Baud Rate Control Register High
SC0BDL	00C1	SCI Baud Rate Control Register Low
SC0CR1	00C2	SCI Control Register 1
SC0CR2	00C3	SCI Control Register 2
SC0SR1	00C4	SCI Status Register 1
SC0SR2	00C5	SCI Status Register 2
SC0DRH	00C6	SCI Data Register High
SC0DRL	00C7	SCI Data Register Low
SC1BDH	00C8	SCI Baud Rate Control Register High
SC1BDL	00C9	SCI Baud Rate Control Register Low
SC1CR1	00CA	SCI Control Register 1
SC1CR2	00CB	SCI Control Register 2
SC1SR1	00CC	SCI Status Register 1
SC1SR2	00CD	SCI Status Register 2
SC1DRH	00CE	SCI Data Register High
SC1DRL	00CF	SCI Data Register Low

On the other hand, some evaluation boards have two serial "D" connectors, one labeled "Terminal" and the other labeled "Host." The one labeled "Terminal" can use a straightthrough cable to the PC because the *RxD* signal will be connected to pin 2 and the *TxD* signal will be connected to pin 3 of the "D" connector. On the other hand the serial port labeled "Host" will have the *RxD* signal connected to pin 3 of the "D" connector and the *TxD* signal connected to pin 2. Thus, for the *TxD* signal from the PC to be connected to the *RxD* signal of the target system, it is necessary to interchange the wires in the cable so that pin 2 at one end is connected to pin 3 at the other end and vice versa. We call this a *null modem*.

The Data Register   The SCI data register low, *SCxDRL*, is shown in Figure 11–3. It is really two separate registers. If you read from this address, you read the *receive data register*, shown in Figure 11–2. If you write to address *SCxDRL*, you write to the *transmit data register*, also shown in Figure 11–2.

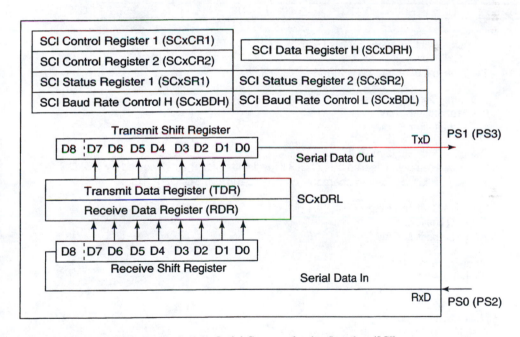

Figure 11–2   Functional Diagram of the Serial Communication Interface (SCI)

	7	6	5	4	3	2	1	0	
$00C7(F)	R7/T7	R6/T6	R5/T5	R4/T4	R3/T3	R2/T2	R1/T1	R0/T0	SCxDRL

Read: Reads the receive data buffer
Write: Writes to the transmit data buffer

Figure 11–3   The SCI Data Register Low

The Status Register The SCI status register 1, *SCxSR1*, is shown in Figure 11–4. Bit 5 of *SCxSR1* is the *receive data register full* (*RDRF*) flag. This bit is set to 1 when the *receive shift register* has filled up with a complete byte and transferred this byte to the *receive data register* (*RDR*) (see Figure 11–2).

Bit 7 of *SCxSR1* is the *transmit data register empty* (*TDRE*) bit. This bit is set to 1 when data from the *transmit data register* (*TDR*) is transferred to the *transmit shift register*. These data are then shifted out through *TxD* at the baud rate, preceded by a start bit and ending with a parity bit (if selected) and a stop bit. While these data are being shifted out, another byte can be stored in the *transmit data register*. When this is done the *TDRE* bit is cleared to zero and will remain zero until the *transmit shift register* has finished shifting out the previous character. When the shift register is free to accept another byte, the contents of the *TDR* are transferred to the shift register and the *TDRE* flag (bit 7) in the status register, *SCxSR1*, is set to 1 again.

	7	6	5	4	3	2	1	0	
$00C4(C)	TDRE	TC	RDRF	IDLE	OR	NF	FE	PF	SCxSR1

TDRE: Transmit Data Register Empty Flag
           0 – SCxDR busy
           1 – Transmit data can be written to SCxDR

TC: Transmit Complete Flag
           0 – Transmitter busy
           1 – Transmitter is idle

RDRF: Receive Data Register Full Flag
           0 – SCxDR empty. Cleared by SCxSR1 read with RDRF set, followed by SCxDR read
           1 – SCxDR full. Received character can be read from SCxDR

IDLE: Idle Line Detected Flag
           0 – RxD line is idle
           1 – RxD line is active

OR: Overrun Error Flag
           0 – No overrun
           1 – Overrun detected

NF: Noise Error Flag
           0 – Unanimous decision
           1 – Noise on a valid start bit, any data bit, or the stop bit

FE: Framing Error Flag
           0 – Stop bit detected
           1 – Zero detected instead of a stop bit

PF: Parity Error Flag
           0 – Correct parity
           1 – Incorrect parity

Figure 11–4   The SCI Status Register 1

You must make sure that you check the *RDRF* flag (bit 5 of *SCxSR1*) often enough so as not to miss any incoming bytes. If the *receive shift register* gets full before the previous data in the *receive data register* has been read, the overrun error flag, *OR* (bit 3), in the status register, *SCxSR1*, will be set to 1. The overrun error flag is cleared by reading *SCxSR1* with the *OR* flag set, followed by a read of *SCxDRL*.

All asynchronous serial data must end with a stop bit. If a stop bit does not occur where expected, a framing error is indicated and the *FE* flag (bit 1) in the status register, *SCxSR1*, is set to 1. This flag is cleared by reading *SCxSR1* with the *FE* flag set, followed by a read of *SCxDRL*.

When a start bit is first detected (by the signal going from high to low), then three samples are measured near the center of the start bit, each successive data bit, and the stop bit. The majority of these three readings is taken to be the data value for that bit. If these three measurements are all the same, then the noise error flag, *NF*, in the status register, *SCxSR1*, is cleared to zero. If anything other than a unanimous decision is detected, then *NF* is set to 1. This flag is cleared by reading *SCxSR1* with the *NF* flag set, followed by a read of *SCxDRL*.

If parity has been set (by setting bit *PE* in the control register, *SCxCR1*, described below), then a parity error will set the parity error flag, *PF*, in *SCxSR1*. This flag is cleared by reading *SCxSR1* with the *PF* flag set, followed by a read of *SCxDRL*.

The second status register, SCxSR2, listed in Table 11–2 has only a single bit, *RAF* (bit 0). This is a receiver active flag that is set to 1 when a character is being received.

The Control Registers   The *SCI control register 1*, *SCxCR1*, is shown in Figure 11–5. The mode flag (bit 4) of *SCxCR1* determines whether the character format is 8 bits or 9 bits. If this bit is set to 1, then the received and transmitted characters will contain 9 bits. These ninth bits (*T8* and *R8*) are stored in bits 6 and 7 of the *SCI data register high*, *SCxDRH*, as shown in Figure 11–6. You will normally use 8-bit data. The 9-bit data format is used when multiple 68HC12s are communicating with each other in a master-slave relationship as will be described in Section 11.4 where the meaning of the WAKE bit in *SCxCR1* will also be explained. For normal 8-bit operation with no parity, you will set all the bits in *SCxCR1* to zero.

Setting the *LOOPS* bit in *SCxCR1* (with *RSRC* = 0) will cause the receiver to be connected internally to the transmitter. This may be useful to test the operation of the SCI port without having to connect it to another source. We will show an example of using this mode in Section 11.3.2.

The bits *PE* (parity enable) and *PT* (parity type) in *SCxCR2* are used to enable parity and set it to odd or even. We will normally operate the SCI port with no parity.

The *SCI control register 2*, *SCxCR2*, is shown in Figure 11–7 where the meaning of each bit is described. Bits 4–7 enable various SCI interrupts that will be described in Section 11.4. The two important bits in this register that must be set are the transmit and receive enable bits, *TE* and *RE*, that enable the transmit and receive portions of the SCI. Therefore, to use the SCI (without interrupts) you must set these two bits to 1 by storing a value of $0C in *SCxCR2*.

	7	6	5	4	3	2	1	0	
$00C2(A)	LOOPS	WOMS	RSRC	M	WAKE	ILT	PE	PT	SCxCR1

LOOPS: SCI Loop Mode/Single Wire Mode Enable
            0 – Normal operation of TxD and RxD
            1 – LOOP mode or single wire mode enabled

WOMS: Wire-Or Mode for Serial Pins
            0 – Pins operate in normal mode
            1 – Pins declared as outputs operate in open drain fashion

RSRC: Receiver Source (LOOPS = 1)
            0 – Receiver input connected to transmitter internally (not TxD pin)
            1 – Receiver input connected to TxD pin (single wire mode)

M: Mode (Select Character Format)
            0 – 8-bit data
            1 – 9-bit data

WAKE: Wakeup by Address Mark/Idle
            0 – Wakeup by IDLE line recognition
            1 – Wakeup by address mark (most significant data bit set)

ILT: Idle Line Type
            0 – Short idle line mode
            1 – Long idle line mode

PE: Parity Enable
            0 – Parity is disabled
            1 – Parity is enabled

PT: Parity Type
            0 – Even parity
            1 – Odd parity

Figure 11–5   The SCI Control Register 1

	7	6	5	4	3	2	1	0	
$00C6(E)	R8	T8	0	0	0	0	0	0	SCxDRH

R8:   Receive Data Bit 8
            If M bit in SCxCR1 is set, R8 stores the ninth bit of the received data

T8:   Transmit Data Bit 8
            If M bit in SCxCR1 is set, T8 stores the ninth bit of the transmitted data

Figure 11–6   The SCI Data Register High

The use of the *RWU* bit will be described in Section 11.4.1 where we will describe the master-slave operation of multiple 68HC12s. A break code (at least 10 or 11 contiguous zeros) can be generated by setting the *SBK* bit in *SCxCR2* to 1. The transmitter will continue to send zeros as long as *SBK* = 1.

	7	6	5	4	3	2	1	0	
$00C3(B)	TIE	TCIE	RIE	ILIE	TE	RE	RWU	SBK	SCxCR2

TIE: Transmit Interrupt Enable
            0 – TDRE interrupts disabled
            1 – TDRE interrupts enabled

TCIE: Transmit Complete Interrupt Enable
            0 – TC interrupts disabled
            1 – TC interrupts enabled

RIE: Receiver Interrupt Enable
            0 – RDRF interrupts disabled
            1 – RDRF and OR interrupts enabled

ILIE: Idle-Line Interrupt Enable
            0 – IDLE interrupts disabled
            1 – IDLE interrupts enabled

TE: Transmitter Enable
            0 – Transmitter disabled
            1 – Transmitter enabled

RE: Receiver Enable
            0 – Receiver disabled
            1 – Receiver enabled

RWU: Receiver Wakeup Control
            0 – Normal SCI Receiver
            1 – Wakeup enabled and receiver interrupts inhibited

SBK: Send Break
            0 – Break generator off
            1 – Break codes generated as long as SBK = 1

Figure 11–7 The SCI Control Register 2

The Baud Rate Control Register The baud rate can be set by selecting the proper bits in the *SCI baud rate control register*, *SCxBDL* and *SCxBDH*, shown in Figure 11–8. We will use 9600 baud when communicating with the PC using WHYP. This baud rate is selected by setting bits SBR[12:0] to 52 = $34 as shown in Table 11–3.

	7	6	5	4	3	2	1	0	
$00C0(8)	BTST	BSPL	BRDL	SBR12	SBR11	SBR10	SBR9	SBR8	SCxBDH

	7	6	5	4	3	2	1	0	
$00C1(9)	SBR7	SBR6	SBR5	SBR4	SBR3	SBR2	SBR1	SBR0	SCxBDL

SBR[12:0]:BR divisor; SCI Baud Rate = MCLK / (16 x BR)

Figure 11–8 The SCI Baud Rate Control Register

Table 11–3 Baud Rate Selection

Desired SCI Baud Rate	BR Divisor for MCLK = 8.0 MHz
110	4545
300	1667
600	833
1200	417
2400	208
4800	104
9600	52
14400	35
19200	26
38400	13

11.2.1 Programming the SCI Port

As an example of programming the SCI port, consider a portion of the WHYP kernel shown in Figure 11–9. This code is found in the file WHYP12.ASM shown in Appendix D. Note that SCI0 is used as the default. To use SCI1 instead, you can change the five *EQU* statements that define the addresses of the SCI registers.

The subroutine *INITSER*, will initialize the SCI port by first clearing *SC0CR1*, shown in Figure 11–5. This will set the 8-bit mode with no parity. The value 52 = \$34 is loaded into register *D* and then stored in the 16-bit SCI baud rate control register, *SC0BDH:SC0BDL*, shown in Figure 11–8. The value \$0C is stored in the SCI control register 2, *SC0CR2*, shown in Figure 11–7. This will enable both the SCI transmitter and receiver.

The subroutine *INCHAR*, shown in Figure 11–9, will wait for a character to be received in *RxD* and then store this 8-bit byte in accumulator *A*. This is done by ANDing the mask \$20 (*RDRF* bit 5) with the contents of the status register, *SC0SR1*. If no character has been received, the *RDRF* bit will be zero and the result of ANDing \$20 with the contents of *SC0SR1* will be zero. The *BEQ* instruction will therefore continue to branch to the beginning of the subroutine until bit 5 (*RDRF*) of *SC0SR1* becomes 1. This will happen when a character has been received, at which point the character value is in the SCI data register, *SC0DRL*. This value is then loaded into accumulator *A*.

The subroutine *OUTPUT* shown in Figure 11–9 will send the byte in accumulator *A* out the transmit line, *TxD*. We first need to wait until the *TDRE* bit in the status register, *SC0SR1*, becomes 1. Note from Figure 11–4 that this is bit 7 of *SC0SR1*. Therefore, when it becomes set to 1, the value in this register will become a negative number. We can therefore use the branching instruction, *BPL* (branch if plus), to continue branching as long as the value in *SC0SR1* is positive, that is, bit 7 is zero. Once *TDRE* (bit 7) becomes 1, then we simply store the byte in *A* in the SCI data register, *SC0DRL*, which will cause the byte to be sent out the *TxD* line.

```
*********************************************************
********  Change the following five addresses   ********
********  for a particular 68HC12 environment    ********
*********************************************************
REGBASE  EQU      $0000              ;register base
RAMBASE  EQU      $0900              ;ram base
EESTART  EQU      $1000              ;start address of EEPROM
EESTOP   EQU      $1FFF              ;stop address of EEPROM
WHYPBASE EQU      $4000              ;start of WHYP kernel


********  To use SCI1 instead of SCI0 change $C0-$C7 *******
********  in the following five lines to $C8-$CF     *******
*********************************************************
SCXBDH   EQU      REGBASE+$C0        ;baud rate control
SCXCR1   EQU      REGBASE+$C2        ;SCI control reg 1
SCXCR2   EQU      REGBASE+$C3        ;SCI control reg 2
SCXSR1   EQU      REGBASE+$C4        ;SCI status reg
SCXDRL   EQU      REGBASE+$C7        ;SCI data reg
RDRF     EQU      $20                ;SCXSR1 mask


;        INITIALIZE SCI
INITSER
         CLR      SCXCR1             ;8 bit
         LDD      #52
         STD      SCXBDH             ;9600 baud
         LDAA     #$0C
         STAA     SCXCR2             ;enable tx & rx
NOOP     RTS


;        INPUT BYTE FROM SERIAL PORT INTO A
INCHAR
         LDAA     SCXSR1             ;check status
         ANDA     #RDRF              ;check rdrf
         BEQ      INCHAR             ;wait for char
         LDAA     SCXDRL             ;get char in A
         RTS


;        OUTPUT BYTE IN A TO SERIAL PORT
OUTPUT
         TST      SCXSR1
         BPL      OUTPUT             ;loop until tdre
         STAA     SCXDRL             ;send A
         RTS
```

Figure 11–9   The 68HC12 SCI Code Used in the WHYP Kernel

11.2.2 The 68HC11 SCI Registers

The 68HC11 has a single SCI port with *RxD* connected to pin *PD0* and *TxD* connected to pin *PD1* of Port D. The 68HC11 SCI registers are listed in Table 11–4. Note that there are only five 8-bit registers compared with the eight in the 68HC12.

The 68HC11 data register and status register are shown in Figure 11–10. The data register, *SCDR*, is the same as register *SCxDRL* in the 68HC12. The status register, *SCSR*, is the same as register *SCxSR1* in the 68HC12 except that there is no parity flag because the 68HC11 SCI does not support parity.

The 68HC11 SCI control register 1, *SSCR1*, is shown in Figure 11–11. Note that this control register contains the two bits, *R8* and *T8*, that were in the SCI data register high, *SCxDRH*, in the 68HC12. The only other bits in *SSCR1* are the *M* and *WAKE* bits.

The 68HC11 SCI control register 2, *SSCR2*, is shown in Figure 11–12. Note that this is the same as control register 2, *SCxCR2*, in the 68HC12 shown in Figure 11–7.

Whereas the baud rate control register in the 68HC12 is a 16-bit register (see Figure 11–8), the 68HC11 has only the 8-bit baud rate control register, *BAUDRC*, shown in Figure 11–13. Note that bits *SCP[1:0]* select the maximum baud rate (for a given crystal frequency) and then bits *SCR[2:0]* further divide the prescaler to determine a final baud rate.

Table 11–4 The 68HC11 SCI Registers

Name	Register Addr	Description
BAUDRC	102B	SCI Baud Rate Control Register
SCCR1	00C2	SCI Control Register 1
SCCR2	00C3	SCI Control Register 2
SCSR	00C4	SCI Status Register
SCDR	00CF	SCI Data Register (Read RDR, Write TDR)

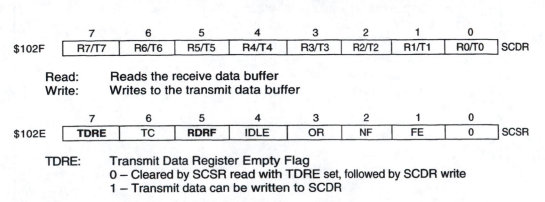

	7	6	5	4	3	2	1	0	
$102F	R7/T7	R6/T6	R5/T5	R4/T4	R3/T3	R2/T2	R1/T1	R0/T0	SCDR

Read: Reads the receive data buffer
Write: Writes to the transmit data buffer

	7	6	5	4	3	2	1	0	
$102E	TDRE	TC	RDRF	IDLE	OR	NF	FE	0	SCSR

TDRE: Transmit Data Register Empty Flag
            0 – Cleared by SCSR read with TDRE set, followed by SCDR write
            1 – Transmit data can be written to SCDR

RDRF: Receive Data Register Full Flag
            0 – Cleared by SCSR read with RDRF set, followed by SCDR read
            1 – Received character can be read from SCDR

Figure 11–10 The 68HC11 SCI Data and Status Registers

$102C	7	6	5	4	3	2	1	0	
	R8	T8	0	M	WAKE	0	0	0	SCCR1

R8:   Receive Data Bit 8
           If M bit is set, R8 stores the ninth bit of the received data

T8:   Transmit Data Bit 8
           If M bit is set, T8 stores the ninth bit of the transmitted data

M: Mode (Select Character Format)
           0 – 8-bit data
           1 – 9-bit data

WAKE: Wakeup by Address Mark/Idle
           0 – Wakeup by IDLE line recognition
           1 – Wakeup by address mark (most significant data bit set)

Figure 11–11   The 68HC11 SCI Control Register 1

$102D	7	6	5	4	3	2	1	0	
	TIE	TCIE	RIE	ILIE	TE	RE	RWU	SBK	SCCR2

Figure 11–12   The 68HC11 SCI Control Register 2

$102B	7	6	5	4	3	2	1	0	
	TCLR	0	SCP1	SCP0	RCKB	SCR2	SCR1	SCR0	BAUDRC

SCP1, SCP0:SCI Baud Rate Prescaler Selects (Specifies highest possible baud rate)

SCP[1:0]	Divide Internal Clock by	Maximum Baud Rate (8 MHz Crystal Freq.)
0 0	1	125.0K
0 1	3	41.67K
1 0	4	31.25K
1 1	13	9600

SCR[2:0]:   SCI Baud Rate Selects (Subdivides highest possible baud rate)

SCR[2:0]	Divide Prescalar by	Baud Rate (9600 Max. Baud Rate)
0 0 0	1	9600
0 0 1	2	4800
0 1 0	4	2400
0 1 1	8	1200
1 0 0	16	600
1 0 1	32	300
1 1 0	64	150
1 1 1	128	75

Figure 11–13   The SCI 68HC11 Baud Rate Control Register

11.3 PROGRAMMING THE SCI IN WHYP

It is a simple matter to program the SCI port in WHYP. Begin by defining *CONSTANT*s for the addresses of the register names. For programming SCI0 you will generally need to use only the five register names shown in Figure 11–14. Similar names and addresses would be used for SCI1 (see Table 11–2).

The WHYP word *SCI0.INIT*, shown in Figure 11–15, can then be used to initialize the SCI0 port. Note that *SC0CR1* is set for 8 bits (see Figure 11–5). The transmitter and receiver are enabled by setting bits *TE* and *RE* in *SC0CR2* (see Figure 11–7). Finally the baud rate is set to 9600 by storing $34 = 52$ in the 16-bit baud rate control register at *SC0BDH* (see Figure 11–8).

The WHYP word *TX! (c --)*, shown in Figure 11–16, will wait for the *TDRE* flag (bit 7 of *SC0SR1*) to go high and then store the character *c* in the *transmit data register (SC0DRL)* which will send the character out the *TxD* pin.

```
\       Serial Communications Interface - SCI
HEX
00C0    CONSTANT    SC0BDH      \ SCI Baud Rate Control
00C2    CONSTANT    SC0CR1      \ SCI Control Register 1
00C3    CONSTANT    SC0CR2      \ SCI Control Register 2
00C4    CONSTANT    SC0SR1      \ SCI Status Register 1
00C7    CONSTANT    SC0DRL      \ SCI Data (Read RDR, Write TDR)
```

Figure 11–14 The SCI Register Names Needed to Program SCI0

```
: SCI0.INIT  ( -- )
             0 SC0CR1 C!       \ 8 data bits
             0C SC0CR2 C!      \ enable TE & RE
             34 SC0BDH ! ;     \ 9600 BAUD
```

Figure 11–15 WHYP Word to Initialize SCI0

```
: TX!        ( c -- )            \ send character
             BEGIN
                7 SC0SR1 ?HI
             UNTIL
             SC0DRL C! ;

: ?RX        ( -- c tf | ff )    \ receive character
             5 SC0SR1 ?HI
             IF
                SC0DRL C@ TRUE
             ELSE
                FALSE
             THEN ;
```

Figure 11–16 Basic WHYP Words for Transmitting and Receiving SCI Data

The *receive data register (RDR)* in Figure 11–2 can be read using the WHYP word *?RX (-- c tf | ff)*, shown in Figure 11–16. Note that this word checks to see if bit 5 of *SC0SR1* is set, and if it is, then the character value is read from the *SC0DRL* register and is left on the stack under a true flag; otherwise, a false flag is left on the stack. The *RDRF* flag in the status register, *SC0SR1*, is cleared by reading the *SC0SR1* register with *RDRF* set followed by a read of the *SC0DRL* register. Note that this is done in the WHYP word *?RX*.

You can set the baud rate to any of the values shown in Table 11–3 using the WHYP word *BAUD (n --)*, shown in Figure 11–17. For example, the statement

```
1200 BAUD
```

will set the baud rate to 1200. Note that the word *BAUD* uses the word *FIND.N* described in Section 5.2.8 (see Figure 5–40) to search the table, *BAUD.RATE*, for

```
DECIMAL
CREATE BAUD.RATE
      110 , 300 , 600 , 1200 , 2400 , 4800 ,
      9600 , 14400 , 19200 , 38400 ,

CREATE BR.DIVISOR
      4545 , 1667 , 833 , 417 , 208 , 104 ,
      52 , 35 , 26 , 13 ,

: FIND.N          ( imax n -- ff | index tf )
            0 SWAP ROT                              \ 0 n imax
            0 DO                                    \ 0 n
                  DUP I BAUD.RATE                   \ 0 n n ix pfa
                  SWAP 2* +                         \ 0 n n pfa+2*ix
                  @ =                               \ 0 n f
                  IF                                \ 0 n
                        DROP I TRUE                 \ 0 ix tf
                        ROT LEAVE                   \ ix tf 0
                  THEN
            LOOP                                    \ 0 n
            DROP ;                                  \ 0 | ix tf

: BAUD   ( n -- )                  ( Ex.   1200 BAUD )
            10 SWAP FIND.N
            IF
                2* BR.DIVISOR + @          \ BR
                SC0BDH !
            THEN ;
```

Figure 11–17   WHYP Word to Set the Baud Rate

1200 and return the corresponding index value which is then used to get the corresponding divisor from the table *BR.DIVISOR*. This value is then stored in the 16-bit baud rate control register, *SC0BDH*.

We will now give three different examples of programming the SCI port in WHYP. These examples are in files on the disk accompanying this book and can be loaded and run.

11.3.1   Communicating with a PC

It is sometimes useful to write a program that will send information from the target HC12 board to a PC. The PC must be running some type of communication program. When running WHYP12 on the PC, if you press function key F7, it turns the PC into a dumb terminal that runs the full-duplex algorithm shown in Figure 11–18. If you press a key, the ASCII code for that key is sent out the serial port to a remote computer. That remote computer will echo the character back to the PC.

For example, the file SCIECHO.WHP contains the program shown in Listing 11–1. The WHYP word *sci.echo (--)*, shown in Listing 11–1, running on a

```
loop:     if key has been pressed
          then send character to remote computer
          if remote computer has sent character
          then display character
repeat loop
```

Figure 11–18   Algorithm for a Dumb Terminal

Listing 11–1   The File SCIECHO.WHP

```
\       Serial Communications Interface - SCI
HEX
00C0    CONSTANT        SC0BDH          \ SCI0 Baud Rate Control
00C2    CONSTANT        SC0CR1          \ SCI0 Control Register 1
00C3    CONSTANT        SC0CR2          \ SCI0 Control Register 2
00C4    CONSTANT        SC0SR1          \ SCI0 Status Register 1
00C7    CONSTANT        SC0DRL          \ SCI0 Data (Read RDR, Write TDR)

: SCI0.INIT     ( -- )
          0 SC0CR1 C!          \ 8 DATA BITS
          0C SC0CR2 C!         \ ENABLE TE & RE
          34 SC0BDH ! ;        \ 9600 BAUD

: TX!           ( c -- )       \ send character
          BEGIN
            7 SC0SR1 ?HI
          UNTIL
          SC0DRL C! ;
```

Listing 11–1   (continued)

```
: ?RX            ( -- c tf | ff )        \ receive character
                 5 SC0SR1 ?HI
                 IF
                    SC0DRL C@ TRUE
                 ELSE
                    FALSE
                 THEN ;

: sci.echo       ( -- )
                 SCI0.INIT
                 BEGIN
                    BEGIN
                       ?RX
                    UNTIL
                    TX!
                 AGAIN ;
```

target HC12 board connected to the PC through the SCI port, will echo all characters received in *RxD* by sending them out *TxD*. To test this out, first load the file SCIECHO.WHP into the 68HC12 memory and then type *sci.echo*. The word *sci.echo* will now be executing, but because it is a *BEGIN...AGAIN* loop, it will seem to be stuck. Press the Esc key to return to WHYP. Then press function key F7 to execute the host terminal program. Anything you now type on the keyboard will make a round trip to the HC12 board and back and be displayed on the PC screen. Press the function key F5 to quit the host terminal program and return to WHYP. You must press the reset button on the 68HC12 board to exit the *sci.echo* word.

11.3.2   Testing SCI1 with the LOOP Function

As a second example we will use the LOOP mode (see Figure 11–5) to test the SCI1 port on a 68HC812A4. Consider the program shown in Listing 11–2 which is available in the file SCILOOP.WHP. Note that in this case we are programming only the SCI1 port. The SCI0 port is being used to communicate with the PC running WHYP.

The word *SCI1.INIT* in Listing 11–2 sets the LOOP mode by setting bit 7 (*LOOPS*) of *SC1CR1* (see Figure 11–5). We also define the words *TX1!* and *?RX1* the same way we did in Figure 11–16 except that we are using the SCI1 registers instead of the SCI0 registers. We also include the words from Figure 11–17 to set the baud rate—again using the SCI1 baud rate register.

The word *sci1.test (--)* begins by putting the ASCII code for *A* on the data stack. Note that the statement *ASCII A* leaves the ASCII code for *A* ($41) on the data stack. (The statement *CONTROL A* would leave the ASCII code for *control-A* = $01 on the data stack.) The *FOR...NEXT* loop will execute 26 times—once for each letter in the alphabet. The ASCII code for *A* is transmitted out *TxD1* using *TX1!* and then received in *RxD1* using *?RX1*. The received character is then sent to

Listing 11–2   The File `SCILOOP.WHP`

```
\       Serial Communications Interface - SCI
\       Works only on a 68HC12A4 using the SCI1 port
HEX
00C8    CONSTANT         SC1BDH          \ SCI1 Baud Rate Control
00CA    CONSTANT         SC1CR1          \ SCI1 Control Register 1
00CB    CONSTANT         SC1CR2          \ SCI1 Control Register 2
00CC    CONSTANT         SC1SR1          \ SCI1 Status Register 1
00CF    CONSTANT         SC1DRL          \ SCI1 Data (Read RDR, Write TDR)

: SCI1.INIT      ( -- )
                 80 SC1CR1 C!            \ 8 DATA BITS - LOOP mode
                 0C SC1CR2 C!            \ ENABLE TE & RE
                 34 SC1BDH ! ;           \ 9600 BAUD

: TX1!     ( c -- )                      \ send character
                 BEGIN
                     7 SC1SR1 ?HI
                 UNTIL
                 SC1DRL C! ;

: ?RX1              ( -- c tf | ff )   \ receive character
                 5 SC1SR1 ?HI
                 IF
                     SC1DRL C@ TRUE
                 ELSE
                     FALSE
                 THEN ;

DECIMAL

CREATE BAUD.RATE
      110 , 300 , 600 , 1200 , 2400 , 4800 ,
      9600 , 14400 , 19200 , 38400 ,

CREATE BR.DIVISOR
      4545 , 1667 , 833 , 417 , 208 , 104 ,
      52 , 35 , 26 , 13 ,

: FIND.N         ( imax n -- ff | index tf )
                 0 SWAP ROT                     \ 0 n imax
                 0 DO                           \ 0 n
                     DUP I BAUD.RATE            \ 0 n n ix pfa
                     SWAP 2* +                  \ 0 n n pfa+2*ix
                     @ =                        \ 0 n f
                     IF                         \ 0 n
                        DROP I TRUE             \ 0 ix tf
                        ROT LEAVE               \ ix tf 0
                     THEN
                 LOOP                           \ 0 n
                 DROP ;                         \ 0 | ix tf
```

Listing 11–2   (*continued*)

```
: BAUD          ( n -- )                    \ Ex. 1200 BAUD
                10 SWAP FIND.N
                IF
                    BR.DIVISOR + @          \ BR
                    SC1BDH !
                THEN ;

: sci1.test     ( -- )
                ASCII A                     \ c
                26 FOR
                    DUP TX1!                \ c
                    BEGIN                   \ wait for char
                        ?RX1
                    UNTIL                   \ c c
                    EMIT                    \ c
                    1+                      \ c'
                NEXT
                DROP ;
```

the PC using the WHYP word *EMIT*. The word *EMIT (c --)* is used to display an ASCII character on the PC screen. The ASCII code (still on the data stack from the *DUP* instruction) is then incremented by 1 to give the ASCII code of the next letter in the alphabet.

You should test this program by first loading the file SCILOOP.WHP. Then type the word *SCI1.INIT* which will initialize the SCI1 port in the loop mode. Then type

```
sci1.test
```

The alphabet should be displayed on the screen. Try changing to a slow baud rate by typing

```
110 BAUD
```

and then again type *sci1.test*. Try some other baud rates.

11.3.3   Sending Register Values to the PC

As a final example of communicating with a PC, suppose you want to display the contents of some of the 68HC12 registers on the PC screen when you press the key *R*. The WHYP word *send.regs (--)*, shown in Listing 11–3, will do this if you are running the host terminal program on the PC by pressing function key F7 when in WHYP. The word *send.regs* continually checks to see if a character has been received in *RxD*. If it has, it then checks to see if it is the ASCII code for *R*. If the *R* key was pressed, then the word *send.regs* will send the contents of Port F, Port G, Port H, Port J, and Port T to the PC separated by the ASCII code for a carriage return ($0D).

Listing 11–3   The File `SCIREG.WHP`

```
\     Serial Communications Interface - SCI

LOAD HEX2ASC.WHP
HEX
00C0  CONSTANT      SC0BDH            \ SCI0 Baud Rate Control
00C2  CONSTANT      SC0CR1            \ SCI0 Control Register 1
00C3  CONSTANT      SC0CR2            \ SCI0 Control Register 2
00C4  CONSTANT      SC0SR1            \ SCI0 Status Register 1
00C7  CONSTANT      SC0DRL            \ SCI0 Data (Read RDR, Write TDR)
0030  CONSTANT      PORTF
0031  CONSTANT      PORTG
0024  CONSTANT      PORTH
0028  CONSTANT      PORTJ
00AE  CONSTANT      PORTT


: SCI0.INIT   ( -- )
          0 SC0CR1 C!               \ 8 DATA BITS
          0C SC0CR2 C!              \ ENABLE TE & RE
          34 SC0BDH ! ;             \ 9600 BAUD


: TX!         ( c -- )          \ send character
          BEGIN
             7 SC0SR1 ?HI
          UNTIL
          SC0DRL C! ;


: ?RX         ( -- c tf | ff )        \ receive character
          5 SC0SR1 ?HI
          IF
             SC0DRL C@ TRUE
          ELSE
             FALSE
          THEN ;


: send.reg    ( n -- )
          DUP 4 RSHIFT              \ high nibble
          hex2asc TX!
          0F AND                   \ low nibble
          hex2asc TX! ;
```

Listing 11–3   (*continued*)

```
: send.regs         ( -- )
                SCI0.INIT
                BEGIN
                  ?RX
                  IF
                    ASCII R =
                    IF
                        0D TX!              \ send CR
                        PORTF C@ send.reg   \ send Port F
                        0D TX!              \ send CR
                        PORTG C@ send.reg   \ send Port G
                        0D TX!              \ send CR
                        PORTH C@ send.reg   \ send Port H
                        0D TX!              \ send CR
                        PORTJ C@ send.reg   \ send Port J
                        0D TX!              \ send CR
                        PORTT C@ send.reg   \ send Port T
                        0D TX!              \ send CR
                    THEN
                  THEN
                AGAIN ;
DECIMAL
```

If the contents of a register is, for example, $3F, and if we just transmit this value, then the PC will display a question mark (?) whose ASCII code is $3F. This is what terminal programs do. They display the characters whose ASCII codes are received in the serial port. To have the PC display 3F, we need to transmit the ASCII code for 3 ($33), followed by the ASCII code of F ($46). The word *send.reg (n --)* shown in Listing 11–3 will do this. This word expects the number to be sent, for example $3F, on the data stack. It first gets the high nibble by shifting this number right 4 bits and then converts this digit to its ASCII value by calling the word *hex2asc*. This word was described in Section 5.2.3 and shown in Figure 5–16. Its definition is in the file HEX2ASC.WHP. Therefore, we can just load this file at the beginning of the program as shown in Listing 11–3. After sending the ASCII code for the high nibble, the low nibble is obtained by ANDing the original number by $0F. This hex value is also converted to ASCII and then transmitted out the serial port.

The host terminal program on the PC will display these five values on five consecutive lines on the screen. To test this program, first load the file SCIREG.WHP and then type *send.regs*. You will need to press *Esc* to return to WHYP and then press function key F7 to execute the host terminal program. When you press an uppercase R, the five register values should be displayed on the screen. Press function key F5 to quit the host terminal program and return to WHYP. You must press the reset button on the 68HC12 board to exit the *send.regs* word.

11.4 SCI INTERFACE USING INTERRUPTS

An example of programming the 68HC12 SCI ports was given in Listing 11–3 where the word *send.regs* sends the contents of five port registers to the PC when the character "R" is received from the PC. The problem with this word is that it takes a fair amount of time to send the contents of all five registers to the PC. If during this time more than one "R" is received, they will overrun each other in the receive shift register shown in Figure 11–2 and one or more will be lost before the *RDRF* flag in the *SCxSR1* register is checked by the word *?RX*. The solution to this problem is to enable receiver interrupts so that an SCI interrupt is generated each time the *RDRF* flag is set. The interrupt service routine can then read the received byte in the receive data register, *SCxDRL*, and store the value in a queue using the word *qstore* (c --) as described in Section 10.6.

To enable receive interrupts, the *RIE* bit in *SCxCR2* must be set as indicated in Figure 11–7. The *TE* and *RE* bits must also be set to enable the transmit and receive subsystems. Therefore, the value $2C is stored in *SC0CR2*, as shown in the word *SCINT.INIT* in Listing 11–4.

Note that the interrupt service routine in Listing 11–4 just reads the receive data register and stores the byte in a queue. The word *main.SCIports* in Listing 11–4 corresponds to the word *send.regs* in Listing 11–3. Note that after initializing the queue and the SCI port for receive interrupts, the program goes into an endless loop where it continually checks the queue, and if an "R" is received, it sends the values

---

Listing 11–4   Using SCI Receive Interrupts

```
\          SCI Interface using interrupts      File: SCIINT.WHP

LOAD HEX2ASC.WHP
LOAD QUEUE.WHP


HEX
00C0      CONSTANT       SC0BDH       \ SCI0 Baud Rate Control
00C2      CONSTANT       SC0CR1       \ SCI0 Control Register 1
00C3      CONSTANT       SC0CR2       \ SCI0 Control Register 2
00C4      CONSTANT       SC0SR1       \ SCI0 Status Register 1
00C7      CONSTANT       SC0DRL       \ SCI0 Data (Read RDR, Write TDR)
0030      CONSTANT       PORTF
0031      CONSTANT       PORTG
0024      CONSTANT       PORTH
0028      CONSTANT       PORTJ
00AE      CONSTANT       PORTT
0B16      CONSTANT       SCI0.IVEC    \ SCI0 user vector address
```

Listing 11–4   (continued)

```
: SCINT.INIT           ( -- )
               0 SC0CR1 C!          \ 8 DATA BITS
               2C SC0CR2 C!         \ ENABLE TE & RE, RX INT
               34 SC0BDH C! ;       \ 9600 BAUD

INT: SCI.INTSER    ( -- )
               5 SC0SR1 ?HI         \ read to clear RDRF flag
               IF
                  SC0DRL C@
                  QSTORE
               THEN
RTI;
: SET.SCI.INTVEC      ( -- )
                 [ ' SCI.INTSER ] LITERAL
                 SCI0.IVEC ! ;

: send.reg          ( n -- )
               DUP 4 RSHIFT          \ high nibble
               hex2asc TX!
               0F AND                \ low nibble
               hex2asc TX! ;

\ Transmit all registers when 'R' is received
: main.SCIports    ( -- )
               SEI
               INITQ
               SCINT.INIT
               SET.SCI.INTVEC
               CLI
               BEGIN
                 CHECKQ
                 IF
                 52 =            \ if R
                 IF
                  0D TX!                     \ send CR
                  PORTF C@ send.reg          \ send Port F
                  0D TX!                     \ send CR
                  PORTG C@ send.reg          \ send Port G
                  0D TX!                     \ send CR
                  PORTH C@ send.reg          \ send Port H
                  0D TX!                     \ send CR
                  PORTJ C@ send.reg          \ send Port J
                  0D TX!                     \ send CR
                  PORTT C@ send.reg          \ send Port T
                  0D TX!                     \ send CR
                 THEN
                 THEN
               AGAIN ;
```

in the five ports to the PC. But now it doesn't matter if more than one "R" comes in before the register values have been sent. All of the "R" values will be waiting in the queue, having been put there by the interrupt service routine that will interrupt the sending of the port values to read the receive data register. Thus each "R" that is received will result in a new set of port data being sent to the PC.

11.4.1 Master-Slave SCI Communications

A single 68HC12 can serve as a master and communicate with several other 68HC12s (or 68HC11s) acting as slaves. The *TxD* pin of the master is connected to the *RxD* pin of each slave and the *RxD* pin of the master is connected to the *TxD* pin of each slave. This means that bytes transmitted by the master will go to all the slaves. An addressing scheme is used from which a slave can determine if a particular message is meant for it.

We will illustrate master-slave communications with a simple example involving only a single slave. The master will send an address of 1 to the slave which will signify to the slave that the message is for that slave (the only one in this example) and that the slave should read its channel 2 A/D converter and send the value to the master. In a more elaborate example the master might send a series of bytes as a message to the addressed slave. Other slaves on the network would want to ignore this message by putting themselves to sleep so that their receive interrupt would be inhibited during the transmission of some other slave's message. When a new message is to be sent to some other slave, there must be a way of waking up the slaves so that they can see if the next message is for them.

Two different methods of waking up a slave are available: idle line or address mark. An idle line condition occurs if the line is in the high state for an entire character time (including the start and stop bit times). In idle-time wakeup, the byte following an idle time is read by all slaves and taken to be the address. In this mode no idle times are allowed during the sending of a message to a slave as this is used to indicate the end of the message.

The other wakeup method uses an address mark and this is the method we will use in our example. An address mark is indicated by setting the most significant bit in a transmitted byte from the master. In order to use all eight data bits we can add a ninth bit to the transmitted data for the address mark. This transmitted ninth bit (bit 8) is stored in the *T8* bit (bit 6) of the *SCxDRH* register (see Figure 11–6) and we must set the *M* bit in *SCxCR1* to 1 to indicate that nine data bits are to be sent as shown in Figure 11–5.

The program for the master is shown in Figure 11–19. Note that the word *SCINIT.MASTER* stores a $10 in *SC0CR1* to select 9-bit data and stores a $40 in *SC0DRH* to set the *T8* bit to 1. This means that in this example all bytes sent by the master will be address bytes. The word *MAIN.MASTER* sends out a 1 (the address of the slave) and then waits for a response. When a byte is received from the slave, it reads it and displays its value on the PC screen. The master continually asks the slave to send its A/D value so that the master can display it.

```
\         MASTER   - SEND 9-BIT REQUEST TO SLAVE 1 FOR ADCONV READ
LOAD SCIREG.WHP      \ SCI registers


: SCINIT.MASTER          ( -- )
            10 SC0CR1 C!                \ 9 data bits
            40 SC0DRH C!                \ set T8
            0C SC0CR2 C!                \ ENABLE TE & RE
            34 SC0BDH C! ;              \ 9600 BAUD


: MAIN.MASTER    ( -- )
            SCINIT.MASTER
            BEGIN
                1 TX!                   \ send 1 with T8 set
                BEGIN
                    5 SC0SR1 ?HI
                UNTIL
                SC0DRL C@ . CR
            AGAIN ;
```

Figure 11–19   Master Program for Master-Slave SCI Example

The program running on the slave must also have the *M* bit in *SC0CR1* set to indicate 9-bit data. The received ninth bit (bit 8) is stored in bit *R8* of *SC0DRH*, as shown in Figure 11–6. The slave must also set the *WAKE* bit in *SC0CR1* (see Figure 11–5) to indicate that it will wake up using an address mark. A byte with the most significant bit set will automatically clear the *RWU* bit in *SC0CR2* (see Figure 11–7) so that the byte will be read as an address by all slaves. The slave will check to see if the address is its address. If it is not, it will set the *RWU* bit in *SC0CR2* which will inhibit the receiver interrupt. In this way it will not respond to any further message bytes in which the most significant bit is zero. However, the next address byte with the most significant bit set to 1 will wake it up and clear the *RWU* bit in *SC0CR2*.

The program for the slave is shown in Figure 11–20. Note how the registers *SC0CR1* and *SC0CR2* are set up. Receiver interrupts are enabled by setting the *RIE* bit in *SC0CR2*. The *RWU* bit in *SC0CR2* is initially set to 1 to put the slave to sleep. It will therefore only respond to an address byte.

The interrupt service routine in Figure 11–20 will be executed each time the master sends a byte with the most significant bit set. The routine checks to see if the address is 1 and if it is, then channel 2 of the A/D converter is read and sent back to the master. If the address is not 1, then the slave puts itself back to sleep by setting the *RWU* bit in *SC0CR2*. Note that the main program in Figure 11–20 just initializes the slave and sets up its interrupt vector. All of the work of the program is done in the interrupt service routine.

```
\         SCI SLAVE - INT ROUTINE WAKE UP - READ ADCONV - SEND

LOAD ATD.WHP           \ for ADCONV
LOAD SCIREG.WHP        \ SCI registers

: SCINIT.SLAVE         ( -- )
            18 SC0CR1 C!              \ 9 DATA BITS - ADDR MARK WAKE
            2E SCCR2 C!               \ ENABLE TE & RE, REI
            34 SC0BDH C! ;            \ 9600 BAUD

INT: SCISL.INTSER ( -- )
            5 SC0SR1 ?HI
            IF
                SC0DRL C@ 1 =        \ if addr = 1
                IF
                    2 ADCONV         \ read A/D
                    TX!              \ and send it
                ELSE                 \ else
                    SC0CR2 1 HI      \ go back to sleep
                THEN
            THEN
RTI;

: SET.SCISL.INTVEC          ( -- )
                [ ' SCISL.INTSER ] LITERAL
                SCI.IVEC ! ;

: MAIN.SLAVE     ( -- )
            SEI
            SCINIT.SLAVE
            SET.SCISL.INTVEC
            CLI ;
```

Figure 11.20 Slave Program for Master-Slave SCI Example

11.5 SUMMARY

This chapter described asynchronous serial communication in Section 11.1 and then showed how it is implemented in the SCI ports on a 68HC12 (and 68HC11) in Section 11.2. The following files contain examples of programming the SCI ports in WHYP that were discussed in Sections 11.3 and 11.4.

SCI12.WHP
Contains the code in Figures 11–14 through 11–17.

Box 11–1   WHYP Words Introduced in Chapter 11

ASCII   (-- ascii_code)
                  Used to find the ASCII code of characters.
                  The statement *ASCII <char>* will leave the ASCII code of *<char>* on
                  the data stack.
                  For example, *ASCII A*, will leave a $41 on the data stack.

CONTROL   (-- control_code)
                  Used to find the ASCII code of control characters.
                  The statement *CONTROL <char>* will leave the ASCII code of
                  ^*<char>* on the data stack.
                  For example, *CONTROL G*, will leave a $07 on the data stack.

EMIT   (c --)
                  Displays the character whose ASCII code is *c* on the PC screen.

SCIECHO.WHP
Any character received in *RxD* on the 68HC12 is retransmitted out *TxD*.

SCILOOP.WHP
The loop mode is used to test the SCI1 port on a 68HC812A4. Provides an example of changing the baud rate.

SCIREG.WHP
The values in five registers are transmitted out the serial port in response to receiving the character *R*.

SCIINT.WHP
SCI receive interrupts are used to store input characters in a queue. If an R is received, the values in five registers are transmitted out the serial port.

SCIMSTR.WHP and SCISLV.WHP
A 1 sent from the master causes the slave to read channel 2 of its A/D converter and send the result to the master.

The second, fourth, and fifth examples require that a host terminal program be running on the PC. While any standard terminal communication program will work, WHYP has such a program built in that is executed by pressing function key F7 in WHYP. To exit this terminal program and return to WHYP, you press function key F5.

The WHYP words given in Box 11–1 were discussed in this chapter.

EXERCISES

Exercise 11.1

The relationship between the *SCI baud rate* and the *BR divisor* in Table 10–3 is given by

```
SCI Baud Rate = MCLK/(16 x BR)
```

where $MCLK = 8.0$ MHz.

    a. Find the baud rates resulting from *BR* divisors of 12, 11, 10, 9, and 8.

    b. Because each character is resynchronized on the start bit (see Figure 10–1), the baud rate of the receiver can differ from that used to send the character by up to about 5 percent before the center-bit sampling will drift out of the bit time by the time the stop bit is reached. Find the ±5% baud rate range for each of the baud rates calculated in part (a).

Exercise 11.2

Write WHYP words *SCINIT (--)*, *TX! (c --)*, and *?RX (-- c tf| ff)* similar to those in Figures 11–15 and 11–16 that will work on a 68HC11.

Exercise 11.3

Rewrite the program shown in Figure 11–17 in such a way that the word *BAUD (n --)* will set the baud rate of the SCI port on a 68HC11.

Exercise 11.4

    a. Write a WHYP word called *send.xx (c --)* that will send the character *c* out the SCI0 port as two ASCII characters plus a blank. For example, the byte 5A would send out the three hex values 35, 41, 20.

    b. Write a WHYP word called *send.4chars (c3 c2 c1 c0 --)* that will send four characters (using *send.xx*) followed by a carriage return out the SCI0 port.

    c. Write a WHYP word called *send.adconv (--)* that will poll the SCI0 port waiting to receive a character. If it receives an "*L*," it should read the lower four channels of the A/D converter and send these four hex bytes so that the data will be displayed on the screen in the following format when the terminal host program (Esc – F7) is run on the PC and an "*L*" is pressed.

```
Channels 0-3: 00 21 4A 05
```

If it receives an "*H*," it should read the higher four channels of the A/D converter and send these four hex bytes so that the data will be displayed on the screen in the following format when the terminal host program (Esc – F7) is run on the PC and an "*H*" is pressed.

```
Channels 4-7: E0 27 3F 85
```

Hint: ." will work with the host program to print the string "Channels 0-3:".

Exercise 11.5

Redo Exercise 11.4 using receive interrupts on SCI0. The interrupt service routine should read a received character and store it in a queue.

Exercise 11.6

Assume C++ (or other language such as Visual Basic) is running on the PC and wants to access the external world through a 68HC12 connected to the PC through an asynchronous serial line. This can be done by sending an 8-bit "opcode" to the 68HC12 SCI port followed by possible parameters and then receiving possible data from the 68HC12. For example, suppose the C++ program wants to read the hex keypad shown in Figure 7–12 that is connected to a

68HC12. The C++ function *int GetHexKey()* might do this by sending the opcode $41 (ASCII code for "A") out the serial port and then wait for the hex key value to be sent from the 68HC12 to the PC. Meanwhile the program running on the 68HC12 will wait to receive an opcode in the SCI0 port. If it receives a $41, it will wait for a key on the keypad to be pressed by calling the word *keypad (-- n)* given in Figure 7–15, and then send the key value, *n*, out the SCI0 port to the PC. We will describe this program running on the 68HC12 by the WHYP word *Get HexKey (--) { $41 -- c }* where the braces contain a description of the bytes sent by the PC and the bytes sent to the PC according to the format { *<bytes from PC to 68HC12> -- <bytes from 68HC12 to PC>* }. The following examples will use a different opcode to perform different 68HC12 I/O operations. When sending 16-bit data from the PC to the 68HC12, send the low byte first. When sending 16-bit data from the 68HC12 to the PC, send the high byte first.

a. Opcode = $41 ("A"): Write a WHYP word called *Get HexKey (--) { $41 -- c }* that will wait for a key to be pressed in response to the opcode $41 and send the hex key value to the PC through the SCI0 port. Use the hex keypad shown in Figure 7–12.

b. Opcode = $42 ("B"): Write a WHYP word called *DotDigit (--) { $42 dig# n -- }* that will display the value *n* (0-F) on the seven-segment digit number *dig#*. Use the word *.digit (dig# n --)* shown in Figure 7–11 for the connection shown in Figure 7–10.

c. Opcode = $43 ("C"): Write a WHYP word called *Hex2LCD (--) { $43 hex -- }* that will display the hex number *hex* on the LCD shown in Figure 7–22. Use the word *hex>lcd (hex --)* given in Listing 7–1.

d. Opcode = $44 ("D"): Write a WHYP word called *Dot4Leds (--) { $44 n -- }* that will display the decimal number *n* on up to four seven-segment displays shown in Figure 8–10. Use the word *.4leds (n --)* given in Figure 8–11.

e. Opcode = $45 ("E"): Write a WHYP word called *D2A (--) { $45 n -- }* that will output a voltage on the D/A converter described in Exercise 8.3 that is proportional to the lower six bit of the byte *n*. Use the word *DACONV (n --)* found in Exercise 8.3(b).

f. Opcode = $46 ("F"): Write a WHYP word called *Write_EEPROM (--) { $46 addr #bytes <bytes> -- }* that will write the #*byte* (up to 32) bytes, *<bytes>*, starting at address, *addr*, to the 25C320 serial EEPROM described in Exercise 8.6.

g. Opcode = $47 ("G"): Write a WHYP word called *Read_EEPROM (--) { $47 addr #bytes -- <bytes> }* that will read the #*bytes* bytes, *<bytes>*, starting at address, *addr*, from the 25C320 serial EEPROM described in Exercise 8.6 and send these bytes to the PC.

h. Opcode = $48 ("H"): Write a WHYP word called *SetR (--) { $48 n -- }* that will set the resistance of the AD7376 Digital Potentiometer described in Exercise 8.7 to *n* ohms.

i. Opcode = $49 ("I"): Write a WHYP word called *Record_ChipCorder (--) { $49 -- }* that will allow you to record a message (starting at address 00) on the ISD4004 ChipCorder described in Exercise 8.8.

j. Opcode = $4A ("J"): Write a WHYP word called *Play_ChipCorder (--) { $4A -- }* that will allow you to play a message (starting at address 00) on the ISD4004 ChipCorder described in Exercise 8.8.

k. Opcode = $4B ("K"): Write a WHYP word called *ReadCompass (--) { $4B -- deg }* that will read the compass direction (0–360°) for the compass transducer shown in Figures 9–11 and 9–12. Use the word *read.compass (-- deg)* given in Listing 9–3.

l. Opcode = $4C ("L"): Write a WHYP word called *GetTemp (--) { $4C -- temp }* that will read the temperature (in degrees Celsius) using the temperature sensor described in either Exercise 9.2 or 9.3.

m. Opcode = $4D ("M"): Write a WHYP word called *GetLevelDegree (--) { $4D -- angle }* that will read the tilt angle, in tenths of a degree, using the ADXL05 accelerometer described in Exercise 9.6.

n. Opcode = $4E ("N"): Write a WHYP word called *GetPressure (--) { $4E -- n }* that will read the pressure, in kPa, using the pressure sensor described in either Exercise 9.7 or 9.8.

o. Opcode = $4F ("O"): Write a WHYP word called *PulseTrain (--) { $4F period width -- }* that will generate the pulse train shown in Figure 10–11 on pin *PT6*. Use the word *PULSE (--)* given in Listing 10–2.

p. Opcode = $50 ("P"): Write a WHYP word called *GetPulseWidth (--) { $50 -- n }* that will read the width of a single pulse connected to pin *PT2* using the word *PULSE.WIDTH (--)* given in Listing 10–3.

q. Opcode = $51 ("Q"): Write a WHYP word called *GetLightLevel (--) { $51 -- n }* that will read the light intensity using the light sensor described in either Exercise 10.6 or 10.7.

r. Opcode = $52 ("R"): Write a WHYP word called *GetPitchRoll (--) { $52 -- pitch roll }* that will read the pitch and roll angles, in tenths of a degree, using the ADXL202 Dual-Axis Accelerometer described in Exercises 10.8 and 10.9.

s. Opcode = $53 ("S"): Write a WHYP word called *GetAngle (--) { $53 -- angle }* that will read the angle (0–360°) of a wheel in the vertical plane using the ADXL202 Dual-Axis Accelerometer as described in Exercise 10.10.

12

Strings and Number Conversions

When you type a number (such as 1234) on the keyboard of the PC, it is stored as a string of characters representing the ASCII codes of each digit in the number. This ASCII number string must first be converted to a binary number before it is stored as an integer in the computer. The C++ WHYP host program automatically handles this conversion for you. Similarly, when you have an integer such as 1234 stored as a binary number in the computer and you want to display this number on the screen, it must first be converted to an ASCII number string. Again the C++ WHYP host program does this conversion for you.

However, if you build a stand-alone system such as a calculator in which you type in numbers from a keypad and display the results of calculations on an LCD display, you will need to do these conversions yourself. In this chapter we will develop a number of WHYP words to help perform these tasks.

In this chapter you will learn

- How strings are stored in WHYP
- How to convert an ASCII number string to a binary number
- How to convert a binary number to an ASCII number string

All of the string WHYP words described in this chapter are available in the file STRING.WHP. To use these words you would load this file at the beginning of your program.

12.1 WHYP STRINGS

Strings are usually specified in one of three ways:

1. A *counted* string in which the first byte contains the number of characters in the string. The string is specified by the address of the count byte (*addr* --).
2. An *address-length* string in which the address of the first character of the string and the length of the string are specified: (*addr len* --).
3. An *ASCIIZ* string is a string specified by the address of the first character (*addr* --). The string is terminated by a *null* character (a zero byte).

A counted string (1) can be converted to an address-length string (2) by using the WHYP word *COUNT* defined in Figure 12–1.

Note that *COUNT* takes the address of a counted string (*addr*) and leaves the address of the first character of the string (*addr*+1) and the length of the string (which it got from the byte at *addr*).

As shown in Box 11–1 in Chapter 11 the WHYP word *EMIT (char --)* will print on the screen the character whose ASCII code is on top of the stack.

The WHYP word *TYPE (addr len --)*, shown in Figure 12–2, prints a string whose address and length are on the stack. Note that the WHYP word *?DUP*

```
: COUNT          ( addr -- addr+1 len )
                 DUP 1+
                 SWAP C@ ;
```

Figure 12–1 *COUNT* converts a counted string to an address-length string.

```
: TYPE           ( addr len -- )
                 ?DUP
                 IF                    \ if len ≠ 0
                   0 DO                \ addr
                       DUP C@          \ addr char
                       EMIT 1+         \ next.addr
                   LOOP
                 THEN
                 DROP ;
```

Figure 12–2 *TYPE* prints an address-length string on the screen.

(*n -- n n | 0*) will duplicate the value on top of the data stack (*len*) only if it is nonzero. Therefore, no characters will be printed for a string of length zero.

Since *TYPE* requires the address and length of the string to be on the stack, to print a counted string you would use

```
COUNT TYPE
```

The WHYP word "quote" (") can be used to generate an address-length string of type 2. For example, if within a colon definition you type

```
"This is a string"
```

then the first double quote will be compiled as a *JSR (DQ)* followed by the counted string. When the instruction *JSR (DQ)* is later executed, it will leave the address and length of the string on the data stack. For example, the word

```
: bar "********" TYPE ;
```

will produce the same result as the word

```
: bar ." ********" ;
```

12.2 ASCII NUMBER STRING TO BINARY CONVERSION

When we enter a number (such as 34671) from the keyboard, the characters in the number are stored in a buffer as an ASCII string. If you were to type such a number on a hex keypad of the type we described in Section 7.4, then you could form an ASCII string by first converting each digit to an ASCII value using *HEX2ASC* (see Figure 5–16). If we want to store the *value* of this number in some register or memory location we must convert the ASCII number string to a binary number. After performing some calculation it will be necessary to convert the binary number to an ASCII number string before the result can be displayed on the screen or on an LCD display.

The decimal value 34671 can be represented as

$$34671 = 3 \times 10^4 + 4 \times 10^3 + 6 \times 10^2 + 7 \times 10 + 1$$
$$= 1 + 10(7 + 10(6 + 10(4 + 10(3)))) \tag{12.1}$$

This form of representing a number can be used to convert an ASCII number string to a binary number. The ASCII code for a given character can be checked to see if it is a valid character in the current base using the WHYP word *DIGIT* shown in Figure 12–3. The current base is stored in the variable *BASE*.

Note that if the character is a valid digit, the contents of *n* left on the data stack under a true flag will contain the valid hex value. For example, if *c* contains $35 (the ASCII code for the character 5) when the word *DIGIT* is called, it will leave the hex

```
DECIMAL

: DIGIT              ( c base -- n f )
                >R                              \ save radix
                48 -                            \ subtract ascii 0
                9 OVER <                        \ if offset > 9
                IF
                    7 -                         \   offset it from A
                    DUP                         \   n n
                    10 <                        \   if n<10, flag is -1
                    OR                          \   OR with n will be -1
                THEN                            \   if n>10, flag=0 and
                DUP                             \   OR will still be n
                R> U< ;                         \ if n>=radix, digit not valid
```

Figure 12–3   *DIGIT* checks to see if *c* is a valid character in the current *base*.

value $05 on the data stack under a true flag. If the character is *not* a valid digit in the current base, a false flag will be left on top of the data stack over a meaningless invalid value of *n*.

The algorithm to convert an ASCII number string to a 32-bit double number is given in Figure 12–4. This algorithm follows from the nested representation of the number given in Eq. (12.1). This algorithm is implemented as the WHYP word *>NUMBER (ud1 addr1 -- ud2 addr2)*, shown in Figure 12–5. This word is called with *ud1* and *addr1* on the data stack where *ud1* is a double word set to zero and *addr1* is the address of the counted number string to be converted.

After the word *>NUMBER* is executed, the values *ud2* and *addr2* will be left on the data stack where *ud2* is the converted double number and *addr2* will point to the first invalid digit in the number string. This will normally be the character following the number and may be a *blank* or a *carriage return*.

```
>NUMBER:   input:    addr1 -> number string
                     ud1 = double number  (0 0)
          output:    addr2 -> first invalid digit
                     ud2 = converted double number

loop:   get next digit
        call DIGIT
while: digit is valid
        multiply ud1 by base and
        add digit value
        store result in ud1
repeat:
```

Figure 12–4   Algorithm to Convert an ASCII String to a 32-Bit Double Number.

```
\               Convert counted string at addr1 to double number ud2
\               ud1 normally zero to begin with
\               addr2 points to first invalid character
: >NUMBER       ( ud1 addr1 -- ud2 addr2 )
                BEGIN
                    1+ DUP >R                \ skip count
                    C@ BASE @ DIGIT          \ convert one digit
                WHILE
                    DUP >R                   \ save digit
                    DUM*                     \ ud1*base
                    0 R> D+                  \ add digit
                    R>                       \ get incremented addr1
                REPEAT
                DROP R> ;
```

Figure 12–5   >NUMBER converts an ASCII string to a 32-bit double number.

12.3   BINARY NUMBER TO ASCII STRING CONVERSION

To display the value of a 32-bit double number on a computer screen or LCD display, it is first necessary to convert this double number to a string of ASCII characters. The steps used to create this string of ASCII characters are illustrated in Figure 12–6. Note that the algorithm consists of dividing the number by the base and converting the remainder to an ASCII character.

Figure 12–7 shows the algorithm for a routine called *sharp* which will convert the next digit of a double number according to the steps in Figure 12–6. The algorithm for the routine *sharps* is also given in Figure 12–7. This subroutine will convert all of the remaining digits in a double number.

The WHYP words shown in Figure 12–8 can be used to perform the conversion described by the algorithm in Figure 12–7. After defining the variables *BASE* and *HLD*, a 16-byte buffer is allocated and the address *PAD* is the address at the end of this buffer. This is the number string buffer in which characters will be stored backward in memory as indicated in Figure 12–6. The variable *HLD* points to the last character stored in the number string.

The word <# ("less-sharp"), shown in Figure 12–8, starts the number conversion which will store the number string in the memory bytes below *PAD*. It simply stores the address, *PAD*, in the variable *HLD*.

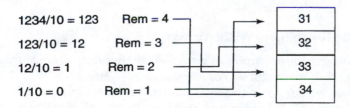

Figure 12–6   Steps for Creating an ASCII Number String.

SHARP   convert the next digit of a double number to ASCII
          input: double number
          output: double quotient after dividing by base
          The digits are converted least significant digit first
          and stored in memory starting at the end of the string.

          Divide double number on data stack by *base*
          If *rem* > 9 **then** add 7 to *rem*
          Add '0' to *rem* to convert to ASCII
          Store ASCII digit in string buffer

SHARPS   convert all (remaining) digits in the double number

          loop: call *SHARP*
          repeat until double number quotient = 0

Figure 12–7   Algorithms to Convert a Double Number to an ASCII String.

The word *HOLD* (*char* --), shown in Figure 12–8, will insert the character *char* in the output string. Recall that the WHYP word *+!* (*n addr* --) adds *n* to the value at *addr*. Thus, in the definition of *HOLD*, the value in *HLD* is decremented by 1 and then the ASCII code *char* is stored in the byte at *HLD*.

The word # (*d1* -- *d2*) ("sharp"), shown in Figure 12–8, converts the next digit by performing the algorithm shown in Figure 12–7. The dividend must be a double number and you must remember to store the current base in the variable *BASE* before calling the word #.

The word #S (*d* -- *0 0*) ("sharp-S"), shown in Figure 12–8, converts the rest of a double number using the algorithm shown in Figure 12–7 and leaves a double zero on the stack.

The word #> (*d* -- *addr len*) ("sharp-greater"), shown in Figure 12–8, completes the conversion by dropping the double zero left by #S and then computing the length of the string by subtracting the address of the first character (now in *HLD*) from the address following the last char (*PAD*). This string length is left on the stack above the string address (in *HLD*).

The word *SIGN* (*n* --) is used to insert a minus sign (−) in an output string if the value on top of the stack is negative.

These words will be used in the next section to display number values on the screen.

12.3.1 Examples of Converting Numbers to ASCII Strings

In this section we will look at some examples of using the number output conversion words shown in Figure 12–8. Four useful words are shown in Figure 12–9.

The word (UD.) (*ud* -- *addr len*) converts an unsigned double number and leaves the address and length of the converted string on the stack. Note how the three WHYP words <# #S #> form a natural sequence for creating the ASCII string.

```
HEX
VARIABLE        BASE    \ the current base
VARIABLE        HLD     \ pointer to next character location
10 VALLOT               \ 16-byte buffer for PAD
VARIABLE        PAD     \ highest address of temporary buffer

: <#            ( -- )
                PAD HLD ! ;

: HOLD          ( char -- )
                -1 HLD +!
                HLD @ C! ;

: #             ( d1 -- d2 )
                BASE @ MU/MOD           \ rem d2
                ROT 9 OVER              \ d2 rem 9 rem
                <
                IF                      \ if 9 < rem
                    7 +                 \    add 7 to rem
                THEN
                30 +                    \ conv. rem to ASCII
                HOLD ;                  \ insert in string

: #S            ( d -- 0 0 )
                BEGIN
                    #                   \ convert next digit
                    2DUP OR 0=          \ continue until
                UNTIL ;                 \ quotient = 0

: #>            ( d -- addr len )
                2DROP                   \ drop 0 0
                HLD @                   \ addr
                PAD OVER                \ addr pad addr
                - ;                     \ addr len

: SIGN          ( n -- )
                0<
                IF
                    ASCII - HOLD
                THEN ;
```

Figure 12–8   WHYP Words Used to Convert a Double Number to an ASCII String

In general, as we will see below, we can include any WHYP words between the <# and #> when converting numbers to ASCII strings.

Once we have produced the ASCII string using *(UD.)*, we can print this string on the screen by executing the word *TYPE* given in Figure 12–2. In fact, the WHYP word *UD.* *(ud--)* could be defined as follows:

```
: UD.           ( ud - )
                (UD.) TYPE 32 EMIT ;
```

where 32 = $20 is the ASCII code for a blank.

```
: (UD.)          ( ud -- addr len )
                 <# #S #> ;

: (U.)           ( u -- addr len )
                 0 <# #S #> ;

: (.)            ( n -- addr len )
                 DUP ABS                    \ n u
                 0 <# #S                    \ n 0 0
                 ROT SIGN #> ;

: (D.)           ( d -- addr len )
                 TUCK DABS                  \ dH ud
                 <# #S ROT SIGN #> ;
```

Figure 12–9   Examples of Converting Numbers to an ASCII String

This definition of *UD.* is not the one actually used by WHYP. Rather WHYP lets the C++ program do the number conversions inasmuch as you will always be running the WHYP host program while connected to the target system. On the other hand, the word *(UD.)* might be useful in a stand-alone system when you want to output a number to a liquid crystal display, for example. You could make your own version of *UD.* which uses a variation of the word *TYPE* (see Section 12.1) that *EMITs* characters to the LCD rather than to the screen (see Exercise 12.1).

The word *(U.)* (*u -- addr len*), shown in Figure 12–9, converts an unsigned single number and leaves the address and length of the converted string on the stack. Remember that <# always expects a double number on the data stack. Therefore, in this case we must add a zero before <# to convert the single word, *u*, to the double word, *0:u*. Again, we could print the unsigned single number on the screen by defining the word *U.* as

```
: U.             ( u -- )
                 (U.) TYPE 32 EMIT ;
```

Recall that the word *(U.)* was used in the word *.4leds* (see Figure 8–11) to convert the number to be displayed on the three seven-segment displays to an ASCII number string.

To print a signed number, we need to insert a minus-sign at the beginning of the string if the number is negative. The word *(.)* (*n -- addr len*), shown in Figure 12–9, will do this. Note that it first saves the signed number, *n*, and then converts the absolute value of *n*. Before terminating the conversion with #>, it uses the word *SIGN* from Figure 12–8 to see if a minus sign needs to be inserted at the beginning of the string.

The word "*dot*" could then be defined as

```
: .              ( n -- )
                 (.) TYPE 32 EMIT ;
```

```
: .$              ( u -- )
                  0 <# # #        \ convert cents
                  ASCII . HOLD    \ add decimal point
                  #S              \ convert dollars
                  ASCII $ HOLD    \ add dollar sign
                  #> TYPE;        \ display
```

Figure 12–10   Example of Formatting an ASCII Number String

Finally, the word *(D.)* *(d -- addr len)*, shown in Figure 12–9, will convert a signed double number. Note that the word *TUCK* saves the high word of *d* which contains the sign bit and is used by *SIGN* to insert a possible minus sign at the beginning of the string.

The conversion words given in Figure 12–8 can be used to provide special formatting for displaying number strings. For example, suppose that *u* is an unsigned number representing an amount of money in cents. We could display this amount in the form $xxx.xx by using the word *.$* *(u --)*, shown in Figure 12–10.

12.4 THE WHYP WORDS CMOVE AND CMOVE>

Sometimes it may be convenient to move a string of bytes from one location in memory to another location. The two WHYP words *CMOVE (ad1 ad2 cnt --)* and *CMOVE> (ad1 ad2 cnt --)*, shown in Box 12–1, make it easy to do this. The word *CMOVE* will move *cnt* consecutive bytes starting at address *ad1* to a new memory location starting at address *ad2*. Note that if address *ad2* is less than *ad1 + cnt*, then the two strings will overlap and the first string will be overwritten before it is completely copied. To prevent this from happening it is necessary to copy the string starting at the last byte in the string. This is what the WHYP word *CMOVE>* does. In this case, *ad1* and *ad2* are the last bytes in the source and destination strings and the bytes are copied downward in memory. The 68HC12 code for the words *CMOVE* and *CMOVE>* is shown in Figure 12–11.

As an example of using *CMOVE*, suppose you want to store a particular path name as an ASCIIZ string in an array called *pathname*. The program shown in Figure 12–12 will do this.

Box 12–1   WHYP Words for Moving Bytes of Data

CMOVE   (ad1 ad2 cnt --)   ("C-move")
             move *cnt* bytes up in memory from addr *ad1* to *ad2*.

CMOVE>   (ad1 ad2 cnt --)   ("C-move-down")
             move *cnt* bytes down in memory from addr *ad1* to *ad2*.

```
;          CMOVE   ( ad1 ad2 cnt -- )
;          move cnt bytes up in memory from addr ad1 to ad2
           LDD     2,X+                  ; D = count
           LDY     2,X+                  ; Y = to address
           PSHX                          ; save X
CMV1       LDX     0,X                   ; X = from address
           MOVB    1,X+,1,Y+             ; move bytes from X to Y
           SUBD    #1                    ; move cnt bytes
           BNE     CMV1
           PULX                          ; restore X
           INX                           ; pop data stack
           INX
           RTS


;          CMOVE>  ( ad1 ad2 cnt -- )
;          move cnt bytes down in memory from addr ad1 to ad2
CMOVEG
           LDD     2,X+                  ; D = count
           LDY     2,X+                  ; Y = to address
           PSHX                          ; save X
           LDX     0,X                   ; X = from address
           INY                           ; move bytes from
           INX                           ;  right to left
CMVG1      MOVB    1,-X,1,-Y             ; move bytes from -X to -Y
           SUBD    #1                    ; move cnt bytes
           BNE     CMVG1
           PULX                          ; restore X
           INX                           ; pop data stack
           INX
           RTS
```

Figure 12–11   68HC12 Code for the WHYP Words CMOVE and CMOVE>

```
VARIABLE pathname 46 VALLOT

: name1 ( -- )
       " c:\prog\whypdata.txt"     \ addr len
       TUCK pathname SWAP          \ len ad1 ad2 len
       CMOVE                       \ len
       0 SWAP pathname + C! ;      \ make asciiz string
```

Figure 12–12   Example of Using the WHYP Word CMOVE

12.5   SUMMARY

In this chapter we saw that WHYP generally specifies strings as either counted strings, in which the first byte at the string address contains the number of characters in the string, or as address-length strings in which both the address and length of the string are specified on the data stack.

We showed how the WHYP words in the file STRING.WHP, shown in Box 12–2, can be used to convert a binary number to an ASCII number string or, conversely, how an ASCII number string can be converted to a binary number (using the words *DIGIT* and *>NUMBER*). The words *COUNT*, *TYPE*, *SPACE*, and *SPACES* are useful for displaying strings on the PC screen.

Box 12–2   WHYP Words Defined in the File STRING.WHP

<# (--) ("less-sharp")
Starts a string conversion.

(d1 -- d2) ("sharp")
Converts the next digit of the double number *d1* by dividing *d1* by the value in the variable *BASE* and converting the remainder to ASCII. The double quotient, *d2*, is left on the data stack.

#S   (d1 -- 0 0) ("sharp-S")
Converts the rest of the double number *d1* and leaves double zero on the data stack.

#>   (d -- addr len) ("sharp-greater")
Completes the string conversion and leaves the address, *addr*, and length, *len*, of the number string on the data stack.

HOLD (char --)
Inserts the character, *char*, in the output string.

SIGN (n --)
Inserts a minus sign (−) in the output string if *n* is negative.

COUNT (addr -- addr+1 len)
Converts a counted string at address, *addr*, to an address-length string at *addr*+1.

TYPE (addr len --)
Prints an address-length string on the screen.

(U.) (u -- addr len) ("paren-U-dot")
Converts an unsigned single number, *u*, and leave the address, *addr*, and length, *len*, of the number string on the data stack.

(.)   (n -- addr len) ("paren-dot")
Converts a signed single number, *n*, and leaves the address, *addr*, and length, *len*, of the number string on the data stack.

(UD.) (ud -- addr len) ("paren-U-D-dot")
Converts an unsigned double number, *ud*, and leaves the address, *addr*, and length, *len*, of the number string on the data stack.

(continued)

Box 12–2   (*continued*)

(D.)	(d -- addr len) ("paren-D-dot")	

Converts a signed double number, *d*, and leaves the address, *addr*, and length, *len*, of the number string on the data stack.

SPACE   (--)
Prints a space on the screen.

SPACES   (n --)
Prints *n* spaces on the screen.

DIGIT   (c base -- n f)
Checks to see if the character, *c*, is a valid digit in the base, *base*. If it is, leaves the valid digit, *n*, and a true flag, *f*, on the data stack; otherwise, leaves a false flag, *f*, and a meaningless value of *n*.

>NUMBER   (ud1 addr1 -- ud2 addr2)
Converts a counted string at address, *addr1*, to the double number, *ud2*. Starts the conversion with *ud1* equal to a double zero. The first invalid character is at address, *addr2*.

EXERCISES

Exercise 12.1

Write a WHYP word called *TYPE.LCD (addr len --)* that will display on an LCD a string of ASCII characters of length, *len*, starting at address, *addr*.

Exercise 12.2

Write a WHYP word called *.xxx.xx (n --)* that will print on the PC screen a positive 16-bit number *n* in a field of width 6 with 2 places after the decimal point. If the number is negative, the word should print 4 spaces followed by --.

Exercise 12.3

Write a WHYP word called *.$x,xxx.xx (d --)* that will print on the PC screen a signed 32-bit number *d* right-justified in a field of width 15 with 2 places after the decimal point and a leading dollar sign. If the number is negative, print the number preceded by a minus sign. If the number represents a value over $1000, include a comma between every three digits to the left of the decimal point. For example, the value 123456789 would be displayed as $1,234,567.89.

Exercise 12.4

Assume that the variable, *DPL*, contains the number of digits following the decimal point in a fixed point double number, *d*. Write a WHYP word called *.fixed (d --)* that will print on the PC screen the number *d* with the decimal point located in the proper place.

Exercise 12.5

Write a WHYP word called *s.type (addr cnt --)* that will expect the address of a string and the number of characters in the string on the data stack and will send this string followed by a carriage return out the serial port SCI0. For example, typing

```
"ATD 3388384" s.type
```

will send the string "ATD 3388384" out the serial port.

Exercise 12.6

Create a ten-byte table containing the ten digits 0123456789.

a. Write a WHYP word that will move the first nine bytes up one byte such that the table will contain the bytes 0012345678.

b. Write a WHYP word that will move the last nine bytes down one byte such that the table will contain the bytes 1234567899.

13

Program Control and Data Structures

WHYP has a special feature that allows you to define what are called *defining words*. These words contain the WHYP words *CREATE . . . DOES>* whose function and implementation are described in Section 13.1. Defining words are used in Section 13.2 to implement jump tables that are useful for maintaining overall control of a program. In Section 13.3 we will look at how WHYP can implement various data structures. We have already seen how we can implement a character queue in Section 10.6. We will see how to implement arrays in Section 13.3.1 and linked lists in Section 13.3.2.

13.1 CREATE . . . DOES>

The WHYP word pair *CREATE . . . DOES>* is used to define *defining words*, that is, words that can define new words. The unique thing about defining words is that at the time they are defined the run-time behavior is specified for all future words that may be defined using this defining word. To illustrate the use of *CREATE . . . DOES>* consider the definition of the defining word *table* shown in Figure 13–1.

This word *table* can be used to define a new word *junk* by typing

```
3 15 7 2 4 table junk
```

```
: table              ( list n +++  )
                     CREATE
                        0 DO
                           C,
                        LOOP
                     DOES>     ( ix pfa -- c )
                        + C@ ;
```

Figure 13–1 Example of a Defining Word Using *CREATE . . . DOES>*

When the word *table* is executed, the WHYP words between *CREATE* and *DOES>* in the definition of *table* are executed. This will cause the word *junk* to be added to the dictionary with the values 2, 7, 15, and 3 stored in memory starting at the *PFA* of *junk* as shown in Figure 13–2.

The address of *junk* contains a *JSR* instruction to machine code (^*DOES*) which will put the *PFA* of *junk* on the data stack and then cause the WHYP words following *DOES>* in the definition of *table* to be executed. Thus, when the word *junk* is executed with an index *ix* on the stack, this index will be added to the *PFA* and then *C@* will fetch the byte at that location.

For example,

```
2 junk .
```

will print 15.

The way *CREATE . . . DOES>* works is as follows. If you define the word *table* as given in Figure 13–1 and then use *see table* and *show table*, you can verify that the following code is produced:

```
table  5000    16  46  93      JSR (CREATE)
       5003    16  45  22      JSR (LIT)
       5006    00  00               0
       5008    16  46  CC      JSR (DO)
       500B    00  0A               10
       500D    16  46  31      JSR C,
       5010    16  47   1      JSR (LOOP)
       5013    FF  FA              -6
       5015    16  46  AE      JSR (;CODE)
       5018    16  46  B5      JSR DODOES
       501B    16  42  E2      JSR +
       501E    16  41  EB      JSR C@
       5021    3D              RTS
```

If you then type

```
3  15  7  2  4 table junk
```

the following code will be added in the 68HC12:

```
JUNK    5022    16  50  18      JSR ^DOES
PFA     5025    02                   2
        5026    07                   7
        5027    0F                  15
        5028    03                   3
```

junk	JSR ^DOES	
PFA	2	ix = 0
	7	ix = 1
	15	ix = 2
	3	ix = 3

Figure 13–2   The Table *junk* Created with the Defining Word *table*

Note that the address of *junk* contains a *JSR* instruction to the instruction *JSR DODOES* at address 5018. How did the address 5018 get inserted at address 5023? When the word *junk* was created by the execution of the word *(CREATE)* at the beginning of *table*, a *JSR DOVAR* instruction was inserted at the address of *junk*. This will normally return the *PFA* of *junk* when *junk* is executed. However, the address of *junk+1* (5023 in the above example) is stored in the WHYP variable *LAST*. When the subroutine *(;CODE)* is executed at line 5015, the code shown in Figure 13–3 is executed. This first pops the address of the next instruction (the address 5018 of *JSR DODOES*) into *D* and then stores this address at the address in *LAST*, which in this case is 5023. It then executes *RTS* which will return to the statement following the call to *table*, because we have popped the address following the *JSR (;CODE)* instruction. This is why when you execute the word *table*, only the words between *CREATE* and *DOES>* will be executed.

Later, when the word *junk* is called, it will execute the statement *JSR $5018*. This has two effects. First, it puts the *PFA* of *junk* on the return stack, and second it executes the statement *JSR DODOES* at address 5018. At this point the two return addresses 5025 and 501B will be on the return (system) stack. The code for the subroutine *DODOES* is shown in Figure 13–3. It first pops the address 501B into *Y*. It then pops the address 5025 (the *PFA* of *junk*) into *D*. It then pushes the address 501B back on the stack so that when the instruction *RTS* is executed at the end of the subroutine *DODOES* control will return to address 501B, the address of the first

```
;           (;CODE)  ( -- )         Compile time code for DOES>
PSCODE
  PULD                        ;get addr of JSR DODOES
  LDY     LAST                ;replace DOVAR with DODOES
  STD     0,Y                 ;at addr in LAST
  RTS                         ;return up one level


;           DODOES  ( -- pfa )    Run time code for DOES>
DODOES
  PULY                        ;Y -> code following DOES>
  PULD                        ;D = pfa of defined word
  PSHY
  STD     2,-X                ;push pfa on data stack
  RTS                         ;return to code after DOES>
```

Figure 13–3   68HC12 Code for the WHYP Words *(;CODE)* and *DODOES*

word following *DOES>* in the definition of *table*. Before executing the *RTS* instructions, *DODOES* will push the *PFA* of *junk* onto the data stack.

Thus when *junk* is executed, the code starting at address 501B will be executed. These are just the statements that were defined following *DOES>* in the definition of *table*. It is important to note that these same WHYP words will be executed each time *any* word defined by *table* is executed. This is a very powerful feature that we will exploit in the following sections to define various types of jump tables.

13.2 PROGRAM CONTROL

Most computer languages have some type of *CASE* (or *SWITCH*) statement that allows you to control program execution by executing different code depending on the value of some expression. In WHYP we can accomplish a similar effect by using a jump table. In Section 13.2.1 we will develop a simple jump table consisting of a list of WHYP word addresses. A more general jump table will be developed in Section 13.2.2 in which an arbitrary 16-bit word (for example, the ASCII or HEX code of a key) can be associated with a particular WHYP word to be executed.

13.2.1 A Simple Jump Table

As an example of using a defining word, suppose you want to create a jump table called *do.key* of the form shown in Figure 13–4. This might be used, for example, if you had a keypad with five keys labeled 0–4 which returned the values 0–4 on the stack when the corresponding key was pressed. You want to execute the WHYP words *0word, 1word, . . . , 4word* when the corresponding key is pressed. The subroutine addresses of these words are to be stored in the jump table.

We will define a defining word called *JUMP.TABLE* that can be used to produce *do.key*, or any other similar jump table. To produce *do.key* you would enter the code shown in Figure 13–5.

The definitions of *JUMP.TABLE* and *',* ("tick-comma") are given in Figure 13–6. This code is available in the file JMPTBL.WHP. At compile time the words between *CREATE* and *DOES>* will be executed. The word *HERE* will leave the *PFA* of *do.key* on the data stack. The statements *0,* will initialize the count of the number of table entries to zero.

do.key	JSR ^DOES	
PFA	5	# of words
	0word	n = 0
	1word	n = 1
	2word	n = 2
	3word	n = 3
	4word	n = 4

Figure 13–4 Structure of a Simple Jump Table

```
JUMP.TABLE do.key
         ', 0word
         ', 1word
         ', 2word
         ', 3word
         ', 4word
    DROP
```

Figure 13–5
WHYP Code Used to Create a
Simple Jump Table

```
: JUMP.TABLE    ( +++  )
     CREATE
        HERE 0 ,
     DOES>          ( n pfa -- )
        SWAP 1+ SWAP              \ n+1 pfa
        2DUP @ >                  \ n+1 pfa (n+1)>nmax
        IF
           2DROP
        ELSE
           SWAP                   \ pfa n+1
           2* +                   \ addr = pfa + 2(n+1)
           @ EXECUTE
        THEN ;

: ',   ( pfa -- pfa )
     ' ,                          \ store addr of word in table
     1 OVER +! ;                  \ increment count at PFA
```

Figure 13–6   Definition of WHYP Words Used to Create a Simple Jump Table

Note that in the definition of the WHYP word ', (*tick-comma*) the *tick* (') in the first line will get the address of the WHYP word following the word *tick-comma* (',) and *comma* it into the table. The statements *1 OVER +!* in the second line will increment the word count at the *PFA* of *do.key*. Note that the *PFA* of *do.key* is maintained on the data stack while all the word addresses are being entered into the jump table. Therefore, at the end of the jump table definition, a *DROP* statement is needed to drop this *PFA* from the data stack.

In the *DOES>* part of the definition of *JUMP.TABLE*, shown in Figure 13–6, the value of n on the data stack is checked to make sure it is less than the number of entries in the jump table. If it is, then the appropriate WHYP word is executed using the WHYP word *EXECUTE (addr --)* that executes the word whose subroutine address is stored on top of the data stack.

13.2.2 A Jump Table with WHYP Words

A limitation of the jump table described in the previous section is that the index into the table must be consecutive integers starting at zero. Often the value one knows is an ASCII code or a hex code corresponding to a key that has been pressed. A more general jump table would involve a key value (e.g., a hex code) plus a subroutine (WHYP word) address for each entry as shown in Figure 13–7.

```
do.key  | JSR ^DOES |
   PFA  |     5     |  # of entries
        |     A     |  choice 1
        |    add    |
        |     B     |  choice 2
        | subtract  |
        |     C     |  choice 3
        | multiply  |
        |     D     |  choice 4
        |  divide   |
        |     E     |  choice 5
        |  enter    |
        |  chrout   |  default
```

Figure 13-7   Structure of a General Jump Table

This table might be used for a *Reverse Polish Notation* (RPN) calculator that had a hex keypad. Pressing key *A* would cause the WHYP word *add* to be executed which would add the top two values on the data stack and leave the sum on the stack and displayed on a Liquid Crystal Display (LCD). Similarly, pressing keys *B*, *C*, and *D* would execute the words *subtract*, *multiply*, and *divide*, respectively. Pressing key *E* would execute the word *enter* which would cause a previously entered number to be converted to an integer and stored on top of the data stack. The default word *chrout* would be executed if no match were found in the jump table. This word might display the digit (0–9) on an LCD display and store it in an input buffer for later conversion to an integer (when key *E* is pressed). The 5 at the *PFA* location is the number of key choices in the table, excluding the default word.

To make this table we will use the defining word *EXEC.TABLE*, as shown in Figure 13–8. Note that any WHYP words, such as \, can be used on any line defining the table. For example, we could use lines such as

```
CONTROL Q  |  quit       \ quit the program
ASCII A    |  printA
HEX 2B     |  escape    DECIMAL
```

where the statement *CONTROL Q* would return $11 and *ASCII A* would return $41.

```
HEX
EXEC.TABLE do.key
        A  |  add          \ addition
        B  |  subtract     \ subtraction
        C  |  multiply     \ multiplication
        D  |  divide       \ division
        E  |  enter        \ store number
  DEFAULT|  chrout         \ display digits
```

Figure 13-8   WHYP Code Used to Create the General Jump Table in Figure 13-7

```
: EXEC.TABLE        ( +++ )
          CREATE
              HERE 0 ,                        \ pfa
          DOES>        ( n pfa -- )
              DUP 2+                          \ n pfa pfa+2
              SWAP @                          \ n pfa+2 cnt
              0 DO                            \ n code.addr
                 2DUP @ =                     \ n addr (n=code)
              IF                              \ n addr
                  NIP 2+
                  LEAVE
              ELSE
                  4 +                         \ n addr'
              THEN
              LOOP
              @ EXECUTE ;

: |    ( addr n -- addr )
          , ' ,                        \ store n and addr in table
          1 OVER +! ;                  \ increment count at PFA

: DEFAULT|    ( addr -- )
          DROP ' , ;
```

Figure 13-9　Definition of WHYP Words Used to Create a General Jump Table

The definition of the word *EXEC.TABLE* used in Figure 13–8 is given in Figure 13–9. This code is available in the file EXECTBL.WHP. Note that the *CREATE* part of *EXEC.TABLE* is the same as that for *JUMP.TABLE* in the previous section. It simply stores a zero in the count field at the *PFA* of the defined word (*do.key*) and leaves this *PFA* value on the data stack. The program then returns to WHYP and will execute whatever WHYP words are on the following lines.

When *do.key* is executed with a key code on the stack, the *DOES>* part of the above definition is executed which will execute either the subroutine address of a key code match or the default word. Note that if the default word is executed, the key code will still be on the stack so that it can be used (for example, to display on an LCD and store in a buffer).

The vertical bar | is a WHYP word defined in Figure 13–9. Note that the first line , ' , (*comma-tick-comma*) will comma the value of *n* (the key code) into the table being created and then the *tick* (') will get the address of the WHYP word following the vertical bar | and comma it into the table. Any other WHYP words on the same line such as \ or *DECIMAL* will just be executed.

The word *DEFAULT|* is defined in Figure 13–9. It just drops the *PFA*, gets the address of the default word (*chrout*), and commas it into the jump table.

13.3　DATA STRUCTURES

A circular queue data structure was described in Section 10.6. In this section we will show how you can use WHYP to create two additional data structures: arrays and linked lists.

13.3.1 Arrays

In Section 4.3.3 we used the WHYP words *VARIABLE* and *VALLOT* to create simple arrays. The data in arrays must be stored in RAM and therefore the memory is allocated using *VALLOT*. Remember that *VALLOT* increments the variable dictionary pointer, *vdp*, while *ALLOT* increments the target dictionary pointer, *tdp*, which, in general, could be in EPROM.

Suppose you want to create an array of a certain size in memory and then use @ and *!* to fetch and store values in this array. One way to do this is to use the defining word, *array*, shown in Figure 13–10. This word, which is available in the file ARRAY.WHP, expects the size (number of 16-bit words) of the array on the stack. Thus, for example, to define an array called *my_array* containing seven words, you would type

```
7 array my_array
```

This will produce the array structure shown in Figure 13–11 (see Figure 4–17).

Recall that *CREATE . . . DOES>* will create a new word (the name of the array) whose *pfa* is put on the data stack when the new word is called (executing the words following *DOES>*). But this *pfa* will, in general, be in EPROM and thus the elements of the array cannot be stored here. Rather we store the starting address of the array at the *pfa* using the WHYP word *VHERE* that puts the current value of *vdp* on the data stack. The word *VALLOT* is used to allocate the number of bytes in the array and this number is also stored in memory following the array address as shown in Figure 13–11.

```
: array     ( size +++ )
            CREATE
               VHERE ,                  \ save vdp ram addr
               2* DUP VALLOT            \ allocate memory
               ,                        \ save #bytes in array
            DOES>  ( ix pfa -- addr )
               @                        \ get array addr
               SWAP 2* + ;              \ get address of element
```

Figure 13–10 Defining Word for Creating Arrays

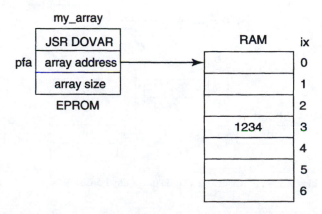

Figure 13–11 Structure of *my_array*
Defined Using *Array*

The word *my_array* will expect an array index value, *ix*, to be on the data stack. When *my_array* is executed, the WHYP words following *DOES>* in Figure 13–10 will cause the address of *my_array[ix]* to be put on the data stack. For example,

```
5 my_array @ .
```

will print the value stored in *my_array[5]*. Similarly,

```
1234 3 my_array !
```

will store 1234 in *my_array[3]*.

We didn't use the array size that we stored at *pfa+2* in Figure 13–11. You could access this in the *DOES>* part of the word *array* in Figure 13–10 to check to make sure that the index, *ix*, is within the bounds of the array. (See Exercise 13.1.) You could also add some code in the *CREATE* part of the word *array* in Figure 13–10 to check that a positive array size is on the data stack. (See Exercise 13.2.)

13.3.2 Linked Lists

In this section we will write a number of words for creating and maintaining linked lists in a 68HC12(11) microcontroller environment. Each node in the linked list will contain four bytes. The first two will be a pointer to the next node and the last two will contain the 16-bit value associated with the node. The last node in the list contains a pointer value of zero. The process of inserting a node into the list is shown in Figure 13–12.

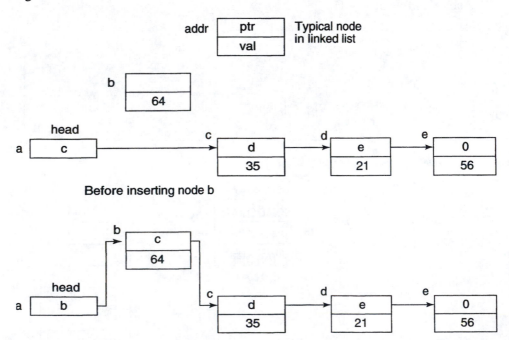

Figure 13–12   Inserting a Node into a Linked List

The file `LINKLIST.WHP`, given in Listing 13–1, contains a series of words that can be loaded into a 68HC12 WHYP system. The address of the first node in the list is contained in the variable *HEAD*. The variable *LPTR* contains the address of the next available free memory from which a new node can be created. It is initially set to *LPTR0* which you should initialize with the *CONSTANT* statement to some free RAM memory area. The variable *FREE* contains the address of the first node in a list of free nodes. Nodes are added to this list when they are removed from the list pointed to by *HEAD*. These same nodes then become available when values are later added to the list.

Listing 13–1   Linked List in WHYP

```
\ LINKLIST.WHP
\ Linked lists for the 68HC12/68HC11
\ Written by Richard E. Haskell
\ -----------------------------------------------------
\ Linked lists
\ Nodes: | ptr | val |

HEX
6000 CONSTANT LPTR0        \ the start of some free ram memory
VARIABLE LPTR              \ list pointer to unused free memory
LPTR0 LPTR !
VARIABLE HEAD              \ list header
0 HEAD !                   \ list initially empty
VARIABLE FREE              \ free list header
0 FREE !                   \ free list initially empty

: LALLOT          ( n -- )
                  LPTR +! ;

\        create a new node
: new.node        ( -- node.addr )
                  LPTR @ 4 LALLOT ;

\ -------------------------------------------------------
\ Node manipulation words

: insert.node  ( node.addr list.addr --- )      \ insert at head of list
                  2DUP @                         \ na la na @la
                  SWAP ! ! ;

: remove.node  ( list.addr -- node.addr )       \ remove 1st node
                  DUP @               \ a b
                  DUP @               \ a b c
                  ROT ! ;             \ b
```

(continued)

Listing 13–1 (*continued*)

```
: get.node     ( -- node.addr )
               FREE @
               IF                        \ if free node available
                   FREE remove.node      \    get it
               ELSE                       \ else
                   new.node              \    make it from new memory
               THEN ;

: delete.node  ( list.addr -- node.addr )
               DUP @                     \ a b
               IF                        \ if list is not empty
                   remove.node           \    remove node from list
                   DUP FREE insert.node  \    and put in free list
               ELSE                      \ if list is empty
                   DROP 0                \    return 0
               THEN ;

\ -------------------------------------------------------
\ Data manipulation words
\              push value at head of list
: push         ( value list.addr -- )
               get.node                  \ get a new node
               DUP ROT insert.node       \ insert it at head of list
               2+ ! ;                    \ store value in node

\              pop value at head of list
: pop          ( list.addr -- value )
               delete.node ?DUP
               IF                        \ node.addr
                   2+ @                  \ get value
               ELSE
                   FFFF                  \ return ffff if list empty
               THEN ;

: ?pop         ( list.addr -- value tf | ff )  \ ff if list is empty
               delete.node ?DUP
               IF                        \ node.addr
                   2+ @ TRUE             \ get value
               ELSE
                   FALSE
               THEN ;

: ?list.empty    ( list.addr -- f )
               DUP ?pop                  \ try to pop
               IF                        \ if something in list
                   SWAP push FALSE       \ push it back - set false
               ELSE
                   DROP TRUE             \ else, set true
               THEN ;
```

Listing 13–1   *(continued)*

```
\ List display and tests

: .all          ( list.addr -- )           \ print list contents
                BEGIN                       \ a
                   @ ?DUP                   \ b b | 0
                WHILE                       \ b
                   DUP 2+ @ .               \ b
                REPEAT ;                    \ b

: get.#nodes    ( list.addr -- n )
                0 SWAP                      \ 0 a
                BEGIN                       \ # a
                   @ ?DUP                   \ 0 b b | 0 0
                WHILE                       \ 0 b
                   SWAP 1+ SWAP             \ # b
                REPEAT ;

\ find position of node after which to insert value
\ so that values will be stored in the list in ascending order

: findpos<      ( val list -- val node )
                BEGIN                       \ v a
                   TUCK @ ?DUP              \ a v b b | a v 0
                WHILE                       \ a v b
                   2+ @                     \ a v v'
                   OVER >                   \ a v f - true if v'>v
                   IF                       \ a v
                      SWAP EXIT             \ v a
                   THEN                     \ a v
                   SWAP @                   \ v n
                REPEAT                      \ v n
                SWAP ;                      \ v n

\ find position of node after which to insert value
\ so that values will be stored in the list in descending order

: findpos>      ( val list -- val node )
                BEGIN                       \ v a
                   TUCK @ ?DUP              \ a v b b | a v 0
                WHILE                       \ a v b
                   2+ @                     \ a v v'
                   OVER <                   \ a v f - true if v'>v
                   IF                       \ a v
                      SWAP EXIT             \ v a
                   THEN                     \ a v
                   SWAP @                   \ v n
                REPEAT                      \ v n
                SWAP ;                      \ v n

DECIMAL
```

Note that the variable *HEAD* is the name of the list. You can have more than one list by creating additional header variables such as *HEAD2* or *LIST3*. Each of these header variables must contain an initial value of zero.

The word *new.node (-- node.addr)* will create a new node from unused memory by incrementing the value of *LPTR* by 4. The WHYP word *insert.node (node.addr list.addr --)* will insert a node with an address *node.addr* (*b* in Figure 13–12) at the head of a list with a header address *list.addr* (*a* in the Figure 13–12). Note from Figure 13–12 that this only requires that the address in the header (*c*) be put in the pointer field of the node to be inserted (at address *b*) and that the address of the node (*b*) be put in the header (at *a*).

The word *remove.node (list.addr -- node.addr)* will remove a node from the head of a list with a header address *list.addr* (*a* in the figure) and leave its *node.addr* (*b* in the figure) on the data stack.

The word *get.node (-- node.addr)* will get a new node either by removing one from the free list if one is available, or by creating a new one by calling *new.node*.

The word *delete.node (list.addr -- node.addr)* will remove a node from a non-empty list and return it to the free list. If the list is empty, then *delete.node* will leave a value of zero on the data stack.

The word *push (n list.addr --)* will push the value *n* on the top of the list. For example, to push the value 5 on the top of the list you would type

```
5 head push
```

The word *pop (list.addr -- value)* will pop the value on the top of the list to the data stack. To pop this value you would type

```
head pop
```

The word *?pop (list.addr -- value tf | ff)* can be used to pop the top of the list if the list is not empty. If the list is empty, this word leaves a false flag on top of the stack. This word is useful if you are not sure when the list will be empty. The word *?list.empty (list.addr -- f)* will return a true flag if the list is empty.

The word *.all (list.addr --)* will print out all values in the list on the screen. To print out the contents of the list you would type

```
head .all
```

The word *get.#nodes (seg list -- n)* will find the number of nodes in the list. To print out the number of nodes in the list you would type

```
head get.#nodes .
```

The word *findpos< (val list -- val node)* will find the address of the node after which to insert a value so that values will be stored in the list in ascending order. For example, to insert the value 35 into the list so that the list is maintained in ascending order, you would type

```
35 head findpos< push
```

The word *findpos> (val list -- val node)* will find the position of the node after which to insert a value so that values will be stored in the list in descending order. For example, to insert the value 35 into the list so that the list is maintained in descending order, you would type

```
35 head findpos> push
```

13.4 SUMMARY

In this chapter we showed how to use the WHYP words *CREATE . . . DOES>*, shown in Box 13–1, to create defining words that can be used to define new classes of words. Examples of using defining words to create jump tables and arrays were given in Sections 13.2 and 13.3.1, respectively. Finally, WHYP words that can be used to create linked lists were discussed in Section 13.3.2 and included in Listing 13–1.

Box 13–1   WHYP Words Introduced in Chapter 13

CREATE . . . DOES> (--)
  Used in the definition of defining words. When the defining word is executed, the words between *CREATE* and *DOES>* are executed. When the word defined by the defining word is executed, the words following *DOES>* (with the *pfa* on the data stack) are executed.

EXECUTE (addr --)
  Executes the 68HC12 (68HC11) code starting at address *addr*.

EXERCISES

Exercise 13.1

Modify the definition of the defining word *array* in Figure 13–10 to make sure that the index *ix* in the *DOES>* part of *array* is within bounds. Note that this will increase the time required to access data in arrays.

Exercise 13.2

Modify the definition of the defining word *array* in Figure 13–10 to make sure that a positive array size is on the data stack when the *CREATE* part of the definition is executed. *Hint:* Use the word *DEPTH* given in Figure 4–16.

Exercise 13.3

Write a defining word called *MATRIX (row col + +) (row col -- addr)* that expects the number of rows and number of columns on the data stack and creates the storage for the matrix elements in memory. The first two elements (starting at the *PFA* of the defined word) should contain the values of *row* and *col*. The matrix data (16-bit values) should then be stored one row at a time. Thus,

```
3 4 MATRIX X
```

would create the matrix X, which contains 3 rows and 4 columns. Executing the word X with a row and column on the stack will return the address of that element. For example,

```
2 1 X @
```

would return the value of $X(2,1)$.

Exercise 13.4

a. Write a defining word called *COUNTER (n ++) (--)* that uses the number on the data stack to initialize its children (i.e., the words defined by *COUNTER*). When the children of *COUNTER* execute, they will modify their own contents to be one greater each time they execute. Thus,

```
0 COUNTER COUNTIT
```

would create *COUNTIT*, which would modify its contents to be 1, 2, 3, and so on, each time *COUNTIT* executes. *Note:* If you insert *COUNTIT* (or any child of *COUNTER*) in the colon definition of a word, you could tell how often that word is used within a program.

b. How would you retrieve the count stored in *COUNTIT*?

Exercise 13.5

a. Write a defining word called *MAKEDATE (month day year ++) (--)* that expects *month*, *day*, and *year* numbers on the data stack and creates children that will display their date with slashes. Thus,

```
7 4 1776 MAKEDATE INDEPENDENCE
```

would create *INDEPENDENCE*, which would display

```
07/04/1776
```

when it executes.

b. Using *MAKEDATE*, define a word called *BIRTHDAY* that will print out your birthday when executed.

Exercise 13.6

Write a defining word called *LINEAR (a b ++) (x -- y)* that can be used to define new words for solving linear equations of the form $y = ax + b$. For example, to solve the equation $y = 2x + 5$, you would type

```
2 5 LINEAR EQ1
```

Then

```
3 EQ1 .
```

would print 11 ($= 2 \times 3 + 5$).

Hint: At compile time store the parameters a and b in the parameter field of *EQ1*.

Exercise 13.7

Write a defining word called *QUADRATIC (a b c ++) (x -- y)* that can be used to define new words for solving quadratic equations of the form $y = ax^2 + bx + c$. For example, to solve the equation $y = 2x^2 + 3x + 4$, you would type

```
2 3 4 QUADRATIC EQ2
```

Then

```
2 EQ2 .
```

would print 18.

Exercise 13.8

Modify the program in Listing 11–3 so as to use a jump table to print the following messages on the PC screen in response to the indicated key pressings:

Key Pressed	Message
F	Port F = xx
G	Port G = xx
H	Port H = xx
J	Port J = xx
T	Port T = xx
Other	Press F,G,H,J,T

In each case the value of *xx* should be the hex value currently stored in the indicated port register.

Exercise 13.9

Design and implement an HP type calculator using the 16-character × 1 line Liquid Crystal Display (LCD) shown in Figure 7–22 and a 4 × 4 keypad of the type shown in Figure 7–12. The calculator should work as follows: Each time you press a digit (0–9), convert the hex digit to ASCII, display it on the LCD, and store it in a buffer. After typing in a number in this fashion, if you press the * key (or E), convert the ASCII number string to a single number (16-bit integer) and push this value on the data stack. Leave the number displayed on the LCD. When you start to type a second number, clear the display and display the first digit of the new number.

Have the following keys perform indicated operations using the values on the data stack:

A Add the top two elements on the stack and leave the sum on top of the stack. Display the sum on the LCD.

B Subtract the top element on the stack from the second element on the stack and leave the difference on top of the stack. Display the difference on the LCD.

C Multiply the top two elements on the stack and leave the product on top of the stack. Display the product on the LCD.

D Divide the second element on the stack by the top element on the stack and leave the quotient on top of the stack. Display the quotient on the LCD.

E or * Make the buffer containing the ASCII codes of entered digits a counted string, append a blank ($20) to the end of the string, and convert the string to a single number that is left on the data stack.

F or # Clear the LCD display.

Hint: Use a jump table *do.key* similar to that shown in Figure 13–8.

Exercise 13.10

Implement a calculator similar to the one in Exercise 13.9 that will perform addition and subtraction of signed real numbers that can include an optional decimal point. Use key C for a negative sign and use key D for the decimal point.

14

Fuzzy Control

Fuzzy logic has been applied successfully to a wide variety of difficult control problems. The input and output control variables are members of fuzzy sets that admit varying degrees of membership. In this chapter we will introduce the basic ideas of fuzzy sets. We will then describe how a fuzzy controller works and present an overall approach to implementing a fuzzy controller on a microcontroller. The 68HC12 has some special instructions which simplify the implementation of a fuzzy controller. We will define some WHYP words that use these 68HC12 instructions to implement a fuzzy controller.

14.1 FUZZY SETS

Lotfi Zadeh introduced the term *fuzzy sets* in 1965.* In normal "crisp" logic the basic assumption is that assertions, or statements, are either *true* or *false*. But this assumption leads to paradoxes. For example, is the sentence in Figure 14–1 true or false? If the sentence is true, then it must be false; but if it is false, then it must be true. There are many such paradoxes in which it appears that true must be equal to false.

*L. Zadeh, "Fuzzy Sets," *Inform. and Contr.*, Vol. 8, pp. 338–353, 1965.

The sentence on the other side
of the line is false

The sentence on the other side
of the line is false

Figure 14–1 Is this sentence *true* or *false*?

Fuzzy logic does not require that everything be either true or false. In normal "crisp" set theory an element either belongs to the set, or it doesn't. However, a little reflection should convince you that most things in the world aren't that black and white. For example, is a given person *young*? We can consider *young* to be a fuzzy set in which we use membership functions to define the degree of membership (between 0 and 1) in the set.

A membership function for the fuzzy set *Young* is shown in Figure 14–2. People who are younger than age *a1* are definitely young (with a degree of membership equal to 1) while people who are older than age *a2* are definitely not young (with a degree of membership equal to 0). However, people with ages between *a1* and *a2* are young to some degree determined by the membership function shown in Figure 14–2.

When applied to fuzzy sets the logic operations *NOT*, *AND*, and *OR* are defined as shown in Table 14–1. These are not the only possible definitions but they are the ones most commonly used. Note that they reduce to the crisp case when *A* and *B* have the binary values 0 and 1.

If we apply the *NOT* operation to the fuzzy set *Young*, we obtain the fuzzy set *NOT Young*, shown in Figure 14–3. In a similar way we could define the fuzzy sets *Old* and *NOT Old*, as shown in Figure 14–4.

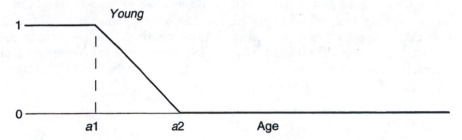

Figure 14–2 Membership Function for the Fuzzy Set *Young*

Table 14–1 Fuzzy Logic Operations

Logic Operation	Fuzzy Logic Operation
NOT A	$1 - A$
A AND B	MIN (A, B)
A OR B	MAX (A, B)

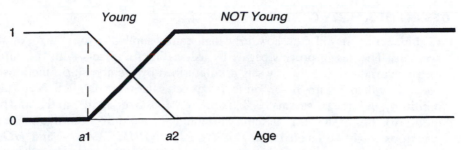

Figure 14–3   *NOT Young = 1 – Young*

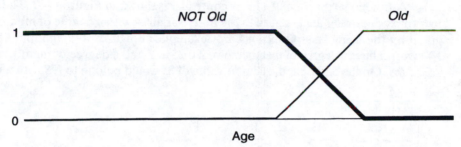

Figure 14–4   Membership Functions for the Fuzzy Sets *Old* and *NOT Old*

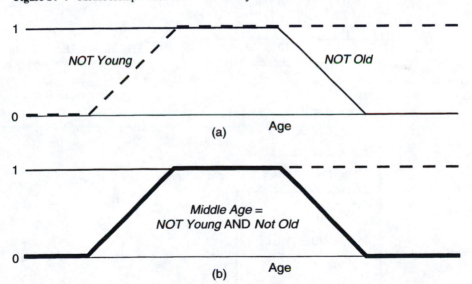

Figure 14–5   Deriving the Membership Function for *Middle Age*

We can use the *AND* operation given in Table 14–1 to define new fuzzy sets. For example, we might define *Middle Age* as *NOT Young AND Not Old*. Taking the minimum of the membership functions for *NOT Young* and *NOT Old* will produce the membership function for *Middle Age*, as shown in Figure 14–5.

14.2 DESIGN OF A FUZZY CONTROLLER

In this section we will show how fuzzy logic can be applied to the control of physical systems. The design process begins by associating fuzzy sets with the input and output variables. These fuzzy sets are described by membership functions of the type shown in Figure 14–6. These fuzzy set values are labeled *NM* (negative medium), *NS* (negative small), *Z* (zero), *PS* (positive small), and *PM* (positive medium). For example, if an input variable is temperature, the five membership functions might be labeled *COLD*, *COOL*, *MEDIUM*, *WARM*, and *HOT*. The shape of the membership functions are, in general, trapezoids that may have no top (triangles) or may have vertical sides as shown in Figure 14–6.

A functional diagram of a fuzzy controller is shown in Figure 14–7. The inputs to a fuzzy controller are assigned to the fuzzy variables with a degree of membership given by the membership functions. For example, in Figure 14–6 an input value of 140 would have a degree of membership of 0.25 in *Z* and a degree of membership of 0.5 in *PS*. On the other hand, an input value of 85 would belong to *NS* with a degree

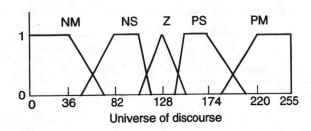

Figure 14–6   Example of Fuzzy Membership Functions

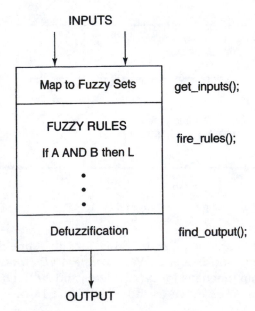

Figure 14–7   Functional Diagram of a Fuzzy Controller

```
do_forever
    {
        get_inputs();
        fire_rules();
        find_output();
    }
```

Figure 14–8 Overall Algorithm of
a Fuzzy Controller

of membership of 1.0. In general, an input value will belong to all fuzzy sets with different degrees of membership (including zero).

The fuzzy controller itself consists of a set of fuzzy rules of the form *if x_1 is PM AND x_2 is Z, then y is NM*, where x_1 and x_2 are inputs, *y* is the output, and *PM, Z,* and *NM* are fuzzy sets of the type shown in Figure 14–6. For example, a fuzzy rule for an air conditioner might be *if temperature is WARM AND change in temperature is ZERO, then motor speed is FAST*. Note that *WARM, ZERO,* and *FAST* are fuzzy sets. After applying all of the fuzzy rules to a given set of input variables, the output (motor speed in this case) will, in general, belong to more than one fuzzy set with different weights. The weighted output fuzzy sets are combined in a manner to be described below and then a centroid defuzzification process is used to obtain a single crisp output value.

The fuzzy controller shown in Figure 14–7 consists of three parts: the fuzzification of inputs, the processing of rules, and the defuzzification of the output. The overall algorithm of a fuzzy controller is shown in Figure 14–8 where each function represents the three parts of the controller shown in Figure 14–7. We will consider each of these parts separately.

14.2.1 Fuzzification of inputs: get_inputs()

For each crisp input x_i a set of weights w_j^i are computed for each membership function such as those shown in Figure 14–6. In general, each input will have a different set and number of membership functions. For input number *i* the weight w_j^i can be stored in a vector $weight_i[j], j = 1, M_i$ where M_i is the number of membership functions for input *i*. Each value in the weight vector is a weight value between 0 and 1 given by the shape of a particular membership function. Typically for a given input the weight vector will contain up to two nonzero entries in adjacent cells.

The purpose of the function *get_inputs()* is to read each input value x_i and fill the weight vector *weight[M_i]* with the degree of membership of x_i in each input fuzzy set. The pseudocode for *get_inputs()* is shown in Figure 14–9. In this figure M_i is the number of membership functions for input *i*.

Figure 14–9 Pseudocode for
get_inputs()

```
get_inputs()
for i = 1, num_inputs
    {
        get_x(i);
        fill_weight(x_i, M_i);
    }
```

The function *get_x(i)* is problem dependent and will consist of reading the input values x_i, $i = 1$, *num_inputs*. The function *fill_weight(x_i, M_i)* will fill the weight vector *weight[M_i]* with the degree of membership of x_i in each of the M_i membership functions for input i. We will now look at how the 68HC12 instruction *MEM* can be used to compute the function *fill_weight(x_i, M_i)*.

The 68HC12 *MEM* Instruction   The first step in designing a fuzzy controller is to define the membership functions for all inputs and the output. Each membership function can be defined by the four parameters *u1*, *u2*, *u3*, and *u4*, shown in Figure 14–10. The *MEM* instruction requires that the values *u1* and *u4* be 8-bit values between $00 and $FF. The weight values also range from $00 to $FF where $FF represents a weight value of 1.0 in Figure 14–10.

The *MEM* instruction does not use the parameters *u1*, *u2*, *u3*, and *u4*, shown in Figure 14–10, to define the membership function. Rather it uses *u1* (called *point_1*) and *u4* (called *point_2*) together with the values of the two slopes, *slope_1* and *slope_2*, shown in Figure 14–10.

The value of *slope_1* is $FF/(*u2* − *u1*) and the value of *slope_2* is $FF/(*u4* − *u3*). These values can range from $01 to $FF. If u1 = u2 or u3 = u4 then the slope is really infinite. In this case the values of *slope_1* and/or *slope_2* are taken to be $00 inasmuch as this value is not used otherwise. A special case is a singleton, or "crisp," membership function. This can be defined by setting *u1* = *u4* and *slope_1* = *slope_2* = $00.

The *MEM* instruction requires accumulator *A* to contain the input value x_i and index register *X* to point to a data structure containing the two points and slopes that define the membership function as shown in Figure 14–11. Index register *Y* points to the element of the array *weight(j)* corresponding to membership function *j*.

The *MEM* instruction will compute the weight value at the input value x_i based on the membership function whose parameters are pointed to by *X*. The computed

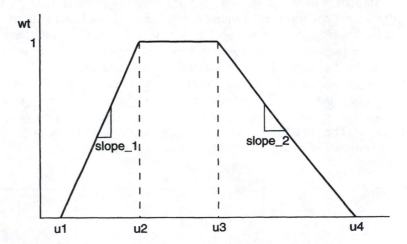

Figure 14–10   A membership function is defined in terms of u1, u2, u3, and u4.

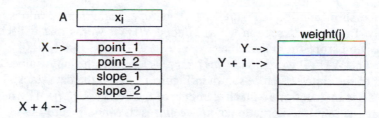

Figure 14–11 Data Structure Used by the 68HC12 MEM Instruction

weight value ($00–$FF) is stored in the byte pointed to by *Y*. After the *MEM* instruction is executed *X* will have been incremented by 4 and *Y* will have been incremented by 1. If the four parameters of all membership functions for a single input are stored in adjacent bytes of memory, then *X* will be pointing to the parameters of the next membership function. Similarly, *Y* will be pointing to the next element in the array *weight(j)*.

Suppose that an input has the five membership functions shown in Figure 14–6. We can store the parameters associated with these five membership functions in the data structure shown in Figure 14–12. We will show in the next section how to generate this data structure by using a simple WHYP-based data entry technique.

The first 16-bit word at address *pfa* in Figure 14–12 contains the number of membership functions. The second 16-bit word contains the address of the array *weight(j)*. The next 20 bytes contain the 4-byte parameters for each of the five membership functions. We have indicated the *point_1* and *point_2* values for each

pfa	5	# mem fncs
	^ wt	pointer to weight array
X -->	0	point_1
	72	point_2
		slope_1
		slope_2
	48	point_1
	116	point_2
		slope_1
		slope_2
	104	point_1
	152	point_2
		slope_1
		slope_2
	140	point_1
	208	point_2
		slope_1
		slope_2
	184	point_1
	255	point_2
		slope_1
		slope_2

Figure 14–12 Data Structure for Storing
Membership Function Parameters

membership function in Figure 14–6. The *slope_1* and *slope_2* values have been left empty. In the next section we will define WHYP words that will compute these values and store them in memory.

The WHYP word *fill.weights (xi pfa --)* expects the input value, x_i, and the address of the data structure shown in Figure 14–12 on the data stack. The word uses the *MEM* instruction to fill all elements of the array *weight(j)*. The 68HC12 assembly language implementation of *fill.weights* is shown in Figure 14–13. Note that the *pfa* in Figure 14–12 is first popped from the data stack into Y and the value of x_i is popped from the data stack into B. The value of Y is transferred to X and then loaded with the address of the array *weight(j)*. The next three statements will load the number of membership functions into B, store x_i in A, and leave X pointing to the first byte of the parameters associated with the first membership function. This is the setup needed for the *MEM* instruction as shown in Figure 14–11.

The *MEM* instruction is then executed B times (five in this example) by using the looping instruction *DBNE B,FW1*. This instruction will decrement B and branch to *FW1* if B is not equal to zero. The net result will be that the five weight values associated with the five membership functions for this particular input value, x_i, will be stored in the array *weight(j)*.

WHYP Words for Defining Membership Functions   In this section we will develop WHYP words that will produce the data structure shown in Figure 14–12. We will consider the example of a fuzzy controller designed to keep a ping-pong ball floating at the center of a vertical, plexiglas cylinder. The inputs to the controller will be the position and speed of the ping-pong ball (measured by the ultrasonic tape measure described in Section 10.10) and the output will be the power to a fan motor at the bottom of the cylinder.

The input, *ball_position*, will have the five fuzzy sets *neg_far*, *neg_close*, *zero_p*, *pos_close*, and *pos_far*. Assume that these membership functions have the same shape as those shown in Figure 14–6. We will enter these membership function parameters by typing their *u1*, *u2*, *u3*, and *u4* values (see Figure 14–10) using the format shown in Figure 14–14.

```
*        Fill Weight Arrays
*        fill.weights  ( xi pfa -- )
FILLWT
        LDY      2,X+            Y = pfa
        LDD      2,X+            B = xi
        PSHX                     save X
        TFR      Y,X             X = pfa
        LDY      2,X             Y -> input weight table
        PSHB                     save xi
        LDD      4,X+            B = #mem functs; X->1st memb fnc
        PULA                     A = xi
FW1     MEM                      fuzzy membership grade
        DBNE     B,FW1
        PULX                     restore X
        RTS
```

Figure 14–13   68HC12 Code for the WHYP Word *fill.weights (xi addr --)*

```
fuzzy.input        ball_position
          0     0    36    72   >m           \ neg_far
         48    82   100   116   >m           \ neg_close
        104   128   128   152   >m           \ zero_p
        140   156   174   208   >m           \ pos_close
        184   220   255   255   >m           \ pos_far
end.input
```

Figure 14–14   Format for Entering Membership Functions

The word *fuzzy.input* is a defining word given in Listing 14–1. The *CREATE* part of the word puts the address, *pfa*, on the data stack (using *HERE*) and then commas in two zeros. These will be the locations for the number of membership functions and the address of *weight(j)* shown in Figure 14–12. Note from the

Listing 14–1   Fuzzy Control in WHYP—Defining Membership Functions

```
\    Fuzzy Logic Control Using WHYP12    File: FUZZY12.WHP
\ **********************************************
\        Fuzzy Control
\ **********************************************

\ ********** Defining word for input **********
: fuzzy.input    ( +++ )
        CREATE
            HERE 0 , 0 ,
        DOES>              ( pfa -- )
          ;

: get.slopes    ( u1 u2 u3 u4 -- )
                3 PICK C,                    \ store point_1
                DUP C,                       \ store point_2
                2SWAP                        \ u3 u4 u1 u2
                SWAP - ?DUP
                IF
                255 SWAP / C,                \ store slope_1
                ELSE
                0 C,                         \ vertical slope
                THEN                         \ u3 u4
                SWAP - ?DUP
                IF
                255 SWAP / C,                \ store slope_2
                ELSE
                0 C,                         \ vertical slope
                THEN ;

: 4DROP         ( n1 n2 n3 n4 -- )
                2DROP 2DROP ;
```

(continued)

Listing 14–1 (continued)

```
: >m      ( pfa u1 u2 u3 u4 -- pfa )
          DUP 255 >
          IF
            4DROP CR
            ." ERROR: u4 > 255"
          ELSE                              \ pfa u1 u2 u3 u4
            2DUP >
            IF
              4DROP CR
              ." ERROR: u3 > u4"
            ELSE                            \ pfa u1 u2 u3 u4
              2OVER >
              IF
                4DROP CR
                ." ERROR: u1 > u2"
              ELSE                          \ pfa u1 u2 u3 u4
                2 PICK 2 PICK >
                IF
                  4DROP CR
                  ." ERROR: u2 > u3"
                ELSE                        \ pfa u1 u2 u3 u4
                  get.slopes
                THEN
              THEN
            THEN
          THEN
          1 OVER +! ;                       \ inc #member fncs
: end.input           ( pfa -- )
          VHERE OVER 2+ !
          @ VALLOT ;
```

definition of *fuzzy.input* that when *ball_position* is executed, it will put its *pfa* on the data stack.

Each of the five rows in Figure 14–14 contains the values of *u1*, *u2*, *u3*, and *u4* for one of the membership functions. The word >m (pfa u1 u2 u3 u4 -- pfa) at the end of each line will check to make sure that $u1 \le u2 \le u3 \le u4 \le 255$ and then computes the slope values and stores the *MEM* parameters in the data structure of Figure 14–12. The definition of >m (pfa u1 u2 u3 u4 -- pfa) is shown in Listing 14–1. The actual calculation of the slopes is done in the word *get.slopes (u1 u2 u3 u4 --)*, shown in Listing 14–1. This word will store the values of *point_1 (u1)*, *point_2 (u4)*, *slope_1*, and *slope_2* in the data structure of Figure 14–12. At the end of the word >m in Listing 14–1, the number of membership functions stored at the *pfa* is incremented.

The word *end.input (pfa --)* used in Figure 14–14 is used to allocate memory for the array *weight(j)* and to store the address of this array in the second word of the data structure in Figure 14–12. As shown in Listing 14–1, the word *end.input* uses the WHYP word *VHERE* to put on the data stack the next available RAM memory address where variables are stored. This will be the address of *weight(j)* and is stored at *pfa+2* in Figure 14–12. The word *VALLOT* is used to allocate a number of bytes equal to the number of membership functions given by the word at *pfa* in Figure 14–12.

In addition to the definition of *ball_position* given in Figure 14–14, a similar definition would be used to define the membership functions of the input *ball_speed*. A complete listing of this example will be given later in this chapter.

14.2.2 Fuzzy Inference

The heart of a fuzzy controller is the list of fuzzy rules. Fuzzy logic inference is used to find a fuzzy output, given a fuzzy input and a list of fuzzy rules. In a fuzzy controller the inputs are normally crisp, nonfuzzy values that must first be fuzzified in the first step of Figure 14–7 as described in Section 14.2.1. The output also needs to be a crisp value used to control some device. Therefore, the fuzzy output resulting from processing the fuzzy rules must be defuzzified as described in the next section. The way fuzzy rules are processed is illustrated in Figure 14–15 where fuzzy sets are represented by their membership functions *m*.

Fuzzy inference involves a set of fuzzy rules of the form

If x_1 is A_1 and x_2 is B_1, then y is L_1.   **Rule 1**

If x_1 is A_2 and x_2 is B_2, then y is L_2.   **Rule 2**

Given the fact that

x_1 is A' and x_2 is B' **Fact**

the problem is to find the conclusion

y is L' **Conclusion**

In this representation of the problem, A_1, A_2, B_1, B_2, A', and B' are input fuzzy sets and L_1, L_2, and L' are output fuzzy sets. Fuzzy reasoning would form the union of the intersection of A' and A_1. This is interpreted as being the maximum (union) of the minimum (intersection) of the membership functions A' and A_1. In Figure 14–15 A' is taken to be the singleton fuzzy set $x_1 = a$. In Rule 1, the maximum of the intersection (minimum) of this singleton with A_1 is the value w_1 shown in Figure 14–15. Similarly, the maximum of the intersection (minimum) of the singleton $x_2 = b$ with B_1 is the value w_2 shown in Figure 14–15. The fact $x_1 = a$ and $x_2 = b$ applied to the antecedent x_1 is A_1 and x_2 is B_1 is interpreted as the intersection (minimum) of w_1 and w_2, that is, w_2 for rule 1 in Figure 14–15. The conclusion of rule 1, y is L_1, is found by taking the intersection (T-norm) of w_2 with L_1. This is normally the minimum operation which would truncate L_1 to the height w_2. However, for fuzzy control it is sometimes advantageous to use a product T-norm for this intersection which would have the effect of multiplying L_1 by w_2 as shown in Rule 1 in Figure 14–15. Thus, Rule 1 in Figure 14–15 will contribute the fuzzy set w_2*L_1 to the conclusion fuzzy set L'. Similarly, Rule 2 in Figure 14–15 will contribute the

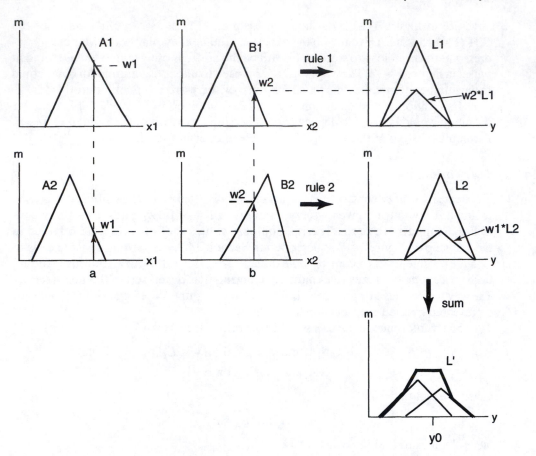

Figure 14–15 Fuzzy Inference

fuzzy set w_1*L_2 to the conclusion fuzzy set L' because w_1 is the minimum of w_1 and w_2 for Rule 2. Note that if L_1 and L_2 are singletons (as is normally the case), then there will be no difference in using the minimum T-norm or the product T-norm.

The conclusion fuzzy set L' is found by forming the T-conorm of w_2*L_1 and w_1*L_2. This is normally the maximum operation which is the one used by the 68HC12 *REV* instruction as we will see below. However, sometimes better results are obtained by taking the sum of w_2*L_1 and w_1*L_2, as shown in Figure 14–15. The difference between these two approaches is shown in Figure 14–16.

If L_1 and L_2 are singletons (the normal case), then taking the maximum or sum of the two rules shown in Figure 14–15 will be the same as shown in Figure 14–16. In general, they won't be the same if more than one rule contribute to the same output fuzzy set L_i. In this case the maximum rule will keep only the maximum value while the sum rule will add the contributions of each. Inasmuch as the 68HC12 *REV* instruction uses the maximum rule, we will use this in our WHYP implementation and leave the case of the sum rule to an exercise (see Exercise 14.7).

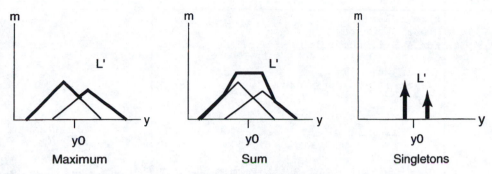

Figure 14–16   Comparing the MAX Rule and the SUM Rule

The conclusion output L' is a fuzzy set shown by the bold-line membership function in Figures 14–15 and 14–16. To obtain a crisp output some type of defuzzification process is required. The most common method is to compute the centroid of the area of L'. We will see that using the sum rule will be helpful in analyzing centroid defuzzification in Section 14.2.4.

14.2.3   Processing the Rules: fire_rules( )

We will use the MIN-MAX rule described in the previous section to find the contribution of each rule to the output. The outputs are assumed to be represented by k singleton membership functions L^k. These membership functions are defined by the singleton centroids, c^k. An output array, $Out(k)$, will contain the maximum over all the rules of the minimum weights from all inputs. The purpose of the function *fire_rules()* is to fill the elements of the output weight vector, $Out(k)$. A fuzzy rule with two inputs can be represented by the triplet $(A^1_j, A^2_j; L_j)$ where the subscript j refers to the jth fuzzy rule. Let the value A^1_j be the address (pointer) of the kth element of the weight vector $weight_1(k)$ for input 1. A^1_j will therefore correspond to one of the membership functions (and therefore one of the fuzzy sets) of input 1. Similarly, A^2_j will be the address of the kth element of the weight vector $weight_2(k)$ for input 2. In general, A^i_j will be the address of the kth element of the weight vector $weight_i(k)$ for input i. The pseudocode for the function *fire_rules()* is given in Figure 14–17. We will next see how this pseudocode can be implemented using the 68HC12 *REV* instruction.

The 68HC12 *REV* Instruction   The setup required for the 68HC12 *REV* instruction is shown in Figure 14–18. Index register Y points to an *in.out.array* that contains the input *weight(j)* arrays allocated in the word *end.input* in Listing 14–1 and ends with the *Out(k)* array described in the previous section. The elements of the *weight(j)* and *Out(k)* arrays are assigned offsets (0–15) which represent the various membership functions such as *neg_far* and *pos_high* as shown in Figure 14–18.

The data structure labeled *rules* in Figure 14–18 contains the number of rules in the first 16-bit word and a pointer to *Out0* in the *in.out.array* in the second word. The byte at *Out0* in the *in.out.array* contains the number of bytes in the *Out* array,

```
fire_rules()
clear Out array;
for j = 1, num_rules
    {
    min_wt = 1;
    for i = 1, num_inputs
        {
        wt = weight_i[A^i_j]
        if wt < min_wt
            min_wt = wt;
        }
    Out[L_j] = MAX(Out[L_j], min_wt);
    }
```

Figure 14–17 Pseudocode for *fire_rules()*

		in.out.array	pfa	#rules	rules
Y--> neg_far 0	weight(1)			Out0	
neg_close 1	--		X-->	0	x1 is neg_far
zero_p 2	--			5	x2 is neg_fast
pos_close 3	--			FE	
pos_far 4	--			15	y is pos_high
neg_fast 5	weight(2)			FE	
neg_slow 6	--			0	x1 is neg_far
zero_s 7	--			6	x2 is neg_slow
pos_slow 8	--			FE	
pos_fast 9	--			15	y is pos_high
10	5	Out0		FE	
neg_high 11	0	Out			
neg_low 12	0				
zero_m 13	0			11	
pos_low 14	0		A =$FF	FF	end of rules
pos_high 15	0				

Figure 14–18 Setup Required for REV Instruction

that is, the number of output membership functions. The remainder of the *rules* data structure is a series of bytes, pointed to by index register X, that contains an encoding of all the rules. Each rule is of the form

```
if x1 is neg_far and x2 is neg_fast then y is pos_high
```

The offsets in the *in.out.array* corresponding to *neg_far* (0) and *neg_fast* (5) are stored in the first two bytes. This is followed by a byte containing $FE which separates the input antecedents from the output consequents. The next byte contains 15, the offset of *pos_high* in the *in.out.array*. This is followed by another $FE which separates the last consequent offset from the first antecedent offset of the next rule. A byte containing $FF marks the end of the rules. This rule encoding scheme will allow any number of inputs and any number of outputs.

In addition to initializing *X* and *Y*, as shown in Figure 14–18, accumulator *A* must be set to $FF and the *Out(k)* array must be initialized to zero before the *REV* instruction is executed. The *REV* instruction will then process all of the rules and fill the *Out(k)* array following the pseudocode shown in Figure 14–17.

You may wonder how the *REV* instruction can tell the difference between the $FE at the end of the antecedents and the $FE at the end of the consequents. The answer is that it uses the overflow bit *V* in the condition code register as a flag to tell the difference. This bit is automatically set to zero when the statement *LDAA #$FF* is executed. The *REV* instruction then toggles this bit to 1 when it encounters the $FE at the end of the antecedents and clears it to zero by reloading accumulator *A* with $FF when it encounters the $FE at the end of the consequents.

The WHYP word *firerules (in.out.array rules --)* implements the pseudocode in Figure 14–17 using the 68HC12 code shown in Figure 14–19. It expects the two addresses, *in.out.array* and *rules*, shown in Figure 14–18 on the data stack. Note that after popping these two addresses into *D* and *Y*, the *Out* array is cleared to zero, *Y* is left pointing to the *in.out.array*, *X* is left pointing to the first rule, accumulator *A* is loaded with $FF, and then *REV* is executed.

WHYP Words for Defining Fuzzy Rules   In this section we will develop WHYP words that will produce the *rules* data structure shown in Figure 14–18. Using the same ping-pong ball example described in Section 14.2.1, we will list the rules in the form of the table shown in Figure 14–20.

The word *make.rules* is a defining word given in Listing 14–2. The *CREATE* part of the word puts the address, *rules*, on the data stack (using *HERE*) and then commas in two zeros. These will be the locations for the number of rules and the

```
*          Fire all rules
*          firerules ( in.out.array rules -- )
FIRERULES
          LDD     2,X+          D -> rules
          LDY     2,X+          Y -> in.out.array
          PSHX
          TFR     D,X           X -> rules
          INX
          INX                   X -> Out0 addr
          PSHY                  save Y
          LDY     2,X+          Y -> Out0, X -> 1st rule
          LDAB    0,Y           B = #out.memb.fncs
FR0       CLR     1,Y+          clear Out array
          DBNE    B, FR0
          PULY                  Y -> in.out.array
          LDAA    #$FF
          REV                   rule evaluation
          PULX
          RTS
```

Figure 14–19   68HC12 Code for WHYP Word *firerules (in.out.array rules--)*

```
make.rules        rules
\          ball_position     ball_speed        motor_power
           neg_far    C,  neg_fast    C:   pos_high  C;
           neg_far    C,  neg_slow    C:   pos_high  C;
           -----                           -----
           -----                           -----
           pos_far    C,  pos_slow    C:   neg_high  C;
           pos_far    C,  pos_fast    C:   neg_high  C.
end.rules
```

Figure 14–20   Format for Defining Fuzzy Rules

address of *Out0*, shown in Figure 14–18. Note from the definition of *make.rules* that when *rules* is executed it will put its address on the data stack.

Each row in the table is one rule. For example, the row

```
neg_far   C, neg_fast   C:   pos_high  C;
```

corresponds to the rule

```
if ball_position is neg_far and ball_speed is neg_fast then
motor_power is pos_high
```

The membership function names such as *neg_far*, *neg_fast*, and *pos_high* will have been assigned the offset values shown in Figure 14–18 using the *CONSTANT* word. The word *C,* will comma in the offset value of *neg_far* (0). The word *C:* (defined in Listing 14–2) will comma in the offset value of *neg_fast* (5) followed by an $FE. The word *C;* (defined in Listing 14–2) will comma in the offset value of *pos_high* (15) followed by an $FE and then increment the number of rules.

The word *C.* defined in Listing 14–2 and used at the end of the last rule in Figure 14–20, will comma in the offset value of *neg_high* (11) followed by an $FF and then increment the number of rules.

The word *end.rules* (*pfa* --) defined in Listing 14–2 and used at the end of Figure 14–20 simply drops the address of *rules* from the data stack.

14.2.4 Centroid Defuzzification

The last step in the fuzzy controller shown in Figure 14–7 is defuzzification. This involves finding the centroid of the net output fuzzy set L' shown in Figures 14–15 and 14–16. Although we have used the MIN-MAX rule in the previous section, we will begin by deriving the centroid equation for the sum rule shown in Figure 14–16. This will illuminate the assumptions made in deriving the defuzzification equation that we will actually use in the fuzzy controller.

Let $L_i(y)$ be the original output membership function associated with rule i where y is the output universe of discourse (see Figure 14–15). After applying rule i, this membership function will be reduced to the value

$$m_i(y) = w_i L_i(y) \tag{14.1}$$

Listing 14–2   Fuzzy Control in WHYP—Making rules

```
\           Fuzzy Logic Control Using WHYP12      File: FUZZY12.WHP
\ ********** Defining word for making rules **********
: make.rules   ( +++ )
            CREATE
               HERE 0 ,              \ leave room for #rules
               0 ,                   \ leave room for ^Out0
            DOES>   ( pfa -- )
               ;

HEX

C:             ( pfa ix -- pfa )
            C, FE C, ;

C;             ( pfa ix -- pfa )
            C, FE C,
            1 OVER +! ;              \ inc #rules

C.             ( pfa ix -- pfa )
            C, FF C,
            1 OVER +! ;              \ inc #rules

DECIMAL

: end.rules    ( pfa -- )
            DROP ;                   \ drop addr of #rules
```

---

where w_i is the minimum weight found by applying rule i. The sum of these reduced output membership functions over all rules is then given by

$$M(y) = \sum_{i=1}^{N} m_i(y) \tag{14.2}$$

where N is the number of rules.

The crisp output value y_0 is then given by the centroid of $M(y)$ from the equation

$$y_0 = \frac{\int y M(y) dy}{\int M(y) dy} \tag{14.3}$$

Note that the centroid of membership function $L_i(y)$ is given by

$$c_i = \frac{\int y L_i(y) dy}{\int L_i(y) dy} \tag{14.4}$$

But

$$I_i = \int L_i(y)dy \qquad (14.5)$$

is just the area of membership function $L_i(y)$. Substituting (14.5) into (14.4) we can write

$$\int y L_i(y)dy = c_i I_i \qquad (14.6)$$

Using Eqs. (14.1) and (14.2) we can write the numerator of (14.3) as

$$
\begin{aligned}
\int y M(y)dy &= \int y \sum_{i=1}^{N} w_i L_i(y) \, dy \\
&= \sum_{i=1}^{N} \int y w_i L_i(y) \, dy \\
&= \sum_{i=1}^{N} w_i c_i I_i \qquad (14.7)
\end{aligned}
$$

where (14.6) was used in the last step. Similarly, using (14.1) and (14.2) the denominator of (14.3) can be written as

$$
\begin{aligned}
\int M(y)dy &= \int \sum_{i=1}^{N} w_i L_i(y) \, dy \\
&= \sum_{i=1}^{N} \int w_i L_i(y) \, dy \\
&= \sum_{i=1}^{N} w_i I_i \qquad (14.8)
\end{aligned}
$$

where (14.5) was used in the last step. Substituting (14.7) and (14.8) into (14.3), we can write the crisp output of the fuzzy controller as

$$y_0 = \frac{\sum_{i=1}^{N} w_i c_i I_i}{\sum_{i=1}^{N} w_i I_i} \qquad (14.9)$$

Equation (14.9) says that we can compute the output centroid from the centroids, c_i, of the individual output membership functions.

Note in Eq. (14.9) the summation is over all N rules. But the number of output membership functions, Q, will, in general, be less than the number of rules, N. This means that in the sums in Eq. (14.9) there will be many terms that will have the same values of c_i and I_i. For example, suppose that rules 2, 3, and 4 in the sum all have the output membership function L^k as the consequent. This means that in the sum

$$w_2 c_2 I_2 + w_3 c_3 I_3 + w_4 c_4 I_4$$

the values c_i and I_i are the same values c^k and I^k because they are just the centroid and area of the kth output membership function. These three terms would then contribute the value

$$(w_2 + w_3 + w_4)c^k I^k = W^k c^k I^k$$

to the sum, where

$$W^k = (w_2 + w_3 + w_4)$$

is the sum of all weights from rules whose consequent is output membership function L^k. This means that the equation for the output value, y_0, given by (14.9) can be rewritten as

$$y_0 = \frac{\sum_{k=1}^{Q} W^k c^k I^k}{\sum_{k=1}^{Q} W^k I^k} \tag{14.10}$$

If the area of all output membership functions I^k are equal, then Eq. (14.10) reduces to

$$y_0 = \frac{\sum_{k=1}^{Q} W^k c^k}{\sum_{k=1}^{Q} W^k} \tag{14.11}$$

Equations (14.10) and (14.11) show that the output crisp value of a fuzzy controller can be computed by summing over only the number of output membership functions rather than over all fuzzy rules. Also, if we use Eq. (14.11) to compute the output crisp value, then we need to specify only the centroids, c^k, of the output fuzzy membership functions. This is equivalent to assuming singleton fuzzy sets for the output.

We will always use singleton fuzzy sets for the output represented by the centroids, c^k. We will also use the MIN-MAX inference rule described in the previous section. It should be clear from Figure 14–16 that in this case the centroid y_0 will still be given by Eq. (14.11) where W^k is now the output array, $Out(k)$, shown in Figure 14–18 and computed by the word *firerules* given in Figure 14–19.

14.2.5   Output Defuzzification: find_output()

Once the function *fire_rules()* has filled the output weight array, $Out(k)$, the function *find_output()* will calculate the centroid y_0 using Eq. (14.11). The pseudocode for the function *find_output()* is given in Figure 14–21. The centroids of the Q output membership functions are stored in the array c^k.

The 68HC12 *WAV* Instruction   The values of *numer* and *denom* in Figure 14–21 can easily be calculated using the 68HC12 *WAV* instruction. If index

```
find_output ()
numer = 0;
denom = 0;
for k = 1, Q
    if Out[k] != 0
        {
        numer = numer + Out[k]*c[k];
        denom = denom + Out[k];
        }
y0 = numer/denom;
```

Figure 14.21 Pseudocode for *find_output()*

register X points to $c[k]$, index register Y points to $Out[k]$, and if accumulator B contains the number of output membership functions, Q, then the 68HC12 *WAV* instruction will compute a 24-bit value for *numer* and store the result in $Y{:}D$ and compute a 16-bit value for *denom* and store this result in X. Therefore, if the *WAV* instruction is followed by the instruction *EDIV* (see Section 3.3.2), then the centroid value y_0 will be left in Y.

The WHYP word *calc.output (rules cent_addr -- output_value)* will expect the address of *rules* (see Figure 14–18) and the address of the centroid array, $c[k]$, on the data stack and will return the crisp output value, y_0. The 68HC12 code for the word *calc.output* is shown in Figure 14–22.

After popping the address of $c[k]$ into D and the address of *rules* into Y, the address of *Out0* in Figure 14–18 is found from the byte at *rules+2*. This is used to load B with the number of output membership functions at *Out0* and to load Y with the address of the *Out* array. The address of the centroid array, $c[k]$, is stored in X and then the two instructions *WAV* and *EDIV* are executed to compute the output, y_0, which is then pushed onto the data stack.

```
*           Find Output value
*           calc.output ( rules   cent_addr -- output_value )
FINDOUT
        LDD     2,X+            D -> cent
        LDY     2,X+            Y -> rules
        PSHX
        TFR     D,X             X -> cent array
        LDY     2,Y             Y -> Out0
        LDAB    0,Y             B = #out.memb.fncs
        INY                     Y -> Out array
        WAV
        EDIV                    Y = quotient
        TFR     Y,D             D = quotient   A = 0, B = output
        PULX
        STD     2,-X
        RTS
```

Figure 14.22 68HC12 Code for *calc.output (rules cent_addr -- output_value)*

14.2.6   A Fuzzy Control Example—Floating Ping-Pong Ball

The complete WHYP example of the fuzzy controller for the floating ping-pong ball is shown in Listing 14–3. The fuzzy controller is designed to keep a ping-pong ball floating at the center of a vertical plexiglas cylinder. The first step is to define the membership functions for the inputs. The two inputs to the controller will be the *ball_position* and *ball_speed* whose membership functions are defined using *fuzzy.input* as described in Section 14.2.1. Note that constants are used to define the names of the input membership functions (such as *neg_far, neg_close, zero_p, pos_close*, and *pos_far*) as equal to their offsets shown in Figure 14–18.

Listing 14–3   Fuzzy Control Example—Ping-Pong Ball

```
\       Fuzzy Control Example      File: PINGPONG.WHP
\       Floating ping-pong ball


LOAD FUZZY12.WHP
\ **********************************************
\       Define inputs
\ **********************************************


\       Ball position
0 CONSTANT    neg_far
1 CONSTANT    neg_close
2 CONSTANT    zero_p
3 CONSTANT    pos_close
4 CONSTANT    pos_far


\       Ball speed
5 CONSTANT    neg_fast
6 CONSTANT    neg_slow
7 CONSTANT    zero_s
8 CONSTANT    pos_slow
9 CONSTANT    pos_fast


\       Define input membership functions

fuzzy.input      ball_position
         0   0  30  50  >m          \ neg_far
        40  60  80 110  >m          \ neg_close
       100 120 135 165  >m          \ zero_p
       155 175 185 210  >m          \ pos_close
       200 220 255 255  >m          \ pos_far
end.input
```

(continued)

Listing 14–3 (*continued*)

```
fuzzy.input        ball_speed
              0    0   20   60 >m          \ neg_fast
             50   70   90  120 >m          \ neg_slow
            100  125  135  155 >m          \ zero_s
            140  170  180  200 >m          \ pos_slow
            190  210  255  255 >m          \ pos_fast
end.input


\ **********************************************
\     Define output
\ **********************************************
5 CONSTANT #out.member.fncs    \ No. of output membership functions
CREATE cent                    \ output centroid array
         5 C, 65 C, 128 C, 175 C, 200 C,
         \ |neg_high|neg_low|zero_m|pos_low|pos_high|

10 CONSTANT       Out0
\     Power percent change to motor
11 CONSTANT       neg_high
12 CONSTANT       neg_low
13 CONSTANT       zero_m
14 CONSTANT       pos_low
15 CONSTANT       pos_high
        ball_position @ 2- VALLOT        \ input 1 weight array
        ball_speed @  VALLOT             \ input 1 weight array
        #out.member.fncs 1+ VALLOT       \ controller output weights


\ **********************************************
\     Define rules
\ **********************************************

make.rules        rules
\       ball_position  ball_speed    motor_power
        neg_far     C,  neg_fast  C:  pos_high C;
        neg_far     C,  neg_slow  C:  pos_high C;
        neg_far     C,  zero_s    C:  pos_high C;
        neg_far     C,  pos_slow  C:  pos_low  C;
        neg_far     C,  pos_fast  C:  zero_m   C;
        neg_close   C,  neg_fast  C:  pos_high C;
        neg_close   C,  neg_slow  C:  pos_high C;
        neg_close   C,  zero_s    C:  pos_low  C;
        neg_close   C,  pos_slow  C:  zero_m   C;
        neg_close   C,  pos_fast  C:  neg_low  C;
        zero_p      C,  neg_fast  C:  pos_high C;
        zero_p      C,  neg_slow  C:  pos_low  C;
        zero_p      C,  zero_s    C:  zero_m   C;
        zero_p      C,  pos_slow  C:  neg_low  C;
```

Listing 14–3   (*continued*)

```
        zero_p     C,   pos_fast  C:   neg_high C;
        pos_close  C,   neg_fast  C:   pos_low  C;
        pos_close  C,   neg_slow  C:   zero_m   C;
        pos_close  C,   zero_s    C:   neg_low  C;
        pos_close  C,   pos_slow  C:   neg_high C;
        pos_close  C,   pos_fast  C:   neg_high C;
        pos_far    C,   neg_fast  C:   zero_m   C;
        pos_far    C,   neg_slow  C:   neg_low  C;
        pos_far    C,   zero_s    C:   neg_high C;
        pos_far    C,   pos_slow  C:   neg_high C;
        pos_far    C,   pos_fast  C:   neg_high C.
end.rules


\   ***********************************************************
\       Implement fuzzy controller
\   ***********************************************************


: init.Out.array     ( -- )
                #out.member.fncs       \ #
                in.out.array Out0 +    \ # Out0
                DUP rules 2+ !         \ store Out0 @rules+2
                C! ;                   \ store # @Out0


\                 Compute output power given input pos and speed
: fuzzy            ( pos speed -- power )
                ball_speed fill.weights
                ball_position fill.weights
                in.out.array rules firerules
                rules cent calc.output ;


: fuzzy_control ( -- )
                init.Out.array
                BEGIN
    \             get.position   \ pos            (user defined)
    \             get.speed      \ pos speed      (user defined)
                  fuzzy          \ power
    \             adjust.motor   \                (user defined)
                AGAIN ;
```

The second step is to define the output. The output membership functions are defined as singletons and stored in the array *cent*. The names of these membership functions (such as *neg_high* and *pos_high*) are assigned the constant values shown in Figure 14–18. Memory in RAM is then allocated for the *in.out.array*.

The third step is to determine the fuzzy rules. These will be common-sense rules based on the two inputs, *ball_position* and *ball_speed*, and the output, *motor_power*. It is convenient to represent these rules in the form of a 5 × 5 fuzzy K-map of the form shown in Figure 14–23. The entries in this fuzzy K-map are the membership functions of the output, *motor_power*.

For example, if the ball_position is *zero_p* (at its desired location) and the *ball_speed* is *zero_s* (it is not moving), then the change in *motor_power* should be *zero_m* (no change). This is the center entry in Figure 14–23.

If the *ball_speed* is *zero_s* (the center row in Figure 14–23) and the *ball_position* is *neg_close* (a little below the desired location), then we should increase the fan speed a little by setting *motor_power* to *pos_low*. If the *ball_position* is *neg_far* (a lot below the desired location), then we should increase the fan speed a lot by setting *motor_power* to *pos_high*. Similar arguments will hold if the *ball_position* is *pos_close* or *pos_far* leading to values of *motor_power* of *neg_low* (decrease fan speed a little) and *neg_high* (decrease fan speed a lot) respectively.

If the *ball_position* is *zero_p* (the center column in Figure 14–23) and the *ball_speed* is *neg_slow* (ball is falling slowly through the desired location), then we should increase the fan speed a little by setting *motor_power* to *pos_low*. If the *ball_speed* is *neg_fast* (ball is falling rapidly through the desired location), then we should increase the fan speed a lot by setting *motor_power* to *pos_high*. Similar arguments will hold if the *ball_speed* is *pos_slow* or *pos_fast*, leading to values of *motor_power* of *neg_low* (decrease fan speed a little) and *neg_high* (decrease fan speed a lot) respectively.

Similar arguments can be made for the four entries in each of the four corners of the fuzzy K-map in Figure 14–23. Note that the same fuzzy output membership function tends to occur on diagonal lines going from the upper-left to bottom-right of the diagram in Figure 14–23. This is typical of many fuzzy controller rules.

The last step in designing the fuzzy controller in Listing 14–3 is to implement the fuzzy controller according to the overall algorithm given in Figure 14–8. The word *fuzzy_control (--)*, given in Listing 14–3, does this. It begins by initializing the

		ball_position				
		neg_far	neg_close	zero_p	pos_close	pos_far
ball_speed	pos_fast	zero_m	neg_low	neg_high	neg_high	neg_high
	pos_slow	pos_low	zero_m	neg_low	neg_high	neg_high
	zero_s	pos_high	pos_low	zero_m	neg_low	neg_high
	neg_slow	pos_high	pos_high	pos_low	zero_m	neg_low
	neg_fast	pos_high	pos_high	pos_high	pos_low	zero_m

Figure 14–23   Fuzzy K-Map for Floating Ping-Pong Ball

Out array by storing the address of *Out0* at the address *rules+2* in Figure 14–18 and storing the number of output membership functions at *Out0*.

The words *get.position* and *get.speed* in the *BEGIN ... AGAIN* loop are user-defined words that will leave the position and speed of the ping-pong ball on the data stack. The position can be measured using the ultrasonic tape measure described in Section 10.10. The speed can be computed by subtracting two successive position measurements.

The word *fuzzy (pos speed -- power)* takes the position and speed on the data stack and returns the motor power by calling *fill.weights* for both inputs, *firerules*, and *calc.output*. The word *adjust.motor (power --)* is a user-defined word that will set the speed of the fan according the value of power on the data stack.

14.3   SUMMARY

In this chapter we introduced the idea of fuzzy sets in Section 14.1 where we saw that fuzzy sets are characterized by membership functions that show how an element belongs to the set with a degree of membership between 0 and 1. We showed in Section 14.2 that a fuzzy controller consists of three parts: (1) an input section in which crisp inputs are mapped to fuzzy sets, (2) in inference section in which fuzzy outputs are inferred from fuzzy inputs using fuzzy rules, and (3) a defuzzification section in which a fuzzy output is converted to a crisp output.

We showed in Section 14.2.1 how the 68HC12 *MEM* instruction can be used to perform the mapping of crisp inputs to fuzzy sets. We also introduced a WHYP defining word called *fuzzy.input (+++)* that made it easy to enter membership functions in a form that could be used by the *MEM* instruction.

Fuzzy inference was described in Section 14.2.2 and the way in which fuzzy rules can be evaluated using the 68HC12 *REV* instruction was discussed in Section 14.2.3. We introduced another WHYP defining word called *make.rules (+++)* that provides an easy way to enter the rules in a format that can be used by the *REV* instruction.

The way in which centroid defuzzification works was described in Section 14.2.4 and we showed in Section 14.2.5 how the 68HC12 *WAV* instruction can be used to compute the output defuzzification.

Finally, in Section 14.2.6 we gave a complete example of how you can use WHYP to design a fuzzy controller that controls a fan at the bottom of a vertical plexiglas tube to maintain a ping-pong ball floating at a predetermined height.

For more information on fuzzy control, you can consult the many books on this topic including

Fuzzy Logic and Control: Software and Hardware Applications, Vol. 2, by M. Jamshidi, N. Vadiee, and T. Ross, Prentice Hall, Upper Saddle River, NJ, 1993.

Applications of Fuzzy Logic: Towards High Machine Intelligence Quotient Systems, by M. Jamshidi, A. Titli, L. Zadeh, and S. Boverie, Prentice Hall, Upper Saddle River, NJ, 1997.

EXERCISES

Exercise 14.1

The fuzzy set *Young* was characterized by the membership function shown in Figure 14–2. We can also represent such a fuzzy set by listing a sequence of (age, degree_of_membership) pairs, as in

$$Y = \{(5, 1.0), (10, 1.0), (15, 0.7), (20, 0.5), (30, 0.2), (40, 0.0)\}$$

This fuzzy set is sometimes represented as

$$Y = 1.0/5 + 1.0/10 + 0.7/15 + 0.5/20 + 0.2/30 + 0.0/40$$

where the / is not division and the + is not addition, but are just used as separators.
    If the universe of discourse is arbitrary as in

$$A = \{(1, .2), (2, .7), (3, .1), (4, .6), (5, .4)\}$$

then we will write the fuzzy set in the simplified form

$$A = \{\,.2\ .7\ .1\ .6\ .4\,\}$$

Consider the two fuzzy sets

$$A = \{\,.2\ .7\ .1\ .6\ .4\,\} \quad \text{and} \quad B = \{\,.4\ .5\ .3\ .9\ .7\,\}$$

a. Find $A' = $ NOT A
b. Find $B' = $ NOT A
c. Find $A \cap B = A$ AND B
d. Find $A \cup B = A$ OR B

Exercise 14.2

Consider the two fuzzy sets

$$A = \{\,.2\ .7\ .1\ .6\ .4\,\} \quad \text{and} \quad B = \{\,.4\ .5\ .3\ .9\ .7\,\}$$

a. Find $(A \cap B)'$
b. Find $A' \cup B'$
c. Find $(A \cup B)'$
d. Find $A' \cap B'$

Exercise 14.3

Prove that the fuzzy sets A and B satisfy the DeMorgan laws

$$(A \cap B)' = A' \cup B'$$

and

$$(A \cup B)' = A' \cap B'$$

Hint: Use the fuzzy definitions of *AND*, *OR*, and *NOT* and consider the three cases of when A (degree of membership) is greater than, equal to, and less than B (see Exercise 14.2).

Exercise 14.4

Consider the two fuzzy sets

$$A = \{\,.2\ .7\ .1\ .6\ .4\,\} \quad \text{and} \quad B = \{\,.4\ .5\ .3\ .9\ .7\,\}$$

    a. Find $A \cap A'$

    b. Find $A \cup A'$

    c. Find $(A \cap A') + (A \cup A')$

    d. Find $B \cap B'$

    e. Find $B \cup B'$

    f. Find $(B \cap B') + (B \cup B')$

Exercise 14.5

Consider the three fuzzy sets

$$A = \{.2\ .7\ .1\ .6\ .4\}$$
$$B = \{.4\ .5\ .3\ .9\ .7\}$$
$$C = \{.8\ .2\ .5\ .7\ .3\}$$

    a. Find $C \cup (A \cap B)$

    b. Find $C \cap (A \cup B)$

    c. Find $C \cup A$

    d. Find $C \cup B$

    e. Find $(C \cup A) \cap (C \cup B)$

    f. Find $C \cap A$

    g. Find $C \cap B$

    h. Find $(C \cap A) \cup (C \cap B)$

Exercise 14.6

Prove that the fuzzy sets A, B, and C satisfy the distributive laws

$$C \cup (A \cap B) = (C \cup A) \cap (C \cup B)$$

and

$$C \cap (A \cup B) = (C \cap A) \cup (C \cap B)$$

(See Exercise 14.5.)

Exercise 14.7

Modify the fuzzy control program so as to implement the sum fuzzy inference rule shown in Figure 14–15 rather than the maximum rule shown in Figure 14–16.

Exercise 14.8

    a. Implement the floating ping-pong ball fuzzy control problem described in this chapter. Use the Polaroid ultrasonic transducer described in Section 10.10 to measure the distance to the ping-pong ball. The difference between two consecutive distance measurements can be used to represent the ball speed. A muffin fan at the bottom of the plexiglas cylinder is used to maintain the ping-pong ball at a fixed height within the cylinder.

    b. Add a dial that you can use to set the height of the ping-pong ball.

    c. Add a mode that has the ping-pong ball move between two different heights every 10 seconds.

    d. Use the ultrasonic tape measure described in Section 10.10 to measure the distance from the floor to your hand. Use the serial port to send this distance to your ping-pong ball setup. Have the ping-pong ball float at the height of your hand above the floor. As you move your hand up and down, the ping-pong ball should follow!

Exercise 14.9

A fuzzy controller is used to maintain the idle speed of an automobile engine. The idle speed can be controlled by varying both the throttle position and the spark advance. In this exercise we will consider only the throttle position. The two inputs will be

$x1$: the RPM error (current RPM − desired RPM)

$x2$: the change in RPM error from one measurement to the next

The output, y, will be a signal to a stepper motor that changes the throttle position. All input and output values are scaled from 0–255 as shown in Figure 14–6. The membership functions for the two inputs are given in the following tables.

Input x1	u1	u2	u3	u4
NM_1	0	0	20	100
NS_1	0	100	100	120
Z_1	100	128	128	156
PS_1	136	156	156	255
PM_1	156	235	255	255

Input x2	u1	u2	u3	u4
NS_2	0	0	64	128
Z_2	64	128	128	192
PS_2	128	192	255	255

The output, y, will have the five centroid values, 10, 80, 128, 176, and 245, corresponding to NM_y, NS_y, Z_y, PS_y, and PM_y.

    a. Make plots of the membership functions for the two inputs, $x1$ and $x2$, and the output, y.

    b. Make up a list of rules that seem sensible to you. For example, one rule might be

```
IF x1 is NS_1 and x2 is Z_2 THEN y is PS_y
```

Make a fuzzy K-map of your rule set similar to the one shown in Figure 14–23.

    c. Write a fuzzy control program for this problem by following the format in Listing 14–3.

Exercise 14.10

Suggest how you might design a fuzzy control system for each of the following applications:

    a. An autofocusing camera.
    b. The braking system of a truck.
    c. A washing machine.
    d. A rain-dependent variable-speed windshield wiper.
    e. An electric oven.
    f. Acceleration and deceleration control of a train.
    g. A robot manipulator.
    h. A laser tracking system.
    i. A refrigerator.
    j. An air conditioner.

15

Special Topics

In this chapter we will consider a number of special topics related to the 68HC12 which are not covered elsewhere in this book. The *Computer Operating Properly* (COP) feature of the 68HC12 (and 68HC11) is a method for checking that the software continues to run as expected and doesn't get lost. This technique, together with a hardware clock monitor feature, is described in Section 15.1. If a 68HC812A4 has been put in the STOP or WAIT mode to save power, a key wakeup interrupt, described in Section 15.2, can be used to wake up the CPU. The steps required to program the flash memory in a 68HC912B32 are described in Section 15.3. Finally, the pulse width modulator module that is available on a 68HC912B32 is discussed in Section 15.4.

15.1 COMPUTER OPERATING PROPERLY (COP)

Two COP (Computer Operating Properly) interrupts are available on the 68HC12 (see Table 6–1) and the 68HC11 (see Table 6–4). The first is the *COP clock monitor fail reset* with the vector address $FFFC–$FFFD. Setting the *CME* bit in the *COP control register, COPCTL*, as shown in Figure 15–1, enables this interrupt. If this interrupt is enabled and the clock stops, or its frequency falls below about 500 KHz, then the code whose address is at $FFFC–$FFFD will be executed. This is often the same as the reset vector so that a system reset will occur.

	7	6	5	4	3	2	1	0	
$0016	CME	FCME	FCM	FCOP	DISR	CR2	CR1	CR0	COPCTL

CME: Clock Monitor Enable
            0 – Clock monitor disabled (FCME = 0)
            1 – Clock monitor enabled (FCME = 0)

FCME: Force Clock Monitor Enable
            0 – Clock monitor follows CME bit
            1 – Clock monitor enabled (Write once in normal modes)

FCM: Force Clock Monitor Reset
            0 – Normal operation (DISR = 0)
            1 – Force a clock monitor reset (if enabled and DISR = 0)

FCOP: Force COP Watchdog Reset
            0 – Normal operation (DISR = 0)
            1 – Force a COP reset (DISR = 0)

DISR: Disable Resets from COP Watchdog and Clock Monitor
            0 – Normal operation
            1 – Disable resets from COP Watchdog and Clock Monitor

CR[2:0]:   COP Watchdog Timer Rate Select

CR[2:0]	Time-Out Period M = 8.0 MHz
0 0 0	OFF
0 0 1	1.024 ms
0 1 0	4.096 ms
0 1 1	16.384 ms
1 0 0	65.536 ms
1 0 1	262.144 ms
1 1 0	512.288 ms
1 1 1	1.048576 s

Figure 15–1 COP Control Register

The second COP interrupt is the *COP failure reset* with the vector address $FFFA–$FFFB as shown in Tables 11–1 and 11–4. This interrupt, which is often a system reset, will occur if a special sequence ($55 followed by $AA) isn't written to the *Arm/Reset COP Timer Register (COPRST)*, shown in Figure 15–2, within a specified time. The maximum time interval that can elapse before the $55–$AA sequence is written to the *COPRST* register is specified by the *CR[2:0]* bits in the *COPCTL* register as shown in Figure 15–1.

As an example of using the COP watchdog consider the digital compass program, shown in Listing 9–3. The main program given by the word *compass* contains a *BEGIN ... AGAIN* loop that itself contains a *FOR ... NEXT* delay loop that delays for about 27.5 ms. By toggling an I/O pin at the beginning of the *BEGIN ... AGAIN* loop we could use an oscilloscope or logic analyzer to measure the time required to go through the loop once. Or we could use trial and error to determine the COP delay to use. In Figure 15–3 we have modified the word *compass*

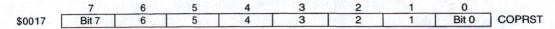

	7	6	5	4	3	2	1	0	
$0017	Bit 7	6	5	4	3	2	1	Bit 0	COPRST

Figure 15-2 Arm/Reset COP Timer Register

```
HEX
0016  CONSTANT  COPCTL
0017  CONSTANT  COPRST

: COP.INIT          ( -- )
                    07 COPCTL C! ;      \ 1 sec. watchdog

: watchdog          ( -- )
                    55 COPRST C!
                    AA COPRST C! ;

DECIMAL
: compass           ( -- )
                    SPI.INIT
                    0 MaxAD !
                    255 MinAD !
                    COP.INIT
                    BEGIN
                        watchdog
                        read.compass
                        359 SWAP - .41eds
                        20000 FOR NEXT
                    AGAIN ;
```

Figure 15-3 Example of Using the COP Watchdog in the Compass Program of Listing 9.3

to produce a COP watchdog interrupt if the time to execute the *BEGIN . . . AGAIN* loop exceeds 1 second. This would indicate that the software got lost somehow and an automatic reset would then take place. It is assumed that the COP failure reset vector address contains the address of the code that resets the microprocessor.

You should note that on reset the 68HC812A4 sets the *COPCTL* register to $07 and the 68HC912B32 sets the *COPCTL* register to $01 which will enable the COP watchdog! However, the D-Bug12 startup code as well as the beginning of the WHYP12.ASM program (see Appendix D) disables the COP watchdog by clearing the *COPCTL* register. This is why you haven't had to worry about it up to this point in this book.

15.2 KEY WAKEUP (68HC812A4 ONLY)

The 68HC12 *STOP* instruction will stack the CPU registers and stop all system clocks, thereby saving power and putting the device in a standby mode. The *STOP* instruction is disabled if the S-bit in the condition code register is set (see Section 1.2.5). A *RESET*, *XIRQ*, or *IRQ* interrupt can be used to exit the standby mode.

The 68HC12 *WAI* (wait for interrupt) instruction is similar to the *STOP* instruction in that it stacks the CPU registers and enters a wait state. However, only the CPU clock is stopped, while other system clocks continue to run. Any non-masked interrupt will cause the CPU to exit the wait state.

The key wakeup feature on a 68HC812A4 can be used to produce an interrupt that will wake the CPU from the *STOP* standby mode or from the wait state. The interrupt is caused by a falling edge on Port H pins or by either a rising or falling edge on Port J pins. (Port D can also be used for key wakeups if the 68HC812A4 is *not* in the wide expanded mode.) The key wakeup interrupt vectors are $FFD0–$FFD1 for Port J and $FFCE–$FFCF for Port H as shown in Table 6–2. (The Port D key wakeup shares the *IRQ* interrupt vector, $FFF2–FFF3, as shown in Table 6–2.)

To enable a key wakeup, a corresponding bit in a key wakeup interrupt enable register (*KWIEH* or *KWIEJ*) must be set as shown in Figure 15–4. For Port J the bits

	7	6	5	4	3	2	1	0	
$0026	Bit 7	6	5	4	3	2	1	Bit 0	KWIEH

KWIEH[7:0]: Key Wakeup Port H Interrupt Enables
          0 – Interrupt for the associated bit is disabled
          1 – Interrupt for the associated bit is enabled

	7	6	5	4	3	2	1	0	
$0027	Bit 7	6	5	4	3	2	1	Bit 0	KWIFH

KWIFH[7:0]: Key Wakeup Port H Flags
          0 – A falling edge on the associated pin has not occurred
          1 – A falling edge on the associated pin has occurred

	7	6	5	4	3	2	1	0	
$002A	Bit 7	6	5	4	3	2	1	Bit 0	KWIEJ

KWIEJ[7:0]: Key Wakeup Port J Interrupt Enables
          0 – Interrupt for the associated bit is disabled
          1 – Interrupt for the associated bit is enabled

	7	6	5	4	3	2	1	0	
$002B	Bit 7	6	5	4	3	2	1	Bit 0	KWIFJ

KWIFJ[7:0]: Key Wakeup Port J Flags
          0 – An active edge on the associated pin has not occurred
          1 – An active edge on the associated pin has occurred

	7	6	5	4	3	2	1	0	
$002C	Bit 7	6	5	4	3	2	1	Bit 0	KPOLJ

KPOLJ[7:0]: Key Wakeup Port J Polarity Select
          0 – A falling edge is the active edge on the associated pin of Port J
          1 – A rising edge is the active edge on the associated pin of Port J

Figure 15–4 Port H and Port J Key Wakeup Registers

in the *KPOLJ* register shown in Figure 15–4 determine the polarity (rising or falling edge). An active edge on a Port H or Port J pin will set the corresponding bit in the key wakeup flag register (*KWIFH* or *KWIFJ*), as shown in Figure 15–4.

15.3 FLASH EEPROM (68HC912B32 ONLY)

The method of erasing and programming the internal EEPROM in a 68HC12 was described in Section 4.5. In this section we will describe the operation of the internal 32–Kbyte flash EEPROM on the 68HC912B32. The flash EEPROM is similar to the smaller internal EEPROM with a few notable differences. Whereas a single byte in the EEPROM described in Section 4.5 can be erased, the flash EEPROM module can only be bulk erased. The flash EEPROM has a minimum program/erase life of 100 cycles, whereas the corresponding value for the internal EEPROM is 10,000 cycles. The flash EEPROM is generally used for storing programs that don't change often, such as the D-Bug12 or WHYP programs. As such, it is important that the flash EEPROM not be erased or programmed inadvertently. There are a number of protection interlocks, described below, to make this unlikely.

The *Miscellaneous Mapping Control Register* (*MISC*) shown in Figure 15–5 can be used to enable the flash EEPROM and locate it in the memory map. On reset

	7	6	5	4	3	2	1	0	
$0013	0	NDRF	RFSTR1	RFSTR0	EXSTR1	EXSTR0	MAPROM	ROMON	MISC

NDRF:
: Narrow Data Bus for Register-Following Map
  0 – 512-byte space following register map acts as a full 16-bit data bus
  1 – 512-byte space following register map acts as an 8-bit data bus

RFSTR[1:0]: Register-Following Stretch Bits 1 and 0

RFSTR[1:0]	E Clocks Stretched
0 0	0
0 1	1
1 0	2
1 1	3

EXSTR[1:0]: External Access Stretch Bits 1 and 0

EXSTR[1:0]	E Clocks Stretched
0 0	0
0 1	1
1 0	2
1 1	3

MAPROM:
: Map Location of Flash EEPROM
  0 – Flash EEPROM is located from $0000 to $7FFF (Default in expanded modes)
  1 – Flash EEPROM is located from $8000 to $FFFF (Default in single-chip modes)

ROMON:
: Enable Flash EEPROM
  0 – Flash EEPROM disabled (Default in expanded modes)
  1 – Flash EEPROM enabled   (Default in single-chip modes)

Figure 15–5 The Miscellaneous Mapping Control Register

in the single–chip mode, the flash EEPROM is enabled ($ROMON = 1$) and mapped to addresses $8000–$FFFF ($MAPROM = 1$). On reset in the expanded mode the flash EEPROM is disabled ($ROMON = 0$) and mapped to addresses $0000–$7FFF ($MAPROM = 0$). In normal modes the $MISC$ register can be written once to change the location of the flash EEPROM. If address conflicts occur when mapping the flash EEPROM, the internal register space, RAM, and EEPROM have precedence over the flash EEPROM. On the other hand, the flash EEPROM has precedence over external memory.

A 2-Kbyte block of memory at the top of the flash EEPROM ($78FF–$7FFF or $F800–$FFFF) can be used for boot routines and is protected from programming and erasure using the $LOCK$ and $BOOTP$ bits in the $FEELCK$ and $FEEMCR$ registers, shown in Figure 15–6. In normal modes the $LOCK$ bit can be written only once after reset. On reset the $BOOTP$ bit is set, which means you are unable to erase or program the bytes in the boot block of the Flash EEPROM.

15.3.1 Erasing and Programming the Flash EEPROM

You will normally erase and program the Flash EEPROM using some vendor-supplied program. For example, the M68EVB912B32 evaluation board from Motorola has two jumpers that allow it to start in the BOOTLOAD mode on reset. This mode executes a bootloader program that is stored in the erase-protected region of the Flash EEPROM starting at $FC00. When this program executes, it gives you a choice to erase the Flash EEPROM (except the erase-protected area), program the Flash EEPROM from an S-record file, or program the internal EEPROM from an S-record file. See Appendix C for more information on programming the Flash EEPROM. In this section we will show you what a program must do to erase and/or program the Flash EEPROM.

Erasing and programming the Flash EEPROM are controlled by the $FEECTL$ register shown in Figure 15–7. The following steps are used to erase the entire Flash EEPROM array (except for an erase-protected boot area as described in Figure 15–6).

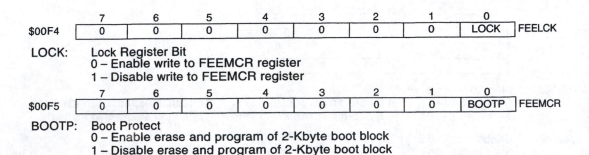

	7	6	5	4	3	2	1	0	
$00F4	0	0	0	0	0	0	0	LOCK	FEELCK

LOCK: Lock Register Bit
        0 – Enable write to FEEMCR register
        1 – Disable write to FEEMCR register

	7	6	5	4	3	2	1	0	
$00F5	0	0	0	0	0	0	0	BOOTP	FEEMCR

BOOTP: Boot Protect
        0 – Enable erase and program of 2-Kbyte boot block
        1 – Disable erase and program of 2-Kbyte boot block

Figure 15–6   The Flash EEPROM Lock Control and Module Configuration Registers

	7	6	5	4	3	2	1	0	
$00F7	0	0	0	FESWAI	SVFP	ERAS	LAT	ENPE	FEECTL

FESWAI: Flash EEPROM Stop in Wait Control
            0 – In wait state do not halt Flash EEPROM clock.
            1 – In wait state halt Flash EEPROM clock.

SVFP: Status of V_{FP} Voltage (read only)
            0 – Voltage of V_{FP} pin is below programming voltage level.
            1 – Voltage of V_{FP} pin is above programming voltage level.

ERAS: Erase Control
            0 – Flash EEPROM configured for programming.
            1 – Flash EEPROM configured for erasure.

LAT: Latch Control
            0 – Programming latches disabled.
            1 – Programming latches enabled. Can only write to if ENPE = 0.

ENPE: Enable Program/Erase
            0 – Disables program/erase voltage to Flash EEPROM
            1 – Applies program/erase voltage to Flash EEPROM

Figure 15–7   The Flash EEPROM Control Register

1. Apply 12 volts to the V_{FP} pin.
2. Set the *ERAS* bit and the *LAT* bit by writing a $06 to the FEECTL register.
3. Write any data to any valid address in the Flash array.
4. Write a 1 to the *ENPE* bit in the *FEECTL* register. Applies erase voltage.
5. Delay 100 milliseconds.
6. Write a 0 to the *ENPE* bit in the *FEECTL* register. Removes erase voltage.
7. Delay 1 millisecond.
8. Read entire array.
   • If any locations are not erased, repeat steps 4 through 7 until all locations are erased, or a maximum of five erase pulses have been applied.
   • If all locations are erased, repeat steps 4 through 7 the same number of times required to erase the Flash EEPROM. This gives a 100 percent margin.
9. Read entire array to verify erasure.
10. Write a 0 to the *LAT* bit in the *FEECTL* register to set normal read mode.
11. Reduce the voltage of the V_{FP} pin from 12 volts to 5 volts (V_{DD}).

The following steps are used to program the Flash EEPROM:

1. Apply 12 volts to the V_{FP} pin.
2. Clear the *ERAS* bit and set the *LAT* bit by writing a $02 to the FEECTL register.

3. Write data to a valid address in the Flash array.

4. Write a 1 to the *ENPE* bit in the *FEECTL* register. Applies programming voltage.

5. Delay 20–25 microseconds.

6. Write a 0 to the *ENPE* bit in the *FEECTL* register. Removes programming voltage.

7. Delay 10 microseconds.

8. Read the address location to verify programming.
   - If the location is not programmed, repeat steps 4 through 7 until the location is programmed, or a maximum of 50 programming pulses have been reached.
   - If the location is programmed, repeat steps 4 through 7 the same number of times required to program the location. This gives a 100 percent margin.

9. Read the address to verify that it is still programmed.

10. Write a 0 to the *LAT* bit in the *FEECTL* register to set normal read mode.

11. Repeat steps 2 through 10 for any other locations to program.

12. Reduce the voltage of the V_{FP} pin from 12 volts to 5 volts (V_{DD}).

15.4 PULSE-WIDTH MODULATOR (68HC912B32 ONLY)

In Sections 10.2.1 and 10.8 we saw how we could produce a Pulse-Width-Modulated (PWM) signal (pulse train) using output compares in the timer module. The 68HC912B32 has a separate pulse-width modulator that is associated with pins *PP0–PP3* of Port P (see Figure 1–4). This module can produce four independent 8-bit PWM waveforms. Alternatively, channels 0 and 1 (and/or channels 2 and 3) can be combined into a single 16-bit PWM channel.

The PWM output can be either left-aligned, as shown in Figure 15–8, or center-aligned as shown in Figure 15–9, depending upon the value of the *CENTR* bit

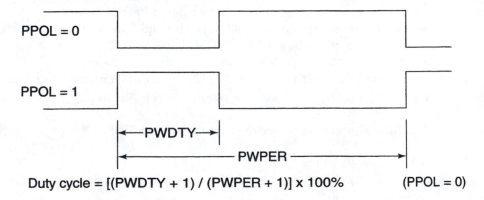

Duty cycle = [(PWDTY + 1) / (PWPER + 1)] x 100%   (PPOL = 0)

Figure 15–8 Left-Aligned PWM Output Signal

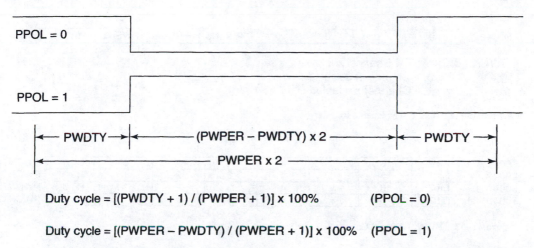

Duty cycle = [(PWDTY + 1) / (PWPER + 1)] x 100%   (PPOL = 0)

Duty cycle = [(PWPER – PWDTY) / (PWPER + 1)] x 100%   (PPOL = 1)

Figure 15–9   Center-Aligned PWM Output Signal

	7	6	5	4	3	2	1	0	
$0054	0	0	0	PSWAI	CENTR	RDPP	PUPP	PSBCK	PWCTL

PSWAI: PWM Halts while in Wait Mode
           0 – Allow PWM main clock generator to continue in wait mode
           1 – Halt PWM main clock generator in wait mode

CENTR: Center-Aligned Output Mode (write CENTR bit only when PWM channels
           are disabled)
           0 – Left-aligned output mode
           1 – Center-aligned output mode

RDPP: Reduced Drive of Port P
           0 – Normal drive capability for Port P output pins
           1 – Reduced drive capability for Port P output pins

PUPP: Pull-Up Port P Enable
           0 – Disable active pull-up for all Port P pins
           1 – Enable active pull-up for all Port P pins

PSBCK: PWM Stops while in Background Mode
           0 – Continue PWM while in background mode
           1 – Disable PWM input clock when in background mode

Figure 15–10   The PWM Control Register

in the PWM control register, *PWCTL*, shown in Figure 15–10. A PWM channel is enabled by setting the appropriate bit in the PWM enable register, *PWEN*, as shown in Figure 15–11.

Consider the left-aligned PWM waveform shown in Figure 15–8. The way that this signal is generated is as follows. An 8-bit PWM channel counter, *PWCNT*, shown in Figure 15–12 is incremented by a clock source. Writing to this register resets the counter to $00. The period, *PWPER*, of the output waveform and the

	7	6	5	4	3	2	1	0	
$0042	0	0	0	0	PWEN3	PWEN2	PWEN1	PWEN0	PWEN

PWENx[3:0]: PWM Channel x Enable
         0 – Channel x disabled
         1 – Channel x enabled

Figure 15–11   The PWM Enable Register

	7	6	5	4	3	2	1	0	
$0048	Bit 7	6	5	4	3	2	1	Bit 0	PWCNT0
$0049	Bit 7	6	5	4	3	2	1	Bit 0	PWCNT1
$004A	Bit 7	6	5	4	3	2	1	Bit 0	PWCNT2
$004B	Bit 7	6	5	4	3	2	1	Bit 0	PWCNT3

Figure 15–12   PWM Channel Counters

duty time, *PWDTY*, shown in Figures 15–8 and 15–9, are determined by the contents of the PWM channel period registers and channel duty registers, shown in Figures 15–13 and 15–14. When the value in the channel counter, *PWCNT*, matches the value in the channel duty register, *PWDTY*, the output changes state (going high if $PPOL = 0$ and going low in $PPOL = 1$). The value of *PPOL* is determined by the channel polarity bits in the *PWPOL* register as shown in Figure 15–15. When the value in the channel counter, *PWCNT*, matches the value in the channel period register, *PWPER*, the output changes state again and the channel counter, *PWCNT*, is reset to $00.

The center-aligned PWM waveform shown in Figure 15–9 is generated in a similar way. In this case when the value in the channel counter, *PWCNT*, matches the value in the channel duty register, *PWDTY*, the output is toggled, and when the value in the channel counter, *PWCNT*, matches the value in the channel period register, *PWPER*, the direction of the up/down channel counter, *PWCNT*, is changed.

Note that the duty cycle of the PWM output is determined only by the values of the 8-bit registers, *PWPER* and *PWDTY*, as shown in Figure 15–8, 15–9, 15–13,

	7	6	5	4	3	2	1	0	
$004C	Bit 7	6	5	4	3	2	1	Bit 0	PWPER0
$004D	Bit 7	6	5	4	3	2	1	Bit 0	PWPER1
$004E	Bit 7	6	5	4	3	2	1	Bit 0	PWPER2
$004F	Bit 7	6	5	4	3	2	1	Bit 0	PWPER3

Figure 15–13   PWM Channel Period Registers

	7	6	5	4	3	2	1	0	
$0050	Bit 7	6	5	4	3	2	1	Bit 0	PWDTY0
$0051	Bit 7	6	5	4	3	2	1	Bit 0	PWDTY1
$0052	Bit 7	6	5	4	3	2	1	Bit 0	PWDTY2
$0053	Bit 7	6	5	4	3	2	1	Bit 0	PWDTY3

Figure 15–14   PWM Channel Duty Registers

	7	6	5	4	3	2	1	0	
$0041	PCLK3	PCLK2	PCLK1	PCLK0	PPOL3	PPOL2	PPOL1	PPOL0	PWPOL

PCLKLx[3:0]: PWM Channel x Clock Select
        0 – Channels 2 and 3 use clock B and channels 0 and 1 use clock A
        1 – Channels 2 and 3 use clock S1 and channels 0 and 1 use clock S0

PPOLx[3:0]: PWM Channel x Polarity
        0 – At duty count the output of channel x goes from low to high
        1 – At duty count the output of channel x goes from high to low

Figure 15–15   The PWM Clock Select and Polarity Register

and 15–14. The actual period of the output waveform will depend on how fast (or slowly) the channel counter, *PWCNT*, shown in Figure 15–12 is counting. This, in turn, is determined by the clock source that increments the counter.

There are two main clock sources, Clock A and Clock B, that are both derived from the system P clock and can have separate prescaled values by setting the appropriate bits in the *PWCLK* register, shown in Figure 15–16. Note that these bits can divide the P clock by a maximum of 128. A separate slower clock, S0, can be generated by dividing clock A by the contents of register *PWSCAL0* shown in Figure 15–17 and then dividing again by two. A write to the *PWSCAL0* register will

	7	6	5	4	3	2	1	0	
$0040	CON23	CON01	PCKA2	PCKA1	PCKA0	PCKB2	PCKB1	PCKB0	PWCLK

CON23:   Concatenate PWM Channels 2 and 3
              0 – Channels 2 and 3 are separate 8-bit PWMs
              1 – Channels 2 and 3 are concatenated to create a single 16-bit PWM channel

CON01:   Concatenate PWM Channels 0 and 1
              0 – Channels 0 and 1 are separate 8-bit PWMs
              1 – Channels 0 and 1 are concatenated to create a single 16-bit PWM channel

PCKA[2:0]: Prescalar for Clock A
PCKB[2:0]: Prescalar for Clock B

PCKA[2:0] (PCKB[2:0])	Value of Clock A (B) P = 8.0 MHz
000	P
001	P/2
010	P/4
011	P/8
100	P/16
101	P/32
110	P/64
111	P/128

Figure 15–16   The PWM Clocks and Concatenate Register

PWM Scale Register 0

7	6	5	4	3	2	1	0	
Bit 7	6	5	4	3	2	1	Bit 0	PWSCAL0

$0044

PWM Scale Counter 0 Value

7	6	5	4	3	2	1	0	
Bit 7	6	5	4	3	2	1	Bit 0	PWSCNT 0

$0045

PWM Scale Register 1 Value

7	6	5	4	3	2	1	0	
Bit 7	6	5	4	3	2	1	Bit 0	PWSCAL 1

$0046

PWM Scale Counter 1 Value

7	6	5	4	3	2	1	0	
Bit 7	6	5	4	3	2	1	Bit 0	PWSCNT1

$0047

Figure 15–17   Scale Registers Used to Determine Frequencies of Clocks S0 and S1

cause the value to be loaded into the down-counter, *PWSCNT0*, shown in Figure 15–17. When this down-counter reaches $00, it reloads the value from the *PWSCAL0* register. If the value in *PWSCAL0* is $00, then clock A is divided by 256 and then divided by 2 to generate clock S0.

Registers *PWSCAL1* and *PWSCNT1*, shown in Figure 15–17, play a similar role with clock B to generate a second slower clock, S1. Channels 0 and 1 can use either clock A or clock S0, and channels 2 and 3 can use either clock B or clock S1, depending upon the *PCLK* bits in the *PWPOL* register shown in Figure 15–15. Note that it is possible to have all four channels using a different clock.

Note that the *PWCLK* register shown in Figure 15–16 is also used to concatenate channels 2 and 3 (or 0 and 1) into a single 16-bit PWM channel. In this case channel 2 (or channel 0) becomes the high-order byte and channel 3 (or channel 1) becomes the low-order byte. The waveform is output from the channel 2 (or channel 0) pin and the clock source is determined by the channel 3 (or channel 1) clock-select control bits.

15.5   SUMMARY

In this chapter we have discussed a number of special topics related to the 68HC12. In Section 15.1 we saw how the Computer Operating Properly (COP) feature can be used to detect when software gets lost and to produce a reset interrupt. The key wakeup feature on a 68HC812A4 was described in Section 15.2. This allows pins on Port H or Port J to wake up the CPU from the STOP or wait state by producing an interrupt on an active edge of the pin.

The method used to program and erase the Flash EEPROM in a 68HC912B32 was described in Section 15.3. Finally, we showed in Section 15.4 how pulse-width modulated signals can be generated by using the special PWM module associated with Port P on a 68HC912B32.

EXERCISES

Exercise 15.1

Add a COP watchdog to the ultrasonic tape measure given in Listing 10–8.

Exercise 15.2

Describe how you would add a COP watchdog to the fuzzy control example given in Listing 14–3.

Exercise 15.3

Add a COP watchdog to the fuzzy control program written in Exercise 14.9.

Exercise 15.4

Add a feature to the calculator in Exercise 13.9 that will allow you to put it in the STOP mode to save power and then wake it up using the key wakeup feature on a 68HC812A4.

Exercise 15.5

a. Write a WHYP program that will erase the Flash EEPROM in a 68HC912B32. Note that WHYP cannot be running in the Flash EEPROM when this program is run!

b. Write a WHYP program that will program the Flash EEPROM in a 68HC912B32. Note that WHYP cannot be running in the Flash EEPROM when this program is run (even if you want to program some other part of the flash array) because bytes cannot be read properly from the array when the programming voltage is on.

Exercise 15.6

Write a program using the PWM module of the 68HC912B32 that will generate the waveform shown in Figure 10–11. The variables *PERIOD* and *P_WIDTH* should contain the values of the period and pulse width in microseconds.

16

WHYP12 C++ Classes

The host program running on the PC is written in C++ and is discussed in Chapter 17. This program contains classes for a character queue, a UART, an S-record file, a linked list, and the WHYP dictionary. These C++ classes are described in this chapter.

It is not necessary to know C++ in order to program the 68HC12 in WHYP. You have been doing it throughout this book. Therefore, these last two chapters are optional and are included so that you can see exactly how the PC side of WHYP works. All C++ files for WHYP are included on the disk accompanying this book. The source files were compiled using Borland C++ Version 5 using a standard DOS console model. All of the classes defined in this chapter, except the WHYP dictionary class, are C++ classes that may be useful in other applications.

16.1 A CHARACTER QUEUE CLASS

A character queue data structure was shown in Figure 10–18 in Section 10.6. The files `queue1.h` and `queue1.cpp`, shown in Listings 16–1 and 16–2, implement this queue in C++. This queue is used by the *uart* class described in Section 16.2 to store the characters received in the serial port by the interrupt service routine.

Listing 16–1   A Character Queue Class—File `queue1.h`

```cpp
// queue1.h
// character queue as an array
// Written by Richard E. Haskell -- November 1994

#ifndef QUEUE1_H_
#define QUEUE1_H_

// character linked list

class   ch_queue                  // character queue
      {
      private:
          int  front;
          int  rear;
          int  size;
          char* qbuff;
          enum{max_size = 4096};
      public:
          ch_queue();                       // constructor
          ~ch_queue();                      // destructor
          bool qstore(char);                // add val to queue
          bool checkq(char&);               // get char from queue
          void display();                   // display entire queue
          int num_in_queue();               // get number of nodes
      };

#endif // QUEUE1_H_
```

Listing 16–2   A Character Queue Class—File `queue1.cpp`

```cpp
// queue1.cpp
// member functions for character queue
// Copyright 1994 by Richard E. Haskell. All rights reserved.
#include <iostream.h>
#include <dos.h>
#include "queue1.h"

// *******************************
// character queue member functions
// *******************************

//    Constructor
ch_queue::ch_queue()
      {
      size = max_size + 1;
      qbuff = new char[size];
      front = 0;
      rear = 0;
      }
```

(continued)

Listing 16–2 (*continued*)

```
//     Class destructor -- delete queue
ch_queue::~ch_queue()                                    // destructor
     {
     delete qbuff;
     }

//     store a value in the queue
bool ch_queue::qstore(char val)
     {
     if(++rear > max_size)
        rear = 0;
     if(front == rear)
        {
        if(--rear < 0)
           rear = max_size;
        return false;
        }
     else
        {
        qbuff[rear] = val;
        return true;
        }
     }

//     check the queue and return value from front of queue
//     return false if queue is empty
bool ch_queue::checkq(char& val)
     {
     if(front != rear)
        {
        if(++front > max_size)
           front = 0;
        val = qbuff[front];
        return true;              // return true if value removed
        }
     else
        return false;              // return false if queue is empty
     }

//     Display all values in queue
void ch_queue::display()          // display all links
     {
     int i;
     if(rear > front)
        for(i = front+1; i <= rear; i++)
           cout << endl << qbuff[i];
     else
        if(rear < front)
```

Listing 16–2 (*continued*)

```
        {
        for(i = front+1; i <= max_size; i++)
           cout << endl << qbuff[i];
        for(i = 0; i <= rear; i++)
           cout << endl << qbuff[i];
        }
     else
        cout << endl << "Queue empty ";
     }

//   Get number of characters in queue
int  ch_queue::num_in_queue()
     {
     if(rear >= front)
        return (rear - front);
     else
        return (max_size - front + rear + 1);
     }
```

The member function *ch_queue::qstore(char val)* implements the algorithm shown in Figure 10–19 to store a character in the queue. The member function *ch_queue::checkq(char & val)* implements the algorithm shown in Figure 10–20 to check to see if a character is in the queue.

16.2 A UART CLASS

The files uart2.h and uart2.cpp, shown in Listings 16–3 and 16–4, define a *uart* class that is used by WHYP to communicate with the target system via the asynchronous serial port. The *uart* class uses the *character queue* class that was defined in Section 16.1. This *uart* class uses a hardware interrupt to detect a character received by the PC. When a character is received, it will produce an interrupt. The interrupt service routine will read the character and put it in a queue.

16.2.1 The 8250 UART

Serial boards in a PC use the INS8250 Universal Asynchronous Receiver/Transmitter (UART) as the basic hardware interface to the serial port. This is a chip that performs the same function as the SCI port in the 68HC12 described in Chapter 11. The functional diagram of the 8250 UART is similar to that shown in Figure 11–2 with a different set of control and status registers. The 8250 UART registers are shown in Table 16–1.

The I/O space addresses of these registers for the two serial ports, COM1 and COM2, are given in Table 16–1. Note that the first three registers in Table 16–1 have the same I/O address. If bit 7 of the *line control register* is set to 1, then the address

Listing 16–3   A UART Class—File `uart2.h`

```
// uart2.h
// 8250 UART of PC
// Written by Richard E. Haskell -- 1994/1996

#ifndef UART1_H_
#define UART1_H_
#include "queue1.h"

enum Com_port {COM1, COM2};

enum    {                               // 8250 Registers
        RxBuff = 0,                     // Receive Buffer (read)
        TxBuff = 0,                     // Transmit Holding (write)
        IntEnable = 1,                  // Interrupt Enable
        IntId = 2,                      // Interrupt Identification (read)
        LineCtl = 3,                    // Line Control
        ModemCtl = 4,                   // Modem Control
        LineStatus = 5,                 // Line Status
        ModemStatus = 6,                // Modem Status
        DivLo = 0,                      // Divisor Latch Low Byte
        DivHi = 1,                      // Divisor Latch High Byte
        };
const int COM_1 = 0x3f8;
const int COM_2 = 0x2f8;
const int int_1 = 0x0c;                 // interrupt number for COM1
const int int_2 = 0x0b;                 // interrupt number for COM2
const int pic_enable4 = 0xef;           // interrupt 4 enable mask
const int pic_disable4 = 0x10;          // interrupt 4 disable mask
const int pic_enable3 = 0xf7;           // interrupt 3 enable mask
const int pic_disable3 = 0x08;          // interrupt 3 disable mask

// 8259A Priority Interrupt Controller registers
const int imask = 0x21;                 // mask reg in PIC
const int eoi = 0x20;                   // end of interrupt value
const int ocw2 = 0x20;                  // PIC ocw2
// Baud rate divisor table
const int baud_items = 9;
// Baud rate divisor table
const unsigned long int baud_rate[baud_items] =
        {300, 600, 1200, 2400, 4800, 9600, 19200, 38400, 57600};
const unsigned int divisor[baud_items] =
        {384, 192, 96, 48, 24, 12, 6, 3, 2};

class  uart
    {
    private:
        int int_num;                    // interrupt number for current COM
        unsigned char pic_enable;       // enable mask for current COM
        unsigned char pic_disable;      // disable mask for current COM
    public:
        uart();                         // constructor
        ~uart();                        // destructor
```

Listing 16–3   (*continued*)

```
        bool setbaud(long int);         // set baud rate - true if ok
        bool set_com(Com_port);         // set COM - true if ok
        void init_term();               // initialize terminal
        void transmit_byte(char);       // transmit character
        bool check_recv(char&);         // get receive char
        void enable_com();
        void disable_com();
        void change_com(int);
    };

#endif // UART1_H_
```

Listing 16–4   A UART Class—File `uart2.cpp`

```cpp
// uart2.cpp
// member functions for 8250 uart
// Written by Richard E. Haskell -- Nov. 1994/Dec. 1996

#include <iostream.h>
#include <dos.h>
#include "uart2.h"

ch_queue q;                 // make a queue object

int COM;                    // COM base address

void interrupt (far *old_handler)(...);    // old handler
void interrupt int_handler(...);                        // new handler

//     Receiver interrupt handler
void   interrupt int_handler(...)
       {
       unsigned char in_byte;
       in_byte = inportb(COM+LineStatus) & 0x01;
       if( in_byte != 0)
         q.qstore(inportb(COM+RxBuff));
       outportb(ocw2,eoi);
       }

// *********************
// uart member functions
// *********************

//     constructor
uart::uart()
       {
       if(set_com(COM1))     // COM1 default
          enable_com();
       else
          cout << endl << "Unable to set COM " << endl;
       }
//     destructor
```

(continued)

Listing 16–4   (continued)

```
uart::~uart()
        {
        disable_com();
        }
//    Set baud rate
bool  uart::setbaud(long int baud)
      {
      int i;
      unsigned short old_lcr, new_lcr;
      i = 0;
      while((baud != baud_rate[i]) && (i != baud_items))
            i++;
      if(i < baud_items)
         {
         old_lcr = inportb(COM+LineCtl);
         new_lcr = old_lcr | 0x80;
         outportb(COM+LineCtl, new_lcr);
         outportb(COM+DivLo, divisor[i] & 0xff);
         outportb(COM+DivHi, (divisor[i] >> 8) & 0xff);
         return true;
         }
      else
         return false;
      }
//    Set COM port
bool  uart::set_com(Com_port Com_x)
      {
      switch(Com_x)
         {
          case 0:                         // COM1
             COM = COM_1;
             int_num = int_1;
             pic_enable = pic_enable4;
             pic_disable = pic_disable4;
             return true;
          case 1:                         // COM2
             COM = COM_2;
             int_num = int_2;
             pic_enable = pic_enable3;
             pic_disable = pic_disable3;
             return true;
          default:
             return false;
         }
      }
//    Initialize terminal
void  uart::init_term()
      {
      outportb(COM+ModemCtl,11);
      // modem ctrl reg out2 lo
      outportb(COM+IntEnable,1);
```

Listing 16–4 (*continued*)

```
        // enable recv interrupt
        old_handler = getvect(int_num);            // save old int vector
        setvect(int_num, int_handler);             // set new int vector
        outportb(imask, inportb(imask) & pic_enable);  // enable PIC irq
        }
//      Transmit character
void    uart::transmit_byte(char val)
        {
        while((inportb(COM+LineStatus) & 32) == 0)
            {}
                        // wait for TBE bit hi
        outportb(COM+TxBuff,val);                  // send byte
        }
//      Receive byte
bool    uart::check_recv(char& ch)
        {
        return q.checkq(ch);
        }
//      enable new com
void    uart::enable_com()
            {
          setbaud(9600);                           // 9600 baud
          outportb(COM+LineCtl, 3);                // 8 bits, no parity
          init_term();
            }
//      disable current com
void          uart::disable_com()
            {
          outportb(imask,inportb(imask) | pic_disable);  // disable PIC irq
          outportb(COM+ModemCtl,0);                // turn off OUT2
          setvect(int_num,old_handler);            // restore old_handler
            }
//      change COM value
void    uart::change_com(int comval)
        {
        disable_com();                             // disable current com
        set_com(comval);                           // set new com
        enable_com();                              // enable it
        }
```

$3F8 (COM1) will be the *divisor low register* (which is used to set the baud rate). On the other hand if bit 7 of the *line control register* is zero, then the address $3F8 (COM1) will be the *receive data buffer* for a read operation and the *transmit data buffer* for a write operation. These are the same as the receive and transmit holding registers in Figure 11–2. The *interrupt enable register* and the *divisor high register* in Table 16–1 also share the same I/O address and are distinguished by the value of bit 7 in the *line control register*.

Table 16–1   8250 UART Registers

Register Addr.		Bit 7	Read/	8250 Register	
COM1	COM2	LCR	Write	Name	C++ Name
$3F8	$2F8	0	R	Receive Data Buffer	RxBuff
$3F8	$2F8	0	W	Transmit Data Buffer	TxBuff
$3F8	$2F8	1	R/W	Divisor Low Register	DivLo
$3F9	$2F9	0	R/W	Interrupt Enable Register	IntEnable
$3F9	$2F9	1	R/W	Divisor High Register	DivHi
$3FA	$2FA	X	R	Interrupt ID Register	IntId
$3FB	$2FB	X	R/W	Line Control Register	LineCtl
$3FC	$2FC	X	R/W	Modem Control Register	ModemCtl
$3FD	$2FD	X	R/W	Line Status Register	LineStatus
$3FE	$2FE	X	R/W	Modem Status Register	ModemStatus

The 8250 *Line Control Register* (LCR) is shown in Figure 16–1 in which bit 7 is used as a register address discrimination bit as described above. The 8250 *Line Status Register* (LSR) is shown in Figure 16–2.

The PC uses an 8259A Priority Interrupt Controller (PIC) to process hardware interrupts. The interrupt line from the 8250 UART chip is connected to the COM1 (*irq4*) line of the PIC as shown in Figure 16–3. Note that this interrupt line goes through a buffer that is enabled when the $\overline{OUT\,2}$ line of the 8250 goes low. This line is controlled by bit 3 in the 8250 *modem control register* that is shown in Figure 16–4. This bit must be set to 1 to enable 8250 interrupts. To have a hardware interrupt occur every time the receive data ready bit in the *line status register* gets set (meaning a new value has been loaded into the *receive data buffer*), we must set bit 0 of the 8250 *interrupt enable register*, shown in Figure 16–5.

Even after setting the *modem control register* and the *interrupt enable register* to the values shown in Figures 16–4 and 16–5, the interrupt signal will still not get

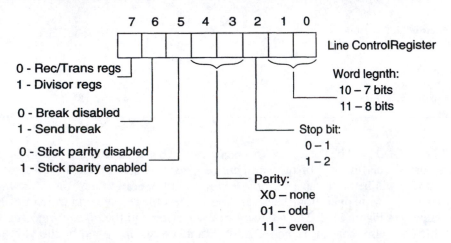

Figure 16–1   The 8250 Line Control Register

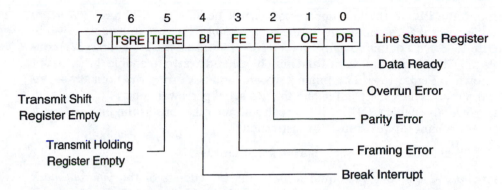

Figure 16–2   The 8250 Line Status Register

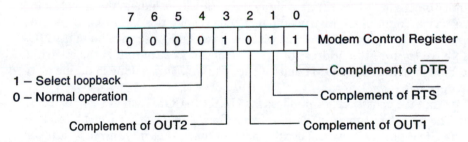

Figure 16–3   The 8250 must have $\overline{\text{OUT2}}$ low to enable COM1 interrupts.

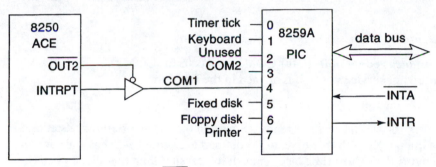

Figure 16–4   The 8250 Modem Control Register

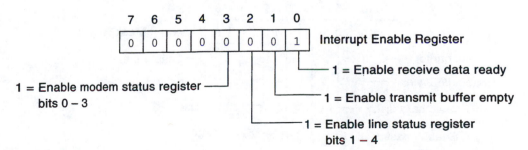

Figure 16–5   The 8250 Interrupt Enable Register

through the PIC to the microprocessor. That is because the PIC has an *interrupt mask register* that can mask any of the eight possible hardware interrupts shown in Figure 16–3. Bit 4 of this *interrupt mask register* (which has the I/O address $21) controls the COM1 interrupt signal and must be cleared to zero to enable this interrupt as shown in Figure 16–6. The timer, keyboard, and disk drives will normally be enabled already while the printer and the two serial ports will generally be masked. Therefore, to enable COM1 while keeping all the other bits in the *interrupt mask register* unchanged, we can use the instruction

```
outportb(imask, inportb(imask) & pic_enable);
```

where *imask* is a constant equal to 0x21, the I/O address of the *interrupt mask register*, and *pic_enable* is equal to 0xef for COM1 (and 0xf7 for COM2). To turn off the COM1 interrupt we can set bit 4 of the *interrupt mask register* with the instruction

```
outportb(imask, inportb(imask) | pic_disable);
```

where *pic_disable* is equal to 0x10 for COM1 (and 0x08 for COM2).

The interrupt service routine is defined in the function

```
void interrupt int_handler(...)
```

given in Listing 16–4. This routine reads the byte in the receive buffer register and stores it in a queue. Note that the queue, as defined in Listing 16–1, has a maximum size of 4096 bytes. This should be large enough to prevent filling the queue when receiving a large number of bytes to be displayed on the screen (for example, displaying memory blocks in D-Bug12). It is always necessary to include at the end of an interrupt service routine an instruction that will output the value 0x20 (end-of-interrupt, *eoi*) to I/O port 0x20 (*ocw2*) which will reset the in-service bit in the PIC. You also have to store the address of the interrupt service routine in the interrupt vector table (Type 0x0c for COM1 and 0x0b for COM2). This is done in the member function *uart::init_term()*.

Note that the constructor initializes the UART to COM1 when a *uart* object is created. The member function *uart::set_com(Com_port Com_x)* can be used to change the COM port. You would use the member function *uart::transmit_byte (char*

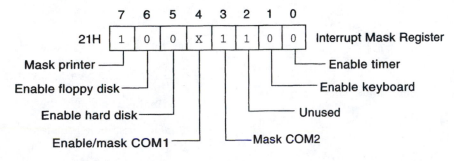

Figure 16–6   The 8259A PIC Interrupt Mask Register

val) to send a byte out the UART transmit line. To check to see if a character has been received you would use the member function *uart::check_recv(char& ch)* which will be true if a character has been found in the queue.

16.3 AN s-RECORD CLASS

The files *srecord.h* and *srecord.cpp*, shown in Listings 16–5 and 16–6, define an *srecord* class that is used by WHYP to produce s-record files. An s-record file is

---

Listing 16–5 An s-Record Class—File `srecord.h`

```
// srecord.h
// srecord class for WHYP
// Written by Richard E. Haskell -- February 1995
#include <iostream.h>

class    srecord            // a Motorola s-record file

    {
    private:
        int checksum;                       // line checksum
    public:
        srecord()                           // constructor
            { }
        ~srecord()                          // destructor
            { }
        void make_srecord_file(FILE *, char*,
                int, int, int);                        // save srecord file
        void send_s9_line(FILE *);
        void send_32bytes(FILE *, char*, int, int, int);
        int hex2asc(int);                              // hex to ascii conv
        void send_ascii_byte(FILE *, int);
        void send_ascii_word(FILE *, int);
    };
```

Listing 16–6 An s-Record Class—File `srecord.cpp`

```
// srecord.cpp
// member functions for s-record files
// Written by Richard E. Haskell -- February 1995

#include <stdio.h>
#include <stdlib.h>
#include <io.h>
#include <string.h>
#include "srecord.h"

// s-record member functions
```

(continued)

Listing 16–6 (*continued*)

```
void srecord::make_srecord_file(FILE * filename, char* vseg,
                    int ix_start, int ix_end, int dest_addr)
    {
    int num_bytes, num_lines, i;
    num_bytes = ix_end - ix_start + 1;
    num_lines = (num_bytes + 31)/32;
    for(i = 0; i < num_lines; i++)
        send_32bytes(filename, vseg, ix_start, i, dest_addr);
    send_s9_line(filename);
    }

void srecord::send_32bytes(FILE * filename,
            char* vseg, int start, int i, int dest_addr)
    {
    int j;
    checksum = 0;
    fprintf(filename, "%c",  'S');                      // send S
    fprintf(filename, "%c", '1');                       // send 1
    send_ascii_byte(filename, 35);                      // send #bytes
    send_ascii_word(filename, dest_addr + i*32);        // send addr
    for(j = 0; j < 32; j++)
        send_ascii_byte(filename, vseg[start + i*32 + j]);  // send data
    send_ascii_byte(filename, ~checksum);
    fprintf(filename, "\n");
    }

void srecord::send_s9_line(FILE * filename)
    {
    checksum = 0;
    fprintf(filename, "%c", 'S');
    // send S
    fprintf(filename, "%c", '9');
    // send 9
    send_ascii_byte(filename, 3);                       // send #bytes
    send_ascii_word(filename, 0);
    // send addr
    send_ascii_byte(filename, ~checksum);               // send checksum
    fprintf(filename, "\n\n");
    }

int srecord::hex2asc(int n)
    {
    if(n > 9)                                           // if n > 9
        n += 0x37;                                      //    add 37H
    else
        n += 0x30;                                      // else add 30H
    return n;
    }

void srecord::send_ascii_byte(FILE * filename, int n)
    {
    int hi_nibble, lo_nibble;
```

Listing 16–6 (*continued*)

```
      checksum += n;                                    // add to checksum
      hi_nibble = (n >> 4) & 0x0f;
      fprintf(filename, "%c", hex2asc(hi_nibble));      // send hi_nibble
      lo_nibble = n & 0x0f;
      fprintf(filename, "%c", hex2asc(lo_nibble));      // send lo_nibble
      }

void srecord::send_ascii_word(FILE * filename, int n)
      {
      int hi_byte, lo_byte;
      hi_byte = (n >> 8) & 0xff;
      send_ascii_byte(filename, hi_byte);
      lo_byte = n & 0xff;
      send_ascii_byte(filename, lo_byte);
      }
```

a format used by Motorola to encode binary data. It is the format used in the .S19 file produced when you assemble a 68HC12 program. A typical S-record file is shown in Figure 16–7. Each line (S-record) in the file has the form shown in - Figure 16–8.

The member function that you would normally use is

```
void srecord::make_srecord_file(FILE * filename, char* vseg,
                int ix_start, int ix_end, int dest_addr)
```

This function will write an S-record file to the file with the path name, *filename*, using the data in the character array, *vseg*, starting at the array index, *ix_start*, and going through the array index, *ix_end*. The starting address in the S-record file will be *dest_addr*.

```
S107000001C001FF37
S123D0008610B710358E01FF3009DF02CE01C0DF008D1718CE100A181F0001037EB6008DC4
S123D0204918AD0086068D1F20F53CCE10006F2CCC300CA72BE72D38393CCE1000A62E840B
S123D0402027FAA62F38393C37CE1000E62E2AFCA72F3338398DE209A7008DDD09A70039CE
S123D060EC0008088DE1178DDE398DCD168DCA188F398DC5168DC28F393C8DF68DEC188F82
S123D080ED0038398DE4183C8DE0188CB600251F8DA7164F0909ED0009091AEF00183C8DCA
S123D0A01F1838180832335A373626E41838398D8818A700180832335A373626F21838395D
S123D0C01AEE00080818A60081FF27028D19EC00080817C602F7103B18A700C603F7103B40
S11ED0E0BDD7B37F103B39C616F7103B18E700C617F7103BBDD7B37F103B3961
S9030000FC
```

igure 16–7 A Typical Motorola S-Record File

TYPE	RECORD LENGTH	ADDRESS	CODE/DATA	CHECKSUM

TYPE: S1 - defines a record with a 2-byte address
              S9 - termination record

RECORD LENGTH: 2 printable characters. Number of character pairs (bytes) in record, excluding the type and record length. For example, 23 means 23 hex or 35 decimal bytes. Note that each byte is represented by two printable characters.

ADDRESS: 4 printable characters. For example, D060 represents the hex address D060.

CODE/DATA: Every 2 printable characters in the CODE/DATA field represent a byte of data to be loaded into memory starting at the address in the ADDRESS field.

CHECKSUM: The last two printable characters on each line represent an 8-bit checksum. This checksum is the least significant byte of the one's complement of the sum of values represented by the pairs of characters making up the record length, the address, and the code/data fields.

Figure 16–8   S-Record Format

16.4   A LINKED LIST CLASS

The file *linklist.h* shown in Listing 16–7 describes a generic linked list class defined in terms of C++ templates. It is used in WHYP to define an integer linked list used as a stack for implementing various immediate compiler words. Note that all the member functions for the linked list are included in the file *linklist.h*. This is because the template classes cannot be precompiled.

Listing 16–7   A Linked List Class—File `linklist.h`

```
// linklist.h
// single linked lists
// Copyright 1996 by Richard E. Haskell -- All rights reserved.
#include <iostream.h>

// generic linked list

template<class T>
class linklist              // a linked list
    {
    private:
        class  list_node                    // one element of list
            {
            public:
                list_node* next;       // ptr to next node
```

Listing 16–7 (continued)

```cpp
                T data;                  // data item
                list_node()              // constructor
                {
                next = NULL;
                }
                ~list_node()             // destructor
                {
                if(next)
                    delete next;
                }
            };
        list_node* first;                // ptr to first node
    public:
        linklist();                      // constructor
        ~linklist();                     // destructor
        void push(T);                    // add val to list
        T pop();                         // pop val from list
        void display();                  // display entire list
        bool is_empty();                 // is list empty?
        int num_nodes();                 // get number of nodes
        void additem_inc(T);             // add value - ascending
        void additem_dec(T);             // add value - descending
    };

//*****************************************************
// member functions for linklist
// Note: Each client must compile template functions
//*****************************************************

//  constructor
template<class T>
linklist<T>::linklist()
        {
        first = NULL;
        }

//  destructor
template<class T>
linklist<T>::~linklist()
    {
    if(first != NULL)
        delete first;
    }

template<class T>
void    linklist<T>::push(T val)
    {
    list_node* newlink = new list_node;  // make a new link
    newlink->data = val;                 // give it data
    newlink->next = first;               // it points to next link
    first = newlink;                     // now first points to this
    }
```

(continued)

Listing 16–7 (*continued*)

```
template<class T>
T       linklist<T>::pop()
        {
        T value = 0;
        list_node* firstnode = first;           // ptr to first node
        if( first != NULL )
           {
           value = first->data;                  // get value
           first = first->next;                  // remove 1st node
           firstnode->next = NULL;                // no more links
           delete firstnode;                      // delete 1st node
           }
        else
           cout << "\nList empty\n";
        return value;                             // pop value
        }

template<class T>
void    linklist<T>::display()                    // display all links
        {
        list_node* current = first ;              // set ptr to 1st link
        while( current != NULL )
           {
           cout << endl << current->data;         // print data
           current = current->next;               // move to next link
           }
        }

template<class T>
bool   linklist<T>::is_empty()
        {
        if( first == NULL )
          return true;
        else
          return false;
        }

template<class T>
int     linklist<T>::num_nodes()
        {
        list_node* current = first;
        int count = 0;
        while( current != NULL )
           {
           count += 1;
           current = current->next;
           }
        return count ;
        }

// add value to list in ascending order
template<class T>
void linklist<T>::additem_inc(T val)
```

Listing 16–7   (*continued***)**

```
    {
    list_node* newlink = new list_node;   // make a new link
    list_node* prevlink, * current;
    newlink->data = val;                   // give it data
    if( first == NULL )                    // if list empty
        {
      newlink->next = first;               // put at head of list
      first = newlink;
        }
    else {
      current = first;
      if( current->data > val )            // if < first item
          {
        newlink->next = first;             // add to head of list
        first = newlink;
          }
      else {
        while( current != NULL )
            {
          if( current->data > val )        // stop when next value > val
             break;
          prevlink = current;
          current = current->next;         // get next link
            }
        newlink->next = prevlink->next;    // add after prev link
        prevlink->next = newlink;
          }
        }
      }

// add value to list in descending order
template<class T>
void linklist<T>::additem_dec(T val)
    {
    list_node* newlink = new list_node;   // make a new link
    list_node* prevlink, * current;
    newlink->data = val;                   // give it data
    if( first == NULL )                    // if list empty
        {
      newlink->next = first;               // put at head of list
      first = newlink;
        }
    else {
      current = first;
      if( current->data < val )            // if > first item
          {
      newlink->next = first;               // add to head of list
      first = newlink;
          }
      else {
```

(*continued*)

Listing 16–7   (*continued*)

```
        while( current != NULL ) {
           if( current->data < val )      // stop when next value < val
              break;
           prevlink = current;
           current = current->next;       // get next link
           }
        newlink->next = prevlink->next;   // add after prev link
        prevlink->next = newlink;
        }
     }
  }
```

The structure of the linked list is the same as that shown in Section 13.3.2 except that the data value can be of different data types. For example, to create a linked list object called *bstack* with integer data types, you would use the following statement:

```
linklist<int> bstack;
```

16.5   A DICTIONARY CLASS

The names of all WHYP words are maintained in the PC in two separate dictionaries. The first dictionary is an object of the C++ class *dict* defined in the files *wdict12.h*, shown in the Listing 16–8, and *wdict12.cpp*, shown in Listing 16–9. In addition to storing header information, this class maintains an image of actual 68HC12 code in the character array *tseg*. The class *dict* contains member functions to perform such operations as adding a word to the dictionary, building the dictionary, loading 68HC12 code from an S-record file into *tseg*, searching for a word in the dictionary, compiling colon definitions in the dictionary, saving *tseg* as an S-record file, and saving the headers in a header file. When WHYP12 is run, it loads in the header file, WHYP12.HED that

Listing 16–8   A Dictionary Class—File wdict12.h

```
// wdict1.h
// linked list dictionary for WHYP
// Copyright 1996 by Richard E. Haskell -- All rights reserved.
#include <iostream.h>
#include <iomanip.h>
#include "srecord.h"

class header        // one entry in dictionary
```

Listing 16–8 (continued)

```
    {
    public:
        header();                    // constructor
        ~header();                   // desctructor
        bool flag;                   // true if word is in target
        int sub;                     // address of 68HC11 code for word
        int size;                    // number of bytes in subroutine
        header* next;                // ptr to next link
        char*  name;                 // pointer to word name
    };

class  dict          // a linked dictionary
    {
    protected:
        header* first;               // ptr to first link
        char* tseg;                  // target segment
        int hdp;                     // tseg dict ptr
        int base_addr;
        int hed_base_addr;
        srecord srec;                // srecord class
    public:
        dict();                      // constructor
        ~dict();                     // destructor - same as kill
        void add_word(char*,int);    // add word to list
        bool is_in_dict(char*, header*&,
            bool&, int&, int&);      // is word in dict?
        bool find_name(int, char*);  // find name from addr
        void load_hc11(FILE *);      // load an s19 file
        int get_hex_byte(FILE *);    // get hex byte from file
        void tcomma(int);            // compile int in tseg
        void tccomma(int);           // compile char in tseg
        void add_string(int, char*); // add string to tseg
        void get_string(int, int, char*&); // get string from tseg
        void get_first_string(char*&);  // get first string from tseg
        void set_address(header*, int);  // set sub address in header
        void set_first_address(int);     // set sub addr in first header
        int get_hdp()                // get current hdp
        int first_size();            // get first->size
        void store(int, int);        // store int in tseg[int]
        void set_flags();            // set all flags true
        void set_hed_base_addr(int); // set hed base address
        void set_base_addr(int);     // set base address
        void build_dict(FILE *);     // build dict from name & srec files
        void compile(int);           // compile JSR int in tseg
        void fix_size();             // fix size of colon def
        void save_tseg();            // save tseg to s-record file
        void save_headers();         // save dictionary headers
    };
```

Listing 16–9   A Dictionary Class—File `wdict12.cpp`

```cpp
// wdict12.cpp
// member functions for WHYP12 dictionary
// Copyright 1996/1998 by Richard E. Haskell -- All rights reserved.

#include <stdio.h>
#include <stdlib.h>
#include <io.h>
#include <string.h>
#include "wdict12.h"

// *************************************
// header member functions
// *************************************
//     constructor for class header
header::header()
    {
    next = NULL;
    name = NULL;
    }

//    destuctor for class header
header::~header()
    {
    if(next)
        delete next;
    if(name)
        delete name;
    }

// *************************************
// linked list dictionary member functions
// *************************************
//    Constructor for class dict
dict::dict()                                    // constructor
    {
    first = NULL;
    tseg = new char[16000];                     // big segment for hc11 code
    hdp = 0;
    base_addr = 0;
    }

//    Destructor for class dict
dict::~dict()                                   // destructor
    {
    delete tseg;
    if(first)
        delete first;
    }
```

Listing 16–9 (*continued*)

```
//    Add a word to the dictionary
void    dict::add_word(char* wordname, int sub_addr)
      {
      header* newlink = new header;          // make a new link
      int length = strlen(wordname);         // length of wordname
      newlink->name = new char[length+1];    // get memory for name
      strcpy(newlink->name,wordname);        // copy wordname to it
      newlink->sub = sub_addr;               // add ptr to hc11 code
      newlink->size = 0;                     // set size to 0
      newlink->flag = false;                 // set flag to false
      newlink->next = first;                 // it points to next link
      first = newlink;                       // now first points to this
      }
//    Load hc12 code words from s19 file
void  dict::load_hc12(FILE * s19file)
      {
      int checksum, count, val, c, i, j;
      i = hdp;
      do
         {
         // look for 'S'
         do
            c = getc(s19file);
         while(c != 'S' && c != EOF);
         if(c == EOF)
            {
            cout << endl << "End of file ";
            break;
            }
         c = getc(s19file);                      // get next char
         if(c == '9')
            break;
         if(c == '1')                            // if '1'
            {
            checksum = 0;                        //    load in line
            count = get_hex_byte(s19file);
            checksum += count;
            count -= 3;                          //   # of bytes
            checksum += get_hex_byte(s19file);   // read addr
            checksum += get_hex_byte(s19file);
            for(j = 0; j < count; j++)
               {
               val = get_hex_byte(s19file);
               checksum += val;
               tseg[i++] = val;
               }
```

(*continued*)

Listing 16–9 (*continued*)

```
            if(get_hex_byte(s19file) != (~checksum & 0xff))
                cout << endl << "Checksum error ";
        }
    }
    while(true);
    hdp = i;                                    // update hdp
    }

//   Get 2-character hex byte from file
int  dict::get_hex_byte(FILE * infile)
    {
    char str[3];
    char* stop_at;
    unsigned long value;
    int radix = 16;                             // hex conversion
    int c;
    c = getc(infile);
    str[0] = c;
    c = getc(infile);
    str[1] = c;
    str[2] = '\0';
    value = strtoul(str, &stop_at, radix);
    return value;
    }


//   Search for word in dictionary
bool dict::is_in_dict(char* wordname, header*& wordhead,
         bool& dwload, int& sub_addr, int& num_bytes)
    {
    header* current = first;
    bool found = false;
    while (current != NULL && !found)
        {
        if(stricmp(wordname, current->name) == 0)
            {
            found = true;
            wordhead = current;
            dwload = current->flag;
            sub_addr = current->sub;
            num_bytes = current->size;
            }
        current = current->next;
        }
    return found;
    }

    //    Search for address in dictionary
bool dict::find_name(int sub_addr, char* wordname)
```

Listing 16–9 (continued)

```
      {
      header* current = first;
      bool found = false;
      while(current != NULL && !found)
          {
          if(sub_addr == current->sub)
              {
              found = true;
              strcpy(wordname, current->name);
              }
          current = current->next;
          }
      return found;
      }

//    Compile int word in tseg
void dict::tcomma(int val)
      {
      int hibyte, lobyte, i;
      i = hdp;
      hibyte = val >> 8;                       // Motorola order
      tseg[i++] = hibyte;
      lobyte = val & 0xff;
      tseg[i++] = lobyte;
      hdp = i;                                 // update hdp
      }

//    Compile byte in tseg
void    dict::tccomma(int val)
      {
      int i;
      i = hdp;
      tseg[i++] = val;                         // compile low byte
      hdp = i;                                 // update hdp
      }

//    Add string to tseg
void dict::add_string(int nbytes, char* str)
      {
      int i, val;
      for(i = 0; i < nbytes; i++)
          {
          val = str[i];
          tccomma(val);
          }
      }
```

(continued)

Listing 16–9 (*continued*)

```
//    Get string from tseg
void  dict::get_string(int nbytes, int start_addr, char* &strbuf)
      {
      int i, j;
      j=0;
      for(i = start_addr; i < start_addr+nbytes; i++)
          strbuf[j++] = tseg[i];
      }

//    Get string from tseg for first word
void  dict::get_first_string(char* &strbuf)
      {
      int i, j;
      j=0;
      for(i = first->sub; i < first->sub+first->size; i++)
          strbuf[j++] = tseg[i];
      }

//    Set target subroutine address in header
void  dict::set_address(header* wordhead, int address)
      {
      wordhead->sub = address;
      wordhead->flag = true;
      }

//    Set target subroutine address in first header
void  dict::set_first_address(int address)
      {
      first->sub = address;
      first->flag = true;
      }

//    Get hdp
int   dict::get_hdp()
      {
      return hdp;
      }

//    Get first size
int   dict::first_size()
      {
      return first->size;
      }

//    Store int val at tseg[addr]
void  dict::store(int val, int addr)
      {
      int hibyte, lobyte;
```

Listing 16–9   *(continued)*

```
        hibyte = val >> 8;                              // Motorola order
        tseg[addr] = hibyte;
        lobyte = val & 0xff;
        tseg[addr+1] = lobyte;
        }
//    Set flag true for all words in dictionary
void    dict::set_flags()
        {
        header* current = first ;                       // set ptr to 1st link
        while( current != NULL )
            {
            current->flag = true;
            current = current->next;                    // move to next link
            }
        }

//    Set hed base address
void        dict::set_hed_base_addr(int val)   // set hed base address
        {
        hed_base_addr = val;
        }

//    Set base address
void        dict::set_base_addr(int val)        // set base address
        {
        base_addr = val;
        }

//    Save tseg as s-record file
void  dict::save_tseg()
        {
        int dest_addr;
        char filename[80];
        FILE * datfile;
        // open file
        cout << endl << "Enter an s19 filename for tseg: ";
        cin >> filename;
        if((datfile = fopen(filename,"w")) == NULL)
            {
            cout << "problem opening file\n";
            exit(1);
            }
        cout << endl << "Enter destination hex address for data: ";
        cout << setiosflags(ios::hex);
        cin >> dest_addr;
```

                                                                (continued)

Listing 16–9 (*continued*)

```
        srec.make_srecord_file(datfile, tseg, 0, hdp-1, dest_addr);
        cout << setiosflags(ios::dec);
        fclose(datfile);
        }

//      Build dictionary from hc11 code words
void dict::build_dict(FILE * namefile)
        {
        int old_addr;
        char old_name[81];
        fscanf(namefile,"%s%x", old_name, &old_addr);
        while( strcmp(old_name, "END") != 0)
            {
            old_addr = hed_base_addr + old_addr;
            add_word(old_name, old_addr);
            fscanf(namefile,"%s%x", old_name, &old_addr);
            }
        }

//      Compile JSR word in tseg
void dict::compile(int val)
        {
        int opcode;
        opcode = 0x16;                          // JSR opcode = 16
        tccomma(opcode);                        // compile it
        tcomma(val);                            // compile address
        }

//      Fix size of colon definition
void dict::fix_size()
        {
        // first points to last word defined
        first->size = hdp + base_addr - first->sub;
        }

//      Save dictionary headers as .sym file
void dict::save_headers()
        {
        char* ps;                               // ptr to string
        int subaddr;
        header* current = first ;               // set ptr to 1st link
        char filename[80];
        FILE * datfile;
        // open file
        cout << endl << "Enter a filename for header names: ";
        cin >> filename;
        if((datfile = fopen(filename,"w")) == NULL)
```

Listing 16–9   (*continued*)

```
    {
    cout << "problem opening file\n";
    exit(1);
    }
while( current != NULL )
    {
    ps = current->name;
    subaddr = current->sub;
    fprintf(datfile, "\n");
    while( *ps )
        // until null char
        fprintf(datfile, "%c", *ps++);        // print characters
    fprintf(datfile, "\t\t%x",
            subaddr);
            // print sub address
    current = current->next;                  // move to next link
    }
fprintf(datfile, "\nEND\t\t%x",0);
fclose(datfile);
}
```

contains the names and addresses of all built-in WHYP words. These words are all stored in a dictionary, *dict*.

A second dictionary is used to store all immediate words. These words are needed only at compile time and therefore all the code associated with these words can be maintained in the PC. This immediate dictionary is implemented in the host C++ program as an array of character strings. This array of strings is searched for a particular parsed word and the word is executed using a switch statement. This immediate dictionary is described in Chapter 17.

16.6   SUMMARY

In this chapter we have discussed and given the C++ code for the following classes that are used in the main WHYP program described in Chapter 17:

- A character queue class in Section 16.1
- A UART class in Section 16.2
- An S-record class in Section 16.3
- A linked list class in Section 16.4
- A dictionary class in Section 16.5

17

WHYP12 C++ Main Program

WHYP is run by typing *WHYP12* for a 68HC12 (or *WHYP11* for a 68HC11) which executes the PC program `WHYP12.EXE` (or `WHYP11.EXE`). The C++ source code for this program is contained in the file `WHYP12.CPP` (or `WHYP11.CPP`). In this chapter we will describe various portions of this C++ program. The program can be run with evaluation boards containing any 68HC12 (or 68HC11) part. It can do this because it first reads a configuration file described in Section 17.1 that configures the program for a particular part.

17.1   COMPILING AND RUNNING THE WHYP HOST PROGRAM

The source code for the C++ host program is given in the file `WHYP12.CPP`. The first part of this file is shown in Listing 17–1. Note that in addition to a number of C++ header files, this program includes the files *uart2.h*, *wdict12.h*, and *linklist.h*, described in Chapter 16. When making the executable file, `WHYP12.EXE`, the file, `WHYP12.CPP`, must be linked with the following files:

```
SRECORD.CPP
WDICT12.CPP
QUEUE1.CPP
UART2.CPP
```

Listing 17–1   Beginning of the WHYP C++ Host—from File `whyp12.cpp`

```
// WHYP12.CPP
// Copyright 1997/1998 by Richard E. Haskell
//      WHYP for the 68HC12 family of microcontrollers

#include <stdio.h>
#include <iostream.h>
#include <iomanip.h>
#include <dos.h>
#include <bios.h>
#include <conio.h>
#include <string.h>
#include <stdlib.h>
#include <limits.h>
#include <math.h>
#include "uart2.h"
#include "wdict12.h"
#include "linklist.h"

// create a uart object
uart uart_8250;

// create a dictionary object
dict dict12;

// create an int linklist object
linklist<int> bstack;

// make an srecord object
srecord srec12;
```

Note that because the linked list class is a template class, the file `linklist.h` contains all the linked list member functions and cannot be precompiled.

17.1.1 The WHYP Configuration File

The configuration file, `WHYP12.CFG`, must be in the directory containing the program `WHYP12.EXE`. The file `WHYP12A4.CFG` shown in Figure 17–1 is the configuration file to use with the Motorola HC12A4EVB evaluation board. The contents of this file must be copied to the file `WHYP12.CFG` when using this board. To use the Axiom CME12B32 development board, you must copy the contents of the file `WB32RAM1.CFG` to the file `WHYP12.CFG`. By modifying this configuration file you can use WHYP12 with any 68HC12 computer system (see Appendix C for several examples).

The subdirectory containing `WHYP12.EXE` must also contain a header file, such as `WHYP12.HED`, that contains the names and addresses of all the WHYP words. The name of this header file is the first entry in the file `WHYP12.CFG` as shown in Figure 17–1.

```
WHYP12.HED
tdp        5000
vdp        800
TORG       4000
HEDBASE  4000
RAMBASE  0900
INCHAR   32
OUTPUT   3B
TPUSH    44
TPOP     4D
INWDY    58
INWDX    61
STOREW   6A
TBLKST   75
SNDSUB   8B2
rts_code     31
EESTART  1000
EESTOP   1FFF
last     be
set_flags   -1
```

Figure 17–1   The Configuration File
WHYP12A4.CFG

The second and third lines in Figure 17–1 contain the default values of the target dictionary pointer, *tdp*, and the variable dictionary pointer, *vdp*. Although you can change these values using function keys F9 and F8, respectively, you can also modify the default values by editing the file WHYP12.CFG. For example, if you wanted new WHYP words to be compiled into the EEPROM at address $1000, you would change the second line in Figure 17–1 to

```
tdp     1000
```

The value of *TORG* in Figure 17–1 is the starting address of the WHYP kernel. This value should be the same as *WHYPBASE* defined by the *EQU* statement at the beginning of the file WHYP12.ASM, given in Appendix D. The value of *HEDBASE* in Figure 17–1 should initially be the same as *TORG*. This is the value added to the addresses in the file WHYP12.HED to give the addresses of each WHYP word. If you want to move all WHYP words to addresses that are different from those in which they were loaded (for example, to an EPROM or flash memory), you can use the WHYP words *load>tseg*, *save.tseg*, and *save.headers*. The word *load>tseg* loads your WHYP file into the C++ *tseg* character array, rather than downloading the code to the 68HC12. The word *save.tseg* will save this character array as an S-record file. The word *save.headers* will create a new *.HED* file. However, this new *.HED* file will contain absolute addresses for all WHYP words, rather that the relative addresses given in *WHYP12.HED* (see, for example, Figure 4–36). You must not only change the name of the *.HED* file in the first line in the configuration file in Figure 17–1, but you must also change the value of *HEDBASE* to 0000. The value of *RAMBASE* in Figure 17–1 is the starting address of a RAM block used by the WHYP kernel. This value should be the same as *RAMBASE* defined by the *EQU* statement at the beginning of the file WHYP12.ASM, given in Appendix D.

The next ten lines in Figure 17–1 are the offset addresses within the kernel of various kernel subroutines. The values of *EESTART* and *EESTOP* are the beginning and ending addresses of the internal EEPROM memory. These should be the same as the corresponding values at the beginning of the file WHYP12.ASM, given in Appendix D. The address of *last* is its offset address (relative to *RAMBASE*) within the 68HC12 RAM. If the value of *set_flags* in Figure 17–1 is −1 (the normal case), then WHYP will assume that all of the WHYP words are already in the target system, as they will be if you have downloaded the file WHYP12.S19 to RAM or stored this code in EPROM or flash memory. If the value of *set_flags* is 0, then all the words are maintained in the PC and downloaded to the target system only as needed.

The parts of the C++ host program used to read the .CFG file are shown in Listing 17–2.

Listing 17–2   Reading the .CFG File—from File whyp12.cpp

```
//         Global variables to read in from .CFG file
//         Target subroutine offset addresses
char       NAME_FILE[14];
int        TORG;
int        HEDBASE;
int        RAMBASE;
int        INCHAR;
int        OUTPUT;
int        TPUSH;
int        TPOP;
int        INWDY;
int        INWDX;
int        STOREW;
int        TBLKST;
int        SNDSUB;

unsigned int        tdp;              // target dictionary pointer
unsigned int        vdp;              // variable dictionary pointer
int                 last;             // address of last
int                 rts_code;         // address of RTS in WKE9.S19
bool                set_flags;        // set flags true for PROM
unsigned int        EESTART;          // EEPROM addresses
unsigned int        EESTOP;

------------------

//         read cfg file
void       read_cfg_file(FILE* cfgfile)
           {
       int addr;
       char int_name[16];
       fscanf(cfgfile,"%s", NAME_FILE);
       cout << "Using " << NAME_FILE;
       while(fscanf(cfgfile,"%s%x", int_name, &addr) != EOF)
           set_int(int_name, addr);
       }
//         set integer values from .cfg file
void       set_int(char* name, int val)
```

(continued)

Listing 17–2 *(continued)*

```
{
if(strcmp(name,"TORG") == 0)
   TORG = val;
else if(strcmp(name,"HEDBASE") == 0)
   HEDBASE = val;
else if(strcmp(name,"RAMBASE") == 0)
   RAMBASE = val;
else if(strcmp(name,"INCHAR") == 0)
   INCHAR = val;
else if(strcmp(name,"OUTPUT") == 0)
   OUTPUT = val;
else if(strcmp(name,"TPUSH") == 0)
   TPUSH = val;
else if(strcmp(name,"TPOP") == 0)
   TPOP = val;
else if(strcmp(name,"INWDY") == 0)
   INWDY = val;
else if(strcmp(name,"INWDX") == 0)
   INWDX = val;
else if(strcmp(name,"STOREW") == 0)
   STOREW = val;
else if(strcmp(name,"TBLKST") == 0)
   TBLKST = val;
else if(strcmp(name,"SNDSUB") == 0)
   SNDSUB = TORG+val;
else if(strcmp(name,"EESTART") == 0)
   EESTART = val;
else if(strcmp(name,"EESTOP") == 0)
   EESTOP = val;
else if(strcmp(name,"tdp") == 0)
   tdp = val;
else if(strcmp(name,"vdp") == 0)
   vdp = val;
else if(strcmp(name,"last") == 0)
   last = RAMBASE+val;
else if(strcmp(name,"rts_code") == 0)
   rts_code = TORG+val;
else if(strcmp(name,"set_flags") == 0)
   set_flags = val;
else
   cout << endl << "Error in .CFG file";
}
```

17.2 THE IMMEDIATE DICTIONARY

The dictionary described by the class *dict* in Section 16.5 contains the WHYP words that get compiled as subroutine jumps in a colon definition. In addition to these words there are a number of *immediate* WHYP words which are executed immediately when they occur within a colon definition. These include, for example, all of the branching words such as *IF* and *UNTIL*. These immediate words are stored in an immediate dictionary in the form of an array of character strings as shown in Listing 17–3.

Listing 17–3   The Immediate Dictionary—from File `whyp12.cpp`

```
// The Immediate Dictionary
const    int nwords = 47;
char*    imed_dict[nwords] = {
               "FOR",              // 0 forr()
               "NEXT",             // 1 next()
               "IF",               // 2 iff()
               "ELSE",             // 3 elsee()
               "THEN",             // 4 thenn()
               "BEGIN",            // 5 begin()
               "AGAIN",            // 6 again()
               "UNTIL",            // 7 until()
               "WHILE",            // 8 whilee()
               "REPEAT",           // 9 repeat()
               "HEX",              // 10 hex()
               "DECIMAL",          // 11 decimal()
               ":",                // 12 colon()
               ";",                // 13 semis()
               "CONSTANT",         // 14 constant()
               "VARIABLE",         // 15 variable()
               "\\",               // 16 backslash()
               "(",                // 17 paren()
               "LOAD",             // 18 load()
               "CREATE",           // 19 create()
               "DOES>",            // 20 does()
               "'",                // 21 tick()
               "[",                // 22 left bracket
               "]",                // 23 right bracket
               "LITERAL",          // 24 literal()
               ".\"",              // 25 dot_quote()
               "SEI",              // 26 sei()
               "CLI",              // 27 cli()
               "INT:",             // 28 int_colon()
               "RTI;",             // 29 rti_semis()
               "BYE",              // 30 bye
               "\n",               // 31 newline  (in files)
               "DO",               // 32 doo()
               "LOOP",             // 33 loop()
               "SAVE.TSEG",        // 34 save_tseg()
               "SAVE.HEADERS",     // 35 save_headers()
               "LOAD>TSEG",        // 36 load_tseg()
               ",",                // 37 comma()
               "C,",               // 38 ccomma()
               "LOAD.S19.FILE",    // 39 load_s19_file()
               "RECURSE",          // 40 recurse()
               "ASCII",            // 41 ascii()
               "CONTROL",          // 42 control()
               "SEE",              // 43 see()
               "SHOW",             // 44 show()
               "STEP",             // 45 step()
               "\""                // 46 quote()
          };
```

(continued)

Listing 17–3 (*continued*)

```
-----------------


//      Check to see if a word is in the immediate dictionary
bool in_imed_dict(char* here, int& ix)
    {
    int i;
    bool found = false;
    for(i = 0; i < nwords; i++)
        {
        if(stricmp(here, imed_dict[i]) == 0)
            {
            found = true;
            ix = i;
            break;
            }
        }
    return found;
    }


---------------


//      Process an immediate word
void    do_imed_word(int ix)
    {
    switch(ix)
        {
        case 0:                 // FOR
            forr();
            break;
        case 1:                 // NEXT
            next();
            break;
        case 2:                 // IF
            iff();
            break;
        case 3:                 // ELSE
            elsee();
            break;
        case 4:                 // THEN
            thenn();
            break;
        case 5:                 // BEGIN
            begin();
            break;
        case 6:                 // AGAIN
            again();
            break;
        case 7:                 // UNTIL
            until();
            break;
```

Listing 17–3 (*continued*)

```
        case 8:                         // WHILE
            whilee();
            break;
        case 9:                         // REPEAT
            repeat();
            break;
        case 10:                        // HEX
            hex();
            break;
        case 11:                        // DECIMAL
            decimal();
            break;
        case 12:                        // :
            colon();
            break;
        case 13:                        // ;
            semis();
            break;
        case 14:                        // CONSTANT
            constant();
            break;
        case 15:                        // VARIABLE
            variable();
            break;
        case 16:                        // \
            backslash();
            break;
        case 17:                        // (
            paren();
            break;
        case 18:                        // LOAD
            load();
            break;
        case 19:                        // CREATE
            create();
            break;
        case 20:                        // DOES>
            does();
            break;
        case 21:                        // ' tick
            tick();
            break;
        case 22:                        // [ left bracket
            compile = false;
            break;
        case 23:                        // ] right bracket
            compile = true;
            break;
        case 24:                        // LITERAL
            literal();
            break;
```

(*continued*)

Listing 17–3 *(continued)*

```
        case 25:              // ."
           dot_quote();
           break;
        case 26:              // SEI
           sei();
           break;
        case 27:              // CLI
           cli();
           break;
        case 28:              // INT:
           int_colon();
           break;
        case 29:              // RTI;
           rti_semis();
           break;
        case 30:              // BYE
           done = true;
           break;
        case 31:              // \n 0x0a
           cout << endl;
           break;
        case 32:              // DO
           doo();
           break;
        case 33:              // LOOP
           loop();
           break;
        case 34:              // SAVE.TSEG
           dict12.save_tseg();
           break;
        case 35:              // SAVE.HEADERS
           dict12.save_headers();
           break;
        case 36:              // LOAD>TSEG
           load_tseg();
           break;
        case 37:              // ,
           comma();
           break;
        case 38:              // C,
           ccomma();
           break;
        case 39:              // LOAD.S19.FILE
           load_s19_file();
           break;
        case 40:              // RECURSE
           recurse();
           break;
        case 41:              // ASCII
           ascii();
           break;
```

Listing 17–3   (continued)

```
        case 42:                    // CONTROL
            control();
            break;
        case 43:                    // SEE
            see();
            break;
        case 44:                    // SHOW
            show();
            break;
        case 45:                    // STEP
            step();
            break;
        case 46:                    // "
            quote();
            break;
        }
    }
```

The immediate dictionary can be searched for the character string *here* using the function *bool in_immed_dict(char* her, int& ix)*, shown in Listing 17–3. This function will be *true* if the character string is found in the dictionary at the index *ix*. This index is then used in the switch statement shown in Listing 17–3 to execute the appropriate function.

17.3   THE WHYP MAIN PROGRAM

The WHYP main program is shown in Listing 17–4. It first reads the configuration (.CFG) file as described in Section 17.1.1. It then reads the header (.HED) file and stores all the words in the dictionary using the function *dict12.build_dict(namefile)*, as described in Section 16.5. It then checks to see if the target board is connected to COM1 or COM2 by calling the function *check_COM_ports()* that will be described in Section 17.3.1.

The *while(!done)* loop, shown in Listing 17–4, is the WHYP outer interpreter. This is the loop that is being executed as you sit at the keyboard. It displays the *ok* prompt and then waits for you to enter a line using the function *queryq()* to be described in Section 17.3.2. After a line has been entered into the buffer *kbuf* (terminated by pressing the *<enter>* key), each word is parsed using the C++ function *strtok(kbuf, tokensep)* for the first word and *strtok(NULL, tokensep)* for the rest of the words in the buffer. In this case the character string *tokensep* is defined as

```
char  tokensep[] = " \t\n";
```

which means that each word will be parsed on a blank, tab, or newline character.

Each parsed word is stored in the string *here* and is then processed using the function *doword(here)* that will be described in Section 17.3.3.

Listing 17–4   The WHYP Main Program—from File `whyp12.cpp`

```cpp
// The WHYP main program
void    main()
    {
    FILE * cfgfile;
    // open files for reading
    if((cfgfile = fopen("WHYP12.CFG", "r")) == NULL)
        {
        cout << "problem opening .CFG file\n";
        exit(1);
        }
    // read .cfg file
    read_cfg_file(cfgfile);
    // close file
    fclose(cfgfile);

    FILE * namefile;
    // open files for reading
    if((namefile = fopen(NAME_FILE, "r")) == NULL)
        {
        cout << "problem opening .HED file\n";
        exit(1);
        }
    // build dictionary
    dict12.set_hed_base_addr(HEDBASE);
    dict12.build_dict(namefile);
    if(set_flags)
        dict12.set_flags();                 // set all flags true
    // close files
    fclose(namefile);
    here = new char[81];
    latest = new char[81];
    check_COM_ports();
    cout << endl << "68HC12 WHYP12 - Version 4.6";
    cout << endl << "Press <Esc> or type BYE to exit" << endl;
    // The outer interpreter
    while(!done)
        {
        skip = false;                       // don't skip
        to_in = 0;                          // reset pointer
        prompt();                           // display 'ok'
        queryq();                           // input a line
        if(done)                            // esc key quits
            break;
        if(skip)                            // function keys skip
            continue;
        here = strtok(kbuf, tokensep);      // parse 1st word
            while(here != NULL)             // while another word
            {
            doword(here);                   // process it
            here = strtok(NULL, tokensep);  // parse next word
            }
        }
    }
```

17.3.1   Checking the COM Port

The function *void check_COM_ports()*, shown in Listing 17–5, is called in the main program shown in Listing 17–4. It checks to see which COM port is connected to the target board by first sending the *rts_code* out COM1. The *rts_code* is the address of an *RTS* (return from subroutine) instruction in the WHYP kernel running on the target board. The value of *rts_code* was read in from the .CFG file (see Listing 17–2).

Listing 17–5   Checking the COM Port—from File `whyp12.cpp`

```
// Check for COM1 or COM2
void   check_COM_ports()
    {
    char recv_val;
    long oldcount, newcount;
    int ticks = 2;                          // > 55 ms delay
    bool ack = false;
    send_int(rts_code);                     // RTS
    oldcount = biostime(0,0L);
    newcount = oldcount;
    while(!ack && (newcount - oldcount) < ticks)
        {
        if(uart_8250.check_recv(recv_val))
            do_recv(recv_val, ack);
        newcount = biostime(0,0L);
        }
    if(ack)
        cout << endl << "Communicating with COM1";
    else
        {
        uart_8250.change_com(1);            // try COM2
        send_int(rts_code);                 // RTS
        oldcount = biostime(0,0L);
        newcount = oldcount;
        while(!ack && (newcount - oldcount) < ticks)
            {
            if(uart_8250.check_recv(recv_val))
              do_recv(recv_val, ack);
            newcount = biostime(0,0L);
            }
        if(ack)
            cout << endl << "Communicating with COM2" << endl;
        else
            {
            cout << endl << "Target board not responding" << endl;
            uart_8250.change_com(0);        // back to COM1
            }
        }
    }
```

If COM1 is connected to the target board, then the 68HC12 will return the acknowledge byte, $06 (see the WHYP12.ASM listing in Appendix D). This will set the *ack* flag to true (see Section 17.4) and the message "Communicating with COM1" will be displayed on the screen. If no acknowledge byte has been received after a delay of about 55 ms (measured using BIOS timer ticks), then the same procedure is followed for COM2.

17.3.2 Getting Input from the Keyboard

The function *void queryq()*, shown in Listing 17–6, is called in the main program, shown in Listing 17–4. It receives individual keystrokes using the function *getkeyq()* and then processes each keystroke by calling the function *dokey (keyval, ix, exit_key)*.

Listing 17–6   Getting Input from the Keyboard—from File `whyp12.cpp`

```
// Wait for key press and return generalized ASCII code
// Check for characters in receive queue
int    getkeyq()
    {
    int keyval, ascii_code, scan_code;
    char recv_val;
    bool ack = false;
    while(!ack)
        {
        if(bioskey(1))
            {
            keyval = bioskey(0);              // scan code in high byte
            scan_code = keyval >> 8;
            ascii_code = keyval & 0xff;       // ascii code in low byte
            if(ascii_code == 0)
                return scan_code | 0x80;      // Generalized ASCII code
            else
                return ascii_code;
            }
        if(uart_8250.check_recv(recv_val))
            do_recv(recv_val, ack);
        }
    return 0;
    }


//     Get a line of input
void   queryq()
    {
    int keyval;
    int ix = 0;
    bool exit_key = false;
    do
```

Listing 17–6 *(continued)*

```
        {
        keyval = getkeyq();
        dokey(keyval, ix, exit_key);
        }
    while(!exit_key);
    }
//      Process key in queryq
void    dokey(int keyval, int& ix, bool& exit_key)
    {
    switch(keyval)
        {
        char keybyte;
        char dp_string[10];
        char* stop_at;
        case 0x1b:                              // esc key
           exit_key = true;
           done = true;
           break;
        case 8:                                 // backspace
           backspace(ix);
           break;
        case 13:                                // enter key
           exit_key = true;
           kbuf[ix++] = 0;
           span = ix;
           cout << " ";
           break;
        case 0xc1:                              // F7 Host terminal
           cout << endl << "Terminal host..." << endl;
           cout << "(Press F5 to return to WHYP)" << endl << endl;
           host();
           break;
        case 0xc2:                              // F8
           cout << setiosflags(ios::hex);
           cout << "Current value of VARIABLE vdp is " << vdp;
           cout << endl << "Enter a new hex value for vdp ("
                     << vdp << "): ";
           gets(dp_string);
           if(strlen(dp_string) > 0)
             vdp = strtoul(dp_string, &stop_at, 16);
           cout << "New value is " << vdp << endl;
           cout << setiosflags(ios::dec);
           break;
        case 0xc3:                              // F9
           cout << setiosflags(ios::hex);
           cout << "Current value of target dp is " << tdp;
           cout << endl << "Enter a new hex value for tdp ("
                     << tdp << "): ";
           gets(dp_string);
           if(strlen(dp_string) > 0)
```

(continued)

Listing 17–6 *(continued)*

```
            tdp = strtoul(dp_string, &stop_at, 16);
          cout << "Value of tdp is " << tdp << endl;
          cout << setiosflags(ios::dec);
          break;
      case 0xc4:                           // F10
          check_COM_ports();               // check connection to target
          break;
      default:
          {
          if(ix > 79)
            cout << "\a";                  // beep
          else
            {
            keybyte = keyval;
            kbuf[ix++] = keybyte;
            cout << keybyte;
            }
          }
      }
   }


//      Handle backspace key
void    backspace(int& ix)
   {
   if(ix == 0)                             // if 1st char
      cout << "\a";                        //      beep
   else
      {
      kbuf[--ix] = ' ';                    // back up & insert blank
      cout << "\b \b";                     // backspace
      }
   }
```

The function *int getkeyq()*, shown in Listing 17–6, will wait for a key to be pressed and will return a generalized ASCII code. For most keys this will be their normal ASCII code. However, for special keys, including the function keys and cursor keys, whose ASCII code is zero, a generalized ASCII code is formed by ORing the key scan code with $80. If while you are waiting to press a key a character is received in the serial port, it will be processed using the function *do_recv(recv_val, ack)*, as will be described in Section 17.4.

The function *void dokey (int keyval, int& ix, bool& exit_key)*, shown in Listing 17–6, will process each keystroke using a *switch* statement. The *esc* key will set the *exit_key* flag to true and thus terminate the function *queryq()*. The *exit_key* flag is also set by pressing the *<enter>* key. Pressing the backspace key will cause a backspace to be implemented using the function *backspace(ix)*. The value of *ix* is the index into the buffer *kbuf* where all nonspecial key values are stored, as shown in the default phrase of the *switch* statement.

Note that four function keys are implemented in *dokey*. Function key F7 switches to the host terminal mode by calling the function *host()* which will be described in Section 17.4.1. Function keys F8 and F9 allow you to change the values of the variable dictionary pointer, *vdp*, and the target dictionary pointer, *tdp*, respectively. Function key F10 checks the COM ports to make sure you're still connected to the target system.

17.3.3   Processing an Input Word

The function *void doword(char* here)*, shown in Listing 17–7, is called in the main program, shown in Listing 17–4. This word implements the following algorithm for processing the character string *here*.

```
if the word here is in the dict12 dictionary         (dict12.is_in_dict)
then    if compiling in a colon definition
        then compile the word                        (dict12.compile)
        else execute the word                        (send.int)
else    if the word is in the immediate dictionary   (in_immed_dict)
        then process the word                        (do_imme_word)
        else  if it is a valid single or double number  (number)
              then push the number on the data stack  (single_number,
                                                        double_number)

              else print <--What? error message
```

The function *dict12.is_in_dict(here, wordhead, dwload, sub_addr, num_bytes)* is a Boolean function given in Listing 16–9. It will search for the word *here* in the dictionary and return a value of true if it finds it. It will also return values for *wordhead* (a pointer to the header of *here*), *dwload* (a flag that is true if the subroutine has already been downloaded to the target system), *sub_addr* (the address of the subroutine, *here*), and *num_bytes* (the number of bytes in the subroutine *here*).

Listing 17–7   Processing an Input Word—from File `whyp12.cpp`

```
//      Process a word from the input line
void    doword(char* here)
        {
        bool single;
        int ix, dpl;
        long value;
        what_flag = false;
        if(dict12.is_in_dict(here, wordhead, dwload,
                        sub_addr, num_bytes))            // if in dict
            if(compile)                                  //    if compiling
                dict12.compile(sub_address(wordhead, dwload,
                        sub_addr, num_bytes));           //       compile
            else
                {                                        //    else
                send_int(sub_address(wordhead, dwload,
                        sub_addr, num_bytes));           //       execute sub
                wait6();                                 //       wait for ack
                }
```

(continued)

Listing 17–7   (continued)

```
        else                                         // else if immed wod
            if(in_imed_dict(here, ix))
                do_imed_word(ix);                    //      process it
            else
                {
                    if(number(here, value, single, dpl))    //      else if number
                        if(single)
                            single_number(int(value));
                        else                          //  push on data stack
                            double_number(value);
                    else
                        {
                        cout << endl << here << " <-What? " << endl;  // else error
                        what_flag = true;
                        }
                }
        }

//      Find subroutine address
int     sub_address(header* wordhead, bool dwload,
                int sub_addr, int num_bytes)
    {
    int newaddr, taddr;
    newaddr = sub_addr;
    if(!dwload && !to_tseg)                     // if word not downloaded & !>tseg
        {                                       //      download it
        taddr = tdp;
        dict12.get_string(num_bytes, sub_addr, strbuf);
        tblock_store(num_bytes, strbuf, taddr);
        dict12.set_address(wordhead, taddr);
        tdp += num_bytes;                       // update tdp
        newaddr = taddr;
        }
    return newaddr;
    }

//     Check to see if a word is a valid number
bool number(char* here, long& value, bool& single, int& dpl)
    {
    char* stop_at;
    long val;
    value = strtol(here, &stop_at, base);
    if(*stop_at == NULL)
        {
        val = value & 0xffff0000;
        if(val == 0 || val == 0xffff0000)
            single = true;
        else
            single = false;
        dpl = 0;
        return true;
        }
    else
```

Listing 17–7 (*continued*)

```
        if(*stop_at == 0x2e)        // decimal point
            {
            single = false;
            return true;
            }
        else
            return false;
    }

//       Handle a single number
void     single_number(int value)
    {
    char str[] = "(LIT)";                                 // compile (LIT)
    if(dict12.is_in_dict(str, wordhead, dwload,
                     sub_addr, num_bytes))                // if in dict
        if(compile
            {                                             // if compiling
            dict12.compile(sub_address(wordhead, dwload,
                     sub_addr, num_bytes));               //    compile
            dict12.tcomma(value);                         // value T,
            }
        else
            tpush(value);                                 // push value on stack
    else
        cout << endl << "Can't find (LIT) in dictionary" << endl;
    }

void     double_number(long value)
    {
    unsigned int hi_word, lo_word;
    char str[] = "(DLIT)";                 .             // compile (DLIT)
    if(dict12.is_in_dict(str, wordhead, dwload,
                     sub_addr, num_bytes))                // if in hc11 dict
        if(compile)
            {                                             // if compiling
            dict12.compile(sub_address(wordhead, dwload,
                     sub_addr, num_bytes));               //   compile
            hi_word = value >> 16;
            lo_word = value & 0xffff;
            dict12.tcomma(hi_word);                       // value T,
            dict12.tcomma(lo_word);                       // value T,
            }
        else
            tpush2(value);                                // push value on stack
    else
        cout << endl << "Can't find (DLIT) in dictionary" << endl;
            }
```

The function *int sub_address(header* wordhead, bool dwload, int sub_addr, int num_bytes)*, given in Listing 17–7, is used to find the target subroutine address of a word in the dictionary with a header pointed to by *wordhead*. If the word is already on the target board (*dwload* = true), then the subroutine address is just the value of *sub_addr* which was already in the dictionary. On the other hand, if the word is not yet in the target system (*dwload* = false), then the function *sub_address* will download the word to the target system and return its new address.

17.4 COMMUNICATING WITH THE TARGET BOARD

All communication with the target board is done over the serial line using the *uart* class described in Section 16.2. When a character is received from the target board, an interrupt routine puts it in a queue of the type described in Section 16.1. The function *int getq()*, shown in Listing 17–8, will get a byte from this receiver queue. If no character is in the queue, it will wait for one to arrive. However, you can exit this function by pressing the *esc* key. The function *int getqword()*, shown in Listing 17–8, will get two bytes from the queue (high byte first) and form them into a 16-bit word.

Listing 17–8   Communicating with the Target Board—File `whyp12.cpp`

```
//        Pop value from target data stack
int       tpop()
          {
          int val;
          val = TORG + TPOP;
          send_int(val);                            // send TPOP addr
          val = getqword();                         // get word from target
          wait6();                        // wait for ack
          return val;
          }
//        Push value on target data stack
void      tpush(int value)
          {
          int val;
          val = TORG + TPUSH;
          send_int(val);                  // send TPUSH addr
          send_int(value);                // send value
          wait6();                        // wait for ack
          }
//        Push double number on target data stack
void      tpush2(long value)
          {
          unsigned int hi_word, lo_word;
          hi_word = value >> 16;
          lo_word = value & 0xffff;
          tpush(lo_word);
          tpush(hi_word);
          }
//        Send 16-bit integer to target
void      send_int(int val)
          {
          unsigned char hi_byte, lo_byte;
          hi_byte = val >> 8;
          lo_byte = val & 0xff;
```

Listing 17–8   (*continued*)

```
        uart_8250.transmit_byte(lo_byte);
        uart_8250.transmit_byte(hi_byte);
        }
//      Store block of bytes in target
void    tblock_store(int nbytes, char* buf, int taddr)
        {
        unsigned int taddru;
        int val, i;
        val = TORG + TBLKST;
        taddru = taddr;
        send_int(val);                              // send TBLKST addr
        send_int(nbytes);                           // send count
        send_int(taddr);                            // send target address
        for(i = 0; i < nbytes; i++)
            {
            uart_8250.transmit_byte(buf[i]);        // sent bytes
            if(taddru >= EESTART && taddru <= EESTOP)
                delay(60);
            }
        wait6();                                    // wait for ack
        }

//      Get word from queue
int     getqword()
        {
        int hi_byte;
        hi_byte = getq() << 8;        // get high byte
        return hi_byte | getq();      // get low byte
        }

//      Get byte from queue
int     getq()
        {
        int keyval, ascii_code, val;
        char recv_val;
        while(!uart_8250.check_recv(recv_val))
            {
            if(bioskey(1))
                {
                keyval = bioskey(0);
                ascii_code = keyval & 0xff;
                if(ascii_code == 0x1b)              // if esc key
                    break;                          //    quit
                }
            }
        val = recv_val & 0xff;
        return val;
        }

//      Wait for acknowledge (6) from target
void    wait6()
        {
        int val;
        do
            val = getkeyq();
        while(val != 0 && val != 0x1b);
        }
```

The function *void send_int(int val)*, shown in Listing 17–8, will send a 16-bit integer (low byte first) to the target system. Recall that the kernel running in the target system is waiting to receive a 16-bit address (low byte first) and then executes the subroutine at that address. Therefore, to execute a subroutine on the target board you just have to send the subroutine address using the function *send_int(addr)*. For example, the function *int tpop()*, shown in Listing 17–8, will send the address of the kernel subroutine *TPOP* which will pop the top of the data stack and send the result to the PC. The function *tpop* then gets this value by calling *getqword()*.

In a similar way the function *void tpush(int value)*, shown in Listing 17–8, will push the 16-bit value on the target data stack by first sending the address of the kernel subroutine, *TPUSH*, followed by the 16-bit word *value*. The function *tpush2(long value)* will push a 32-bit double number onto the target data stack.

The function *void tblock_store(int nbytes, char* buf, int taddr)*, shown in Listing 17–8, will store a block of *nbytes* bytes from the character array, *buf*, in the target memory starting at address *taddr*. It does this by first sending the address of the kernel subroutine, *TBLKST*, followed by the number of bytes, followed by the target address, followed the string of bytes. The subroutine *TBLKST* that is executed on the target system then takes care of reading the bytes and storing them into the memory.

The function *void wait6()*, shown in Listing 17–8, will wait for the acknowledge byte ($06) to be sent from the target system. Note that it does this by waiting for the value returned by *getkeyq()* in Listing 17–6 to be zero. This happens when the *ack* flag becomes true, which it does when a $06 is received from the target board as will be shown in Listing 17–12 in Section 17.6.

17.4.1 The Terminal Host Function

As shown in Listing 17–6, pressing function key F7 will call the function *host()*, shown in Listing 17–9. This function implements a full-duplex terminal program that just alternates between checking the keyboard and checking the receive serial line. If a key is pressed, its ASCII code is sent out the serial line. If a character is received in the serial line, it is displayed on the screen. The function is exited by pressing function key F5.

Listing 17–9   The Terminal Host Function—File `whyp12.cpp`

```
//  Terminal host program entered with F7
void    host()
     {
     int keyval, ascii_code, scan_code;
     char recv_val;
     unsigned char out_byte;
     bool F5key = false;
     while(!F5key)
```

Listing 17–9   (continued)

```
        {
    if(bioskey(1))
        {
        keyval = bioskey(0);
        scan_code = keyval >> 8;
        ascii_code = keyval & 0xff;
        if(ascii_code == 0)
            ascii_code = scan_code | 0x80;
        if(ascii_code == 0xbf)      // F5 key
            F5key = true;
        else
            {
            out_byte = ascii_code;
            uart_8250.transmit_byte(out_byte);
            }
        }
    if(uart_8250.check_recv(recv_val))
        {
        if(recv_val == 0x0d)        // CR
            cout << endl;
        if(recv_val >= 0x20)
            cout << recv_val;
        }
    }
    cout << endl << "Returning to WHYP" << endl;
    }
```

17.5   COMPILER WORDS

The immediate dictionary was described in Section 17.2 where we saw that the *switch* statement, shown in Listing 17–3, called a different function for each immediate word. In this section we will show a couple of examples of how these immediate, or compiler, words do their job. To see how the other compiler words work, consult the complete C++ source code in the file WHYP12.CPP.

17.5.1   Branching Words

As an example of how branching words get compiled, consider the functions *begin()*, *again()*, and *until()*, shown in Listing 17–10, which get called when the words *BEGIN*, *AGAIN*, and *UNTIL* are encountered in a colon definition.

As a colon definition is being compiled, an image of the final 68HC12 code is built up in the character array *tseg*. The dictionary pointer within this array is called *hdp*. The word *BEGIN* just pushes this value of *hdp* on a local stack so that its

Listing 17–10 Example of Compiling Branching Words—File `whyp12.cpp`

```
//        BEGIN  ( -- )
void      begin()
          {
          bstack.push(dict12.get_hdp());          // push hdp
          }
//        AGAIN  ( -- )
void      again()
          {
          int displ, xhere1;
          if(compile)
              {                                   // if compiling
              // compile LBRA inline
              dict12.add_string(2, LBRA);          // complile LBRA
              xhere1 = bstack.pop();
              displ = xhere1 - dict12.get_hdp() - 2;
              dict12.tcomma(displ);                // complile displ
              }
          else
              cout << endl << "AGAIN must be in colon definition" << endl;
          }
void      until()
          {
          int displ, xhere1;
          if(compile)
              {                                   // if compiling
              // compile LDD 2,X+ LBEQ inline
              dict12.add_string(4, LBEQ);
              xhere1 = bstack.pop();
              displ = xhere1 - dict12.get_hdp() -2;
              dict12.tcomma(displ);                // complile displ
              }
          else
              cout << endl << "UNTIL must be in colon definition" << endl;
          }
```

address can be remembered when a matching word such as *AGAIN* or *UNTIL* is encountered. The local stack is implemented using the *linklist* class described in Section 16.4.

Recall from Figure 5–25 that the *AGAIN* word will compile a *LBRA* instruction followed by the two's complement displacement. Note how the function *again()* does this in Listing 17–10. The character string, *LBRA*, is defined as

```
char      LBRA[] = "\x18\x20";          // LBRA -- --
```

and contains the opcode for the *LBRA* instruction. This is compiled in-line using the function *dict12.add_string(2, LBRA)*. The displacement is computed by subtracting the current value of *hdp* from the value pushed on the local stack by *BEGIN* minus 2. This displacement is then compiled in-line using the function *dict12.tcomma(displ)*.

An example of a compiled *BEGIN . . . UNTIL* loop was given in Figure 5–28. Recall that *UNTIL* gets compiled as the statement *LDD 2,X+* (which pops the flag from the data stack) followed by an *LBEQ* instruction. This will cause the branch to occur if the flag is false. Note how the function *until()* does this in Listing 17–10. It is similar to the function *again()* except that the string compiled is now the string *LBEQ* given by

```
char    LBEQ[] = "\xec\x31\x18\x27";          // LDD 2,X+ LBEQ -- --
```

Other branching words are compiled in a similar fashion. Refer to the listing in the file WHYP12.CPP for more details.

17.5.2 Compiling Colon Definitions

As another example of how compiler words work, consider the functions *colon()* and *semis()*, shown in Listing 17–11, that get executed when a colon (:) and semi-colon (;) are encountered in the input stream.

Listing 17–11   Compiling Colon Definitions—File whyp12.cpp

```
//       Colon definition
void     colon()
         {
         int subaddr;
         compile = true;
         // get next word
         here = strtok(NULL, tokensep);
         if(to_tseg)
             subaddr = dict12.get_hdp() + base_addr;
         else
             subaddr = dict12.get_hdp();
         this_addr = subaddr;             // remember for recurse
         strcpy(latest, here);            // remember name
         // make a header
         dict12.add_word(here, subaddr);
         }

//       Semi-colon
void     semis()
         {
         compile = false;
         dict12.tccomma(0x3d);            // compile RTS
         dict12.fix_size();
         download_word();                 // download word to HC11
         }

//       download word at end of semis
void     download_word()
         {
         int word_addr;
         if(dict12.is_in_dict(latest, wordhead, dwload,
                         sub_addr, num_bytes))    // if in dict
```

(continued)

Listing 17–11   (*continued*)

```
          word_addr = sub_address(wordhead, dwload,
                      sub_addr, num_bytes);         //      download
    }

//      RECURSE
void    recurse()
    {
    int displ;
    int opcode;
    opcode = 0x07;                                  // BSR opcode
    dict12.tccomma(opcode);                         // compile BSR
    displ = this_addr - dict12.get_hdp() - 1;
    dict12.tccomma(displ);                          // compile displacement
    }
```

The function *colon()* gets the next word in the input stream and adds it to the dictionary using the function *dict12.add_word(here, subaddr)*. The variable *subaddr* contains the local address of the subroutine within the *tseg* character array that is being used to create an image of the final 68HC12 code to be downloaded into the target system. This address is stored in the global variable, *this_addr*, that is used by the function *recurse()*, shown in Listing 17–11, to compute the displacement for the *BSR* instruction that gets compiled by the word *RECURSE* (see Figure 5–43).

The function *semis()*, shown in Listing 17–11, completes the colon definition by compiling the opcode for the *RTS* instruction in-line, computing the number of bytes in the subroutine by calling the function *dict12.fix_size()*, and then downloading all of the code for the new colon definition to the target board using the function *download_word()* shown in Listing 17–11.

17.6 PROCESSING CHARACTERS RECEIVED FROM THE TARGET

We saw in Listing 17–6 that the function *getkeyq()* called the function *do_recv(recv_val, ack)* if a character had been received on the serial line. This function consists of a large *switch* statement as shown in Listing 17–12. There are a number of WHYP words that are resident on the target system that need to either send or receive data to or from the PC when the word is executed. To do this, it sends a kind of opcode to the PC to tell the PC what it is to do. These opcodes are the values of *recv_val* that show up in the switch statement, shown in Listing 17–12.

For example, when the word "dot" (.) is executed on the 68HC12, it sends the opcode 1 plus the 16-bit value to be displayed on the screen. The C++ program then executes the code shown under case 1: in Listing 17–12 which prints the value of the 16-bit integer on the screen followed by a blank space.

As another example, consider the words *HERE* and *VHERE* which put the values of *tdp* and *vdp* on the data stack. However, the current values of *tdp* and *vdp* are maintained in the C++ program on the PC. But the data stack is on the 68HC12! Therefore, when the words *HERE* and *VHERE* are executed, the 68HC12

Listing 17–12 Processing Received Characters—File `whyp12.cpp`

```cpp
//      ***********************************************************
//      Process receive value
//      ***********************************************************
void    do_recv(char recv_val, bool &ack)
        {
        switch(recv_val)
          {
          case 1:                                   // .  dott
            {
              int val1 = getqword();
              cout << val1 << " ";                  // add blank
              break;
            }
          case 2:                                   // U.  udott
            {
              unsigned int val2 = getqword();
              cout << val2 << " ";                  // add blank
              break;
            }
          case 3:                                   // D.  ddott
            {
              long val3 = getqword();               // high word
              long val31 = getqword();              // low word
              val31 = val31 & 0x0000ffff;           // mask sign ext
              val3 = val3 << 16;                     // high word
              val3 = val3 | val31;                   // plus low word
              cout << val3 << " ";                  // add blank
              break;
            }
          case 4:                                   // UD.  uddott
            {
              unsigned long val4 = getqword();      // high word
              unsigned long val41 = getqword();     // low word
              val41 = val41 & 0x0000ffff;           // mask sign ext
              val4 = val4 << 16;                     // high word
              val4 = val4 | val41;                   // plus low word
              cout << val4 << " ";                  // add blank
              break;
            }
          case 5:                                   // EMIT
            {
              char val5 = getqword();
              cout << val5;
              break;
            }
          case 6:                                   // ACK
            ack = true;
            break;
          case 7:                                   // .S
            _dots();                                // display data stack
            break;
```

(continued)

Listing 17–12   (*continued*)

```
      case 8:                       // .R
        _dotr();                    // display return stack
        break;
      case 9:                       // ."
        _dot_quote();               // display string
        break;
      case 10:                      // linefeed
        break;                      //  let CR do it
      case 11:                      // ,
        send_int(tdp);
        tdp +=2;
        break;
      case 12:                      // C,
        send_int(tdp++);
        break;
      case 13:                      // CR
        cout << endl;
        break;
      case 14:                      // .REG
        _dot_regs();                // display registers
        break;
      case 15:                      // CREATE
        _create();
        break;
      case 16:                      // HERE ( -- n )
        _here();
        break;
      case 17:                      // '   ( -- cfa )
        _tick();
        break;
      case 18:                      // S.FILE ( start.addr end.addr -- )
        _sfile();
        break;
      case 19:                      // VHERE ( -- n )
        _vhere();
        break;
      case 20:                      // ALLOT ( -- n )
        _allot();
        break;
      case 21:                      // VALLOT ( -- n )
        _vallot();
        break;
      case 22:                      // DARK ( -- )
        clrscr();                   // clear screen
        break;
      case 23:                      // AT ( col row-- )
        {
        int row = getqword();
        int col = getqword();
        gotoxy(col, row);           // set cursor
        break;
        }
```

Listing 17–12   (*continued*)

```
        default:
            cout << setw(2) << recv_val;
        }
    }


----------------------------

//      HERE ( -- n )
void    _here()
        {
        send_int(tdp);
        }

//      VHERE ( -- n )
void    _vhere()
        {
        send_int(vdp);
        }

//      ALLOT ( n -- )
void    _allot()
        {
        tdp += getqword();
        }

//      VALLOT ( n -- )
void    _vallot()
        {
        vdp += getqword();
        }
```

subroutines *HERE* and *VHERE*, shown in Figure 17–2, are executed. These subroutines send an opcode to the PC (16 and 19) and then wait for a value to be sent from the PC to push on the data stack. Meanwhile, when the opcode (16 or 19) is received by the PC the function *_here()* or *_vhere()*, shown in Listing 17–12, is executed. This function just sends the appropriate value (*tdp* or *vdp*) to the target system.

The words *ALLOT*, and *VALLOT*, shown in Figure 17–2, work in a similar way. In this case the number of bytes needed by the PC is on the target data stack. Therefore, the subroutines *ALLOT* and *VALLOT*, shown in Figure 17–2, send an opcode (20 or 21) to the PC followed by the number that is popped from the data stack. Meanwhile, when the opcode (20 or 21) is received by the PC, the function *_allot()*, or *_vallot()*, shown in Listing 17–12, is executed. This function just increments the appropriate variable (*tdp* or *vdp*) by the 16-bit number sent by the target system.

```
;       HERE    (  -- n )
HERE
        LDAA    #16             ;opcode = 16
        JSR     OUTPUT          ;get tdp
        JSR     INWDY
        STY     2,-X            ;push on stack
        RTS


;       VHERE   (  -- n )
VHERE
        LDAA    #19             ;opcode = 19
        JSR     OUTPUT          ;get vdp
        JSR     INWDY
        STY     2,-X            ;push on stack
        RTS


;       ALLOT ( n -- )              ;allocate n bytes in code (tdp) space

ALLOT
        LDAA    #20             ;opcode = 20
        JSR     OUTPUT          ;send to host
        JSR     TPOP            ;send top of stack
        RTS


;       VALLOT ( n -- )             ;allocate n bytes in ram (vdp) space

VALLOT
        LDAA    #21             ;opcode = 21
        JSR     OUTPUT          ;send to host
        JSR     TPOP            ;send top of stack
        RTS
```

Figure 17–2 Portion of the 68HC12 Code from the File WHYP12.ASM

17.7 SUMMARY

In this chapter we have provided a detailed look inside the C++ program that is running on the PC when you run WHYP. This should give you a complete picture of how WHYP works and how an assembly language program running on a target 68HC12 board can communicate with a C++ program running on the PC.

You now have all the tools you need to write sophisticated programs on a 68HC12 microcontroller. Feel free to modify and extend WHYP to suit your own needs. Remember that WHYP is your personal language which you can use to enhance you own productivity.

Appendix A

68HC12 Instruction Set

Table A-1 Instruction Set Summary

Source Form	Operation	Addr. Mode	Machine Coding (hex)	~	S	X	H	I	N	Z	V	C
ABA	(A) + (B) ⇒ A Add Accumulators A and B	INH	18 06	2	–	–	Δ	–	Δ	Δ	Δ	Δ
ABX	(B) + (X) ⇒ X *Translates to* LEAX B,X	IDX	1A E5	2	–	–	–	–	–	–	–	–
ABY	(B) + (Y) ⇒ Y *Translates to* LEAY B,Y	IDX	19 ED	2	–	–	–	–	–	–	–	–
ADCA *opr*	(A) + (M) + C ⇒ A Add with Carry to A	IMM DIR EXT IDX IDX1 IDX2 [D,IDX] [IDX2]	89 ii 99 dd B9 hh ll A9 xb A9 xb ff A9 xb ee ff A9 xb A9 xb ee ff	1 3 3 3 3 4 6 6	–	–	Δ	–	Δ	Δ	Δ	Δ
ADCB *opr*	(B) + (M) + C ⇒ B Add with Carry to B	IMM DIR EXT IDX IDX1 IDX2 [D,IDX] [IDX2]	C9 ii D9 dd F9 hh ll E9 xb E9 xb ff E9 xb ee ff E9 xb E9 xb ee ff	1 3 3 3 3 4 6 6	–	–	Δ	–	Δ	Δ	Δ	Δ
ADDA *opr*	(A) + (M) ⇒ A Add without Carry to A	IMM DIR EXT IDX IDX1 IDX2 [D,IDX] [IDX2]	8B ii 9B dd BB hh ll AB xb AB xb ff AB xb ee ff AB xb AB xb ee ff	1 3 3 3 3 4 6 6	–	–	Δ	–	Δ	Δ	Δ	Δ
ADDB *opr*	(B) + (M) ⇒ B Add without Carry to B	IMM DIR EXT IDX IDX1 IDX2 [D,IDX] [IDX2]	CB ii DB dd FB hh ll EB xb EB xb ff EB xb ee ff EB xb EB xb ee ff	1 3 3 3 3 4 6 6	–	–	Δ	–	Δ	Δ	Δ	Δ
ADDD *opr*	(A:B) + (M:M+1) ⇒ A:B Add 16-Bit to D (A:B)	IMM DIR EXT IDX IDX1 IDX2 [D,IDX] [IDX2]	C3 jj kk D3 dd F3 hh ll E3 xb E3 xb ff E3 xb ee ff E3 xb E3 xb ee ff	2 3 3 3 3 4 6 6	–	–	–	–	Δ	Δ	Δ	Δ

Table A-1 Instruction Set Summary (Continued)

Source Form	Operation	Addr. Mode	Machine Coding (hex)	~	S	X	H	I	N	Z	V	C
ANDA opr	(A) • (M) ⇒ A Logical And A with Memory	IMM DIR EXT IDX IDX1 IDX2 [D,IDX] [IDX2]	84 ii 94 dd B4 hh ll A4 xb A4 xb ff A4 xb ee ff A4 xb A4 xb ee ff	1 3 3 3 3 4 6 6	–	–	–	–	Δ	Δ	0	–
ANDB opr	(B) • (M) ⇒ B Logical And B with Memory	IMM DIR EXT IDX IDX1 IDX2 [D,IDX] [IDX2]	C4 ii D4 dd F4 hh ll E4 xb E4 xb ff E4 xb ee ff E4 xb E4 xb ee ff	1 3 3 3 3 4 6 6	–	–	–	–	Δ	Δ	0	–
ANDCC opr	(CCR) • (M) ⇒ CCR Logical And CCR with Memory	IMM	10 ii	1	⇓	⇓	⇓	⇓	⇓	⇓	⇓	⇓
ASL opr ASLA ASLB	Arithmetic Shift Left Arithmetic Shift Left Accumulator A Arithmetic Shift Left Accumulator B	EXT IDX IDX1 IDX2 [D,IDX] [IDX2] INH INH	78 hh ll 68 xb 68 xb ff 68 xb ee ff 68 xb 68 xb ee ff 48 58	4 3 4 5 6 6 1 1	–	–	–	–	Δ	Δ	Δ	Δ
ASLD	Arithmetic Shift Left Double	INH	59	1	–	–	–	–	Δ	Δ	Δ	Δ
ASR opr ASRA ASRB	Arithmetic Shift Right Arithmetic Shift Right Accumulator A Arithmetic Shift Right Accumulator B	EXT IDX IDX1 IDX2 [D,IDX] [IDX2] INH INH	77 hh ll 67 xb 67 xb ff 67 xb ee ff 67 xb 67 xb ee ff 47 57	4 3 4 5 6 6 1 1	–	–	–	–	Δ	Δ	Δ	Δ
BCC rel	Branch if Carry Clear (if C = 0)	REL	24 rr	3/1	–	–	–	–	–	–	–	–
BCLR opr, msk	(M) • (mm̄) ⇒ M Clear Bit(s) in Memory	DIR EXT IDX IDX1 IDX2	4D dd mm 1D hh ll mm 0D xb mm 0D xb ff mm 0D xb ee ff mm	4 4 4 4 6	–	–	–	–	Δ	Δ	0	–
BCS rel	Branch if Carry Set (if C = 1)	REL	25 rr	3/1	–	–	–	–	–	–	–	–
BEQ rel	Branch if Equal (if Z = 1)	REL	27 rr	3/1	–	–	–	–	–	–	–	–
BGE rel	Branch if Greater Than or Equal (if N ⊕ V = 0) (signed)	REL	2C rr	3/1	–	–	–	–	–	–	–	–
BGND	Place CPU in Background Mode see Background Mode section.	INH	00	5	–	–	–	–	–	–	–	–
BGT rel	Branch if Greater Than (if Z + (N ⊕ V) = 0) (signed)	REL	2E rr	3/1	–	–	–	–	–	–	–	–
BHI rel	Branch if Higher (if C + Z = 0) (unsigned)	REL	22 rr	3/1	–	–	–	–	–	–	–	–

Table A-1 Instruction Set Summary (Continued)

Source Form	Operation	Addr. Mode	Machine Coding (hex)	~	S	X	H	I	N	Z	V	C
BHS *rel*	Branch if Higher or Same (if C = 0) (unsigned) same function as BCC	REL	24 rr	3/1	–	–	–	–	–	–	–	–
BITA *opr*	(A) • (M) Logical And A with Memory	IMM	85 ii	1	–	–	–	–	Δ	Δ	0	–
		DIR	95 dd	3								
		EXT	B5 hh ll	3								
		IDX	A5 xb	3								
		IDX1	A5 xb ff	3								
		IDX2	A5 xb ee ff	4								
		[D,IDX]	A5 xb	6								
		[IDX2]	A5 xb ee ff	6								
BITB *opr*	(B) • (M) Logical And B with Memory	IMM	C5 ii	1	–	–	–	–	Δ	Δ	0	–
		DIR	D5 dd	3								
		EXT	F5 hh ll	3								
		IDX	E5 xb	3								
		IDX1	E5 xb ff	3								
		IDX2	E5 xb ee ff	4								
		[D,IDX]	E5 xb	6								
		[IDX2]	E5 xb ee ff	6								
BLE *rel*	Branch if Less Than or Equal (if Z + (N ⊕ V) = 1) (signed)	REL	2F rr	3/1	–	–	–	–	–	–	–	–
BLO *rel*	Branch if Lower (if C = 1) (unsigned) same function as BCS	REL	25 rr	3/1	–	–	–	–	–	–	–	–
BLS *rel*	Branch if Lower or Same (if C + Z = 1) (unsigned)	REL	23 rr	3/1	–	–	–	–	–	–	–	–
BLT *rel*	Branch if Less Than (if N ⊕ V = 1) (signed)	REL	2D rr	3/1	–	–	–	–	–	–	–	–
BMI *rel*	Branch if Minus (if N = 1)	REL	2B rr	3/1	–	–	–	–	–	–	–	–
BNE *rel*	Branch if Not Equal (if Z = 0)	REL	26 rr	3/1	–	–	–	–	–	–	–	–
BPL *rel*	Branch if Plus (if N = 0)	REL	2A rr	3/1	–	–	–	–	–	–	–	–
BRA *rel*	Branch Always (if 1 = 1)	REL	20 rr	3	–	–	–	–	–	–	–	–
BRCLR *opr, msk, rel*	Branch if (M) • (mm) = 0 (if All Selected Bit(s) Clear)	DIR	4F dd mm rr	4	–	–	–	–	–	–	–	–
		EXT	1F hh ll mm rr	5								
		IDX	0F xb mm rr	4								
		IDX1	0F xb ff mm rr	6								
		IDX2	0F xb ee ff mm rr	8								
BRN *rel*	Branch Never (if 1 = 0)	REL	21 rr	1	–	–	–	–	–	–	–	–
BRSET *opr, msk, rel*	Branch if ($\overline{M}$) • (mm) = 0 (if All Selected Bit(s) Set)	DIR	4E dd mm rr	4	–	–	–	–	–	–	–	–
		EXT	1E hh ll mm rr	5								
		DX	0E xb mm rr	4								
		IDX1	0E xb ff mm rr	6								
		IDX2	0E xb ee ff mm rr	8								
BSET *opr, msk*	(M) + (mm) ⇒ M Set Bit(s) in Memory	DIR	4C dd mm	4	–	–	–	–	Δ	Δ	0	–
		EXT	1C hh ll mm	4								
		IDX	0C xb mm	4								
		IDX1	0C xb ff mm	4								
		IDX2	0C xb ee ff mm	6								
BSR *rel*	(SP) – 2 ⇒ SP; $RTN_H:RTN_L$ ⇒ $M_{(SP)}:M_{(SP+1)}$ Subroutine address ⇒ PC Branch to Subroutine	REL	07 rr	4	–	–	–	–	–	–	–	–

Table A-1 Instruction Set Summary (Continued)

Source Form	Operation	Addr. Mode	Machine Coding (hex)	~	S	X	H	I	N	Z	V	C
BVC rel	Branch if Overflow Bit Clear (if V = 0)	REL	28 rr	3/1	–	–	–	–	–	–	–	–
BVS rel	Branch if Overflow Bit Set (if V = 1)	REL	29 rr	3/1	–	–	–	–	–	–	–	–
CALL opr, page	$(SP) - 2 \Rightarrow SP$; $RTN_H:RTN_L \Rightarrow M_{(SP)}:M_{(SP+1)}$ $(SP) - 1 \Rightarrow SP$; $(PPG) \Rightarrow M_{(SP)}$; pg $\Rightarrow$ PPAGE register; Program address $\Rightarrow$ PC Call subroutine in extended memory (Program may be located on another expansion memory page.)	EXT IDX IDX1 IDX2	4A hh ll pg 4B xb pg 4B xb ff pg 4B xb ee ff pg	8 8 8 9	–	–	–	–	–	–	–	–
CALL [D,r] CALL [opr,r]	Indirect modes get program address and new pg value based on pointer. r = X, Y, SP, or PC	[D,IDX] [IDX2]	4B xb 4B xb ee ff	10 10	–	–	–	–	–	–	–	–
CBA	(A) – (B) Compare 8-Bit Accumulators	INH	18 17	2	–	–	–	–	Δ	Δ	Δ	Δ
CLC	$0 \Rightarrow C$ Translates to ANDCC #$FE	IMM	10 FE	1	–	–	–	–	–	–	–	0
CLI	$0 \Rightarrow I$ Translates to ANDCC #$EF (enables I-bit interrupts)	IMM	10 EF	1	–	–	–	0	–	–	–	–
CLR opr	$0 \Rightarrow M$ Clear Memory Location	EXT IDX IDX1 IDX2 [D,IDX] [IDX2]	79 hh ll 69 xb 69 xb ff 69 xb ee ff 69 xb 69 xb ee ff	3 2 3 3 5 5	–	–	–	–	0	1	0	0
CLRA	$0 \Rightarrow A$ Clear Accumulator A	INH	87	1								
CLRB	$0 \Rightarrow B$ Clear Accumulator B	INH	C7	1								
CLV	$0 \Rightarrow V$ Translates to ANDCC #$FD	IMM	10 FD	1	–	–	–	–	–	–	0	–
CMPA opr	(A) – (M) Compare Accumulator A with Memory	IMM DIR EXT IDX IDX1 IDX2 [D,IDX] [IDX2]	81 ii 91 dd B1 hh ll A1 xb A1 xb ff A1 xb ee ff A1 xb A1 xb ee ff	1 3 3 3 3 4 6 6	–	–	–	–	Δ	Δ	Δ	Δ
CMPB opr	(B) – (M) Compare Accumulator B with Memory	IMM DIR EXT IDX IDX1 IDX2 [D,IDX] [IDX2]	C1 ii D1 dd F1 hh ll E1 xb E1 xb ff E1 xb ee ff E1 xb E1 xb ee ff	1 3 3 3 3 4 6 6	–	–	–	–	Δ	Δ	Δ	Δ

Table A-1 Instruction Set Summary (Continued)

Source Form	Operation	Addr. Mode	Machine Coding (hex)	~°	S	X	H	I	N	Z	V	C
COM opr	$(\overline{M}) \Rightarrow M$ equivalent to \$FF – (M) $\Rightarrow$ M 1's Complement Memory Location	EXT	71 hh ll	4	–	–	–	–	Δ	Δ	0	1
		IDX	61 xb	3								
		IDX1	61 xb ff	4								
		IDX2	61 xb ee ff	5								
		[D,IDX]	61 xb	6								
		[IDX2]	61 xb ee ff	6								
COMA	$(\overline{A}) \Rightarrow A$ Complement Accumulator A	INH	41	1								
COMB	$(\overline{B}) \Rightarrow B$ Complement Accumulator B	INH	51	1								
CPD opr	(A:B) – (M:M+1) Compare D to Memory (16-Bit)	IMM	8C jj kk	2	–	–	–	–	Δ	Δ	Δ	Δ
		DIR	9C dd	3								
		EXT	BC hh ll	3								
		IDX	AC xb	3								
		IDX1	AC xb ff	3								
		IDX2	AC xb ee ff	4								
		[D,IDX]	AC xb	6								
		[IDX2]	AC xb ee ff	6								
CPS opr	(SP) – (M:M+1) Compare SP to Memory (16-Bit)	IMM	8F jj kk	2	–	–	–	–	Δ	Δ	Δ	Δ
		DIR	9F dd	3								
		EXT	BF hh ll	3								
		IDX	AF xb	3								
		IDX1	AF xb ff	3								
		IDX2	AF xb ee ff	4								
		[D,IDX]	AF xb	6								
		[IDX2]	AF xb ee ff	6								
CPX opr	(X) – (M:M+1) Compare X to Memory (16-Bit)	IMM	8E jj kk	2	–	–	–	–	Δ	Δ	Δ	Δ
		DIR	9E dd	3								
		EXT	BE hh ll	3								
		IDX	AE xb	3								
		IDX1	AE xb ff	3								
		IDX2	AE xb ee ff	4								
		[D,IDX]	AE xb	6								
		[IDX2]	AE xb ee ff	6								
CPY opr	(Y) – (M:M+1) Compare Y to Memory (16-Bit)	IMM	8D jj kk	2	–	–	–	–	Δ	Δ	Δ	Δ
		DIR	9D dd	3								
		EXT	BD hh ll	3								
		IDX	AD xb	3								
		IDX1	AD xb ff	3								
		IDX2	AD xb ee ff	4								
		[D,IDX]	AD xb	6								
		[IDX2]	AD xb ee ff	6								
DAA	Adjust Sum to BCD Decimal Adjust Accumulator A	INH	18 07	3	–	–	–	–	Δ	Δ	?	Δ
DBEQ cntr, rel	(cntr) – 1 $\Rightarrow$ cntr if (cntr) = 0, then Branch else Continue to next instruction Decrement Counter and Branch if = 0 (cntr = A, B, D, X, Y, or SP)	REL (9-bit)	04 lb rr	3	–	–	–	–	–	–	–	–
DBNE cntr, rel	(cntr) – 1 $\Rightarrow$ cntr If (cntr) not = 0, then Branch; else Continue to next instruction Decrement Counter and Branch if $\neq$ 0 (cntr = A, B, D, X, Y, or SP)	REL (9-bit)	04 lb rr	3	–	–	–	–	–	–	–	–

Table A-1 Instruction Set Summary (Continued)

Source Form	Operation	Addr. Mode	Machine Coding (hex)	~	S	X	H	I	N	Z	V	C
DEC opr	(M) – $01 ⇒ M Decrement Memory Location	EXT	73 hh ll	4	–	–	–	–	Δ	Δ	Δ	–
		IDX	63 xb	3								
		IDX1	63 xb ff	4								
		IDX2	63 xb ee ff	5								
		[D,IDX]	63 xb	6								
		[IDX2]	63 xb ee ff	6								
DECA	(A) – $01 ⇒ A Decrement A	INH	43	1								
DECB	(B) – $01 ⇒ B Decrement B	INH	53	1								
DES	(SP) – $0001 ⇒ SP *Translates to* LEAS –1,SP	IDX	1B 9F	2	–	–	–	–	–	–	–	–
DEX	(X) – $0001 ⇒ X Decrement Index Register X	INH	09	1	–	–	–	–	–	Δ	–	–
DEY	(Y) – $0001 ⇒ Y Decrement Index Register Y	INH	03	1	–	–	–	–	–	Δ	–	–
EDIV	(Y:D) ÷ (X) ⇒ Y Remainder ⇒ D 32 × 16 Bit ⇒ 16 Bit Divide (unsigned)	INH	11	11	–	–	–	–	Δ	Δ	Δ	Δ
EDIVS	(Y:D) ÷ (X) ⇒ Y Remainder ⇒ D 32 × 16 Bit ⇒ 16 Bit Divide (signed)	INH	18 14	12	–	–	–	–	Δ	Δ	Δ	Δ
EMACS sum	$(M_{(X)}:M_{(X+1)}) \times (M_{(Y)}:M_{(Y+1)}) + (M \sim M+3) \Rightarrow$ M~M+3 16 × 16 Bit ⇒ 32 Bit Multiply and Accumulate (signed)	Special	18 12 hh ll	13	–	–	–	–	Δ	Δ	Δ	Δ
EMAXD opr	MAX((D), (M:M+1)) ⇒ D MAX of 2 Unsigned 16-Bit Values N, Z, V and C status bits reflect result of internal compare ((D) – (M:M+1))	IDX	18 1A xb	4	–	–	–	–	Δ	Δ	Δ	Δ
		IDX1	18 1A xb ff	4								
		IDX2	18 1A xb ee ff	5								
		[D,IDX]	18 1A xb	7								
		[IDX2]	18 1A xb ee ff	7								
EMAXM opr	MAX((D), (M:M+1)) ⇒ M:M+1 MAX of 2 Unsigned 16-Bit Values N, Z, V and C status bits reflect result of internal compare ((D) – (M:M+1))	IDX	18 1E xb	4	–	–	–	–	Δ	Δ	Δ	Δ
		IDX1	18 1E xb ff	5								
		IDX2	18 1E xb ee ff	6								
		[D,IDX]	18 1E xb	7								
		[IDX2]	18 1E xb ee ff	7								
EMIND opr	MIN((D), (M:M+1)) ⇒ D MIN of 2 Unsigned 16-Bit Values N, Z, V and C status bits reflect result of internal compare ((D) – (M:M+1))	IDX	18 1B xb	4	–	–	–	–	Δ	Δ	Δ	Δ
		IDX1	18 1B xb ff	4								
		IDX2	18 1B xb ee ff	5								
		[D,IDX]	18 1B xb	7								
		[IDX2]	18 1B xb ee ff	7								
EMINM opr	MIN((D), (M:M+1)) ⇒ M:M+1 MIN of 2 Unsigned 16-Bit Values N, Z, V and C status bits reflect result of internal compare ((D) – (M:M+1))	IDX	18 1F xb	4	–	–	–	–	Δ	Δ	Δ	Δ
		IDX1	18 1F xb ff	5								
		IDX2	18 1F xb ee ff	6								
		[D,IDX]	18 1F xb	7								
		[IDX2]	18 1F xb ee ff	7								
EMUL	(D) × (Y) ⇒ Y:D 16 × 16 Bit Multiply (unsigned)	INH	13	3	–	–	–	–	Δ	Δ	–	Δ
EMULS	(D) × (Y) ⇒ Y:D 16 × 16 Bit Multiply (signed)	INH	18 13	3	–	×	–	–	Δ	Δ	–	Δ

Table A-1 Instruction Set Summary (Continued)

Source Form	Operation	Addr. Mode	Machine Coding (hex)	~	S	X	H	I	N	Z	V	C
EORA opr	(A) ⊕ (M) ⇒ A Exclusive-OR A with Memory	IMM DIR EXT IDX IDX1 IDX2 [D,IDX] [IDX2]	88 ii 98 dd B8 hh ll A8 xb A8 xb ff A8 xb ee ff A8 xb A8 xb ee ff	1 3 3 3 3 4 6 6	–	–	–	–	Δ	Δ	0	–
EORB opr	(B) ⊕ (M) ⇒ B Exclusive-OR B with Memory	IMM DIR EXT IDX IDX1 IDX2 [D,IDX] [IDX2]	C8 ii D8 dd F8 hh ll E8 xb E8 xb ff E8 xb ee ff E8 xb E8 xb ee ff	1 3 3 3 3 4 6 6	–	–	–	–	Δ	Δ	0	–
ETBL opr	(M:M+1)+ [(B)×((M+2:M+3) – (M:M+1))] ⇒ D 16-Bit Table Lookup and Interpolate Initialize B, and index before ETBL. <ea> points at first table entry (M:M+1) and B is fractional part of lookup value (no indirect addr. modes allowed)	IDX	18 3F xb	10	–	–	–	–	Δ	Δ	–	?
EXG r1, r2	(r1) ⇔ (r2) (if r1 and r2 same size) or $00:(r1) ⇒ r2 (if r1=8-bit; r2=16-bit) or (r1low) ⇔ (r2) (if r1=16-bit; r2=8-bit) r1 and r2 may be A, B, CCR, D, X, Y, or SP	INH	B7 eb	1	–	–	–	–	–	–	–	–
FDIV	(D) ÷ (X) ⇒ X; r ⇒ D 16 × 16 Bit Fractional Divide	INH	18 11	12	–	–	–	–	–	Δ	Δ	Δ
IBEQ cntr, rel	(cntr) + 1 ⇒ cntr If (cntr) = 0, then Branch else Continue to next instruction Increment Counter and Branch if = 0 (cntr = A, B, D, X, Y, or SP)	REL (9-bit)	04 lb rr	3	–	–	–	–	–	–	–	–
IBNE cntr, rel	(cntr) + 1 ⇒ cntr if (cntr) not = 0, then Branch; else Continue to next instruction Increment Counter and Branch if ≠ 0 (cntr = A, B, D, X, Y, or SP)	REL (9-bit)	04 lb rr	3	–	–	–	–	–	–	–	–
IDIV	(D) ÷ (X) ⇒ X; r ⇒ D 16 × 16 Bit Integer Divide (unsigned)	INH	18 10	12	–	–	–	–	–	Δ	0	Δ
IDIVS	(D) ÷ (X) ⇒ X; r ⇒ D 16 × 16 Bit Integer Divide (signed)	INH	18 15	12	–	–	–	–	Δ	Δ	Δ	Δ

Table A-1 Instruction Set Summary (Continued)

Source Form	Operation	Addr. Mode	Machine Coding (hex)	~*	S	X	H	I	N	Z	V	C
INC opr	(M) + $01 ⇒ M Increment Memory Byte	EXT IDX IDX1 IDX2 [D,IDX] [IDX2]	72 hh ll 62 xb 62 xb ff 62 xb ee ff 62 xb 62 xb ee ff	4 3 4 5 6 6	–	–	–	–	Δ	Δ	Δ	–
INCA INCB	(A) + $01 ⇒ A Increment Acc. A (B) + $01 ⇒ B Increment Acc. B	INH INH	42 52	1 1								
INS	(SP) + $0001 ⇒ SP *Translates to* LEAS 1,SP	IDX	1B 81	2	–	–	–	–	–	–	–	–
INX	(X) + $0001 ⇒ X Increment Index Register X	INH	08	1	–	–	–	–	–	Δ	–	–
INY	(Y) + $0001 ⇒ Y Increment Index Register Y	INH	02	1	–	–	–	–	–	Δ	–	–
JMP opr	Subroutine address ⇒ PC Jump	EXT IDX IDX1 IDX2 [D,IDX] [IDX2]	06 hh ll 05 xb 05 xb ff 05 xb ee ff 05 xb 05 xb ee ff	3 3 3 4 6 6	–	–	–	–	–	–	–	–
JSR opr	(SP) − 2 ⇒ SP; RTN$_H$:RTN$_L$ ⇒ M$_{(SP)}$:M$_{(SP+1)}$; Subroutine address ⇒ PC Jump to Subroutine	DIR EXT IDX IDX1 IDX2 [D,IDX] [IDX2]	17 dd 16 hh ll 15 xb 15 xb ff 15 xb ee ff 15 xb 15 xb ee ff	4 4 4 4 5 7 7	–	–	–	–	–	–	–	–
LBCC rel	Long Branch if Carry Clear (if C = 0)	REL	18 24 qq rr	4/3	–	–	–	–	–	–	–	–
LBCS rel	Long Branch if Carry Set (if C = 1)	REL	18 25 qq rr	4/3	–	–	–	–	–	–	–	–
LBEQ rel	Long Branch if Equal (if Z = 1)	REL	18 27 qq rr	4/3	–	–	–	–	–	–	–	–
LBGE rel	Long Branch Greater Than or Equal (if N ⊕ V = 0) (signed)	REL	18 2C qq rr	4/3	–	–	–	–	–	–	–	–
LBGT rel	Long Branch if Greater Than (if Z + (N ⊕ V) = 0) (signed)	REL	18 2E qq rr	4/3	–	–	–	–	–	–	–	–
LBHI rel	Long Branch if Higher (if C + Z = 0) (unsigned)	REL	18 22 qq rr	4/3	–	–	–	–	–	–	–	–
LBHS rel	Long Branch if Higher or Same (if C = 0) (unsigned) same function as LBCC	REL	18 24 qq rr	4/3	–	–	–	–	–	–	–	–
LBLE rel	Long Branch if Less Than or Equal (if Z + (N ⊕ V) = 1) (signed)	REL	18 2F qq rr	4/3	–	–	–	–	–	–	–	–
LBLO rel	Long Branch if Lower (if C = 1) (unsigned) same function as LBCS	REL	18 25 qq rr	4/3	–	–	–	–	–	–	–	–
LBLS rel	Long Branch if Lower or Same (if C + Z = 1) (unsigned)	REL	18 23 qq rr	4/3	–	–	–	–	–	–	–	–
LBLT rel	Long Branch if Less Than (if N ⊕ V = 1) (signed)	REL	18 2D qq rr	4/3	–	–	–	–	–	–	–	–
LBMI rel	Long Branch if Minus (if N = 1)	REL	18 2B qq rr	4/3	–	–	–	–	–	–	–	–
LBNE rel	Long Branch if Not Equal (if Z = 0)	REL	18 26 qq rr	4/3	–	–	–	–	–	–	–	–
LBPL rel	Long Branch if Plus (if N = 0)	REL	18 2A qq rr	4/3	–	–	–	–	–	–	–	–
LBRA rel	Long Branch Always (if 1=1)	REL	18 20 qq rr	4	–	–	–	–	–	–	–	–

Table A-1 Instruction Set Summary (Continued)

Source Form	Operation	Addr. Mode	Machine Coding (hex)	~*	S	X	H	I	N	Z	V	C
LBRN *rel*	Long Branch Never (if 1 = 0)	REL	18 21 qq rr	3	–	–	–	–	–	–	–	–
LBVC *rel*	Long Branch if Overflow Bit Clear (if V=0)	REL	18 28 qq rr	4/3	–	–	–	–	–	–	–	–
LBVS *rel*	Long Branch if Overflow Bit Set (if V = 1)	REL	18 29 qq rr	4/3	–	–	–	–	–	–	–	–
LDAA *opr*	(M) ⇒ A Load Accumulator A	IMM	86 ii	1	–	–	–	–	Δ	Δ	0	–
		DIR	96 dd	3								
		EXT	B6 hh ll	3								
		IDX	A6 xb	3								
		IDX1	A6 xb ff	3								
		IDX2	A6 xb ee ff	4								
		[D,IDX]	A6 xb	6								
		[IDX2]	A6 xb ee ff	6								
LDAB *opr*	(M) ⇒ B Load Accumulator B	IMM	C6 ii	1	–	–	–	–	Δ	Δ	0	–
		DIR	D6 dd	3								
		EXT	F6 hh ll	3								
		IDX	E6 xb	3								
		IDX1	E6 xb ff	3								
		IDX2	E6 xb ee ff	4								
		[D,IDX]	E6 xb	6								
		[IDX2]	E6 xb ee ff	6								
LDD *opr*	(M:M+1) ⇒ A:B Load Double Accumulator D (A:B)	IMM	CC jj kk	2	–	–	–	–	Δ	Δ	0	–
		DIR	DC dd	3								
		EXT	FC hh ll	3								
		IDX	EC xb	3								
		IDX1	EC xb ff	3								
		IDX2	EC xb ee ff	4								
		[D,IDX]	EC xb	6								
		[IDX2]	EC xb ee ff	6								
LDS *opr*	(M:M+1) ⇒ SP Load Stack Pointer	IMM	CF jj kk	2	–	–	–	–	Δ	Δ	0	–
		DIR	DF dd	3								
		EXT	FF hh ll	3								
		IDX	EF xb	3								
		IDX1	EF xb ff	3								
		IDX2	EF xb ee ff	4								
		[D,IDX]	EF xb	6								
		[IDX2]	EF xb ee ff	6								
LDX *opr*	(M:M+1) ⇒ X Load Index Register X	IMM	CE jj kk	2	–	–	–	–	Δ	Δ	0	–
		DIR	DE dd	3								
		EXT	FE hh ll	3								
		IDX	EE xb	3								
		IDX1	EE xb ff	3								
		IDX2	EE xb ee ff	4								
		[D,IDX]	EE xb	6								
		[IDX2]	EE xb ee ff	6								
LDY *opr*	(M:M+1) ⇒ Y Load Index Register Y	IMM	CD jj kk	2	–	–	–	–	Δ	Δ	0	–
		DIR	DD dd	3								
		EXT	FD hh ll	3								
		IDX	ED xb	3								
		IDX1	ED xb ff	3								
		IDX2	ED xb ee ff	4								
		[D,IDX]	ED xb	6								
		[IDX2]	ED xb ee ff	6								
LEAS *opr*	Effective Address ⇒ SP Load Effective Address into SP	IDX	1B xb	2	–	–	–	–	–	–	–	–
		IDX1	1B xb ff	2								
		IDX2	1B xb ee ff	2								

Table A-1 Instruction Set Summary (Continued)

Source Form	Operation	Addr. Mode	Machine Coding (hex)	~˙	S	X	H	I	N	Z	V	C
LEAX opr	Effective Address ⇒ X Load Effective Address into X	IDX IDX1 IDX2	1A xb 1A xb ff 1A xb ee ff	2 2 2	–	–	–	–	–	–	–	–
LEAY opr	Effective Address ⇒ Y Load Effective Address into Y	IDX IDX1 IDX2	19 xb 19 xb ff 19 xb ee ff	2 2 2	–	–	–	–	–	–	–	–
LSL opr LSLA LSLB	 Logical Shift Left same function as ASL Logical Shift Accumulator A to Left Logical Shift Accumulator B to Left	EXT IDX IDX1 IDX2 [D,IDX] [IDX2] INH INH	78 hh ll 68 xb 68 xb ff 68 xb ee ff 68 xb 68 xb ee ff 48 58	4 3 4 5 6 6 1 1	–	–	–	–	Δ	Δ	Δ	Δ
LSLD	 Logical Shift Left D Accumulator same function as ASLD	INH	59	1	–	–	–	–	Δ	Δ	Δ	Δ
LSR opr LSRA LSRB	 Logical Shift Right Logical Shift Accumulator A to Right Logical Shift Accumulator B to Right	EXT IDX IDX1 IDX2 [D,IDX] [IDX2] INH INH	74 hh ll 64 xb 64 xb ff 64 xb ee ff 64 xb 64 xb ee ff 44 54	4 3 4 5 6 6 1 1	–	–	–	–	0	Δ	Δ	Δ
LSRD	 Logical Shift Right D Accumulator	INH	49	1	–	–	–	–	0	Δ	Δ	Δ
MAXA	MAX((A), (M)) ⇒ A MAX of 2 Unsigned 8-Bit Values N, Z, V and C status bits reflect result of internal compare ((A) – (M)).	IDX IDX1 IDX2 [D,IDX] [IDX2]	18 18 xb 18 18 xb ff 18 18 xb ee ff 18 18 xb 18 18 xb ee ff	4 4 5 7 7	–	–	–	–	Δ	Δ	Δ	Δ
MAXM	MAX((A), (M)) ⇒ M MAX of 2 Unsigned 8-Bit Values N, Z, V and C status bits reflect result of internal compare ((A) – (M)).	IDX IDX1 IDX2 [D,IDX] [IDX2]	18 1C xb 18 1C xb ff 18 1C xb ee ff 18 1C xb 18 1C xb ee ff	4 5 6 7 7	–	–	–	–	Δ	Δ	Δ	Δ
MEM	μ (grade) ⇒ $M_{(Y)}$; (X) + 4 ⇒ X; (Y) + 1 ⇒ Y; A unchanged if (A) < P1 or (A) > P2 then μ = 0, else μ = MIN[((A) – P1)×S1, (P2 – (A))×S2, $FF] where: A = current crisp input value; X points at 4-byte data structure that de- scribes a trapezoidal membership function (P1, P2, S1, S2); Y points at fuzzy input (RAM location). See instruction details for special cases.	Special	01	5	–	–	?	–	?	?	?	?

Table A-1 Instruction Set Summary (Continued)

Source Form	Operation	Addr. Mode	Machine Coding (hex)	~	S	X	H	I	N	Z	V	C
MINA	MIN((A), (M)) ⇒ A MIN of Two Unsigned 8-Bit Values N, Z, V and C status bits reflect result of internal compare ((A) − (M)).	IDX IDX1 IDX2 [D,IDX] [IDX2]	18 19 xb 18 19 xb ff 18 19 xb ee ff 18 19 xb 18 19 xb ee ff	4 4 5 7 7	–	–	–	–	Δ	Δ	Δ	Δ
MINM	MIN((A), (M)) ⇒ M MIN of Two Unsigned 8-Bit Values N, Z, V and C status bits reflect result of internal compare ((A) − (M)).	IDX IDX1 IDX2 [D,IDX] [IDX2]	18 1D xb 18 1D xb ff 18 1D xb ee ff 18 1D xb 18 1D xb ee ff	4 5 6 7 7	–	–	–	–	Δ	Δ	Δ	Δ
MOVB opr1, opr2	(M₁) ⇒ M₂ Memory to Memory Byte-Move (8-Bit)	IMM-EXT IMM-IDX EXT-EXT EXT-IDX IDX-EXT IDX-IDX	18 0B ii hh ll 18 08 xb ii 18 0C hh ll hh ll 18 09 xb hh ll 18 0D xb hh ll 18 0A xb xb	4 4 6 5 5 5	–	–	–	–	–	–	–	–
MOVW opr1, opr2	(M:M+1₁) ⇒ M:M+1₂ Memory to Memory Word-Move (16-Bit)	IMM-EXT IMM-IDX EXT-EXT EXT-IDX IDX-EXT IDX-IDX	18 03 jj kk hh ll 18 00 xb jj kk 18 04 hh ll hh ll 18 01 xb hh ll 18 05 xb hh ll 18 02 xb xb	5 4 6 5 5 5	–	–	–	–	–	–	–	–
MUL	(A) × (B) ⇒ A:B 8 × 8 Unsigned Multiply	INH	12	3	–	–	–	–	–	–	–	Δ
NEG opr	0 − (M) ⇒ M or ($\overline{M}$) + 1 ⇒ M Two's Complement Negate	EXT IDX IDX1 IDX2 [D,IDX] [IDX2]	70 hh ll 60 xb 60 xb ff 60 xb ee ff 60 xb 60 xb ee ff	4 3 4 5 6 6	–	–	–	–	Δ	Δ	Δ	Δ
NEGA	0 − (A) ⇒ A equivalent to ($\overline{A}$) + 1 ⇒ B Negate Accumulator A	INH	40	1								
NEGB	0 − (B) ⇒ B equivalent to ($\overline{B}$) + 1 ⇒ B Negate Accumulator B	INH	50	1								
NOP	No Operation	INH	A7	1	–	–	–	–	–	–	–	–
ORAA opr	(A) + (M) ⇒ A Logical OR A with Memory	IMM DIR EXT IDX IDX1 IDX2 [D,IDX] [IDX2]	8A ii 9A dd BA hh ll AA xb AA xb ff AA xb ee ff AA xb AA xb ee ff	1 3 3 3 3 4 6 6	–	–	–	–	Δ	Δ	0	–
ORAB opr	(B) + (M) ⇒ B Logical OR B with Memory	IMM DIR EXT IDX IDX1 IDX2 [D,IDX] [IDX2]	CA ii DA dd FA hh ll EA xb EA xb ff EA xb ee ff EA xb EA xb ee ff	1 3 3 3 3 4 6 6	–	–	–	–	Δ	Δ	0	–
ORCC opr	(CCR) + M ⇒ CCR Logical OR CCR with Memory	IMM	14 ii	1	⇑	–	⇑	⇑	⇑	⇑	⇑	⇑

Table A-1 Instruction Set Summary (Continued)

Source Form	Operation	Addr. Mode	Machine Coding (hex)	~	S	X	H	I	N	Z	V	C
PSHA	$(SP) - 1 \Rightarrow SP; (A) \Rightarrow M_{(SP)}$ Push Accumulator A onto Stack	INH	36	2	–	–	–	–	–	–	–	–
PSHB	$(SP) - 1 \Rightarrow SP; (B) \Rightarrow M_{(SP)}$ Push Accumulator B onto Stack	INH	37	2	–	–	–	–	–	–	–	–
PSHC	$(SP) - 1 \Rightarrow SP; (CCR) \Rightarrow M_{(SP)}$ Push CCR onto Stack	INH	39	2	–	–	–	–	–	–	–	–
PSHD	$(SP) - 2 \Rightarrow SP; (A:B) \Rightarrow M_{(SP)}:M_{(SP+1)}$ Push D Accumulator onto Stack	INH	3B	2	–	–	–	–	–	–	–	–
PSHX	$(SP) - 2 \Rightarrow SP; (X_H:X_L) \Rightarrow M_{(SP)}:M_{(SP+1)}$ Push Index Register X onto Stack	INH	34	2	–	–	–	–	–	–	–	–
PSHY	$(SP) - 2 \Rightarrow SP; (Y_H:Y_L) \Rightarrow M_{(SP)}:M_{(SP+1)}$ Push Index Register Y onto Stack	INH	35	2	–	–	–	–	–	–	–	–
PULA	$(M_{(SP)}) \Rightarrow A; (SP) + 1 \Rightarrow SP$ Pull Accumulator A from Stack	INH	32	3	–	–	–	–	–	–	–	–
PULB	$(M_{(SP)}) \Rightarrow B; (SP) + 1 \Rightarrow SP$ Pull Accumulator B from Stack	INH	33	3	–	–	–	–	–	–	–	–
PULC	$(M_{(SP)}) \Rightarrow CCR; (SP) + 1 \Rightarrow SP$ Pull CCR from Stack	INH	38	3	Δ	⇓	Δ	Δ	Δ	Δ	Δ	Δ
PULD	$(M_{(SP)}:M_{(SP+1)}) \Rightarrow A:B; (SP) + 2 \Rightarrow SP$ Pull D from Stack	INH	3A	3	–	–	–	–	–	–	–	–
PULX	$(M_{(SP)}:M_{(SP+1)}) \Rightarrow X_H:X_L; (SP) + 2 \Rightarrow SP$ Pull Index Register X from Stack	INH	30	3	–	–	–	–	–	–	–	–
PULY	$(M_{(SP)}:M_{(SP+1)}) \Rightarrow Y_H:Y_L; (SP) + 2 \Rightarrow SP$ Pull Index Register Y from Stack	INH	31	3	–	–	–	–	–	–	–	–
REV	MIN-MAX rule evaluation Find smallest rule input (MIN). Store to rule outputs unless fuzzy output is already larger (MAX). For rule weights see REVW. Each rule input is an 8-bit offset from the base address in Y. Each rule output is an 8-bit offset from the base address in Y. $FE separates rule inputs from rule outputs. $FF terminates the rule list. REV may be interrupted.	Special	18 3A	3** per rule byte	–	–	–	–	–	–	Δ	–

Table A-1 Instruction Set Summary (Continued)

Source Form	Operation	Addr. Mode	Machine Coding (hex)	~	S	X	H	I	N	Z	V	C
REVW	MIN-MAX rule evaluation Find smallest rule input (MIN), Store to rule outputs unless fuzzy output is already larger (MAX). Rule weights supported, optional. Each rule input is the 16-bit address of a fuzzy input. Each rule output is the 16-bit address of a fuzzy output. The value $FFFE separates rule inputs from rule outputs. $FFFF terminates the rule list. REVW may be interrupted.	Special	18 3B	3" per rule byte; 5 per wt.	–	–	?	–	?	?	Δ	!
ROL opr	 Rotate Memory Left through Carry	EXT IDX IDX1 IDX2 [D,IDX] [IDX2]	75 hh ll 65 xb 65 xb ff 65 xb ee ff 65 xb 65 xb ee ff	4 3 4 5 6 6	–	–	–	–	Δ	Δ	Δ	Δ
ROLA	Rotate A Left through Carry	INH	45	1								
ROLB	Rotate B Left through Carry	INH	55	1								
ROR opr	 Rotate Memory Right through Carry	EXT IDX IDX1 IDX2 [D,IDX] [IDX2]	76 hh ll 66 xb 66 xb ff 66 xb ee ff 66 xb 66 xb ee ff	4 3 4 5 6 6	–	–	–	–	Δ	Δ	Δ	Δ
RORA	Rotate A Right through Carry	INH	46	1								
RORB	Rotate B Right through Carry	INH	56	1								
RTC	$(M_{(SP)}) \Rightarrow PPAGE; (SP) + 1 \Rightarrow SP;$ $(M_{(SP)}:M_{(SP+1)}) \Rightarrow PC_H:PC_L;$ $(SP) + 2 \Rightarrow SP$ Return from Call	INH	0A	6	–	–	–	–	–	–	–	–
RTI	$(M_{(SP)}) \Rightarrow CCR; (SP) + 1 \Rightarrow SP$ $(M_{(SP)}:M_{(SP+1)}) \Rightarrow B:A; (SP) + 2 \Rightarrow SP$ $(M_{(SP)}:M_{(SP+1)}) \Rightarrow X_H:X_L; (SP) + 4 \Rightarrow SP$ $(M_{(SP)}:M_{(SP+1)}) \Rightarrow PC_H:PC_L; (SP) - 2 \Rightarrow SP$ $(M_{(SP)}:M_{(SP+1)}) \Rightarrow Y_H:Y_L;$ $(SP) + 4 \Rightarrow SP$ Return from Interrupt	INH	0B	8	Δ	⇓	Δ	Δ	Δ	Δ	Δ	Δ
RTS	$(M_{(SP)}:M_{(SP+1)}) \Rightarrow PC_H:PC_L;$ $(SP) + 2 \Rightarrow SP$ Return from Subroutine	INH	3D	5	–	–	–	–	–	–	–	–
SBA	$(A) - (B) \Rightarrow A$ Subtract B from A	INH	18 16	2	–	–	–	–	Δ	Δ	Δ	Δ

Table A-1 Instruction Set Summary (Continued)

Source Form	Operation	Addr. Mode	Machine Coding (hex)	~ˑ	S	X	H	I	N	Z	V	C
SBCA opr	(A) − (M) − C ⇒ A Subtract with Borrow from A	IMM DIR EXT IDX IDX1 IDX2 [D,IDX] [IDX2]	82 ii 92 dd B2 hh ll A2 xb A2 xb ff A2 xb ee ff A2 xb A2 xb ee ff	1 3 3 3 3 4 6 6	−	−	−	−	Δ	Δ	Δ	Δ
SBCB opr	(B) − (M) − C ⇒ B Subtract with Borrow from B	IMM DIR EXT IDX IDX1 IDX2 [D,IDX] [IDX2]	C2 ii D2 dd F2 hh ll E2 xb E2 xb ff E2 xb ee ff E2 xb E2 xb ee ff	1 3 3 3 3 4 6 6	−	−	−	−	Δ	Δ	Δ	Δ
SEC	1 ⇒ C Translates to ORCC #$01	IMM	14 01	1	−	−	−	−	−	−	−	1
SEI	1 ⇒ I; (inhibit I interrupts) Translates to ORCC #$10	IMM	14 10	1	−	−	−	1	−	−	−	−
SEV	1 ⇒ V Translates to ORCC #$02	IMM	14 02	1	−	−	−	−	−	−	1	−
SEX r1, r2	$00:(r1) ⇒ r2 if r1, bit 7 is 0 or $FF:(r1) ⇒ r2 if r1, bit 7 is 1 Sign Extend 8-bit r1 to 16-bit r2 r1 may be A, B, or CCR r2 may be D, X, Y, or SP Alternate mnemonic for TFR r1, r2	INH	B7 eb	1	−	−	−	−	−	−	−	−
STAA opr	(A) ⇒ M Store Accumulator A to Memory	DIR EXT IDX IDX1 IDX2 [D,IDX] [IDX2]	5A dd 7A hh ll 6A xb 6A xb ff 6A xb ee ff 6A xb 6A xb ee ff	2 3 2 3 3 5 5	−	−	−	−	Δ	Δ	0	−
STAB opr	(B) ⇒ M Store Accumulator B to Memory	DIR EXT IDX IDX1 IDX2 [D,IDX] [IDX2]	5B dd 7B hh ll 6B xb 6B xb ff 6B xb ee ff 6B xb 6B xb ee ff	2 3 2 3 3 5 5	−	−	−	−	Δ	Δ	0	−
STD opr	(A) ⇒ M, (B) ⇒ M+1 Store Double Accumulator	DIR EXT IDX IDX1 IDX2 [D,IDX] [IDX2]	5C dd 7C hh ll 6C xb 6C xb ff 6C xb ee ff 6C xb 6C xb ee ff	2 3 2 3 3 5 5	−	−	−	−	Δ	Δ	0	−

Table A-1 Instruction Set Summary (Continued)

Source Form	Operation	Addr. Mode	Machine Coding (hex)	~*	S	X	H	I	N	Z	V	C
STOP	$(SP) - 2 \Rightarrow SP$; $RTN_H:RTN_L \Rightarrow M_{(SP)}:M_{(SP+1)}$; $(SP) - 2 \Rightarrow SP$; $(Y_H:Y_L) \Rightarrow M_{(SP)}:M_{(SP+1)}$; $(SP) - 2 \Rightarrow SP$; $(X_H:X_L) \Rightarrow M_{(SP)}:M_{(SP+1)}$; $(SP) - 2 \Rightarrow SP$; $(B:A) \Rightarrow M_{(SP)}:M_{(SP+1)}$; $(SP) - 1 \Rightarrow SP$; $(CCR) \Rightarrow M_{(SP)}$; STOP All Clocks If S control bit = 1, the STOP instruction is disabled and acts like a two-cycle NOP. Registers stacked to allow quicker recovery by interrupt.	INH	18 3E	9** +5 or +2**	–	–	–	–	–	–	–	–
STS *opr* Store Stack Pointer	$(SP_H:SP_L) \Rightarrow M:M+1$	DIR EXT IDX IDX1 IDX2 [D,IDX] [IDX2]	5F dd 7F hh ll 6F xb 6F xb ff 6F xb ee ff 6F xb 6F xb ee ff	2 3 2 3 3 5 5	–	–	–	–	Δ	Δ	0	–
STX *opr* Store Index Register X	$(X_H:X_L) \Rightarrow M:M+1$	DIR EXT IDX IDX1 IDX2 [D,IDX] [IDX2]	5E dd 7E hh ll 6E xb 6E xb ff 6E xb ee ff 6E xb 6E xb ee ff	2 3 2 3 3 5 5	–	–	–	–	Δ	Δ	0	–
STY *opr* Store Index Register Y	$(Y_H:Y_L) \Rightarrow M:M+1$	DIR EXT IDX IDX1 IDX2 [D,IDX] [IDX2]	5D dd 7D hh ll 6D xb 6D xb ff 6D xb ee ff 6D xb 6D xb ee ff	2 3 2 3 3 5 5	–	–	–	–	Δ	Δ	0	–
SUBA *opr* Subtract Memory from Accumulator A	$(A) - (M) \Rightarrow A$	IMM DIR EXT IDX IDX1 IDX2 [D,IDX] [IDX2]	80 ii 90 dd B0 hh ll A0 xb A0 xb ff A0 xb ee ff A0 xb A0 xb ee ff	1 3 3 3 3 4 6 6	–	–	–	–	Δ	Δ	Δ	Δ
SUBB *opr* Subtract Memory from Accumulator B	$(B) - (M) \Rightarrow B$	IMM DIR EXT IDX IDX1 IDX2 [D,IDX] [IDX2]	C0 ii D0 dd F0 hh ll E0 xb E0 xb ff E0 xb ee ff E0 xb E0 xb ee ff	1 3 3 3 3 4 6 6	–	–	–	–	Δ	Δ	Δ	Δ

Table A-1 Instruction Set Summary (Continued)

Source Form	Operation	Addr. Mode	Machine Coding (hex)	~	S	X	H	I	N	Z	V	C
SUBD opr	(D) − (M:M+1) ⇒ D Subtract Memory from D (A:B)	IMM DIR EXT IDX IDX1 IDX2 [D,IDX] [IDX2]	83 jj kk 93 dd B3 hh ll A3 xb A3 xb ff A3 xb ee ff A3 xb A3 xb ee ff	2 3 3 3 3 4 6 6	–	–	–	–	Δ	Δ	Δ	Δ
SWI	$(SP) - 2 \Rightarrow SP$; $RTN_H:RTN_L \Rightarrow M_{(SP)}:M_{(SP+1)}$; $(SP) - 2 \Rightarrow SP$; $(Y_H:Y_L) \Rightarrow M_{(SP)}:M_{(SP+1)}$; $(SP) - 2 \Rightarrow SP$; $(X_H:X_L) \Rightarrow M_{(SP)}:M_{(SP+1)}$; $(SP) - 2 \Rightarrow SP$; $(B:A) \Rightarrow M_{(SP)}:M_{(SP+1)}$; $(SP) - 1 \Rightarrow SP$; $(CCR) \Rightarrow M_{(SP)}$ $1 \Rightarrow I$; (SWI Vector) $\Rightarrow$ PC Software Interrupt	INH	3F	9	–	–	–	1	–	–	–	–
TAB	(A) ⇒ B Transfer A to B	INH	18 0E	2	–	–	–	–	Δ	Δ	0	–
TAP	(A) ⇒ CCR *Translates to* TFR A , CCR	INH	B7 02	1	Δ	⇓	Δ	Δ	Δ	Δ	Δ	Δ
TBA	(B) ⇒ A Transfer B to A	INH	18 0F	2	–	–	–	–	Δ	Δ	0	–
TBEQ cntr, rel	If (cntr) = 0, then Branch; else Continue to next instruction Test Counter and Branch if Zero (cntr = A, B, D, X,Y, or SP)	REL (9-bit)	04 lb rr	3	–	–	–	–	–	–	–	–
TBL opr	$(M) + [(B) \times ((M+1) - (M))] \Rightarrow A$ 8-Bit Table Lookup and Interpolate Initialize B, and index before TBL. <ea> points at first 8-bit table entry (M) and B is fractional part of lookup value. (no indirect addressing modes allowed.)	IDX	18 3D xb	8	–	–	–	–	Δ	Δ	–	?
TBNE cntr, rel	If (cntr) not = 0, then Branch; else Continue to next instruction Test Counter and Branch if Not Zero (cntr = A, B, D, X,Y, or SP)	REL (9-bit)	04 lb rr	3	–	–	–	–	–	–	–	–
TFR r1, r2	(r1) ⇒ r2 or $00:(r1) ⇒ r2 or (r1[7:0]) ⇒ r2 Transfer Register to Register r1 and r2 may be A, B, CCR, D, X, Y, or SP	INH	B7 eb	1	– or Δ	⇓	Δ	Δ	Δ	Δ	Δ	Δ
TPA	(CCR) ⇒ A *Translates to* TFR CCR , A	INH	B7 20	1	–	–	–	–	–	–	–	–

Table A-1 Instruction Set Summary (Continued)

Source Form	Operation	Addr. Mode	Machine Coding (hex)	~	S	X	H	I	N	Z	V	C
TRAP	$(SP) - 2 \Rightarrow SP$; $RTN_H:RTN_L \Rightarrow M_{(SP)}:M_{(SP+1)}$; $(SP) - 2 \Rightarrow SP$; $(Y_H:Y_L) \Rightarrow M_{(SP)}:M_{(SP+1)}$; $(SP) - 2 \Rightarrow SP$; $(X_H:X_L) \Rightarrow M_{(SP)}:M_{(SP+1)}$; $(SP) - 2 \Rightarrow SP$; $(B:A) \Rightarrow M_{(SP)}:M_{(SP+1)}$; $(SP) - 1 \Rightarrow SP$; $(CCR) \Rightarrow M_{(SP)}$ $1 \Rightarrow I$; (TRAP Vector) $\Rightarrow$ PC Unimplemented opcode trap	INH	18 tn tn = $30–$39 or $40–$FF	10	–	–	–	1	–	–	–	–
TST opr	(M) – 0 Test Memory for Zero or Minus	EXT IDX IDX1 IDX2 [D,IDX] [IDX2]	F7 hh ll E7 xb E7 xb ff E7 xb ee ff E7 xb E7 xb ee ff	3 3 3 4 6 6	–	–	–	–	Δ	Δ	0	0
TSTA	(A) – 0 Test A for Zero or Minus	INH	97	1								
TSTB	(B) – 0 Test B for Zero or Minus	INH	D7	1								
TSX	$(SP) \Rightarrow X$ *Translates to TFR SP,X*	INH	B7 75	1	–	–	–	–	–	–	–	–
TSY	$(SP) \Rightarrow Y$ *Translates to TFR SP,Y*	INH	B7 76	1	–	–	–	–	–	–	–	–
TXS	$(X) \Rightarrow SP$ *Translates to TFR X,SP*	INH	B7 57	1	–	–	–	–	–	–	–	–
TYS	$(Y) \Rightarrow SP$ *Translates to TFR Y,SP*	INH	B7 67	1	–	–	–	–	–	–	–	–
WAI	$(SP) - 2 \Rightarrow SP$; $RTN_H:RTN_L \Rightarrow M_{(SP)}:M_{(SP+1)}$; $(SP) - 2 \Rightarrow SP$; $(Y_H:Y_L) \Rightarrow M_{(SP)}:M_{(SP+1)}$; $(SP) - 2 \Rightarrow SP$; $(X_H:X_L) \Rightarrow M_{(SP)}:M_{(SP+1)}$; $(SP) - 2 \Rightarrow SP$; $(B:A) \Rightarrow M_{(SP)}:M_{(SP+1)}$; $(SP) - 1 \Rightarrow SP$; $(CCR) \Rightarrow M_{(SP)}$; WAIT for interrupt	INH	3E	8** (in) + 5 (int)	– or – or –	– – 1	–	1 1	–	–	–	–
WAV	$$\sum_{i=1}^{B} S_i F_i \Rightarrow Y{:}D$$ $$\sum_{i=1}^{B} F_i \Rightarrow X$$ Calculate Sum of Products and Sum of Weights for Weighted Average Calculation Initialize B, X, and Y before WAV. B specifies number of elements. X points at first element in S_i list. Y points at first element in F_i list. All S_i and F_i elements are 8-bits. If interrupted, six extra bytes of stack used for intermediate values	Special	18 3C	8** per lable	–	–	?	–	?	Δ	?	?

Table A-1 Instruction Set Summary (Continued)

Source Form	Operation	Addr. Mode	Machine Coding (hex)	~*	S	X	H	I	N	Z	V	C
wavr pseudo-instruction	*see* WAV Resume executing an interrupted WAV instruction (recover intermediate results from stack rather than initializing them to zero)	Special	3C	**	–	–	?	–	?	Δ	?	?
XGDX	(D) ⇔ (X) *Translates to* EXG D, X	INH	B7 C5	1	–	–	–	–	–	–	–	–
XGDY	(D) ⇔ (Y) *Translates to* EXG D, Y	INH	B7 C6	1	–	–	–	–	–	–	–	–

NOTES:
 *Each cycle (~) is typically 125 ns for an 8-MHz bus (16-MHz oscillator).
 **Refer to detailed instruction descriptions for additional information.

Appendix B

68HC11 Instruction Set

Table 10-1. MC68HC11A8 Instructions, Addressing Modes, and Execution Times (Sheet 1 of 7)

Source Form(s)	Operation	Boolean Expression	Addressing Mode for Operand	Machine Coding (Hexadecimal) Opcode	Operand(s)	Bytes	Cycle	Cycle by Cycle*	S	X	H	I	N	Z	V	C
ABA	Add Accumulators	A + B → A	INH	1B		1	2	2-1	-	-	$\updownarrow$	-	$\updownarrow$	$\updownarrow$	$\updownarrow$	$\updownarrow$
ABX	Add B to X	IX + 00:B → IX	INH	3A		1	3	2-2	-	-	-	-	-	-	-	-
ABY	Add B to Y	IY + 00:B → IY	INH	18 3A		2	4	2-4	-	-	-	-	-	-	-	-
ADCA (opr)	Add with Carry to A	A + M + C → A	A IMM	89	ii	2	2	3-1	-	-	$\updownarrow$	-	$\updownarrow$	$\updownarrow$	$\updownarrow$	$\updownarrow$
			A DIR	99	dd	2	3	4-1								
			A EXT	B9	hh ll	3	4	5-2								
			A IND,X	A9	ff	2	4	6-2								
			A IND,Y	18 A9	ff	3	5	7-2								
ADCB (opr)	Add with Carry to B	B + M + C → B	B IMM	C9	ii	2	2	3-1	-	-	$\updownarrow$	-	$\updownarrow$	$\updownarrow$	$\updownarrow$	$\updownarrow$
			B DIR	D9	dd	2	3	4-1								
			B EXT	F9	hh ll	3	4	5-2								
			B IND,X	E9	ff	2	4	6-2								
			B IND,Y	18 E9	ff	3	5	7-2								
ADDA (opr)	Add Memory to A	A + M → A	A IMM	8B	ii	2	2	3-1	-	-	$\updownarrow$	-	$\updownarrow$	$\updownarrow$	$\updownarrow$	$\updownarrow$
			A DIR	9B	dd	2	3	4-1								
			A EXT	BB	hh ll	3	4	5-2								
			A IND,X	AB	ff	2	4	6-2								
			A IND,Y	18 AB	ff	3	5	7-2								
ADDB (opr)	Add Memory to B	B + M → B	B IMM	CB	ii	2	2	3-1	-	-	$\updownarrow$	-	$\updownarrow$	$\updownarrow$	$\updownarrow$	$\updownarrow$
			B DIR	DB	dd	2	3	4-1								
			B EXT	FB	hh ll	3	4	5-2								
			B IND,X	EB	ff	2	4	6-2								
			B IND,Y	18 EB	ff	3	5	7-2								
ADDD (opr)	Add 16-Bit to D	D + M:M + 1 → D	IMM	C3	jj kk	3	4	3-3	-	-	-	-	$\updownarrow$	$\updownarrow$	$\updownarrow$	$\updownarrow$
			DIR	D3	dd	2	5	4-7								
			EXT	F3	hh ll	3	6	5-10								
			IND,X	E3	ff	2	6	6-10								
			IND,Y	18 E3	ff	3	7	7-8								
ANDA (opr)	AND A with Memory	A•M → A	A IMM	84	ii	2	2	3-1	-	-	-	-	$\updownarrow$	$\updownarrow$	0	-
			A DIR	94	dd	2	3	4-1								
			A EXT	B4	hh ll	3	4	5-2								
			A IND,X	A4	ff	2	4	6-2								
			A IND,Y	18 A4	ff	3	5	7-2								
ANDB (opr)	AND B with Memory	B•M → B	B IMM	C4	ii	2	2	3-1	-	-	-	-	$\updownarrow$	$\updownarrow$	0	-
			B DIR	D4	dd	2	3	4-1								
			B EXT	F4	hh ll	3	4	5-2								
			B IND,X	E4	ff	2	4	6-2								
			B IND,Y	18 E4	ff	3	5	7-2								
ASL (opr)	Arithmetic Shift Left	(diagram) C b7 b0	EXT	78	hh ll	3	6	5-8	-	-	-	-	$\updownarrow$	$\updownarrow$	$\updownarrow$	$\updownarrow$
			IND,X	68	ff	2	6	6-3								
			IND,Y	18 68	ff	3	7	7-3								
ASLA			A INH	48		1	2	2-1								
ASLB			B INH	58		1	2	2-1								
ASLD	Arithmetic Shift Left Double	(diagram) C b15 b0	INH	05		1	3	2-2	-	-	-	-	$\updownarrow$	$\updownarrow$	$\updownarrow$	$\updownarrow$
ASR (opr)	Arithmetic Shift Right	(diagram) b7 b0 C	EXT	77	hh ll	3	6	5-8	-	-	-	-	$\updownarrow$	$\updownarrow$	$\updownarrow$	$\updownarrow$
			IND,X	67	ff	2	6	6-3								
			IND,Y	18 67	ff	3	7	7-3								
ASRA			A INH	47		1	2	2-1								
ASRB			B INH	57		1	2	2-1								
BCC (rel)	Branch if Carry Clear	? C = 0	REL	24	rr	2	3	8-1	-	-	-	-	-	-	-	-
BCLR (opr) (msk)	Clear Bit(s)	M•($\overline{mm}$) → M	DIR	15	dd mm	3	6	4-10	-	-	-	-	$\updownarrow$	$\updownarrow$	0	-
			IND,X	1D	ff mm	3	7	6-13								
			IND,Y	18 1D	ff mm	4	8	7-10								
BCS (rel)	Branch if Carry Set	? C = 1	REL	25	rr	2	3	8-1	-	-	-	-	-	-	-	-
BEQ (rel)	Branch if = Zero	? Z = 1	REL	27	rr	2	3	8-1	-	-	-	-	-	-	-	-

*Cycle-by-cycle number provides a reference to Tables 10-2 through 10-8 which detail cycle-by-cycle operation.
  Example: Table 10-1 Cycle-by-Cycle column reference number 2-4 equals Table 10-2 line item 2-4.

Table 10-1. MC68HC11A8 Instructions, Addressing Modes, and Execution Times (Sheet 2 of 7)

Source Form(s)	Operation	Boolean Expression	Addressing Mode for Operand	Opcode	Operand(s)	Bytes	Cycle	Cycle by Cycle*	S	X	H	I	N	Z	V	C
BGE (rel)	Branch if ≥ Zero	? N ⊕ V = 0	REL	2C	rr	2	3	8-1	-	-	-	-	-	-	-	-
BGT (rel)	Branch if > Zero	? Z + (N ⊕ V) · 0	REL	2E	rr	2	3	8-1	-	-	-	-	-	-	-	-
BHI (rel)	Branch if Higher	? C · Z ÷ 0	REL	22	rr	2	3	8-1	-	-	-	-	-	-	-	-
BHS (rel)	Branch if Higher or Same	? C = 0	REL	24	rr	2	3	8-1	-	-	-	-	-	-	-	-
BITA (opr)	Bit(s) Test A with Memory	A•M	A IMM	85	ii	2	2	3-1	-	-	-	-	↕	↕	0	-
			A DIR	95	dd	2	3	4-1								
			A EXT	B5	hh ll	3	4	5-2								
			A IND,X	A5	ff	2	4	6-2								
			A IND,Y	18 A5	ff	3	5	7-2								
BITB (opr)	Bit(s) Test B with Memory	B•M	B IMM	C5	ii	2	2	3-1	-	-	-	-	↕	↕	0	-
			B DIR	D5	dd	2	3	4-1								
			B EXT	F5	hh ll	3	4	5-2								
			B IND,X	E5	ff	2	4	6-2								
			B IND,Y	18 E5	ff	3	5	7-2								
BLE (rel)	Branch if ≤ Zero	? Z - (N ⊕ V) = 1	REL	2F	rr	2	3	8-1	-	-	-	-	-	-	-	-
BLO (rel)	Branch if Lower	? C · 1	REL	25	rr	2	3	8-1	-	-	-	-	-	-	-	-
BLS (rel)	Branch if Lower or Same	? C + Z = 1	REL	23	rr	2	3	8-1	-	-	-	-	-	-	-	-
BLT (rel)	Branch if < Zero	? N ⊕ V = 1	REL	2D	rr	2	3	8-1	-	-	-	-	-	-	-	-
BMI (rel)	Branch if Minus	? N = 1	REL	2B	rr	2	3	8-1	-	-	-	-	-	-	-	-
BNE (rel)	Branch if Not = Zero	? Z ÷ 0	REL	26	rr	2	3	8-1	-	-	-	-	-	-	-	-
BPL (rel)	Branch if Plus	? N · 0	REL	2A	rr	2	3	8-1	-	-	-	-	-	-	-	-
BRA (rel)	Branch Always	? 1 · 1	REL	20	rr	2	3	8-1	-	-	-	-	-	-	-	-
BRCLR(opr) (msk) (rel)	Branch if Bit(s) Clear	? M• mm = 0	DIR	13	dd mm rr	4	6	4-11	-	-	-	-	-	-	-	-
			IND,X	1F	ff mm rr	4	7	6-14								
			IND,Y	18 1F	ff mm rr	5	8	7-11								
BRN (rel)	Branch Never	? 1 = 0	REL	21	rr	2	3	8-1	-	-	-	-	-	-	-	-
BRSET(opr) (msk) (rel)	Branch if Bit(s) Set	? ($\overline{M}$)•mm · 0	DIR	12	dd mm rr	4	6	4-11	-	-	-	-	-	-	-	-
			IND,X	1E	ff mm rr	4	7	6-14								
			IND,Y	18 1E	ff mm rr	5	8	7-11								
BSET(opr) (msk)	Set Bit(s)	M + mm → M	DIR	14	dd mm	3	6	4-10	-	-	-	-	↕	↕	0	-
			IND,X	1C	ff mm	3	7	6-13								
			IND,Y	18 1C	ff mm	4	8	7-10								
BSR (rel)	Branch to Subroutine	See Special Ops	REL	8D	rr	2	6	8-2	-	-	-	-	-	-	-	-
BVC (rel)	Branch if Overflow Clear	? V ÷ 0	REL	28	rr	2	3	8-1	-	-	-	-	-	-	-	-
BVS (rel)	Branch if Overflow Set	? V = 1	REL	29	rr	2	3	8-1	-	-	-	-	-	-	-	-
CBA	Compare A to B	A - B	INH	11		1	2	2-1	-	-	-	-	↕	↕	↕	↕
CLC	Clear Carry Bit	0 → C	INH	0C		1	2	2-1	-	-	-	-	-	-	-	0
CLI	Clear Interrupt Mask	0 → I	INH	0E		1	2	2-1	-	-	-	0	-	-	-	-
CLR (opr)	Clear Memory Byte	0 → M	EXT	7F	hh ll	3	6	5-8	-	-	-	-	0	1	0	0
			IND,X	6F	ff	2	6	6-3								
			IND,Y	18 6F	ff	3	7	7-3								
CLRA	Clear Accumulator A	0 → A	A INH	4F		1	2	2-1	-	-	-	-	0	1	0	0
CLRB	Clear Accumulator B	0 → B	B INH	5F		1	2	2-1	-	-	-	-	0	1	0	0
CLV	Clear Overflow Flag	0 → V	INH	0A		1	2	2-1	-	-	-	-	-	-	0	-
CMPA (opr)	Compare A to Memory	A - M	A IMM	81	ii	2	2	3-1	-	-	-	-	↕	↕	↕	↕
			A DIR	91	dd	2	3	4 1								
			A EXT	B1	hh ll	3	4	5-2								
			A IND,X	A1	ff	2	4	6-2								
			A IND,Y	18 A1	ff	3	5	7-2								

*Cycle-by-cycle number provides a reference to Tables 10-2 through 10-8 which detail cycle-by-cycle operation.
   Example: Table 10-1 Cycle-by-Cycle column reference number 2-4 equals Table 10-2 line item 2-4.

Table 10-1. MC68HC11A8 Instructions, Addressing Modes, and Execution Times (Sheet 3 of 7)

Source Form(s)	Operation	Boolean Expression	Addressing Mode for Operand	Machine Coding (Hexadecimal) Opcode	Operand(s)	Bytes	Cycle	Cycle by Cycle*	S	X	H	I	N	Z	V	C
CMPB (opr)	Compare B to Memory	B – M	B IMM	C1	ii	2	2	3-1	-	-	-	-	↕	↕	↕	↕
			B DIR	D1	dd	2	3	4-1								
			B EXT	F1	hh ll	3	4	5-2								
			B IND,X	E1	ff	2	4	6-2								
			B IND,Y	18 E1	ff	3	5	7-2								
COM (opr)	1's Complement Memory Byte	$FF – M → M	EXT	73	hh ll	3	6	5-8	-	-	-	-	↕	↕	0	1
			IND,X	63	ff	2	6	6-3								
			IND,Y	18 63	ff	3	7	7-3								
COMA	1's Complement A	$FF – A → A	A INH	43		1	2	2-1	-	-	-	-	↕	↕	0	1
COMB	1's Complement B	$FF – B → B	B INH	53		1	2	2-1	-	-	-	-	↕	↕	0	1
CPD (opr)	Compare D to Memory 16-Bit	D – M:M + 1	IMM	1A 83	jj kk	4	5	3-5	-	-	-	-	↕	↕	↕	↕
			DIR	1A 93	dd	3	6	4-9								
			EXT	1A B3	hh ll	4	7	5-11								
			IND,X	1A A3	ff	3	7	6-11								
			IND,Y	CD A3	ff	3	7	7-8								
CPX (opr)	Compare X to Memory 16-Bit	IX – M:M + 1	IMM	8C	jj kk	3	4	3-3	-	-	-	-	↕	↕	↕	↕
			DIR	9C	dd	2	5	4-7								
			EXT	BC	hh ll	3	6	5-10								
			IND,X	AC	ff	2	6	6-10								
			IND,Y	CD AC	ff	3	7	7-8								
CPY (opr)	Compare Y to Memory 16-Bit	IY – M:M + 1	IMM	18 8C	jj kk	4	5	3-5	-	-	-	-	↕	↕	↕	↕
			DIR	18 9C	dd	3	6	4-9								
			EXT	18 BC	hh ll	4	7	5-11								
			IND,X	1A AC	ff	3	7	6-11								
			IND,Y	18 AC	ff	3	7	7-8								
DAA	Decimal Adjust A	Adjust Sum to BCD	INH	19		1	2	2-1	-	-	↕	↕	↕	↕	↕	
DEC (opr)	Decrement Memory Byte	M – 1 → M	EXT	7A	hh ll	3	6	5-8	-	-	-	-	↕	↕	↕	-
			IND,X	6A	ff	2	6	6-3								
			IND,Y	18 6A	ff	3	7	7-3								
DECA	Decrement Accumulator A	A – 1 → A	A INH	4A		1	2	2-1	-	-	-	-	↕	↕	↕	-
DECB	Decrement Accumulator B	B – 1 → B	B INH	5A		1	2	2-1	-	-	-	-	↕	↕	↕	-
DES	Decrement Stack Pointer	SP – 1 → SP	INH	34		1	3	2-3	-	-	-	-	-	-	-	-
DEX	Decrement Index Register X	IX – 1 → IX	INH	09		1	3	2-2	-	-	-	-	-	↕	-	-
DEY	Decrement Index Register Y	IY – 1 → IY	INH	18 09		2	4	2-4	-	-	-	-	-	↕	-	-
EORA (opr)	Exclusive OR A with Memory	A ⊕ M → A	A IMM	88	ii	2	2	3-1	-	-	-	-	↕	↕	0	-
			A DIR	98	dd	2	3	4-1								
			A EXT	B8	hh ll	3	4	5-2								
			A IND,X	A8	ff	2	4	6-2								
			A IND,Y	18 A8	ff	3	5	7-2								
EORB (opr)	Exclusive OR B with Memory	B ⊕ M → B	B IMM	C8	ii	2	2	3-1	-	-	-	-	↕	↕	0	-
			B DIR	D8	dd	2	3	4-1								
			B EXT	F8	hh ll	3	4	5-2								
			B IND,X	E8	ff	2	4	6-2								
			B IND,Y	18 E8	ff	3	5	7-2								
FDIV	Fractional Divide 16 by 16	D/IX → IX; r → D	INH	03		1	41	2-17	-	-	-	-	-	↕	↕	↕
IDIV	Integer Divide 16 by 16	D/IX → IX; r → D	INH	02		1	41	2-17	-	-	-	-	-	↕	0	↕
INC (opr)	Increment Memory Byte	M + 1 → M	EXT	7C	hh ll	3	6	5-8	-	-	-	-	↕	↕	↕	-
			IND,X	6C	ff	2	6	6-3								
			IND,Y	18 6C	ff	3	7	7-3								
INCA	Increment Accumulator A	A + 1 → A	A INH	4C		1	2	2-1	-	-	-	-	↕	↕	↕	-
INCB	Increment Accumulator B	B + 1 → B	B INH	5C		1	2	2-1	-	-	-	-	↕	↕	↕	-
INS	Increment Stack Pointer	SP + 1 → SP	INH	31		1	3	2-3	-	-	-	-	-	-	-	-

*Cycle-by-cycle number provides a reference to Tables 10-2 through 10-8 which detail cycle-by-cycle operation.
    Example: Table 10-1 Cycle-by-Cycle column reference number 2-4 equals Table 10-2 line item 2-4.

Table 10-1. MC68HC11A8 Instructions, Addressing Modes, and Execution Times (Sheet 4 of 7)

Source Form(s)	Operation	Boolean Expression	Addressing Mode for Operand	Machine Coding (Hexadecimal) Opcode	Operand(s)	Bytes	Cycle	Cycle by Cycle*	S	X	H	I	N	Z	V	C
INX	Increment Index Register X	IX + 1 → IX	INH	08		1	3	2-2	-	-	-	-	-	↕	-	-
INY	Increment Index Register Y	IY + 1 → IY	INH	18 08		2	4	2-4	-	-	-	-	-	↕	-	-
JMP (opr)	Jump	See Special Ops	EXT	7E	hh ll	3	3	5-1	-	-	-	-	-	-	-	-
			IND,X	6E	ff	2	3	6-1								
			IND,Y	18 6E	ff	3	4	7-1								
JSR (opr)	Jump to Subroutine	See Special Ops	DIR	9D	dd	2	5	4-8	-	-	-	-	-	-	-	-
			EXT	BD	hh ll	3	6	5-12								
			IND,X	AD	ff	2	6	6-12								
			IND,Y	18 AD	ff	3	7	7-9								
LDAA (opr)	Load Accumulator A	M → A	A IMM	86	ii	2	2	3-1	-	-	-	-	↕	↕	0	-
			A DIR	96	dd	2	3	4-1								
			A EXT	B6	hh ll	3	4	5-2								
			A IND,X	A6	ff	2	4	6-2								
			A IND,Y	18 A6	ff	3	5	7-2								
LDAB (opr)	Load Accumulator B	M → B	B IMM	C6	ii	2	2	3-1	-	-	-	-	↕	↕	0	-
			B DIR	D6	dd	2	3	4-1								
			B EXT	F6	hh ll	3	4	5-2								
			B IND,X	E6	ff	2	4	6-2								
			B IND,Y	18 E6	ff	3	5	7-2								
LDD (opr)	Load Double Accumulator D	M → A, M + 1 → B	IMM	CC	jj kk	3	3	3-2	-	-	-	-	↕	↕	0	-
			DIR	DC	dd	2	4	4-3								
			EXT	FC	hh ll	3	5	5-4								
			IND,X	EC	ff	2	5	6-6								
			IND,Y	18 EC	ff	3	6	7-6								
LDS (opr)	Load Stack Pointer	M:M + 1 → SP	IMM	8E	jj kk	3	3	3-2	-	-	-	-	↕	↕	0	-
			DIR	9E	dd	2	4	4-3								
			EXT	BE	hh ll	3	5	5-4								
			IND,X	AE	ff	2	5	6-6								
			IND,Y	18 AE	ff	3	6	7-6								
LDX (opr)	Load Index Register X	M:M + 1 → IX	IMM	CE	jj kk	3	3	3-2	-	-	-	-	↕	↕	0	-
			DIR	DE	dd	2	4	4-3								
			EXT	FE	hh ll	3	5	5-4								
			IND,X	EE	ff	2	5	6-6								
			IND,Y	CD EE	ff	3	6	7-6								
LDY (opr)	Load Index Register Y	M:M + 1 → IY	IMM	18 CE	jj kk	4	4	3-4	-	-	-	-	↕	↕	0	-
			DIR	18 DE	dd	3	5	4-5								
			EXT	18 FE	hh ll	4	6	5-6								
			IND,X	1A EE	ff	3	6	6-7								
			IND,Y	18 EE	ff	3	6	7-6								
LSL (opr)	Logical Shift Left		EXT	78	hh ll	3	6	5-8	-	-	-	-	↕	↕	↕	↕
			IND,X	68	ff	2	6	6-3								
			IND,Y	18 68	ff	3	7	7-3								
LSLA			A INH	48		1	2	2-1								
LSLB			B INH	58		1	2	2-1								
LSLD	Logical Shift Left Double		INH	05		1	3	2-2	-	-	-	-	↕	↕	↕	↕
LSR (opr)	Logical Shift Right		EXT	74	hh ll	3	6	5-8	-	-	-	-	0	↕	↕	↕
			IND,X	64	ff	2	6	6-3								
			IND,Y	18 64	ff	3	7	7-3								
LSRA			A INH	44		1	2	2-1								
LSRB			B INH	54		1	2	2-1								
LSRD	Logical Shift Right Double		INH	04		1	3	2-2	-	-	-	-	0	↕	↕	↕
MUL	Multiply 8 by 8	A x B → D	INH	3D		1	10	2-13	-	-	-	-	-	-	-	↕

*Cycle-by-cycle number provides a reference to Tables 10-2 through 10-8 which detail cycle-by-cycle operation.
Example: Table 10-1 Cycle-by-Cycle column reference number 2-4 equals Table 10-2 line item 2-4.

Table 10-1. MC68HC11A8 Instructions, Addressing Modes, and Execution Times (Sheet 5 of 7)

Source Form(s)	Operation	Boolean Expression	Addressing Mode for Operand	Opcode	Operand(s)	Bytes	Cycle	Cycle by Cycle*	S	X	H	I	N	Z	V	C
NEG (opr)	2's Complement Memory Byte	$0 - M \rightarrow M$	EXT	70	hh ll	3	6	5-8	-	-	-	-	↕	↕	↕	↕
			IND,X	60	ff	2	6	6-3								
			IND,Y	18 60	ff	3	7	7-3								
NEGA	2's Complement A	$0 - A \rightarrow A$	A INH	40		1	2	2-1	-	-	-	-	↕	↕	↕	↕
NEGB	2's Complement B	$0 - B \rightarrow B$	B INH	50		1	2	2-1	-	-	-	-	↕	↕	↕	↕
NOP	No Operation	No Operation	INH	01		1	2	2-1	-	-	-	-	-	-	-	-
ORAA (opr)	OR Accumulator A (Inclusive)	$A + M \rightarrow A$	A IMM	8A	ii	2	2	3-1	-	-	-	-	↕	↕	0	-
			A DIR	9A	dd	2	3	4-1								
			A EXT	BA	hh ll	3	4	5-2								
			A IND,X	AA	ff	2	4	6-2								
			A IND,Y	18 AA	ff	3	5	7-2								
ORAB (opr)	OR Accumulator B (Inclusive)	$B + M \rightarrow B$	B IMM	CA	ii	2	2	3-1	-	-	-	-	↕	↕	0	-
			B DIR	DA	dd	2	3	4-1								
			B EXT	FA	hh ll	3	4	5-2								
			B IND,X	EA	ff	2	4	6-2								
			B IND,Y	18 EA	ff	3	5	7-2								
PSHA	Push A onto Stack	$A \rightarrow Stk, SP = SP - 1$	A INH	36		1	3	2-6	-	-	-	-	-	-	-	-
PSHB	Push B onto Stack	$B \rightarrow Stk, SP = SP - 1$	B INH	37		1	3	2-6	-	-	-	-	-	-	-	-
PSHX	Push X onto Stack (Lo First)	$IX \rightarrow Stk, SP = SP - 2$	INH	3C		1	4	2-7	-	-	-	-	-	-	-	-
PSHY	Push Y onto Stack (Lo First)	$IY \rightarrow Stk, SP = SP - 2$	INH	18 3C		2	5	2-8	-	-	-	-	-	-	-	-
PULA	Pull A from Stack	$SP = SP + 1, A \leftarrow Stk$	A INH	32		1	4	2-9	-	-	-	-	-	-	-	-
PULB	Pull B from Stack	$SP = SP + 1, B \leftarrow Stk$	B INH	33		1	4	2-9	-	-	-	-	-	-	-	-
PULX	Pull X from Stack (Hi First)	$SP = SP + 2, IX \leftarrow Stk$	INH	38		1	5	2-10	-	-	-	-	-	-	-	-
PULY	Pull Y from Stack (Hi First)	$SP = SP + 2, IY \leftarrow Stk$	INH	18 38		2	6	2-11	-	-	-	-	-	-	-	-
ROL (opr)	Rotate Left		EXT	79	hh ll	3	6	5-8	-	-	-	-	↕	↕	↕	↕
			IND,X	69	ff	2	6	6-3								
			IND,Y	18 69	ff	3	7	7-3								
ROLA		☐─⟦⟧⟧─☐ C b7 ← b0 C	A INH	49		1	2	2-1								
ROLB			B INH	59		1	2	2-1								
ROR (opr)	Rotate Right		EXT	76	hh ll	3	6	5-8	-	-	-	-	↕	↕	↕	↕
			IND,X	66	ff	2	6	6-3								
			IND,Y	18 66	ff	3	7	7-3								
RORA		☐─⟦⟧⟧─☐ C b7 → b0 C	A INH	46		1	2	2-1								
RORB			B INH	56		1	2	2-1								
RTI	Return from Interrupt	See Special Ops	INH	3B		1	12	2-14	↕	↕	↕	↕	↕	↕	↕	↕
RTS	Return from Subroutine	See Special Ops	INH	39		1	5	2-12	-	-	-	-	-	-	-	-
SBA	Subtract B from A	$A - B \rightarrow A$	INH	10		1	2	2-1	-	-	-	-	↕	↕	↕	↕
SBCA (opr)	Subtract with Carry from A	$A - M - C \rightarrow A$	A IMM	82	ii	2	2	3-1	-	-	-	-	↕	↕	↕	↕
			A DIR	92	dd	2	3	4-1								
			A EXT	B2	hh ll	3	4	5-2								
			A IND,X	A2	ff	2	4	6-2								
			A IND,Y	18 A2	ff	3	5	7-2								
SBCB (opr)	Subtract with Carry from B	$B - M - C \rightarrow B$	B IMM	C2	ii	2	2	3-1	-	-	-	-	↕	↕	↕	↕
			B DIR	D2	dd	2	3	4-1								
			B EXT	F2	hh ll	3	4	5-2								
			B IND,X	E2	ff	2	4	6-2								
			B IND,Y	18 E2	ff	3	5	7-2								
SEC	Set Carry	$1 \rightarrow C$	INH	OD		1	2	2-1	-	-	-	-	-	-	-	1
SEI	Set Interrupt Mask	$1 \rightarrow I$	INH	OF		1	2	2-1	-	-	-	1	-	-	-	-
SEV	Set Overflow Flag	$1 \rightarrow V$	INH	OB		1	2	2-1	-	-	-	-	-	-	1	-

*Cycle-by-cycle number provides a reference to Tables 10-2 through 10-8 which detail cycle-by-cycle operation.
    Example: Table 10-1 Cycle-by-Cycle column reference number 2-4 equals Table 10-2 line item 2-4.

Table 10-1. MC68HC11A8 Instructions, Addressing Modes, and Execution Times (Sheet 6 of 7)

Source Form(s)	Operation	Boolean Expression	Addressing Mode for Operand	Opcode	Operand(s)	Bytes	Cycle	Cycle by Cycle*	S	X	H	I	N	Z	V	C
STAA (opr)	Store Accumulator A	A → M	A DIR	97	dd	2	3	4-2	-	-	-	-	↕	↕	0	-
			A EXT	B7	hh ll	3	4	5-3								
			A IND,X	A7	ff	2	4	6-5								
			A IND,Y	18 A7	ff	3	5	7-5								
STAB (opr)	Store Accumulator B	B → M	B DIR	D7	dd	2	3	4-2	-	-	-	-	↕	↕	0	-
			B EXT	F7	hh ll	3	4	5-3								
			B IND,X	E7	ff	2	4	6-5								
			B IND,Y	18 E7	ff	3	5	7-5								
STD (opr)	Store Accumulator D	A → M, B → M + 1	DIR	DD	dd	2	4	4-4	-	-	-	-	↕	↕	0	-
			EXT	FD	hh ll	3	5	5-5								
			IND,X	ED	ff	2	5	6-8								
			IND,Y	18 ED	ff	3	6	7-7								
STOP	Stop Internal Clocks		INH	CF		1	2	2-1	-	-	-	-	-	-	-	-
STS (opr)	Store Stack Pointer	SP → M:M + 1	DIR	9F	dd	2	4	4-4	-	-	-	-	↕	↕	0	-
			EXT	BF	hh ll	3	5	5-5								
			IND,X	AF	ff	2	5	6-8								
			IND,Y	18 AF	ff	3	6	7-7								
STX (opr)	Store Index Register X	IX → M:M + 1	DIR	DF	dd	2	4	4-4	-	-	-	-	↕	↕	0	-
			EXT	FF	hh ll	3	5	5-5								
			IND,X	EF	ff	2	5	6-8								
			IND,Y	CD EF	ff	3	6	7-7								
STY (opr)	Store Index Register Y	IY → M:M + 1	DIR	18 DF	dd	3	5	4-6	-	-	-	-	↕	↕	0	-
			EXT	18 FF	hh ll	4	6	5-7								
			IND,X	1A EF	ff	3	6	6-9								
			IND,Y	18 EF	ff	3	6	7-7								
SUBA (opr)	Subtract Memory from A	A − M → A	A IMM	80	ii	2	2	3-1	-	-	-	-	↕	↕	↕	↕
			A DIR	90	dd	2	3	4-1								
			A EXT	B0	hh ll	3	4	5-2								
			A IND,X	A0	ff	2	4	6-2								
			A IND,Y	18 A0	ff	3	5	7-2								
SUBB (opr)	Subtract Memory from B	B − M → B	B IMM	C0	ii	2	2	3-1	-	-	-	-	↕	↕	↕	↕
			B DIR	D0	dd	2	3	4-1								
			B EXT	F0	hh ll	3	4	5-2								
			B IND,X	E0	ff	2	4	6-2								
			B IND,Y	18 E0	ff	3	5	7-2								
SUBD (opr)	Subtract Memory from D	D − M:M + 1 → D	IMM	83	jj kk	3	4	3-3	-	-	-	-	↕	↕	↕	↕
			DIR	93	dd	2	5	4-7								
			EXT	B3	hh ll	3	6	5-10								
			IND,X	A3	ff	2	6	6-10								
			IND,Y	18 A3	ff	3	7	7-8								
SWI	Software Interrupt	See Special Ops	INH	3F		1	14	2-15	-	-	-	1	-	-	-	-
TAB	Transfer A to B	A → B	INH	16		1	2	2-1	-	-	-	-	↕	↕	0	-
TAP	Transfer A to CC Register	A → CCR	INH	06		1	2	2-1	↕	↕	↕	↕	↕	↕	↕	↕
TBA	Transfer B to A	B → A	INH	17		1	2	2-1	-	-	-	-	↕	↕	0	-
TEST	TEST (Only in Test Modes)	Address Bus Counts	INH	00		1	**	2-20	-	-	-	-	-	-	-	-
TPA	Transfer CC Register to A	CCR → A	INH	07		1	2	2-1	-	-	-	-	-	-	-	-
TST (opr)	Test for Zero or Minus	M − 0	EXT	7D	hh ll	3	6	5-9	-	-	-	-	↕	↕	0	0
			IND,X	6D	ff	2	6	6-4								
			IND,Y	18 6D	ff	3	7	7-4								
TSTA		A − 0	A INH	4D		1	2	2-1	-	-	-	-	↕	↕	0	0
TSTB		B − 0	B INH	5D		1	2	2-1	-	-	-	-	↕	↕	0	0
TSX	Transfer Stack Pointer to X	SP + 1 → IX	INH	30		1	3	2-3	-	-	-	-	-	-	-	-
TSY	Transfer Stack Pointer to Y	SP + 1 → IY	INH	18 30		2	4	2-5	-	-	-	-	-	-	-	-

*Cycle-by-cycle number provides a reference to Tables 10-2 through 10-8 which detail cycle-by-cycle operation.
   Example: Table 10-1 Cycle-by-Cycle column reference number 2-4 equals Table 10-2 line item 2-4.

Table 10-1. MC68HC11A8 Instructions, Addressing Modes, and Execution Times (Sheet 7 of 7)

Source Form(s)	Operation	Boolean Expression	Addressing Mode for Operand	Machine Coding (Hexadecimal) Opcode	Operand(s)	Bytes	Cycle	Cycle by Cycle*	S	X	H	I	N	Z	V	C
TXS	Transfer X to Stack Pointer	IX − 1 → SP	INH	35		1	3	2-2	-	-	-	-	-	-	-	-
TYS	Transfer Y to Stack Pointer	IY − 1 → SP	INH	18 35		2	4	2-4	-	-	-	-	-	-	-	-
WAI	Wait for Interrupt	Stack Regs & WAIT	INH	3E		1	***	2-16	-	-	-	-	-	-	-	-
XGDX	Exchange D with X	IX → D, D → IX	INH	8F		1	3	2-2	-	-	-	-	-	-	-	-
XGDY	Exchange D with Y	IY → D, D → IY	INH	18 8F		2	4	2-4	-	-	-	-	-	-	-	-

* Cycle-by-cycle number provides a reference to Tables 10-2 through 10-8 which detail cycle-by-cycle operation.
Example: Table 10-1 Cycle-by-Cycle column reference number 2-4 equals Table 10-2 line item 2-4.

** Infinity or Until Reset Occurs

*** 12 Cycles are used beginning with the opcode fetch. A wait state is entered which remains in effect for an integer number of MPU E-clock cycles (n) until an interrupt is recognized. Finally, two additional cycles are used to fetch the appropriate interrupt vector (14 + n total).

dd = 8-Bit Direct Address ($0000 – $00FF) (High Byte Assumed to be $00)
ff = 8-Bit Positive Offset $00 (0) to $FF (255) (Is Added to Index)
hh = High Order Byte of 16-Bit Extended Address
ii = One Byte of Immediate Data
jj = High Order Byte of 16-Bit Immediate Data
kk = Low Order Byte of 16-Bit Immediate Data
ll = Low Order Byte of 16-Bit Extended Address
mm = 8-Bit Bit Mask (Set Bits to be Affected)
rr = Signed Relative Offset $80 (– 128) to $7F (+ 127)
(Offset Relative to the Address Following the Machine Code Offset Byte)

Appendix C

Loading WHYP on 68HC12 and 68HC11 Evaluation Boards

This appendix describes how to load WHYP into some specific 68HC12 and 68HC11 evaluation boards. You can download the latest versions of WHYP and find methods of loading WHYP into other evaluation boards by going to the Web site *www.secs.oakland.edu/~haskell.*

C.1 68HC12 BOARDS

In this section we will show you how to load WHYP into four different evaluation boards: two containing the 68HC812A4 microcontroller and two containing the 68HC912B32 microcontroller. Two of the evaluation boards are from Motorola (*http://www.mcu.motsps.com/dev_tools/index.html*) and two are from Axiom Manufacturing (*http://www.axman.com*). These procedures can be modified to load WHYP into any 68HC12 evaluation board.

Setting up WHYP on a particular 68HC12 board consists of the following steps:

1. Generate the appropriate WHYP12.S19 file by either assembling the `WHYP12.ASM` file in Appendix D, or by copying an existing .S19 file to `WHYP12.S19`.

2. Download the file `WHYP12.S19` to the target board, or use this file to program EPROM or flash memory.

3. Copy the appropriate file to WHYP12.CFG in the current directory (see Appendix F).

4. Make sure that the header file WHYP12.HED, is present in the current directory (see Appendix E).

5. Run WHYP12.EXE from a DOS prompt.

C.1.1   The Motorola M68HC12A4EVB Evaluation Board

The Motorola M68HC12A4EVB evaluation board contains the 68HC812A4 micro-controller and has the memory map shown in Table C–1. The WHYP kernel fits in less than 2.5 Kbytes of memory. It can be stored in the external RAM or in the external EPROM. We will consider each of these possibilities separately and discuss the advantages and disadvantages of each.

Note that although there is room in the internal EEPROM of the 68HC812A4 to store WHYP this is not a good idea because bytes in the EEPROM cannot be read while the *EEPGM* bit in the *EEPROG* register is set (see Figure 4–28). This means that you can't program other parts of the EEPROM from a program that is running in the EEPROM itself.

Loading WHYP into RAM   The easiest thing to do is to store the WHYP kernel, shown in Appendix D, in RAM starting at address $4000. This is the default code stored in the file WHYP12.S19 and also in the file WA4RAM4.S19.

To load WHYP into RAM starting at address $4000 do the following:

1. Copy file WA4RAM4.S19 to WHYP12.S19.
2. Copy file WA4RAM4.CFG to WHYP12.CFG.
3. Connect the M68HC12A4EVB to one of the COM ports of the PC.
4. Apply power to the M68HC12A4EVB.
5. From the DOS prompt, type *HOST* followed by *<enter>*. If you are connected to COM2 you will need to press F10 to change the COM port.
6. Type *LOAD* followed by *<enter>*.
7. Press function key F6 and type WHYP12.S19 followed by *<enter>*.
8. Type *G 4000*. This will execute the WHYP kernel.
9. Press the *ESC* key to return to DOS prompt.
10. Type *WHYP12* to execute WHYP on the PC.

Table C–1   Memory Map for the M68HC12A4EVB

Address Range	Memory Type
$0000–$01FF	On-chip I/O registers
$0800–$0BFF	1K on-chip RAM
$1000–$1FFF	4K on-chip EEPROM
$4000–$7FFF	16K external RAM
$8000–$FFFF	32K external EPROM

The disadvantage of loading WHYP into RAM is that you have to do it every time you turn on power to the evaluation board. To avoid this you can load WHYP into the external EPROM.

Loading WHYP into the EPROM   If you want to make a turnkey system that will run your WHYP program stored in the internal EEPROM on reset, you will need to store the WHYP kernel in the external EPROM that holds the D-Bug12 monitor. The D-Bug12 program starts at address $A000 in the EPROM. Addresses $8000–$9FFF are available for user programs. To store the WHYP kernel in the external EPROM, one needs to reassemble the file WHYP12.ASM, shown in Appendix D, with the value of *WHYPBASE* changed to $8000. We have done this and stored the resulting .S19 file in the file WA4EPROM.S19.

The external EPROM consists of two 32K × 8 chips (27256) with the even addresses in chip U9A and the odd addresses in chip U7 as shown in Figure C–1. The first half of each chip is not programmed and must be filled with all 1's.

The logical address of the WHYP kernel will be $8000–$8972. You will program the even addresses in this range in chip U9A starting at the physical address $4000. You will program the odd addresses in this range in chip U7 starting at the physical address $4000. The code from the D-Bug12 chips from the physical addresses $5000–$7FFF should be copied to your chips. Do not reprogram the original EPROMs that came with the board.

The specific steps required to program the EPROMs will depend on your particular PROM programmer. In general, you should do the following:

1. Copy file WA4EPROM.S19 to WHYP12.S19.
2. Copy file WA4EPROM.CFG to WHYP12.CFG.

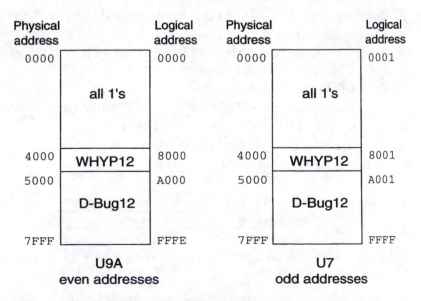

Figure C–1   Memory Map of Two EPROM Chips

3. Load the contents of chip U9A into your PROM programmer memory.

4. Load the even addresses of file WHYP12.S19 into your PROM programmer memory starting at address $4000.

5. Program your new U9A chip.

6. Load the contents of chip U7 into your PROM programmer memory.

7. Load the odd addresses of file WHYP12.S19 into your PROM programmer memory starting at address $4000.

8. Program your new U7 chip.

9. Install the new U9A and U7 chips on the evaluation board.

10. Connect the M68HC12A4EVB to one of the COM ports of the PC.

11. Apply power to the M68HC12A4EVB.

12. From the DOS prompt, type *HOST* followed by <*enter*>. If you are connected to COM2, you will need to press F10 to change the COM port.

13. Type *G 8000*. This will execute the WHYP kernel.

14. Press the *ESC* key to return to the DOS prompt.

15. Type *WHYP12* to execute WHYP on the PC.

Running WHYP from Reset   Moving jumper W20 from pins 2–3 to pins 1–2 will cause the program at the beginning of the on-chip EEPROM to be executed on reset. If you put the instruction *JMP $8000* (06 80 00) at address $1000 in the EEPROM, then the WHYP kernel at address $8000 will be executed on reset. However, on reset the D-Bug12 startup code will jump to the EEPROM address $1000 before it sets the registers that allow access to the external RAM. Therefore, in order to be able to enter your programs into the external RAM, you will need to add the startup code shown in Listing C–1 starting at address $1000 by doing the following:

1. From the DOS prompt, type *HOST* followed by <*enter*>. If you are connected to COM2, you will need to press F10 to change the COM port.

2. Type *LOAD 4000* followed by <*enter*>. This will load the .S19 file into RAM with an offset of $4000. The startup code shown in Listing C–1 will therefore start at $5000.

3. Press function key F6 and type STARTA4.S19 followed by <*enter*>.

4. Type *MOVE 5000 5015 1000* followed by <*enter*>. This will move the startup code from external RAM to the on-chip EEPROM. It will take a short time for this to occur and for the prompt to reappear.

5. Move jumper W20 from pins 2–3 to pins 1–2. When you press the reset button, the WHYP kernel in the external EPROM will execute.

6. Press the *ESC* key to return to the DOS prompt.

7. Type *WHYP12* to execute WHYP on the PC.

Now when you press the reset button WHYP will be executed. You can always go back to D-Bug12 on reset by moving jumper W20 to pins 2–3.

Listing C–1   Startup Code for Accessing WHYP from Reset—File `startA4.lst`

```
                          ; From D-Bug12 Startup Code
                          ; See Appendix of 68HC12 User Manual

000a               PEAR   EQU    $0A     Port E assignment register
000b               MODE   EQU    $0B     Mode register
003c               CSCTL0 EQU    $3C     Chip select control register 0
003d               CSCTL1 EQU    $3D     Chip select control register 1
003e               CSSTR0 EQU    $3E     Chip select stretch register 0
8000               WHYP   EQU    $8000

1000                      ORG    $1000
1000 86 2c                LDAA   #$2C
1002 5a 0a                STAA   PEAR
1004 4c 0b 08             BSET   MODE,$08
1007 86 30                LDAA   #$30
1009 5a 3c                STAA   CSCTL0
100b 86 10                LDAA   #$10
100d 5a 3d                STAA   CSCTL1
100f 86 05                LDAA   #$05
1011 5a 3e                STAA   CSSTR0
1013 06 80 00             JMP    WHYP
                          END
```

Making a Turnkey System   After you have written a program and loaded your WHYP words in the EEPROM, you may want to make a turnkey system that will execute your main WHYP word on reset. You need to execute the beginning of the WHYP kernel (see Appendix D) which will initialize the return and data stack pointers, enable the EEPROM, disable the COP watchdog, and initialize the SCI port. The program then jumps to *START* which is normally the WHYP loop that polls the SCI port. You also need to execute the startup code shown in Listing C–1. We have combined this D-Bug12 startup code with the WHYP startup code in the file `startup.asm` shown in Listing C–2. This includes the code at the beginning of the WHYP kernel shown in Appendix D and has been assembled starting at the first address of the EEPROM. This startup code is in the file `startup.asm` and the assembled machine code is in the file `startup.s19`.

Listing C–2   Startup Code for a Turnkey System—File `startup.lst`

```
        ;     Startup code FOR WHYP12
        ;     Includes code from D-Bug12 startup
        ;     This code can be downloaded to the internal
        ;     EEPROM to be executed on reset in a turnkey
        ;     system. Control can be passed to either WHYP
        ;     or your main program.
        ;     Copyright 1998 by Richard E. Haskell
        ;     CSE Dept., Oakland University
        ;     Rochester, Michigan 48309
```

Listing C–2   (continued)

```
                  ***********************************************************
                  ********* Change the following five addresses  *********
                  ********* for a particular 68HC12 environment  *********
                  ***********************************************************
0000              REGBASE EQU    $0000              ;register base
0900              RAMBASE EQU    $0900              ;ram base
1000              EESTART EQU    $1000              ;start address of EEPROM
8000              WHYPBASE EQU   $8000              ;start of WHYP kernel in EPROM

                  ********* To make a turnkey system change START *******
                  ********* to the address of your main word.    *******
                  ********* The default, MN1, will run WHYP.     *******
                  ***********************************************************
8017              START   EQU    MN1
8017              MN1     EQU    WHYPBASE+$17
8021              INITSER EQU    WHYPBASE+$21
0016              COPCTL  EQU    REGBASE+$16        ;COP control reg
00f1              EEPROT  EQU    REGBASE+$F1        ;EEPROM Block Protect reg
09a0              STACK   EQU    RAMBASE+$A0        ;initial system stack pointer
0970              DATSTK  EQU    RAMBASE+$70        ;initial data stack pointer

0948                      ORG    RAMBASE+$48
0948 09 70        SP0     DW     DATSTK             ;initial data stack pointer
094a 09 a0        RP0     DW     STACK              ;initial return stack pointer
000a              PEAR    EQU    $0A       Port E assignment register
000b              MODE    EQU    $0B       Mode register
003c              CSCTL0  EQU    $3C       Chip select control register 0
003d              CSCTL1  EQU    $3D       Chip select control register 1
003e              CSSTR0  EQU    $3E       Chip select stretch register 0

                  **********************************************
                  *        WHYP Startup code
                  **********************************************

1000                      ORG    EESTART            ;load code at start of EEPROM
                  STARTUP
1000 86 2c                LDAA   #$2C               ;from D-Bug12 startup
1002 5a 0a                STAA   PEAR
1004 4c 0b 08             BSET   MODE,$08
1007 86 30                LDAA   #$30
1009 5a 3c                STAA   CSCTL0
100b 86 10                LDAA   #$10
100d 5a 3d                STAA   CSCTL1
100f 86 05                LDAA   #$05
1011 5a 3e                STAA   CSSTR0
1013 cf 09 a0             LDS    #STACK             ;initialize system stack
1016 7f 09 4a             STS    RP0
1019 ce 09 70             LDX    #DATSTK            ;initialize data stack
101c 7e 09 48             STX    SP0
101f 79 00 f1             CLR    EEPROT             ;enable EEPROM writes
1022 79 00 16             CLR    COPCTL             ;disable COP watchdog
1025 16 80 21             JSR    INITSER            ;initialize sci
1028 06 80 17             JMP    START              ;change for turnkey
```

To make a turnkey system that will execute your program on reset, do the following:

1. Program the WHYP kernel in the external EPROMs as described above.
2. From the DOS prompt, type *HOST* followed by *<enter>*. If you are connected to COM2, you will need to press F10 to change the COM port.
3. Type *LOAD 4000* followed by *<enter>*. This will load the .S19 file into RAM with an offset of $4000. The startup code shown in Listing C–2 will therefore start at $5000.
4. Press function key F6 and type STARTUP.S19 followed by *<enter>*.
5. Type *MOVE 5000 502A 1000* followed by *<enter>*. This will move the startup code from external RAM to the on-chip EEPROM. It will take a short time for this to occur and for the prompt to reappear.
6. Move jumper W20 from pins 2–3 to pins 1–2. When you press the reset button the WHYP kernel in the external EPROM will execute.
7. Press the *ESC* key to return to the DOS prompt.
8. Type *WHYP12* to execute WHYP on the PC.
9. Press function key F9 and change the target dictionary pointer, *tdp*, to $1030. This will cause your WHYP code to be loaded in the EEPROM beyond the startup code.
10. Type *LOAD* <name>.whp to load your WHYP program into the EEPROM memory.
11. Use *tick* to find the hex address, *main_addr*, of the word you want to execute on reset.
12. Type

    ```
    HEX <main_addr> 1029 EE!
    ```

    to replace the address of *START* in the *JMP START* instruction in Listing C–2.
13. Press the reset button to execute your program.

To return to WHYP move jumper W20 from pins 1–2 back to pins 2–3. Pressing reset will execute D-Bug12. Carry out steps 12–15 in the previous section. You can now type

```
HEX 8017 1029 EE!
```

to reset the address of *START* in the *JMP START* instruction in Listing C–2 to the address of *MN1* in the WHYP kernel.

C.1.2   The Axiom CME12A4 Development Board

The Axiom CME12A4 development board contains the 68HC812A4 microcontroller and has the memory map shown in Table C–2. This board comes with 64 Kbytes of on-board memory that can be expanded using memory expansion address

Table C–2 Memory Map for the Axiom CME12A4

Address Range	Memory Type
$0000–$01FF	On-chip I/O registers
$0800–$0BFF	1K on-chip RAM
$1000–$1FFF	4K on-chip EEPROM
$0200–$07FF	32K external RAM
$0C00–$0FFF	
$2000–$7FFF	
$8000–$FFFF	32K external EEPROM

windows. The board contains three 32-pin memory sockets: one for RAM, one for EEPROM, and one for either RAM or EEPROM. Jumpers allow you to select various sized RAM, EEPROM, or flash memory chips.

You can load WHYP into RAM at location $4000 using the same procedure described in Section C.1.1. You can also use the utilities that come with the board to load WHYP into an external EEPROM. For more details on using the CME12A4 development board, see the Web site, *www.secs.oakland.edu/~haskell.*

C.1.3 The Axiom CME12B32 Development Board

The Axiom CME12B32 development board contains the 68HC912B32 microcontroller and has the memory map shown in Table C–3. The WHYP kernel can be stored in the external RAM or in the internal flash EEPROM. The internal flash EEPROM occupies addresses $8000–$FFFF in the single-chip mode (set by jumpers). However, in the single-chip mode not only is the external EPROM containing the D-Bug12 monitor removed from the memory map, but also the external RAM is no longer in the memory map. This leaves only the 768 bytes of on-chip EEPROM and 1 Kbyte of on-chip RAM from program development. Some of the on-chip RAM must be used for variables and the return and data stacks. In the single-chip mode it will therefore be necessary to develop a large program in parts, moving new WHYP words to the flash EEPROM after they have been tested in the on-chip RAM or EEPROM.

A more convenient development environment is to load WHYP into the external RAM starting at address $1000 and then load your WHYP words into

Table C–3 Memory Map for the CME12B32

Address Range	Memory Type
$0000–$01FF	On-chip I/O registers
$0800–$0BFF	1K on-chip RAM
$0D00–$0FFF	768 bytes of on-chip EEPROM
$1000–$7FFF	28K external RAM
$8000–$FFFF	32K external EPROM
	(Expanded Wide Mode)
	32K internal FLASH EEPROM
	(Single Chip Mode)

the external RAM between addresses $2000–$7FFF. This provides up to 24 Kbytes of memory for your program. To make a single-chip turnkey system your entire program including the WHYP kernel is moved to the internal flash EEPROM using the method described later in this section.

Loading WHYP into RAM   To store the WHYP kernel in RAM on the CME12B32 board starting at address $1000, one needs to reassemble the file WHYP12.ASM, shown in Appendix D, with the value of *WHYPBASE* changed to $1000 and the values of *EESTART* and *EESTOP* changed to $0D00 and $0FFF, respectively. We have done this and stored the resulting .S19 file in the file WB32RAM1.S19.

To load WHYP into RAM starting at address $1000 do the following:

1. Copy file WB32RAM1.S19 to WHYP12.S19.
2. Copy file WB32RAM1.CFG to WHYP12.CFG.
3. Connect the CME12B32 to one of the COM ports of the PC.
4. Apply power to the CME12B32.
5. From the DOS prompt, type *HOST* followed by *<enter>*. If you are connected to COM2 you will need to press F10 to change the COM port.
6. Type *LOAD* followed by *<enter>*.
7. Press function key F6 and type WHYP12.S19 followed by *<enter>*.
8. Type *G 1000*. This will execute the WHYP kernel.
9. Press the *ESC* key to return to DOS prompt.
10. Type *WHYP12* to execute WHYP on the PC.

Making a Turnkey System   After you have written a program and tested it in the external RAM, you may want to make a turnkey system that will execute your main WHYP word on reset. You need to execute the beginning of the WHYP kernel (see Appendix D) which will initialize the return and data stack pointers, enable the EEPROM, disable the COP watchdog, and initialize the SCI port. The program then jumps to *START* which is normally the WHYP loop that polls the SCI port. You will need to change the address of *START* to the address of your main word. You will also need to change the value of *WHYPBASE* (see Appendix D) to $8000 because that is where you are going to store the WHYP kernel.

However, before you do this you need to load your program in such a way that it starts at address $9000 and references all the words in the WHYP kernel with their addresses in the $8000 block of memory. You can do this by running WHYP with the value of *HEDBASE* in the configuration file WHYP.CFG set to $8000. This will load all of the WHYP words from the file WHYP12.HED with dictionary addresses starting at address $8000. Of course, the codes for these words are not yet at those addresses so you cannot execute regular WHYP words at this point. However, you can execute the word *load>tseg <filename>* which will load your program into the *tseg* array in the PC with the proper $8000 addresses for the built-in WHYP words. You will then be able to generate an S-record file of your program by executing the word *save.tseg*. The word *save.headers* will save all of your current header names if you want to execute WHYP from the flash memory.

Finally, you will need to include the proper reset and interrupt vector addresses at the top of the flash memory so that the beginning of the **WHYP** kernel at address $8000 is executed on reset and that all of your interrupt routines execute properly.

Therefore, to make a turnkey system you will need to create the following three S-record files:

1. **myprog.s19.** This file will contain the code for all of your WHYP words and will start at address $9000. The steps used to create this file are described below.

2. **WHYPFLSH.s19.** This file is created by assembling the source file WHYPFLSH.ASM which is a copy of the file WHYP12.ASM given in Appendix D in which *WHYPBASE* has been changed to $8000, and *EESTART* and *EESTOP* have been changed to $0D00 and $0FFF, respectively. You will need to change the value of *START* in this program to be the address of the **WHYP** word you want to execute on reset. The steps required to do this are described below.

3. **ivecb32.s19.** This file contains the interrupt vectors to be stored at the top of the flash memory. It is generated by assembling the file ivecb32.asm which will produce the listing file shown in Listing C–3. Note that the reset vector at addresses $FFFE–$FFFF contains $8000 which will be the start of the **WHYP** kernel. Also note that each interrupt vector points to some code between $FF60 and $FFD0 that will cause an indirect jump to your interrupt service routines whose addresses you have stored in RAM addresses between $0B10 and $0B39, as shown in Tables 6–5 and 6–7 in Chapter 6.

Listing C–3   Interrupt Vector Jump Table for 68HC912B32—File ivecb32.1st

```
8000                        WHYP     EQU    $8000

ff60                                 ORG    $FF60
                            *** Vector jump table ***
ff60  cd 0b 10              JBDLC    LDY    #$0B10
ff63  05 eb 00 00           JUMP     JMP    [0,Y]
ff67  cd 0b 12              JATD     LDY    #$0B12
ff6a  20 f7                          BRA    JUMP
ff6c  cd 0b 14              JRES     LDY    #$0B14
ff6f  20 f2                          BRA    JUMP
ff71  cd 0b 16              JSCI     LDY    #$0B16
ff74  20 ed                          BRA    JUMP
ff76  cd 0b 18              JSPI     LDY    #$0B18
ff79  20 e8                          BRA    JUMP
ff7b  cd 0b 1a              JPAIE    LDY    #$0B1A
ff7e  20 e3                          BRA    JUMP
ff80  cd 0b 1c              JPAO     LDY    #$0B1C
ff83  20 de                          BRA    JUMP
ff85  cd 0b 1e              JTOF     LDY    #$0B1E
ff88  20 d9                          BRA    JUMP
ff8a  cd 0b 20              JTC7     LDY    #$0B20
ff8d  20 d4                          BRA    JUMP
```

(continued)

Listing C–3 *(continued)*

```
ff8f cd 0b 22          JTC6    LDY     #$0B22
ff92 20 cf                     BRA     JUMP
ff94 cd 0b 24          JTC5    LDY     #$0B24
ff97 20 ca                     BRA     JUMP
ff99 cd 0b 26          JTC4    LDY     #$0B26
ff9c 20 c5                     BRA     JUMP
ff9e cd 0b 28          JTC3    LDY     #$0B28
ffa1 20 c0                     BRA     JUMP
ffa3 cd 0b 2a          JTC2    LDY     #$0B2A
ffa6 20 bb                     BRA     JUMP
ffa8 cd 0b 2c          JTC1    LDY     #$0B2C
ffab 20 b6                     BRA     JUMP
ffad cd 0b 2e          JTC0    LDY     #$0B2E
ffb0 20 b1                     BRA     JUMP
ffb2 cd 0b 30          JRTI    LDY     #$0B30
ffb5 20 ac                     BRA     JUMP
ffb7 cd 0b 32          JIRQ    LDY     #$0B32
ffba 20 a7                     BRA     JUMP
ffbc cd 0b 34          JXIRQ   LDY     #$0B34
ffbf 20 a2                     BRA     JUMP
ffc1 cd 0b 36          JSWI    LDY     #$0B36
ffc4 20 9d                     BRA     JUMP
ffc6 cd 0b 38          JILLOP  LDY     #$0B38
ffc9 20 98                     BRA     JUMP


ffd0                           ORG     $FFD0
                       *** Vectors ***
ffd0 ff 60             VBDLC   FDB     JBDLC
ffd2 ff 67             VATD    FDB     JATD
ffd4 ff 6c             VRES    FDB     JRES
ffd6 ff 71             VSCI    FDB     JSCI
ffd8 ff 76             VSPI    FDB     JSPI
ffda ff 7b             VPAIE   FDB     JPAIE
ffdc ff 80             VPAO    FDB     JPAO
ffde ff 85             VTOF    FDB     JTOF
ffe0 ff 8a             VTC7    FDB     JTC7
ffe2 ff 8f             VTC6    FDB     JTC6
ffe4 ff 94             VTC5    FDB     JTC5
ffe6 ff 99             VTC4    FDB     JTC4
ffe8 ff 9e             VTC3    FDB     JTC3
ffea ff a3             VTC2    FDB     JTC2
ffec ff a8             VTC1    FDB     JTC1
ffee ff ad             VTC0    FDB     JTC0
fff0 ff b2             VRTI    FDB     JRTI
fff2 ff b7             VIRQ    FDB     JIRQ
fff4 ff bc             VXIRQ   FDB     JXIRQ
fff6 ff c1             VSWI    FDB     JSWI
fff8 ff c6             VILLOP  FDB     JILLOP
fffa 80 00             VCOP    FDB     WHYP
fffc 80 00             VCLM    FDB     WHYP
fffe 80 00             VRST    FDB     WHYP
```

Therefore, to make a turnkey system that will execute your program on reset, do the following:

1. Load WHYP into RAM as described above in this section.
2. Make sure the target dictionary pointer, *tdp*, is set to 2000 using function key F9.
3. Load your program into RAM using *LOAD <filename>* and make sure your program is working properly.
4. Find the hex address of your main word, say *main*, you want to execute on reset by typing

   ```
   hex ' main u.
   ```

   Remember this address. If it is 2A3C, then its address in the flash memory will be 9A3C.
5. Type *bye* to quit **WHYP**.
6. Copy file `WB32FLSH.CFG` to `WHYP12.CFG`. This will change the value of *HEDBASE* to 8000.
7. Type WHYP12 to execute WHYP.
8. Type *LOAD>TSEG <filename>* where *<filename>* is the name of the file containing your WHYP words. In response to "Enter base address: " type 9000. This will be the starting hex address of your words in the flash memory.
9. Type *SAVE.TSEG*.
   In response to "Enter an s19 filename for tseg: " type `myprog.s19` (or any other *.s19* file name you want).
   In response to "Enter destination hex address for data: " type 9000.
10. Type *SAVE.HEADERS*.
    In response to "Enter a filename for header names: " type `myprog.hed` (or any other *.hed* file name you want).
11. Type *bye* to quit **WHYP**.
12. Open the file `WHYPFLSH.ASM` in an editor and change the *START* address to the address in flash memory of your main word that you found in step 4. For example, if the address is 9A3C, then the *START* line at the beginning of the program should read

    ```
    START    EQU    $9A3C
    ```

13. Assemble the file `WHYPFLSH.ASM` using a 68HC12 assembler. For example, if you are using `AS12.EXE` you would type

    ```
    as12 whypflsh.asm >whypflsh.lst
    ```

    This will produce a listing file called `whypflsh.lst` as well as the .s19 file, `whypflsh.s19`.

14. You now have the three .s19 files, `myprog.s19`, `whypflsh.s19`, and `ivecb32.s19` (provided on the `disk` with the book). You should merge these three files into a single .s19 file called `flash.s19` by doing the following:
    a. Copy the file `whypflsh.s19` to `flash.s19`.
    b. Copy only the lines in file `myprog.s19` that begin with *S1* to the clipboard and paste them in the file `flash.s19` just before the last line that begins with *S9*.
    c. Copy only the lines in file `ivecb32.s19` that begin with *S1* to the clipboard and paste them in the file `flash.s19` just before the last line that begins with *S9*.

    Make sure that no blank lines remain in the file `flash.s19` and that the last line begins with S9.

15. Program the internal flash memory with the data in the file `flash.s19` by using the utilities provided in the Axiom program `ax12.exe`. When you switch to the single-chip mode by removing jumpers A and B and press reset, your program should execute.

C.1.4 The Motorola M68EVB912B32 Evaluation Board

The Motorola M68EVB912B32 evaluation board contains the 68HC912B32 microcontroller and has the memory map shown in Table C–4. This board operates in the single-chip mode and contains no external memory. The WHYP kernel must therefore be stored in the internal flash EEPROM. This flash EEPROM normally contains the D-Bug12 monitor that will be overwritten when you store the WHYP kernel in the flash memory.

Because there is no external memory, you will have only the 768 bytes of on-chip EEPROM and 1 Kbyte of on-chip RAM for program development. This means that you must develop large programs in parts, moving new WHYP words to the flash EEPROM after they have been tested in the on-chip RAM or EEPROM. Although we have developed large programs in WHYP using this method, it is not as convenient as using the external RAM on the CME12B32 board described in Section C.1.3.

The WHYP kernel in the file `WHYPFLSH.ASM` described in the previous section can be loaded into the flash EEPROM using the EEPROM bootloader described in Appendix E of the Motorola M68EVB912B32 Evaluation Board User's Manual. This bootloader resides in 2 Kbytes of erase-protected memory in the internal Flash EEPROM from addresses $F800–$FFFF. Therefore, your total program, including the WHYP kernel can occupy memory between $8000 and $F7FF.

Table C–4 Memory Map for the M68EVB912B32

Address Range	Memory Type
$0000–$01FF	On-chip I/O registers
$0800–$0BFF	1K on-chip RAM
$0D00–$0FFF	768 bytes of on-chip EEPROM
$8000–$FFFF	32K internal FLASH EEPROM

However, the erase-protected memory area includes the addresses between $FFD0 and $FFFF that contain the interrupt vectors shown in Listing C–2, but we can no longer store the file `ivecb32.s19` (generated from Listing C–2) in that protected memory region. The interrupt vectors that are stored from $FFD0 to $FFFF are pointers to a secondary jump table in the user-programmable flash EEPROM starting at address $F7D0. That is, the reset vector at $FFFE–$FFFF is $F7FE and the BDLC interrupt vector at $FFD0–$FFD1 is $F7D0. This means that if you assemble the file shown in Listing C–2 with the first ORG statement changed to $F760 and the second ORG statement changed to $F7D0, then you can merge the resulting .S19 file with the `WHYPFLSH.S19` file, as described in the previous section to create a resulting .S19 file that you can use to program the flash EEPROM. All of the interrupt vectors shown in Listing C–2 will then be mapped to the RAM area between $0B10 and $0B38, as described in Chapter 6.

To give yourself some more RAM memory, you may want to change the value of *RAMBASE* in the file `WHYPFLSH.ASM` to $0800 (see Appendix D) and change the size of the data and return stacks by changing the values in *STACK* and *DATSTK*. Be careful to change the value of *vdp* in the .CFG file so that your variables don't conflict with the system variables or your two stacks.

As WHYP words are developed and tested they can be moved to the flash EEPROM using the WHYP words *LOAD>TSEG*, *SAVE.TSEG*, and *SAVE.HEADERS*, as described in the previous section.

C.2   68HC11 BOARDS

WHYP was first developed for the 68HC11 and has been used with a wide variety of 68HC11 parts. A version of WHYP called WHYP11 can be used with most 68HC11 parts. This section describes how to load WHYP11 into two Motorola evaluation boards: the M68HC11EVB that uses a 68HC11A8 chip, and the M68HC11EVBU that uses a 68HC711E9 chip. Similar procedures can be used to load WHYP11 into many other 68HC11 systems.

C.2.1   The Motorola M68HC11EVB Evaluation Board

The Motorola M68HC11EVB evaluation board contains the 68HC11A8 microcontroller and has the memory map shown in Table C–5. The WHYP11 kernel fits in less than 4 Kbytes of memory. It can be stored in the external RAM between $D000

Table C–5   Memory Map for the M68HC11EVB

Address Range	Memory Type
$0000–$00FF	256 bytes of on-chip RAM
$1000–$103F	On-chip I/O registers
$4000	PD0/Host(pin 3) flip-flop
$6000–$7FFF	Optional 8K external RAM
$9800–$9801	ACIA registers
$B600–$B7FF	512 bytes on-chip EEPROM
$C000–$DFFF	8K external RAM
$E000–$FFFF	8K external EPROM

and $DFFF. Alternatively, you can program the last half of an 8-KByte EPROM (2764), starting at the physical address $1000 with the WHYP kernel and replace the $C000–$DFFF RAM (U5) with this EPROM.

Loading WHYP11 into RAM   The file WHYP11.ASM contains the WHYP11 kernel and the default ORG address is $D000. To load WHYP11 into RAM starting at address $D000 do the following:

1. Make sure the files WHYP11.CFG and WHYP11.HED are in the current directory.
2. Connect the HOST port of the M68HC11EVB to one of the COM ports of the PC using a null modem. This means that in the connecting cable pins 2 and 3 must be crossed. That is, pin 2 on one end must be connected to pin 3 on the other end, and vice versa. A straightthrough cable will not work.
3. Apply power to the M68HC11EVB. Note that it requires ±12 volts as well as +5 volts and ground.
4. From the DOS prompt, type *HOST* followed by <*enter*>. If you are connected to COM2, you will need to press F10 to change the COM port.
5. Type *LOAD* followed by <*enter*>.
6. Press function key F6 and type WHYP11.S19 followed by <*enter*>.
7. Type *G D000*. This will execute the WHYP kernel.
8. Press the *ESC* key to return to DOS prompt.
9. Type *WHYP11* to execute WHYP on the PC.

Loading WHYP11 into an External EPROM   If you want to make a turnkey system that will run your WHYP program when you press reset, you will need to store the WHYP kernel in an external EPROM. Your WHYP words can then be stored in the internal EEPROM, or if you need more room, they can be added to the external EPROM.

The specific steps required to program the EPROM will depend on your particular PROM programmer. In general, you should do the following:

1. Make sure the EPROM (a 2764) is erased.
2. Load the contents of the file WHYP11.S19 into your PROM programmer memory starting at address $1000. This is the physical address of the 8K EPROM. Addresses $0000–$0FFF should be filled with all ones (FF). Addresses $1000–$1FFF will contain the WHYP kernel.
3. Program the 2764 chip.
4. Remove the 8K RAM from the U5 socket and install the 2764 in its place.
5. Connect the HOST port of the M68HC11EVB to one of the COM ports of the PC using a null modem. This means that in the connecting cable pins 2 and 3 must be crossed. That is, pin 2 on one end must be connected to pin 3 on the other end, and vice versa. A straightthrough cable will not work.

6. Apply power to the M68HC11EVB. Note that it requires ±12 volts as well as +5 volts and ground.

7. From the DOS prompt, type *HOST* followed by *<enter>*. If you are connected to COM2, you will need to press F10 to change the COM port.

8. Type *G D000*. This will execute the WHYP kernel.

9. Press the *ESC* key to return to DOS prompt.

10. Type *WHYP11* to execute WHYP on the PC.

Making a Turnkey System with Your Program in EEPROM   After you have written a program, you may want to make a turnkey system that will execute your main WHYP word on reset. You need to execute the beginning of the WHYP kernel (see the file WHYP11.ASM) which will initialize the return and data stack pointers, enable the EEPROM (on the E9 part), and initialize the SCI port. The program then jumps to *START* which is normally the WHYP loop that polls the SCI port. One possibility is to change the address of *START* to the address of your main word. This, however, would require reprogramming the EPROM.

Alternatively, you can store the startup code given in the file start11.s19 at the beginning of the internal EEPROM. This is the 23 bytes at the beginning of the WHYP kernel given in the file WHYP11.ASM that has been assembled starting at the first address of the EEPROM. This startup code is in the file start11.asm and the machine code is given in the file start11.lst.

If all of your program fits in the internal EEPROM starting at address $B620, then you can make a turnkey system that will execute your program on reset by doing the following:

1. Program the WHYP kernel in an external EPROM as described in the previous section.

2. From the DOS prompt, type *HOST* followed by *<enter>*. If you are connected to COM2, you will need to press F10 to change the COM port.

3. Type *MM B600* followed by *<enter>* to modify the memory in the EEPROM starting at address $B600. Enter the 23 bytes from address $B600 to address $B616 in the startup code given in the file start11.lst.

4. Move jumper J4 from pins 1–2 to pins 2–3. When you press the reset button, the code at the beginning of the EEPROM at address $B600 will be executed. This will execute the startup code and then jump to the WHYP kernel in the external EPROM.

5. Press the *ESC* key to return to the DOS prompt.

6. Type *WHYP11* to execute WHYP on the PC.

7. Press function key F9 and change the target dictionary pointer, *tdp*, to $B620. This will cause your WHYP code to be loaded in the EEPROM beyond the startup code.

8. Type *LOAD* <name>.whp to load your WHYP program into the EEPROM memory. Make sure that the ending address is not beyond $B7FF.

9. Use *tick* to find the hex address, *main_addr*, of the word you want to execute on reset.

10. Type

```
HEX <main_addr> B615 EE!
```

to add the address of your main word to the *JMP* instruction in `start11.lst`.

11. Press the reset button to execute your program.

To return to WHYP, move jumper J4 from pins 2–3 back to pins 1–2. Pressing reset will execute the Buffalo monitor. Carry out steps 7–10 in the previous section. You can now type

```
HEX D017 B615 EE!
```

to reset the address of *MN1* in the *JMP START* instruction in the code given in the file *start11.lst* to the address of *MN1* in the WHYP11 kernel.

Making a Turnkey System with Your Program in EPROM   If your program is too large to fit in the EEPROM, then you can load it into RAM and later replace the RAM with an EPROM. If your program is less that 4 Kbytes in length, then you can load it starting at address \$C000 and include it in the same EPROM as the WHYP kernel. If it is larger than 4 Kbytes, then you can load up to 8 Kbytes into RAM U4 starting at address \$6000. An additional 4 Kbytes can then be stored in RAM U5 starting at address \$C000.

Specifically, to make a turnkey system that will execute a program less than 4 Kbytes long on reset, do the following:

1. Load WHYP into RAM as described above in this section.

2. Make sure the target dictionary pointer, *tdp*, is set to C000 using function key F9.

3. Load your program into RAM using *LOAD <filename>* and make sure your program is working properly.

4. Find the hex address of your main word, say *main*, you want to execute on reset by typing

```
hex ' main u.
```

Remember this address.

5. Type

```
hex C000 CFFF s.file
```

In response to "Enter an s19 filename: " type `myprog.s19` (or any other *.s19* file name you want). This will create an S-record file of all bytes in RAM between addresses \$C000 and \$CFFF. You can replace the address \$CFFF in the above statement with the address of the last byte in your program.

6. Store the instruction *JMP $D000* at the beginning of the EEPROM by typing

```
HEX
7E B600 EEC!
D000 B601 EE!
```

7. Type *bye* to quit **WHYP**.

8. Make a copy of the file `WHYP11.ASM` and open this copy in an editor. Change the statement *JMP MN1* in the main program to *JMP <main>* where *<main>* is the address of your main word that you found in step 4.

9. Assemble the edited file `WHYP11.ASM` to produce a new .S19 file, `WHYP11.S19`.

10. You now have the two .19 files, `myprog.s19`, and `whyp11.s19`. You should merge these two files into a single .s19 file called `eprom.s19` by doing the following:

    a. Copy the file `whyp11.s19` to `eprom.s19`.

    b. Copy only the lines in file `myprog.s19` that begin with *S1* to the clipboard and paste them in the file `eprom.s19` just after the first line that begins with *S0* and just before the first *S1* line in the file `eprom.s19`.

    Make sure that no blank lines remain in the file `eprom.s19` and that the last line begins with S9.

11. Program a 2764 EPROM with the data in the file `eprom.s19` using a prom programmer.

12. Turn off the power to the EVB board. Remove the 8K RAM from the U5 socket and install the 2764 in its place. Move jumper J4 from pins 1–2 to pins 2–3. When you turn on the power to the EVB board, or press the reset button, your program should execute.

Similar steps can be carried out to program the U4 RAM chip where you would load your program starting at address $6000.

C.2.2   The Motorola M68HC11EVBU Evaluation Board

The Motorola M68HC11EVBU evaluation board contains the 68HC11E9 micro-controller and has the memory map shown in Table C–6. It is designed to operate in the single-chip mode. The 68HC11E9 on the board contains the Buffalo monitor in its 12-Kbyte internal ROM. A separate 68HC711E9 microcontroller is also included

Table C–6   Memory Map for the M68HC11EVBU

Address Range	Memory Type
$0000–$01FF	512 bytes of on-chip RAM
$1000–$103F	On-chip I/O registers
$B600–$B7FF	512 bytes on-chip EEPROM
$D000–$FFFF	12K internal ROM/EPROM

with the board. This is a version of the 'E9 part that contains a 12 Kbyte erasable EPROM instead of the Buffalo monitor ROM. You can program the WHYP11 kernel in the EPROM of the 68HC711E9, load your programs into the on-chip RAM and EEPROM, and then add your words to the on-chip EPROM.

To store the WHYP11 kernel in the EPROM of the 68HC711E9, you need to combine the S-record files from WHYP11.S19 and the interrupt vectors from INTVECE9.S19 shown in Listing 6–1. We have done this and stored the resulting .S19 file in the file WHYP11E9.S19. This WHYP11 kernel will occupy less than 4 Kbytes of memory starting at address $D000. You will be able to add your own words starting at address $E000.

The easiest way to do this is to use an external PROM programmer that will program 68HC711E9 chips. To run WHYP, just power up the board or press the reset button and type *WHYP11*.

The specific steps required to program the 68HC711E9 will depend on your particular PROM programmer. In general, you should do the following:

1. Copy file WHYP11E9.CFG to WHYP11.CFG.
2. Use the file WHYP11E9.S19 to program the 68HC711E9.
3. With the power to the board turned off, replace the 68HC11E9 chip on the board with the 68HC711E9 containing the WHYP kernel.
4. Apply power to the board. Pressing the reset button will execute the WHYP kernel.
5. From the DOS prompt, type *WHYP11*.

Adding Your Own Words to the EPROM To add your own words to the 68HC711E9 EPROM starting at $E000, do the following:

1. Make sure your words work properly by first loading them into RAM or EEPROM and testing them.
2. Exit WHYP and then type *WHYP11* to execute WHYP.
3. Type *LOAD>TSEG <filename>* where *<filename>* is the name of the file containing your WHYP words. In response to "Enter base address: " type E000. This will be the starting hex address of your words in the EPROM.
4. Type *SAVE.TSEG*.
   In response to "Enter an s19 filename for tseg: " type myprog.s19 (or any other *.s19* file name you want).
   In response to "Enter destination hex address for data: " type E000.
5. Type *SAVE.HEADERS*.
   In response to "Enter a filename for header names: " type myprog.hed (or any other *.hed* file name you want).
6. Type *bye* to quit WHYP.
7. In the file WHYP11.CFG change the first line to myprog.hed (the one you just saved) and change the value of *HEDBASE* to 0000.

8. Remove power from the board and remove the 68HC711E9 chip.

9. Program the 68HC711E9 chip with the file `myprog.s19`. To do this you will normally need to load the current contents of the chip into the programmer memory, and then load the data from the file `myprog.s19` into the programmer memory. When you program the chip, only the new values that are different from what is currently on the chip will be programmed. This will add your words to the existing EPROM starting at address $E000. This part of the EPROM should contain all FFs before you program it.

10. With the power to the board turned off, replace the 68HC11E9 chip on the board with the 68HC711E9 containing the WHYP kernel.

11. Apply power to the board. Pressing the reset button will execute the WHYP kernel.

12. From the DOS prompt, type *WHYP11*. Your new words are now a permanent part of the system.

Making a Turnkey System   To make a turnkey system that will execute your program on reset do the following:

1. Add all of your words to the 68HC711E9 EPROM as described in the previous section.

2. Type *WHYP11* to execute WHYP on the PC.

3. Press function key F9 and change the target dictionary pointer, *tdp*, to $B600. Type *LOAD* `START11.WHP`. This will cause the first 21 bytes of the startup code shown in file `start11.asm` to be loaded into the EEPROM starting at address $B600.

4. Use *tick* to find the hex address, *main_addr*, of the word you want to execute on reset.

5. Type

```
HEX <main_addr> B615 EE!
```

to add the address of your main word to the JMP instruction in `start11.lst`.

6. Move jumper J2 from pins 2–3 to pins 1–2. When you press the reset button, the code at the beginning of the EEPROM at address $B600 will be executed. This will execute the startup code and then jump to your main word in the 68HC711E9 EPROM.

To return to WHYP just move jumper J2 from pins 1–2 back to pins 2–3. Pressing reset will now execute WHYP.

Appendix D

WHYP12.ASM File

```
;       68HC12 KERNEL FOR WHYP12
;       Copyright 1998 by Richard E. Haskell
;       CSE Dept., Oakland University
;       Rochester, Michigan 48309


***********************************************************
********  Change the following five addresses    *********
********  for a particular 68HC12 environment     *********
***********************************************************
REGBASE  EQU     $0000              ;register base
RAMBASE  EQU     $0900              ;ram base
EESTART  EQU     $1000              ;start address of EEPROM
EESTOP   EQU     $1FFF              ;stop address of EEPROM
WHYPBASE EQU     $4000              ;start of WHYP kernel


********  To make a turnkey system change START   *******
********  to the address of your main word.       *******
********  The default, MN1, will run WHYP.         *******
***********************************************************
START    EQU     MN1
```

(continued)

```
******** To use SCI1 instead of SCI0 change $C1-$C7 *******
******** in the following five lines to $C9-$CF      *******
**************************************************************
SC0BDL    EQU    REGBASE+$C1    ;baud rate control
SC0CR1    EQU    REGBASE+$C2    ;SCI control reg 1
SC0CR2    EQU    REGBASE+$C3    ;SCI control reg 2
SC0SR     EQU    REGBASE+$C4    ;SCI status reg
SC0DR     EQU    REGBASE+$C7    ;SCI data reg

COPCTL    EQU    REGBASE+$16    ;COP control reg
EEPROT    EQU    REGBASE+$F1    ;EEPROM Block Protect reg
EEPROG    EQU    REGBASE+$F3    ;EEPROM programming control reg
RDRF      EQU    $20            ;SCSR mask
STACK     EQU    RAMBASE+$100   ;system (return) stack
DATSTK    EQU    RAMBASE+$80    ;data stack
******    WHYP System Variables  ******
SP0       EQU    RAMBASE        ;initial data stack pointer
RP0       EQU    RAMBASE+$02    ;initial return stack pointer
LAST      EQU    RAMBASE+$04    ;address called by CREATE


***********************************************
*         WHYP Kernel
***********************************************

          ORG    WHYPBASE       ;beginning of whyp kernel
MAIN
          LDS    #STACK         ;initialize system (return) stack
          STS    RP0
          LDX    #DATSTK        ;initialize data stack
          STX    SP0
          CLR    EEPROT         ;enable EEPROM writes
          CLR    COPCTL         ;disable COP watchdog
          BSR    INITSER        ;initialize sci
          JMP    START          ;default=MN1, change for turnkey
MN1       BSR    INWDY          ;input word to Y
          JSR    0,Y            ;execute subroutine
          LDAA   #6
          BSR    OUTPUT           ;send ACK
          BRA    MN1

;         INITIALIZE SCI
INITSER
          CLR    SC0CR1         ;8 bit
          LDD    #$340C
          STAA   SC0BDL         ;9600 baud
          STAB   SC0CR2         ;enable tx & rx
NOOP      RTS

;         INPUT BYTE FROM SERIAL PORT
INCHAR
          LDAA   SC0SR          ;check status
          ANDA   #RDRF          ;check rdrf
```

(continued)

(continued)

```
            BEQ      INCHAR              ;wait for char
            LDAA     SC0DR               ;get char in A
            RTS


;          OUTPUT BYTE TO SERIAL PORT
OUTPUT
            TST      SC0SR
            BPL      OUTPUT              ;loop until tdre
            STAA     SC0DR               ;send A
            RTS


;          PUSH INPUT WORD ON STACK
;          LOW BYTE SENT FIRST
;          ( w -- )
TPUSH
            BSR      INCHAR              ;get low byte
            STAA     1,-X                ;push on data stack
            BSR      INCHAR              ;get high byte
            STAA     1,-X                ;push on data stack
            RTS


;          POP STACK TO SERIAL PORT
;          UPLOAD HIGH BYTE FIRST
;          ( -- w )
TPOP
            PSHD
            LDD      2,X+                ;pop top of stack into D
            BSR      OUTPUT              ;send high byte
            TBA
            BSR      OUTPUT              ;send low byte
            PULD
            RTS


;          INPUT WORD TO Y
;          LOW BYTE SENT FROM HOST FIRST
INWDY
            BSR      INCHAR
            TAB                          ;B=low byte
            BSR      INCHAR              ;D=word
            XGDY                         ;Y=word
            RTS


;          INPUT WORD TO X
INWDX
            BSR      INCHAR
            TAB                          ;B=low byte
            BSR      INCHAR              ;D=word
            XGDX                         ;X=word
            RTS
```

(continued)

```
;          STORE 'WORD' AT ADDR
;          ( addr word -- )
STOREW
        PSHX                            ;save X
        BSR     INWDX                   ;X = addr
        BSR     INWDY                   ;Y = word
        XGDY                            ;D = word
        STD     0,X                     ;store it
        PULX                            ;restore X
        RTS


;          STORE 'COUNT' BYTES AT ADDR IN EEPROM
;          ( #bytes addr sequence_of_bytes -- )
TBLKST
        BSR     INWDY                   ;Y = count
        PSHY                            ;count on stack
        BSR     INWDY                   ;Y = addr
        CPY     #EESTART
        BLO     TBS2                    ;If in eeprom
        CPY     #EESTOP
        BHI     TBS2
TBS1    BSR     INCHAR                  ;get next byte
        BSR     EESTA                   ;store it in eeprom
        INY                             ;inc addr
        PULD
        DECB                            ;dec count
        PSHD                            ;save count
        BNE     TBS1                    ;do all 'count' bytes
        PULY                            ;fix stack
        RTS
TBS2    BSR     INCHAR                  ;else
        STAA    0,Y                     ;save in ram
        INY                             ;inc addr
        PULD                            ;get count
        DECB                            ;dec count
        PSHD                            ;save count
        BNE     TBS2                    ;do all 'count' bytes
        PULY                            ;fix stack
        RTS

;          EEPROM PROGRAMMING ROUTINES
;          STORE BYTE A AT ADDRESS Y
EESTA
        PSHA                            ;save byte
        LDAA    0,Y                     ;if @addr != FF
        CMPA    #$FF
        BEQ     EEB1
        BSR     BYTEE                   ;erase byte
EEB1    PULA                            ;get byte
        LDAB    #$02
        STAB    EEPROG                  ;set EELAT bit
```

(continued)

(continued)

```
        STAA    0,Y             ;store data to EEPROM addr
        LDAB    #$03
        STAB    EEPROG           ;set EEPGM bit (EELAT=1)
        JSR     DLY10           ;10 msec delay
        LDAB    #$02
        STAB    EEPROG          ;turn off hi voltage
        CLR     EEPROG          ;clear EELAT bit
        RTS


;       ERASE BYTE AT ADDRESS Y
BYTEE
        LDAB    #$16
        STAB    EEPROG          ;set to byte erase mode
        STAB    0,Y             ;write any data to addr to erase
        LDAB    #$17
        STAB    EEPROG          ;turn on high voltage
        JSR     DLY10           ;10 msec delay
        LDAB    #$16
        STAB    EEPROG          ;turn off hi voltage
        CLR     EEPROG          ;clear EELAT bit
        RTS


;       STORE WORD D AT ADDRESS Y AND Y+1
EESTD
        PSHB
        BSR     EESTA
        INY
        PULA
        BSR     EESTA
        RTS


***************************************
*       WHYP WORDS
***************************************


;       10MS.DELAY ( -- )       ; 8 MHz clock
DLY10                           ; 4*N + 12 = 80000
        PSHX                    ; 2 cycles
        LDX     #19997          ; 2  "      N = 19997
DL1     DEX                     ; 1  "
        BNE     DL1             ; 3  "
        PULX                    ; 3  "
        RTS                     ; 5  "


;       EEC! ( c addr -- )
EECST
        LDY     2,X+
        LDD     2,X+
        TBA
        JSR     EESTA
        RTS
```

(continued)

```
;        EE!   ( n addr -- )
EEST
        LDY       2,X+
        LDD       2,X+
        JSR       EESTD
        RTS


;        ERASE.BULK        ( -- )
BULKE
        LDAB      #$06
        STAB      EEPROG            ;set to bulk erase mode
        STAB      EESTART           ;write any data to EEPROM
        LDAB      #$07
        STAB      EEPROG            ;turn on high voltage
        BSR       DLY10             ;10 msec delay
        LDAB      #$06
        STAB      EEPROG            ;turn off high voltage
        CLR       EEPROG            ;clear EELAT bit
        RTS


**************************************************
* 68HC12          WHYP Stack Words
**************************************************

; DUP ( w -- w w )
; Duplicate the top stack item.
DUPP
        MOVW 0,X,2,-X
        RTS

; SWAP ( w1 w2 -- w2 w1 )
; Exchange top two stack items.
SWAP
        LDD 0,X
        MOVW 2,X,0,X
        STD 2,X
        RTS

; OVER ( w1 w2 -- w1 w2 w1 )
; Copy second stack item to top.
OVER
        MOVW 2,X,2,-X
        RTS

; DROP ( w -- )
; Discard top stack item.
DROP
        INX
        INX
        RTS
```

(continued)

(continued)

```
;       ROT       ( n1 n2 n3 -- n2 n3 n1 )
ROT
        LDD       0,X                 ;D = n3
        MOVW      4,X,0,X             ;n1 n2 n1
        MOVW      2,X,4,X             ;n2 n2 n1
        STD       2,X                 ;n2 n3 n1
        RTS

;       -ROT      ( n1 n2 n3 -- n3 n1 n2 )
MROT
        LDD       0,X                 ;D = n3
        MOVW      2,X,0,X             ;n1 n2 n2
        MOVW      4,X,2,X             ;n2 n1 n2
        STD       4,X                 ;n3 n1 n2
        RTS

;       NIP       ( n1 n2 -- n2 )
NIP
        MOVW      2,X+,0,X
        RTS

;       TUCK      ( n1 n2 -- n2 n1 n2 )
TUCK
        MOVW      0,X,2,-X            ;n1 n2 n2
        MOVW      4,X,2,X             ;n1 n1 n2
        MOVW      0,X,4,X             ;n2 n1 n2
        RTS

;       2DROP     ( n1 n2 -- )
DROP2
        INX
        INX
        INX
        INX
        RTS

;       2DUP      ( n1 n2 -- n1 n2 n1 n2 )
DUP2
        MOVW      2,X,2,-X
        MOVW      2,X,2,-X
        RTS

;       2SWAP     ( a b c d -- c d a b )
SWAP2
        LDD       0,X                 ;D = d
        MOVW      4,X,0,X             ;a b c b
        STD       4,X                 ;a d c b
        LDD       2,X                 ;D = c
        MOVW      6,X,2,X             ;a d a b
        STD       6,X                 ;c d a b
        RTS
```

(continued)

```
;         2OVER    ( a b c d -- a b c d a b )
OVER2
          MOVW     6,X,2,-X
          MOVW     6,X,2,-X
          RTS


;         FLIP     ( ab -- ba )      flip bytes
FLIP
          LDD      0,X
          STAB     0,X             ;bb
          STAA     1,X             ;ba
          RTS


;         PICK     ( n1 -- n2 )      copy n1th element to top
PICK
          LDD      2,X+            ;D = n1
          NOP
          LSLD
          MOVW     D,X,2,-X
          RTS


;         ROLL     ( n -- )
ROLL
          LDD      0,X             ;D = n
          NOP
          LSLD
          LEAY     2,X             ;Y -> top of stack
          LEAY     D,Y             ;Y -> n1th element
          LSRB                     ;B = n
          MOVW     0,Y,0,X         ;save n1th element
          TSTB
          BEQ      RL2             ;move all elements
RL1       MOVW     2,-Y,2,Y        ; up 2 bytes
          DECB
          BNE      RL1
RL2       MOVW     2,X+,0,Y        ;move 1st element
          RTS


;         ?DUP     ( n -- 0 | n n )
QDUP
          LDAA     0,X             ;if n <> 0
          ORAA     1,X
          BEQ      QD1
          MOVW     0,X,2,-X        ;DUP
QD1       RTS


;         SP@ ( -- a )
; Push the current data stack pointer.
SPAT
          PSHX
```

(*continued*)

(continued)

```
        PULY                        ;Y = X = a
        STY      2,-X               ;push on data stack
        RTS

;       SP! ( a -- )
; Set the data stack pointer.
SPSTO
        LDX     0,X                 ;X = a
        RTS

;       >R ( w -- )                 ( R:   -- w )
; Push the data stack to the return stack.
TOR
        PULY                        ;save return addr
        LDD      2,X+               ;D = w
        PSHD                        ;push D on ret stack
        PSHY                        ;restore return addr
        RTS

;       R> ( -- w )      ( R: w -- )
; Pop the return stack to the data stack.
RFROM
        PULY                        ;save return addr
        PULD                        ;D = ret stack val, w
        STD      2,-X               ;push w on data stack
        PSHY                        ;restore return addr
        RTS

;       R@    ( -- w ) ( R: w -- w )
; Copy top of return stack to the data stack.
RAT
        TSY                         ;SP+1 -> Y
        LDD      2,Y                ;D = ret stack val, w
        STD      2,-X               ;push w on data stack
        RTS

;       R>DROP           ( R: sys -- )
RFDROP
        PULY                        ;save return addr
        PULD                        ;pop sys
        PSHY                        ;restore return addr
        RTS

;       RP@  ( -- a )
; Push the current RP to the data stack.
RPAT
        PULD                        ;save return addr
        TFR     SP,Y                ;SP -> Y
        STY      2,-X               ;push Y to data stack
        PSHD                        ;restore return addr
        RTS
```

(continued)

```
;         RP!        ( a -- )
; Set the return stack pointer.
RPSTO
        PULD                         ;save return addr
        LDY        2,X+              ;Y=a
        TFR        Y,SP              ;Y -> SP, SP = a
        PSHD                         ;restore return addr
        RTS


**************************************************
*       68HC12   WHYP Memory Access Words
**************************************************


;         !        ( w a -- )
STORE
        LDY        2,X+              ;Y=a, pop data stack in Y
        MOVW       2,X+,0,Y          ;store w at a
        RTS


;         @        ( a -- w )
AT
        LDY        0,X               ;Y = a
        MOVW       0,Y,0,X           ;w = @Y
        RTS


;         C!       ( c b -- )
CSTOR
        LDY        2,X+              ;Y=b
        LDD        2,X+              ;D = c
        STAB       0,Y               ;store c at b
        RTS


;         C@       ( b -- c )
CAT
        LDY        0,X               ;Y=b
        CLRA
        LDAB       0,Y
        STD        0,X
        RTS


**************************************************
*       68HC12   WHYP Logic Words
**************************************************


; AND ( w w -- w )
; Bitwise AND.
ANDD
        LDD        2,X+              ;D=w, pop data stack into D
        ANDA       0,X
        STAA       0,X
```

(continued)

(continued)

```
        ANDB    1,X
        STAB    1,X
        RTS


; OR ( w w -- w )
; Bitwise inclusive OR.
ORR
        LDD     2,X+            ;D=w
        ORAA    0,X
        STAA    0,X
        ORAB    1,X
        STAB    1,X
        RTS


; XOR ( w w -- w )
; Bitwise exclusive OR.
XORR
        LDD     2,X+            ;D=w
        EORA    0,X
        STAA    0,X
        EORB    1,X
        STAB    1,X
        RTS


;       INVERT  ( n -- 1's_compl_of_n )
INVERT
        COM     0,X
        COM     1,X
        RTS


;       TRUE = -1 = $FFFF
TRUE
        LDD     #-1
        STD     2,-X
        RTS


;       FALSE = 0
FALSE
        LDD     #0
        STD     2,-X
        RTS


**************************************************
*    68HC12  WHYP Relational Operator Words
**************************************************


;       0< ( n -- t )
; Return true if n is negative.
ZLESS
        LDY     #$FFFF         ;true
        LDD     0,X            ;if not negative
```

(continued)

```
        BMI     ZL1
        LDD     #0000        ;false
ZL1     STY     0,X
        RTS

;       0= ( n -- t )
; Return true if n is zero
ZEQ
        LDY     #$FFFF                ;true
        LDD     0,X               ;if not zero
        BEQ     ZE1
        LDY     #0000             ;false
ZE1     STY     0,X               ;push flag on stack
        RTS

;       < ( n1 n2 -- t )
; Return true if n1 is less than n2.
LT
        LDY     #$FFFF            ;true
        LDD     2,X+              ;D = n2
        CPD     0,X               ;if n2 <= n1
        BGT     LT1
        LDY     #0                ;set false
LT1     STY     0,X               ;set flag
        RTS

;       = ( n1 n2 -- t )
; Return true if n1 is equal to n2.
EQ
        LDY     #$FFFF            ;true
        LDD     2,X+              ;D = n2
        CPD     0,X               ;if n2 <> n1
        BEQ     EQ1
        LDY     #0                ;set false
EQ1     STY     0,X               ;set flag
        RTS

;       0> ( n -- t )
; Return true if n is greater than zero
ZGT
        LDY     #$FFFF            ;true
        LDD     0,X               ;if <= zero
        BGT     ZG1
        LDY     #0000             ;false
ZG1     STY     0,X               ;push flag on stack
        RTS

;       > ( n1 n2 -- t )
; Return true if n1 is greater than n2.
GT
        LDY     #$FFFF            ;true
```

(continued)

(continued)

```
        LDD     2,X+            ;D = n2
        CPD     0,X             ;if n2 >= n1
        BLT     GT1
        LDY     #0              ;set false
GT1     STY     0,X             ;set flag
        RTS

;       >= ( n1 n2 -- t )
; Return true if n1 is greater than or equal to n2.
GTE
        LDY     #$FFFF          ;true
        LDD     2,X+            ;D = n2
        CPD     0,X             ;if n2 > n1
        BLE     GTE1
        LDY     #0              ;set false
GTE1    STY     0,X             ;set flag
        RTS

;       <= ( n1 n2 -- t )
; Return true if n1 is less than or equal to n2.
LTE
        LDY     #$FFFF          ;true
        LDD     2,X+            ;D = n2
        CPD     0,X             ;if n2 < n1
        BGE     LTE1
        LDY     #0              ;set false
LTE1    STY     0,X             ;set flag
        RTS

;       <> ( n1 n2 -- t )
; Return true if n1 is not equal to n2.
NEQ
        LDY     #$FFFF          ;true
        LDD     2,X+            ;D = n2
        CPD     0,X             ;if n2 = n1
        BNE     NEQ1
        LDY     #0              ;set false
NEQ1    STY     0,X             ;set flag
        RTS

;       U< ( u1 u2 -- t )
; Return true if u1 is less than u2.
ULT
        LDY     #$FFFF          ;true
        LDD     2,X+            ;D = u2
        CPD     0,X             ;if u2 <= u1
        BHI     ULT1
        LDY     #0              ;set false
ULT1    STY     0,X             ;set flag
        RTS
```

(continued)

```
;        U> ( u1 u2 -- t )
; Return true if u1 is greater than u2.
UGT
        LDY       #$FFFF          ;true
        LDD       2,X+            ;D = u2
        CPD       0,X             ;if u2 >= u1
        BLO       UGT1
        LDY       #0              ;set false
UGT1    STY       0,X             ;set flag
        RTS


;        U<= ( u1 u2 -- t )
; Return true if u1 is less than or equal to u2.
ULE
        LDY       #$FFFF          ;true
        LDD       2,X+            ;D = u2
        CPD       0,X             ;if u2 < u1
        BHS       ULE1
        LDY       #0              ;set false
ULE1    STY       0,X             ;set flag
        RTS


;        U>= ( u1 u2 -- t )
; Return true if u1 is greater than or equal to u2.
UGE
        LDY       #$FFFF          ;true
        LDD       2,X+            ;D = u2
        CPD       0,X             ;if u2 > u1
        BLS       UGE1
        LDY       #0              ;set false
UGE1    STY       0,X             ;set flag
        RTS


**************************************************
*       68HC12 WHYP Arithmetic Words
**************************************************


;        + ( X Y -- X+Y )
PLUS
        LDD       2,X+
        ADDD      0,X
        STD       0,X
        RTS


;        - ( X Y -- X-Y )
MINUS
        LDD       2,X
        SUBD      2,X+
        STD       0,X
        RTS
```

(continued)

(continued)

```
;         D+ ( d1 d2 -- d3 )
DPLUS
        LDAA    7,X
        ADDA    3,X
        STAA    7,X
        LDAA    6,X
        ADCA    2,X
        STAA    6,X
        LDAA    5,X
        ADCA    1,X
        STAA    5,X
        LDAA    4,X
        ADCA    0,X
        STAA    4,X
        LEAX    4,X
        RTS

;         D- ( d1 d2 -- d3 )
DMINUS
        LDAA    7,X
        SUBA    3,X
        STAA    7,X
        LDAA    6,X
        SBCA    2,X
        STAA    6,X
        LDAA    5,X
        SBCA    1,X
        STAA    5,X
        LDAA    4,X
        SBCA    0,X
        STAA    4,X
        LEAX    4,X
        RTS

;    UM*          ( u u -- ud )   16 x 16 = 32
;                Unsigned multiply. Return double product.
UMSTA
        LDD     2,X+
        LDY     2,X+
        EMUL
        STD     2,-X
        STY     2,-X
        RTS

*        M*          ( n n -- d )   16 x 16 = 32
*     Signed multiply. Return double product.
MSTAR
        LDD     2,X+
        LDY     2,X+
        EMULS
        STD     2,-X
        STY     2,-X
        RTS
```

(continued)

```
*          *            ( n n -- n )   16 x 16 = 16
*          Signed multiply. Return single product. (UM* DROP)
STAR
          LDD       2,X+
          LDY       2,X+
          EMUL
          STD       2,-X
          RTS


;          DUM*     ( ud un -- ud )   32 x 16 = 32
;          Unsigned multiply of double number by single number.
;          Returns a double unsigned number, pcL pcH.
;          A B x C = pH pL   (drop high 16 bits of product, ACH)
;          pL = BCL, pH = BCH + ACL
DUMST
          LDD       0,X             ;D = un (C)
          LDY       2,X             ;Y = udH (A)
          EMUL                      ;Y = ACH, D = ACL
          STD       2,X             ;save ACL
          LDD       0,X             ;D = un (C)
          LDY       4,X             ;Y = udL (B)
          EMUL                      ;Y = BCH, D = BCL
          STD       4,X             ;save pL = BCL
          TFR       Y,D             ;D = BCH
          ADDD      2,X             ;D = BCH+ACL = pH
          STD       2,X             ;save pH
          LEAX      2,X             ;fix data stack
          RTS


*          UM/MOD        ( udl udh un -- ur uq )   32/16 = 16:16
*          Unsigned divide of a double by a single. Return mod and
quotient.
UMMOD
          PSHX
          LDY       2,X
          LDD       4,X
          LDX       0,X
          EDIV
          BCS       UM1             ;if div by 0
          BVC       UM2             ; or overflow
UM1       LDD       #$FFFF          ; rem = $FFFF
          LDY       #$FFFF          ; quot = $FFFF
UM2       PULX
          LEAX      2,X
          STD       2,X
          STY       0,X
          RTS


*          M/MOD        ( dl dh n -- r q )   32/16 = 16:16
*          Signed divide of a double by a single. Return mod and quotient.
MMOD
```

(continued)

(continued)

```
        PSHX
        LDY     2,X
        LDD     4,X
        LDX     0,X
        EDIVS
        BCS     MM1                 ;if div by 0
        BVC     MM2                 ; or overflow
MM1     LDD     #$FFFF              ; rem = $FFFF
        LDY     #$FFFF              ; quot = $FFFF
MM2     PULX
        LEAX    2,X
        STD     2,X
        STY     0,X
        RTS

*       /MOD      ( n n -- r q )    16/16 = 16:16
*       Signed divide of a single by a single. Return mod and quotient.
SMOD
        PSHX
        LDD     2,X
        LDX     0,X
        IDIVS
        TFR     X,Y
        BCS     SM1                 ;if div by 0
        BVC     SM2                 ; or overflow
SM1     LDD     #$FFFF              ; rem = $FFFF
        LDY     #$FFFF              ; quot = $FFFF
SM2     PULX
        STD     2,X
        STY     0,X
        RTS

*       /         ( n n --  q )     16/16 = 16
*       Signed divide of a single by a single. Return quotient.
SLASH
        PSHX
        LDD     2,X
        LDX     0,X
        IDIVS
        TFR     X,Y
        BCS     SL1                 ;if div by 0
        BVC     SL2                 ; or overflow
SL1     LDD     #$FFFF              ; rem = $FFFF
        LDY     #$FFFF              ; quot = $FFFF
SL2     PULX
        LEAX    2,X
        STY     0,X
        RTS

*       U/        ( u u --  q )     16/16 = 16
*       Unsigned divide of a single by a single. Return quotient.
USLASH
```

(continued)

```
         PSHX
         LDD      2,X
         LDX      0,X
         IDIV
         TFR      X,Y
         PULX
         LEAX     2,X
         STY      0,X
         RTS
*        MOD      ( n n -- r )    16/16 = 16
*        Signed divide of a single by a single. Return remainder.
MOD
         PSHX
         LDD      2,X
         LDX      0,X
         IDIVS
         TFR      X,Y
         BCS      MD1              ;if div by 0
         BVC      MD2              ; or overflow
MD1      LDD      #$FFFF           ; rem = $FFFF
MD2      PULX
         LEAX     2,X
         STD      0,X
         RTS
*        */       ( n1 n2 n3 -- n1*n2/n3 )    star-slash
*        Signed multiply-divide  n1*n2 double
STARSL
         PSHX
         LDD      4,X
         LDY      2,X
         EMULS
         LDX      0,X
         EDIVS
         BCS      SS1              ;if div by 0
         BVC      SS2              ; or overflow
SS1      LDY      #$FFFF           ; quot = $FFFF
SS2      PULX
         LEAX     4,X
         STY      0,X
         RTS
; IDIV    ( num denom -- rem quot )
;               Integer divide 16 by 16
IDIVV
         PSHX
         LDD      2,X
         LDX      0,X
         IDIV                      ;X=quot,D=rem
         TFR      X,Y
```

(*continued*)

(continued)

```
        BCC     ID1                 ;div by 0
        LDD     #$FFFF              ;quot already $FFFF
ID1     PULX
        STD     2,X
        STY     0,X
        RTS


;   FDIV          ( num denom -- rem quot )
;                 Fractional divide 16 by 16
FDIVV
        PSHX
        LDD     2,X
        LDX     0,X
        FDIV                        ;X=quot,D=rem
        TFR     X,Y
        BCS     FD1                 ;if div by 0
        BVC     FD2                 ; or numer > denom
FD1     LDD     #$FFFF              ; rem = $FFFF
        LDY     #$FFFF              ; quot = $FFFF
FD2     PULX
        STD     2,X
        STY     0,X
        RTS


;       MU/MOD  ( ud un -- urem udquot )
;       Unsigned divide of a double by a single.
;       Return remainder and double quotient.
MUMOD
        LDD     0,X
        STD     2,-X                ; dup un
        PSHX
        LDD     4,X                 ;D = udH
        LDY     #0                  ;0:udH / un
        LDX     0,X
        EDIV                        ;Y = quotH, D = remH
        BCC     MU1                 ;if div by 0
        PULX
        LEAX    2,X
        LDD     #$FFFF              ; rem, quot = $FFFF
        STD     0,X
        STD     2,X
        STD     4,X
        RTS
MU1     PULX
        STY     2,X                 ;quotH
        STD     4,X                 ;remH
        LDY     4,X                 ;Y = remH
        LDD     6,X                 ;D = udL
        PSHX
        LDX     0,X                 ;X = un
        EDIV                        ;Y = quotL, D = remL
```

(continued)

```
        PULX
        STD      6,X                  ;remL
        STY      4,X                  ;quotL
        LEAX     2,X
        RTS


;       MIN      (n1 n2 -- min )
MIN
        LDY      2,X+                 ;Y = n2
        CPY      0,X                  ;if n2 < n1
        BGE      MIN1
        STY      0,X                  ;leave n2 on stack
MIN1    RTS                            ;else leave n1


;       MAX      (n1 n2 -- min )
MAX
        LDY      2,X+                 ;Y = n2
        CPY      0,X                  ;if n2 > n1
        BLE      MX1
        STY      0,X                  ;leave n2 on stack
MX1     RTS                          ;else leave n1


;       NEGATE   ( n -- -n )
NEGATE
        NEG      1,X                  ;negate low byte
        BEQ      NG1                  ;if not zero
        COM      0,X                  ;complement high byte
        RTS
NG1     NEG      0,X                  ;else, negate high byte
        RTS


;       ABS      ( n -- |n| )
ABS
        TST      0,X                  ;if negative
        BPL      AB2                  ;negate:
        NEG      1,X                  ;negate low byte
        BEQ      AB1                  ;if not zero
        COM      0,X                  ;complement high byte
        RTS
AB1     NEG      0,X                  ;else, negate high byte
AB2     RTS


;       1+       ( n -- n+1 )
ONEP
        LDD      0,X
        ADDD     #1
        STD      0,X
        RTS


;       2+       ( n -- n+2 )
```

(continued)

```
TWOP
        LDD     0,X
        ADDD    #2
        STD     0,X
        RTS


;       1-      ( n -- n-1 )
ONEM
        LDD     0,X
        SUBD    #1
        STD     0,X
        RTS


;       2-      ( n -- n-2 )
TWOM
        LDD     0,X
        SUBD    #2
        STD     0,X
        RTS


;       2*      ( n -- 2*n )
TWOT
        ASL     1,X             ;arith shift left
        ROL     0,X
        RTS


;       2/      ( n -- n/2 )
TWOS
        ASR     0,X             ;arith shift right
        ROR     1,X
        RTS


;       U2/     ( u -- u/2 )
U2S
        LSR     0,X
        ROR     1,X             ;logic shift right
        RTS


;       +!      ( n addr -- )      add n to @addr
PSTORE
        LDY     2,X+            ;Y = addr
        LDD     0,Y             ;D = @addr
        ADDD    2,X+            ;add n to @addr
        STD     0,Y
        RTS


;       LSHIFT          ( n1 n2 -- n1 )
;               Left shift bits of n1 n2 times
LSHIFT
        LDY     2,X+            ;Y = n2
LS1     ASL     1,X             ;arith shift left
```

(continued)

```
          ROL       0,X                    ; n2 bits
          DEY
          BNE       LS1
          RTS


;         RSHIFT         ( n1 n2 -- n1 )
;                   Right shift bits of n1 n2 times
RSHIFT
          LDY       2,X+                   ;Y = n2
RS1       LSR       0,X                    ;arith shift right
          ROR       1,X                    ; n2 bits
          DEY
          BNE       RS1
          RTS


;         ?NEGATE ( n1 n2 -- n3 )  if n2 < 0, negate n1
QNEGATE
          TST       0,X                    ;if n2 < 0
          BPL       QN2
          NEG       3,X                    ;negate n1
          BEQ       QN1
          COM       2,X
          BRA       QN2
QN1       NEG       2,X
QN2       INX                              ;leave only n3
          INX
          RTS


;         DNEGATE ( d -- d )
DNEGATE
          NEG       3,X                    ;dnegate
          BNE       DN1
          NEG       2,X
          BNE       DN2
          NEG       1,X
          BNE       DN3
          NEG       0,X
          RTS
DN1       COM       2,X
DN2       COM       1,X
DN3       COM       0,X
          RTS


;         DABS      ( d -- |d| )
DABS
          TST       0,X                    ;if d negative
          BPL       DA4
          NEG       3,X                    ;dnegate
          BNE       DA1
          NEG       2,X
```

(continued)

(continued)

```
        BNE     DA2
        NEG     1,X
        BNE     DA3
        NEG     0,X
        RTS
DA1     COM     2,X
DA2     COM     1,X
DA3     COM     0,X
DA4     RTS


;       S>D     ( n -- d )       sign extend
STOD
        LDD     #$FFFF          ;negative extend
        DEX
        DEX
        TST     2,X             ;if n positive
        BMI     SD1
        LDD     #$0000          ;extend zeros
SD1     STD     0,X             ;else extend 1's
        RTS


***************************************************
*       68HC12  WHYP Number I/O & Display
***************************************************


;       (LIT)   ( -- n )
;               Runtime routine for single literals
LIT
        PULY                    ;Y -> number
        LDD     0,Y             ;Push number
        STD     2,-X            ;on data stack
        INY                     ;jump over number
        INY
        PSHY
        RTS


;       (DLIT)  ( -- d )
;               Runtime routine for double literals
DLIT
        PULY                    ;Y -> number
        LDD     2,Y             ;Push number
        STD     2,-X            ;on data stack
        LDD     0,Y
        STD     2,-X
        INY                     ;jump over number
        INY
        INY
        INY
        PSHY
        RTS
```

(continued)

```
;       . ( n -- )                    ;print top of stack
DOTT
        LDAA     #1                   ;opcode = 1
        JSR      OUTPUT               ;send to host
        JSR      TPOP                 ;send top of stack
        RTS

;       U. ( n -- )                   ;print unsigned number
UDOTT
        LDAA     #2                   ;opcode = 2
        JSR      OUTPUT               ;send to host
        JSR      TPOP                 ;send top of stack
        RTS

;       D. ( d -- )                   ;print double number
DDOTT
        LDAA     #3                   ;opcode = 3
        JSR      OUTPUT               ;send to host
        JSR      TPOP                 ;send double number
        JSR      TPOP
        RTS

;       UD. ( d -- )                  ;print unsigned dnumber
UDDOTT
        LDAA     #4                   ;opcode = 4
        JSR      OUTPUT               ;send to host
        JSR      TPOP                 ;send double number
        JSR      TPOP
        RTS

;       EMIT    ( c -- )              ;display ascii char
EMIT
        LDAA     #5                   ;opcode = 5
        JSR      OUTPUT               ;send to host
        JSR      TPOP                 ;send top of stack
        RTS

;       .S      ( -- )    Display contents of stack
DOTS
        LDAA     #7
        JSR      OUTPUT               ;host code = 7
        STX      2,-X                 ;save data stack ptr
        LDD      SP0
        SUBD     0,X                  ;#bytes = SP0 - X
        ASRA
        RORB                          ;B = #stack items
        TBA
        JSR      OUTPUT               ;send #items
        TSTB
        BLE      DS2                  ;while B > 0
        LDY      SP0                  ; send bottom of stack 1st
```

(continued)

(continued)

```
DS1     PSHB
        LDD     2,-Y
        JSR     OUTPUT          ; send D
        TBA
        JSR     OUTPUT
        PULB
        DECB
        BNE     DS1             ; send all stack items
DS2     LEAX    2,X             ;fix data stack
        RTS


;       .R      ( -- )      Display contents of return stack
DOTR
        LDAA    #8
        JSR     OUTPUT          ;host code = 8 (DOTS)
        TFR     SP,Y             ;Y = RP
        INY
        INY
        STY     2,-X            ;save return stack ptr
        LDD     RP0
        SUBD    0,X             ;#bytes = RP0 - RP
        ASRA
        RORB                    ;B = #stack items
        TBA
        JSR     OUTPUT          ;send #items
        TSTB
        BLE     DR2             ;while B > 0
        LDY     RP0             ; send bottom of stack 1st
DR1     PSHB
        LDD     2,-Y
        JSR     OUTPUT          ; send D
        TBA
        JSR     OUTPUT
        PULB
        DECB
        BNE     DR1             ; send all stack items
DR2     LEAX    2,X             ;fix data stack
        RTS


;       (.")       ( -- ) Run-time routine for ."
PDOTQ
        LDAA    #9
        JSR     OUTPUT          ;send 9
        PULY
        LDAA    0,Y
        JSR     OUTPUT          ;send count
        TAB                     ;B = count
DQ1     INY
        LDAA    0,Y             ;get next char
        JSR     OUTPUT          ;& send it
        DECB
```

(continued)

```
        BNE     DQ1                     ;do all chars
        INY
        PSHY                            ;skip over string
        RTS


;       S.FILE  ( start.addr end.addr -- )
;       send data for making s-record file
SFILE
        LDAA    #18
        JSR     OUTPUT                  ;send code 18
SF1     JSR     INCHAR
        CMPA    #6
        BNE     SF1                     ;wait for ACK
        LDD     2,X                     ;send start.addr
        JSR     OUTPUT
        TBA
        JSR     OUTPUT
        LDD     0,X                     ;send #bytes
        SUBD    2,X
        ADDD    #1
        JSR     OUTPUT
        TBA
        JSR     OUTPUT
        LDY     2,X                     ;Y -> start.addr
SF2     LDAA    0,Y
        JSR     OUTPUT                  ;send next byte
        INY
        CPY     0,X                     ;repeat until
        BLS     SF2                     ; Y >= end.addr
        INX
        INX                             ;pop data stack
        INX
        INX
        RTS


;       (,)         ( n -- )
COMMA
        LDAA    #11                      ; send code 11
        JSR     OUTPUT                  ;get tdp
        JSR     INWDY                   ;Y = tdp
        LDD     2,X+
        CPY     #$1000
        BLO     CMA1                    ;if in eeprom
        CPY     #$1FFF
        BHI     CMA1
        JSR     EESTD                   ; do eeprom store
        RTS                             ;else
CMA1    STD     0,Y                     ; store tos at tdp in ram
        RTS
```

(continued)

(continued)

```
;        (C,)      ( c -- )
CCOMMA
        LDAA     #12              ; send code 12
        JSR      OUTPUT           ;get tdp
        JSR      INWDY            ;Y = tdp
        LDD      2,X+
        CPY      #$1000
        BLO      CCA1             ;if in eeprom
        CPY      #$1FFF
        BHI      CCA1
        TBA
        JSR      EESTA            ; do eeprom store
        RTS                       ;else
CCA1    STAB     0,Y              ;store char at tdp in ram
        RTS


;       CR      Carriage Return
CR
        LDAA     #$0D             ; send 13
        JSR      OUTPUT
        RTS


;        .REG   ( -- )
;        Display registers
DOTREG
        PSHY
        PSHX
        PSHB
        PSHA
        TPA
        PSHA                      ;push CCR
        BSR      DOTREGS
        PULA
        PULA
        PULB
        PULX
        PULY
        RTS


;       .REGS   ( -- )
;       Send register values to host
;       Pushed on stack by SWI
DOTREGS
        LDAA     #14
        JSR      OUTPUT           ;Code = 14
        TSY
        XGDY
        ADDD     #10              ;D = orig SP
        JSR      OUTPUT
        TBA
        JSR      OUTPUT           ;send SP
```

(continued)

```
        TSY
        INY
        INY                         ;Y -> CCR
        LDAB    #9                  ;9 bytes on stack
DRG1:   LDAA    0,Y
        JSR     OUTPUT              ;send 9 bytes on stack
        INY
        DECB
        BNE     DRG1
        LDY     2,-Y                ;get addr of next word
        LDD     0,Y                 ; JSR D
        JSR     OUTPUT              ;send ^sub
        TBA
        JSR     OUTPUT
        RTS


*************************************************
*       68HC12 WHYP  -- CREATE ... DOES>
*************************************************
;       (CREATE)        ( +++ )        Run time for CREATE
PCREATE
        LDAA    #15                 ;code 15
        JSR     OUTPUT
PC1     JSR     INWDY               ;read word
        CPY     #6                  ;if 6, exit
        BEQ     PC2
        JSR     0,Y                 ;else, execute sub
        LDAA    #6
        JSR     OUTPUT              ;send ACK
        BRA     PC1
PC2     RTS

;       DOVAR   ( -- a )        (leave pfa on data stack)
                                ;Run time code for CREATE
DOVAR
        PULY                        ;get return addr (pfa)
        STY     2,-X                ;push on data stack
        RTS                         ;return one level up

;       (;CODE)  ( -- )     Compile time code for DOES>
PSCODE
        PULD                        ;get addr of JSR DODOES
        LDY     LAST                ;replace DOVAR with DODOES
        STD     0,Y                 ;at addr in LAST
        RTS                         ;return up one level

;       DODOES  ( -- pfa )  Run time code for DOES>
DODOES
        PULY                        ;Y -> code following DOES>
        PULD                        ;D = pfa of defined word
        PSHY
```

(continued)

```
        STD     2,-X                ;push pfa on data stack
        RTS                         ;return to code after DOES>

**************************************************
*       68HC12  WHYP Branching Words
**************************************************

;       EXIT    ( -- ), Exit the current word (subroutine)
EXIT
        PULY
        RTS
;         EXECUTE ( ca -- )
EXECUTE
        LDY     2,X+
        JMP     0,Y

;       I       ( -- n )            Index in DO loop
I
        TSY                         ;Y -> ret addr
        INY
        INY
        LDD     0,Y                 ;D = index - (limit+$8000)
        ADDD    2,Y                 ;D = index
        STD     2,-X                ;push index
        RTS

;       (DO)    Run time code for DO
PDO
        TSY
        LDD     0,Y                 ;D = ret addr
        XGDY                        ;Y = ret addr, D = SP+1
        SUBD    #6
        XGDY                        ;D = ret addr, Y = SP+1-6
        STD     0,Y                 ;put back ret addr
        TYS                         ;move SP to new ret addr
        INY
        INY                         ;Y -> return stack
        LDD     2,X                 ;D = limit
        ADDD    #$8000              ;D = (limit + $8000)
        STD     2,Y                 ;2nd element on ret stack
        STD     2,-X                ;save in temp storage
        LDD     2,X                 ;D = index
        SUBD    0,X                 ;D = index - (limit+$8000)
        STD     0,Y                 ;1st element on ret stack
        PULY
        PSHY                        ;Y = next addr
        PSHY
        PULD                        ;D = next addr
        ADDD    0,Y                 ;get xhere2
        TSY                         ;Y -> ret addr
        STD     6,Y                 ;3rd element on ret stack
        INX
```

(continued)

```
        INX                         ;pop temp storage
        INX
        INX
        INX
        INX                         ;pop index & limit
        PULY
        INY                         ;jump over displ
        INY
        PSHY
        RTS                         ;go to next sub

;       (LOOP)            Run time code for LOOP
PLOOP
        TSY
        LDD     2,Y                 ;inc top of ret stack
        ADDD    #1
        BVS     LP1                 ;if no overflow
        STD     2,Y
        PULY                        ; keep looping
        PSHY                        ;Y -> displ
        PULD
        ADDD    0,Y                 ;D -> sub after DO
        PSHD
        RTS                         ;jump there
LP1     LDD     0,Y                 ;if overflow
        XGDY
        INY                         ;jump over displ
        INY
        ADDD    #6                  ;rewind ret stack
        XGDY
        STD     0,Y
        TYS
        RTS                         ;& quit loop

;       LEAVE    ( -- )
LEAVE
        PULY                        ;jump
        TSY
        INY
        INY
        INY
        INY                         ;Y -> xhere2
        LDD     2,Y+                ;D = addr after LOOP
        TYS                         ;pop return stack
        PSHB
        PSHA                        ;push D
        RTS                         ;jump past LOOP

;       DONEXT   ( -- )            run time code for NEXT
DONEXT
        TSY
```

(continued)

```
        LDD     0,Y             ;dec RP
        SUBD    #1
        STD     0,Y
        FCB     $26             ;BNE opcode

*************************************************
*       Misc. words
*************************************************

;       MASK    8-bit byte
;        INPUT: B = bit no.
;        OUTPUT; B = mask = 2^bit#
MASK
        PSHY                    ;save Y
        BSR     MSK1
        DB      1
        DB      2
        DB      4
        DB      8
        DB      16
        DB      32
        DB      64
        DB      128
MSK1    PULY                    ;addr of DB  1
        ABY
        LDAB    0,Y             ;get mask
        PULY                    ;restore Y
        RTS

;       HI      ( b# addr -- )
;       set bit number b# of byte at address addr to 1
HI
        LDY     2,X+            ;Y = addr
        LDD     2,X+            ;B = b#
        BSR     MASK            ;B = mask
        STAB    1,-X            ;push B on data stack
        LDAA    0,Y             ;A = @Y
        ORAA    1,X+            ;OR with mask and pop mask
        STAA    0,Y             ;store back at addr
        RTS

;       LO      ( b# addr -- )
;       clear bit number b# of byte at address addr to 0
LO
        LDY     2,X+            ;Y = addr
        LDD     2,X+            ;B = b#
        BSR     MASK            ;B = mask
        COMB                    ;complement mask
        STAB    1,-X            ;push B on data stack
        LDAA    0,Y             ;A = @Y
        ANDA    1,X+            ;AND with mask and pop mask
```

(continued)

```
        STAA    0,Y                 ;store back at addr
        RTS


;       ?HI     ( b# addr -- f )
;       leave a true flag if bit number b# of byte at addr is high
QHI
        LDY     2,X+                ;Y = addr
        LDD     2,X+                ;B = b#
        BSR     MASK                ;b = mask
        STAB    1,-X                ;push B on data stack
        LDAA    0,Y                 ;A = @Y
        ANDA    1,X+                ;AND with mask and pop mask
        BEQ     QH1                 ;if not zero
        LDD     #$FFFF              ; leave true flag
        BRA     QH2
QH1     LDD     #$0000              ;else leave false flag
QH2     STD     2,-X                ;push flag on stack
        RTS


;       HERE    ( -- n )
HERE
        LDAA    #16
        JSR     OUTPUT              ;get tdp
        JSR     INWDY
        STY     2,-X                ;push on stack
        RTS


;       [']             Run-time of 'tick' in colon defn
BTICKB
        LDAA    #17                 ;code 16
        JSR     OUTPUT
BT1     JSR     INWDY               ;read word
        CPY     #6                  ;if 6, exit
        BEQ     BT2
        JSR     0,Y                 ;else, execute sub
        LDAA    #6
        JSR     OUTPUT              ;send ACK
        BRA     BT1
BT2     RTS


;       DEPTH ( -- n )              return #items on stack
DEPTH
        STX     2,-X                ;save data stack ptr
        LDD     SP0
        SUBD    0,X                 ;#bytes = SP0 - X
        ASRA
        RORB                        ;D = #stack items
        STD     0,X                 ; if neg, underflow
        RTS
;       MOVE  ( from to cnt -- )
```

(continued)

(continued)

```
MOVE
        LDD     2,X+                ; D = count
        LDY     2,X+                ; Y = to address
        PSHX                        ; save X
        LDX     0,X                 ; X = from address
MV1     MOVW    2,X+,2,Y+           ; move words from X to Y
        SUBD    #1                  ; move cnt words
        BNE     MV1
        PULX                        ; restore X
        INX                         ; pop data stack
        INX
        RTS

;           CMOVE   ( ad1 ad2 cnt -- )
;           move cnt bytes up in memory from addr ad1 to ad2
CMOVE
        LDD     2,X+                ; D = count
        LDY     2,X+                ; Y = to address
        PSHX                        ; save X
        LDX     0,X                 ; X = from address
CMV1    MOVB    1,X+,1,Y+           ; move bytes from X to Y
        SUBD    #1                  ; move cnt bytes
        BNE     CMV1
        PULX                        ; restore X
        INX                         ; pop data stack
        INX
        RTS

;           CMOVE>  ( ad1 ad2 cnt -- )
;           move cnt bytes down in memory from addr ad1 to ad2
CMOVEG
        LDD     2,X+                ; D = count
        LDY     2,X+                ; Y = to address
        PSHX                        ; save X
        LDX     0,X                 ; X = from address
        INY                         ; move bytes from
        INX                         ;   right to left
CMVG1   MOVB    1,-X,1,-Y           ; move bytes from -X to -Y
        SUBD    #1                  ; move cnt bytes
        BNE     CMVG1
        PULX                        ; restore X
        INX                         ; pop data stack
        INX
        RTS

*********************************
*       DEBUG WORDS
*********************************

*       HEX2ASC
*       input:  A = hex value
*       output: A = ASCII value
```

(continued)

```
HEX2ASC
        ANDA       #$0F
        CMPA       #9
        BLS        HA1
        ADDA       #$37
        RTS
HA1     ADDA       #$30
        RTS


*       EMIT blank space
BLANK
        MOVW       #$20,2,-X
        JSR        EMIT
        RTS


*       EMIT hex value in A
DOTXX
        PSHB
        PSHA
        LSRA
        LSRA
        LSRA
        LSRA
        BSR        HEX2ASC
        TAB
        CLRA
        STD        2,-X
        JSR        EMIT
        PULA
        BSR        HEX2ASC
        TAB
        CLRA
        STD        2,-X
        JSR        EMIT
        PULB
        RTS


*       EMIT 4 hex digit address in D
DOTADDR
        BSR        DOTXX
        TBA
        BSR        DOTXX
        RTS


*       DUMP16            Print out 1 line from 16 addresses
*       Input:  Y = addr
*       Output: Y = addr+16
DUMP16
        PSHD
        TFR        Y,D
        PSHY
```

(continued)

```
        BSR     DOTADDR
        BSR     BLANK
        BSR     BLANK
        LDAB    #16
DP161   LDAA    1,Y+
        BSR     DOTXX
        BSR     BLANK
        DECB
        BNE     DP161
        BSR     BLANK
        LDAB    #16
        PULY
DP162   LDAA    1,Y+
        CMPA    #$20
        BHI     DP163
        LDAA    #$20
DP163   STAA    1,-X
        MOVB    #0,1,-X
        JSR     EMIT
        DECB
        BNE     DP162
        JSR     CR
        PULD
        RTS


*       HEAD16              ." dump header "
HEAD16
        JSR     PDOTQ
        DB      54      # of chars
        FCC     '    0 1 2 3 4 5 6 7 8 9 A B C D E F'
        RTS


*       DUMP    ( addr cnt -- )
DUMP
        JSR     CR
        BSR     HEAD16
        JSR     CR
        LDD     2,X+            count
        LDY     2,X+            addr
        ADDD    #15
        LSRD                    B = # of 16-byte lines
        LSRD
        LSRD
        LSRD
DMP1    JSR     DUMP16
        DECB
        BNE     DMP1
        RTS


*       Send subroutine code to PC
*       SNDSUB  ( addr num_bytes -- )
SNDSUB
        LDD     2,X+            ;B = num_bytes
```

(continued)

```
        LDY     2,X+                ;Y = addr
SSB1    LDAA    0,Y
        JSR     OUTPUT
        INY
        DECB
        BNE     SSB1
        RTS

*************************************************************
*       Fuzzy Control
*************************************************************

*       Fill Weight Arrays
*       fill.weights ( xi memfunc_addr -- )
FILLWT
        LDY     2,X+                Y -> input membership functions
        LDD     2,X+                B = xi
        PSHX                        save X
        TFR     Y,X                 X -> membership functions
        LDY     2,X                 Y -> input weight table
        PSHB                        save xi
        LDD     4,X+                B = #mem functs; X->1st memb fnc
        PULA                        A = xi
FW1     MEM                         fuzzy membership grade
        DBNE    B,FW1
        PULX                        restore X
        RTS

*       Fire all rules
*       firerules ( in.out_addr rules_addr -- )
FIRERULES
        LDD     2,X+                D -> rules
        LDY     2,X+                Y -> in.out.array
        PSHX
        TFR     D,X                 X -> rules
        INX
        INX                         X -> Wout addr
        PSHY                        save Y
        LDY     2,X+                Y -> Wout, X -> 1st rule
        LDAB    0,Y                 B = #out.memb.fncs
FR0     CLR     1,X+                 clear W array
        DBNE    B, FR0
        PULY                        Y -> in.out.array
        LDAA    #$FF
        REV                         rule evaluation
        PULX
        RTS

*       Find Output value
*       calc.output ( rules  cent_addr -- output_value )
FINDOUT
        LDD     2,X+                D -> cent
        LDY     2,X+                Y -> rules
```

(continued)

```
        PSHX
        TFR     D,X                   X -> cent array
        LDY     2,Y                   Y -> Warray
        LDAB    0,Y                   B = #out.memb.fncs
        INY                           Y -> W array
        WAV
        EDIV                          Y = quotient
        TFR     Y,D                   D = quotient  A = 0, B = output
        PULX
        STD     2,-X
        RTS


;       VHERE    ( -- n )
VHERE
        LDAA    #19                   ;opcode = 19
        JSR     OUTPUT                ;get vdp
        JSR     INWDY
        STY     2,-X                  ;push on stack
        RTS


;       ALLOT ( n -- )                ;allocate n bytes in code (tdp) space
ALLOT
        LDAA    #20                   ;opcode = 20
        JSR     OUTPUT                ;send to host
        JSR     TPOP                  ;send top of stack
        RTS


;       VALLOT ( n -- )               ;allocate n bytes in ram (vdp) space
VALLOT
        LDAA    #21                   ;opcode = 21
        JSR     OUTPUT                ;send to host
        JSR     TPOP                  ;send top of stack
        RTS


;       2!  ( d a -- )                store double word
        LDY     2,X+                  ;Y = a
        MOVW    2,X+,2,Y+             ;store dH
        MOVW    2,X+,0,Y             ;store dL
        RTS


;       2@  ( a -- d )                fetch double word
        LDY     2,X+                  ;Y = a
        MOVW    2,Y,2,-X             ;push dL on data stack
        MOVW    0,Y,2,-X             ;push dH on data stack
        RTS


;       (")   ( -- )  Run-time routine for "
PQUOTE
        PULY                          ;get addr of cnt
        LDAB    0,Y
        CLRA                          ;D = count
```

(continued)

```
            INY                         ;Y = addr
            STY     2,-X                ;push addr on data stack
            STD     2,-X                ;push len on data stack
            ABY                         ;add len to addr
            PSHY                        ;skip over string
            RTS

;           DARK  ( -- )                 ;clear the PC screen
DARK
            LDAA    #22                 ;opcode = 22
            JSR     OUTPUT              ;send to host
            RTS

;           AT ( col row -- )           ;set cursor on PC screen to col, row
ATXY
            LDAA    #23                 ;opcode = 23
            JSR     OUTPUT              ;send to host
            JSR     TPOP                ;send row
            JSR     TPOP                ;send col
            RTS

;           SP0 ( -- addr )             ;get data stack pointer for empty stack
SPP0
            LDD     #SP0
            STD     2,-X
            RTS

;           RP0 ( -- addr )             ;get return stack pointer for empty stack
RPP0
            LDD     #RP0
            STD     2,-X
            RTS

;           B.LOOKUP  ( addr frac -- interp )   ;8-bit table lookup wrapper
BLOOKUP
            LDD     2,X+
            LDY     0,X
            TBL     0,Y
            TAB
            LDAA    #0
            STD     0,X
            RTS

;           W.LOOKUP  ( addr frac -- interp )   ;16-bit table lookup wrapper
WLOOKUP
            LDD     2,X+
            LDY     0,X
            ETBL    0,Y
            STD     0,X
            RTS

END         FCB     0
```

Appendix E

WHYP12.HED Header File

The file `WHYP12.HED` contains a list of all WHYP words that have been stored in memory on a 68HC12 evaluation board. Each line in the file contains the name of the word and the offset address of the subroutine that is called when the word is executed. The offset address is relative to the value of *HEDBASE* in the file `WHYP12.CFG`. Both files, `WHYP12.HED` and `WHYP12.CFG`, must be in the current subdirectory when the program `WHYP12.EXE` is executed. The program reads this file and uses the information to build the WHYP dictionary.

WHYP12.HED (sorted by address)					
		ROT	117	?DUP	197
		-ROT	124	SP@	1a2
		NIP	131	SP!	1a7
10MS.DELAY	d1	TUCK	136	>R	1aa
EEC!	da	2DROP	143	R>	1b0
EE!	e4	2DUP	148	R@	1b6
ERASE.BULK	ec	2SWAP	151	R>DROP	1bd
DUP	101	2OVER	162	RP@	1c1
SWAP	106	FLIP	16b	RP!	1c8
OVER	10f	PICK	172	!	1cf
DROP	114	ROLL	17b	@	1d6

C!	1dd	2/	4a4	calc.output	8e7
C@	1e4	U2/	4a9	VHERE	8fc
AND	1ec	+!	4ae	ALLOT	907
OR	1f7	LSHIFT	4b7	VALLOT	910
XOR	202	RSHIFT	4c1	2!	919
INVERT	20d	?NEGATE	4cb	2@	924
TRUE	212	DNEGATE	4dc	(")	92f
FALSE	218	DABS	4f2	DARK	93c
0<	21e	S>D	50c	AT	942
0=	22b	(LIT)	51b	SP0	94e
<	238	(DLIT)	524	RP0	954
=	247	.	533	B.LOOKUP	95a
0>	256	U.	53c	W.LOOKUP	968
>	263	D.	545	END	0
>=	272	UD.	551		
<=	281	EMIT	55d		
<>	290	.S	566		
U<	29f	.R	591		
U>	2ae	(.")	5c0		
U<=	2bd	S.FILE	5d7		
U>=	2cc	(,)	60f		
+	2db	(C,)	62a		
-	2e2	CR	647		
D+	2e9	.REG	64d		
D-	304	(CREATE)	68c		
UM*	31f	DOVAR	6a3		
M*	329	(;CODE)	6a7		
*	334	DODOES	6ae		
DUM*	33c	EXIT	6b4		
UM/MOD	353	EXECUTE	6b6		
M/MOD	36d	I	6ba		
/MOD	388	(DO)	6c4		
/	3a1	(LOOP)	6fa		
U/	3ba	LEAVE	71c		
MOD	3c9	DONEXT	72a		
*/	3df	HI	746		
IDIV	3f7	LO	755		
FDIV	40b	?HI	765		
MU/MOD	424	HERE	77e		
MIN	455	[']	789		
MAX	45e	DEPTH	7a0		
NEGATE	467	MOVE	7ac		
ABS	471	CMOVE	7c0		
1+	47f	CMOVE>	7d4		
2+	487	DUMP	891		
1-	48f	SNDSUB	8ab		
2-	497	fill.weights	8b9		
2*	49f	firerules	8cd		

WHYP12.HED

(sorted by name)

!	1cf
(")	92f
(,)	60f
(.")	5c0
(;CODE)	6a7
(C,)	62a
(CREATE)	68c
(DLIT)	524
(DO)	6c4
(LIT)	51b
(LOOP)	6fa
*	334
*/	3df
+	2db
+!	4ae
-	2e2
-ROT	124
.	533
.R	591
.REG	64d
.S	566
/	3a1
/MOD	388
0<	21e
0=	22b
0>	256
1+	47f
1-	48f
2*	49f
2+	487
2-	497

2/	4a4	DNEGATE	4dc	OR	1f7		
2!	919	DODOES	6ae	OVER	10f		
2@	924	DONEXT	72a	PICK	172		
2DROP	143	DOVAR	6a3	R>	1b0		
2DUP	148	DROP	114	R>DROP	1bd		
2OVER	162	DUM*	33c	R@	1b6		
2SWAP	151	DUMP	891	ROLL	17b		
10MS.DELAY	d1	DUP	101	ROT	117		
<	238	EE!	e4	RP!	1c8		
<=	281	EEC!	da	RP@	1c1		
<>	290	EMIT	55d	RP0	954		
=	247	ERASE.BULK	ec	RSHIFT	4c1		
>	263	EXECUTE	6b6	S.FILE	5d7		
>=	272	EXIT	6b4	S>D	50c		
>R	1aa	FALSE	218	SNDSUB	8ab		
?DUP	197	FDIV	40b	SP!	1a7		
?HI	765	fill.weights	8b9	SP@	1a2		
?NEGATE	4cb	firerules	8cd	SP0	94e		
@	1d6	FLIP	16b	SWAP	106		
ABS	471	HERE	77e	TRUE	212		
ALLOT	907	HI	746	TUCK	136		
AND	1ec	I	6ba	U.	53c		
AT	942	IDIV	3f7	U/	3ba		
B.LOOKUP	95a	INVERT	20d	U2/	4a9		
C!	1dd	LEAVE	71c	U<	29f		
C@	1e4	LO	755	U<=	2bd		
calc.output	8e7	LSHIFT	4b7	U>	2ae		
CMOVE	7c0	M*	329	U>=	2cc		
CMOVE>	7d4	M/MOD	36d	UD.	551		
CR	647	MAX	45e	UM*	31f		
D+	2e9	MIN	455	UM/MOD	353		
D-	304	MOD	3c9	VALLOT	910		
D.	545	MOVE	7ac	VHERE	8fc		
DABS	4f2	MU/MOD	424	W.LOOKUP	968		
DARK	93c	NEGATE	467	XOR	202		
DEPTH	7a0	NIP	131	[']	789		

WHYP12.CFG
Configuration File

The file WHYP12.CFG contains configuration information for a particular 68HC12 evaluation board. A specific .CFG file must be copied to the file WHYP12.CFG as described in Appendix C. This file must be in the current subdirectory when the program WHYP12.EXE is executed.

```
WA4RAM4.CFG

WHYP12.HED
tdp        5000
vdp        800
TORG       4000
HEDBASE    4000
RAMBASE    0900
INCHAR     2C
OUTPUT     35
TPUSH      3D
TPOP       46
INWDY      51
INWDX      5A
STOREW     63
TBLKST     6E
SNDSUB     8AB
EESTART    1000
EESTOP     1FFF
last       04
rts_code       2B
set_flags      -1
```

```
WB32RAM1.CFG

WHYP12.HED
tdp        2000
vdp        800
TORG       1000
HEDBASE    1000
RAMBASE    0900
INCHAR     2C
OUTPUT     35
TPUSH      3D
TPOP       46
INWDY      51
INWDX      5A
STOREW     63
TBLKST     6E
SNDSUB     8AB
EESTART    0D00
EESTOP     0FFF
last       04
rts_code       2B
set_flags      -1
```

```
WA4EPROM.CFG

WHYP12.HED
tdp        5000
vdp        800
TORG       8000
HEDBASE    8000
RAMBASE    0900
INCHAR     2C
OUTPUT     35
TPUSH      3D
TPOP       46
INWDY      51
INWDX      5A
STOREW     63
TBLKST     6E
SNDSUB     8AB
EESTART    1000
EESTOP     1FFF
last       04
rts_code       2B
set_flags      -1
```

```
WB32FLSH.CFG

WHYP12.HED
tdp        2000
vdp        800
TORG       1000
HEDBASE    8000
RAMBASE    0900
INCHAR     2C
OUTPUT     35
TPUSH      3D
TPOP       46
INWDY      51
INWDX      5A
STOREW     63
TBLKST     6E
SNDSUB     8AB
EESTART    0D00
EESTOP     0FFF
last       04
rts_code       2B
set_flags      -1
```

Appendix G

WHYP Glossary

!	(n addr --) ("store")	

Stores the 16-bit value of *n* at address *addr*.

" (-- addr len) ("quote")
Leaves the address, *addr*, and length, *len*, of a string consisting of characters to closing ".

\# (d1 -- d2) ("sharp")
Converts the next digit of the double number *d1* by dividing *d1* by the value in the variable *BASE* and converting the remainder to ASCII. The double quotient, *d2*, is left on the data stack. Must be loaded from file STRING.WHP.

\#> (d -- addr len) ("sharp-greater")
Completes the string conversion and leaves the address, *addr*, and length, *len*, of the number string on the data stack. Must be loaded from file STRING.WHP.

\#S (d1 -- 0 0) ("sharp-S")
Converts the rest of the double number *d1* and leaves double zero on the data stack. Must be loaded from file STRING.WHP.

' (-- cfa) ("tick" -- a single quote)
The statement ' *<name>* will leave the CFA of *<name>* on the data stack.

(continued)

(continued)

((-- n)   ("paren")
All characters between (and a closing) are treated as a comment.

(.)   (n -- addr len)   ("paren-dot")
Converts a signed single number, *n*, and leaves the address, *addr*, and length, *len*, of the number string on the data stack. Must be loaded from file STRING.WHP.

(D.)   (d -- addr len)   ("paren-D-dot")
Converts a signed double number, *d*, and leaves the address, *addr*, and length, *len*, of the number string on the data stack. Must be loaded from file STRING.WHP.

(U.)   (u -- addr len)   ("paren-U-dot")
Converts an unsigned single number, *u*, and leaves the address, *addr*, and length, *len*, of the number string on the data stack. Must be loaded from file STRING.WHP.

(UD.)   (ud -- addr len)   ("paren-U-D-dot")
Converts an unsigned double number, *ud*, and leaves the address, *addr*, and length, *len*, of the number string on the data stack. Must be loaded from file STRING.WHP.

*   (n1 n2 -- n3)
Leaves the 16-bit product, n1*n2, on the stack.

*/   (n1 n2 n3 -- n4)
Leaves n4 = n1*n2/n3, on the stack. Keeps n1*n2 as an intermediate 32-bit value.

+   (n1 n2 -- n3)   ("plus")
Adds top two elements on data stack and leaves the sum. *n3 = n1 + n2*.

+!   (n addr --)   ("plus-store")
Adds *n* to the value at address *addr*.

,   (n --)   ("comma")
Stores the value *n* at the location pointed to by the target dictionary pointer, *tdp*, and increments *tdp* by 2. Will comma data into EEPROM.

−   (n1 n2 -- n3)   ("minus")
Subtracts top element from second element on data stack and leaves the difference. *n3 = n1 – n2*.

-ROT   (n1 n2 n3 -- n3 n1 n2)
Rotates the top three elements on the stack backwards. The top element is rotated to third place.

.   (n --)   ("dot")
Pops the top element on the data stack and displays its value on the PC screen.

."   (--)   ("dot-quote")
Prints a string consisting of characters to closing ".

.R   (--)   ("dot-R")
Displays the contents of the return stack nondestructively.

There are, in fact, eight conversion complete flags, *CCFx*, one for each of the eight channels. Normally, we are interested in when an entire sequence consisting of four or eight conversions has been completed. The sequence complete flag, *SCF*, shown in Figure 9–7, is used to test this condition.

The *ADPU* bit used to enable the A/D converter has been moved from the *OPTION* register in the 68HC11 to the new *ATDCTL2* control register, shown in Figure 9–8. This control register also contains an *AFFC* bit which, when set, will cause the *CCF* flags to be cleared automatically when a result register is read (see Figure 9–7).

There are no interrupts associated with the A/D converter on the 68HC11. However, it is possible to produce a hardware interrupt on the 68HC12 when the A/D conversion sequence is complete. This interrupt is enabled with the *ASCIE* bit in the *ATDCTL2* control register, shown in Figure 9–8. The interrupt vector addresses associated with this ATD interrupt are shown in Tables 6–6 and 6–7 in Chapter 6.

If *MULT* = 1, *S8CM* = 0, and *SCAN* = 0 in the *ATDCTL5* control register in Figure 9–7, then a single separate conversion is done on each of four separate channels just as in the 68HC11 as shown in Figure 9–9. On the other hand, if *MULT* = 1 and *S8CM* = 1, then a single separate conversion can be done on each of the eight separate channels with the results stored in the eight A/D result registers, as indicated in Figure 9–10.

	7	6	5	4	3	2	1	0	
$0062	ADPU	AFFC	AWAI	0	0	0	ASCIE	ASCIF	ATDCTL2

ADPU: A/D Power Up
            0 – A/D disabled
            1 – A/D enabled

AFFC: A/D Fast Flag Clear All
            0 – A/D flag clearing operates normally
            1 – Uses fast clear sequence for A/D conversion complete flags
                (Any access to result register will cause the associated CCF to clear
                automatically.)

AWAI: A/D Wait Mode
            0 – A/D continues to run in wait mode
            1 – A/D stops to save power in wait mode

ASCIE: A/D Sequence Complete Interrupt Enable
            0 – A/D interrupt disabled
            1 – A/D interrupt (on sequence complete) enabled

ASCIF: A/D Sequence Complete Interrupt Flag
            0 – No A/D interrupt occurred
            1 – A/D sequence complete

Figure 9–8   The 68HC12 ATD Control Register 2

CD	CC	CB	CA	Channel Signal	MULT = 1
0	0	0	0	AN0	ADR0
0	0	0	1	AN1	ADR1
0	0	1	0	AN2	ADR2
0	0	1	1	AN3	ADR3
0	1	0	0	AN4	ADR0
0	1	0	1	AN5	ADR1
0	1	1	0	AN6	ADR2
0	1	1	1	AN7	ADR3
1	0	0	0	Reserved	ADR0
1	0	0	1	Reserved	ADR1
1	0	1	0	Reserved	ADR2
1	0	1	1	Reserved	ADR3
1	1	0	0	V_H	ADR0
1	1	0	1	V_L	ADR1
1	1	1	0	$(V_H + V_L)/2$	ADR2
1	1	1	1	Reserved	ADR3

Figure 9–9   The 68HC12 A/D Channel Assignments (S8CM = 0)

CD	CC	CB	CA	Channel Signal	MULT = 1
0	0	0	0	AN0	ADR0
0	0	0	1	AN1	ADR1
0	0	1	0	AN2	ADR2
0	0	1	1	AN3	ADR3
0	1	0	0	AN4	ADR4
0	1	0	1	AN5	ADR5
0	1	1	0	AN6	ADR6
0	1	1	1	AN7	ADR7
1	0	0	0	Reserved	ADR0
1	0	0	1	Reserved	ADR1
1	0	1	0	Reserved	ADR2
1	0	1	1	Reserved	ADR3
1	1	0	0	V_H	ADR4
1	1	0	1	V_L	ADR5
1	1	1	0	$(V_H + V_L)/2$	ADR6
1	1	1	1	Reserved	ADR7

Figure 9–10   The 68HC12 A/D Channel Assignments (S8CM = 1)

(continued)

AGAIN   (--)
        Used in *BEGIN . . . AGAIN* loop: *BEGIN* <words> *AGAIN*
        Execute <words> forever.

ALLOT   (n --)
        Allocates *n* bytes of memory by incrementing *tdp* by *n*.

AND   (n1 n2 -- and)
        Leaves n1 AND n2 on top of the stack. This is a bitwise AND.

ASCII   (-- ascii_code)
        Used to find the ASCII code of characters.
        The statement *ASCII* <char> will leave the ASCII code of <char> on the data stack.
        For example, *ASCII A*, will leave a $41 on the data stack.

B.LOOKUP (addr frac -- interp)
        8-bit table lookup wrapper

BEGIN   (--)
        Used in *BEGIN . . . UNTIL, BEGIN . . . AGAIN*, and *BEGIN . . . WHILE . . .*
        *REPEA*T statements.

C!   (c addr --)   ("C-store")
        Stores the Least Significant Byte (LSB) of the value on top of the stack at address *addr*.

C,   (c --)   ("C-comma")
        Stores the byte *c* at the location pointed to by the target dictionary pointer, *tdp*, and
        increments *tdp* by 1. Will C-comma data into EEPROM.

C@   (addr -- c)   ("C-fetch")
        Reads the byte at address *addr* and leaves it as the Least Significant Byte (LSB) on top
        of the stack.

CLI   (--)
        Compiles the opcode for *CLI* ($10EF) in-line within a colon definition.

CMOVE   (ad1 ad2 cnt --)   ("C-move")
        Moves *cnt* bytes up in memory from addr *ad1* to *ad2*.

CMOVE>   (ad1 ad2 cnt --)   ("C-move-down")
        Moves *cnt* bytes down in memory from addr *ad1* to *ad2*.

CONSTANT   (n --)
        n CONSTANT <name> will define <name> to be a constant with value *n*.

CONTROL   (-- control_code)
        Used to find the ASCII code of control characters.
        The statement *CONTROL* <char> will leave the ASCII code of ^<char> on the data
        stack. For example, *CONTROL G*, will leave a $07 on the data stack.

COUNT   (addr -- addr+1 len)
        Converts a counted string at address, *addr*, to an address-length string at *addr*+1. Must
        be loaded from file STRING.WHP.

(continued)

(continued)

CR   (--)   ("carriage return")
Produces a "carriage return" and line feed on the screen.

CREATE   (--)
CREATE <name> will add *<name>* to the dictionary and compile a *JSR DOVAR* at its
CFA. Executing *<name>* will put its PFA on the data stack.

CREATE...DOES>   (--)
Used in *CREATE ... DOES>* to create defining words. When the defining word is
executed, the words between *CREATE* and *DOES>* are executed. When the word
defined by the defining word is executed, the words following *DOES>* (with the *pfa* on
the data stack) are executed.

D+   (d1 d2 -- d3)   ("D-plus")
Adds top two double numbers on data stack and leaves the double sum. $d3 = d1 + d2$.

D-   (d1 d2 -- d3)   ("D-minus")
Subtracts top double number from second double number on data stack and leaves the
difference. $d3 = d1 - d2$.

D.   (d --)   ("D-dot")
Pops the top double number on the data stack and displays its signed value on the PC
screen.

DECIMAL (--)
Changes display mode to decimal.

DEPTH   (-- n)
Returns the number of items on the data stack.

DIGIT   (c base -- n f)
Checks to see if the character, *c*, is a valid digit in the base, *base*. If it is, leaves the valid
digit, *n*, and a true flag, *f*, on the data stack; otherwise, leaves a false flag, *f*, and a
meaningless value of *n*. Must be loaded from file STRING.WHP.

DO   (limit index --)
Used in *DO ... LOOP*: *<limit> <index> DO <WHYP statements> LOOP*.
Executes *<WHYP statements>* as long as *<index>* is less than *<limit>*;
LOOP increments *<index>* by 1.

DOES>   (pfa --)
Used in *CREATE ... DOES>* to create defining words. When the defining word is
executed, the words between *CREATE* and *DOES>* are executed. When the word
defined by the defining word is executed, the words following *DOES>* (with the *pfa* on
the data stack) are executed.

DROP   (n --)
Removes the top element from the stack.

DUM*   (ud un -- ud)
Unsigned multiply of 32 × 16. Leaves the 32-bit product, ud*un, on the stack.

(continued)

DUMP   (addr len --)
            Displays a block of memory of length *len* starting at address *addr*. The value of *len* is the number of bytes to display; however, *DUMP* always displays multiples of 16 bytes.

DUP   (n -- n n)
            Duplicates the top element on the stack

EE!   (n addr --)   ("E-E-store")
            Stores the 16-bit value of *n* at the EEPROM address *addr*.

EEC!   (c addr --)   ("E-E-C-store")
            Stores the Least Significant Byte (LSB) of the value on top of the stack at the EEPROM address *addr*.

ELSE   (--)
            Used in *IF ... ELSE ... THEN* statement
            <flag> IF <true statements> ELSE <false statements> THEN

EMIT   (c --)
            Displays the character whose ASCII code is *c* on the PC screen.

ERASE.BULK   (--)
            Erases the entire EEPROM by storing $FF in all EEPROM addresses.

EXECUTE   (addr --)
            Executes the 68HC12 (68HC11) code starting at address *addr*.

FDIV   (u1 u2 -- rem quot)
            Fractional division. Divides unsigned 16-bit u1 by unsigned 16-bit u2 and leaves the unsigned 16-bit quotient over the unsigned 16-bit remainder on the stack. u1 must be less than u2.

FLIP   (ab -- ba)
            Exchanges the bytes of the top element on the stack.

FOR   (n --)
            Used in *FOR ... NEXT* statement: *n FOR <WHYP statements> NEXT*
            Execute *<WHYP statements> n* times.

HERE   (-- n)
            Puts the current value of the target dictionary pointer, *tdp*, on the data stack.

HEX   (--)
            Changes display mode to hexadecimal.

HI   (b# addr --)
            Sets bit number *b#* of the byte at address *addr* to 1.

HOLD   (char --)
            Inserts the character, *char*, in the output string. Must be loaded from file STRING.WHP.

IDIV   (u1 u2 -- rem quot)
            Divides unsigned 16-bit u1 by unsigned 16-bit u2 and leaves the unsigned 16-bit quotient over the unsigned 16-bit remainder on the stack.

(continued)

(continued)

IF (flag --)
Used in *IF . . . ELSE . . . THEN* statement
<flag> IF <true statements> ELSE <false statements> THEN

INT: (--)
Used in place of : to define a high-level WHYP word that is an interrupt service routine.

INVERT (n -- 1's_comp)
Leaves the bitwise 1's complement of n on top of the stack.

LEAVE (--)
Immediately exits a *DO* loop.

LITERAL (n --)
Compiles *n* as a literal within a colon definition. Compiles *JSR (LIT)* followed by *n*.

LO (b# addr --)
Clears bit number *b#* of the byte at address *addr* to 0.

LOAD (--)
LOAD <filename> will load the file *<filename>* containing colon definitions.

LOOP (--)
Used in *DO . . . LOOP*: *<limit> <index> DO <WHYP statements> LOOP*
Execute *<WHYP statements>* as long as *<index>* is less than *<limit>*;
LOOP increments *<index>* by 1.

LSHIFT (n1 n2 -- n3)
Shifts bits of n1 left n2 times.

M* (n1 n2 -- d)
Signed multiply. Leaves the 32-bit product, n1*n2, on the stack.

M/MOD (d n -- rem quot)
Divides 32-bit signed d by 16-bit signed n and leaves the 16-bit signed quotient over the 16-bit signed remainder on the stack.

MAX (n1 n2 -- n3)
Leaves the larger of *n1* and *n2* on the stack.

MIN (n1 n2 -- n3)
Leaves the smaller of *n1* and *n2* on the stack.

MOD (n1 n2 -- rem)
Leaves on the stack the remainder of dividing signed 16-bit n1 by signed 16-bit n2.

MU/MOD (ud un -- urem udquot)
Divides 32-bit unsigned ud by 16-bit unsigned un and leaves the 32-bit unsigned quotient over the 16-bit unsigned remainder on the stack.

NEGATE (n -- -n)
Changes the sign of *n*.

(*continued*)

NEXT   (--)
        Used in *FOR . . . NEXT* statement: *n FOR <WHYP statements> NEXT*
        Execute *<WHYP statements> n* times.

NIP   (n1 n2 -- n2)
        Removes the second element from the stack. This is equivalent to *SWAP DROP.*

NOT   (n -- not)
        Leaves the logical NOT of n on top of the stack. NOT is equivalent to 0=.

OR   (n1 n2 -- or)
        Leaves n1 OR n2 on top of the stack. This is a bitwise OR.

OVER   (n1 n2 -- n1 n2 n1)
        Duplicates the second element on the stack.

PICK   (n1 -- n2)
        Duplicates the value at position n1 from the top of the stack
        (not counting n1). The top of the stack corresponds to n1 equal to 0.
        0 *PICK* is the same as *DUP*. 1 *PICK* is the same as *OVER*

R>   (-- n)   (R: n --)   ("from-R")
        Pops the top element of the return stack and pushes it onto the data stack.

R>DROP   (--)   (R: n --)   ("from-R-DROP")
        Pops the top element of the return stack and throws it away.

R@   (-- n)   (R: n -- n)   ("R-fetch")
        Copies the top element of the return stack to the top of the parameter stack.

RECURSE   (--)
        Executes the current word recursively.

REPEAT   (--)
        Used in *BEGIN . . . WHILE . . . REPEAT* statement.
        BEGIN <words1> <flag> WHILE <words2> REPEAT
        Executes *<words1>*; if *<flag>* is true, execute *<words2>* and branches back to
        <words1>; if *<flag>* is false, exits loop.

ROLL   (n --)
        Rotates the value at position n (not counting n) to the top of the stack.
        n must be greater than 0.
        1 *ROLL* is the same as *SWAP*. 2 *ROLL* is the same as *ROT*

ROT   (n1 n2 n3 -- n2 n3 n1)
        Rotates the top three elements on the stack. The third element becomes the first
        element.

RP!   (n --)   (R: --)   ("RP-store")
        Sets the return stack pointer (the system SP).

(*continued*)

(continued)

RP@   (-- n)   (R: --)   ("RP-fetch")
           Pushes the current RP (system SP) to the data stack.

RSHIFT   (n1 n2 -- n3)
           Shifts bits of n1 right n2 times.

RTI;   (--)
           Used to end a high-level WHYP word defined using *INT:*. Compiles the opcode
           for the *RTI* instruction ($0B) inline.

S>D   (n -- d)
           Sign extends a single to a double.

SEE   (--)
           SEE <name> will decompile the WHYP definition of *<name>*.

SEI   (--)
           Compiles the opcode for *SEI* ($1410) in-line within a colon definition.

SHOW   (--)
           SHOW <name> will display the machine code of *<name>*.

SIGN   (n --)
           Inserts a minus sign (−) in the output string if *n* is negative.
           Must be loaded from file STRING.WHP.

SP!   (a --)   ("SP-store")
           Sets the data stack pointer, *X*, to the value on top of the data stack.

SP@   (-- a)   ("SP-fetch")
           Pushes the current data stack pointer (index register *X*) onto the data stack.

SPACE   (--)
           Prints a space on the screen. Must be loaded from file STRING.WHP.

SPACES   (n --)
           Print *n* spaces on the screen. Must be loaded from file STRING.WHP.

STEP   (<name_stack> --)
           STEP <name> will single-step through the WHYP words making up *<name>*.
           The data stack must contain the values expected by *<name>* before *STEP* is called.
           Pressing the space bar single-steps the next instruction. Pressing *q* quits *STEP*.

SWAP   (n1 n2 -- n2 n1)
           Interchanges the top two elements on the stack.

THEN   (--)
           Used in *IF . . . ELSE . . . THEN* statement
           <flag> IF <true statements> ELSE <false statements> THEN

TUCK   (n1 n2 -- n2 n1 n2)
           Duplicates the top element on the stack under the second element.
           This is equivalent to *SWAP OVER*.

(continued)

TYPE	(addr len --) Prints an address-length string on the screen. Must be loaded from file STRING.WHP.
U.	(u --) ("U-dot") Pops the top element on the data stack and displays its unsigned value on the PC screen.
U/	(u1 u2 -- uquot) Divides 16-bit unsigned u1 by 16-bit unsigned u2 and leaves the 16-bit unsigned quotient, u1/u2, on the stack.
U2/	(u -- u/2) Divides the unsigned value on top of the stack by 2 by performing a logic shift right one bit.
U<	(u1 u2 -- f) ("U-less-than") Flag, f, is true if u1 is less than u2.
U<=	(u1 u2 -- f) ("U-less-than or equal") Flag, f, is true if u1 is less than or equal to u2.
U>	(u1 u2 -- f) ("U-greater-than") Flag, f, is true if u1 is greater than u2.
U>=	(u1 u2 -- f) ("U-greater-than or equal") Flag, f, is true if u1 is greater than or equal to u2.
UD.	(ud --) ("U-D-dot") Pops the top unsigned double number on the data stack and displays its unsigned value on the PC screen.
UM*	(u1 u2 -- ud) Unsigned multiply. Leaves the 32-bit product, u1*u2, on the stack.
UM/MOD	(ud un -- urem uquot) Divides 32-bit unsigned ud by 16-bit unsigned un and leaves the 16-bit unsigned quotient over the 16-bit unsigned remainder on the stack.
UNTIL	(flag --) Used in *BEGIN . . . UNTIL* statement *BEGIN <words> <flag> UNTIL* Executes *<words>* until *<flag>* is true.
VALLOT	(n --) Allocates *n* bytes of RAM memory by incrementing *vdp* by *n*.
VARIABLE	(--) *VARIABLE <name>* will define *<name>* to be a variable.
VHERE	(-- n) Puts the current value of the variable dictionary pointer, *vdp*, on the data stack.

(continued)

(*continued*)

W.LOOKUP   (addr frac -- interp)
        16-bit table lookup wrapper

WHILE   (flag --)
        Used in *BEGIN . . . WHILE . . . REPEAT* statement
        BEGIN <words1> <flag> WHILE <words2> REPEAT
        Executes *<words1>*; if *<flag>* is true, executes *<words2>* and branches back to
        <words1>; if *<flag>* is false, exits loop.

XOR   (n1 n2 -- xor)
        Leaves n1 XOR n2 on top of the stack. This is a bitwise XOR.

[(--)   ("left-bracket")
        Turns off the compiler within a colon definition.

\   (-- n)   ("backslash")
        All characters following \ to the end of the line are treated as a comment.

]   (--)   ("right-bracket")
        Turns on the compiler within a colon definition.

Appendix H

The WHYP Disk

The disk that accompanies this book contains the WHYP programs WHYP12 and WHYP11 for the 68HC12 and 68HC11 microcontrollers, respectively. All of the assembly language and C++ programs are included on the disk together with many of the WHYP programs described in this book. For a complete listing of all the files on the disk, see the README file on the disk.

The latest versions of WHYP can be downloaded from the Web site *www.secs. oakland.edu/~haskell.*

Index

The 68HC12 A/D converter has two additional control registers, *ATDCTL3* and *ATDCTL4*, shown in Table 9–2. The control register *ATDCTL3* has two bits that control the response of the A/D converter when a breakpoint occurs in the background debug mode. The default is to continue the conversion.

We saw in Section 9.2 that a single 8-bit A/D conversion on the 68HC11 took 32 clock periods. In the 68HC12 the default 8-bit conversion time is 18 ATD clock periods at a conversion frequency of 2 MHz. This means that the total conversion time for four conversions is 36 μsec compared to the 64 μsec on the 68HC11. The total 8-bit conversion time is programmable up to a maximum of 32 ATD clock periods and the ATD clock frequency is programmable from 500 KHz to 2 MHz using the control register *ATDCTL4*. In this book we will always use the default value.

9.3.1 WHYP Words for the 68HC12 A/D Converter

The file ATD.WHP contains the WHYP words for accessing the A/D converter on the 68HC12 and is shown in Listing 9–2. These are the same words that we developed for the 68HC11 in Listing 9–1. Note that only four of the A/D registers in Table 9–2 need to be defined as *CONSTANT*s at the beginning of the file.

Listing 9–2   68HC12 A/D Converter

```
\       68HC12 Analog-to-Digital Converter -- File: ATD.WHP
HEX

0062    CONSTANT        ATDCTL2         \ ATD Control Register 2
0065    CONSTANT        ATDCTL5         \ ATD Control Register 5
0066    CONSTANT        ATDSTAT         \ ATD Status Register
0070    CONSTANT        ADR0H           \ A/D Result Register 0

: ADCONV.ON      ( -- )
      C0 ATDCTL2 C! ;                   \ Set ADPU and AFFC

: ADCONV.OFF     ( -- )
      0 ATDCTL2 C! ;                    \ Clear ADPU

: WAIT.FOR.CONV  ( -- )
            BEGIN
              7 ATDSTAT ?HI
            UNTIL ;

: AVG4           ( -- n )               \ Average 4 values in ADR0H-ADR3H
            0 ADR0H 2-
            4 FOR                       \ sum addr
              DUP R@ 2* + C@            \ sum addr val
```

CD	CC	CB	CA	Channel Signal	MULT = 1
0	0	0	0	AN0	ADR0
0	0	0	1	AN1	ADR1
0	0	1	0	AN2	ADR2
0	0	1	1	AN3	ADR3
0	1	0	0	AN4	ADR0
0	1	0	1	AN5	ADR1
0	1	1	0	AN6	ADR2
0	1	1	1	AN7	ADR3
1	0	0	0	Reserved	ADR0
1	0	0	1	Reserved	ADR1
1	0	1	0	Reserved	ADR2
1	0	1	1	Reserved	ADR3
1	1	0	0	V_H	ADR0
1	1	0	1	V_L	ADR1
1	1	1	0	$(V_H + V_L)/2$	ADR2
1	1	1	1	Reserved	ADR3

Figure 9–9   The 68HC12 A/D Channel Assignments (S8CM = 0)

CD	CC	CB	CA	Channel Signal	MULT = 1
0	0	0	0	AN0	ADR0
0	0	0	1	AN1	ADR1
0	0	1	0	AN2	ADR2
0	0	1	1	AN3	ADR3
0	1	0	0	AN4	ADR4
0	1	0	1	AN5	ADR5
0	1	1	0	AN6	ADR6
0	1	1	1	AN7	ADR7
1	0	0	0	Reserved	ADR0
1	0	0	1	Reserved	ADR1
1	0	1	0	Reserved	ADR2
1	0	1	1	Reserved	ADR3
1	1	0	0	V_H	ADR4
1	1	0	1	V_L	ADR5
1	1	1	0	$(V_H + V_L)/2$	ADR6
1	1	1	1	Reserved	ADR7

Figure 9–10   The 68HC12 A/D Channel Assignments (S8CM = 1)

The 68HC12 A/D converter has two additional control registers, *ATDCTL3* and *ATDCTL4*, shown in Table 9–2. The control register *ATDCTL3* has two bits that control the response of the A/D converter when a breakpoint occurs in the background debug mode. The default is to continue the conversion.

We saw in Section 9.2 that a single 8-bit A/D conversion on the 68HC11 took 32 clock periods. In the 68HC12 the default 8-bit conversion time is 18 ATD clock periods at a conversion frequency of 2 MHz. This means that the total conversion time for four conversions is 36 μsec compared to the 64 μsec on the 68HC11. The total 8-bit conversion time is programmable up to a maximum of 32 ATD clock periods and the ATD clock frequency is programmable from 500 KHz to 2 MHz using the control register *ATDCTL4*. In this book we will always use the default value.

9.3.1 WHYP Words for the 68HC12 A/D Converter

The file ATD.WHP contains the WHYP words for accessing the A/D converter on the 68HC12 and is shown in Listing 9–2. These are the same words that we developed for the 68HC11 in Listing 9–1. Note that only four of the A/D registers in Table 9–2 need to be defined as *CONSTANT*s at the beginning of the file.

Listing 9–2   68HC12 A/D Converter

```
\        68HC12 Analog-to-Digital Converter -- File: ATD.WHP
HEX

0062    CONSTANT        ATDCTL2         \ ATD Control Register 2
0065    CONSTANT        ATDCTL5         \ ATD Control Register 5
0066    CONSTANT        ATDSTAT         \ ATD Status Register
0070    CONSTANT        ADR0H           \ A/D Result Register 0

: ADCONV.ON       ( -- )
      C0 ATDCTL2 C! ;                   \ Set ADPU and AFFC

: ADCONV.OFF      ( -- )
      0 ATDCTL2 C! ;                    \ Clear ADPU

: WAIT.FOR.CONV   ( -- )
          BEGIN
             7 ATDSTAT ?HI
          UNTIL ;

: AVG4            ( -- n )              \ Average 4 values in ADR0H-ADR3H
          0 ADR0H 2-
          4 FOR                        \ sum addr
             DUP R@ 2* + C@            \ sum addr val
```